www.wadsworth.com

Personality
Sixth Edition

Jerry M. Burger

Santa Clara University

THOMSON

WADSWORTH

Australia • Canada • Mexico • Singapore • Spain
United Kingdom • United States

Acquisitions Editor: Michele Sordi
Assistant Editor: Dan Moneypenny
Editorial Assistant: Chelsea Junget
Technology Project Manager: Darin Derstine
Marketing Manager: Chris Caldeira
Marketing Assistant: Laurel Anderson
Advertising Project Manager: Brian Chaffee
Project Manager, Editorial Production: Ritchie Durdin
Print / Media Buyer: Rebecca Cross
Permissions Editor: Elizabeth Zuber

Production Service: G & S Typesetters, Inc.
Text Designer: Carolyn Deacy
Photo Researcher: Terri Wright
Copy Editor: Anne Marie Walker
Illustrator: Glenda Barlow
Cover Designer: Roger Knox
Cover Image: © Trevor Wood / Getty Images
Cover Printer: Phoenix Color Corp
Compositor: G & S Typesetters, Inc.
Printer: Phoenix Color Corp

Printed in the United States of America
1   2   3   4   5   6   7   07   06   05   04   03

For more information about our products, contact us at:
Thomson Learning Academic Resource Center
1-800-423-0563
For permission to use material from this text, contact us by:
Phone: 1-800-730-2214
Fax: 1-800-730-2215
Web: http://www.thomsonrights.com

Library of Congress Control Number: 2002116012

ISBN: 0-534-52796-5

Wadsworth / Thomson Learning
10 Davis Drive
Belmont, CA 94002-3098
USA

Asia
Thomson Learning
5 Shenton Way #01-01
UIC Building
Singapore 068808

Australia / New Zealand
Thomson Learning
102 Dodds Street
Southbank, Victoria 3006
Australia

Canada
Nelson
1120 Birchmount Road
Toronto, Ontario M1K 5G4
Canada

Europe / Middle East / Africa
Thomson Learning
High Holborn House
50/51 Bedford Row
London WC1R 4LR
United Kingdom

Latin America
Thomson Learning
Seneca, 53
Colonia Polanco
11560 Mexico D.F.
Mexico

Spain / Portugal
Paraninfo
Calle / Magallanes, 25
28015 Madrid, Spain

To Marlene

Brief Contents

Contents

The Behavioral/Social Learning Approach

Preface

 Lately, each time I cross the Golden Gate Bridge, I think about this book. The bridge spans 8,981 feet across the entrance to the San Francisco Bay, with towers that rise 1,120 feet above the water. By popular lore, the painters hired to maintain the bridge's famous orange appearance have been handed a never-ending task. Because fog and wind and sea hammer the bridge daily, it's said that when the painters finally finish the job, it's time to start over. Although smaller in scope, this book has come to require a similar never-ending maintenance. Today, personality is a vibrant and healthy field that spills into other areas of psychology as well as into other disciplines. As a result, chronicling developments in the field becomes a year-round commitment. However, perhaps also like the bridge, the underlying structure of the book remains the same. Briefly, here's what's new this time around, as well as what's stayed the same.

What's New?

As in previous revisions, each chapter has been updated to reflect new research findings and new developments in the field. More than 300 new references have been added to this edition. Developments in the field are also reflected in the three new personality inventories in the sixth edition—the Achievement Goals Questionnaire (Chapter 8), the Distress Disclosure Index (Chapter 12), and the Relationship-Interdependent Self-Construal Scale (Chapter 16).

Of course, some sections of the book require more revision than others. Those familiar with the previous edition will notice extensive changes in a number of places. Chapter 5 includes more analysis of reliability and validity for the Myers-Briggs Type Indicator, reflecting some of the growing criticism of the scale. A new research topic in Chapter 6, "Psychoanalytic Concepts and Aggression," incorporates many concepts covered in previous editions—frustration, displacement, catharsis—but focuses more on recent research findings and less on the original frustration-aggression hypothesis. Chapter 8 now includes an extensive discussion of achievement goals, an elaboration on research tying anger and hostility to health problems, and a presentation of the recent debate on the relation between positive and negative affect. New longitudinal research examining the relation between temperament and personality is presented in Chapter 9. New developments in research on self-disclosure have been added to Chapter 12. In particular, you'll find a discussion on whether therapists should disclose personal information to their clients and recent studies exploring the reasons why disclosing traumatic experiences has health and psychological benefits. Chapter 13 has been rewritten to place less emphasis on behaviorism and more on the bridge between traditional behaviorism and cognitive approaches to personality. New developments in learned helplessness research, especially findings from neuropsychology, are reviewed in Chapter 15. A rewritten Chapter 16 places more emphasis on cognitive representations of the self than previous editions, including a presentation of Higgins' self-discrepancy theory. Finally, the assessment section in that chapter has been expanded to cover repertory grid techniques beyond the REP test.

What's the Same?

The philosophy that guided the organization and writing of the first five editions remains. I wrote this book to organize within one textbook the two approaches typically taken by instructors of undergraduate personality courses. Many instructors focus on the great theories and theorists—Freud, Jung, Rogers, Skinner, and so on. Students in these classes gain insight into the structure of the mind and issues of human nature, as well as a background for understanding psychological disorders and psychotherapy. However, these students are likely to be puzzled when they pick up a current journal of personality research only to find they recognize few, if any, of the topics. Other instructors emphasize personality research. Students learn about current studies on individual differences and personality processes. But they probably see little relationship between the abstract theories they may touch upon in class and the research topics that are the focus of the course.

However, these two approaches to teaching the course do not represent separate disciplines that happen to share the word *personality* in their titles. Indeed, the structure of this book is designed to demonstrate that the classic theories stimulate research and that the research findings often shape the development and acceptance of the theories. Limiting a student's attention to either theory or research provides an unfortunately narrow view of the field.

Something else that remains from the earlier editions is my belief that students learn about research best by seeing *programs* of research rather than a few isolated examples. Twenty-six research programs are covered in the seven research chapters in this edition. In each case I have tried to illustrate how the questions being investigated are connected to a larger theory, how early researchers developed their initial hypotheses and investigations, and how experimental findings led to new questions, refined hypotheses, and ultimately a greater understanding of the topic. Through this process, students are exposed to some of the problems researchers encounter, the fact that experimental results are often equivocal, and a realistic picture of researchers who don't always agree on how to interpret findings.

I have also retained and expanded many of the features of the previous editions in this sixth edition. Each of the theory chapters contains a section on application and a section on assessment. These sections demonstrate how the sometimes abstract theories relate to everyday concerns and issues and how each approach to understanding personality brings with it unique assumptions and problems when measuring relevant personality variables. I've retained the personality tests students can take and score themselves. There are now 15 "Assessing Your Own Personality" boxes scattered throughout the book. I've discovered in my own teaching that discussions about social anxiety mean a lot more to students when they know first how they scored on a social anxiety test. This hands-on experience not only gives students a better idea of how personality assessment works, but often generates a little healthy skepticism about relying too heavily on such measures. I've retained the biographies of the prominent personality theorists in this edition. Feedback from students indicates that knowing something about the person behind the theory helps to make the theory come alive. I've noticed how my own students enjoy speculating about how the theorist's life affected the development of the theory. Students and instructors also tell me they like the "In the News" boxes I introduced two editions ago. Consequently, these have been retained as well.

Acknowledgments

Thanks are extended to all the people who helped with the production of this book. This includes the many colleagues who reviewed various parts of the manuscript: Jason Baker, Texas Tech University; Linda Crothers, Humboldt State University; Howard Ehrlichman, Queens College; Joseph Fitzgerald, Wayne State University; and James Reid, Washington University in St. Louis. And, as always, I thank Marlene and Adam, whose understanding and support through all six editions have made this book possible.

 *About the Author*

Jerry M. Burger is professor of psychology at Santa Clara University. He is the author of dozens of journal articles and book chapters and the 1992 book *Desire for Control: Personality, Social and Clinical Perspectives.* He has been on the editorial board of the *Journal of Personality* and the *Personality and Social Psychology Bulletin* and has served as an associate editor for the "Personality Processes and Individual Difference" section of the *Journal of Personality and Social Psychology.* In his spare time he likes to run, read, and write. You can send comments about the book to him via e-mail at jburger@scu.edu.

Credits

This page constitutes an extension of the copyright page. We have made every effort to trace the ownership of all copyrighted material and to secure permission from copyright holders. In the event of any question arising as to the use of any material, we will be pleased to make the necessary corrections in future printings. Thanks are due to the following authors, publishers, and agents for permission to use the material indicated.

Photographs

Chapter 1 **9:** Photo courtesy of Emily Murphy. **16:** Jerry Burger.

Chapter 2 **23:** Jerry Burger.

Chapter 3 **44:** © Hulton-Deutsch Collection / CORBIS. **50:** Photo by Marlene Somsak. **54, 55, 62:** Jerry Burger.

Chapter 4 **86, 91:** Jerry Burger.

Chapter 5 **102:** © Bettmann / CORBIS. **105, 107:** Jerry Burger. **108:** © Bettmann / CORBIS. **111:** © Ted Streshinsky / CORBIS. **116:** Jerry Burger. **118:** © Bettmann / CORBIS. **122:** © Bettmann / CORBIS. **126:** © Bettmann / CORBIS. **127:** Photo by Marlene Somsak. **129:** Jerry Burger.

Chapter 6 **141:** Photo by Kathryn MacLean. **149, 155:** Jerry Burger.

Chapter 7 **170:** © Bettmann / CORBIS. **174:** © Bettmann / CORBIS. **176:** Reproduced by permission of the Cattell Family.

Chapter 8 **205, 207, 214, 222:** Jerry Burger.

Chapter 9 **250:** Reproduced by permission from The H. J. Eysenck Memorial Fund. **252:** Photo by Marlene Somsak. **258, 269:** Jerry Burger

Chapter 10 **280, 288:** Jerry Burger

Chapter 11 **308:** © Roger Ressmeyer / CORBIS. **311:** Jerry Burger **313:** © Bettmann / CORBIS. **327:** Jerry Burger

Chapter 12 **340, 349. 367:** Jerry Burger

Chapter 13 **374:** © Underwood & Underwood / CORBIS. **376:** © Bettmann / CORBIS. **379:** Jerry Burger **385:** University of Connecticut, Department of Psychology. **390:** Stanford University New Service. **402:** Photo by Marlene Somsak.

Chapter 14 **411, 421:** Jerry Burger **430:** Photo by Marlene Somsak. **437:** Photo by Kathryn MacLean.

Chapter 15 **445:** National Library of Medicine.

Literary Acknowledgments

Chapter 3 **60:** Excerpts from COLLECTED PAPERS, Vol.3, by Sigmund Freud, authorized translation by Alix and James Strachey. Published by Basic Books, Inc., by arrangement with the Hogarth Press Ltd. and The Institute of Psycho-Analysis, London. Reprinted by permission of Basic Books, a division of HarperCollins Publishers. **64:** From Koppitz, E. M. (1968), PSYCHOLOGICAL EVALUATION OF CHILDREN'S HUMAN FIGURE DRAWINGS. Reprinted by permission of Grune & Stratton, Inc., and the author.

Chapter 4 **75:** From "'A Ubiquitous Sex Difference in Dreams' revisited," by C. S. Hall, *Journal of Personality and Social Psychology, 46* (1984), 1109–1117. Reprinted by permission of D. Hall Busch. **82:** From "Evidence for change in children's use of defense mechanisms," by Phebe Cramer, *Journal of Personality, 65* (1997), 233–247. Used by permission of the author.

Chapter 5   115: From "Cross-cultural Investigation of the Validity of Erikson's Theory of Personality Development," by R. Ochse and C. Plug, *Journal of Personality and Social Psychology, 50* (1986), 1240–1252. Copyright © 1986 American Psychological Association. Reprinted by permission of the authors.

Chapter 6   143: From "Personal and Contextual Determinants of Coping Strategies," by C. J. Holahan and R. H. Moos, *Journal of Personality and Social Psychology, 52* (1987), 946–955. Copyright © 1987 by the American Psychological Association. Reprinted with permission. **150:** From Harris, M. B. (1974), Mediators between frustration and aggression in a field experiment, *Journal of Experimental and Social Psychology, 10,* 561–571. Reprinted by permission of Plenum. **152:** From Konecni, V. J., & Doob, A. N. (1972), Catharsis through displacement of aggression, *Journal of Personality and Social Psychology, 23,* 379–387. Reprinted by permission of the author. **154:** From Geen, R. G., Stonner, D., & Shope, G. L. (1975), The facilitation of aggression by aggression: Evidence against the catharsis hypothesis, *Journal of Personality and Social Psychology, 31,* 721–726. Reprinted by permission of Russell G. Geen. **161:** Adapted from "Behavioral and experiential patterns of avoidantly and securely attached women across adulthood," by Eva C. Klohnen, *Journal of Personality and Social Psychology, 74* (1998), 211–223. Copyright © 1998 American Psychological Association. Reprinted by permission of the author.

Chapter 7   172: From EXPLORATIONS IN PERSONALITY by Henry A. Murray, copyright 1938, renewed 1966 by Henry A. Murray. Used by permission of Oxford University Press, Inc. **178:** Reprinted by permission of the Institute of Personality and Ability Testing. **179:** Adapted from "Clinical Assessment Can Benefit from Recent Advances in Personality Psychology," by R. R. McCrae and P. T. Costa, *American Psychologists, 41* (1986), 1001–1003. Copyright © 1986 American Psychological Association. Reprinted by permission of the author. **181:** From "The development of markers for the Big-Five structure," by Lewis R. Goldberg, *Psychological Assessment, 4* (1992), 26–42. Reprinted by permission of the author. **188:** From Bem, D. J., and Allen, A. (1974), On predicting some of the people some of the time: The search for cross-situational consistencies in behavior, *Psychological Review, 81,* 506–520. Adapted and reprinted by permission of Daryl J. Bem. **194:** MINNESOTA MULTIPHASIC PERSONALITY INVENTORY. Copyright © The University of Minnesota 1943, renewed 1970. This profile from 1948, 1976, 1982. Reprinted by permission of the University of Minnesota Press. **198:** From SELF-DECEPTION: AN ADAPTIVE MECHANISM? by Joan S. Lockard and Delroy L. Paulhus (Eds.), Prentice-Hall, 1988.

Chapter 8   216: From Holmes, D. S., et al. (1984), Task-related arousal of Type A and Type B persons: Level of challenge and response specificity, *Journal of Personality and Social Psychology, 46,* 1322–1327. Reprinted by permission of the David Holmes. **220:** From "Trait hostility and ambulatory cardiovascular activity: Responses to social interaction," by M. Guyll and R. J. Contrada in *Health Psychology, 17* (1998), 30–39. Copyright © 1998 by the American Psychological Association. Adapted with permission. **224:** From "Social Anxiousness: The Construct and Its Measurement," by M. R. Leary, *Journal of Personality Measurement, 47* (1986), 71. Reprinted by permission of Lawrence Erlbaum Associates, Inc., and the author. **232:** Adapted from "The Stability of Mood Variability: A Spectral Analytic Approach to Daily Mood

Assessments," by R. J. Larsen, *Journal of Personality and Social Psychology, 52* (1987), 1195–1204. Copyright © 1987 by the American Psychological Association. Reprinted by permission of the author. **235:** From "Individual Differences in Dispositional Expressiveness: Development and Validation of the Emotional Expressivity Scale" by A. M. Kring, D. A. Smith, and J. M. Neale, *Journal of Personality and Social Psychology, 66* (1994), 934–949. Copyright © 1994 by the American Psychological Association. Reprinted with permission. **238:** Adapted from "Dispositional optimism and primary and secondary appraisal of a stressor," by E. C. Chang, *Journal of Personality and Social Psychology, 74* (1998), 1109–1120. Copyright © 1998 by the American Psychological Association. Reprinted by permission of the author. **242:** Adapted from "Strategy-dependent Effects of Reflecting on Self and Tasks: Some Implications of Optimism and Defensive Pessimism," by J. K. Norem and S. S. Illingworth, *Journal of Personality and Social Psychology, 65* (1993), 822–835. Copyright © 1993 by the American Psychological Association. Adapted with permission.

Chapter 9   249: From Eysenck, H. J., & Eysenck, B. G. (1968), MANUAL FOR THE EYSENCK PERSONALITY INVENTORY (San Diego: EDITS). Reprinted by permission of Educational and Industrial Testing Service. **256:** From TEMPERAMENT: EARLY DEVELOPING PERSONALITY TRAITS by A. H. Buss and R. Plomin, Copyright © 1984 Lawrence Erlbaum Associates, Inc. Reprinted with permission. **260:** From Reznick, J. S., et al. (1986), Inhibited and uninhibited children: A follow-up study, *Child Development, 57,* 660–680. Reprinted by permission of The Society for Research in Child Development, Inc.

Chapter 10   282: From "Genetic and environmental influences on personality: A study of twins reared together using self- and peer-report NEO-FFI Scales," by R. Riemann, A. Angleitner, and J. Stretlau, *Journal of Personality, 65* (1997), 449–475. Copyright © 1997 Blackwell Publishers. Reprinted with permission. **283:** From Rowe, D. C. (1987), Resolving the person-situation debate: Invitation to an interdisciplinary dialogue, *American Psychologist, 42,* 218–227. Reprinted by permission of David C. Rowe. **287:** From Pedersen, N. L. Plomin, R., McClearn, G. E., & Friberg, L. (1988), Neuroticism, extraversion, and related traits in adult twins reared apart and reared together, *Journal of Personality and Social Psychology, 55,* 950–957. Reprinted by permission of the author. **295, 298:** From Buss, D. M. (1989), Sex differences in human mate preferences: Evolutionary hypotheses tested in 37 cultures, *Behavioral and Brain Sciences, 12,* 1–49. Reprinted by permission of the author and Cambridge University Press.

Chapter 11   316: From "Validation of a Short Index of Self-Actualization," by A. Jones and R. Crandall, *Personality and Social Psychology Bulletin, 12* (1986), 63–73. Copyright © 1986 by Sage Publications. Reprinted by permission of Sage Publications and the authors. **331:** From Rogers, C. R. (1955), Personality change in psychotherapy, *Journal of Social Psychiatry, 1,* 31–41. Reprinted by permission of The Avenue Publishing Company.

Chapter 12   341: From Davis, J. D. (1976), Self-disclosure in an acquaintance exercise: Responsibility for level of intimacy, *Journal of Personality and Social Psychology, 33,* 787–792. Reprinted by permission of the author. **345:** From "Measuring the tendency to conceal versus disclose psychological distress," by J. H. Kahn and R. M. Hessling, *Journal of Social and Clinical Psychology, 20* (2001),

41–65. Copyright © 2001 Guilford Publications, Inc. **352:** From Schmidt, N., & Sermat, V. (1983), Measuring loneliness in different relationships, *Journal of Personality and Social Psychology, 44,* 1038–1047. Reprinted by permission of Vello Sermat. **362:** Adapted from "Multiple facets of self-esteem and their relations to depressive symptoms," by M. H. Kernis et al., *Personal and Social Psychological Bulletin, 24* (1998), 657–668. Copyright © 1998 by Sage Publications, Inc. Reprinted by permission of Sage Publications. **364:** Adapted from "Is there a universal need for positive self-regard?" by S. J. Heine et al., *Psychological Review, 106* (1999), 766–794. Copyright © 1999 by the American Psychological Association. Adapted by permission of the American Psychological Association and the author.

Chapter 13 **393:** From Bandura, A. (1965), Influence of models' reinforcement contingencies on the acquisition of imitative responses, *Journal of Personality and Social Psychology, 1,* 589–595. Reprinted by permission of the author. **401:** From Swan, G. E., & MacDonald, M. L. (1978), Behavior therapy in practice: A national survey of behavior therapists, *Behavior Therapy, 9,* 799–807. Reprinted by permission of the Association for the Advancement of Behavior Therapy. **404:** From Rathus, S. A. (1973), A 30-item schedule for assessing assertive behavior, *Behavior Therapy, 4,* 398–406.

Chapter 14 **418:** From Ickes, W., & Barnes, R. D. (1978), Boys and girls together—and alienated: On enacting stereotyped sex roles in mixed-sex dyads, *Journal of Personality and Social Psychology, 36,* 669–683. Reprinted by permission of William Ickes. **422:** From Slife, B. D., & Rychlak, J. F. (1982), Role of affective assessment in modeling aggressive behavior, *Journal of Personality and Social Psychology, 43,* 861–868. Reprinted by permission of Brent D. Slife. 435: From Paulhus, D. (1983), Sphere-specific measures of perceived control, *Journal of Personality and Social Psychology, 44,* 1253–1265. Reprinted by permission of the author.

Chapter 15 **447:** From A THEORY OF PERSONALITY: THE PSYCHOLOGY OF PERSONAL CONSTRUCTS by George A. Kelly. Copyright © 1955, 1963 by George A. Kelly, renewed 1983, 1991 by Gladys Kelly. Used by permission of W. W. Norton & Company, Inc. **450:** From "A Cognitive-affective System Theory of Personality: Reconceptualizing Situations, Disposotion, Dynamics, and Invariance in Personality Structure," by W. Mischel and Y. Shoda, *Psychological Review, 102* (1995), 246–148. Copyright © 1995 American Psychological Association. Reprinted by permission. **451:** Adapted from "A Cognitive-affective System Theory of Personality: Reconceptualizing Situations, Disposotion, Dynamics, and Invariance in Personality Structure," by W. Mischel and Y. Shoda, *Psychological Review, 102* (1995), 246–148. Copyright © 1995 American Psychological Association. Reprinted by permission. **455:** From Markus, H. (1977), Self-schemata

and processing information about the self, *Journal of Personality and Social Psychology, 35,* 63–78. Reprinted by permission of the author. **456:** From Rogers et al. (1977), Self-reference and the encoding of personal information, *Journal of Personality and Social Psychology, 35,* 677–688. Reprinted by permission of T. B. Rogers. **461:** From Ellis, A. E. (1987), The impossibility of achieving consistently good mental health, *American Psychologist, 42,* 364–375. Reprinted by permission of the author. **467:** The Role Construct Repertory (REP) Test from A THEORY OF PERSONALITY: THE PSYCHOLOGY OF PERSONAL CONSTRUCTS by George A. Kelly. Copyright © 1955, 1963 by George A. Kelly, renewed 1983, 1991 by Gladys Kelly. Used by permission of W. W. Norton & Company, Inc.

Chapter 16 **474:** Table from p. 481 of "Transference in Interpersonal Relations: Inferences and Affect," by S. M. Andersen and A. Baum, in *Journal of Personality, 62* (1994). Reprinted by permission of Blackwell Publishers. **477:** Adaptation of Table 2 on p. 587 of "Repression and the inaccessibility of affective memories," by P. J. Davis, *Journal of Personality and Social Psychology, 53* (1987), 585–593. Reprinted by permission of the author. **481:** From Bem, S. L. (1981), Gender schema theory: A cognitive account of sex typing, *Psychological Review, 88,* 354–364. Reprinted by permission of the author. **483:** Adapted from "Sex differences in the recall of affective experience," by L. Seidlitz and E. Diener, *Journal of Personality and Social Psychology, 74* (1998), 262–271. Copyright © 1998 by the American Psychological Association. Adapted with permission of the APA and the author. **484:** Adapted from "Gender differences in autobiographical memory of childhood emotional experience," by P. J. Davis in *Journal of Personality and Social Psychology, 76* (1999), 498–510. Copyright © 1999 by the American Psychological Association. Adapted with permission of APA and the author. **485:** From "The relational-interdependent self-construal and relationships," by Cross, S. E., Bacon, P. L., & Morris, M. L. (2000), *Journal of Personality and Social Psychology, 78,* 791–808. Copyright © 2000 by the American Psychological Association. Reprinted with permission. **486:** Adapted from "Photographic depictions of the self: Gender and age differences in social connectedness," by S. M. Clancy and S. J. Dollinger, *Sex Roles, 29* (1993), 477–495. Copyright © 1993 by Plenum Publishing Corporation. Reprinted by permission of Stephen J. Dollinger, Ph.D. **489:** From Derry, P. A., & Kuiper, N. A. (1981), Schematic processing and self-reference in clinical depression, *Journal of Abnormal Psychology, 90,* 286–297. Reprinted with permission of Nicholas A. Kuiper. **490:** From Clark, D. M., & Teasdale, J. D. (1982), Diurnal variation in clinical depression and accessibility of memories of positive and negative experiences, *Journal of Abnormal Psychology, 91,* 87–95. Reprinted by permission of the authors. **493:** From Abramson, L. Y., Seligman, M. E. P., & Teasdale, J. D. (1978), Learned helplessness in humans: Critique and reformulation, *Journal of Abnormal Psychology, 87,* 49–74. Reprinted by permission of Lyn Y. Abramson.

TO THE OWNER OF THIS BOOK:

I hope that you have found *Personality*, Sixth Edition useful. So that this book can be improved in a future edition, would you take the time to complete this sheet and return it? Thank you.

School and address: _____

_____

Department: _____

Instructor's name: _____

1. What I like most about this book is: _____

_____

_____

2. What I like least about this book is: _____

_____

_____

3. My general reaction to this book is: _____

_____

_____

4. The name of the course in which I used this book is: _____

_____

5. Were all of the chapters of the book assigned for you to read? _____

   If not, which ones weren't? _____

6. In the space below, or on a separate sheet of paper, please write specific suggestions for improving this book and anything else you'd care to share about your experience in using this book.

_____

_____

_____

OPTIONAL:

Your name: _____ Date: _____

May we quote you, either in promotion for *Personality*, Sixth Edition, or in future publishing ventures?

Yes: _____ No: _____

Sincerely yours,

Jerry M. Burger

‖‖‖‖

**NO POSTAGE
NECESSARY
IF MAILED
IN THE
UNITED STATES**

BUSINESS REPLY MAIL
FIRST CLASS   PERMIT NO. 34   BELMONT, CA

POSTAGE WILL BE PAID BY ADDRESSEE

ATTN: *Psychology/Michele Sordi*

WADSWORTH / THOMSON LEARNING
10 DAVIS DRIVE
BELMONT, CA   94002-9801

Chapter 1

What Is Personality?

The Person and the Situation
Defining Personality
Six Approaches to Personality
Personality and Culture
The Study of Personality: Theory, Application, Assessment, and Research
Summary

On the morning of September 11, 2002, Americans everywhere paused. Throughout the country, citizens shared a moment of silence at 8:46 A.M. EST, exactly one year after the first hijacked airliner crashed into the North Tower of the World Trade Center in New York. Family members of the victims gathered near the area now known as Ground Zero. As a lone performer played Bach's Cello Suite in C Minor, the names of the 2,801 people killed in the New York attack were read aloud. Similar ceremonies were held at the Pentagon in Washington and in Pennsylvania, where the other two hijacked planes had crashed during the attacks. In hundreds of communities across the country and in many other nations, people gathered to observe the anniversary and honor the victims. It was a day to mourn, to remember, and to reflect.

The September 11 terrorist attacks united Americans like no event since the bombing of Pearl Harbor. From the moment of the first news reports, Americans from all regions of the country—from all ethnic groups and religious backgrounds—shared the horror and disbelief. They bought flags, donated blood, sent donations, and shared their emotions. Businesses and schools closed, sports and entertainment events were canceled. A nation grieved.

Powerful events like the September 11 attacks have a way of bringing out similar reactions in people. Someone might point to this tragedy to illustrate how much alike each of us really is, how all people are basically the same. Yet if we look

1

a little more closely, even in this situation, we can see that not everyone reacted in the same way to the tragedy. In the days following the attack, many Americans were glued to their television sets, eagerly following each new development. But others turned their sets off, unable to watch the unsettling images any longer. Some citizens were overcome with anger and vowed revenge. But others focused on the victims and asked how they could help. Some people gathered at public events where they shared feelings and consoled their neighbors, whereas others sought solitude and quiet reflection. Many people turned to their religion to find meaning and comfort, but some struggled to find the hand of God in so much suffering. One year later, many people talked about how much had changed, yet others marveled at the nation's ability to return to normalcy. Some people found hope in the new beginning promised by the anniversary. For others, the day triggered painful memories and renewed fears.

In many ways, the reactions to the September 11 attacks are typical of people who are suddenly thrown into a unique and tragic situation. At first, the demands of the situation overwhelm individual differences. But soon each person's characteristic way of dealing with the situation and the emotional aftermath begins to surface. The more we look, the more we see that not all people are alike. The closer we look, the more we begin to see characteristic differences between people. These characteristic differences are the focus of this book. They are part of what we call personality. Moreover, many of the topics and issues that surface as we look at the September 11 tragedy have already been studied by personality psychologists. Coping with stress, disclosing to others, emotions, religion, anxiety, solitude, and many other relevant topics are covered in various places in this book.

The Person and the Situation

Is our behavior shaped by the situation we are in or by the type of person we are? In the September 11 tragedy, did people act the way they did because of the events surrounding them, or were their reactions more the result of the kind of people they were before the incident? This is one of the enduring questions in psychology. The generally agreed-upon answer today is that both the situation and the person contribute to behavior. Certainly, we don't act the same way in all situations. Depending on where we are and what is happening, each of us can be outgoing, shy, aggressive, friendly, depressed, frightened, or excited. But it is equally apparent that not everyone at the same party, the same ball game, or the same shopping center behaves identically. The debate among psychologists has now shifted to the question of *how* the situation influences our behavior as well as how our behavior reflects the individual.

"The outstanding characteristic of man is his individuality. There was never a person just like him, and there never will be again."
GORDON ALLPORT

We can divide the fields of study within psychology along the answer to this question. Many psychologists concern themselves with how people *typically* respond to environmental demands. These researchers recognize that not everyone in a situation reacts the same, but their objective is to identify patterns that generally describe what most people will do. Thus, a social psychologist might create several different situations in which participants view a person in need of help. The purpose of this research is to identify the kinds of situations that increase or decrease helping behavior. However, personality psychologists turn this way of thinking completely around. We know there are typical response patterns to situations, but what we find more interesting is why Peter tends to help more than Paul, even when both are presented with the same request.

You may have heard the axiom "There are few differences between people, but what differences there are really matter." That tends to sum up the personality psychologists' viewpoint. They want to know what makes you different from the person sitting next to you. Why do some people make friends easily, whereas others are lonely? Why are some people prone to bouts of depression? Can we predict who will rise to the top of the business ladder and who will fall short? Why are some people introverted, whereas others are so outgoing? We explore each of these questions in this book. Other topics covered include how your personality is related to hypnotic responsiveness, reactions to stress, how well you do in school, and even your chances of having a heart attack.

This is not to say that situations are unimportant or of no interest to personality psychologists. Indeed, as discussed in Chapter 7, many of the questions posed by personality researchers concern how a certain kind of person behaves in a particular situation. However, the emphasis of this book is on what makes you different from the next person—that is, your personality. But before addressing that question, we should start by defining what we mean by personality.

Defining Personality

Anyone who has been in college a while can probably anticipate the topic of the first lecture of the term. The philosophy professor asks, "What is philosophy?" The first class meeting in a communication course centers on the question: What is communication? Those who teach geography, history, and calculus have similar lectures. And so, for traditional and practical reasons, psychology professors too begin with the basic question: What is personality?

Although a definition follows, bear in mind that psychologists do not agree on a single answer to this question. In fact, personality psychologists are engaged in an ongoing and perhaps never-ending discussion of how to describe human personality and what topics belong within this subfield of psychology (Mayer, 1998; McAdams & Emmons, 1995; Sarason, Sarason, & Pierce, 1996). Personality theorists have different ideas about what personality psychologists ought to study. Whereas one theorist points to unconscious mechanisms, another looks at learning histories, and still another at the way people organize their thoughts. Although some students might find this lack of agreement frustrating, let me suggest from the outset that these different viewpoints provide a rich and exciting framework within which to explore the complexities of the individual.

Personality can be defined as *consistent behavior patterns and intrapersonal processes originating within the individual.* Several aspects of this simple definition need elaboration. Notice that there are two parts to it. The first part is concerned with consistent patterns of behavior. Personality researchers often refer to these as *individual differences.* The important point here is that personality is *consistent.* We can identify these consistent behavior patterns across time and across situations. We expect someone who is outgoing today to be outgoing tomorrow. Someone who is competitive at work is also quite likely competitive in sports. We acknowledge this consistency in character when we say, "It was just like her to do that" or, "He was just being himself." Of course, this does not mean an extraverted person is boisterous and jolly all the time, on solemn occasions as well as at parties. Nor does it mean people cannot change. But if personality exists and behavior is not just a reflection of whatever situation we find ourselves in, then we must expect some consistency in the way people act.

The second part of the definition concerns intrapersonal processes. In contrast to *interpersonal* processes, which take place between people, *intrapersonal* processes include all the emotional, motivational, and cognitive processes that go on inside of us that affect how we act and feel. Thus, you will find that many personality psychologists are interested in such topics as depression, information processing, happiness, and denial. Of course, some of these processes are shared by all people. For example, according to some theorists, each of us has a similar capacity to experience anxiety or similar processes for dealing with threatening events. However, how we use these processes and how they interact with individual differences play a role in determining our individual character.

It also is important to note that, according to the definition, these consistent behavior patterns and intrapersonal processes originate within the individual. This is not to say that external sources do not influence personality. Certainly, the way parents raise their children affects the kind of adult the child becomes. And, of course, the emotions we experience are often a reaction to the events we encounter. But the point is that behavior is not solely a function of the situation. The fear we experience while watching a frightening movie is the result of the film, but the different ways we each express or deal with that fear come from within.

Six Approaches to Personality

What are the sources of consistent behavior patterns and intrapersonal processes? This is the basic question asked by personality theorists and researchers. One reason for the length of this book is that personality psychologists have answered this question in many different ways. To help make sense of the wide range of personality theories proposed over the past century, we'll look at six general approaches to explaining personality. These are the psychoanalytic approach, the trait approach, the biological approach, the humanistic approach, the behavioral/social learning approach, and the cognitive approach. Although the fit is not always perfect, each of the major theories of personality can be placed into one of these six general approaches.

But why so many theories of personality? This question can be answered by way of analogy. Nearly everyone has heard the story about the five blind men who encounter an elephant. Each feels a different part of the animal and then tries to explain to the others what an elephant is like. The blind man feeling the leg describes the elephant as tall and round. Another feels the ear and claims an elephant is thin and flat, whereas another, holding onto the trunk, describes the animal as long and slender. The man feeling the tail and the one touching the elephant's side have still different images. The point to this story, of course, is that each man knows only a part of the whole animal. Because there is more to the elephant than what he has experienced, each man's description is correct but incomplete.

In one sense, the six approaches to personality are analogous to the blind men. That is, each approach does seem to correctly identify and examine an important aspect of human personality. For example, psychologists who subscribe to the *psychoanalytic approach* argue that people's unconscious minds are largely responsible for important differences in their behavior styles. Other psychologists, those who favor the *trait approach*, identify where a person might lie along a continuum of various personality characteristics. Psychologists advocating the *biological approach* point to inherited predispositions and physiological processes to explain individual differences in personality. In contrast, those promoting the *humanistic approach* identify personal responsibility and feelings of self-acceptance as the key causes of differences in personality. *Behavioral/social learning* theorists explain consistent behavior patterns as the result of conditioning and expectations. Those promoting the *cognitive approach* look at differences in the way people process information to explain differences in behavior.

It's tempting to suggest that by combining all six approaches we can obtain the larger, accurate picture of why people act they way they do. Unfortunately, the blind men analogy is only partially applicable to the six approaches to personality. Although different approaches to a given issue in personality often vary only in emphasis—with each providing a legitimate, compatible explanation—in many instances, the explanations of two or more approaches appear entirely incompatible. Thus, people who work in the field often align themselves with one or another of the six approaches as they decide which of the competing explanations they accept.

Returning to the blind men and the elephant, suppose someone were to ask how an elephant moves. The man feeling the trunk might argue that the elephant slithers along the ground like a snake. The man holding the elephant's ear might disagree, saying that the elephant must fly like a bird with its big, floppy wings. The man touching the leg would certainly have a different explanation. Although in some instances more than one of these explanations might be accurate (for example, a bird can both walk and fly), it should be obvious that at times not every theory can be right. It also is possible that one theory is correct in describing one part of human personality, whereas another theory is correct in describing other aspects.

No doubt some theories will make more sense to you than others. But it is worth keeping in mind that each approach has been developed and promoted by a large number of respected psychologists. Although not all of these men and women are correct about every issue, each approach has something of value to offer in our quest to understand what makes each of us who we are.

Two Examples: Aggression and Depression

To get a better idea of how the six approaches to understanding personality provide six different, yet legitimate, explanations for consistent patterns of behavior, let's look at two common examples. Because aggressive behavior and the suffering that comes from depression are widespread problems in our society, we should not be surprised that psychologists from many different perspectives have looked into the causes of aggression and depression.

Example 1: Aggression. We have all seen or read about people who consistently engage in aggressive behavior. Adults arrested for assault typically have a history of aggressive behavior that goes back to playground fights in childhood. Why are some people consistently more aggressive than others? Each of the six approaches to personality provides at least one answer. As you read these answers, you might want to think about an aggressive person you have encountered. Which of the six explanations seems to do the best job of explaining that person's behavior?

The classic psychoanalytic explanation of aggression points to an unconscious death instinct. That is, we are all said to possess an unconscious desire to self-destruct. However, because people with a healthy personality do not hurt themselves, these self-destructive impulses may be unconsciously turned outward and expressed against others in the form of aggression. Other psychoanalysts argue that aggression results when we are blocked from reaching our goals. A person who experiences a great deal of frustration, perhaps someone who is constantly falling short of a desired goal, is a likely candidate for persistent aggressive behavior. In most cases, the person is unaware of the real reasons for the aggression.

Personality theorists who follow the trait approach focus on individual differences and the stability of aggressive behavior. For example, one team of researchers measured aggressiveness in eight-year-old children (Huesmann, Eron, & Yarmel, 1987). The investigators interviewed the participants again when the participants were 30 years old. The researchers discovered that the children identified as aggressive in elementary school were likely to have become aggressive adults. The children who pushed and shoved their classmates often grew into adults who abused their spouses and engaged in violent criminal behavior.

Personality psychologists from the biological perspective also are interested in stable patterns of aggressive behavior. They point to a genetic predisposition to act aggressively as one reason for this stability. Evidence now suggests that some people inherit more of a proclivity toward aggression than others (Miles & Carey, 1997). That is, some people may be born with aggressive dispositions that, depending on their upbringing, result in their becoming aggressive adults. Other psychologists explain aggression in terms of evolutionary theory (Cairns, 1986). For example, the fact that men tend to be more aggressive than women might be explained by the man's inherited need to exercise control over rivals in order to survive and pass along his genes. Still other researchers have implicated differences in testosterone level to explain aggressive behavior (DiLalla & Gottesman, 1991), although the evidence on this point is still uncertain (Geen, 1998).

Psychologists with a humanistic approach to personality explain aggressive behavior in yet another way. These theorists deny that some people are born to be aggressive. In fact, many argue that people are basically good. They believe all individuals can become happy, nonviolent adults if allowed to grow and develop in an enriching and encouraging environment. Problems develop when something interferes with this natural growth process. Aggressive children often come from homes in which basic needs are frustrated. If the child develops a poor self-image, he or she may strike out at others in frustration.

The behavioral /social learning approach contrasts in many ways with the humanistic view. According to these psychologists, people learn to be aggressive the same way they learn other behaviors. Playground bullies find that aggressive behavior is rewarded. They get to bat first and have first choice of playground equipment because other children fear them. The key to the behavioral interpretation is that rewarded behavior will be repeated. Thus, the playground bully probably will continue this aggressive behavior and try it in other situations. If the aggression is continually met with rewards instead of punishment, the result will be an aggressive adult.

People also learn from watching models. Children may learn from watching aggressive classmates that hurting others is sometimes useful. As discussed in Chapter 14, many people are concerned that the aggressive role models children routinely watch on television may be responsible for increasing the amount of violence in society.

Cognitive psychologists approach the question of aggressive behavior from yet another perspective. Their main focus is on the way aggressive people process information. To better understand this concept, imagine that you are walking alone through a park. Two teenage boys who are walking about 30 feet behind you suddenly quicken their pace and draw closer to you. What is your reaction? Perhaps the boys are in a hurry to get somewhere; perhaps they are simply more energetic and walk faster than you do. Maybe they are interested in catching up to you to ask you for the time or for directions to the library. Or maybe they want to harm you. This situation, like many we encounter, contains a fair degree of ambiguity, and people react to it differently.

Cognitive personality psychologists argue that how you respond to this situation depends on how you interpret it (Dill, Anderson, & Anderson, 1997; Zelli, Cervone, & Huesmann, 1996). Whether you see the circumstances as threatening, annoying, or benign will cause you to run away, prepare to fight, or move out of the way. The cognitive approach proposes that some people are more likely than others to interpret ambiguous situations as threatening. These people also are more likely to respond by acting aggressively. The cognitive approach can help us understand why some adolescent boys act more aggressively than others (Dodge & Crick, 1990; Hubbard, Dodge, Cillessen, Coie, & Schwartz, 2001). Researchers find that aggressive elementary school boys frequently interpret innocent actions by others as personally threatening (Dodge & Somberg, 1987; Lochman, 1987). An accidental bump in the hallway might be misinterpreted as an attempt to start a fight. It's not difficult to see why a boy who believes others are constantly threatening and challenging him would often respond aggressively.

Now, let's return to the original question: Why do some people show a consistent pattern of aggressive behavior? Each of the six approaches to personality offers a different explanation. Which is correct? One possibility is that only one is correct and that future research will identify that theory. A second possibility is that each approach is partially correct. There may be six (or more) different causes of aggressive behavior. Still a third possibility is that the six explanations do not contradict one another but rather differ only in their focus. That is, it's possible that aggressiveness is relatively stable and reflects an aggressive trait (the trait approach). But it might also be the case that some people tend to interpret ambiguous events as threatening (the cognitive explanation) because of past experiences in which they were assaulted (the behavioral/social learning explanation). These people may have been born with a tendency to respond to threats in an aggressive manner (the biological approach), but perhaps if they had been raised in a nonfrustrating environment (the psychoanalytic approach) or in a supportive home in which their basic needs were met (the humanistic approach), they would have overcome their aggressive tendencies. The point is that each approach appears to contribute something to our understanding of aggression.

Example 2: Depression. Most of us know what it is like to be depressed. We have all had days when we feel a little blue or melancholy. Like many college students, you may also have suffered through longer periods of intense sadness and a general lack of motivation to do anything. Although most of us fluctuate through changing moods and levels of interest and energy, some people seem more prone to depression than others. Once again, each of the six approaches to personality has a different explanation for depression.

According to Sigmund Freud, the founder of the psychoanalytic approach, depression is anger turned inward. That is, people suffering from depression hold unconscious feelings of anger and hostility. For example, they may want to strike

Photo courtesy of Emily Murphy

What causes depression? Depending on which approach to personality you adopt, you might explain depression in terms of anger turned inward, a stable trait, an inherited predisposition, low self-esteem, a lack of reinforcers, or negative thoughts.

out at family members. But a healthy personality does not express such feelings overtly. In addition, psychoanalysts argue that each of us has internalized the standards and values of society, which typically discourage the expression of hostility. Therefore, these angry feelings are turned inward, and people take it out on themselves. As with most psychoanalytic explanations, this takes place at an unconscious level.

Trait theorists are concerned with identifying depression-prone people. Researchers find that a person's general emotional level today is a very good indicator of that person's emotions, including depression, in the future. One team of investigators measured depression levels in a group of men when they were middle-aged and again 30 years later (Leon, Gillum, Gillum, & Gouze, 1979). The researchers found an impressively high correlation between the men's depression levels at the two different times. Yet another study found that depression levels in 18-year-olds could be predicted from looking at participants' behavior from as early as 7 years old (Block, Gjerde, & Block, 1991).

Biological personality psychologists point to evidence that some people may inherit a genetic susceptibility to depression (McGue & Christensen, 1997; Wender et al., 1986). A person born with this vulnerability faces a much greater likelihood than the average individual of reacting to stressful life events with depression. Because of this inherited tendency, some of these people experience repeated bouts of depression throughout their lives.

Humanistic personality theorists explain depression in terms of self-esteem. That is, people who frequently suffer from depression are those who have failed to develop a good sense of their self-worth. A person's level of self-esteem is established while growing up and, like other personality concepts, is fairly stable across time and situations. The ability to accept oneself, even one's faults and weaknesses, is an important goal for humanistic therapists when dealing with clients suffering from depression.

The behavioral/social learning approach examines the type of learning history that leads to depression. Behaviorists argue that depression results from a lack of positive reinforcers in a person's life. That is, you may feel down and unmotivated because you see few activities in your life worth doing. A more extensive behavioral model of depression, covered in Chapter 14, proposes that depression develops from experiences with aversive situations over which people have little control. This theory maintains that exposure to uncontrollable events creates a perception of helplessness that is generalized to other situations and may develop into classic symptoms of depression.

Some cognitive personality psychologists have taken this explanation one step further. These psychologists argue that whether people become depressed depends on how they interpret their inability to control events. For example, people who attribute their inability to get a promotion to a temporary economic recession will not become as depressed as people who believe it is the result of personal inadequacies. Other cognitive psychologists propose that we use something like a depressive filter to interpret and process information. That is, depressed people are prepared to see the world in the most depressing terms possible. For this reason, depressed people can easily recall depressing experiences. People and places they encounter are likely to remind them of some sad or unpleasant time. In short, people become depressed because they are prepared to generate depressing thoughts.

Which of these accounts of depression strikes you as the most accurate? If you have been depressed, was it because of your low self-esteem, because you experienced an uncontrollable situation, or because you tend to look at the world through depressing lenses? As in the aggression example, more than one of these approaches may be correct. You may have found that one theory could explain an experience you had with depression last year, whereas another seems to better account for a more recent bout. In addition, the theories can at times complement one another. For example, people might interpret events in a depressing way because of their low self-esteem.

One more lesson can be taken from these two examples: You need not align yourself with the same approach to personality when explaining different phenomena. For example, you may have found that the cognitive explanation for aggression made the most sense to you, but that the humanistic approach provided the best account of depression. This observation demonstrates the main point of this section: Each of the six approaches has something to offer the student interested in understanding personality.

Personality and Culture

Psychologists have recently recognized the important role culture plays in understanding personality. To some students, this observation at first seems inconsistent with the notion of personality as distinct from situational influences on behavior. However, personality psychologists in Western developed countries increasingly recognize that many of the assumptions underlying the way we describe and study personality may not apply when dealing with people from different cultures (Church, 2001; Kanagawa, Cross, & Markus, 2001; Kitayama & Markus, 1994). It is not just that different experiences in different cultures affect how personalities develop. Rather, psychologists have come to see that people and their personalities exist within a cultural context.

Perhaps the most important distinction cross-cultural researchers make is between individualistic cultures and collectivist cultures (Triandis, 1989, 2001). **Individualistic cultures,** which include most Northern European countries and the United States, place great emphasis on individual needs and accomplishments. People in these cultures like to think of themselves as independent and unique. In contrast, people in **collectivist cultures** are more concerned about belonging to a larger group, such as a family, tribe, or nation. These people are more interested in cooperation than competition. They obtain satisfaction when the group does well rather than from individual accomplishments. Many Asian, African, Central American, and South American countries fit the collectivist culture description. Consequently, concepts commonly studied by Western personality psychologists often take on very different meanings when people from collectivist cultures are studied. For example, research reviewed in Chapter 12 suggests that the Western notion of self-esteem is based on assumptions about personal goals and feelings of uniqueness that may not make sense to citizens of other countries (Markus & Kitayama, 1991).

Moreover, the kinds of behaviors examined in personality research can take on different meanings depending on the culture. For example, for many years personality psychologists have been concerned with achievement behavior. Traditionally, this means trying to predict which individuals will get ahead in academic or business situations. However, this definition of achievement and success is not shared universally (Salili, 1994). In some collectivist cultures, success means cooperation and group accomplishments. Personal recognition may even be frowned upon by people living in these cultures. Similarly, we need to consider the culture a person comes from when identifying and treating psychological disorders (Fischer, Jome, & Atkinson, 1998; Lewis-Fernandez & Kleinman, 1994; Okazaki, 1997). For example, behavior that suggests excessive dependency or exaggerated egotism in one culture might reflect good adjustment in another.

Thus, it is worth remembering that most of the theories and much of the research covered in this book are based on observations in individualistic cultures. In fact, most of the research was conducted in the United States, the country that was found to be the most individualistic of 41 nations examined in one study (Suh, Diener, Oishi, & Triandis, 1998). This does not mean the research findings should be dismissed. Rather, we should keep in mind that whether a particular description applies to people in all cultures remains an open question. In some cases, such as the research on dream content presented in Chapter 4 and the studies on marriage patterns presented in Chapter 10, investigators find nearly identical results across very different cultural groups. In other cases, such as in the self-esteem and achievement examples, they find important differences between cultures. Identifying the cultural limitations or universality of various phenomena provides additional insight into the nature of the concepts we study.

The Study of Personality: Theory, Application, Assessment, and Research

"*There can scarcely be anything more familiar than human behavior. Nor can there be anything more important. Nonetheless, it is certainly not the thing we understand best.*"

B. F. SKINNER

If you spend a few minutes looking through the table of contents at the beginning of this book, you will notice that the book is divided into sections. Each section presents one of the different approaches to personality. Each of these sections is divided into four parts (in two chapters). These divisions represent the four components necessary for a complete understanding of personality. We begin each section with a presentation of *theory*. Each of the personality theorists covered in these pages presents a comprehensive model for how human personality is structured and how it operates. But psychologists have never been content to simply describe personality. Rather, we have a long history of applying the information we gain from theories and research to questions and issues that directly affect people's lives. These *applications* include psychotherapy, education, and behavior in the workplace. An example of how psychologists apply their theories to these settings is presented for each approach. Psychologists working within each of the approaches also must develop ways to measure the personality constructs they study and use. Thus, *assessment* is another important area of personality psychology covered within each approach. Examples of personality assessment procedures are scattered throughout this book. If you take the time to try each of these inventories, not only will you obtain a better understanding of how psychologists from the different approaches measure personality, but you will also gain insight into your own personality. In addition, within each section, an entire chapter is devoted to *research* relevant to that approach to personality. Personality psychology is, after all, a science. By examining a few research topics in depth for each of the approaches, you will see how theories generate research and how the findings from one study typically lead to new questions and more research.

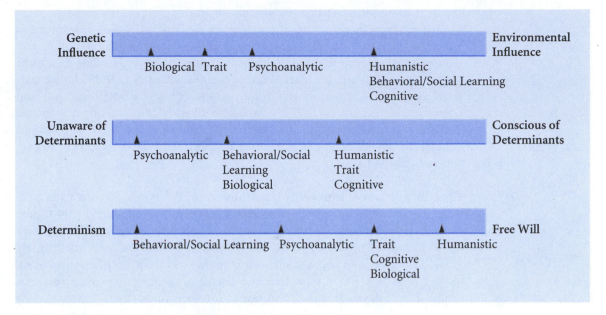

Figure 1.1
Position of the Six Approaches to Personality on Three Theory Issues

Theory

Each approach to understanding personality begins with a theory. This theory usually comes from the writings of several important psychologists who provide their own descriptions of consistent patterns of behavior and intrapersonal processes. They explain the mechanisms that underlie human personality and how these mechanisms are responsible for creating behaviors unique to a given individual. In most cases, theorists also attempt to explain how differences in personality develop. Many also describe methods for changing personality based on their theories.

Although each theory tends to emphasize a different aspect of personality, each theorist must wrestle with several issues when describing the nature of human personality. A few of these issues are introduced in the following sections. The way theorists from each of the six approaches generally deal with these issues is diagrammed in Figure 1.1.

Genetic Versus Environmental Influences. Are people born with the seeds for their adult personalities already intact? Or are they born with no inherited personality orientation, with each healthy baby just as likely as any other to become a great humanitarian, a criminal, a leader, or a helpless psychotic? Naturally, there is plenty of room for opinions in between these two views. But most personality theorists address this question: To what extent are our personalities the result of inherited predispositions, and to what extent are they shaped by the environment in which we grow up? Many biological and trait theorists argue that too often psychologists fail to recognize the importance of inherited predispositions. To a lesser degree, psychoanalytic theorists also emphasize innate needs and behavior patterns, albeit unconscious. However, humanistic, behavioral/social learning, and cognitive theorists are less likely to emphasize inherited influences on personality. To some extent, the answer to this question is an empirical one. A growing amount of research implicates at least some inherited factors in the development of personality (Chapter 10).

Conscious Versus Unconscious Determinants of Behavior. To what extent are people aware of the causes of their behavior? Psychoanalyst Sigmund Freud argued that much of what we do is under the control of unconscious forces, those that by definition we are not aware of. B.F. Skinner, an influential behavior theorist, argued that people assume they understand the reasons for their actions, when in reality they do not. In contrast, trait and cognitive theorists rely heavily on self-report data in developing their theories and in their research. For example, they assume people can identify and report their level of social anxiety or how they organize information in their minds. However, these psychologists hedge away from an extreme position on this issue. Increasingly, cognitive psychologists recognize that much information processing takes place at a level below awareness. Humanistic theorists often take a middle-ground position on this issue. Although these theorists argue that no one knows us better than ourselves, they also acknowledge that many people do not understand why they act the way they do.

Free Will Versus Determinism. To what extent do we decide our own fate, and to what extent are our behaviors determined by forces outside our control? This is an old issue in psychology that has spilled over from even older discussions in philosophy and theology. On one extreme we find theorists from the behavioral/ social learning approach called radical behaviorists. Perhaps most outspoken on this issue was B. F. Skinner, who argued that our behavior is not freely chosen but rather the direct result of the environmental stimuli to which we have been exposed. Skinner called freedom a myth. Psychoanalytic theorists typically take a less extreme position but still emphasize innate needs and unconscious mechanisms that leave much of human behavior outside of our control. At the other end of the spectrum are the humanistic theorists, who often identify personal choice and responsibility as the cornerstones of mental health. Humanistic psychotherapists frequently encourage clients to recognize the extent to which they are responsible for their own lives.

Although less clear on this issue, trait, biological, and cognitive theorists probably fall somewhere between these others. Trait theorists and biological theorists often emphasize genetic predispositions that tend to limit development in certain areas. But none of these psychologists would argue that personality is completely dictated by these predispositions. Similarly, cognitive psychotherapists often encourage their clients to recognize how they cause many of their own problems and help them to develop strategies to avoid future difficulties.

Application

The most obvious way personality psychologists use their theories to address personal and social needs is through psychotherapy. Many of the major personality theorists were also therapists who developed and refined their ideas about human personality as they worked with clients. Psychotherapy comes in many different styles, each reflecting assumptions the therapist makes about the nature of personality. For example, psychoanalytic therapists attend to unconscious causes of the problem behavior. Humanistic therapists are more likely to work in a nondirective manner to provide the proper atmosphere in which clients can explore their own feelings. Cognitive therapists try to change the way their clients process information, whereas behaviorists typically structure the environment so that desired behaviors increase in frequency and undesired behaviors decrease. Personality theory and research are also used by psychologists working in educational, organizational, and counseling settings. In the following chapters, you will see what personality theorists have said about religion, effective teaching, and choosing a career.

Assessment

How psychologists measure personality depends on which of the six approaches they adhere to. For example, many personality researchers commonly use self-report inventories, in which test takers answer a series of questions about themselves. But psychoanalytic psychologists are more interested in what people are unable to describe directly. They learn about some of these unconscious thoughts by asking test takers to respond to ambiguous stimuli, which a trained psychologist then interprets. Traditional behavioral psychologists often take another tactic in assessing personality. They're not interested in structures and concepts that supposedly exist within peoples' minds. To determine consistent behavior patterns, these psychologists observe behavior. For example, behavioral psychologists who want to measure cooperation might observe people working on a group task. A person who engages in a large number of cooperative behaviors (for example, helping others in the group, complimenting others on their work, and so on) would be identified as a cooperative person. In short, how a psychologist measures personality depends on what he or she thinks personality is.

"Everyone else probably understands us better than we do ourselves."
CARL JUNG

Research

Although the focus thus far has been on the differences among the six approaches, one feature they all have in common is that each generates a great deal of relevant research. As you will see, sometimes this research tests principles and assumptions

It's difficult to make it through college without taking a personality test somewhere along the way. One reason that self-report inventories are frequently used in personality research can be seen here—researchers can quickly collect information from a large number of people.

central to the theory. Other times researchers are interested in further exploring some of the concepts introduced by a personality theory. Several psychology journals are devoted to publishing research on personality, and many more publish articles relevant to the topics examined in this book. The topics that interest personality researchers fluctuate as new theories are introduced, and new findings stimulate additional studies (Sherman, Buddie, Dragan, End, & Finney, 1999).

Psychology researchers employ a large number of methods in their efforts to uncover information about personality (Craik, 1986; Endler & Speer, 1998; Mallon, Kingsley, Affleck, & Tennen, 1998). You won't need a complete understanding of these procedures to appreciate the research covered in this book. But it will help if you have a grasp of the hypothesis-testing approach and a few of the common procedures used by personality researchers. These topics are addressed in the next chapter.

 ## *Summary*

1.   Personality psychology is concerned with the differences among people. Although there is no agreed-upon definition, personality is defined here as consistent behavior patterns and intrapersonal processes originating within the individual.

2.   For convenience, the many theories of personality are divided into six general categories: the psychoanalytic, trait, biological, humanistic, behavioral/social learning, and cognitive approaches. Each approach provides a different focus for explaining individual differences in behavior. The six approaches can be thought of as complementary models for understanding human personality, although occasionally they present competing accounts of behavior.

3.   In recent years, personality psychologists have become aware of the need to consider the culture an individual comes from. Most of the findings reported in this book are based on research in individualistic cultures, such as the United States. However, these results don't always generalize to people in collectivist cultures.

4.   A thorough understanding of human personality requires more than the study of theory. Consequently, we'll also examine how each of the approaches is applied to practical concerns, how each deals with personality assessment, and some of the research relevant to the issues and topics addressed by the theories.

InfoTrac Key Terms

For additional readings go to http://www.infotrac-college.com/wadsworth and enter a search term related to your interest. Use the key terms suggested here to pull up several related articles. Also see the text Web site at http://psychology.wadsworth.com for more suggested readings and interactive quizzes to test your knowledge.

Behavioral/social learning approach
Collectivist culture
Determinism
Free will

Individualistic culture
Personality
Psychoanalysis

Chapter 2

Personality Research Methods

The Hypothesis-Testing Approach
The Case Study Method
Statistical Analysis of Data
Personality Assessment
Summary

Not long ago, "Desperate in Dallas" wrote to a newspaper advice columnist about her husband's 16-year-old cousin, who was living with them. The boy didn't want to work, didn't want to go to school, and generally was a very messy houseguest. What was she to do? The columnist explained to "Desperate" that the boy's real problem was the rejection he had received from his parents earlier in his life. These early childhood experiences were responsible for the boy's lack of motivation. Within the next few weeks, the advisor also explained to "Wondering in Boston" that a five-year-old boy became aggressive from watching too many violent programs on television. She told "Anonymous in Houston" that her five-year-old daughter was going to be a leader, and "Intrigued in Norfolk" that, although some people are routinely incapacitated with minor aches and pains, others are capable of ignoring them.

In each of these examples, the columnist was explaining why a certain person engages in consistent behavior patterns—that is, the causes of that person's personality. Millions of people seem to think this columnist has something to say about human behavior. But how does she know? Experience? Intelligence? A keen insight into human nature? Perhaps. In a way, advice columnists represent one avenue for understanding personality—through expert opinion. In some ways, the columnist is similar to the great personality theorists who study the works of others, make their own observations, and then explain what they believe are the causes of the phenomena they study. For example, as you will see in the next chapter, Sigmund Freud proposed many groundbreaking ideas about personality. Freud read widely about what his contemporaries were saying about human behavior. He worked and consulted with some of the great thinkers of the day who also were concerned about psychological phenomena. Freud also carefully observed his patients, who came to him with a variety of psychological problems. From the information gathered from all of these sources, Freud developed a new conception of human personality that he spent the rest of his career promoting.

Although more scholarly and rigorous than a columnist's one-paragraph diagnoses, Freud's writings often evoke a similar response: How does he know? Freud's ideas are intriguing, and his arguments at times persuasive, but most personality psychologists want more than an expert's viewpoint before they accept a personality theory. They want empirical research. They want studies examining key predictions from the theory. They want some hard numbers providing strong evidence in support of the theory. This is not because an expert's views are of no value. Quite the contrary, the views and observations of personality theorists form the backbone of this book. But theories alone provide only part of the picture. Understanding the nature of human personality also requires an examination of what psychologists have learned from rigorous empirical investigations.

This chapter presents a brief introduction to personality research. We begin with a description of some basic concepts associated with the hypothesis-testing approach to research, with an emphasis on issues particularly relevant for personality researchers. Then we look at a research procedure that has played a significant role in the history of personality psychology—the case study method. Next, we briefly touch on what you will need to know about statistical analysis of data. Finally, because personality psychologists often rely on personality assessment, we quickly review some of the concepts associated with measuring individual differences in personality.

The Hypothesis-Testing Approach

Each of us on occasion speculates about the nature of personality. You may have wondered why you seem to be more self-conscious than others, why a friend seems to be depressed so often, or why you have so much trouble making friends when doing this comes so easily to others. In the latter case, you may have watched the way a popular student interacts with people she meets and compared her behavior with the way you act around strangers. If you are like most people, you may have even tried to change your behavior to be more like hers and then watched to see if this affected how people reacted to you.

In essence, the difference between this process and that used by personality psychologists lies only in the degree of sophistication. Like all of us, personality researchers speculate about the nature of personality. From observations, knowledge about previous theory and research, and careful speculation, these researchers generate hypotheses about why certain people behave the way they do. Then, using rigorous experimental methods, investigators collect data to see if their explanations about human behavior are correct. Like pieces in a large jigsaw puzzle, each study makes another contribution to our understanding of personality. However, by the time you get to the end of this book, it should be clear that this is one puzzle that will never be finished.

Theories and Hypotheses

Most personality research begins with a **theory**—a general statement about the relationship between constructs or events. Theories differ in the range of events or phenomena they explain. Some, such as the major personality theories discussed in this book, are very broad. For example, psychologists have used Freud's psychoanalytic theory to explain topics as diverse as what causes psychological disorders, why people turn to religion, and why certain jokes are funny. However, personality researchers typically work with theories considerably narrower in application. For example, they might be concerned with the reasons some people are more motivated to achieve than others or with the relationship between a parent's behavior and a child's level of self-esteem. It might be useful to think of the larger theories, such as Freud's, as collections of more specific theories that share certain assumptions about the nature of human personality.

A good theory possesses at least two characteristics. First, a good theory is *parsimonious.* Scientists generally operate under the "law of parsimony"—that is, the simplest theory that can explain the phenomenon is the best one. As you will see throughout this book, several theories can be generated to explain any one behavior. Some can be quite extensive, including many concepts and assumptions, whereas others explain the phenomenon in relatively simple terms. Which theory is better? Although it sometimes seems that scientists enjoy wrapping their work in fancy terms and esoteric concepts, the truth is that if two theories can account for the phenomenon equally well, the simpler explanation is preferred.

Second, a good theory is *useful.* More specifically, unless a theory can generate testable hypotheses, it will be of little or no use to scientists. Ideas that cannot be tested are not necessarily incorrect. It's just that they do not lend themselves to scientific investigation. For example, throughout history people have explained psychological disorders in terms of invisible demons taking over a person's body. This may or may not be a correct statement about the causes of disorders. But unless this explanation is somehow testable, the theory cannot be examined through scientific methods and therefore holds little value for scientists.

However, theories themselves are never tested. Instead, investigators derive from the theory hypotheses that can then be tested in research. A **hypothesis** is a formal prediction about the relationship between two or more variables that is logically derived from the theory. Let's illustrate this with an example. As discussed in Chapter 12, many psychologists are interested in individual differences in loneliness. That is, they want to know why some people frequently suffer from feelings

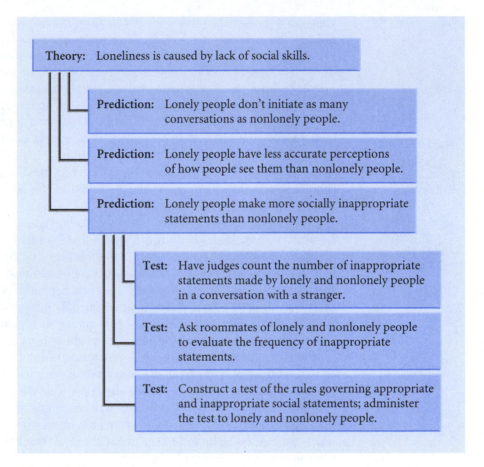

Figure 2.1

Example of the Hypothesis-Testing Approach

of loneliness, whereas others rarely feel lonely. One theory proposes that lonely people lack the social skills necessary to develop and maintain satisfying relationships. Because this is a useful theory, many predictions can be logically derived from it, as shown in Figure 2.1. For example, if the theory correctly describes a cause of loneliness, we might expect consistently lonely people to make fewer attempts to initiate conversations than those who are not lonely. Another prediction might be that these lonely people have a poor idea of how they are being perceived by others. Yet another prediction might maintain that lonely people make more socially inappropriate statements than nonlonely people when they do engage in conversations.

Each of these predictions can be tested. For example, we might test the last prediction by recording conversations lonely and nonlonely people have with new acquaintances. Judges could evaluate the conversations in terms of number of appropriate responses, number of appropriate questions, and so on. If people who identify themselves as lonely make fewer appropriate responses during the conversation, the prediction is confirmed. We then say we have support for the theory. But notice that the theory itself is not tested directly. In fact, theories are never proved or disproved. Rather, a theory is more or less supported by the research and therefore is more or less useful to scientists trying to understand the phenomenon. The more often research confirms a prediction derived from a theory, the more faith psychologists have that the theory is accurately describing the nature of things. However, if empirical investigations consistently fail to confirm predictions, we are much less likely to accept the theory. In these cases, scientists typically generate a new theory or modify the old one to better account for the research findings.

One aspect of hypothesis testing needs to be highlighted here. Most of the research reported in this book began with a theory from which predictions were derived and tested. However, not all research operates this way. Beginning researchers are sometimes tempted to start this process from the bottom, making specific predictions about how one variable affects another without any theoretical reason for why the variables might be related. For example, you might observe while jogging one day that you feel less pain and exhaustion on the days you think about something other than jogging. This might spawn the prediction that running while thinking about something distracting makes the running more bearable. You might even design an experiment in which some people jog while concentrating on their running, whereas others jog while solving math problems in their heads. But even if your prediction were confirmed, what would this tell you? The information might be of some value to runners. However, without a larger theory you would be unable to say much about human behavior outside of this situation.

But suppose you began your research with a theory concerning the relationship between the focus of attention and the impact of stressors. One prediction derived from this theory might be that distraction during physical exertion makes the effort less painful. This prediction could be tested with the running study just described. The results from the study might confirm the prediction and give support to the larger theory. In addition, predictions might be derived from this theory concerning the use of defense mechanisms to deal with anxiety, or how hypnosis helps people overcome pain, or why certain exercises help women reduce the discomfort of childbirth.

This is not to say that atheoretical research is meaningless. Many times psychologists working in applied areas are interested in understanding specific behaviors in specific situations. For example, market researchers may want to know if people are more likely to buy an orange box or a blue box of detergent. However, even in this case, the researchers will be better able to apply their findings to other products if they begin with a theory about how colors are related to emotions.

Many personality researchers conduct laboratory studies to test their hypotheses. These investigations typically take place in university settings, often with under-graduate students as participants and graduate students as experimenters.

Experimental Variables

Good research progresses from theory to prediction to experiment. The basic elements of an experiment are the experimental variables, which are divided into two types: independent variables and dependent variables. An **independent variable** determines how the groups in the experiment are divided. Often, this is manipulated by the experimenter, such as when participants are randomly assigned to different experimental conditions. An independent variable might be the amount of a drug each group receives, how much anxiety is created in each group, or the type of story each group reads. For example, if level of anxiety is the independent variable, a researcher might tell Group A that they will give a speech in front of a dozen critical people, Group B that they will give a speech in front of a few supportive people, and Group C nothing about a speech. Because each of the groups created by the independent variable receives a slightly different treatment, some researchers refer to the independent variable as the *treatment* variable.

A **dependent variable** is measured by the investigator and used to compare the experimental groups. In a well-designed study, differences among groups on the dependent variable can be attributed to the different levels of the independent variable. Returning to the anxiety example, suppose the researcher's hypothesis was that people reduce anxiety about upcoming events by obtaining as much information about the situation as possible. The researcher might use level of anxiety as the independent variable, creating high-, moderate-, and low-anxiety conditions. The three groups might be compared on how many questions they ask the experimenter about the upcoming event. In this case, the number of questions is the dependent variable. The results of such an experiment might look like this:

	High Anxiety	Moderate Anxiety	Low Anxiety
Average number of questions	5.44	3.12	1.88

If the experiment has been designed correctly, the investigator will attribute the difference in the dependent variable (the number of questions) to the different levels of the independent variable (anxiety). Because experimenters want to say that differences in the dependent variable are the result of the different treatment each of the groups received, some researchers refer to the dependent variable as the *outcome* variable.

However, most personality research is more elaborate than this example indicates. Researchers typically use more than one independent variable. In the information-seeking example, an experimenter might want to further divide participants into groups according to how shy they typically are. The researcher might predict that anxiety leads to a search for information, but only among people who are not shy. Shy people don't turn to others as a means of alleviating their anxiety. Researchers in this hypothetical study might use two independent variables to divide participants into groups. They might randomly assign participants to either an anxiety (anticipates speech) or a no-anxiety group, and within each of these groups identify those who are shy and those who are not. If the dependent variable remains the number of questions asked of the experimenter, the results might turn out like those shown in Figure 2.2. This figure illustrates what is called an **interaction.** That is, how one independent variable affects the dependent variable depends on the other independent variable. In this example, whether anxiety leads to an increase in questions depends on whether the participant is high or low in shyness.

Manipulated Versus Nonmanipulated Independent Variables

Sometimes personality researchers randomly assign participants to conditions, such as putting them into anxiety or no-anxiety groups. However, other times they simply identify which group the participant already belongs to, such as whether the person is shy or not shy. The significance of this difference is illustrated in the following example.

Suppose you are interested in the effect violent television programs have on the amount of aggression people display in real life. You recruit two kinds of participants—those who watch a lot of violent TV shows and those who watch relatively few. You then measure the participants' level of aggression in a number of situations. Consistent with the hypothesis, you find people who watch a lot of violent television are more aggressive than those who watch relatively little violent TV. You might be tempted to conclude that watching violent television programs

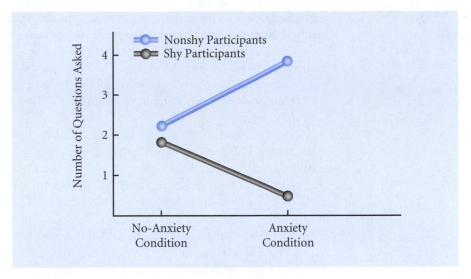

Figure 2.2

An Interaction Between Two Independent Variables

causes people to be more aggressive. However, based on this study alone, such a conclusion must be tempered. For example, it's possible that these people watch violent TV shows precisely because they are aggressive. Perhaps they are more entertained by programs that include shootings, stabbings, and other violent acts. Thus, although the findings are consistent with the hypothesis, statements about cause-and-effect relationships must be qualified.

This example illustrates the fundamental difference between research using manipulated independent variables and research using nonmanipulated independent variables. An investigator who uses a **manipulated independent variable** begins with a large number of participants and randomly assigns them to experimental groups. That is, each person has an equally likely chance of being assigned to Condition A as to Condition B (or C, or D, and so on). Investigators know all participants are not exactly alike at the beginning of the study. Some are naturally more aggressive than others, some more anxious, some more intelligent. Each has different life experiences that might affect what he or she does in the study. However, by using a large number of participants and randomly assigning them to conditions, researchers assume that all of these differences will be evened out. Thus, although within any given condition there are people who are typically high or low in aggressiveness, each condition should have the same *average* level of aggressiveness at the beginning of the experiment.

The researcher then introduces the independent variable. For example, one group might be shown 30 minutes of violent television programming, another group might watch a baseball game, and still another group might sit quietly and watch no television. Because we assume participants in each condition are nearly identical on average at the start of the study, any differences among the groups *after* watching the program can be attributed to the independent variable. That is, if participants who watched the violent TV shows are more aggressive than those who watched the nonviolent shows or those who watched no TV, we have confidence in concluding that watching the violent TV shows *caused* the participants to act more aggressively.

This procedure contrasts with the use of nonmanipulated variables. A **nonmanipulated independent variable** (sometimes referred to as a *subject variable*) exists without the researcher's intervention. For example, researchers might divide people into high self-esteem and low self-esteem groups, or into first-born, middle-born, or last-born categories. In these cases, the investigator does not randomly assign participants to a condition. Returning to the earlier example, the researcher who compared frequent and infrequent television viewers did not manipulate participants into those two categories. Instead, the participants had already determined which of the groups they belonged to without any action on the researcher's part.

The difficulty with this and other nonmanipulated independent variables is that the researcher cannot assume the people in the two groups are nearly identical on average at the beginning of the experiment. For example, people who watch relatively little television might be more intelligent or come from a higher socioeconomic level. We can be fairly certain that they have more time for activities besides television, such as reading or interacting with friends. The two kinds of participants also might differ in terms of self-esteem, diet, and most notably, their level of aggression prior to participating in the experiment. Thus, any differences we find between the two groups could be caused by any of these differences, and not necessarily by the number of violent TV shows each group watches.

Because it is difficult to determine cause-and-effect relationships with nonmanipulated independent variables, researchers generally prefer to manipulate variables. However, doing so is not always possible. Sometimes manipulating the variable is too expensive, too difficult, or unethical. This is a particular problem in personality research because many of the variables researchers want to study simply cannot be manipulated. Returning to the violent television example, it would be next to impossible to tell some participants, "You watch a lot of violent television during the next few years," and tell others, "You watch no violent television until I tell you it's okay." Instead, if we want to know about the long-term effects of exposure to violent TV, we have to accept the participants as they are, understanding that many group differences exist at the outset of the study. Sometimes investigators try to control some of these known differences, such as by comparing the education levels of the two groups. However, researchers can never be sure that they have controlled all relevant variables.

This is not to say that research with nonmanipulated independent variables is useless. On the contrary, personality psychologists often find that relying on nonmanipulated variables is the only way to examine a topic of interest. How else can we study the differences between introverts and extraverts or differences between men and women? Much of what we know of personality comes from such research. Nonetheless, investigators who conduct this research must remain cautious when making statements about cause-and-effect relationships.

Prediction Versus Hindsight

Which person do you find more impressive: the one who can explain *after* a basketball game why the winning team was victorious, or the one who accurately tells you *before* the game which team will win and why? Most of us are more impressed with the second person. After all, anyone can come up with an explanation after the facts are in. But people who really understand the game can make reasonable guesses about what will happen when two teams meet.

In a similar manner, if a scientist has a legitimate theory, we can expect him or her to make reasonably accurate predictions of what will happen in a study before the data are in. Remember, the purpose of research is to provide support for a hypothesis. Researchers generate a theory, make a hypothesis, and collect data that either support or do not support the hypothesis. Suppose a researcher examines the relationship between self-esteem and helping behavior, but the investigator has no clear prediction beforehand of what this relationship might be. If the study finds that high self-esteem people help more than low self-esteem people, the researcher might conclude that this is because people who feel good about themselves maintain that positive evaluation by doing good things. The explanation sounds reasonable, but in this case do the data support the hypothesis? From a scientific standpoint, the answer is no because the hypothesis was generated *after* the results were seen. With that sequence, there is no way the hypothesis would not be supported. If the study found that low self-esteem people help more, the same researcher might conclude that this is because these people are trying to improve their self-image by doing good things. With no possibility that the hypothesis might not be supported, the hypothesis has not really been tested.

This is not to say researchers should ignore findings they haven't predicted. On the contrary, such findings are often the basis for future hypotheses and further research. But explaining everything after the results are in explains nothing. You can hear examples of this problem at the close of the stock market each day. If the president of the United States gives a speech and the stock market goes down, analysts tell us it was because of the speech. However, if the stock market goes up, no doubt the analysts would attribute the rise to the speech as well.

Replication

When investigators conduct a well-designed study and uncover statistically significant results, they usually report the findings in a journal or perhaps at a professional conference. Sometimes the findings are cited as something researchers *know* about the topic they investigate. But psychologists are becoming increasingly cautious of relying on one research finding when drawing conclusions about human behavior.

There are many reasons a researcher might find a statistically significant effect in a given study. There could be something peculiar about the people in the sample. There might be something special about the time the research was conducted—perhaps an unusual mood in the country or on campus, caused by an important event. Or the finding could be the result of some unknown and inadvertent aspect of the particular experimental procedure. Whatever the reason, it is dangerous to assume that a significant finding from one study provides reliable evidence of a phenomenon.

The way to deal with this problem is **replication.** The more often an effect is found in research, the more confidence we have that it reflects a genuine relationship. Replications often examine participant populations different from those used in the original research. This helps to determine whether the effect applies to a larger number of people or is limited to the kind of individuals used in the original sample. Yet determining the strength of an effect by how often it is replicated is not always easy. One difficulty has been called the "File Drawer" problem (Rosenthal, 1979). That is, investigators tend to publish and report research only when they find significant effects. When an attempt at replication fails, the researcher may decide something has gone wrong—perhaps the wrong materials were used, perhaps something was not done the way the original researcher did it, and so on. And so the research is stored away in a file drawer and never reported. The result is that a well-known research finding may, in fact, be difficult to replicate. But because the failures at replication are stored away in file drawers, we might not realize the problem exists.

The Case Study Method

Like a carpenter or a physician, personality researchers must use many different tools to be effective in their job. Although most personality psychologists rely on empirical studies with large numbers of participants to test their ideas, there are other ways to examine individual differences and personality processes. One procedure occasionally used by personality researchers is the **case study method,** an in-depth evaluation of a single individual (or sometimes a few individuals). Most typically, the participant in a case study is a psychotherapy client suffering from a problem of interest to the investigator. The researcher records in great detail the person's history, current behavior, and changes in behavior over the course of the investigation, which often lasts for years. Case study data are usually descriptive. That is, rather than reporting a lot of numbers and statistical analyses, investigators describe their impressions of what the person did and what the behavior means. Researchers occasionally include quantitative assessments, such as recording how many times the person washes his or her hands in a 24-hour period. However, numbers from another group or from another person with which to compare these data are rarely reported.

As you will see throughout this book, case studies have played an important role in the history of personality psychology. Sigmund Freud relied almost exclusively on his own in-depth analysis of patients when formulating ideas about personality. In fact, many of Freud's initial insights into the functions of the human mind came from his observations of one early patient, Anna O., whose story is told in Chapter 3. Gordon Allport, the first psychologist to promote the concept of traits, argued that we cannot capture the essence of a whole personality without an in-depth analysis of a single individual. Humanistic theorists, most notably Carl Rogers, developed their unique concept of human nature through the extensive evaluation of psychotherapy clients. Behaviorists also sometimes rely on case studies to illustrate various aspects of their theories and the effectiveness of their therapies. For example, in Chapter 13, we will review John B. Watson's work with an orphaned infant named "Little Albert." This famous case study has been widely cited as evidence for the behaviorist explanation of abnormal behaviors.

Limitations of the Case Study Method

The widespread use of the case study method by prominent psychologists may surprise you at first, given some of the obvious weaknesses of this method. First is the problem of generalizing from any one case to other people. Just because one person reacts to events in a certain way does not mean all people do. In fact, many case study participants come to the attention of personality theorists when they seek out psychotherapy, often because they feel different from others. One reason researchers randomly assign many people to conditions in their studies is to eliminate the bias that comes from examining just a few people who may or may not represent a larger population.

Second is the problem of determining cause-and-effect relationships with the case study method. For example, a client with a fear of water may recall a traumatic experience of nearly drowning as a child. Although we can speculate that this earlier event is responsible for the fear, we cannot be certain that the fear wouldn't have developed without the experience. For this reason, researchers using case studies must be cautious when speculating about the causes of the behaviors they see.

Third, investigators' subjective judgments can often interfere with scientific objectivity in case study work. The expectancies researchers bring to a case study may cause them to see that which confirms their hypotheses and to overlook that which does not. It's possible that a different psychologist working with the same individual might come to different conclusions. As you will see in the next chapter, Freud in particular has been criticized for approaching his cases with his own biases.

Strengths of the Case Study Method

With all these weaknesses, why do personality researchers occasionally use the case study method? One reason is that many personality concepts are not easily examined with other methods. For example, Freud's concern with the deeper understanding of an individual's unconscious mind is not easily examined in other ways. The richness of a single person's life can be lost when he or she is reduced to a few numbers that are then added to other participant's numbers. This was one reason a team of researchers conducted a case study on Dodge Morgan, who at age 54 sailed around the globe by himself (Nasby & Read, 1997). The detailed analysis of Morgan's behavior and personality provides insights and an appreciation unavailable through other methods. The case study method is also valuable for generating hypotheses about the nature of human personality. Researchers sometimes follow up case studies with more traditional scientific investigations.

The case study method is a particularly useful research tool in at least four situations. It is the most appropriate method when examining a rare case. Suppose you wanted to investigate the personalities of political assassins. You probably would be limited to exploring the background and perhaps current behavior of only a handful of people who fall into this category. Similarly, therapists working with patients described as having multiple personalities often report their observations in a case study manner when recording information about what is probably a once-in-a-lifetime encounter.

The case study method is also appropriate when the researcher can argue that the individual being studied is essentially no different from all normal people on the dimension of interest. For example, case studies of "split-brain" patients have uncovered important information about the functioning of the human brain. Participants in these studies have had the corpus callosum (which connects the right and left halves of the cerebral hemisphere) severed as part of treatment for severe epilepsy. Because the physical functions of the brain are basically alike for all normally functioning people, studying the behavior of these few patients tells us much about the way our right and left brains would operate if not connected by the corpus callosum.

Still another appropriate use of the case study is to illustrate a treatment. Therapists often describe in detail the procedures they used to treat a particular client and the apparent success or failure of the therapy. A prudent therapist will not argue that all people suffering from the disorder should be treated in this way but rather will use the case study to suggest treatment programs other therapists might explore with their clients. A therapy procedure is most effectively demonstrated when the client's progress is compared at various stages of the treatment, such as comparing a no-treatment period with a treatment stage.

Finally, an investigator might choose the case study method simply to demonstrate possibilities. For example, a researcher using one or two easily hypnotizable people might demonstrate impressive changes in behavior. Some deeply hypnotizable people have been reported to change skin temperature on one part of the body but not on another or form blisters on their hands when imagining their hands are on fire. These studies are not intended to argue that all people are able to do these things but rather to illustrate some of the possibilities obtainable with hypnosis.

Statistical Analysis of Data

Suppose a waitress wants to know, for obvious reasons, what kind of behavior elicits the largest tips from customers. Her hypothesis is that smiling and acting in a friendly manner will result in better tips than acting in a more professional and reserved manner. She tests her hypothesis by alternating between the friendly and professional styles each night for 14 nights. At the end of each evening, she counts her tips and records the data. Suppose these are her findings:

Friendly Approach	*Professional Approach*
$31.50	$36.90
42.75	31.75
39.60	38.00
32.00	32.25
41.10	33.60
29.45	39.30
30.20	30.60
$35.23 average	$34.63 average

Let's also suppose that the waitress concludes from this study that the friendly approach indeed works best, and she changes to a friendly waitressing style from then on. But is this conclusion justified? We can see from her numbers that the friendly style came up with a higher average tip than the professional style. But by now you probably have already wondered if an average of $35.23 is reliably different from an average of $34.63. Because of naturally occurring variation in the amount of tips made in an evening, we would not expect the averages to come out exactly the same, even if the waitress never changed her style. One *condition* in this study would almost always come out at least a little higher than the other. So the question becomes this: How much higher must one of the averages be before we conclude that the difference is not just a chance fluctuation, but in fact represents a real difference between the two styles of waitressing? This is the question of statistical significance.

Statistical Significance

How can researchers tell if different group averages on their dependent variables represent real effects or just chance fluctuations? Fortunately, statisticians have developed formulas that allow us to estimate the likelihood that the difference between the averages could have occurred by chance alone. There are many types of statistical tests, each appropriate for different types of data and different research designs. Some of the more common tests are an *analysis of variance,* a *chi-square test,* and a *correlation coefficient.*

Returning to the waitress example, if the two averages differed by an amount so small that it could have been caused by a chance fluctuation, we say the difference has not reached **statistical significance.** Conversely, if the difference is so large that in all likelihood it was not caused by chance but reflects a true difference between the two waitressing styles, we say the difference is statistically significant. In the latter case, the conclusion would be that one style of waitressing does seem to result in better tips than the other style.

However, statistical tests do not really provide a yes or no answer to our question. All they tell us is the statistical probability that the difference between the groups was caused by chance. For example, suppose we apply a statistical test to the waitress's data and find that a difference this large would occur by chance one out of every four times. What could we conclude from this? That the different averages represent a real effect? It would be difficult to have much confidence in such a statement. We might have found a real difference, but there is a considerably high probability that the finding is just a fluke. So when can we say we have a real difference? Traditionally, the significance level used by psychologists is .05. This means that if the difference between the scores is so large that it would occur less than 5% of the time by chance, the difference is probably genuine.

When reviewing studies throughout this book, when we say a difference was found between groups, it means researchers conducted appropriate statistical tests and found a statistically significant difference. But keep in mind that such findings are not necessarily "significant" in all ways. When researchers use a large number of participants, even small differences can be *statistically* significant. Whether the difference is large enough to be important is another question. In response to this concern, investigators often examine and report the size of the difference through statistical procedures known as *effect size* indicators.

Correlation Coefficients

The **correlation coefficient** is a favorite statistic among personality researchers, and one that will pop up from time to time as we examine personality research in this book. The correlation coefficient is the appropriate statistical test when we want to understand the relationship between two measures. For example, we might be interested in the relationship between loneliness and depression. We could ask a large number of people to complete a loneliness scale as well as a depression inventory. If loneliness and depression are related, we would expect people who score high on loneliness to also score high on depression. Similarly, those who score low on loneliness should score low on depression.

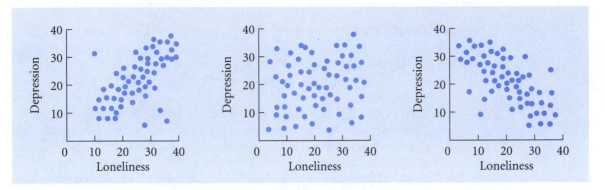

Figure 2.3

Three Possible Relations Between Loneliness and Depression

Figure 2.3 presents three possible outcomes from this research. Each point on the figure represents one participant's scores on both scales. The first outcome (left) indicates that a person's score on one scale is a fairly good predictor of that person's score on the other scale. In this case, if we know someone is high on loneliness, we know that person is probably going to score high on depression as well. The second outcome (center) indicates little or no relationship between the measures. Knowing a person's score on one scale does not provide any information about what the other score will be. The third outcome (right), like the first, indicates that knowing a person's loneliness score will help predict the depression score, but not in the way we might have anticipated. Here, a high score on one measure predicts a low score on the other.

After conducting the appropriate statistical test, we can reduce the data in each of the relationships shown in the figure to a single number, the correlation coefficient. This number can range from 1.00 to −1.00. The closer the coefficient is to either of the extremes, 1.00 or −1.00 (and thus the farther away from 0), the stronger the relationship between the two measures. Returning to the figure, the first outcome indicates a fairly strong relationship between loneliness and depression. The correlation coefficient for this figure might be .60. Because a high score on one measure indicates a high score on the other measure, this is a *positive correlation.* For the second outcome, the correlation coefficient approaches .00, indicating no relationship between the measures. The third outcome might yield a correlation of −.60, also indicating a fairly strong relationship between the variables. Note that the third outcome is a *negative correlation,* but this does not mean it is less important than a positive correlation of the same magnitude. For example, if we had compared scores on a loneliness scale with scores on a sociability measure, we probably would have anticipated that a high score on one would predict a low score on the other.

In the News

First They Tell You One Thing; Then They Tell You Another

Until recently, those of us who try to keep up with the latest developments in nutrition were certain that a high-fiber diet would significantly reduce our chances of contracting colon cancer. Then I picked up a current newspaper and read about a team of researchers who found no evidence that fiber guards against colon cancer (Mestel, 2000). It was a familiar experience. Just like the advice on oat bran, salt, and red wine, what researchers once told us suddenly seemed not to be the case (at least for now). Little wonder that an increasing number of Americans are ignoring expert advice about dietary choices (New York Times, 2001). Personality researchers have little reason to feel smug about this. As discussed in Chapter 8, psychologists in the 1970s warned of the health consequences from a Type A lifestyle. But research in the 1980s suggested that the warnings may have been premature. Similarly, the latest advice on how to lose weight, raise your children, and relate to your romantic partner often shifts with each new discovery. What's going on here? Perhaps, as a friend suggested recently, news media should stop reporting research findings until the investigators agree on what they know.

But the problem is not that researchers can't make up their minds. Rather, consumers of scientific information may need a better understanding of how science works. A single study—even one reported with great fanfare in the news media—is but one step in a long-term, ongoing process. As revealed throughout this book, an important research finding does not merely provide data on an interesting question. It also raises new questions and stimulates new research. To understand what researchers know about a topic, we have to look at *programs* of research, not just isolated studies. Moreover, psychologists know that behavior is the result of many causes, and untangling the complex relationships between variables is a challenging task.

Sometimes, findings can't be replicated. Sometimes, additional information changes the interpretation of earlier results. If we look at research findings over a long period of time, we often see an impressive amount of progress. But a closer inspection reveals that science moves in fits and starts. As a result, highly publicized "discoveries" often turn out to be incorrect. One journalist looked at 12 discoveries in the field of high-energy physics that were important enough to be reported in the New York Times the previous decade (Taubes, 1998). He determined that 9 of the 12 discoveries were later found to be inaccurate.

What's the lesson here? First, scientific understanding of any interesting question comes from a series of investigations, not just one study. Second, the subject matter of this book—personality and behavior—is complex, and good psychological research is difficult. Third, recent findings represent our knowledge at the moment. It would be foolish to dismiss this information. But it would be equally ill-advised to assume the most recent study is the last word.

Personality Assessment

Sometimes Americans seem obsessed with measuring personality. Popular magazines often promote short tests, or quizzes, to measure how good a roommate you are, what type of romantic partner you need, or the type of vacation spot that matches your personality. Although the magazines rarely claim their tests are based on any scientific investigations, the popularity of these tests suggests that readers find them at least interesting, if not believable. There is something about calculating a score that gives credibility to an untested 10-item quiz.

On a more sophisticated level, personality psychologists also have been accused of sometimes putting too much faith in the numbers generated by their personality tests. Personality assessment is a central part of much personality research. If we are going to study achievement motivation, self-esteem, social anxiety, and so on, we need to measure these concepts as accurately as possible. Similarly, psychologists working in education, personnel, and counseling often rely on personality tests to determine if a child should be placed in a special class, if an employee should be promoted to a new position, or if a client needs admission to a psychiatric hospital.

In each case, it is the responsibility of the people using the test to see that it accurately measures the concept they are interested in. Unfortunately, not all personality tests are as good as psychologists would prefer, and even the best tests can be used inappropriately. So how can we tell a good test from a bad one or determine if the test measures what we want to measure? Before using any standardized test, we need to examine its *reliability* and *validity*.

"The man with creative ideas in philosophy or art can give wings to them at once; but in science . . . extensive painstaking experiment has to be done."
RAYMOND CATTELL

Reliability

Suppose you took a personality test today and it indicated that, compared to others your age, you were high on the trait *independence*. That is, more than most people, you enjoy being on your own and making your own decisions. However, suppose next week you take the test again, and this time your score indicates you are relatively low on independence. Which of these scores reflects your true personality? Unfortunately, you have no way of knowing from this test whether you are an independent or a dependent person. The test suffers from poor reliability.

A test has good **reliability** when it measures consistently. One indication of a test's reliability is how consistently the test measures over time. In the independence test example, there is little consistency and therefore low reliability. Many factors can contribute to poor consistency over time. For example, the test questions or the scoring procedures might be vague. Perhaps test responses are dependent on recent events or simply fluctuate depending on the person's mood. Nonetheless, because personality is assumed to be relatively consistent over time, tests designed to measure personality must provide consistent scores over time.

The most common way to determine a test's consistency over time is with a **test-retest reliability** coefficient. To determine this coefficient, researchers first administer the test to a large number of people. Sometime later, usually after a few weeks, the same people take the test again. The scores from the first administration are correlated with those from the second with a simple correlation procedure. Recall that correlation coefficients can range from 1.00 to −1.00. The higher the correlation coefficient, the better the reliability.

Unfortunately, a reliability coefficient does not provide a simple answer to the question of whether or not the test is reliable. Determining a test's reliability is not a yes-or-no question. On the one hand, a test-retest coefficient of .90 is probably reliable enough to meet most people's needs (although not if extremely high reliability is required). On the other hand, a reliability coefficient of .20 is no doubt too low for most purposes. But what about something in between? Is a test with a reliability coefficient of .50 or .60 acceptable? The answer depends on the researcher's needs and the availability of alternative, more reliable tests. Sometimes the nature of the concept being measured contributes to low reliability. For example, tests given to young children often have lower than desirable levels of reliability. The test might be used anyway because typical fluctuations in a child's mood, attention, or effort during testing create inconsistencies in answers and therefore limit the reliability of any test.

Another aspect of reliability is **internal consistency.** A test is internally consistent when all the items on the test measure the same thing. Let's say 10 items on a 20-item test of extraversion accurately measure the extent to which a test taker is an extraverted person. Because half the items measure extraversion, the overall score probably is somewhat indicative of the person's true level on this dimension. But because half the items measure something besides extraversion, the usefulness of the score is limited. This test suffers from poor internal consistency.

Statistical tests can be used to determine how well the responses on each test item correlate with the responses on other items. A statistic called an *internal consistency coefficient* can be calculated. A high coefficient indicates that most of the items are measuring the same concept; a low coefficient suggests items are measuring more than one concept. A careful test maker calculates the test's internal consistency and includes in the final version only those items that "hang together" to measure the same concept.

Validity

Reliability alone does not determine a test's usefulness. Information about a test's reliability only reveals that a test is measuring something consistently. But it tells us nothing about *what* the test is measuring. That is why psychologists also examine data concerning the test's validity. **Validity refers to the extent to which a test measures what it is designed to measure.** As with reliability, the question is not whether a test does or does not have validity. Rather, the question is how well the validity of the test has been demonstrated.

Validity is relatively easy to determine for some kinds of tests. For example, if the purpose of a test is to predict how well students will do on an upcoming task, researchers simply compare the test scores with the task scores to determine what is called the *predictive validity* of the test. Unfortunately, it is not as easy to establish validity for most of the tests personality researchers use. These psychologists are usually interested in measuring hypothetical constructs, such as intelligence, masculinity, or social anxiety. *Hypothetical constructs* are useful inventions researchers employ to describe concepts that have no physical reality. That is, no one can be shown an *intelligence.* We can see behaviors and test performances that suggest a high intellectual functioning, but intelligence remains a theoretical entity.

The problem for personality researchers, then, is how to demonstrate that a test measures something that, in reality, is but a useful abstract invention. How can researchers know if a test is measuring self-esteem? People who agree with the test item, "I am not as competent as most people in sporting events," might have low self-esteem. Then again, they might just have poor athletic ability, or they might be depressed. The task facing personality researchers is establishing the test's **construct validity.** That is, researchers want to demonstrate that the test accurately gauges the personality dimension being measured. Fortunately, there is much a researcher can do to determine the construct validity of a test. Unfortunately, deciding whether there is enough evidence to establish a test's validity comes down to a subjective judgment by the test user. Some of the information psychologists use to answer this question are described next. This information includes the test's face validity, congruent validity, discriminant validity, and behavioral validation.

Face Validity. Perhaps the most obvious way to decide if a test measures what it says it measures is to look at the test items. Most of us would accept that a test asking people, "Do you feel nervous interacting with others?" or "Are you uncomfortable meeting new people?" is probably measuring something like social anxiety. The test would have good **face validity.** That is, on the face of it, the test appears to be measuring social anxiety.

Although most tests probably have high face validity, not all do. Some hypothetical constructs don't lend themselves to these kinds of obvious questions. For example, how would you design a test to measure creativity? Asking people, "Are you creative?" probably won't help much. Instead, you might ask people to write an ending to a story or to name as many uses as they can think of for an ordinary object. These tests might be good measures of creativity, but the face validity would be less certain than with more straightforward measurement procedures.

Congruent Validity. Suppose you are interested in using a new intelligence test that reportedly takes less time to administer and is more economical than the more commonly used tests. You'd probably want to see how scores from this new test compare with scores on an established intelligence test. But suppose you gave both tests to a group of people and found a correlation between the test scores of only .20. Because scores on the two tests are not highly correlated, a person could attain a high score on one intelligence test and a low score on the other, leaving you to wonder which is the true measure of intelligence. This is not to say that the old scale is measuring intelligence and the new scale is not, but rather that they cannot both be measuring the same construct.

The *congruent validity* of a test, sometimes called *convergent validity,* is the extent to which scores from the test correlate with other measures of the same construct. If two tests are measuring the same thing, scores from the two tests should be highly correlated. However, congruent validity data are not limited to correlations with other personality tests. For example, if you wanted to determine the construct validity of a new measure for anxiety, you might compare test scores with anxiety levels as rated by a team of professional psychologists.

Discriminant Validity. In contrast to congruent validity, **discriminant validity** refers to the extent to which a test score does *not* correlate with the scores of theoretically unrelated measures. Let's return to the problem of designing a creativity test. It is important to show that the test measures only creativity and not something that resembles creativity, such as intelligence. To establish discriminant validity, you might give both the creativity test and a standard intelligence test to a group of people. If scores from the two tests are highly correlated, someone could argue that your creativity test does not measure creativity at all, but simply intelligence. If the correlation between the two tests is low, you have evidence that the two tests measure different constructs. Notice that a low correlation does not tell you what the test measures, but only what it does not measure. Nonetheless, this is an important step in establishing the construct validity of the test.

Behavioral Validation. Suppose you used scores on an assertiveness scale to predict how people respond when they receive poor service or when someone cuts in front of them in line. Naturally, you would expect high-assertiveness individuals to complain about the service or ask the intruder to move to the end of the line and low-assertiveness people to tolerate these inconveniences. But what if the test scores were completely unrelated to assertiveness behavior? What if people with low scores on the scale acted just as assertively as those with high scores? In this case, the validity of the test would be in doubt.

Another step in determining the construct validity of a test is **behavioral validation.** In other words, it is important that test scores predict relevant behavior. In the case of the assertiveness scale, it is possible that test takers respond to test items by indicating how they think they would act or wish they would act. But people who describe themselves as quite assertive might in fact act rather meekly when a real need for assertion arises. Therefore, it is possible for a test to have face validity, congruent validity, and discriminant validity, and still have questionable construct validity. If test scores cannot predict behavior, the usefulness of the test must be questioned. However, note that a failure to predict behavior from a test score can be caused by many other factors, such as measuring the wrong behavior or measuring the behavior incorrectly. This issue is discussed again in Chapter 7.

 *Summary*

1.   Personality psychologists examine personality processes through scientific research. Most of this research is based on the hypothesis-testing approach, in which hypotheses are derived logically from theories. These hypotheses are then tested in studies, and the theory either is or is not supported. A good theory is parsimonious and capable of generating many testable hypotheses.

2.   The basic elements of a research design are the independent and dependent variables. One important distinction in personality research concerns whether independent variables are manipulated by the researcher. When researchers examine nonmanipulated variables, they have less confidence in making statements about cause and effect. Predicted results are better than those explained in hindsight because the latter approach does not allow for hypothesis testing. Researchers are becoming increasingly aware of the need to replicate their findings, but obtaining reliable information about how often an effect is replicated is a problem.

3.   Many personality researchers use the case study method. Although case studies have some limitations, such as questionable generalizability to other populations, they also possess some unique advantages over other methods.

4.   Researchers use statistical tests to determine if the differences they find between groups are the result of chance fluctuations or if they represent genuine effects. Personality researchers often use correlation coefficients when analyzing their data. A correlation coefficient identifies the direction and size of a relationship between two measures.

5.   Personality researchers often use personality tests in their work. To determine the usefulness of a test, researchers look at evidence for the test's reliability and validity. Reliability can be gauged through test-retest correlations and internal consistency coefficients. Validity is determined through face validity, congruent validity, discriminant validity, and behavioral validation. Researchers must use subjective judgments in deciding if tests are reliable and valid enough for their needs.

Test-retest

InfoTrac Key Terms

 For additional readings go to http://www.infotrac-college.com/wadsworth and enter a search term related to your interest. Use the key terms suggested here to pull up several related articles. Also see the text Web site at http://psychology .wadsworth.com for more suggested readings and interactive quizzes to test your knowledge.

Case study	Hypothetical constructs
Correlation coefficient	Statistical hypothesis testing

Chapter 3

The Psychoanalytic Approach

Freudian Theory, Application, and Assessment

Although people have speculated about the nature of personality for years, the first acknowledged personality theorist did not emerge until the late 1800s. Then an Austrian neurologist began proposing such outrageous notions as the existence of sexual desires in young children, unconscious causes for baffling physical disorders, and treatment through a time-consuming, expensive procedure in which patients lie on a couch while the doctor listens to them talk about seemingly irrelevant topics. That neurologist, Sigmund Freud, continued to develop, promote, and defend his ideas despite intense criticism. By the time of his death in 1939, Freud had written numerous volumes, was recognized as the leader

41

of an important intellectual movement, and had changed the thinking of psychologists, writers, parents, and laypeople for years to come.

Freud's influence on psychology and twentieth-century thought is so widespread that most of us underestimate the effect his theory has had on our thinking. For example, if you are like most adults in this culture, you freely accept the idea that what you do is sometimes influenced by an unconscious part of your mind. Most of us have said something like, "I must have done that unconsciously" or pondered what sort of hidden psychological conflict might be behind a friend or loved one's unusual behavior. Although Freud was not the first to talk about the unconscious, no one before or since has placed so much emphasis on unconscious processes in explaining human behavior. Similarly, when we wonder if our dreams reveal inner fears and desires, we are espousing an idea that Freud popularized. Again, although people have been interpreting dreams for thousands of years, Freud was the first to incorporate dream interpretation into a larger psychological theory.

References to Freudian theory permeate our culture. As one writer put it, "Freud's theories of the subconscious mind . . . have had a dramatic impact on contemporary film, theater, novels, political campaigning, advertising, legal argument and even religion" (Fisher, 1995). English students learn Freudian psychology when studying the themes in great literature; theology students debate Freud's views on religion. Even our language has not escaped. It is not uncommon to hear people mention *Freudian slips, denial, libido, repression,* and other Freudian concepts in everyday conversations. But perhaps the most telling tribute to Freud's impact is that nearly every major theorist covered in this book has felt compelled to use Freud's works as a point of comparison for his or her own ideas about the nature of personality. Appropriately, this chapter begins with an examination of Freud's theory of personality.

Freud Discovers the Unconscious

How did a Viennese neurologist come to change the way we think of humankind? There is little in Freud's early history to indicate that greatness awaited him. Although Freud was a respected member of the medical community, his interests began to drift. In 1885 he went to Paris to study with another neurologist, Jean-Martin Charcot. Charcot was experimenting with early versions of hypnosis and its use in curing what were then believed to be unusual physiological problems. Shortly thereafter, Freud returned to Vienna and began work with a prominent physician, Joseph Breuer. Like Charcot, Breuer was using hypnosis to treat hysterical patients. Hysteria is a disorder that consists of a variety of physical symptoms. Patients often display blindness, deafness, an inability to walk or to use an arm, and so on. Most physicians of that day treated hysteria as if it were a physically based illness. However, Breuer and Freud developed another interpretation.

Discussions about one of Breuer's patients, a woman with the pseudonym Anna O., probably set the direction for the rest of Freud's career. According to Breuer, Anna O. experienced a number of hysterical symptoms, including paralysis of her left arm, hallucinations, and the ability to speak only in English even though her native tongue was German. Under hypnosis, Anna O. would talk about her daydreams and hallucinations, and about past traumatic events. During her final hypnosis session, she discussed her experiences with her dying father and some associated hallucinations about a black snake. After this session, the paralysis in her arm was gone and she could once again speak German.

In 1895 Freud and Breuer published *Studies in Hysteria,* in which they presented the case of Anna O. and discussed their use of hypnosis in treating hysteria. Freud continued to use hypnosis to treat his hysterical patients but soon grew disillusioned with its limitations and began looking for alternative methods. Slowly he recognized the importance of allowing patients to say whatever came into their mind. He discovered that, even without hypnosis, under the right circumstances patients would describe previously hidden material that seemed related to the causes and cure of their hysterical symptoms. The development of this technique, called **free association,** was a significant step in the development of Freud's theory.

One startling discovery Freud reported in his early patients was that memories uncovered during free association often concerned traumatic sexual experiences, many of which supposedly had occurred in early childhood. He gradually concluded that these early sexual experiences were responsible for the hysterical symptoms expressed by his adult patients. At this point, Freud was well along the way in his transition from neurologist to psychologist. He continued to work with hysterical patients and wrote about his observations and the development of his theories, convinced that he was on the threshold of important psychological discoveries.

Yet Freud's writings sold poorly at first. In fact, his work met with great opposition in the academic and medical communities. Freud's open discussion of infantile sexuality and omnipresent sexual motives did not sit well with the puritanical standards of Victorian Europe. His approach to treatment was so radical that many respected physicians considered it absurd. Nonetheless, Freud continued his work and his writing and soon developed a small following of scholars who traveled to Vienna to study with him. These scholars formed the Vienna Psychoanalytic Society, with Freud as its great figurehead and leader. Later, many members of this society would come to disagree with Freud and leave the ranks to develop their own personality theories and form their own professional organizations. However, as later chapters will reveal, the flavor of their theories remained unmistakably Freudian.

Gradually, Freud's theory gained acceptance within the growing field of psychology. In 1909 Freud was invited to the United States to present a series of lectures on psychoanalysis at Clark University. For Freud, the occasion marked the beginning of international recognition of his work. However, resistance to psychoanalysis by academic psychologists kept Freud's theory out of American text-

Sigmund Freud

1856–1939

Sigmund Freud was born in 1856 in Freiberg, Moravia (now part of the Czech Republic). In 1860 his family moved to Vienna, where Freud spent virtually the rest of his life. Freud's ambition to amount to something important surfaced early. He typically excelled in school, and while in medical school at the University of Vienna was determined to make an important discovery and thereby a name for himself. He began his quest while working in his instructor's medical laboratory. But immediate scientific breakthroughs were not forthcoming, and he soon became discouraged at his chances for advancement. In addition, he had fallen in love with Martha Bernays and wanted to earn enough money to marry her and give her a comfortable lifestyle. So, upon completing his degree, Freud left the lab and went into private practice.

During his subsequent four-year engagement to Bernays (they were finally married in 1886), Freud won a research grant to travel to Paris to observe Jean-Martin Charcot's work with hypnosis. It was also during this time that he began to develop his ideas about the power of the unconscious mind. His work with Joseph Breuer, observations of his own patients, and a great deal of introspection finally blossomed into his 1900 book *The Interpretation of Dreams*. Although it took several years to sell the 600 original printings of the book, it signaled the beginning of the professional recognition that Freud had sought back in medical school.

Something about Sigmund Freud has attracted the attention of numerous biographers. The most complete of these is the three-volume biography by Ernest Jones (1953–1957). Although he sought fame, in many ways Freud was a private person. Consequently, most biographers have glued together the facts we have about Freud's life with a large amount of speculation. Perhaps the most interesting part of this speculation concerns the extent to which Freud's description of human personality reflects his own personality and life experiences. Not surprisingly, Freud's relationship with his parents is of particular interest. Although his father had several children from an earlier marriage, Sigmund was his mother's first child and apparently the apple of her eye. His mother was only 21 when he was born and almost as close in age to her son as she was to her husband. Biographers agree that an especially close relationship was formed. Freud's mother sometimes referred to him as her "Golden Sigi." In contrast, Freud's relationship with his father appears to have been cold, if not occasionally hostile. Freud arrived late to his father's funeral, something he later identified as unconsciously motivated. Freud reported struggling with guilt feelings over his relationship with his father many years after his father's death.

It is not difficult to see how Freud's description of the Oedipus complex—sexual attraction for the mother and competitive hostility toward the father—may have been a kind of projection of his own feelings toward his parents. Freud hints at this insight at many places in his writings. Indeed, he often relied on his own introspection to test the accuracy of his clinical intuition. He is reported to have reserved a half hour each night for this self-analysis.

(continues)

Sigmund Freud (continued)

Freud's marriage was a long and relatively happy one, producing six children. The youngest child, Anna, held a special place in her father's heart. She followed in his professional footsteps, eventually taking over a leadership role in the psychoanalytic movement and becoming a respected psychoanalytic theorist in her own right.

Freud created a situation filled with interesting Oedipal possibilities when he conducted Anna's psychoanalysis himself.

Freud and his family fled from their home and Nazi persecution when Germany invaded Austria in 1938. They escaped to London, where Freud died of cancer the following year.

books for another quarter of a century (Fancher, 2000). Freud continued to develop his theory and write about psychoanalysis until his death in 1939. Many consider Freud the most influential psychologist in the relatively short history of the field. A *Time* magazine cover story in 1999 featured a picture of Albert Einstein and Sigmund Freud, identifying the two as "The Century's Greatest Minds."

We will begin our examination of this influential perspective by looking at classic Freudian theory. Contemporary advocates of the psychoanalytic approach vary in the degree to which they agree with Freud's initial descriptions of personality (Westen, 1998). Most accept key psychoanalytic concepts, such as the importance of unconscious thoughts. But psychoanalytic psychologists typically back away from other aspects of Freudian theory, such as his description of infantile sexuality. Nonetheless, you need to understand what Freud said before deciding which parts make sense to you and which parts to jettison. A century after introducing psychoanalysis to the world, the Viennese neurologist still casts a shadow across the field of personality.

The Freudian Theory of Personality

The Topographic Model

The starting point for understanding the Freudian approach is the division of the human personality into three parts. Freud originally divided personality into the *conscious,* the *preconscious,* and the *unconscious.* This division is known as the **topographic model.** The **conscious** contains the thoughts you are currently aware of. This material changes constantly as new thoughts enter your mind and others pass out of awareness. When you say something is "on your mind," you probably mean the conscious part of your mind. However, the conscious can deal with only a tiny percentage of all the bits of information stored in your mind. You *could* bring an uncountable number of thoughts into consciousness fairly easily if you wanted to. For example, what did you have for breakfast? Who was your third-grade teacher? What did you do last Saturday night? This large body of retrievable information makes up the **preconscious.**

Although many people consider the material in the conscious and preconscious to be fairly exhaustive of the thoughts in their minds, Freud described these as merely the tip of the iceberg. The vast majority of thoughts, and the most important from a psychoanalytic viewpoint, are found in the **unconscious.** This is the material to which you have no immediate access. According to Freud, you cannot bring unconscious material into consciousness except under certain extreme situations. Nonetheless, this unconscious material is responsible for much of your everyday behavior. Understanding the influence of the unconscious on behavior, particularly what might be termed abnormal behavior, is the key to appreciating the psychoanalytic perspective.

The Structural Model

Freud soon discovered that the topographic model provided a limited description of human personality. He therefore added the **structural model,** which divides personality into the *id,* the *ego,* and the *superego.* Just as you often say, "One part of me wants to do one thing, and another part of me wants to do something else," so did Freud conceive of the personality as made up of parts often not at peace with one another.

Freud maintained that at birth there is but one personality structure, the **id.** This is the selfish part of you, concerned only with satisfying your personal desires. Actions taken by the id are based on the *pleasure principle.* In other words, the id is concerned only with what brings immediate personal satisfaction regardless of any physical or social limitations. When babies see something they want, they reach for it. It doesn't matter whether the object belongs to someone else or may be harmful. And this *reflexive action* doesn't disappear when we become adults. Rather, Freud maintained, our id impulses are ever present, held in check by the other parts of a healthy adult personality.

Obviously, our pleasure impulses would be frustrated most of the time if the id were to rely on reflexive action to get what it wants. Therefore, Freud proposed that the id also uses *wish fulfillment* to satisfy its needs. That is, if the desired object is not available, the id will imagine what it wants. If a baby is hungry and doesn't see food nearby, the id imagines the food and thereby at least temporarily satisfies the need. As discussed later in this chapter, Freud argued that our dreams also are a type of wish fulfillment.

If you react skeptically to the idea of id impulses and wish fulfillment operating within your own mental system, this may be because Freud described the id as buried entirely in the unconscious. As shown in Figure 3.1, id impulses remain out of our awareness. Indeed, because many of these impulses center on themes of sexuality and aggression, it is probably good that we are not aware of this unconscious material.

As children interact with their environment during the first two years of life, the second part of the personality structure gradually develops. The actions of the **ego** are based on the reality principle. That is, the primary job of the ego is to sat-

> **"***I**n its relation to the id, [the ego] is like a man on horseback, who has to hold in check the superior strength of the horse, [but] is obliged to guide it where it wants to go."*
> SIGMUND FREUD

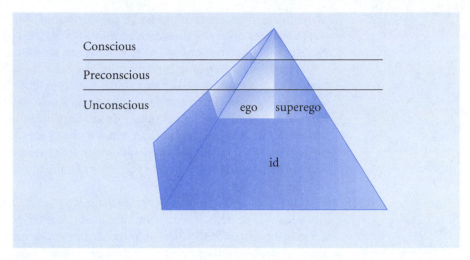

Figure 3.1

Relationship of the Id, Ego, and Superego to the Three Levels of Awareness

isfy id impulses, but in a manner that takes into consideration the realities of the situation. Because id impulses tend to be socially unacceptable, they are threatening to us. The ego's job is to keep these impulses in the unconscious. Unlike the id, your ego moves freely among the conscious, preconscious, and unconscious parts of your mind.

However, the ego's function is not simply to frustrate the aims of the id. Freud maintained that human behavior is directed toward reducing tension, such as the tension we feel when an impulsive need is unmet. Very young children might be allowed to grab food off their parents' plates and thereby reduce tension. But as infants mature, they learn the physical and social limits on what they can and cannot do. If you are hungry, your id impulse may be to grab whatever food is around. But your ego understands this action is unacceptable. The ego tries to satisfy the wants of the id, and thus lessen tension, but in a way that considers the consequences of the action.

By the time a child is about five years old, the third part of the personality structure is formed. The superego represents society's—and, in particular, the parents'—values and standards. The superego places more restrictions on what we can and cannot do. If you see a $5 bill sitting on a table at a friend's house, your id impulse might be to take the money. Your ego, aware of the problems this might cause, attempts to figure out how to get the $5 without being caught. But even if there is a way to get the money without being seen, your superego will not allow the action. Stealing money is a violation of society's moral code, even if you don't get caught. The primary weapon the superego brings to the situation is guilt. If you take the money anyway, you'll probably feel bad about it later and may lose a few nights' sleep before returning the $5 to your friend. Some people have roughly translated the concept of the superego into what is called *conscience.*

But the superego does not merely punish us for moral violations. It also provides the ideals the ego uses to determine if a behavior is virtuous and therefore worthy of praise. Because of poor child-rearing practices, some children fail to fully develop their superegos. As adults, these people have little inward restraint from stealing from or lying to others. In other people, the superego can become too powerful, or supermoral, and burden the ego with impossible standards of perfection. Here the person could suffer from relentless *moral anxiety*—an ever-present feeling of shame and guilt—for failing to reach standards no human can meet.

Like forces pulling at three corners to form a triangle, the desires of the id, ego, and superego complement and contradict one another. In the healthy individual, a strong ego does not allow the id or the superego too much control over the personality. But the battle is never ending. In each of us, somewhere below our awareness, there exists an eternal state of tension between a desire for self-indulgence, a concern for reality, and the enforcement of a strict moral code.

Libido and Thanatos

The topographic model provides the playing field; the structural model provides the characters. But what sets Freud's system in motion? Freud maintained that human behavior is motivated by strong internal forces he called *Triebe,* roughly translated as drives, or instincts. Freud identified two major categories of instincts: the life or sexual instinct, generally referred to as **libido,** and the death or aggressive instinct, known as **Thanatos.** Although Freud originally maintained that the two forces were in opposition, he later suggested that the two often combine, thus intertwining much of what we do with both erotic and aggressive motives.

Freud attributed most human behavior to the life or sexual instinct. However, he used this description in a very broad sense. Sexually motivated behaviors not only include those with obvious erotic content but also nearly any action aimed at receiving pleasure. Late in his career Freud added the death instinct—the desire we all have to die and return to the earth. However, this unconscious motive is rarely expressed in the form of obvious self-destruction. Most often, the death instinct is turned outward and expressed as aggression against others. The wish to die remains unconscious.

Freud was greatly influenced by much of the scientific thought of his day. Among the ideas he adapted from other sciences was the notion of a limited amount of energy. Energy within a physical system does not disappear but exists in finite amounts. Similarly, Freud argued that we each have a finite amount of *psychic energy* that more or less powers the psychological functions. This means that energy spent on one part of psychological functioning is not available for other uses. Thus, if the ego has to expend large amounts of energy to control the id, it has little energy left to carry out the rest of its functions efficiently. One goal of

Freudian psychotherapy is to help troubled clients release unconscious impulses being held in check, thereby freeing up the energy available for daily functioning.

Defense Mechanisms

Freud's description of the thoughts we carry around in our unconscious minds can be a bit unsettling. Classic psychoanalytic cases involve such unconscious themes as hatred for one's parents, aggression toward one's spouse, incestuous thoughts, memories of traumatic childhood experiences, and similar notions too threatening for awareness. The ego attempts to reduce or avoid anxiety by keeping this material out of consciousness. Occasionally, people experience what Freud called *neurotic anxiety.* These are vague feelings of anxiety sparked by the sensation that unacceptable unconscious thoughts are about to burst through the awareness barrier and express themselves in consciousness.

Fortunately, the ego has many techniques at its disposal to deal with unwanted thoughts and desires. These are known collectively as **defense mechanisms.** Some of the principal defense mechanisms are reviewed in the following sections. Freud touched on each of these concepts at various places in his works. However, descriptions of many of the defense mechanisms were developed more completely by some of Freud's followers. Among the later psychoanalysts who elaborated on Freud's writings about defense mechanisms was Anna Freud, Sigmund's daughter.

Repression. Freud called repression "the cornerstone on which the whole structure of psychoanalysis rests" (1914/1963, p. 116). It is clearly the most important of the defense mechanisms. **Repression** is an active effort by the ego to push threatening material out of consciousness or to keep such material from ever reaching consciousness. For example, one night a boy sees his father physically assault his mother. When later asked about the experience, the boy insists he has never seen anything at all like that. He may not be lying. Instead, he may have found the scene too horrifying to accept and therefore simply repressed it out of consciousness. According to Freud, each of us uses repression, for we all have material in our unconscious mind we would rather not bring into awareness. As efficient as this seems, it is not without cost. Because repression is a constant, active process, it requires that the ego constantly expend energy. Repressing a large number of powerful thoughts and impulses leaves our ego with little remaining energy with which to function. And without a strong ego, the battle for a stable personality can be lost.

Sublimation. Unlike repression, which drains our ability to function, the more we use sublimation, the more productive we become. Thus, psychoanalysts often refer to sublimation as the only truly successful defense mechanism. When using **sublimation,** the ego channels threatening unconscious impulses into socially acceptable actions. For example, aggressive id impulses can be sublimated into playing hockey or football. In our society, aggressive athletes are often considered heroes

According to Freud, participation in aggressive sports allows the expression of unconscious aggressive impulses in a socially acceptable manner. Football players might be engaging in sublimation with each tackle.

Photo by Marlene Somsak

and rewarded for their actions. The sublimation is productive because the id is allowed to express its aggression, the ego doesn't have to tie up energy holding back the impulses, and the athlete is loved and admired for aggressive play.

Displacement. Like sublimation, **displacement** involves channeling our impulses to nonthreatening objects. Unlike sublimation, although safe, displaced impulses don't lead to social rewards. For example, as the result of mistreatment or abuse, a woman might carry around a great deal of unconscious anger. If expressing that anger toward her abuser is unacceptable or dangerous, she might instead direct her emotions toward her coworkers or children. Although doing so can create other problems, angry outbursts aimed at these less-threatening people may protect unacceptable thoughts from conscious expression. Freud maintained that many of our apparently irrational fears, or phobias, are merely symbolic displacements. For example, Freud once speculated that a fear of horses expressed by a client's son was really a displaced fear of the father.

Denial. When we use **denial,** we simply refuse to accept that certain facts exist. This is more than saying we do not remember, as in repression. Rather, we insist that something is not true, despite all evidence to the contrary. For example, a widower who loved his wife deeply may act as if she were still alive long after her death. He may set a place for her at the table or tell friends that she is just away visiting a relative. To the widower, this charade is more acceptable than admitting consciously that his wife has died. Obviously, denial is an extreme form of defense. The more we use it, the less in touch with reality we are and the more difficulty we have functioning. Nonetheless, in some cases the ego will resort to denial rather than allow certain thoughts to reach consciousness.

Reaction Formation. When using **reaction formation,** we hide from a threatening unconscious idea or urge by acting in a manner opposite to our unconscious desires. Thus, a young woman who constantly tells people how much she loves her mother could be masking strong unconscious hatred for the mother. People who militantly get involved with antipornography crusades may hold a strong unconscious interest in pornography. It is as if the thought is so unacceptable that the ego must prove how incorrect the notion is. How could a woman who professes so much love for her mother really hate her deep inside?

Intellectualization. One way the ego handles threatening material is to remove the emotional content from the thought before allowing it into awareness. By considering something in a strictly intellectual, unemotional manner, we can bring previously difficult thoughts into consciousness without anxiety. For example, under the guise of unemotionally pondering the importance of wearing seat belts, a woman might imagine her husband in a gruesome automobile accident. A Freudian therapist might guess that the woman holds some unconscious hostility toward her spouse.

Projection. Sometimes we attribute an unconscious impulse to other people instead of to ourselves. This defense mechanism is called **projection.** By projecting the impulse onto another person, we free ourselves from the perception that we are the one who actually holds this thought. For example, the woman who thinks everyone in her neighborhood is committing adultery may be harboring sexual desires for the married man living next door. The man who declares that the world is full of distrustful and cheating people may unconsciously know that he is distrustful and a cheater.

Psychosexual Stages of Development

One of Freud's most controversial contributions to psychology is his theory of personality development. Freud argued that the adult personality is formed by experiences from the first five or six years of life. Although adults sometimes blossom into seemingly different kinds of people than they were in childhood, Freud maintained that the roots of this adult personality were formed during the early years. In addition, Freud often interpreted psychological phenomena within a sexual framework. Consequently, his explanation of early personality development largely centered on sexual themes. According to Freud, each of us progresses through a series of developmental stages during childhood. Because the chief identifying character of each stage is the primary erogenous zone, and because each

In the News

Repressed Memories

One afternoon in 1969, eight-year-old Susan Nason disappeared on her way to visit a neighbor in Foster City, California. Two months later her body was found in a nearby reservoir. The coroner concluded that Susan had died from a fractured skull. An investigation followed, but with little evidence to go on, police never found the killer. Twenty years later, Eileen Franklin-Lipsker, a childhood friend of the victim's, sat with her daughter in her Los Angeles home. Suddenly Franklin-Lipsker recalled images of Susan's death. She could see a man sexually assaulting the girl and then smashing her head with a rock. Franklin-Lipsker also knew the identity of the man in her memories—it was her own father, George Franklin.

Based on little more than his daughter's testimony, George Franklin was tried and convicted for Susan Nason's murder in 1990. Jurors who listened to Franklin-Lipsker's testimony were convinced she could not have known the details she provided unless she had been at the scene of the crime. But why had the memories taken 20 years to surface? The prosecution argued that the nature of the memories was so traumatic Franklin-Lipsker had repressed them into an unconscious part of her mind. It was noticing the physical similarity between her daughter and Susan that triggered the long-repressed images and allowed them to enter consciousness. Superior Court Judge Thomas Smith called George Franklin "wicked and depraved" and sentenced him to life in prison. Franklin thus became the first person to be convicted on the basis of "repressed" memories.

The Franklin verdict provides an egregious example of how psychological principles can be misused. In this case, a handful of psychotherapists tore apart thousands of families by misapplying the psychoanalytic notion of repression (Brody, 2000). During a period of several years, a huge number of adults going through psychotherapy suddenly "recalled" childhood memories of being victimized by parents, often sexually. In virtually every case, the client had not been aware of any such events until they were suggested by the therapist. In response to the near epidemic of repressed memory cases, many personality psychologists and memory researchers raised questions about the accuracy of the clients' claims. Researchers demonstrated that people often have great confidence in the accuracy of repressed memories that could not possibly have been true.

The fall of the repressed memory epidemic came quickly. Parents and family members falsely accused of abuse as a result of repressed memories formed the False Memory Syndrome Foundation. Within the first year, the organization grew to include more than 3,000 families. Hundreds of clients came to see that their memories of abuse were in fact fictional creations and retracted their stories (de Riviera, 1997). In response to increased doubt about the validity of repressed memory claims, courts dismissed cases based on repressed memories and began

(continues)

Repressed Memories (continued)

awarding damages to those who were falsely accused. Soon professional organizations warned practitioners against the use of "memory recovery techniques," such as hypnosis and guided imagery, when looking for evidence of sexual abuse (Brody, 2000).

In 1996, after spending more than five years in prison, George Franklin was granted a new trial. His attorneys argued that the jury in the first case should have been allowed to see newspaper and television reports of Susan's death. Those reports contained details of the crime that could have been the basis of Franklin-Lipsker's memories. Prosecutors responded to new information by dropping the charges. On July 3, 1996, George Franklin was released from prison. One year later, he filed a civil suit against the prosecutor, the witnesses, and his daughter, a suit that was eventually dismissed by the court after three years of litigation (*San Jose Mercury News,* 2000).

stage has an influence on adult personality, they have been labeled the **psychosexual stages of development.**

The significance of the developmental stages lies in the concept of **fixation.** Remember that Freud believed personality operates on psychic energy called libido. In Freud's view, children must resolve certain challenges or crises as they pass through each of the psychosexual stages. Unfortunately, small amounts of libido are used up resolving each crisis. In most people this still leaves an adequate amount of psychic energy to operate the adult personality. But occasionally a child encounters a particularly traumatic experience (or sometimes an excessive amount of satisfaction) during one particular stage. This results in tying up, or fixating, a large amount of libido. Consequently, the ego has less energy available for normal adult functioning. Moreover, as described next, the adult expresses characteristics reminiscent of the stage at which the energy is fixated.

The first stage each child goes through is the **oral stage.** During this period, which spans approximately the first 18 months of life, the mouth, lips, and tongue are the primary erogenous zones. You need only watch a six-month-old baby for a few minutes to realize that everything must go into the mouth. Traumatic experiences during this time, such as traumatic weaning or feeding problems, may result in fixating psychic energy and the development of oral-personality characteristics. People who develop oral personalities are said to be dependent on others as adults, although fixation that occurs after the child has teeth may result in excessive aggression as an adult. Because of the fixation, these people often express the infantile need for oral satisfaction. Adults who smoke or drink excessively, or who constantly put their hands to their mouth, might be diagnosed as oral personalities.

When children reach the age of about 18 months, they enter the **anal stage** of development. According to Freud, the anal region becomes the most important erogenous zone during this period. Not coincidentally, it is during this stage that

According to Freud, adult oral personalities develop when traumatic childhood experiences cause the fixation of an excessive amount of psychic energy at the oral stage of development. Smoking, drinking, and excessive eating are characteristic of an oral personality.

most children are toilet trained. Traumatic toilet training may result in fixation and an anal personality. People with an anal personality may be excessively orderly, stubborn or generous, depending on how their toilet training progressed.

The most important psychosexual stage, the **phallic stage,** occurs when the child is approximately three to six years old. During this period, the penis or clitoris becomes the most important erogenous zone. It is during the later part of this stage that the child goes through the *Oedipus complex,* named for the Greek mythological character who unknowingly marries his mother. Freud argued that children at this age develop a sexual attraction for their opposite-sex parent. Thus, young boys have strong incestuous desires toward their mothers, whereas young girls have these feelings toward their fathers.

Youngsters are not without their share of fear about this situation. Boys develop *castration anxiety,* the fear that their father will discover their thoughts and cut off the son's penis. If the boy has seen his sister's genitals, he is said to conclude that this fate has already befallen her. Girls, upon seeing male genitals, are said to

After resolution of the Oedipus complex, children pass into the latency stage. For several years boys will prefer to play with other boys, and girls with other girls. All of this ends with puberty.

develop *penis envy.* This is a desire to have a penis, coupled with feelings of inferiority and jealousy because of its absence. How do children resolve this situation? Freud's explanation very neatly ties up several psychological questions. Children eventually repress their desire for their opposite-sex parent (whom they realize they probably can never have as long as the other parent is around). Then, as a type of reaction formation, children identify with the parent of the same sex.

The resolution of the Oedipus complex serves a number of important functions. By identifying with the same-sex parent, boys begin to take on masculine characteristics, whereas girls acquire feminine characteristics. Identification with the parents also fits nicely with the development of the superego. This is the age at which the child adopts the values and standards of the parents, in the form of the superego. However, Oedipal desires are repressed, not eliminated. Thus, Freud maintained, they can still influence our behavior in a number of unsuspected ways.

After resolution of the Oedipus complex, the child passes into the **latency stage,** the time before puberty. Sexual desires abate during these years, only to return strongly when the child reaches puberty and the **genital stage,** the final stage of sexual development. Boys and girls seem fairly uninterested in each other during the latency stage. A look at any playground will verify that boys play with other boys and girls play with other girls. Once the child reaches puberty, the erogenous urges return and are focused in the adult genital regions. If a child has progressed to this stage without leaving large amounts of libido fixated at earlier stages, normal sexual functioning is possible.

Getting at Unconscious Material

If we accept the Freudian notion that the largest and most important part of our mind is unconscious and thereby outside our awareness, another problem soon becomes evident. That is, how useful is it for psychologists to talk about unconscious aspects of personality if such things remain unavailable for our inspection? Not surprisingly, Freud had an answer to this dilemma. He maintained that strong id impulses do not simply disappear when they are pushed out of consciousness. Although the true nature of these impulses is repressed by a strong ego, they are often expressed in a disguised or somewhat altered form. If psychologists know what to look for, they can get a glimpse of unconscious thoughts in a number of seemingly innocent behaviors. The following are seven techniques a Freudian psychologist might use to get at unconscious material.

Dreams. Freud called dreams the "royal road to the unconscious." In 1900 he published *The Interpretation of Dreams,* presenting for the first time a psychological theory to explain the meaning of these nighttime dramas. According to Freud, dreams provide id impulses with a stage for expression. They are, in fact, a type of wish fulfillment. In other words, our dreams represent the things and events we desire. This is not to say that we should take each dream as a literal wish for what we have imagined in our sleep. Overt expression of many of our unconscious desires would be difficult to face upon waking; that's why they were repressed in the first place. Therefore, Freud maintained, these ideas are expressed in disguised form in our dreams. Freud distinguished the *manifest content* of a dream (what the dreamer sees and remembers) from the *latent content* (what is really being said). This is why we often laugh about silly and absurd dreams. They may seem like nonsense to us, but to a Freudian therapist they may be filled with valuable clues about our unconscious thinking.

The key to Freudian dream interpretation is understanding that many of our unconscious thoughts and desires are represented symbolically. For example, dreams involving penises, sexual intercourse, and vaginas might be disturbing to us, whereas we probably wouldn't feel threatened by a dream about a fountain, an airplane ride, or a cave. At an unconscious level, we take the threatening content and translate it into symbols before it appears in our dreams. In this manner, the impulses are expressed, and the conscious mind is not threatened. "The dreamer does know what his dream means," Freud wrote. "Only he does not know that he knows it and for that reason thinks he does not know it" (1916/1961, p. 101).

Freud believed a trained psychoanalyst could identify many of the obvious and widely used symbols that appear in our dreams. Thus, the therapist recognizes that a house represents the human body, one's parents are disguised as a king and a queen, children are represented as small animals, birth is associated with water, a train journey is a symbol for dying, and clothes and uniforms represent nakedness.

"Innocent dreams . . . are wolves in sheep's clothing. They turn out to be quite the reverse when we take the trouble to analyze them."

SIGMUND FREUD

Predictably, the vast majority of Freudian dream symbols are sexual. According to Freud, male genitals are represented by objects with a similar shape. Freud (1916/1961) listed several such common symbols, including sticks, umbrellas, trees, knives, rifles, pencils, and hammers. Female genitals are symbolically represented by bottles, boxes, rooms, doors, and ships. Sexual intercourse is hidden in such activities as dancing, riding, and climbing. In fact, reading Freud's long list of sexual symbols, it's hard to think of many dreams that can't be interpreted sexually.

Projective Tests. Children often play a game of describing what they see in the formation of clouds in the sky. One child might see a ship on the ocean, another a lion, and still another the face of a famous person. Of course, there are no real pictures in the clouds. But where are these images coming from? The answer, from a Freudian perspective, is that these responses come from the children's own minds and reflect what they see but ordinarily might not describe. Descriptions of what we find in vague objects like clouds represent another way of getting at unconscious material.

Projective tests present test takers with ambiguous stimuli and ask them to respond with a story, the identification of objects, or perhaps a drawing. As with the cloud formations, there are no right or wrong answers. Rather, responses are individual and may indicate what is going on in the unconscious. Some of the different projective tests used by psychologists are reviewed later in this chapter.

Free Association. Take a few minutes to clear your mind of thoughts. Then allow whatever comes into your mind to enter. Say whatever you feel like saying, even if it is not what you expect and even if you are a little surprised or embarrassed by what comes out. If you are successful in allowing these free-flowing ideas into your awareness, you have experienced what some call the fundamental rule of psychoanalysis: *free association.* During psychoanalysis, the client is encouraged to use free association to temporarily bypass the censoring mechanism the ego employs. Ordinarily we block out distasteful, seemingly trivial or silly thoughts to protect ourselves from this material or to keep from sounding foolish. However, according to Freud, such intrusions contain valuable psychological material. Because these thoughts are normally excluded from consciousness, they provide keen insight into that part of the mind not seen in our everyday censored conversations.

But free associations are not easy to tap. The ego has activated considerable energy to repress certain thoughts and is not likely to let this material just ease into consciousness. Sometimes clients simply slip into long silences and report that nothing comes to mind or cunningly describe all kinds of unimportant ideas in an effort to avoid the crucial but threatening material. But if the client truly expresses whatever enters consciousness, both client and therapist could be surprised by what comes out.

Freudian Slips. We all occasionally make slips of the tongue. A husband might refer to his wife by her maiden name or say that her mind is really her "breast" feature. These slips can be embarrassing and funny, but to Freud they were insightful. The husband who refers to his wife by her maiden name may unconsciously wish he'd never married this woman. Although the statement sounds innocent, it may be loaded with underlying feelings. We call these misstatements **Freudian slips.**

Hypnosis. Freud's early experiences with hypnosis sparked his curiosity about the unconscious. Freud believed that the ego was somehow put into a suspended state during a deep hypnotic trance. A hypnotist could thus bypass the ego's censoring process and get directly to unconscious material. Early experiences with hypnosis told Freud there was more to the human mind than what people can bring into awareness. When people asked him for proof of the unconscious, he often pointed to hypnosis. "Anyone who has witnessed such an experiment," he wrote, "will receive an unforgettable impression and a conviction that can never be shaken" (1938/1964, p. 285).

Because Freud envisioned hypnosis as a pipeline to the unconscious, it is easy to see how hypnosis would be a valuable tool for psychotherapists seeking to uncover unconscious material. Yet Freud was quick to acknowledge some of the drawbacks of hypnosis. Chief among these is that not all clients are responsive to hypnotic suggestion. In addition, as discussed in the next chapter, not all psychologists agree with Freud's description of hypnosis as a pathway to the unconscious.

Accidents. Suppose you are having an argument with a friend and you "accidentally" knock off a shelf an irreplaceable statue belonging to your friend. The statue shatters beyond repair. You apologize, saying that you did not mean to do it. But is this really an accident? In Freud's view, many apparent accidents are in fact intentional actions stemming from unconscious impulses. Freud might argue that you were expressing an unconscious desire to hurt your friend when you broke the statue. Clients who claim they accidentally forgot their regular meeting with a therapist might be displaying what Freud called *resistance.* Consciously, the clients believe they simply did not remember the appointment. Unconsciously, there has been a deliberate effort to thwart a therapist who may be close to uncovering threatening unconscious material. Similarly, reckless drivers might be setting themselves up for an accident to satisfy an unconscious desire to harm themselves. To Freudian psychologists, many unfortunate events are accidents in the sense that people do not consciously intend them, but not in the sense that they are unintended.

Symbolic Behavior. Just as our dreams can be interpreted as symbolic representations of unconscious desires, many of our daily behaviors might be seen as symbolic gestures of unconscious thoughts. Behaviors acted out symbolically pose no threat to the ego because they are not perceived for what they are. But these actions do allow the expression of unconscious desires. An excellent example is found in the case of a client who held a great deal of hostility toward his mother, although not at a conscious level. To the therapist, this unconscious hostility was the root of the client's problems and was expressed through an interesting doormat the client purchased for his home. The doormat was decorated with pictures of daisies. Not coincidentally, the client's mother had a favorite flower, the daisy. She had daisies on her dishes and pictures of daisies all around the house. In short, the daisies symbolized the mother. The good son enjoyed rubbing his feet and stomping on the daisies—symbolically acting out his hostility toward his mother—every time he entered the house.

When we apply Freud's dream symbols to everyday behaviors, we can see psychologically significant behavior seemingly everywhere. What can we say about the woman who joins the rifle team? The man who explores caves? The person who constantly borrows pencils without returning them? It is interesting to note that Freud was a habitual cigar smoker who, despite painful operations for cancer of the jaw, continued to smoke until his death. Although the cigar is an obvious phallic symbol, Freud reportedly answered a query about his habit by saying, "Sometimes a cigar is just a cigar."

Application: Psychoanalysis

Not only was Freud the father of psychoanalytic theory, but he was also the first person to outline and advocate a system of psychotherapy to treat psychological disorders. During his early years with Breuer, Freud recognized that many disorders were psychological rather than physical in origin. Through his experimentation with hypnosis, he came to see that the causes of these disorders were buried in a part of the mind not easily accessible to awareness. Slowly Freud developed various methods to get at this material, beginning with hypnosis and gradually changing to free association. As he gained insights into the causes of his clients' disorders and the structure and functioning of human personality, Freud developed a system of therapy to treat various psychological problems.

This system of psychotherapy is called **psychoanalysis.** Its goal is to bring crucial unconscious material into consciousness, where it can be examined in a rational manner. Once the unconscious material surfaces into consciousness, it must be dealt with in such a way that it does not manifest itself in some new disorder. The therapist and the client work together to help the ego once again exercise appropriate control over the id impulses and the oppressive superego. In some ways, the therapist and the client are like explorers searching through the client's mind for crucial unconscious material. But the therapist also is like a detective, who must evaluate cryptic messages about the underlying cause of the disorder as the client unconsciously, and sometimes cunningly, works to mislead and frustrate the therapist's search.

Typically, psychoanalysis clients lie on a couch while the therapist sits behind them, out of sight. The client is encouraged to speak freely, without any distractions from the room or the therapist that might inhibit free association.

Unfortunately, the process of digging through layers of conscious and unconscious material, as well as avoiding the obstacles and misdirection thrown in the way by the threatened ego, is a lengthy one. Clients usually require several hour-long therapy sessions a week for a period of perhaps several years. Consequently, traditional psychoanalysis is expensive and usually limited to those who can afford it.

The bulk of time spent in psychoanalysis is devoted to getting at the crucial unconscious material causing the disorder. Because the ego has devoted so much energy and is so strongly motivated to repress this material, this part of therapy can be difficult. Freud used a variety of methods to get at unconscious material, including free association, dream interpretation, and hypnosis. Unlike later systems of psychotherapy, in psychoanalysis the therapist actively interprets for clients the significance of their statements, behaviors, and dreams. But Freud cautioned that therapists should not reveal true meanings too soon. Beginning therapists are often tempted to interpret the unconscious meaning behind an act or a statement to a client as soon as they understand it themselves. However, this could be threatening for the client's ego, causing him or her to construct new and stronger defenses for the unconscious material.

Nonetheless, when the timing is right, the psychoanalyst's job is to interpret statements and dream symbols for clients until they understand their true meaning. An excellent example of this is found in one of Freud's famous case studies, the case of Dora. Dora was an 18-year-old patient from an affluent family. She complained of headaches and other physical problems. One area of trauma for Dora concerned a married couple, who Freud referred to as Mr. and Mrs. K. Mrs. K. was having an affair with Dora's father, and to make things more complicated, Mr. K. had made sexual advances toward Dora, to which she reacted with disgust and anger. One day during therapy, Dora related the following dream:

> A house was on fire. My father was standing beside my bed and woke me up. I dressed quickly. Mother wanted to stop and save her jewel-case; but Father said: "I refuse to let myself and my two children be burnt for the sake of your jewel-case." We hurried downstairs, and as soon as I was outside I woke up. (1901/1953, p. 64)

To the untrained listener, this dream seems innocent and meaningless enough, similar to dreams we all have experienced and given little thought to. But for Freud, it was filled with clues about the causes of Dora's problems. With a little questioning, Freud learned that shortly before the dream had occurred, Mr. K. had given Dora an expensive jewel case as a present. With this information, Freud had all the pieces he needed to understand the dream. As he explained to Dora,

> Perhaps you do not know that "jewel-case" is a favourite expression for the female genitals. . . . The meaning of the dream is now becoming even clearer. You said to yourself: "This man is persecuting me; he wants to force his way into my room. My 'jewel-case' is in danger, and if anything happens it will be Father's fault." For that reason in the dream you chose a situation which expresses the opposite—a danger from which your father is saving you. Mr. K. is to be put in the place of your father just as he was in the matter of standing beside your bed. He gave you a jewel-case; so you are to give him your jewel-case. . . . So you are ready to give Mr. K. what his wife withholds from

him. That is the thought which has had to be repressed with so much energy, and which has made it necessary for every one of its elements to be turned into its opposite. The dream confirms once more what I had already told you before you dreamt it—that you are summoning up your old love for your father in order to protect yourself against your love for Mr. K. (p. 69)

Freud interpreted several important psychoanalytic concepts for Dora. He identified her use of symbols and repression of her true desires. He explained how she used reaction formation—dreaming the opposite of what she really wanted—and how her repressed desires for her father affected her behavior. Not surprisingly, Dora had difficulty accepting this interpretation at first. As this example shows, clients must obtain a reasonable understanding of psychoanalytic theory before they can appreciate the therapist's interpretation of their dreams, thoughts, and behaviors.

Ironically, one of the first signs that therapy is progressing is the development of *resistance.* For example, clients might decide that the sessions aren't helping them and that they want to discontinue therapy. Or they might lapse into long silences, return to material already discussed, miss appointments, or insist that certain topics aren't worth exploring. These attempts at resistance may indicate that the therapist and client are getting close to the crucial material. The threatened ego is desperately attempting to defend against the approaching demise of its defenses as crucial unconscious material is almost ready to burst into consciousness.

Another necessary step in traditional psychoanalysis is the development of **transference.** Here the emotions associated with other people in past situations are displaced onto the therapist. For example, a client might talk to and act toward the therapist as if the therapist were a deceased parent. Unconscious emotions and previously undelivered speeches buried deep and long are unleashed, feelings that often lie at the heart of the client's disorder. Freud warned that handling transference was a delicate and crucial part of the therapy process. He also cautioned therapists against *countertransference,* in which therapists displace their own feelings toward other people onto the client.

The bulk of time spent in psychoanalysis is devoted to bringing the unconscious conflict to the surface. At this point, the therapist works with the emotionally vulnerable client to resolve the conflict at a conscious level and integrate it into the new personality. Successful treatment releases the psychic energy the ego has expended in repressing the conflict. Once freed, the client can live a happy, normal life.

Assessment: Projective Tests

Psychoanalysts are faced with a unique problem when developing ways to measure the personality constructs of interest to them. By definition, the most important concepts are those the test taker is unable to report directly. If a client can readily describe a psychological conflict, that conflict obviously is not buried deeply in the unconscious and thus is unlikely to be the key to understanding the person's problem. So how can psychoanalytic therapists and researchers measure unconscious material? The solution is to bypass direct reporting altogether. Projective tests are designed to generate seemingly uninformative responses from test takers that can then be interpreted by a trained psychologist.

As mentioned earlier in this chapter, projective tests present people with ambiguous stimuli, such as inkblots or vague pictures. Test takers respond by describing what they see, telling stories about the pictures, or somehow providing a reaction to the material. The tests are designed to provide no clues about correct or incorrect answers. Therefore, responses tend to be highly idiosyncratic. One person may see a bat and an elephant, whereas another identifies a classroom and a woman in mourning. As the name implies, psychoanalysts consider these responses projections from the unconscious. The ambiguous material gives test takers an opportunity to express pent-up impulses. However, as with other expressions of unconscious impulses, the significance of the response is not apparent to the test taker.

Types of Projective Tests

In 1921 Hermann Rorschach published a paper in which he described a procedure for predicting behavior from responses to a series of inkblots. Although Rorschach died the next year at age 38, his work stimulated other psychologists who continued to develop the test that still bears its creator's name. The **Rorschach inkblot test** consists of 10 cards, each containing nothing more than a blot of ink, some-

This psychologist is administering one of the most widely used personality tests: the Rorschach inkblot test. The participant tells him what she sees on the card, but whether these responses provide a valid assessment of her personality remains a controversy.

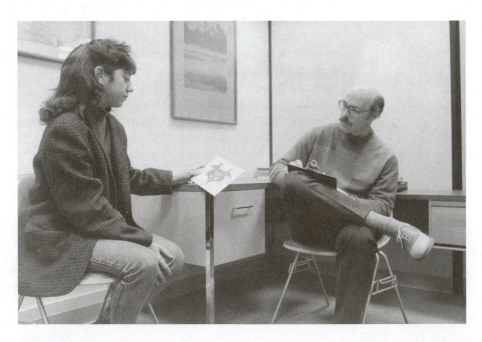

times in more than one color. Test takers are instructed to describe what they see in the inkblot. They are free to use any part of the inkblot and are usually allowed to give several responses to each card. Although some of the cards may be quite suggestive, they are in fact nothing more than inkblots.

Inkblot test responses can be analyzed with any of several scoring systems developed over the years. However, most psychologists probably rely on their personal insights and intuition when interpreting responses. Unusual answers and recurring themes are of particular interest, especially if they are consistent with information revealed during therapy sessions. For example, most therapists would probably take note if a client sees nothing but dead bodies, graves, and tombstones on each card. Similarly, clients who see suicidal acts, bizarre sexual behavior, or violent images probably provide therapists with topics to explore in the next session.

Another widely used projective test is the **Thematic Apperception Test** (TAT). The test was designed by Henry Murray (Chapter 7) and consists of a series of ambiguous pictures. Test takers are asked to tell a story about each picture—who the people are, what is going on, what has led up to the scene, and what the outcome is going to be. Although most of the pictures contain images of people, facial expressions and the nature of the relationship between the people are intentionally vague. Thus, test takers may see love, guilt, anger, or grief in the people's faces. The characters may be fighting, plotting, loving, or unaware of each other. They may be in for a happy, sad, horrifying, or disappointing end to their situation. What the test taker sees in the picture provides clues to the person's personality. Although therapists often rely on their intuition when interpreting TAT responses, many use relatively objective scoring procedures. Examples of how psychologists use the TAT in research are provided in Chapters 4 and 8.

Yet another projective test used by many therapists is the **Human Figure Drawing test.** Although initially developed in the 1920s as a measure of intelligence, psychologists soon recognized that the test also seemed to measure important personality constructs (Handler, 1996). The ambiguous stimulus here consists of a blank piece of paper and the instructions to draw a picture for the psychologist. In many cases, test takers are simply instructed to draw a person, but sometimes psychologists ask them to draw a family or a tree. The Human Figure Drawing test has many uses, including a measure of intelligence in children. However, most often it is used as an indicator of psychological problems, particularly in children (Bardos & Powell, 2001; Matto, 2002). Psychoanalysts often view the person drawn by the test taker as a symbolic representation of the self.

The notion that children's drawings provide a peephole into their inner thoughts and feelings has strong intuitive appeal. Schoolteachers often take note of children who never seem to draw smiles on the faces of the characters they sketch. Similarly, children who frequently draw monsters or ghoulish creatures could be expressing some disturbing inward feelings. A glance at the drawings by emotionally disturbed children presented in Figure 3.2 makes a persuasive case that children sometimes express through drawing what they otherwise might not put into words.

Figure 3.2

Human Figure Drawings by Emotionally Disturbed Children

Source: From Koppitz (1968); reprinted by permission of Grune & Stratton, Inc., and the author.

Evaluation of Projective Tests

Like most things related to psychoanalytic theory, a great deal of controversy surrounds the use of projective tests, particularly the Rorschach inkblot test. Hundreds of studies have been conducted with the inkblot test, using responses to predict everything from intelligence to sexual orientation. Unfortunately, psychologists disagree on how to interpret this research. Critics point to unacceptably low indices of reliability and frequent failures to find evidence for the validity of the scale (Wood, Nezworski, & Stejskal, 1996, 1997). One team of reviewers concluded that "there is currently no scientific basis for justifying the use of Rorschach scales in psychological assessment" (Hunsley & Bailey, 1999, p. 266). Another said bluntly that the Rorschach inkblot test was "not a valid test of anything" (Dawes, 1994, p. 146). Because of concerns about the validity of the test, some psychologists challenge whether the inkblot procedure should be treated as a test at all. They argue that the Rorschach is more accurately characterized as a highly structured interview.

However, there is another side to this controversy. Advocates of the Rorschach test raise several important points in its defense. First, one needs to separate good studies designed to test appropriate predictions from poor studies that attempt to tie test responses to any and all behaviors (Weiner, 1995, 1996). When reviewers look at results from sound studies making reasonable predictions, they find evidence for the usefulness of the test (Meyer, 1997; Parker, Hanson, & Hunsley, 1988; Viglione, 1999; Weiner, 1996). Moreover, newer, more rigorous systems for coding Rorschach responses have proved far more reliable than earlier methods (Viglione & Hilsenroth, 2001; Weiner, 2001). Second, establishing good validity data for projective tests is more difficult than when using other kinds of personality measures. In particular, how can we demonstrate empirically that a Rorschach assessment is accurate? If a therapist concludes from an inkblot test that a client has a certain unconscious conflict, what objective criterion does the researcher use to establish the validity of this claim? Indeed, if objective indicators existed, therapists wouldn't need to use projective tests in the first place.

Despite the controversy, the Rorschach and many other projective tests continue to be widely used psychological instruments (Camara, Nathan, & Puente, 2000; Watkins, Campbell, Nieberding, & Hallmark, 1995). One reason for this widespread use is that the tests may uncover information not easily obtainable in other ways. For example, therapists working with children sometimes allow a child to play with a family of dolls. Imagine a child who acts out a drama in which the mother and father dolls are cruel to the child doll. That child might be expressing something about how he or she perceives parents and home in a way that isn't easily expressed through other means.

Then again, many psychologists warn against overinterpreting responses to projective tests. The child in the previous example could merely be acting out a scene from a recent television program. Because the validity of projective tests remains open to challenge, psychologists usually are advised not to rely heavily on the tests when making diagnoses (Wood, Garb, Lilienfeld, & Nezworski, 2002). Instead, projective test results should be viewed as but one source of information about a client. They should be taken into consideration along with information collected through interviews, observation, case histories, and other psychological tests.

Strengths and Criticisms of Freud's Theory

None of the approaches to personality covered in this book can spark an argument as quickly as Freudian theory. Every clinical psychologist and personality researcher has an opinion on the value and accuracy of Freud's theory. Although few accept all of Freud's observations and postulates unquestioningly, adherents of the Freudian view strongly defend the basic assumptions Freud made about the nature of human functioning. Critics tend to be equally passionate in their evaluations.

Strengths

"Freud's greatest achievement probably consisted in taking neurotic patients seriously."
CARL JUNG

Even if all of Freud's ideas were to be rejected by modern personality theorists, he would still deserve an important place in the history of psychology. Freud's was the first comprehensive theory of human behavior and personality. Most subsequent personality theorists have found it necessary to point out where their theories differ from or correct weaknesses in Freud's works. Many of these psychologists built their theories on the foundation laid by Freud, borrowing key psychoanalytic concepts and assumptions. As discussed in Chapter 5, many of those who studied Freud or were trained in the Freudian tradition went on to develop and promote their own versions of psychoanalytic theory. Most psychology historians credit psychoanalytic theory with setting the direction for personality theory for many decades to follow. Thus, the shape of more recent approaches to personality, even though far removed from psychoanalytic theory, has probably been influenced in many ways by Freud's vision of personality.

Freud also can be credited with developing the first system of psychotherapy. Today, treating psychological disorders through discussions with a therapist is an accepted and widely practiced procedure. Although psychotherapy might have evolved without Freud, it certainly would not have evolved the way it did. Such techniques as free association, hypnosis, and dream interpretation have become standard tools for many therapists. Indeed, some clients are disappointed to find their therapist has no couch and does not plan to hypnotize them or interpret their dreams. Nonetheless, surveys reveal that a large number of young as well as experienced psychotherapists identify their perspective as "psychoanalytic" (Mayne, Norcross, & Sayette, 1994; Smith, 1982; Spett, 1983).

In addition, Freud can be credited with popularizing and promoting important psychological principles and concepts. For example, anxiety has played a key role in the work of many psychotherapists, personality theorists, and researchers from numerous areas of psychology. As discussed in Chapters 4, 6, and 16, many of the topics researched by psychologists today have their roots in one or more of Freud's concepts, even if they no longer carry much of the Freudian flavor. The point is that by placing these concepts onto the menu of psychological topics many years ago, Freud influenced the subject matter of personality research today.

Criticisms

Although Freud's ideas were so revolutionary that they were rejected by many in the medical and academic communities at the time, some writers have argued that Freud's ideas may not have been so original or groundbreaking after all. For example, one investigator discovered that between 1870 and 1880 at least seven books were published in Europe that included the word *unconscious* in the title (Whyte, 1978). Because the educated elite in Europe was relatively small, another researcher concluded that "at the time Freud started his clinical practice every educated person must have [been] familiar with the idea of the unconscious" (Jahoda, 1977, p. 132). Other historians point out that Freud probably had access to the works of people already writing about different levels of consciousness, free association, and infantile sexuality (Jahoda, 1977; Jones, 1953–1957). In addition, many Freudian ideas appear in literature that predates Freud's work. For example, the Russian novelist Fyodor Dostoyevski, who died in 1881, described in his writing such things as unconsciously motivated behaviors, erotic symbolism in dreams, intrapsychic conflict, and even hints of an Oedipus complex.

Thus, a case can be made that Freud's "revolutionary" ideas were not so new and foreign to European thinking at the time. Three points can be offered in Freud's defense. First, Freud often cited earlier works on topics similar to the ones he was introducing. This is especially true in his early writings. Second, Freud was the first person to organize many loosely related ideas into one theory of human behavior. Without a unified theory detailing the relationship among the unconscious, dream interpretation, and infantile sexuality, it is doubtful whether any of these notions would have been developed much further by the scientists who were familiar with them. Third, Freud initiated a lifelong program of investigating the various concepts in his theory. The work Freud and his followers did with their clients provided the data on which psychoanalytic theory was developed. Although many of Freud's major contributions may have had precedents in earlier writings, there is a large difference between introducing an idea and organizing, integrating, and developing many ideas into a comprehensive model of human behavior.

A second criticism often made of Freudian theory is that many of the hypotheses generated from the theory are not testable. Recall that one criterion for a valuable scientific theory is that it can generate hypotheses that can be either supported or not supported. But critics point to the difficulty of finding evidence that would fail to support Freud's theory. For example, if a Freudian therapist concludes that a client has a strong unconscious hatred for her sister, what sort of evidence would demonstrate that the conclusion is incorrect? What if the client says she cannot remember any negative feelings toward her sister? The client is obviously repressing them. What if the client describes how much she loves her sister? Obviously, this is a reaction formation. And if the client admits she harbors negative feelings toward her sister? Then the therapist has been successful in bringing the material into consciousness. If the hypothesis cannot be unsupported, neither can it be truly supported. This makes the theory considerably less useful to scientists.

In Freud's defense, he can hardly be accused of being unconcerned with finding evidence to support his theory. Indeed, he referred to many parts of his theory as "discoveries," the products of detailed examinations of clients' statements during various stages of psychoanalysis. Although some aspects of Freudian theory may be difficult to test, part of the difficulty may be researchers' failure to develop adequate experimental methods. However, as shown in the next chapter, some clever methods for examining various Freudian concepts have been devised in recent years, and others no doubt will be developed in the future.

Freud relied heavily on case study data as evidence for various aspects of his theory. However, this is the basis of another criticism. These data were almost certainly biased. First, Freud's patients hardly represented typical adults. Not only did they come from relatively wealthy and well-educated European families, but they also were suffering from psychological disorders at the time. It is a large leap to say that the minds of these clients function the same as the mind of the average psychologically healthy adult. Second, all information we have about these clients was filtered through Freud. Thus, it is possible that Freud recognized and recorded only those statements and behaviors that supported his theory and ignored or failed to notice those that did not. Third, it is possible that (consciously or unconsciously) Freud caused his patients to say the things he wanted to hear. Psychotherapy clients can at times be highly vulnerable to accepting whatever a person in a position of authority tells them and may be highly motivated to please that person. For example, it is interesting to note that when interpreting Dora's dream, Freud wrote that the dream only confirmed what he already knew. Of course, this criticism is not limited to Freud but applies to all case studies based on private interactions between therapists and their clients. Unless the therapist records or invites others to listen in on the sessions and form their own impressions, the data will almost always be subject to the interpretation and influence of the therapist.

A final group of criticisms concerns disagreements with the points of emphasis and tone of Freud's theory. Many of Freud's early followers eventually broke away from the group and developed their own theories because they felt Freud ignored or deemphasized important influences on personality. For example, some were concerned about Freud's failure to recognize how experiences beyond the first five years of life could affect personality. Others disagreed with Freud's emphasis on an instinctual basis for personality at the expense of important social and cultural influences. Still others took issue with Freud's tendency to concentrate on psychological disorders rather than on daily functioning and positive aspects of personality. As discussed in Chapter 5, many subsequent psychoanalytic thinkers developed theories that corrected some of these limitations and omissions.

Summary

1. The first comprehensive theory of personality was developed by Sigmund Freud about 100 years ago. After working with hypnosis to help patients suffering from hysteria, Freud came to understand the power of unconscious influences on behavior. According to his theory, human personality can be divided into conscious, preconscious, and unconscious parts. In addition, personality can be divided into the id, ego, and superego. Psychological activity is powered by psychic energy, called libido. Intrapsychic conflict creates tension, and the goal of human behavior is to return to a tensionless state.

2. Within Freud's theory, a healthy personality is one in which the ego controls id impulses and superego demands. To this end, the ego often uses defense mechanisms. These include repression, in which traumatic information is pushed out of awareness. Other defense mechanisms include sublimation, displacement, reaction formation, denial, intellectualization, and projection. With the exception of sublimation, the ego uses these defense mechanisms at a cost.

3. Among the most controversial aspects of Freud's theory is his description of the psychosexual stages of development. Freud maintained that young children pass through stages of development characterized by the primary erogenous zone for each stage. Children pass through oral, anal, and phallic stages on their way to healthy sexual expression in the genital stage. Excessive trauma during these early years may cause psychic energy to become fixated, and the adult personality will reflect the characteristics of the fixated stage of development. An important step in the development of adult personality takes place with the resolution of the Oedipus complex at the end of the phallic stage.

4. Psychoanalysts have developed several methods for getting at unconscious material. Freud called dreams the "royal road to the unconscious." He interpreted the symbols in his patients' dreams to understand unconscious impulses. In addition, Freudian psychologists use projective tests, free association, and hypnosis to get at this material. Clues about unconscious feelings also may be expressed in Freudian slips, accidents, and symbolic behavior.

5. Freud also developed the first system of psychotherapy, called psychoanalysis. Most of the time in this lengthy therapy procedure is spent bringing the unconscious sources of the clients' problems into awareness. A Freudian therapist actively interprets the true (unconscious) meanings of the clients' words, dreams, and actions for them. One of the first signs that psychoanalysis is progressing is resistance, in which a client stops cooperating with the therapeutic process in order to halt the therapist's threatening efforts to bring out key hidden material.

6. Many Freudian psychologists rely on projective tests to measure the concepts of interest to them. Typically, test takers are asked to respond to ambiguous stimuli, such as inkblots. Because there are no real answers, responses are assumed to reflect unconscious associations. The use of projective tests is controversial. Critics point to unacceptably low indicators of reliability and validity. However, if used correctly, these tests may provide insights into clients' personalities and sources of psychological problems.

7. Among the strengths of the Freudian approach is the tremendous influence Freud had on personality theorists for many years to follow. In addition, Freud developed the first system of psychotherapy and introduced many concepts into the domain of scientific inquiry. Critics point out that many of Freud's ideas were not new and that many aspects of his theory are not testable. Others criticize his use of biased data in developing his theory. Many of those who studied with Freud also disliked his emphasis on instinctual over social causes of psychological disorders and the generally negative picture he painted of human nature.

InfoTrac Key Terms

For additional readings go to http://www.infotrac-college.com/wadsworth and enter a search term related to your interest. Use the key terms suggested here to pull up several related articles. Also see the text Web site at http://psychology.wadsworth.com for more suggested readings and interactive quizzes to test your knowledge.

Defense mechanism (psychology)   Psychosexual development
Dreams-interpretation   Rorschach inkblot test
Hypnosis   Sigmund Freud
Libido   Unconscious
Oedipus complex

Chapter 4

The Freudian Approach

Relevant Research

Dream Interpretation
Defense Mechanisms
Humor
Hypnosis
Summary

When I describe Freud's theory to undergraduates, I typically find two different reactions. On one hand, some students are impressed with Freud's insight into human behavior. Psychoanalytic theory helps them understand some of their own feelings and behaviors and the conflicts they wrestle with. "It really applies to me," a student told me, "Now I see why I do some of the things I do. Now I understand how symbolic some of my behaviors are."

On the other hand, some students eye Freudian theory with skepticism and even ridicule. Sexual feelings in children, unconscious meanings in dreams, Oedipal desires for one's opposite-sex parent and the like strike these students as little more than a Freudian fantasy taken too seriously. Although we probably embrace the personality theories that fit our own perceptions of human behavior, a scientific approach requires more than faith in one theory over another. What we need is evidence that Freud was correct in his characterization of human nature and psychological processes. In short, we need research.

Critics of the psychoanalytic approach sometimes charge that Freud was unconcerned with validating his theory. But that is not entirely correct. Freud's writings are filled with "a passionate desire to discover ways in which the validity of psychoanalytic findings could be established," wrote one historian. "The search for validation pervaded his entire work" (Jahoda, 1977, p. 113). However, Freud sought validation through methods other than empirical research. Fortunately, many psychologists have taken on the challenge of testing many of Freud's ideas through more rigorous experimental procedures. Although some aspects of Freud's theory do not easily translate into experiments, researchers have succeeded in deriving several testable hypotheses from Freud's writings. In addition to direct tests of Freudian theory, a great deal of research has been conducted on topics either introduced or popularized by Freud. That is, many phenomena of interest to Freud—hypnosis, slips of the tongue, anxiety, early developmental experiences—have been studied in depth by personality psychologists. The results from these investigations often elaborate upon or provide insight into some of the processes described by Freud.

In this chapter, we'll examine four areas of research relevant to Freud's theory. It begins with research on dream interpretation, with an eye to Freud's notions about the meaning and function of our dreams. Next, we look at how researchers study some of the defense mechanisms proposed by Freud and his followers, and how these defense mechanisms change as we move from childhood into adults. This work is followed by research on Freud's theory of humor. According to psychoanalytic theory, unconscious motives are often expressed through jokes, cartoons, and the things we find funny. Finally, we look at the phenomenon that first piqued Freud's curiosity about the unconscious—hypnosis. What is this fascinating phenomenon, and why are some people more responsive to a hypnotist's suggestions than others?

> "*[F]reud was a person with a passionate thirst for truth, unbounded faith in reason, and unflinching courage to stake everything on this faith.*"
>
> ERICH FROMM

Dream Interpretation

Next time you want to liven up a dull social gathering ask the people around you to describe a recent dream. Although some of us remember dreams better than others, most people have little trouble recalling a funny, bizarre, or frightening dream they've experienced—sometimes more than once. In my dreams, I've walked on clouds, been visited by cartoon characters, and interacted with talking clocks. Friends have described dreams in which they fly like Superman, discover lost cities under the sea, live inside a potato and fight with giant spiders. When unrestricted by the laws of time and physics, nearly anything is possible in our nighttime dramas.

If you are like most people, you probably wonder from time to time just what your dreams really mean. Your curiosity reflects one of Freud's legacies to twentieth-century Western culture. The notion that dreams contain hidden psychological meaning was promoted and popularized by Freud. Freud interpreted his patients' dreams in an effort to understand their unconscious conflicts and desires. Today, therapists from various schools of thought use dream interpretation as one of their therapeutic tools. But how accurate is dream interpretation? One problem patients sometimes encounter is that different therapists develop entirely different interpretations of the same dream. Still other psychologists deny that dreams have any significance at all, or they challenge the ability of therapists to understand the significance of dreams. Who is correct?

Although conducting research on dreams presents many challenges, a large number of investigators have studied this universal but mystical phenomenon. We'll look at two questions addressed in this research, with a particular eye on what the findings tell us about Freud's theory. First, *what* do people dream about? Can we use psychoanalytic theory to predict the content of our dreams? Second, *why* do people dream? Freud had some definite hypotheses about this, and researchers have produced findings relevant to some of these ideas. However, like other aspects of Freudian psychology, this research still leaves much room for interpretation by believers and skeptics.

"Dreams are never concerned with trivialities: we do not allow our sleep to be disturbed by trifles."
SIGMUND FREUD

The Meaning of Dream Content

According to Freud, the content of our dreams provides clues about what's in our unconscious. Occasionally, a dream contains images or evokes emotions that we feel must mean something. But for the most part, our dreams are absurd, vague, or just silly images that seemingly have no relation to anything. Of course, Freud might say the important unconscious material has been disguised through symbolism. If you were to describe one of your dreams to a traditional Freudian therapist, you would likely be told that the objects and people in your dreams are symbols, which in the Freudian tradition usually means sexual symbols. For example, you might be told that dancing and flying represent sexual intercourse, guns and tanks are penises, and caves are wombs. Later psychoanalytic theorists have argued that dreams represent unconscious preoccupations (Hall, 1953). That is, our unresolved conflicts surface during our sleeping hours. According to this interpretation, a therapist who knows what his or her client dreams about has an important clue about the client's unconscious conflicts.

Dream researchers have developed various procedures to record and interpret the content of our dreams (Domhoff, 1996, 1999a; Hill, 1996). Sometimes sleepers are awakened when physiological measures indicate they are probably dreaming. Other investigators rely on participants to record their dreams first thing in the morning in diaries they keep next to their beds. Still others simply ask participants to describe a recent dream or a recurrent dream.

Consistent with Freud's intuition, investigations using a variety of methods find that the content of our dreams is not random. Although there may be no apparent explanation for some of the bizarre material that makes its way into our nighttime productions, there is evidence that dream content is often influenced by the fears, problems, and issues that captured our thoughts before we went to bed (Domhoff, 2001; Foulkes & Cavallero, 1993). For example, one team of researchers found that people with a high need to take care of others often had dreams in which they experienced intimacy with another person (Evans & Singer, 1995).

Participants in another study spent several nights in a sleep laboratory (Nikles, Brecht, Klinger, & Bursell, 1998). First, participants were awakened during the

Figure 4.1

Appearance of
Current Concern
in Dreams

Source: Adapted from
Nikles, et al. (1998).

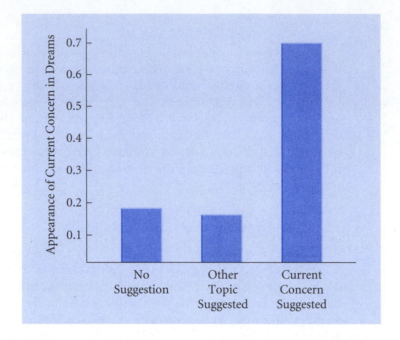

night and asked to describe their dreams. Prior to sleep the next two nights, participants were given suggestions to dream either about a current problem in their lives (such as conflict with a family member) or something that was not a problem for them. Again, participants were awakened during the night and asked to describe their dreams. As shown in Figure 4.1, many participants dreamed about the problem that was bothering them, even when it was not suggested. The current problem was especially likely to make its way into the participants' dream when they were reminded of the problem right before bed time. Clearly, the content of the dream provided information about what was going on in the participant's life.

But what about unconscious conflicts? Can issues we are not even aware of also make their presence known in our dreams? Some research findings suggest they can. Consider a series of investigations comparing how often male and female characters appear in dreams. Think of a recent dream of your own. Were there more male or female characters in your dream? The answer will depend in part on your own gender. Several investigations find that women typically have an equal number of male and female characters in their dreams. However, despite stereotypes about men dreaming only of beautiful women, in truth men are much more likely to dream about male characters (Hall, 1984; Hall & Domhoff, 1963). As shown in Table 4.1, this difference is found at all ages and in nearly every culture. The combined findings of all these studies suggest that males make up about 50% of the characters in women's dreams, but about 65% of the characters in men's dreams.

Age of Participants	Country/ Culture	Percent Male Characters	
		Men	*Women*
2–4	United States	59	49
7–12	United States	67	54
10–13	United States	69	52
	Guatemala	72	43
	Peru	68	50
14–17	United States	66	56
	Guatemala	68	46
	Peru	59	57
	Zulu	81	49
	Cuna	59	55
College	United States*	60	48
	Australia	55	48
	Mexico	59	61
	Peru*	34	39
	Zulu	82	54
	India	71	46
	Nigeria	81	50
Adult	United States	66	52
	Ifaluk	80	53
	Tinguian	61	66
	Alor	68	58
	Skolt	73	48
	Hopi	63	51

Table 4.1 **Percentage of Male Dream Characters for Men and Women**

*Figures combined from more than one sample.

Source: From Hall (1984), with permission.

But why are nearly two-thirds of the characters in men's dreams other males? One explanation relates back to the Oedipus complex and its female counterpart, the Electra complex (Hall, 1984). According to Freudian theory, men never completely overcome their conflicts with their fathers. Because some of these feelings are displaced onto other males, men typically experience more conflict with the men they encounter than do women. If men are preoccupied with this conflict at an unconscious level, as a psychoanalytic psychologist might guess, then this preoccupation should surface in the form of male characters in their dreams.

Can we say then that the universal prevalence of male characters in men's dreams proves this part of Freud's theory correct? Not entirely. Unfortunately, other interpretations are possible. For example, men may dream about males more than about women because they come into contact with more men during the day (Urbina & Grey, 1975). And even if we accept that men have more conflicts with men than with women, it is still an open question as to whether this conflict is a manifestation of unresolved Oedipal feelings. Nonetheless, we can say that the findings from these studies are at least consistent with predictions from Freud's theory.

Another phenomenon of interest to dream researchers is the *recurrent dream.* Most of us have experienced a dream that we believe we have had before. For some people, the same dream occurs every night for several nights in a row. Sometimes a dream appears off and on for months or even years. From a psychoanalytic perspective, the dream reappears night after night because the conflict expressed in the dream is important yet remains unresolved. This helps to explain why recurrent dreamers also are more likely to suffer from anxiety and generally poor adjustment during waking hours than people not experiencing recurrent dreams (Brown & Donderi, 1986; Zadra, O'Brien, & Donderi, 1998). The unconscious conflict surfaces in the dream at night but is expressed in the form of anxiety during the day.

But what of the most provocative aspect of Freud's dream interpretation theory—that seemingly innocent objects and actions are symbolic representations of sexuality and sexual activity? According to some psychoanalytic researchers, people who are anxious about sexual matters are unable to express their sexual desires directly. Instead, these individuals are left to express their sexual feelings through dream symbols. To test this hypothesis, one team of researchers asked participants to keep diaries of their dreams and their daily level of anxiety for 10 days (Robbins, Tanck, & Houshi, 1985). Consistent with the psychoanalytic position, the higher the participants' anxiety level, the more often classic Freudian sexual symbols (pencils, boxes, flying) appeared in their dreams. Although researchers sometimes find results like these consistent with Freud's theory, direct and convincing tests of the notion that dream images are sexual symbols remain elusive. Most dream researchers agree that the content of our dreams is not random, but determining why some images appear in our dreams more often than others remains a challenge.

The Function of Dreams

A more challenging question than what people dream is *why* people dream at all. Freud maintained that unconscious impulses cannot be suppressed forever. Therefore, one of the major functions of dreams is to allow the symbolic expression of these impulses. Dreams provide a safe and healthy outlet for expressing unconscious conflicts. But researchers had to wait for technology to catch up with theory before they could investigate this aspect of Freud's theory.

In the 1950s, researchers discovered that mammals experience two distinctly different kinds of sleep (Aserinsky & Kleitman, 1953). Each night we alternate between periods of *REM* and *non-REM sleep.* The acronym REM derives from the phrase *rapid eye movement,* because this period is usually accompanied by rapidly moving eyes underneath closed lids. REM sleep is sometimes called *paradoxical sleep* because, although our muscles are especially relaxed during this time, our brain activity, as measured by an instrument called an *electroencephalograph,* is similar to that of the waking state. Most adults spend $1\frac{1}{2}$ to 2 hours a night in REM sleep, spread over several periods.

The significance of this discovery for personality researchers is that REM sleep is filled with dreams, whereas non-REM sleep has significantly fewer dreams. Thus, the discovery of REM sleep created new opportunities for dream researchers. For example, researchers could look at the effects of depriving people of REM sleep, they could correlate psychological variables with the length and amount of REM sleep, and they could wake people during REM sleep to capture dreams that might be lost by morning (Arkin, Antrobus, & Ellman, 1978; Cohen, 1979).

What did REM sleep research reveal about the relationship between dreaming and mental health? Early researchers maintained that REM sleep, and therefore dreaming, was necessary for maintaining one's mental health and that depriving someone of REM sleep might create serious psychological disturbances. However, subsequent research challenged this conclusion (Hoyt & Singer, 1978; Vogel, 1975). Nevertheless, dreaming does seem to have some positive psychological effects. For example, REM sleep appears to prepare us for dealing with anxiety-arousing or ego-threatening material. People deprived of REM sleep have more difficulty with potentially stressful tasks (McGrath & Cohen, 1978). Moreover, people deprived of REM sleep one night typically respond by increasing their amount of REM sleep the next night (Bulkeley, 1997). This *rebound effect* also suggests that REM sleep serves some important function.

The psychological value of REM sleep was demonstrated in one experiment in which participants were shown a film about autopsy procedures before and after a night's sleep (Greenberg, Pillard, & Pearlman, 1978). The film, depicting a physician performing an autopsy in gruesome detail, was selected for the study because it invariably created high levels of anxiety in viewers. Participants deprived of REM sleep had a more difficult time coping with their anxiety than participants not deprived of REM sleep. The participants allowed to dream between showings of the film were significantly less disturbed by the film the second time they saw it.

Other research suggests that dreams also may allow us to work through unresolved problems while we sleep. Participants in one study were told just before going to sleep that they had performed poorly on an IQ test (Cohen & Cox, 1975). The participants who reported dreaming about the experiment during the night were in a better mood the next day than were those who did not. This suggests that by dreaming about the problem, the participants were able to somehow resolve it or deal with it better. Consistent with Freud's observations, the dreams appeared to have a positive function.

Although some research findings suggest that Freud was correct when he argued that dreaming was necessary for healthy psychological functioning, other studies challenge Freud's position. For example, why do newborn babies experience as much as eight hours of REM sleep per day? What unconscious conflicts are they working out? For that matter, REM sleep has been found in nearly all mammals and possibly even in human fetuses (Crick & Mitchison, 1983). At best, we can say that REM sleep also serves functions other than dreaming and the unconscious release of tension.

At this point, what can we say about the experimental support for Freud's theory of dream interpretation? Researchers have produced a number of findings consistent with Freud's speculations. The content of our dreams is not random, and dreaming appears to serve some positive psychological functions. However, in almost all cases, psychologists can account for the findings without relying on Freudian concepts. Moreover, occasionally researchers uncover results that are difficult to explain within Freudian theory. In short, the search for definitive answers to some of the questions Freud raised continues. Most of us have a difficult time abandoning the feeling that at least some of our dreams contain important psychological messages and that dreaming serves some important psychological function. Understanding the silly and frightening stories that play in our mind while we sleep no doubt will remain one of the irresistible mysteries for personality researchers for many years to come.

Defense Mechanisms

Among the discoveries Freud encountered when he first began to peek under the surface of human consciousness were the curious ways his patients dealt with emotional pain. As early as 1894, Freud wrote about his patients' unconscious efforts to conceal painful thoughts and described many of their neurotic symptoms as manifestations of defense mechanisms. Freud eventually identified the defense mechanism *repression* as the cornerstone of psychoanalysis. However, it was left to some of Freud's followers to fully develop the notion of defense mechanisms and to explore their psychological origins and function. In particular, Freud's daughter Anna identified 10 defense mechanisms depicted either directly or vaguely in her father's writings. She also described five additional mechanisms on her own, and subsequent psychoanalytic writers have added to the list. Thus, within the psychoanalytic approach, the ego has many tools at its disposal to fend off anxiety and guilt.

Defense mechanisms remain one of the most intriguing yet elusive aspects of Freud's theory. This is because we are said to regularly employ a wide range of defense strategies, yet, by definition, we have no awareness that we are doing so. This is not to say that we are unaware of the behaviors that stem from these defenses. I may be quite in touch with my intense desire to compete, the anger I express at the grocery clerk, and the excuses I make to avoid my parents. But the defensive function that drives these behaviors remains at a level below consciousness. Of course, friends and family members often see the connection. Indeed, we frequently accuse other people of being in denial, projecting their feelings onto others, or rationalizing away their bad habits. Most of us can think of times when friends displaced their anger onto us instead of to whatever or whomever was really upsetting them. It also is the case that we often use anxiety-reducing techniques quite consciously. For example, you might deliberately distract yourself by going to a movie rather than thinking about an upcoming job interview. However, these conscious efforts to reduce anxiety are not the same as the unconscious defense mechanisms we are considering here (Cramer, 2000). The coping strategies we deliberately employ to reduce anxiety are covered in Chapter 6.

Identifying and Measuring Defense Mechanisms

Psychologists investigating defense mechanisms face the same set of problems that confront other researchers studying psychoanalytic concepts. Because such mechanisms operate at a level below consciousness, we cannot simply ask people to describe their defense mechanisms to us. Rather, investigators must rely on less direct methods to determine when and how often research participants use the various mechanisms identified by psychoanalysts (Davidson & MacGregor, 1998).

Not surprisingly, many of these researchers have turned to projective tests. Some investigators interpret responses to Rorschach inkblots (Lerner & Lerner, 1990) or to stories (Ihilevich & Gleser, 1993) to measure defense mechanisms. Others use the stories participants create in response to Thematic Apperception Test (TAT) picture cards (Cramer, 1991; Cramer & Blatt, 1990; Hibbard et al., 1994).

To get an idea of how researchers derive information about defense mechanisms from projective tests, consider the response one psychiatric patient gave to a TAT card. The picture on the card features a boy and an unplayed violin. As with most projective stimuli, what the boy is feeling or thinking and his connection to the musical instrument is deliberately left unclear. The patient provided the following story:

> There's something wrong with this boy physically and mentally. He's unhappy. He wants to play the violin, and he can't. Maybe he's deaf. Somebody else was in the room earlier and put it in front of him, and left. He's not the kind of person who would pick it up and break it or anything. Is that enough? I don't know what the placemat's doing. It's obviously not something to eat. (Cramer, Blatt, & Ford, 1988, p. 611)

Researchers have developed detailed coding systems to turn this kind of response into numerical values (Cramer, 1991). They derive scores from the stories to indicate the extent to which the test taker uses various defense mechanisms. In this example, the investigators found evidence of denial ("He's not the kind of person who would pick it up and break it") and projection ("Something's wrong with this boy physically and mentally"). The more frequently test takers make these kinds of statements, the more they are assumed to use defense mechanisms when dealing with the anxiety they face in their own lives.

Consider an investigation in which college freshmen and sophomores receive some threatening information about their masculinity and femininity (Cramer, 1998b). The researcher reasoned that gender-related behavior is a particularly important aspect of identity for young men and women. In other words, it is important for most men entering adulthood to think of themselves as masculine, and for women to believe they are feminine. Information that threatens this part of the self-concept is potentially quite anxiety provoking. The investigator predicted that students would deal with this anxiety by using the defense mechanism *identification*. People who use identification associate themselves with powerful and successful people. For example, a young man might think about his association with a military leader or successful athlete. By unconsciously identifying with powerful others, we are said to fend off feelings of inadequacy and helplessness. Moreover, psychoanalysts argue that identification plays a particularly important role in the development of gender identity. Young men are said to identify with their father, whereas young women identify with their mother as they develop gender-related characteristics. Thus, when one's masculinity or femininity is threatened, the ego is likely to turn to identification to defend against the resulting anxiety.

To test this prediction, the investigator analyzed participants' stories for three TAT cards. The students then completed a short personality test, one presumably measuring their masculinity and femininity. Shortly thereafter, the students were given bogus feedback on the test. Half the men were told they had scored high in masculinity. However, the other half were told they scored high in femininity. Similarly, half the women were told they were feminine and half that they were masculine. The students were then asked to provide three more stories from another set of TAT cards.

How did the participants respond to the threatening test feedback? As shown in Figure 4.2, men receiving the bogus feedback had a particularly strong emotional reaction. As predicted, they reacted to this threatening information by resorting to more identification. The use of identification was particularly strong for those men who considered themselves highly masculine. In other words, to ward off this overt challenge to their sense of masculinity, the men unconsciously identified with powerful others, presumably masculine men. That the students became defensive in this study was illustrated well by the reaction of one male participant. When asked how he felt after being told he was feminine, he replied, "I didn't feel angry." Of course, no one had suggested that he was.

Developmental Differences

Which defense mechanisms people use depends not only on the kind of threat, but also on the age of the individual. Researchers find that defense mechanisms tend to follow a developmental pattern (Cramer, 1991; Vaillant, 1992). That is, some

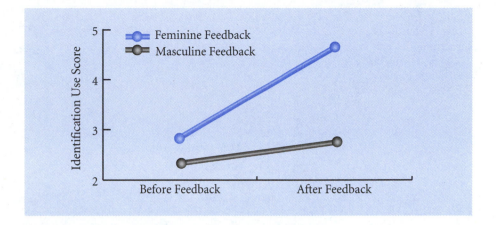

Figure 4.2

Men's Use of Identification as a Function of Feedback

Source: Adapted from Cramer (1998b).

defense mechanisms are more likely to be used by young children, whereas others show up more frequently in older children and adults.

Because they lack some of the complex cognitive skills available to older children, preschool and early elementary-age children often rely on unsophisticated defense mechanisms such as denial to ward off feelings of anxiety. *Denial* consists of disavowing certain facts, from failure to see reality to distorting one's memory ("No, that's not what happened"). Denying the existence of the threatening event reduces the anxiety associated with it. Several studies find that young children rely heavily on denial (Brody, Rozek, & Muten, 1985; Cramer, 1997b; Cramer & Brilliant, 2001). Children who experience severe traumas and threats to their wellbeing may have no other way to deal with their emotional reactions than to deny the events ever took place. When one team of researchers asked kindergarten children if they had ever felt like a sad and crying boy in a drawing, they found that few of the children acknowledged *ever* feeling sad (Glasberg & Aboud, 1982).

However, as children mature they find that outright denial of facts and feelings is increasingly ineffective. By the time they enter the middle elementary school years, the children's increased cognitive skills help them understand that refusing to admit a fact does not make it go away. Unfortunately, the anxieties that brought about the use of denial do not go away with these insights. Rather, the child comes to rely on more sophisticated methods of defense. In particular, older children often turn to projection to alleviate their anxieties and inward fears. *Projection* protects the individual from threatening anxiety by attributing the unacceptable thoughts and feelings to someone else, in a sense moving the anxiety-provoking material outside of the person. We recognize selfish behavior and sinister motives in others, but not in ourselves.

To examine this hypothesized shift from simple denial to more sophisticated defense mechanisms, researchers in one study gathered and coded TAT stories from children at several different times between the ages of six and a half and nine and a half (Cramer, 1997b). As shown in Figure 4.3, the children's use of denial and

Figure 4.3

Use of Defenses as a
Function of Age

Source: Cramer (1997b).
Used by permission of
P. Cramer.

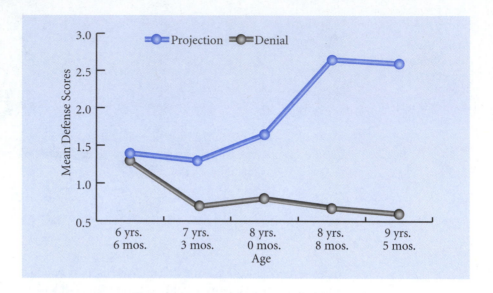

projection perfectly fit the expectations of the investigators. The children used increasingly less denial as they moved through these years, but came to use projection more. Similar outcomes have been obtained by researchers using different measures (Smith & Rossman, 1986) and when comparing the responses of children at different ages (Cramer & Gaul, 1988).

But projection also has its limitations. As they move into young adulthood, men and women begin to rely on even more sophisticated defense mechanisms. In fact, the use of defense mechanisms such as identification instead of denial and projection is sometimes seen as an indicator of emotional maturity (Cramer, 1998a). For example, one team of investigators found that young men still working through adolescent gender issues used projection and other immature defense mechanisms more often than men who had already come to accept their masculinity and the masculine role (Mahalik, Cournoyer, DeFranc, Cherry, & Napolitano, 1998). In short, the tools used by the ego may change as we move through the childhood years and into adulthood, but the need to protect ourselves from unacceptable levels of anxiety remains.

Individual Differences

We all know people who seem to be masters at rationalizing away their misdeeds and mistakes. You also may know someone who frequently displaces his anger onto employees, waiters, and telephone solicitors, or who constantly projects her own suspicions and fears onto others. Consistent with these observations, researchers find that each of us tends to rely on some defense mechanisms more than others (Bond, 1992; Vaillant, 1992). These psychologists sometimes refer to such individual patterns as our *defensive style.* Moreover, because some defense mechanisms are regarded as more effective and more mature than others, identifying a person's defensive style may tell us something about his or her general level of well being. Freud often pointed to defense mechanisms to explain neurotic behavior. However, it is not clear whether he thought the use of defense mechanisms was necessarily pathological. Later psychoanalytic writers have argued that on occasion defense mechanisms can be normal and even adaptive (Fenichel, 1945; Vaillant, 1977, 1992). For example, *sublimation*—turning the unconscious impulse into a socially acceptable action—may serve the dual function of relieving anxiety and improving the person's life situation.

Whether a defense mechanism is adaptive or maladaptive may be a function of how often the person relies on it and how old that person is. Anna Freud (1965) suggested that defense mechanisms are maladaptive when used past an appropriate age. As mentioned earlier, children often rely on denial and projection to deal with their anxieties. Five-year-olds may deny they did something unpleasant and still continue to function well. But adults who use the same defense strategy ("I never said that") may find it more and more difficult to interact with others or to make sense of their own behavior.

Why do some adults continue to rely on immature defense mechanisms like denial despite their ineffectiveness? According to Freud, adult defenses are related to early childhood experiences. One team of investigators tested this notion (Cramer & Block, 1998). The researchers began by measuring the amount of stress experienced by a group of three-year-olds. They then waited 20 years before contacting the participants again and examining the kinds of defense mechanisms used by the now 23-year-old adults. As expected, the men who as adults frequently relied on denial were the participants who had experienced the highest levels of stress in their early childhood. The researchers reasoned that the men had relied heavily on the age-appropriate defense mechanism of denial when they were young. Because denial helped the boys deal with their psychological distress, they continued to rely on this defense mechanism as adults.

Unfortunately, in the real world we cannot simply insist that a problem does not exist. Not surprisingly, investigators often find that the use of immature defenses is associated with problems in psychological functioning (Cramer, 1999, 2000, 2002; Kwon, 2000; Vaillant, 1992). Researchers in one study examined the use of defense mechanisms by parents during a particularly stress-filled time in their lives—the months immediately before the birth of their first child and the first year of the child's life (Ungerer, Waters, & Barnett, 1997). The demands of a newborn, coupled with the financial and personal burdens that come with parenthood, can be a major source of stress and anxiety. New parents who fail to deal with these stressors often experience a decline in their general satisfaction with their relationship. Consistent with these observations, the investigators found that parents who typically relied on immature defense mechanisms such as denial and projection were less happy with their partners as they faced the anxieties of parenting. On the other hand, mothers and fathers who relied on more mature defense mechanisms, such as sublimation, remained satisfied with their relationship despite the challenges and anxieties the baby brought into their lives.

Humor

On January 28, 1986, the space shuttle *Challenger* exploded 73 seconds after liftoff. Debris from the flaming craft scattered into the Atlantic Ocean. All seven crewmembers died. Millions watched television replays of the accident in shock and disbelief. Many cried openly. A nation went into mourning.

Why bring up this tragic incident as an introduction to a section on humor? Because within two days of the disaster I had probably heard more than a halfdozen *Challenger* jokes. Many people I encountered were eager to be the first to tell me the latest one. A radio disc jockey was suspended from his job when he shared a series of *Challenger* jokes on the air.

What is it that brings out this tasteless humor? Every highly publicized tragedy seems to be followed by a series of related jokes. This type of humor has taken many forms over the years but never seems to disappear or go out of style. In recent years cruel, tasteless humor has shown up as "dead baby" jokes, "Helen Keller" jokes, and "Mommy Mommy" jokes. In Freud's day they took the form of "marriage broker" jokes, which always began with a young man visiting a broker to arrange a marriage with a young woman. For example,

> The bridegroom was most disagreeably surprised when the bride was introduced to him, and drew the broker on the one side and whispered his remonstrances: "She's ugly and old, she squints and has bad teeth and bleary eyes. . . ."
> "You needn't lower your voice," interrupted the broker, "she's deaf as well." (Freud, 1905/1960, p. 64)

The typical response to this humor is laughter or a smile, followed by a half-serious complaint about the joke being in poor taste. Yet these jokes remain popular and continue to proliferate in different forms. Why?

Freud's Theory of Humor

In his 1905 book *Jokes and Their Relation to the Unconscious,* Freud presented an extensive analysis of humor. Although he recognized "innocent" jokes, such as puns and clever insights, Freud was more concerned with *tendentious* jokes—the ones that provide insight into the unconscious of the joke teller as well as the person who laughs. Predictably, Freud saw two kinds of tendentious jokes, those dealing with hostility and those dealing with sex.

At first glance, it is difficult to understand how aggression can be funny. What is it about insults and biting satire that attracts and amuses us? Why do we laugh at another person's humiliation and embarrassment? According to Freud, aggres-

"*A person who laughs at [an obscene joke] . . . is laughing as though he were the spectator of an act of sexual aggression.*"
SIGMUND FREUD

sive jokes allow the expression of impulses ordinarily held in check. Although we may have unconscious urges to attack certain people or groups of people, our egos and superegos are generally effective in preventing outward acts of violence. But a good insulting joke allows us to express these same aggressive desires in a socially appropriate manner. And, after all, who can take offense at an innocent joke? As Freud (1905/1960) wrote, "[b]y making our enemy small, inferior, despicable or comic, we achieve in a roundabout way the enjoyment of overcoming him" (p. 103).

Similarly, we can discuss taboo sexual topics through the socially appropriate outlet of sexual humor. Open discussions of sex are inappropriate in many social settings. Yet jokes on sex are often not only tolerated but encouraged and rewarded. I have seen normally conservative and proper people who would never bring up the topic of sex in public deal with all kinds of taboo topics simply by repeating a joke "someone told me." One team of researchers found that sexual jokes provided adolescent girls with an easy way to introduce otherwise embarrassing topics into their lunchtime conversations (Sanford & Eder, 1984).

Freud noticed that the laughter following a hostile or sexual joke is rarely justified by the humor content of the joke. If you stop to consider the next sexually oriented joke you hear, you'll probably notice that the joke actually contains very little humor. So why do we laugh? Freud explained our reaction in terms of tension reduction, or **catharsis.** The description of aggression or sexual behavior at the beginning of the joke creates tension. The punch line allows a release of that tension. We get pleasure from many jokes not because they are clever or witty, but because they reduce tension and anxiety. Freud might have interpreted the jokes following the *Challenger* tragedy in terms of the tension generated by the sudden awareness of death and unpredictable disaster. "Strictly speaking, we do not know what we are laughing at," Freud explained. "The technique of such jokes is often quite wretched, but they have immense success in provoking laughter" (1905/1960, p. 102).

Research on Freud's Theory of Humor

Look at the picture on page 86. Think of a caption that is as humorous or funny as possible. When researchers asked high school students to write funny captions to such pictures, they were surprised at what they found (Nevo & Nevo, 1983). The students gave responses filled with aggressive and sexual themes. Interestingly, the students made almost no references to sex or aggression when asked what they might say if actually in that situation. According to the researchers, the students "used Freud's techniques as if they had read his writings." For example, one picture depicted only that a man was late for an appointment. Although the picture contained no obvious sexual or hostile content, students still came up with captions such as "I was late because I was with your wife."

Was Freud correct when he wrote that people find aggressive and sexual humor funny? Several investigations support this suggestion (Deckers & Carr, 1986;

Kuhlman, 1985; McCauley, Woods, Coolidge, & Kulick, 1983; Pinderhughes & Zigler, 1985). Research participants typically rate cartoons containing aggression or sex as funnier than cartoons without these themes. Common observations point to the same conclusion. From one stooge poking another in the eye to cartoon characters being flattened by anvils, examples of pain and suffering permeate many sources of humor. And it's a rare situation comedy that goes more than a few minutes these days without a reference to sex.

Several other hypotheses derived from Freud's theory of humor have been supported in empirical studies. For example, if hostile humor allows us to satisfy aggressive impulses, we should find a joke funnier when it pokes fun at a person or group we don't like. Several studies find support for this prediction (Wicker, Barron, & Willis, 1980; Zillmann, Bryant, & Cantor, 1974). For example, one team of researchers presented men and women with a series of hostile jokes and cartoons (Mundorf, Bhatia, Zillmann, Lester, & Robertson, 1988). Some of the material ridiculed men, whereas other jokes and cartoons made fun of women. Consistent with Freud's theory, men found humor that targeted women funnier than humor that aimed at men, whereas the women enjoyed humor that put down men more than humor that made fun of women.

Two predictions from Freud's theory of humor are particularly intriguing, because at first glance they appear to defy common sense. First, would you tell a hostile joke to someone who is already dangerously angry? Most of us assume that

Write a funny caption for this picture.

hostile humor would only fan the flames and create a situation that could lead to violence. But Freud said the opposite reaction is more likely. Second, how much do people enjoy humor when they are nervous and maybe even a little frightened? Common sense says that anxiety interferes with having a good time, and that people are more likely to enjoy a good joke when they are comfortable and relaxed. Again, Freud disagreed. As you might expect, researchers have examined each of these questions.

Reducing Aggression with Hostile Humor. We've often heard that humor can turn away anger. Suppose you were confronted with an angry person and wanted to defuse the situation with a joke. What kind would you tell—one with obvious hostile content or an innocent, nonhostile joke? Common sense tells you to try the nonhostile joke. But remember, Freud said hostile humor provides a cathartic release of tension. Therefore, the way to reduce the angry person's aggressive impulses might be to reduce that tension. If that is the case, hostile humor should do the trick better than nonhostile humor.

Although surprising at first, several investigations find the predicted decrease in hostility after exposing participants to hostile humor. Participants in one study were insulted by the investigator and then read a series of either hostile or nonhostile jokes (Leak, 1974). When later asked what they thought about the insulting investigator, the participants who read the hostile jokes had gotten over their anger more than those who read the nonhostile jokes. Angry participants in another study read cartoons that expressed hostility toward women (Baron, 1978b). Later, these participants were given the opportunity to administer electric shocks to a woman under the guise of a learning experiment. Once again, these participants gave less intense and shorter shocks than angry participants who had not seen the cartoons.

These findings suggest Freud may have been correct about hostile humor reducing the likelihood of aggression. In some cases, exposing people to hostile humor seems to provide an outlet for tension reduction that lowers the need to aggress. Unfortunately, the relationship between humor and aggression is more complex than this. Other studies not only fail to find support for the Freudian position, they actually produce results in the opposite direction. For example, angry participants exposed to a hostile comedy routine in one study became *more* hostile toward a person who had insulted them (Berkowitz, 1970). In another study, angry participants allowed to shock an unseen victim gave more electric shocks after reading hostile cartoons than those who read nonhostile cartoons (Baron, 1978a). Thus, sometimes hostile humor reduces aggressiveness, yet other times it increases it.

What's going on here? What can we conclude about this prediction from Freudian theory? Quite possibly, hostile humor defuses aggressive tendencies in some situations. But hostile humor has the potential to do more than reduce tension. For example, as discussed in Chapter 14, people often imitate aggressive models. Thus, the aggression described in hostile jokes or shown in cartoons might be imitated by an angry reader. In addition, hostile humor may be arousing, and arousal has been identified as a contributing factor in aggression (Zillmann, 1979). In short, although Freud may be correct about the tension-reducing capabilities of hostile humor, people need to be cautious about using such humor when dealing with an angry audience.

Level of Tension and Funniness.   Observe a group of listeners the next time a good storyteller tells an obscene joke. Skilled joke tellers elaborate on the details. They allow the tension level to build gradually as they set up the punch line. Listeners smile or blush slightly as the joke progresses. According to Freud, this long buildup creates greater tension and thus a louder and longer laugh when the punch line finally allows a tension release.

Freud said the more tension people experience before a punch line, the funnier they'll find the joke. Thus, a nervous and slightly frightened person is more vulnerable to a funny joke than someone who is calm and therefore tensionless. This prediction was tested in a study in which people were asked to work with a laboratory rat (Shurcliff, 1968). Participants in the low-tension condition were asked to hold the rat for five seconds. They were told, "These rats are bred to be docile and easy to handle, and I don't think you will have any trouble." In the moderate-tension condition, people were asked to take a small sample of the rat's blood. They were told the task was easier than it looked. Participants in the high-tension group were given a bottle and syringe and asked to take two cubic centimeters of blood from the rat. The experimenter stressed the difficulties involved and warned the rat might bite.

The punch line occurred when participants reached into the cage and discovered a toy rat. Consistent with Freud's theory, participants in the high-tension group thought the situation was funnier than participants in the other conditions (Figure 4.4). The pleasure they derived from the release of tension apparently led to their enjoyment of the joke.

Interpreting the Findings

Although inconsistencies exist, researchers have uncovered some evidence in support of Freud's theory of humor. People often find jokes and cartoons funnier when they contain sexual and aggressive themes. We also appear to enjoy hostile humor more when it is aimed at someone we dislike. Hostile humor may reduce tension, although this does not necessarily reduce hostility, and jokes are funnier when the listener's tension level is built up before the punch line. Less direct tests of Freud's theory also suggest that laughter serves important psychological functions. For example, several studies find evidence to support the widely held belief that laughter is an effective means to combat daily tension and stressful events (Krokoff, 1990; Kuiper & Martin, 1998; Kuiper, McKenzie, & Belanger, 1995; Lefcourt, Davidson, Prkachin, & Mills, 1997). Some psychologists have even incorporated humor into their therapy procedures (McGuire, 1999).

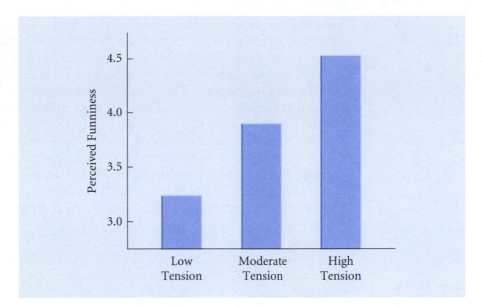

Figure 4.4

Perceived Funniness as a Function of Tension

Source: Based on Shurcliff (1968).

Does all of this mean that Freud was correct in his description of humor? Perhaps. One problem researchers face when interpreting these studies is that alternative explanations are often possible (Kuhlman, 1985; Nevo & Nevo, 1983). For example, many findings can be explained in terms of incongruity (McGhee, 1979). According to this analysis, humor results from an inconsistency between what we expect in a situation and what happens in the joke. Thus, the reason people find sexual and aggressive humor funny may be because sex and aggression are out of place in the joke setting. For example, imagine a movie scene in which two sophisticated women bump into each other at a department store. Imagine further that they either get into a physical fight or say something with sexual connotations. We may find this situation funny for the reasons outlined by Freud. But it might also bring a laugh because we do not expect women to act this way when shopping. Thus, although we can say that some research supports Freud's theory, it is probably best to conclude that much more needs to be learned about what people find funny and why. At any rate, Freud's interpretation has met one criterion for a good theory: It has generated a number of hypotheses and a significant amount of research.

Hypnosis

A psychologist is giving a classroom demonstration of hypnosis. Several student volunteers sit in the front of the room. They are told to relax and that they are becoming drowsy. The hypnotist tells them they are in a state of deep hypnosis and that they will do whatever he says. Soon the students close their eyes and sit peacefully yet attentively in their chairs. The hypnotist begins the demonstration by asking them to extend their left arm and to imagine a weight is pulling it down. Suddenly the arms of several students begin to move downward, just as if a weight were pulling on the arms. A few arms drop immediately; others drop slowly over several repetitions of the instructions. Still other students remain unaffected, with arms extended straight out. Later the hypnotist tells the students a fly is buzzing around their head. Some react swiftly, perhaps swatting at the imaginary fly, others react slowly or only slightly, and others continue to sit calmly. Before taking them out of hypnosis, the psychologist tells the students they won't remember what has happened until they are told to. When later asked about what they recall, some remember nothing, others a few details, and others practically everything that happened.

This description of a hypnotic induction and responsiveness test is typical of those used in hypnosis research. Although considerable disagreement remains over the nature of hypnosis, most researchers agree that hypnosis includes an induction procedure in which people are told they are going to be hypnotized, followed by suggestions to perform certain tasks. These tasks range from the simple ones used in hypnosis research, such as dropping your arm, to the entertaining performances of stage hypnosis participants, such as yelling like Tarzan or trotting up and down the aisles warning that the British are coming.

Although modern hypnosis has existed in some form for more than 200 years, it remains an intriguing and often misunderstood phenomenon shrouded in mysticism and curiosity. Yet hypnosis also carries a number of potentially useful applications. For example, many people have dental work performed under hypnosis, and thus don't need painkillers. Police investigators sometimes use hypnosis to help witnesses remember crime details. And many psychoanalytically oriented therapists believe hypnosis can uncover unconscious material crucial to overcoming patients' problems. Despite these many uses, psychologists still quarrel about just what they are dealing with. We'll explore some of the different opinions on this matter in the next section, followed by an examination of individual differences in hypnotic responsiveness.

What Is Hypnosis?

There is no shortage of theories about the nature of hypnosis. Although these different theories have traditionally been described as opposing camps, more recently hypnosis researchers have placed the various explanations for hypnosis along a continuum (Kirsch & Lynn, 1995). At one end of this continuum we find psychologists who describe hypnosis in a manner similar to the way Freud did. They believe hypnosis taps an aspect of the human mind that is otherwise difficult to reach. These theorists sometimes say that hypnotic participants fall into a trance or that they experience an altered state of consciousness, like sleeping. On the other

Like the volunteers in this classroom demonstration, most people respond to simple suggestions during hypnosis. However, why these subjects go along with the hypnotist's suggestions remains a matter of controversy.

end of the continuum we find theorists who reject the notion that hypnotized people operate under an altered state of awareness. They skeptically maintain there is nothing mysterious about hypnotic phenomena—that all the amazing things people do under hypnosis can be explained in terms of basic psychological processes applicable to hypnotized and nonhypnotized people. Many hypnosis practitioners and researchers fall somewhere between these two positions. It also may be the case that *psychoanalytic* and *social-cognitive* descriptions of hypnosis are both correct, and that each explains different aspects of the hypnotic experience (Kihlstrom, 1998b). But for convenience' sake, we'll examine the two opposing viewpoints in this debate in depth. At one end we find explanations of hypnosis influenced by psychoanalytic theory, and at the other, theories that emphasize the role of cognitive and social processes.

"From being in love to hypnosis is evidently only a short step. There is the same humble subjection, the same compliance, the same absence of criticism toward the hypnotist as toward the love object."

SIGMUND FREUD

Psychoanalytically Influenced Theories. Freud saw hypnosis as a passkey to a highly hypnotizable patient's unconscious mind. Somehow the barrier to the unconscious is weakened during hypnosis, allowing easier access to crucial unconscious material. Many psychoanalytic therapists still use hypnosis this way (Fromm & Nash, 1997). For example, Milton Erickson (1967) developed several techniques to confuse and distract the conscious so that contact with the unconscious could be made. One team of psychologists proposed that the ego forms a new subsystem during hypnosis (Gill & Brenman, 1967). According to this theory, the ego creates a kind of pocket in which the formerly unconscious material that surfaces during hypnosis is stored. The ego monitors this pocket of information during hypnosis, but keeps it out of conscious awareness once hypnosis is terminated.

A more recent explanation of hypnosis with a psychoanalytic flavor is called **neodissociation theory** (Hilgard, 1973, 1992, 1994). According to this explanation, deeply hypnotized people experience a division of their conscious. Part of their conscious enters a type of altered state, but part remains aware of what is going on during the hypnotic session. This second part is said to act as a "hidden observer" monitoring the situation. The hypnotized part of the conscious is unaware of the observer part.

Advocates of the neodissociation theory use *pain analgesia* experiments to illustrate how the hidden observer works. Highly responsive participants in one study were hypnotized and told they would not experience pain (Hilgard, 1977). Their arms were then lowered into ice water for several seconds. Like any of us, when not hypnotized, these people reported severe pain almost as soon as their arms touched the water. However, when hypnotized, they appeared to withstand the icy water with little evidence of suffering.

But this ability to withstand pain under hypnosis has been demonstrated before. The new twist the investigator added was then asking participants to report their experiences through *automatic writing* or *automatic talking*. The researcher found that people could keep one arm in the cold water while writing with the other arm that the experience is quite painful. Advocates of neodissociation theory interpret this as a demonstration of the division of consciousness that occurs under hypnosis. The hypnotized part denies the pain, but the hidden observer is aware of what is going on.

Socio-Cognitive Theories of Hypnosis. In response to the psychoanalytic theories that once dominated the field of hypnosis, some psychologists began to challenge the notion that hypnosis participants experience a state of consciousness different from being awake (Barber, 1969; Sarbin, 1950). They pointed out there is nothing a person can do under hypnosis that cannot be done without hypnosis. For example, people who are relaxed but not hypnotized, and who are asked to imagine a weight pulling their arms down, will experience increased heaviness in their arms.

But how do these skeptical psychologists explain some of the unusual things people do when hypnotized? Most use concepts such as expectancy, motivation, and concentration to explain hypnotic phenomena (Barber, 1999; Coe & Sarbin, 1991; Kirsch, 2000; Lynn & Sherman, 2000; Spanos, 1991). For example, I sometimes ask a few students in my class to stand up and spin like a top. In every case the students comply. When I ask why they are doing this, they say it is because I asked them to. None have ever said it was because they were hypnotized. Yet most people who see hypnosis participants stand and spin like tops at the hypnotist's request say the people act that way because they are hypnotized. What is the difference between these two situations? Does the hypnotist use certain magical words that suddenly transform the people into a trance? Socio-cognitive theorists argue that hypnotized and nonhypnotized people stand up and spin for the same reason: They think they are supposed to.

These theorists are also critical of "hidden observer" demonstrations (Spanos & Katsanis, 1989; Stava & Jaffa, 1988). They argue that the highly responsive people in these experiments are told their hidden observer is supposed to feel pain, and they consequently experience the pain they expect. When researchers told participants in one study that their hidden observer would experience less pain, the hidden observers indeed reported less, not more, pain (Spanos & Hewitt, 1980).

Socio-cognitive theorists also argue that the psychoanalytic position sometimes can become circular. That is, if we ask why hypnosis participants run around making chicken noises, we are told it is because they are hypnotized. But if we ask how we can tell that people are hypnotized, we are shown how they run around making chicken noises. The concept becomes inarguable and therefore useless in explaining the phenomenon.

Which side is correct? Although many psychoanalytic therapists continue to promote the notion of an altered state of consciousness as an explanation of hypnotic behavior, in recent years there has been a growing consensus among researchers that the hypnotic trance notion does a poor job of explaining why hypnosis participants act the way they do (Kirsch, 2000; Kirsch & Lynn, 1998). Although psychoanalytic theorists point to unusual behavior under hypnosis, such as pain analgesia, deafness, and age regression, socio-cognitive theorists counter with demonstrations of the same phenomena without hypnosis, or they challenge the accuracy of the participants' description. For example, people who claim to go back to an earlier age typically do a poor job of re-creating what they were really like at that time (Nash, 1987). Another example of how socio-cognitive theorists have challenged seemingly incredible behavior under hypnosis can be found in the research on posthypnotic amnesia, covered next.

Posthypnotic Amnesia. Hypnosis participants are often told they will not remember what has happened during hypnosis until the hypnotist tells them to. Indeed, many of these people recall little or nothing of the experience until given permission. Posthypnotic amnesia has not escaped the attention of novelists and scriptwriters, whose characters sometimes engage in all manner of heinous acts while seemingly under the control of an evil hypnotist. Although there is no evidence that hypnosis can be used this way, some people do claim to forget what they did when hypnotized. Why?

Psychoanalytically oriented theorists explain that the experience either has been repressed out of consciousness or has been recorded in a part of the mind not accessible to consciousness. For example, some psychologists maintain that information about the hypnotic experience is held in a pocket of the mind created by the ego during the hypnosis (Gill & Brenman, 1967). This information is said to remain inaccessible until the ego allows it to enter awareness. However, socio-cognitive theorists argue that hypnosis participants expect not to recall what happens to them and therefore make no effort to remember (Coe, 1989; Sarbin &

Coe, 1979; Spanos, Radtke, & Dubreuil, 1982). These researchers argue that under the right circumstances people can be convinced to make the effort to recall. For example, how long would posthypnotic amnesia continue if participants were offered $1,000 each to describe what happened while they were hypnotized?

A team of researchers found a less expensive way to test this possibility (Howard & Coe, 1980; Schuyler & Coe, 1981). Some highly hypnotizable people were connected to a physiograph machine and told the instrument could tell when they were lying. The experimenter explained that the machine "is very sensitive and functions in the same manner as a lie detector. It can tell if you are withholding information." In truth, the machine had no such capabilities, but the participants believed that it did. Although they were told under hypnosis they would remember nothing, when it came time to report what they could remember about the hypnotic experience, participants in the "lie detector" condition remembered significantly more than people in a control condition. Apparently, they believed they would be caught for saying they could not remember when they really could. Other methods to encourage participants to breach posthypnotic amnesia also demonstrate that the "forgotten" information is more accessible than psychoanalytic theorists acknowledge (Coe & Sluis, 1989).

Although these studies challenge the psychoanalytically influenced theories of hypnosis, they do not dispute the usefulness of hypnosis or the honesty of the participants. Few people believe they are intentionally deceiving the hypnotist. Rather, they are responding to normal social-psychological influences. Just as you act the way you believe a student is supposed to act when in school, hypnosis participants behave the way they believe people are supposed to when under hypnosis.

Hypnotic Responsiveness

Not everyone responds the same to a hypnotist's suggestions. Some people sing like Frank Sinatra, stick their arms in ice water, or report seeing objects that aren't really there. Others begrudgingly close their eyes but fail to react to any of the hypnotist's requests. Most people fall somewhere in between. One of the first things students ask me after a hypnosis demonstration is why some people are so responsive and others are not. What makes a good hypnotist? What kind of person makes the best participant?

Despite stage hypnotists' claims to be the best at their trade, research shows hypnotic responsiveness is largely a participant variable. The difference between hypnotists for the most part lies in showmanship (Meeker & Barber, 1971). Highly responsive people respond to anyone they perceive to be a legitimate hypnotist. In fact, to standardize procedures, many researchers put hypnotic induction procedures on tape. Research assistants play the tape for participants with no apparent loss in responsiveness. Beginning hypnotists are sometimes disappointed when people fail to respond to their suggestions, wondering what they did wrong. Had they given intelligence tests, they probably would not blame themselves for a test taker who did poorly. But so many performers have promoted the idea of good and bad hypnotists that it is a difficult concept to shake.

Hypnotists can use a few techniques to increase responsiveness, especially among people who are a bit skeptical at the beginning of the experience (Lynn et al., 1991). People are more responsive to hypnotic suggestions when the situation is defined as hypnosis and when their cooperation is secured and trust established before beginning. But most hypnotists use these techniques routinely and still find large differences in responsiveness. More evidence that hypnosis is a participant variable comes from the finding that hypnotic responsiveness is a fairly stable individual difference. People who are highly responsive to one hypnotist's suggestions will probably be responsive to those of another hypnotist. Moreover, how responsive you are to hypnotic suggestions today is an excellent predictor of how responsive you will be years from now (Spanos, Liddy, Baxter, & Burgess, 1994). One team of researchers found an impressive correlation of .71 between hypnotic responsiveness scores taken 25 years apart (Piccione, Hilgard, & Zimbardo, 1989). The question then becomes: What kind of person makes the most responsive participant?

Early research in this area looked for personality trait measures that correlated with hypnotic responsiveness. Researchers speculated that the most responsive participants might score high on measures of sensation seeking, imagination, or intelligence and low on measures of dogmatism, independence, extraversion, and so on. Unfortunately, very few correlations were found, and replications were seldom reported (Kihlstrom, 1985; Kirsch & Council, 1992). Short of hypnotizing the person, no measure was found that reliably predicted responsiveness to hypnosis. Even Freud could not tell beforehand which patients would be highly responsive. He only observed that "neurotics can only be hypnotized with great difficulty and the insane are completely resistant" (1905/1960, pp. 294–295).

However, later research identified a few personality variables other than neurosis and insanity that predict hypnotic responsiveness. These studies succeeded where earlier efforts had failed because investigators measured traits that more directly relate to the hypnotic experience. For example, a person's ability to become immersed in a role is related to hypnotic responsiveness (Sarbin & Coe, 1972). This may be why drama students are more responsive to hypnotic suggestions than other students are (Coe & Sarbin, 1991).

The most successful efforts to predict hypnotic responsiveness from personality traits come from work on a trait called **absorption** (Tellegen & Atkinson, 1974). People who score high on measures of absorption have the ability to become highly involved in sensory and imaginative experiences. They are open to new experiences and are prone to fantasies and daydreams (Roche & McConkey, 1990). Numerous studies find that people who score high on measures of absorption are more responsive to hypnotic suggestions than those who score low (Glisky, Tataryn, Tobias, Kihlstrom, & McConkey, 1991; Nadon, Hoyt, Register, & Kihlstrom, 1991). Thus, if you are the kind of person who gets involved in a good book or a movie and blocks out all experiences around you, you probably can be responsive to hypnotic suggestions.

Beyond this, three important variables affect hypnotic responsiveness: attitude, motivation, and expectancy (Barber, 1999). People with a positive attitude toward hypnosis are more responsive than are those who view hypnosis with suspicion and mistrust. In addition, the more motivated people are to experience hypnosis, the more responsive they will be. Finally, what people expect to happen during the hypnotic experience affects their responsiveness (Braffman & Kirsch, 1999; Kirsch, Silva, Comey, & Reed, 1995). Participants told in one study that responding to suggestions was difficult were not as responsive as those told it was easy (Barber & Calverley, 1964). Similarly, students who first watched a highly responsive participant were more responsive to hypnotic suggestions than those who watched a nonresponsive model (Klinger, 1970). In short, people tend to act under hypnosis the way they think they are supposed to act. This is why people who expect to see bizarre behavior at a hypnosis show tend to act bizarrely when they are brought up on stage and hypnotized.

Studies demonstrating the researcher's ability to increase hypnotic responsiveness by changing expectations raise another question. Although hypnotic responsiveness is a fairly stable personality variable, is it possible to train people to be more responsive to hypnotic suggestions?

Personality traits and the ability to become absorbed in a situation are not changed easily. However, a person's attitudes, expectancies, and motivations may be. Several investigations report success in training initially unresponsive hypnotic people to increase their level of responsiveness (Gfeller, Lynn, & Pribble, 1987; Gorassini & Spanos, 1986; Spanos, Burgess, Roncon, Wallace-Capretta, & Cross, 1993; Spanos, Robertson, Menary, Brett, & Smith, 1987). In each of these investigations, people who were not very responsive to suggestions initially participated in training procedures. This training included the development of positive attitudes toward hypnosis and changing the person's expectancy about hypnosis from one of passively receiving suggestions to one of actively taking part in responding. One investigation found that people who had gone through this training still showed signs of elevated responsiveness when hypnotized a year later (Gorassini, Sowerby, Creighton, & Fry, 1991). In short, if you are fairly unresponsive to hypnotic suggestions, there may be something you can do to better experience hypnosis. However, how responsive you become is still probably limited by your ability to become absorbed in the situation.

 *Summary*

1.   A common thread runs through the four topics covered in this chapter. In each case, evidence supporting the Freudian position has been produced by researchers, yet questions about how to interpret these findings remain. Although it

seems fair to conclude that some empirical support has been obtained for Freud's theory, in no case is this support clear and unequivocal.

2.   Researchers examining the content of dreams find that men tend to dream about male characters twice as often as they dream about female characters. Some researchers interpret this finding as evidence of men's preoccupation with other men, a holdover from unresolved Oedipal impulses. The discovery of REM sleep allowed investigators to better examine the function of dreams. Although it is not clear that deprivation of REM sleep is related to psychological disorders, some research indicates that dreaming may help the sleeper work through ongoing problems.

3.   Researchers use projective tests and other procedures to determine which defense mechanisms people use. Studies find young children tend to rely on unsophisticated defense mechanisms, such as denial, whereas adults more often use defense mechanisms like identification. Researchers also find individual differences in preferred defense mechanisms. People who rely heavily on immature defense mechanisms may have more difficulties with personal adjustment and well-being than those who use more efficient and productive defense mechanisms.

4.   Freud outlined a theory of humor, arguing that sexual and aggressive themes underlie much of what we find funny. In support of his theory, researchers find that people think hostile humor is funnier when it is aimed at someone they dislike. In addition, some research indicates that hostile humor reduces the likelihood of aggression, as Freud predicted. However, other studies find the opposite. Moreover, the more tension people experience before receiving a punch line, the funnier they find a joke. Although many research findings are consistent with Freud's theory, many also are open to alternative interpretations.

5.   Many researchers and therapists explain hypnosis in a manner similar to Freud's description. Although hypnotic participants often behave as if they are in an altered state of consciousness, skeptical researchers explain these phenomena in terms of expectancies, motivations, and relaxation. Hypnotic responsiveness is largely a participant variable. People who are generally able to become absorbed in a situation tend to be responsive to hypnotic suggestions. In addition, attitudes, expectancies, and motivations play a role. Some evidence that people can increase their responsiveness with training exists, but how much this helps is probably limited.

InfoTrac Key Terms

 For additional readings go to http://www.infotrac-college.com/wadsworth and enter a search term related to your interest. Use the key terms suggested here to pull up several related articles. Also see the text Web site at http://psychology .wadsworth.com for more suggested readings and interactive quizzes to test your knowledge.

Catharsis	REM sleep
Humor	Repressed memory
Hypnosis	

Chapter 5

The Psychoanalytic Approach

Neo-Freudian Theory, Application, and Assessment

Historians, scholars, teachers, and textbook writers use a number of images and metaphors to describe Sigmund Freud's work and influence. Some picture Freud defiantly marching against the stream of contemporary thought and values. Others describe him as a pioneer blazing new trails into the previously unknown territory of the unconscious mind. I've also seen Freud compared with a diligent detective piecing together clues about the true nature of the human mind or a shrewd lawyer cutting away the ego's defenses one by one. But the metaphor I like best compares Freud with a tree. Like a giant oak standing in the middle of a grove, Freud's theory is the oldest and most formidable of the many psychoanalytic approaches to understanding personality. Just as the oak drops acorns that sprout into their own trees, so did Freud's Psychoanalytic Society generate several scholars who went on to develop their own theories of personality. However, like the surrounding saplings that resemble the great oak, the ancestry of these later personality theories is clearly Freudian.

The collection of scholars who gathered in Vienna to study with Freud included some of the leading thinkers of the day. Not surprisingly, many of these psychologists eventually developed their own ideas about the nature of personality. Unfortunately, Freud and some of his followers often viewed these contributions as more than elaborations or professional disagreements. Sometimes the failure to adhere strictly to psychoanalytic theory as espoused by Freud was seen as blasphemy. Freud apparently viewed almost any deviation from or disagreement with his works as something akin to treason. Gradually, many followers left the Psychoanalytic Society, sometimes forming their own associations and new schools of psychology.

Although none of the theorists described in this chapter ever developed as much fame or influence as Freud, each made a substantial contribution to the psychoanalytic approach to personality theory. Although at the time their differences with Freud may have seemed great, with the perspective of time, we can see that their contributions were more accurately elaborations of Freud's theory rather than radically new approaches to personality. Hence, these theorists have come to be known as the *neo-Freudians.* For the most part, the neo-Freudian theorists retained the unconscious as a key determinant of behavior. Most also agreed with Freud about the impact of early childhood experiences on personality development, although many felt that later experiences also influenced adult personality. Most of these theorists also readily accepted such Freudian concepts as defense mechanisms and dream interpretation. In short, the neo-Freudian theories should be viewed as different perspectives within the general psychoanalytic approach to personality.

One feature that remains from the tradition of loyalty and divisions found in that early group of theorists is the tendency to treat the theory's developer more as a prophet than a theorist. For example, people often identify themselves as a Jungian or an Adlerian psychologist. Although space doesn't allow more than a brief examination of a few of the major theorists' contributions, students often find that one or two of the neo-Freudians have a grasp on the nature of human personality that is particularly insightful and thought-provoking for them. In that spirit, the following brief presentation serves as a starting point for future reading and thought.

Limits and Liabilities of Freudian Theory

If you were to plow through the many volumes written by Sigmund Freud, you would most certainly find parts of his theory difficult to accept or in need of some elaboration. Although later students of psychoanalysis disagreed with many as-

pects of Freud's thinking, three of the theory's limits and liabilities often played key roles in the development of the neo-Freudians' approaches.

First, many of these theorists rejected the idea that the adult personality is formed almost in its entirety by experiences in the first five or six years of life. Most neo-Freudians acknowledged that early childhood experiences have a significant effect on personality development. But many argued that later experiences, particularly in adolescence and early adulthood, are also important in shaping personality. Has your personality developed or changed during the past 10 or 15 years? Many of us can point to such changes. Yet, according to Freud, the roots of our personalities today lie in our childhood, not in later experiences.

Second, many neo-Freudians challenged Freud's emphasis on instinctual influences on personality. They argued that he failed to recognize many of the important social and cultural forces that shape who we are. For example, Freud attributed many of the differences he saw between the personalities of men and women to inherent biological differences between the sexes. Later theorists, most notably Karen Horney, argued that the culture we grow up in plays a large role in creating these differences. Of course, Freud did not ignore social influences altogether. But he failed to give them enough attention to satisfy many of his detractors.

Third, many theorists disliked the generally negative tone of Freudian theory. They argued that Freud concentrated on the dark side of human personality. At times he painted a pessimistic and in some ways degrading picture of human nature—people largely controlled by instincts and unconscious forces. Later theorists, both psychoanalytic and otherwise, presented a more positive view of humankind and human personality. For example, many addressed the constructive functions of the ego and emphasized the role of conscious rather than unconscious determinants of behavior. Many spoke of growth experiences and the satisfaction people obtain from reaching their potential. These alternative views can be uplifting to those who find the Freudian perspective just a little depressing.

Alfred Adler

Alfred Adler was the first member of the psychoanalytic group to break with Freud. The year was 1911, and it was clear to both men that their differences were fundamental. Unfortunately, the professional dispute became personal as well. Freud saw Adler's disagreements more as defections than points of discussion. When Adler left the Vienna group, several members left with him. Friendships were severed, and accusations were tossed about. Adler went on to develop his own society, establish his own journal, and even select a name for his new psychology. He called his approach *individual psychology*. Among Adler's important contributions to our understanding of personality are the notion of striving for superiority, the role of parental influence on personality development, and the effects of birth order.

Alfred Adler

1870–1937

Alfred Adler's career provides an excellent example of one man's lifelong striving to overcome feelings of inferiority. Adler was born in Vienna in 1870, the third of six children (one older brother and one older sister). Alfred spent much of his childhood in his older brother's shadow. A series of childhood illnesses, particularly rickets, left Adler physically unable to keep up with his brother and other playmates in athletic and outdoor games. He almost died of pneumonia at age four and twice was nearly killed when run over by carts in the streets. Because of his physical inferiority, Adler received special treatment from his mother. However, this ended with the birth of his brother. "During my first two years my mother pampered me," he recalled. "But when my younger brother was born she transferred her attention to him, and I felt dethroned" (in Orgler, 1963, p. 2).

Adler also experienced feelings of inferiority in the classroom. He achieved only mediocre grades and did so poorly at mathematics one year he had to repeat the course. His teacher advised his father to take the boy out of school and find him an apprenticeship as a shoemaker. But this episode only seemed to motivate Adler. He stud-ied furiously and soon became the best mathematics student in the class. He went on to receive his medical degree from the University of Vienna in 1895.

Adler never studied under Freud, nor did he ever undergo psychoanalysis, as required for becoming a practicing psychoanalyst (Orgler, 1963). The two theorists' association began in 1902 when Freud invited Adler to attend his discussion group after Adler had defended Freud's theory of dream interpretation against attacks in the local newspaper. Adler eventually was named the first president of the group in 1910.

However, growing disagreements with Freud led to Adler's resignation in 1911. Several members joined Adler in forming what was originally called the Society for Free Psychoanalytic Research—a name intended to express their objection to Freud's required adherence to his theory. Adler later changed the name of the association to Individual Psychology, established a journal, and received wide acceptance for his alternate interpretation of strict Freudian theory. As in his earlier battles to overcome feelings of inferiority, Adler devoted much of his professional life to catching and trying to surpass Sigmund Freud.

Striving for Superiority

Adler maintained that each of us begins life with a sense of inferiority. This is to be expected from a weak and helpless child, dependent for survival on larger and stronger adults. According to Adler, this perception marks the beginning of a lifelong struggle to overcome feelings of inferiority. He called this struggle a *striving for superiority*. Whereas Freud described motivation in terms of sexual and aggressive themes, Adler maintained that striving for superiority was *the* motivating force in life. All other motives could be subsumed within this single construct. "I began to see clearly in every psychological phenomenon the striving for superiority," Adler wrote. "It lies at the root of all solutions of life's problems and is manifested in the way in which we meet these problems. All our functions follow its direction" (in Ansbacher & Ansbacher, 1956, p. 103).

Thus, for Adler, virtually everything we do is designed to establish a sense of superiority over life's obstacles and thereby overcome our feelings of inferiority. Why do we work so hard to obtain good grades, to excel at athletics, to reach a position of power? Because achieving these things moves us a step further away from our feelings of inferiority. Moreover, the more inferior we see ourselves, the stronger our striving for superiority. For example, Franklin Roosevelt was disabled by polio. Nonetheless, perhaps *because* of this disability, he aspired to become one of the most influential figures of the twentieth century. However, in some cases excessive feelings of inferiority can have the opposite effect. Some people develop an **inferiority complex,** a belief that they are vastly inferior to everyone else. The result is feelings of helplessness rather than an upward drive to establish superiority.

But Adler did not equate achievement with mental health. Instead, he argued that well-adjusted people express their striving for superiority through concern for the *social interest.* Successful businesspeople achieve a sense of superiority and personal satisfaction through their accomplishments, but only if they reach these goals with consideration for the welfare of others. Success means providing consumers with a good product at a fair price that will make everyone's life a little happier. In contrast, poorly adjusted people express their striving for superiority through selfishness and a concern for personal glory at the expense of others. Politicians who seek public office for personal gain and a sense of power are poorly adjusted. Those who seek office to help right some of society's wrongs exhibit well-adjusted superiority striving.

Parental Influence on Personality Development

Like Freud, Adler believed the first few years of life are extremely important in the formation of the adult personality. However, Adler also placed great emphasis on the role of the parents in this process. He identified two parental behaviors in particular that are almost certain to lead to personality problems for the child later in life. First, parents who give their children too much attention and overprotection run the risk of *pampering*. Pampering robs the child of independence, may add to feelings of inferiority, and creates the basis for several personality problems. For example, parents may protect the child from fast rides, aggressive playmates, and scary movies. As a result, the child grows up unable to deal with many of life's problems. You may know some of these formerly pampered children who have difficulty living on their own, making their own decisions, and dealing with the daily hassles and frustrations we all encounter. Allowing children to struggle with problems and make some of their own decisions, even if this means making mistakes, is good for them in the long run.

Parents can avoid pampering by allowing children the independence to make many of their own choices. However, it is also possible to do this too much. The second major mistake parents make is to *neglect* their children. Children who receive too little attention from their parents grow up cold and suspicious. As adults, they are incapable of warm personal relationships. They are uncomfortable with intimacy and may be ill at ease with closeness or touching. As you will see in the next chapter, many other psychologists have explored this connection between parent-child bonds and the ability to establish satisfying adult relationships.

Birth Order

Adler was the first psychologist to emphasize the role of *birth order* in shaping personality. That is, first-born children in a family are said to be different in personality from middle-born children, who are different from last-borns. According to Adler, first-born children are subjected to excessive attention from their parents and thus to pampering. First-time parents rarely seem to have enough film and seldom miss an opportunity to tell friends and relatives about the new arrival. However, this pampering is short-lived. With the arrival of the second child, the first-born is "dethroned." Now attention must be shared with, if not relinquished to, the newest member of the family. As a result, the first-born's perception of inferiority is likely to be strong. Adler suggested that among first-borns we often find "problem children, neurotics, criminals, drunkards, and perverts."

On the other hand, Adler's assessment of middle children—Adler himself was a middle child—was more positive. These children are never afforded the luxury of being pampered, for even when they are the youngest there is always another sibling or two around demanding much of the parents' time. Adler argued that middle children develop a strong superiority striving. As a child, the middle-born is not quite as strong, not quite as fast, not quite as smart as older brothers and sisters. The sense that they are always just a step behind stays with middle-born children into adulthood. As a result, they are always looking at the person just a little ahead of them in school or in the office, always putting in the extra effort to close the gap. Consequently, middle-born children are the highest achievers.

Although Adler believed first-borns made up the greatest proportion of difficult children, he felt last-borns also had their problems. Last-born children are pampered throughout their childhood by all members of the family. Older children often complain that their little brother or sister "gets away with murder," which would not have happened "when I was that age." However, Adler argued that this special treatment carries a definite price. A spoiled child is a very dependent child—a child without personal initiative. Last-born children also are vulnerable to strong inferiority feelings, for everyone in their immediate environment is older and stronger.

According to Adler, secondborn children will spend a lifetime trying to catch up with their older siblings.

Before applying Adler's theory to the members of your own family, you should note that studies do not always support Adler's predictions. Birth order often does not predict how people will score on personality measures (Jefferson, Herbst, & McCrae, 1998; Parker, 1998), and effects found in one study frequently fail to replicate in another (Michalski & Shackelford, 2002). Moreover, the structure and dynamics of the typical family have changed dramatically since Adler's time. Adler's descriptions may fit some families, but there are many exceptions. In short, although Adler's theorizing triggered a great deal of research, most likely the impact of birth order on personality and intellectual development is far more complex than he imagined (Hoffman, 1991; Rodgers, Cleveland, van den Oord, & Rowe, 2000; Zajonc, 2001; Zajonc & Mullally, 1997).

As this brief taste of his theory makes clear, Adler's description of personality contrasts sharply with Freud's on several important points. For example, Freud described the motives driving the successful businessperson in terms of sublimation. Freud also might say that defeating business rivals, particularly businessmen, satisfies an unconscious desire to compete with and defeat one's father, a motive left over from the Oedipus complex. In contrast, Adler saw business success as an expression of superiority striving. He also might have guessed that these high achievers are middle-born children.

Carl Jung

Perhaps the most bitter of the defections from the Freudian camp was Carl Jung's break with the psychoanalytic circle. In Freud's eyes, Jung was the heir apparent to the leadership of the movement. Jung served as the first president of the International Psychoanalytic Association. However, in 1914, after long and intense disagreement with some of the basic aspects of Freud's theory, Jung resigned from the association. In the years that followed, he continued his work as a psychotherapist, traveled extensively around the world to observe other cultures, and eventually established his own school of psychology, named *analytic psychology.*

Some students find Jung's ideas confusing at first blush. Part of the problem lies in Jung's frequent reliance on ancient mythology and Eastern religious views in his writings. The unfamiliar terms and abstract concepts can be perplexing to people reading Jung the first time. However, once the initial difficulty with terms and unusual concepts passes, many students find Jung's work among the most intriguing and thought-provoking of the personality theories.

The Collective Unconscious

If you were like most newborn children, you had no difficulty recognizing and developing a strong attachment to your mother. When you were a little older, you most likely expressed at least some fear of the dark. When you became older yet, you probably had no difficulty accepting the idea that there was a God, or at least some superhuman existence that created and controlled nature. According to Jung, all people have these experiences. If we were to examine history, talk with people from other societies, and thumb through legends and myths of the past, we would find these same themes and experiences throughout various cultures, past and present. Why is this?

Jung's answer was that we all have a part of our mind that Freud neglected to talk about. He called this part the **collective unconscious,** as distinguished from the *personal unconscious.* Like the unconscious Freud talked about, the collective unconscious consists of thoughts and images that are difficult to bring into awareness. However, these thoughts were never repressed out of consciousness. Instead, each of us was born with this unconscious material, and it is basically the same for all people. According to Jung, just as we inherit physical characteristics from our ancestors, we also inherit unconscious psychic characteristics.

The collective unconscious is made up of **primordial images.** Jung described these images in terms of a potential to respond to the world in a certain way. Thus, newborns react so quickly to their mother because the collective unconscious holds an image of a mother for each of us. Similarly, we react to the dark or to God because of unconscious images inherited from our ancestors. Jung referred to these images collectively as **archetypes.** Among the many archetypes Jung described were the mother, the father, the wise old man, the sun, the moon, the hero,

God, and death. The list is almost inexhaustible. Jung maintained there are "as many archetypes as there are typical situations in life."

Jung was aware of how mystical this theory sounds to many people encountering it for the first time. Some students scoff at the idea that each of us is born with a collection of unconscious material that directs our actions and that, like all unconscious material, we have no direct access to. However, Jung argued that the collective unconscious was no more mysterious than the concept of instincts. People are comfortable saying a baby "instinctually" finds its mother or that humans "naturally" share a fear of darkness. He might add that many other theorists describe aspects of personality that we cannot perceive directly. Although the number of archetypes may be limitless, a few are particularly important in Jung's writings. Among the more interesting are the anima, the animus, and the shadow.

Some Important Archetypes

The **anima** is the feminine side of the male, the **animus** is the masculine side of the female. According to Jung, deep inside every masculine man is a feminine counterpart. Deep inside every feminine woman is a masculine self. A principal function of these archetypes is to guide the selection of a romantic partner and the course of the subsequent relationship. According to Jung, we look for a romantic partner by projecting our anima or animus onto potential mates. In his words, "a man, in his love choice, is strongly tempted to win the woman who best corresponds to his own unconscious femininity—a woman, in short, who can

What attracts this woman and man to each other? According to Jung, these two have projected their anima and animus onto the partner and have apparently found a good fit.

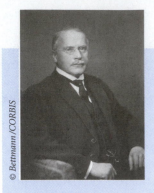

Carl Gustav Jung

1875–1961

Whereas biographers debate the extent to which Freud's personality theory reflected his own unconscious, Carl Jung candidly described how his ideas about personality came from introspection and his own experiences. Jung was born in 1875 in Kesswil, a small town in Switzerland. He was a highly introspective child who kept to himself, largely because he felt no one would understand the inner experiences and thoughts with which he was preoccupied. Jung spent many childhood hours pondering the meaning of the dreams and supernatural visions he experienced. When he was 10, he carved a two-inch human figure out of wood. He kept the figure hidden, spoke to it when alone, and sometimes wrote to it in secret codes. During his teenage years, he was preoccupied with the feeling that he was someone else. He began a lifelong search to identify what he called his "Number Two" personality.

Jung's desire to understand himself led him to the young field of psychiatry. He earned his medical degree from the University of Basel in 1900, and then went to Zurich to study with Eugen Bleuler, a leading authority on schizophrenia. Later he worked in Paris with Pierre Janet, who was conducting pioneering work on consciousness and hypnosis. Naturally, Jung's curiosity about the human mind soon brought him into contact with Freud's work. After reading *The Interpretation of Dreams,* Jung began a correspondence with Freud. When they finally met in 1907, the two men are said to have engaged in a conversation that lasted 13 hours. Jung

soon became a close colleague of Freud's, even accompanying him on his 1909 trip to lecture at Clark University. It was during this trip that Jung came to appreciate how intolerant Freud was of their disagreements about the nature of personality. Jung formally parted with the Vienna group in 1914.

Jung spent the next seven years in virtual isolation, exploring the depths of his own unconscious. He immersed himself in his fantasies, dreams, and visions in an effort to discover the true nature of personality. Scholars disagree on whether this was a period of voluntary introspection or a lengthy psychotic episode. Jung's autobiography, published just before his death, provides evidence for both interpretations. "An incessant stream of fantasies had been released, and I did my best not to lose my head but to find some way to understand these strange things," he wrote. "From the beginning . . . I had an unswerving conviction that I was obeying a higher will" (1961, pp. 176–177).

Jung reports visits by various figures and images during these years. He came to see these figures as the archetypal characters that make up the collective unconscious. Jung described in detail conversations with a figure he called Philemon. "I held conversations with him, and he said things which I had not consciously thought," Jung wrote. "For I observed clearly that it was he who spoke, not I. . . . I went walking up and down the garden with him, and to me he was what the Indians call a guru" (1961, p. 183).

Jung emerged from these years of introspection with a new theory of personality. He devoted the rest of his career to private practice, travel,

(continues)

Carl Gustav Jung (continued)

reading, and studying. His observations during these experiences, combined with his continued introspection, resulted in numerous volumes and lectures. Many of Jung's writings have been controversial, including those that some say hint at anti-Semitism (Noll, 1997). Nonetheless, his ideas about human personality continue to mystify and excite readers from around the world.

unhesitatingly receive the projection of his soul" (1928/1953, p. 70). Less poetically, Jung is saying that each of us holds an unconscious image of the man or woman we are looking for. The more someone matches our projected standards, the more we'll want to develop a relationship with that person. Whereas people in love might prefer to "count the ways," Jung believed the real reason for romance lies in the hidden part of our minds inherited from our ancestors through the centuries.

Although the name may be a bit melodramatic, the **shadow** contains the unconscious part of ourselves that is essentially negative, or to continue the metaphor, the dark side of our personalities. It is the evil side of humankind. The shadow is located partly in the personal unconscious in the form of repressed feelings and partly in the collective unconscious. Jung pointed out that evil is personified in the myths and stories of all cultures. In Judeo-Christian writings, this archetype is symbolized as the Devil. Good versus evil is perhaps the most common theme in literature from all cultures, because the collective unconscious of all people readily grasps the concept. Jung maintained that well-adjusted people incorporate their good and evil parts into a wholeness of self. Otherwise, we may project our evil thoughts. Similar to Freud's description of projection, Jung said we sometimes see our own objectionable characteristics in other people.

Evidence for the Collective Unconscious

One criticism sometimes directed at Jung's ideas is that his theory is difficult to examine with scientific research. However, Jung did not create his ideas out of sheer fantasy. Rather, through a lifelong study of modern and ancient cultures, and through his career as a psychotherapist, Jung arrived at what was for him indisputable evidence for the collective unconscious and the other constructs in his theory.

However, Jung's evidence does not consist of hard data from rigorous laboratory experiments. Instead, Jung examined mythology, cultural symbols, dreams, and the statements of schizophrenics. The logic behind this approach is that if a collective unconscious exists that is basically the same for each of us, the primordial images should be found in some form in all cultures and across time. Jung argued that primordial images are often expressed in dreams. But they also serve as symbols in art, folklore, and mythology. People suffering from psychosis also are said to describe archetype-based images.

As evidence for the collective unconscious, Jung provides the recurrence of certain images and symbols in all of these sources. For example, why does a symbol like a vulture appear in the dreams of people today in the same basic way it appears in religious writings and ancient mythologies of cultures unknown to the dreamer? Jung described an early discovery of such a coincidence when he talked with a mental patient suffering from a type of schizophrenia:

> One day I came across him there, blinking through the window up at the sun, and moving his head from side to side in a curious manner. He took me by the arm and said he wanted to show me something. He said I must look at the sun with eyes half shut, and then I could see the sun's phallus. If I moved my head from side to side the sun-phallus would move too, and that was the origin of the wind. (1936/1959, p. 51)

A few years later, while reading Greek mythology, Jung came across a description of a tubelike element hanging from the sun. According to the myth, the tube was responsible for the wind. How could such an image appear in both the hallucinations of the patient and the stories of the ancient Greeks? Jung maintained that the image existed in the collective unconscious of the Greek storytellers as well as in those of psychotic patients, and therefore in the collective unconscious of us all.

Jung was probably the most prolific writer among the neo-Freudians. Like Freud, he eventually managed to touch on most aspects of human behavior. His description of personality types and his views on religion are reviewed later in this chapter. Although most of the neo-Freudians wrote of personality in less mysterious and more tangible terms than Freud, Jung's thinking took him in the opposite direction. Perhaps the unique flavor of his theory is what has kept his writings so popular for so many years.

Erik Erikson

In the summer of 1927, a young artist wandering about Europe took a job in a school established for the children of Sigmund Freud's patients and friends. This artist, Erik Homburger, who never received a university degree, became friendly with the psychoanalysts and was later trained by them. After changing his name from Homburger to Erikson, he began to practice psychotherapy and eventually to espouse his own views on the nature of human personality. Although Erikson retained several Freudian ideas in his theory, his own contributions to the psychoanalytic approach were numerous. We will discuss two of these contributions here: his description of the ego and his model of personality development throughout the life cycle.

Erikson's Concept of the Ego

Whereas Freud saw the ego as the mediator between id impulses and superego demands, Erikson believed the ego performed many constructive functions. To Erikson, the ego is a relatively powerful, independent part of personality that works

Erik Homburger Erikson

1902–1994

It is difficult to imagine a life filled with more identity issues than the one handed to Erik Erikson. Reflecting back on his formative years, Erikson observed that "it seems all too obvious . . . that such an early life would predispose a person to a severe identity crisis" (1975, p. 31). Indeed, Erikson's struggle with his identity led him to behavior he would later identify as somewhere between neurotic and psychotic. Yet these struggles also provided him with a keen insight into the problems associated with identity, particularly among adolescents and young adults.

Erik was born in Frankfurt, Germany, in 1902. His Danish father abandoned the family before Erik was born. Three years later his mother married a Jewish physician, Theodor Homburger, and for many years told her son that Dr. Homburger was his real father. It was not until he was an adolescent that Erikson learned the truth—that his birth was the result of an extramarital affair, a fact Erikson kept secret until he was 68 (Hopkins, 1995). Erikson's identity was further confused by his physical features. Although living in a Jewish family, he retained most of the physical features of his Scandinavian father—tall, blond hair, blue eyes. "Before long, I was referred to as 'goy' in my stepfather's temple," he wrote, "while to my schoolmates I was a 'Jew'" (1975, p. 27). World War I broke out during Erik's early adolescence, leaving the boy with torn feelings of loyalty between Germany and his growing identity as a Dane.

Erik's need to find his own identity erupted upon graduation from public school. His stepfather pushed medical school, but Erik resisted. He decided instead that he was an artist and spent the next few years wandering about Europe. His travels eventually brought him to Vienna and into contact with Anna Freud, Sigmund's daughter and a noted psychoanalyst herself. Except for a Montessori teaching credential, his psychoanalytic training with Anna Freud was the only formal education he received after leaving home. Somewhere during these years, Erik changed his name to Erik Homburger Erikson, obviously reflecting his changing sense of identity.

Erikson fled the rise of the Nazis in 1933 and settled in Boston. He held positions with numerous universities, including Harvard, Yale, the University of California at Berkeley and the University of Pennsylvania. His first book, *Childhood and Society,* was not published until 1950, when Erikson was nearly 50 years old. Like the mature adults he wrote about, Erikson continued his personal and professional development well into the later years of his life.

toward such goals as establishing one's identity and satisfying a need for mastery over the environment. Appropriately, Erikson's approach to personality has been called *ego psychology.*

According to Erikson, the principal function of the ego is to establish and maintain a sense of identity. He described identity as a complex inner state that includes a sense of our individuality and uniqueness, as well as a sense of wholeness and continuity with the past and the future. The often overused and misused term

identity crisis comes from Erikson's work. He used this phrase to refer to the confusion and despair we feel when we lack a strong sense of identity. Perhaps you have experienced a time when you felt uncertain about who you were, what your values were, or the direction your life was headed. Episodes of identity crises are typical in adolescence but are by no means limited to young people. Many middle-aged people experience similar trying periods.

Personality Development Throughout the Life Cycle

Freud's descriptions of personality development for the most part end when the superego appears at about age six. Within Freud's theory, the essential features of our adult personalities are intact at that time. In contrast, Erikson (1950/1963) maintained that personality development continues throughout a person's lifetime. He outlined eight stages we all progress through, each crucial in the development of personality (Figure 5.1).

Erikson's description of personality development brings to mind the image of a path. We continue down this path from infancy to old age, but at eight different

Figure 5.1

Erikson's Eight Stages of Development

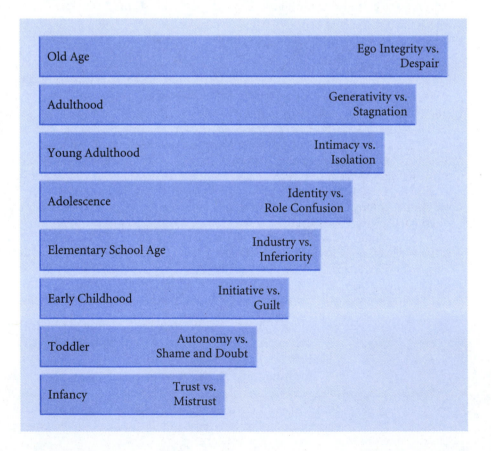

Old Age	Ego Integrity vs. Despair
Adulthood	Generativity vs. Stagnation
Young Adulthood	Intimacy vs. Isolation
Adolescence	Identity vs. Role Confusion
Elementary School Age	Industry vs. Inferiority
Early Childhood	Initiative vs. Guilt
Toddler	Autonomy vs. Shame and Doubt
Infancy	Trust vs. Mistrust

points along the way we encounter a fork—two directions in which to proceed. In Erikson's model, these forks in the path represent turning points in personality development. He called these points *crises.* How we resolve each crisis determines the direction our personality development will take and influences how we resolve later crises. Of the two alternatives for resolving each crisis, one is said to be adaptive, the other not. As you read about these stages, you may want to recall how you resolved the crises for the stages you have already passed through, and perhaps reflect on the stage you now find yourself in.

Basic Trust Versus Mistrust. During the first year or so of life, newborns are almost totally at the mercy of those around them. Whether infants are given loving care and have their needs met or whether their cries go unnoticed is the first turning point in the development of personality. The child whose needs are met develops a sense of *basic trust.* For this child, the world is a good place and people are loving and approachable. Unfortunately, some infants never receive the loving care they need. As a result, they develop a sense of *basic mistrust.* These children begin a lifelong pattern of estrangement and withdrawal, trusting neither themselves nor other people.

Autonomy Versus Shame and Doubt. By the second year of life, children want to know who they are relative to the rest of the world. Is the world something they control or something that controls them? Most children come through this stage with a sense of *autonomy.* They feel powerful and independent. They have a strong sense of personal mastery. People with a sense of autonomy are confident that they can navigate their way through the sea of obstacles and challenges life has in store. However, just as Adler warned against pampering, Erikson observed that overly protective parents can hinder development at this age. If not allowed to explore and exercise influence over the objects and events in their world, children develop feelings of *shame and doubt.* They are unsure of themselves and become dependent on others.

Initiative Versus Guilt. As children begin to interact with other children, they face the challenges that come with living in a social world. Children must learn how to play and work with others and how to resolve the inevitable conflicts. Children who seek out playmates and who learn how to organize games and other social activities develop a sense of *initiative.* They learn how to set goals and tackle challenges with conviction. They develop a sense of ambition and purpose. Children who fail to develop a sense of initiative come through this stage with feelings of *guilt and resignation.* They may lack a sense of purpose and show few signs of initiative in social or other situations.

Industry Versus Inferiority. Most children enter elementary school thinking there is little they can't do. But soon they find themselves in competition with other children—for grades, popularity, teachers' attention, victories in sports and games, and so on. Inevitably, they compare their talents and abilities with other children their age. If children experience success, feelings of competence grow that set them well on their way to becoming active and achieving members of society. But experiences with failure lead to feelings of inadequacy and to a poor prognosis for productivity and happiness. It is during this time, before the turmoil of puberty and the teenage years, that we develop either a sense of *industry* and a belief in our strengths and abilities or a sense of *inferiority* and a lack of appreciation for our talents and skills.

Identity Versus Role Confusion. At last—or perhaps too soon—we reach the teenage years, a time of rapid changes and relatively short preparation for adulthood. Adolescence may be the most difficult time of life. The turmoil of transcending from playground concerns and simple solutions to a sudden bout with life's important questions can be disturbing, and maybe a little cruel. Erikson was well aware of the significance of these years. Young men and women begin to ask the all-important question: "Who am I?" If the question is answered successfully, they develop a sense of *identity.* They make decisions about personal values and religious questions. They understand who they are and accept and appreciate themselves. Unfortunately, many teens fail to develop this strong sense of identity and instead fall into *role confusion.*

In this search for identity, adolescents may join cliques, commit to causes, or drop out of school and drift from one situation to another. A friend of mine from high school bounced from devout Christianity to alcohol and drugs, to Eastern religions, to social causes, and to conservative politics—all during his high school years—in an effort to "find" himself. Ten years later, at our class reunion, I learned that he had spent the decade drifting to different parts of the country, different jobs, several colleges, and was currently thinking of becoming a rock star. His failure to develop a strong sense of identity clearly impeded subsequent personality development.

Intimacy Versus Isolation. The teen years dissolve swiftly into young adulthood and the next challenge in Erikson's model: developing intimate relationships. Young men and women search for that special relationship within which to develop *intimacy* and grow emotionally. Although these relationships typically result in marriage or a romantic commitment to one person, this is not always the case. One can share intimacy without marriage and, unfortunately, marriage without intimacy. People who fail to develop intimacy during this stage face *emotional isolation.* They may pass through many superficial relationships without finding the satisfaction of closeness promised by genuine relationships. Indeed, they may avoid emotional commitment. The single-person's lifestyle has its advantages and may be pleasant for a while, but failure to move beyond this lifestyle can seriously inhibit emotional growth and happiness.

Generativity Versus Stagnation. As men and women approach the middle years of life, they develop a concern for guiding the next generation. Parents find their

Assessing Your Own Personality

A Sense of Personal Identity

Indicate how often each statement applies to you, using the following point scale: 1 = Never applies to me, 2 = Only occasionally or seldom applies to me, 3 = Fairly often applies to me, 4 = Very often applies to me.

_____ 1. I wonder what sort of person I really am.

_____ 2. People seem to change their opinion of me.

_____ 3. I feel certain about what I should do with my life.

_____ 4. I feel uncertain as to whether something is morally right or wrong.

_____ 5. Most people seem to agree about what sort of person I am.

_____ 6. I feel my way of life suits me.

_____ 7. My worth is recognized by others.

_____ 8. I feel freer to be my real self when I am away from those who know me very well.

_____ 9. I feel that what I am doing in life is not really worthwhile.

_____ 10. I feel I fit in well in the community in which I live.

_____ 11. I feel proud to be the sort of person I am.

_____ 12. People seem to see me very differently from the way I see myself.

_____ 13. I feel left out.

_____ 14. People seem to disapprove of me.

_____ 15. I change my ideas about what I want from life.

_____ 16. I am unsure as to how people feel about me.

_____ 17. My feelings about myself change.

_____ 18. I feel I am putting on an act or doing something for effect.

_____ 19. I feel proud to be a member of the society in which I live.

To obtain your score, first reverse the values you assigned to items 1, 2, 4, 8, 9, 12, 13, 14, 15, 16, 17, and 18. That is, for these items only, 1 = 4, 2 = 3, 3 = 2, 4 = 1. The values for the remaining items stay the same. Then add the values for all 19 items. Ochse and Plug (1986) found average scores for this scale of around 57 when they administered it to South African citizens between the ages of 15 and 60. The standard deviation for this score was around 7, indicating that the majority of people obtain scores that fall within 7 points of the average score. Scores considerably higher than this average range indicate a particularly well-developed sense of identity, whereas significantly lower scores suggest the test taker is still progressing.

Scale: *Identity versus Identity Diffusion Scale*

Source: *Ochse and Plug* (1986).

lives enriched by the influence they have on their children. Adults without their own children find this enrichment through interactions with young people, perhaps working with youth groups or playing an active role in raising nieces and nephews. Adults who fail to develop this sense of *generativity* may suffer from a sense of *stagnation*—a feeling of emptiness and questioning one's purpose in life. We've all seen parents whose lives are filled with continued meaning and interests through raising their children. Unfortunately, we've also seen parents who obtain little pleasure from this process. As a result, they become bored and generally dissatisfied with their lives. Failure to see the potential for personal growth in the development of their children is tragic for parent and child alike.

Ego Integrity Versus Despair. Inevitably, most of us keep our appointment with old age. But, according to Erikson, we still have one more crisis to resolve. Reflections on past experiences and the inevitability of life's end cause us to develop either a sense of *integrity* or *feelings of despair*. Men and women who look back on their lives with satisfaction will pass through this final developmental stage with a sense of integrity. "It is the acceptance of one's one and only life cycle . . . as something that had to be and that, by necessity, permitted of no substitution," Erikson wrote (1968, p. 139). People who fail to develop this sense of integrity fall into despair. They realize that time is now all too short, that the options and opportunities available to younger people are no longer there. A life has passed, and those who wish they could do it all differently will express their despair through disgust and contempt for others. Although few things in life are sadder than an older person filled with despair, few things are more satisfying than an elderly person filled with a sense of integrity.

Karen Horney

Unlike many neo-Freudians, Karen Horney (pronounced Horn-Eye) was not a student of Freud's. Instead, Horney studied Freud's work indirectly and later taught psychoanalysis at the Berlin Psychoanalytic Institute and the New York Psychoanalytic Institute. But, like many psychoanalysts, she began to question some of the basic tenets of Freudian theory. In particular, Horney found she could not accept some of Freud's views concerning women. Freud maintained that men and women were born with different personalities. But Horney argued that cultural and social forces are far more responsible than biology for some of the apparent differences between the genders.

Eventually Horney became so disenchanted with the Freudian position that she and the members of the New York Psychoanalytic Institute agreed she should leave the institute. She resigned in 1941 and founded her own American Institute for Psychoanalysis. Horney explored cultural and social influences on personality development throughout her career. The prominent role she gave to social influences over innate causes of behavior can be seen in two of her contributions to the psychoanalytic approach: her views on neurosis and what she called "feminine psychology."

Neurosis

We all know people who fit Horney's description of neurotic. Let me give three examples of people I have met. One is a woman who at first appears friendly and warm. She's always involved in social activities and is quick to pass along a compliment. But people soon find that her attention turns into demands. She can't stand to be alone, can't accept the idea that her friends or romantic partners would be interested in doing anything without her. Although her relationships never work out for long, she inevitably "falls in love" almost as soon as she meets the next man. The second example is a man who was disliked by almost everyone he went to college with. Few people escaped his sarcastic, sometimes biting, comments. He seemed to hold everyone he encountered with contempt. I never heard him say a nice thing about anyone. Today he is a cutthroat—albeit successful—businessman. The third example is a woman who works in a small office tabulating figures. She rarely socializes with the other employees, so now most of them have stopped asking her to join them. She has few friends and spends most of her evenings by herself.

According to Horney, what these three people have in common is that each is desperately fighting off feelings of inadequacy and insecurity. Although they eventually drive people away with their behavior, on the inside they are scared and

© *Bettmann / CORBIS*

Karen Horney

1885–1952

Karen Danielsen was born in Hamburg, Germany, the daughter of a sea captain and his young, second wife. From her earliest years on, she faced the injustices and rejection that came from being a rebellious woman in a man's world. Her father was a strict authoritarian who used Bible verse to promote his views on the superiority of men. Karen's older brother, Berndt, was awarded opportunities, including college and an eventual law degree that her father believed unnecessary for a female. Karen responded to these inequities by vowing in elementary school to always be first in her class, and at age 12 decided she would one day go to medical school.

Karen's mother persuaded her father to allow Karen to go to college, where she met and married Oskar Horney in 1909. In 1915 she received her medical degree from the University of Berlin, one of the very few female students in one of the few schools to accept women. She underwent psychoanalysis as part of her psychoanalytic training but found it insufficient for dealing with her lifelong bouts with depression. At one point,

her husband was reported to have rescued her from a suicide attempt (Rubins, 1978). Despite her depression, her doubts about psychoanalysis, and a number of personal problems—including the premature death of her brother, a strained marriage, and eventual divorce—her career prospered. She worked at the Berlin Psychoanalytic Institute and later immigrated to America, where she joined the New York Psychoanalytic Institute in 1934.

However, it was not in Horney's character to check her growing dissatisfaction with several important aspects of Freud's theory. This open questioning created great strain with the other members of the institute, who in 1941 voted to disqualify her as an instructor. According to most reports of this event, Horney received the vote in a dramatically silent room. She responded by leaving the meeting in a dignified and proud manner, without uttering a word. Horney went on to establish her own highly successful American Institute for Psychoanalysis. By the time of her death, in 1952, it was clear she had made great progress in her battle against the male-dominated and paternalistic psychoanalytic school of thought.

pitiful individuals. Horney would have identified all three of these people as *neurotic*. The key characteristic of neurotics in her theory is that they are trapped in a self-defeating interpersonal style. That is, the way these people interact with others prevents them from developing the social contact they unconsciously crave. Ironically, their destructive interpersonal style is a type of defense mechanism intended to ward off their feelings of anxiety.

What is it in the backgrounds of these people that brought them to the sad situations they find themselves in today? Freud explained neurosis in terms of fixated energy and unconscious battles between various aspects of the personality. But

Horney pointed to disturbed interpersonal relationships during childhood. In particular, she believed children too often grow up in homes that foster feelings of anxiety. The ways parents can generate these feelings are almost endless:

> direct or indirect domination, indifference, erratic behavior, lack of respect for the child's individual needs, lack of real guidance, disparaging attitudes, too much admiration or the absence of it, lack of reliable warmth, having to take sides in parental disagreements, too much or too little responsibility, overprotection, isolation from other children, injustice, discrimination, unkept promises, hostile atmosphere, and . . . [a] sense of lurking hypocrisy in the environment. (1945/1966, p. 41)

In short, parenting is not an easy job. Although raising children is one of the most important tasks we face, there is practically no training for the job and few restrictions on who can raise children and how they should be raised. And so we end up with children who lack a sense of personal worth, who are afraid and unsure of how to deal with their parents, who fear unjust punishment from their parents for reasons they can't understand, who feel insecure and inadequate, and who desperately want but fail to receive the warmth and support they need. These children are confused, afraid, and anxious.

How do children deal with this anxiety? According to Horney, children growing up in anxiety-generating situations develop strategies for dealing with threatening people. On the positive side, these strategies usually succeed in alleviating anxiety in the short run. On the downside, these individuals can come to rely on these strategies even when dealing with people outside the family. As adults, their childhood fear of interacting with other people continues. In essence, these people have learned that social relationships are a source of anxiety. As a result, they develop neurotic interaction styles to fend off the anxiety.

Horney identified three interaction styles neurotics adopt in their efforts to avoid anxiety-provoking experiences. She called these styles *moving toward people,* *moving against people,* and *moving away from people.* As you read about these styles, you'll no doubt see a little of yourself in each. That is healthy. Horney explained that most people use each of the three strategies on occasion to combat anxiety. In contrast, neurotic people inflexibly rely on just one of these styles for virtually all their social interactions.

Moving Toward People. Some children deal with anxiety by emphasizing their helplessness. They become dependent on others, compulsively seeking affection and acceptance from their parents and caregivers. The sympathy they receive provides temporary relief from their anxiety, but the children run the risk of relying on this strategy in later relationships. As adults, these people have an intense need to be loved and accepted. They often believe that if only they can find love, everything else will be all right. They may indiscriminately attach themselves to whomever is available, believing that any relationship is better than loneliness and feeling unwanted. If you've ever been involved with someone who meets this description, you probably can appreciate the futility of pursuing a long-term relationship. These people don't love, they cling. They don't share affection, they can only demand it. Because of this neurotic style, each new relationship is almost certainly doomed.

Moving Against People. One way to handle anxiety is to cling to others, another is to fight. Some children find aggressiveness and hostility are the best way to deal with a poor home environment. They compensate for feelings of inadequacy and insecurity by pushing around other children. They are rewarded with a fleeting sense of power and respect from classmates, but no real friendships. This neurotic style takes on more sophisticated forms when these children become adults. They may take advantage of business partners and lash out at others with hurtful comments. In both child and adult, we find an ever-present need to exploit others. Horney argued that this neurotic style is characterized by *externalization,* similar to Freud's concept of projection. That is, these individuals took from their childhood encounters with adults that all people are basically hostile and out to get what they can. They respond to this perception by doing unto others before others can do unto them. They enter into relationships only when there is something to be gained. Consequently, relationships with these people are necessarily shallow, unfulfilling, and ultimately painful.

Moving Away from People. Some children adopt a third strategy to deal with their anxiety. Instead of interacting with others in a dependent or hostile manner, the child may simply tune out the world. Who needs them? The child's desire for privacy and self-sufficiency can be intense. As adults, these neurotics seek out jobs requiring little interaction with other people. As a rule, they avoid affection, love, and friendship. Because emotional attachment might lead to the kind of pain they remember from childhood, they develop a numbness to emotional experiences. The safest way to avoid anxiety is simply to avoid involvement. This is certainly the wrong person to fall in love with. Affection cannot be returned, because it is not even experienced. Thus, for both participants, the relationship will be shallow and unrewarding.

Feminine Psychology

As a psychoanalyst in the 1930s, Horney found herself a woman in a man's world. Many of her initial doubts about Freudian theory began with some of Freud's disparaging views of women. For example, Freud described *penis envy*—the desire every young girl has to be a boy. Horney (1967) countered this male-flattering position with the concept of *womb envy*—men's envy of women's ability to bear and nurse children. Horney did not suggest that men are therefore dissatisfied with themselves, but rather that each gender has attributes that the other admires. However, she did suggest that men compensate for their inability to have children through achievement in other domains.

Horney also pointed out that Freud's observations and writings took place at a time when society often placed women in inferior positions. If a woman living in that era wished she were a man, it was probably because of the restrictions and burdens placed on her by the culture, not because of inherent inferiorities. In a society where both men and women are free to become whatever they desire, there is little reason to think that girls would want to be boys, or vice versa. In many ways, we can see that Horney's thinking was well ahead of its time. Horney's death in 1952 did not allow her to see how feminists would later use many of her ideas to promote the cause of gender equality.

Harry Stack Sullivan

Unlike the other neo-Freudian theorists covered in this chapter, Harry Stack Sullivan was born and trained in America. After a rather poor education—Sullivan flunked out of college and obtained a medical degree from a soon defunct medical school—he went to work as a psychoanalyst. From his experience with psychoanalysis, particularly in treating schizophrenic patients, Sullivan developed his own theory of personality. In many ways, the link with Freudian theory is apparent. Sullivan retained concepts like anxiety and the unconscious. However, he also placed more emphasis on the interpersonal causes and consequences of these Freudian mechanisms than most psychoanalytic writers. This emphasis places Sullivan's approach somewhere between that of Freudian psychoanalysis and the more recent social-learning theorists (Chapter 13).

According to Sullivan, personality does not even exist in the absence of interpersonal relations, whether real or imagined. A personality "can never be isolated from the complex of interpersonal relations in which the person lives and has his being" (Sullivan, 1953, p. 10). Instead, we can understand people only by observing how they respond to various types of interpersonal situations. Under Sullivan's system, the concept of "self" has meaning only within relations with other people. Two of Sullivan's contributions that illustrate his blend of Freudian theory with a more social orientation are presented in the following sections. These are his concept of personifications and his description of the stages of personality development.

Personifications

Like Freud, Sullivan placed heavy emphasis on the role of anxiety in his theory. However, whereas Freud was concerned with intrapsychic causes of anxiety, Sullivan pointed to our relationships with significant others. Poor social relationships lead to feelings of insecurity and anxiety. This process can begin as early as the first few months of life. Mothers who feel tense when interacting with their babies communicate their feelings of anxiety to the child. At first, children have no way to deal with these feelings. However, as Horney observed, children soon learn techniques for reducing their anxiety. One particularly useful mechanism is

© Bettmann /CORBIS

Harry Stack Sullivan

1892–1949

Perhaps more than with any other theorist, Harry Stack Sullivan's descriptions of personality development seem distinctly autobiographical. Sullivan's emphasis on the importance of good interpersonal relations particularly during the adolescent years, seem to reflect some of his own difficulties and traumas. For example, when Sullivan proposed that a mother's anxiety is transferred to her child, he was probably aware of his troubled relationship with his own mother. Sullivan's mother appears to have suffered from depression. His childhood was a lonely and isolated one. He was an only child (two older brothers died in infancy) and the only Irish Catholic in a Protestant neighborhood.

Sullivan's emphasis on the importance of adolescent relationships probably reflects his turbulent teenage years. When Sullivan was 8, he developed a strong friendship with a 13-year-old, Clarence Bellinger. Biographers disagree on whether this was a homosexual relationship but

acknowledge that it was generally perceived to be (Chapman, 1976; Perry, 1984). It is interesting that Bellinger also became a psychiatrist. However, their relationship was terminated after Sullivan's adolescent years.

Sullivan's academic background was hardly the stuff great scholars are made of. He was suspended his first year at Cornell University in 1909, after failing all his classes. A few years later, without an undergraduate degree, he entered the Chicago College of Medicine and Surgery, a school of questionable academic quality. Sullivan's diploma was held up a few years until he could make his final tuition payment, and the school folded shortly thereafter. Nonetheless, following World War I, he developed a reputation for his successful treatment of schizophrenic patients in private hospitals in Baltimore and Washington, D.C. In 1927 Sullivan unofficially adopted one of these patients, 15-year-old James, who lived with Sullivan the rest of his life. Sullivan never married. He died from a brain hemorrhage in 1949 at age 56.

---

selective inattention. Children and adults use selective inattention when they simply ignore or reject anxiety-provoking information. For example, a woman's sense of security might be threatened after a fight with her spouse. She controls her mounting anxiety by thinking of something less threatening. However, like the defense mechanisms described by Freud, the short-term gain in reduced anxiety comes at a price. By paying less and less attention to relevant information, people develop false impressions of reality. As you will see in the next chapter, research on coping strategies confirms that this kind of tactic is ultimately ineffective for dealing with our problems.

Another consequence of relying on anxiety-reducing strategies like selective inattention is that people soon develop a false sense of who they are. This process is important in shaping what Sullivan called **personifications**—mental images we have of other people and ourselves. Here Sullivan begins to sound like contemporary cognitive personality theorists who study mental representations of our selves (Chapter 15). However, Sullivan's descriptions also retain a psychoanalytic flavor. According to Sullivan, our self-images fall into three basic categories. The *good-me* personification consists of those aspects of ourselves that we feel good about, that have been rewarded in the past. Most important, these are the behaviors associated with feelings of security or, put another way, without feelings of anxiety. In contrast, the *bad-me* personification reflects those parts of our experiences that we would rather not think about, that have not been rewarded. These behaviors are associated with anxiety.

We can easily think of examples of these first two personifications. Sometimes we feel content and pleased with our actions. Other times we wince in shame and embarrassment when thinking about regrettable things we've done. In other words, in Sullivan's theory, the good-me and bad-me personifications exist largely at the conscious level. But Sullivan also identified a third self-personification, the *not-me*. This represents those aspects of ourselves that are so threatening that we *dissociate* them from the self system and keep them in our unconscious. According to Sullivan, people are aware of and experience their not-me personification only when sleeping or when schizophrenic. Dissociation is similar to Freud's concept of repression. Like repression, dissociation requires constant effort to keep unacceptable thoughts out of awareness.

Developmental Epochs

Like other psychoanalysts, Sullivan identified the importance of early childhood experiences in the development of adult personality. He was particularly interested in mother-child relationships. However, like Erikson, Sullivan argued that personality development continues well beyond the first few years of life. Sullivan identified seven distinct stages of personality development—what he called **developmental epochs** (Table 5.1). He called these *infancy, childhood, the juvenile era, preadolescence, early adolescence, late adolescence,* and *adulthood*. Unlike Freud, who described developmental stages in terms of an innate biological clock, Sullivan maintained that developmental epochs are largely determined by social situations. Children go through a particular stage in a particular way partly because of biological changes associated with the stage, but partly because of the typical circumstances they find themselves in at that age. Thus, children growing up in significantly different cultures probably go through quite different developmental stages.

A key feature of Sullivan's developmental scheme is the significance ascribed to the adolescent years, comprising three of the seven stages. Sullivan argued that what happens during the preadolescent and teenage years is crucial for the development of satisfying adult relationships. He traced many of the psychological disorders his patients suffered as adults back to their failure to form satisfying relationships during these early years. Let's look more closely at the three adolescent stages.

Table 5.1 Sullivan's Developmental Epochs	
Epoch	**Appearance Signaled by**
Infancy (0–1 year)	Birth
Childhood (1–5)	Acquisition of early speech
Juvenile era (6–8)	Need for playmates
Preadolescence (9–12)	Need for an intimate relationship with a same-gender friend
Early adolescence (13–17)	Puberty and a sex drive; need for an intimate relationship with a member of the opposite sex
Late adolescence (18–early 20s)	Interest in developing a long-term sexual relationship; interest in career and financial matters
Adulthood	Establishment of career, adult friendships, and long-term sexual relationship

The *preadolescent epoch,* the fourth stage of personality development in Sullivan's theory, begins around eight or nine years of age. This stage is characterized by a strong need to develop an intimate relationship with a peer. Most of us have seen children this age who become inseparable buddies. Sometimes they form larger same-gender cliques or groups, but Sullivan argued that even within these larger groups we can still identify sets of two. This special friendship serves some important psychological functions. It is where the child first develops a sensitivity to other people's needs. In addition, the friendship validates the child's sense of worth. Within this relationship the child feels acceptable and likable. Children who fail to develop a special relationship may experience painful feelings of loneliness. People who never experience this preadolescent friendship may have difficulty forming intimate relationships later in life.

With the onset of puberty comes the *early adolescent epoch.* Along with physical changes, teens must deal with newfound feelings of sexual attraction. For many adolescents, feelings of self-worth take a beating during these years. Too often, self-worth becomes synonymous with sexual attraction and performance. Thus, teenagers who feel they are not sexually attractive or who lag behind their peers in sexual activity may experience low self-esteem. Further conflicts come from parents, who often don't know how to deal with their children's sexual maturity. Sullivan noted that too often parents resort to ridicule or other types of interference that further shatters the sensitive adolescent's self-image.

At the end of the teenage years we reach the *late adolescent epoch.* Here the concern is with developing satisfying sexual activity, presumably within a long-term relationship. This stage also marks the transition to adult concerns like finding a job and handling finances. It is during the late adolescent stage that people often pay for earlier anxiety-reducing tactics. Those who have relied heavily on selective inattention will have extremely distorted self-personifications. Because they have a poor idea of who they are, these people will find it difficult to select an appropriate occupation or the right romantic partner.

Erich Fromm

If you are like most people, you have occasionally found life's problems a little overwhelming. You may recall a time when you just wanted someone stronger and wiser to suddenly appear and take care of you and all your concerns. Maybe you've thought about how nice it would be to become a child again, to be free from the worries and responsibilities of adulthood. Erich Fromm, a German-born psychologist and relative latecomer to the psychoanalytic field, centered his theory of personality around these feelings of anxiety and the desire to escape. His interest in this phenomenon was triggered in part when observing the Nazi party's rise to power in Germany in the 1930s. What would cause people to identify with and carry out the desires of the Nazi leaders? Fromm explained this phenomenon within the context of his theory of personality in his book *Escape from Freedom* (1941/1965), published at the beginning of World War II.

According to Fromm, the rise of modern democracy freed humankind in the sense that we no longer are forced into a certain niche in a larger feudal system. Within obvious limits, today most of us are free to be and do whatever we please. Yet it is this very freedom that creates the greatest problem for us. Freedom can be frightening. It forces each of us to face important personal decisions that we alone must take responsibility for. Fromm described freedom as an "unbearable state of powerlessness and aloneness." As we grow up and develop a sense of individuality, we become aware of all that we cannot control and come painfully face to face with our insignificance. According to Fromm, we respond to this perception of insignificance in one of two ways: We either escape from freedom, or we progress toward "positive freedom."

Fromm identified three main strategies people use to overcome the feelings of powerlessness and anxiety that accompany freedom. Some people turn to **authoritarianism.** That is, they associate themselves with stronger people or forces as a way of feeling powerful themselves. Fromm argued that *authoritarian characters* possess an ironic combination of striving for submission as well as striving for domination. On the one hand, authoritarian characters overcome their feelings of inferiority by abandoning their individuality and joining powerful people or organizations. On the other hand, they obtain a sense of power by dominating and exploiting weaker people. It is just this two-sided authoritarianism that Fromm observed in members of the Nazi party, obedient to authorities but sadistic to their victims. According to Fromm, both the tendency to submit to higher forces and

© Bettmann /CORBIS

Erich Fromm

1900–1980

Personal experiences with war and anti-Semitism prompted Erich Fromm's curiosity about human behavior. Fromm was born at the turn of the century in Frankfurt, Germany. He grew up as a Jewish child in an anti-Semitic environment. World War I broke out in Europe when Fromm was 14. As an adolescent, he was overwhelmed by the irrationality and destructiveness of the war that surrounded him. These experiences left him with a lifelong curiosity about the nature of human beings. "When the war ended," he later wrote, "I was a deeply troubled young man who was obsessed by the question of how war was possible, by the wish to understand the irrationality of human mass behavior, by a passionate desire for peace and international understanding" (Fromm, 1962, p. 9).

Fromm sought and found answers to his questions from two sources. Freud helped him understand individual personalities, and Karl Marx explained the sociopolitical influences on behavior. Fromm studied Freud and Marx extensively while in school. He received his Ph.D. from the University of Heidelberg in 1922 and studied psychoanalysis at the Berlin Psychoanalytic Institute. Then came the rise of the Nazis in Germany. Fromm watched the increase in militaristic, anti-Jewish sentiment in his homeland until 1934, when living in Germany had become too dangerous. Fromm immigrated to the United States and observed the developments in Europe from abroad.

Fromm's interests in psychoanalysis and social issues merged in his 1941 book *Escape from Freedom*. The book explained the Nazi movement with what some have called a "sociopsychoanalytic" interpretation—a blend of classic psychoanalysis and political theories. Fromm's career reflected that same blend of psychoanalysis and socialism found in his writings. He taught at a number of universities, including Columbia, Bennington College, Yale, Michigan State, New York University, and the National University of Mexico in Mexico City. At the same time, he maintained an active interest in political philosophy and was often involved in social and political issues.

the need to express power over subordinates are elaborate defenses against feelings of powerlessness. And because they are mere defenses, they are ultimately inadequate. Aligning oneself with powerful people and exploiting others may succeed in generating a sense of personal strength, but authoritarian characters pay the unacceptable price of relinquishing their individuality and true sense of self-worth.

Fromm identified *destructiveness* as a second mechanism of escape. Here the person attempts to overcome life's threatening situations by destroying them. Although destructiveness is unconsciously motivated, individuals who actively work to destroy the people and circumstances they find threatening usually rationalize away these antisocial actions. They often invoke religion, duty, or patriotism to justify actions taken against people they dislike. Thus, people who say they are fighting for love of country or out of a sense of duty may in reality be unconsciously striving to overcome feelings of powerlessness and isolation.

Fortunately, not everyone turns to authoritarianism or destructiveness as a means of escaping reality. Rather, Fromm argued that most people fall into what he called *automaton conformity*. To avoid the anxiety associated with freedom, most of us eagerly adopt the role and predictable lifestyle society has selected for us. In a sense, we return to the safe niche our ancestors owned back in the feudal system. We find a secure job and routine where we can become a cog in a larger machine. By acting as everyone else acts, we temporarily escape our sense of individuality and thereby escape the anxiety that comes with the awareness of personal freedom. We often hear commentators lament the lack of individuality in modern society. We are accused of following the same fads, adopting the same values, and buying the same products as the people around us. Even "nonconformists" often adopt the nonconformist styles of others.

To this point, Fromm's description of the human condition seems rather grim. However, he also described a healthy response for dealing with the awareness of personal freedom. Like the humanistic psychologists who would follow (Chapter 10), Fromm maintained that knowing and being oneself is the key to happiness. Instead of escaping freedom, we can choose to embrace it. The key to developing

Photo by Marlene Somsak

Fromm's most important book, Escape from Freedom, *was written in part to explain the rise of totalitarianism in Nazi Germany. According to Fromm, citizens joined the Nazi party as an escape from their perception of personal freedom.*

positive freedom is spontaneity—experiencing and expressing our true desires. We express these inner feelings when we figure out what it is we want to do rather than what we are supposed to do. Fromm referred to this experience as *individuation*.

Application: Psychoanalytic Theory and Religion

> *"The religions of mankind must be classed among the mass-delusions. No one, needless to say, who shares a delusion ever recognizes it as such."*
> SIGMUND FREUD

The psychoanalytic theorists did more than describe personality and develop treatments for psychological disorders. These writers also offered an important new perspective on humankind and answers to some enduring philosophical questions about the human condition. Inevitably, their concerns overlapped with some of those traditionally addressed by theologians: Are people inherently good or bad? Should we sacrifice personal pleasure for the common good? Is the source of happiness within each of us or found in powers greater than our own?

In a style that typified his career, Freud directly challenged conventional thinking about many religious issues. Two books in particular, *The Future of an Illusion* and *Civilization and Its Discontents,* assaulted widely held religious beliefs. Although Freud understood that organized religion provided solace for the uneducated, he lamented its widespread acceptance by intelligent people. "The whole thing is so patently infantile, so foreign to reality," Freud wrote, "that to anyone with a friendly attitude to humanity it is painful to think that the great majority of mortals will never be able to rise above this view of life" (1930/1961, p. 21).

Why, then, do so many people believe? According to Freud, religious behavior represents a form of neurosis. It begins with the baby's feelings of helplessness and longing for a powerful protector, presumably the father. Freud called religion a type of collective wish fulfillment. To protect ourselves from a threatening and unpredictable world, we project our imagined savior from this predicament outward in the form of a God. Thus, to Freud, God is but an unconscious father figure generated in an infantile way to provide us with feelings of security.

Not surprisingly, Freud's views on religion have generated considerable reaction from theologians. Some see merit in a few of his points, but most argue against them. Several neo-Freudian theorists also addressed religious questions in their writings. The neo-Freudian theorist who stimulated the most discussion about the intersection between psychology and religion was Carl Jung.

Jung, whose father was a minister in the Swiss Reformed Church, discussed religion in numerous places in his writings. It is apparent from these references that Jung struggled with religious issues throughout much of his life, often wavering between favorable and unfavorable impressions of modern religion. He once referred to "the religious myth," yet at another point he described religious experience as "a great treasure" providing "a source of life, meaning, and beauty" (Bechtle, 1984).

Why do people feel deeply about their religious beliefs? This is one of the questions addressed by Freud and many of the neo-Freudian theorists. Freud declared religion a delusion, while Jung pondered over the nature of religious experiences throughout his career.

Jung often insisted that the question of God's existence was outside the realm of science and hence nothing he could provide answers about. His interest was with humankind's eternal need to find religion. Why does religion surface in all cultures? Why is some entity similar to the Judeo-Christian God found in each of these cultures? Jung's answer was that each of us inherits a God archetype in our collective unconscious. This primordial image causes God-like images to surface in the dreams, folklore, artwork, and experiences of people everywhere. We can easily conceive of a God, find evidence for His existence, and experience deep religious feelings because we were born with a kind of unconscious predisposition for Him. Scholars continue to debate if Jung meant by this that God exists only in our collective unconscious and therefore that the traditional description of God as an external entity is a myth (Bianchi, 1988). Although at times Jung does appear to argue that God exists only in the human mind, other references suggest he was not ready to make such a bold statement.

Jung maintained that organized religions often took advantage of powerful archetypal symbols in promoting themselves to followers. Indeed, he described Christ as a symbol, with the four points on the cross representing the good-versus-bad and the spiritual-versus-material aspects of our being. In addition to religious art and scripture, Jung said, religious symbols are often found in our dreams and in the hallucinations of psychotic patients.

Toward the end of his career, Jung seemed to take a more favorable approach to organized religion. He acknowledged that religion often provides followers with a sense of purpose and feelings of security. According to Jung, many people seek out psychotherapy when their religion fails to provide reassurance. Thus, modern psychotherapy has taken on the role once reserved for the clergy. Of particular importance for many of Jung's patients was the need to resolve the good and evil sides of their personalities. Psychologists try to help these patients through a variety of therapy techniques. However, Jung argued, modern religions have developed their own practices to achieve the same end. For example, churches use confession, absolution, and forgiveness to symbolically help followers reconcile the evil side of their selves with the good.

Erich Fromm also was fascinated by the seemingly universal human need for religion (Fromm, 1950, 1966). He explained this need within his theory of escape from freedom. People turn to the powerful authority of the church to escape the sense of powerlessness and loneliness that accompanies their awareness of individuality. "People return to religion . . . not as an act of faith but in order to escape an intolerable doubt," Fromm wrote. "They make this decision not out of devotion but in search of security" (1950, p. 4). The notion that we are individuals, responsible for ourselves and for finding our own meaning in life, is frightening to many people. Religion provides an escape from these fears. Thus, the same anxieties and insecurities that cause some people to align themselves with powerful political and social forces lead other people to religion. Submission to an authoritarian leader gives many people a sense of strength and security. Similarly, surrendering oneself to a God provides a sense of protection.

However, Fromm also drew a distinction between *authoritarian religions* and *humanistic religions.* The former emphasize that we are under the control of a powerful God, whereas in the latter God is seen as a symbol of our own power. Fromm argued that authoritarian religions deny people their personal identity, but humanistic religions provide an opportunity for personal growth. Thus, while condemning some religions, Fromm recognized the potential for individuation and finding happiness within others.

Today, the writings of Freud, Jung, Fromm, and other psychoanalytic theorists are studied and debated by theology students around the world. Some scholars have even looked into these theorists' backgrounds to understand what in their childhoods might have generated such hostility toward modern religion (Meissner, 1984). Although most theologians probably reject psychoanalytic interpretations of religious behavior, few are able to ignore them.

Assessment: Measuring Types

Because most neo-Freudian theorists did not fall far from the Freudian tree, they share many assumptions about personality assessment with Freudian psychologists. For example, most agree that crucial information about psychological disorders is often buried in the unconscious. Therefore, many neo-Freudian psychologists rely on the Rorschach inkblot test and other projective measures described in Chapter 3 to tap into otherwise inaccessible regions of the mind.

However, many neo-Freudians do not limit their assessment of personality to projective measures. One example of this is the identification of psychological types, as described by Carl Jung. Although Jung maintained that the roots and structure of different personality types are based in the unconscious, later Jungian psychologists found they could identify these types through clients' self-reports of their overt behaviors and feelings. The use of Jung's type theory and the inventory designed to measure personality types have become quite popular in such areas as psychological counseling, career counseling, and education.

Jung's Theory of Psychological Types

Like many early psychologists, Carl Jung was struck by individual differences in personality. As he struggled to make sense of the many different personalities he encountered in his practice and travels, Jung eventually arrived at an important distinction. "There is a whole class of men who at . . . a given situation at first draw back a little as if with an unvoiced 'no,' and only after that are able to react," he wrote. "And there is another class who, in the same situation, come forward with an immediate reaction, apparently confident that their behavior is obviously right" (1933, p. 85). You can probably think of examples of these two types. We all know people who are apprehensive about entering a social gathering. They are likely to wait for someone to approach them rather than initiating a conversation themselves. We also know people who can enter the same gathering and begin interacting with no hesitation.

This distinction reflects what Jung identified as the two *basic attitudes.* The former he called *introversion,* in which the dominant tendency is to channel psychic energy inward. Introverts tend to focus their attention on their inner worlds. They typically are introspective and socially withdrawn. For other people, the dominant tendency is to focus psychic energy outward. *Extraversion* is characterized by an outgoing, active style and an interest in people and the external world.

But Jung soon recognized that there were more than two types of people in the world. He began to look at the relationship between a person's consciousness and experience—that is, how we perceive and make sense of the world. Jung identified what he called the four *basic functions:* sensing, intuition, thinking, and feeling. He argued that each of us adopts one of these four as our dominant mode of experience. If *sensing* is your dominant mode, you tend to focus on the immediate experience. You probably have developed excellent powers of observation and a keen memory for detail. However, if *intuition* is dominant, you are more likely to perceive experience in terms of possibilities. You rely on insight and hunches, and are often imaginative and abstract. On the other hand, people with a dominant *thinking* function analyze information in a logical, objective manner. These people actively and critically dissect arguments and logic when coming to a decision. If your dominant function is *feeling,* you interpret information in terms of values and

Table 5.2 Jung's Eight Psychological Types		

	Attitude	
Function	**Extraversion**	**Introversion**
Thinking	Focus is on learning about the external world. Practical, objective thinker. Interested in facts. Sometimes appears cold and impersonal. Makes a good scientist. Interested in using logic and applying rules.	Interested in understanding own ideas. Reflective, interested in philosophical issues and the meaning of one's own life. May be stubborn, distant, or arrogant. More interested in understanding himself or herself than in examining other people.
Feeling	Likely to be moody, capricious. Easily conforms to the group norm. Likes to follow fads and fashions. Can be highly emotional at times. Can change emotions quickly in a new situation.	Has deep emotional experiences, but keeps them to himself or herself. May appear silent and perhaps self-assuredly cold, but actually hiding strong emotions just under the surface. Often a nonconformist.
Sensing	Interested in experiencing the external world. Often sensual and can become obsessed with pleasure seeking. May live life for the pleasure of the moment.	More interested in own thoughts and inner sensations than external objects. May be able to express himself or herself only through an outlet such as art or music, and these expressions are typically not understood by many.
Intuitive	Constantly seeking new challenges and interests in the external world. Gets bored easily with jobs and relationships. Enjoys novel situations. Tends to be unstable and flighty.	Likes to explore new and different ideas but has difficulty developing insights or communicating them to other people. May consider self a prophet or dreamer whose ideas will be carried out by others. Often fails to understand reality or social norms, thus totally impractical in planning.

subjective impressions. You usually consider the human element rather than logic or principles when making decisions.

The two attitudes and four functions create eight different personality types. Although Jung acknowledged that not all people within a category are identical, he nonetheless maintained that the two-by-four framework represents distinctions inherent in the structure of the human psyche. Prototypic descriptions of the eight kinds of people in this system are presented in Table 5.2.

Measuring Psychological Types: The Myers-Briggs Type Indicator

By far the most popular method for measuring Jung's psychological types is the *Myers-Briggs Type Indicator* (Myers & McCaulley, 1985). Approximately two million people take this personality test each year. The full version of the measure asks test takers to describe themselves on 166 items. In keeping with Jungian theory, the measure is designed to identify which type category the test taker belongs to.

The Myers-Briggs Type Indicator divides people into categories along four dimensions. Jung's eight personality types are created by dividing people into *Extraversion-Introversion, Sensing-Intuitive,* and *Thinking-Feeling* categories. In addition, the test makers have included a *Judgment-Perception* division. People with a *judging* attitude tend to ignore new information as soon as they have enough facts to make up their minds. People with a *perceptive* attitude are open to new information. They are curious and inquisitive. By dividing people along each of these four lines, test makers can identify 16 personality types. Thus, someone who is extraverted, intuitive, feeling, and perceptive is said to be distinctively different from someone who is extraverted, intuitive, thinking, and judging.

The Myers-Briggs test has been most widely used among counselors in nonclinical settings, such as career counseling and education (DeVito, 1985). For example, many counselors find scores on the Myers-Briggs useful in helping clients select careers. An extravert will probably not be happy in a job requiring long hours of isolated work, whereas an introvert might not do well in a job requiring a great deal of socializing and group activity. A list of the kinds of jobs best suited for the different personality types is shown in Table 5.3. Similarly, education researchers find that extraverts do better than introverts in learning groups (Haber, 1980), whereas intuitive people do best when allowed to study what they want at their own pace (Carlson & Levy, 1973).

Table 5.3   **Optimal Career Settings for Personality Types**

Type	Career Setting
Extraverts	Work requiring group interactions, meeting with people, and social gatherings. Lots of travel, speeches, variety.
Introverts	Quiet, solitary desk work. Few interruptions. Jobs requiring concentration and thinking.
Thinking	Work including a lot of problem solving, especially when logic is required. Work with numbers, problems with clear solutions.
Feeling	Service jobs, especially those that benefit underprivileged groups. Work provides personal satisfaction.
Sensing	Work requiring attention to details. Short-term, tangible, and immediate goals and relevance.
Intuitive	Nonrepetitive tasks with new challenges. Abstract problems requiring insight and contemplation.
Judging	Highly organized and structured work. Tasks that can be completed before new ones are begun.
Perceptive	Work requiring an ability to adapt to new circumstances. Tasks calling for new, open-minded approaches to problems.

The popularity of the Myers-Briggs test probably lies in its simplicity (Lanning, 2003). As discussed in Chapter 7, most personality psychologists prefer to describe individual differences in terms of where people fall along a dimension of personality rather than to think of people as falling into only one of two categories. Thus, instead of identifying someone as either an extravert or an introvert, most researchers prefer to know where the person lies on a continuum of possible scores ranging from extreme extraversion to extreme introversion. On the other hand, it probably is easier for most clients to understand that they are a *type* of person than to fully grasp the meaning of percentile scores and normal distributions.

Unfortunately, this ease of understanding comes at a price, and that price appears to be accuracy. Researchers find little evidence that personality can be divided into the neat categories identified by the Myers-Briggs (Bess & Harvey, 2002; Lanning, 2003). Rather, scores generated from the scale are more useful when treated as dimensions rather than types (Mastrangelo, 2001). Worse, because most people have scores that fall very close to the cut-off point for determining which category they belong to, a different answer on one or two items can throw a test taker into a different type. As a result, about a third of the people who take the Myers-Briggs test a second time come away with a different type classification, even when the gap between tests is only a few weeks (Fleenor, 2001; Mastrangelo, 2001).

Strengths and Criticisms of Neo-Freudian Theories

Strengths

The primary strength of the neo-Freudian theories is their elaboration of important concepts that Freud had ignored or deemphasized. For example, most of these theorists identified the role played by social factors in the formation and change of personality. Many, most notably Erikson and Sullivan, described the ways personality develops beyond the first few years of life. And many theorists presented a much more optimistic and flattering picture of humankind than Freud had. Most described the positive functions served by the ego rather than restricting its role to arbitrator between the demanding id and superego.

The neo-Freudians also introduced many new concepts into the psychological literature. For example, birth order, archetypes, authoritarian personality, and personifications can be traced directly to some of the neo-Freudian theorists. As with Freudian theory, many of these ideas have made their way into our everyday language. People speak of identity crises, introversion, and inferiority complexes without recognizing the references to Erikson, Jung, and Adler.

Another gauge of the usefulness of a personality theory is the extent to which it influences later theorists and psychotherapists. In this respect, the neo-Freudian contributions can claim some success. The optimistic tone about humans that characterized many neo-Freudians' views helped pave the way for the humanistic personality theories. Similarly, the emphasis on social aspects of personality development was undoubtedly a considerable step in the evolution of social learning approaches to personality. And the techniques and approaches developed by each of the neo-Freudians have been adopted or adapted by many contemporary psychotherapists.

In short, the neo-Freudian theorists did much to make parts of the psychoanalytic approach palatable to psychologists and nonpsychologists. In fact, these theories provide a bridge between Freud's concepts and many later personality theories. However, no individual neo-Freudian theorist, or even the theories taken as a whole, has ever reached the level of acclaim that Freud did. Part of this can be explained through some limitations in the theories, as described next.

Criticisms

Many of the limitations critics point to in Freud's theory also are present in some of the neo-Freudian works. For example, like Freudian theory, some of the neo-Freudian theories are supported with questionable evidence. In particular, many of Jung's conclusions about the nature of the collective unconscious are based on myths, legends, dreams, occult phenomena, and artwork. Fromm's work has been criticized for being more descriptive than scientific. Fromm's interpretation of history, which he uses to support his theory, has also been challenged. Many neo-Freudians based their conclusions about human personality largely on data from patients undergoing psychotherapy. As such, there are questions about biased interpretations and applicability to normal, functioning adults.

A second problem with the neo-Freudians as a group is that they often oversimplified or ignored important concepts. None dealt with so many topics in so much depth as Freud. Consequently, the neo-Freudians sometimes failed to effectively address concepts central to psychoanalytic theory. This observation has led some people to criticize neo-Freudian works as incomplete or limited accounts of personality and human behavior. For example, Erikson has been criticized for what some consider a superficial treatment of anxiety's role in the development of psychological disorders. Sullivan has been attacked for not giving enough attention to hereditary factors in the schizophrenics he studied. Similarly, Fromm has been criticized for placing too much emphasis on the role of social forces. Indeed, some of the strongest criticisms of Fromm's work center on his recommendation for sweeping social reforms he claimed would improve the lot of humankind. And Adler has been accused of oversimplifying in his attempt to explain many complex behaviors in terms of a single concept, the striving for superiority.

Summary

1.   Many psychologists who studied with Freud eventually broke away from the Vienna group to develop their own theories of personality and establish their own schools of psychology. Collectively, these theorists are known as the neo-Freudians because they retained many basic Freudian concepts and assumptions. Among the limits they saw in Freud's theory were his failure to recognize personality change after the first few years of life, his emphasis on instinctual over social influences, and the generally negative picture he painted of human nature.

2.   Alfred Adler introduced the concept of striving for superiority to account for most human motivation. He argued that we are motivated to overcome feelings of helplessness that begin in infancy. Adler also identified parental pampering and neglect as two sources of later personality problems. He argued that middle-born children were the most achieving and were less likely to experience psychological disorders than were first-borns or last-borns.

3.   Carl Jung proposed the existence of a collective unconscious that houses primordial images he called archetypes. The collective unconscious contains material each of us inherited from past generations and is basically the same for all people. Among the most important of the archetypes are the anima, the animus, and the shadow. Jung pointed to the recurrent surfacing of archetypal symbols in folklore, art, dreams, and psychotic patients as evidence for their existence.

4.   Erik Erikson emphasized the positive functions of the ego in his theory. One of the ego's most important functions is to develop and maintain a sense of identity. Erikson outlined eight stages of personality development that we pass through during our lifetimes. At each stage we are faced with a crisis and two means to resolve the crisis.

5.   Karen Horney rejected Freud's emphasis on instinctual causes of personality development. She argued that the differences Freud saw between the personalities of men and women were more likely the result of social factors than inherited predispositions. Horney maintained that neurotic behavior is the result of interpersonal styles developed in childhood to overcome anxiety. She identified three neurotic styles, which she called moving toward people, moving against people, and moving away from people.

6.   Among Harry Stack Sullivan's contributions to psychoanalytic theory is the notion of personifications. These are mental images we have of others and ourselves. Of particular importance are the personifications Sullivan called the good-me, the bad-me, and the not-me. Sullivan also outlined stages of personality development that extend well past the first few years of life. In particular, he emphasized the importance of the adolescent years.

7.   Erich Fromm argued that many people are motivated to escape from their awareness of personal freedom and individuality. Some escape through authoritarianism, identifying with a powerful figure but also assaulting those with less power. Other mechanisms of escape include destructiveness and automaton conformity. In the latter case, people accept the norms handed to them by society and erase their feelings of uniqueness and individuality.

8.   Freud was highly critical of organized religion, calling it wish fulfillment and a type of neurosis. Jung explained humankind's persistent need for religion in terms of a God archetype. He saw modern psychotherapists taking the place of religious leaders when patients become disenchanted with the answers provided by their religion. Fromm argued that the universal need for religion stems from the need to escape from freedom.

9.   Among the personality assessment instruments to come out of the neo-Freudian theories is the Myers-Briggs Type Indicator. This test measures psychological types, as outlined by Jung. Test scores divide people into types along four dimensions: extraversion-introversion, sensing-intuitive, thinking-feeling, and judgment-perception. Researchers have challenged the way the test divides people into categories.

10.   Among the strengths of the neo-Freudian theories are the contributions they made to psychoanalytic theory. In addition to correcting some of the limitations they found in Freud's work, many of the theorists introduced important concepts to the field of psychology. Many later approaches to personality were no doubt influenced by one or more of these theorists. Criticisms of the neo-Freudians include their use of biased and questionable data to support the theories. In addition, critics have charged that some of the theories are oversimplified and incomplete.

InfoTrac Key Terms

For additional readings go to http://www.infotrac-college.com/wadsworth and enter a search term related to your interest. Use the key terms suggested here to pull up several related articles. Also see the text Web site at http://psychology .wadsworth.com for more suggested readings and interactive quizzes to test your knowledge.

Alfred Adler	Erich Fromm
Archetype	Erik Erikson
Birth order	Individual psychology
Carl Jung	Karen Horney
Ego-psychology	

Chapter 6

The Neo-Freudian Theories

Relevant Research

Anxiety and Coping Strategies
Psychoanalytic Concepts and Aggression
Attachment Style and Adult Relationships
Summary

Decades have passed since many of the neo-Freudian theorists broke away from the Freudian pack, allowing us to see how much more these theorists had in common with Freud than they probably realized at the time. Just as their theories are better thought of as elaborations of Freud's basic psychoanalytic approach, so is the research covered in this chapter relevant for both Freudian and neo-Freudian approaches to personality. In each case, researchers began with concepts introduced by psychoanalytic theory, but, much like the theorists who followed Freud, soon took their thinking in new directions.

We begin by examining research on anxiety and coping strategies. Although most psychoanalytic theorists emphasize unconscious sources of anxiety and defense mechanisms, more recent research has centered on anxiety people are aware of and the conscious efforts people make to reduce or eliminate it. We'll look at some of the ways people cope with stressful events and individual differences in coping styles.

Several decades ago, researchers interested in the causes of aggression reinterpreted some of Freud's concepts to explain the relationship between frustration and aggression. These psychologists retained many Freudian terms—sublimation, displacement, catharsis—in their writings. Although subsequent research on frustration and aggression eventually took investigators far from these psychoanalytic roots, the legacy is clear.

We'll also examine the connection between infant-parent relationships and attachment styles in adults. Borrowing from a neo-Freudian approach known as object relations theory, researchers have identified certain ways people relate to their romantic partners that theoretically have their origin in the early childhood attachment those adults felt with their parents. Studies suggest individual differences in attachment style can influence adult romantic relationships.

Anxiety and Coping Strategies

Are we, as some popular writers suggest, in an "age of anxiety"? Have the good old days of afternoon strolls in the park and summer evenings on the porch been replaced with ever-present pressure to work harder and faster and be better than everyone else? The ubiquitous ads for massages, meditation, anti-anxiety drugs, get-away vacations, and the like seem to say that most people today have been pushed near some sort of anxiety breaking point. Are we more anxious today, or do we just complain more? To answer this question, one investigator examined average anxiety scores reported in published studies from the 1950s through the 1990s (Twenge, 2000). Not only did anxiety scores rise throughout the five decades, but by the 1980s the average American child reported higher levels of anxiety than child psychiatric patients in the 1950s. The data suggest that we may indeed have entered an age of anxiety.

Anxiety and strategies for alleviating anxiety have played an important role in the works of many psychoanalytic theorists. Although anxiety has been defined in many different ways (Monat & Lazarus, 1985), most researchers would probably agree that it is above all else an unpleasant emotional experience. When you experience anxiety, you have feelings of worry, panic, fear, and dread. It is probably the emotional experience you would have if you were suddenly arrested or if you discovered that a diary containing some of your deepest secrets had been passed around among friends.

Although he changed his thinking about anxiety several times during his career, Freud identified three types of anxiety in his last major writing in this area. First, there is *reality anxiety,* or objective anxiety, which is a response to a perceived threat in the real world. You probably experienced this type of anxiety if you ever felt you were being followed by a stranger or if you narrowly escaped a serious automobile accident. In cases of reality anxiety, you are aware of the dangerous situation responsible for your emotional reaction.

Predictably, conscious thoughts were not particularly interesting to Freud. Thus, he devoted more attention to two other types of anxiety: neurotic anxiety and moral anxiety. In neither case are we consciously aware of the source of our anxiety. *Neurotic anxiety* is experienced when unacceptable id impulses are dangerously close to breaking into consciousness. It is this type of anxiety that leads the ego to use defense mechanisms. *Moral anxiety* is brought about by the superego in response to id impulses that violate the superego's strict moral code. Generally, this is experienced as guilt.

Many neo-Freudian theorists adopted and adapted Freud's ideas about anxiety in their writings. For example, Sullivan (1953) considered anxiety a cornerstone of his theory. The neurotic coping styles described by Horney are also said to develop in an effort to reduce and avoid anxiety. These theorists accepted the Freudian notion that some experiences with anxiety stem from unconscious conflicts, although they emphasized the interpersonal and cultural role in this process more than Freud did. For example, Sullivan said anxiety could be overcome by developing solid relationships with others, what he called interpersonal security. Horney agreed that unconscious impulses often triggered anxiety, but largely because they came into conflict with cultural standards.

Eventually, Adler, Anna Freud, and other neo-Freudian psychologists expanded anxiety-fighting tactics to include the conscious and deliberate methods people use to deal with their anxiety (Snyder, 1988). As if to acknowledge the Freudian legacy, these theorists often retained the names of the unconscious defense mechanisms when describing conscious efforts to cope with anxiety. Thus, today we speak of someone being "in denial" even when the person is fully aware of the problem and trying to ignore it. This section reviews research on the deliberate steps people take to deal with the sources of stress in their lives.

Coping with Anxiety

What do you do when faced with a potentially stressful situation, such as waiting for your dentist to start drilling or getting ready for a job interview? If you are like most people, you don't just accept the potential pain or fear as part of life. Rather, researchers find that people typically respond to stress-provoking situations with calculated efforts to reduce their anxiety (Lazarus, 1968, 1974). For example, participants in one study were shown a rather grisly film on industrial safety (Koriat, Melkman, Averill, & Lazarus, 1972). The film depicted several serious accidents, including a scene in which a saw drove a board through the abdomen of a workman who died writhing and bleeding on the floor. How did participants react to the film? As you might expect, each of them tried a number of tactics to reduce their discomfort. The most common strategy was to remind themselves that what they were seeing was only a film, not a real accident. Another common strategy was to watch the film in an emotionally detached manner, focusing on the technical aspects of the production rather than the gruesome content. Interestingly, these two approaches sound similar to two Freudian defense mechanisms: denial and intellectualization. Psychologists refer to these efforts to cope with anxiety in the face of a perceived threat as **coping strategies.**

The number of strategies people use when faced with a threatening situation is almost endless. People work long hours, talk to friends with similar problems, collect more information, meet with professional counselors, drink alcohol, attack the source of the problem, ignore the source of the problem, exercise, avoid

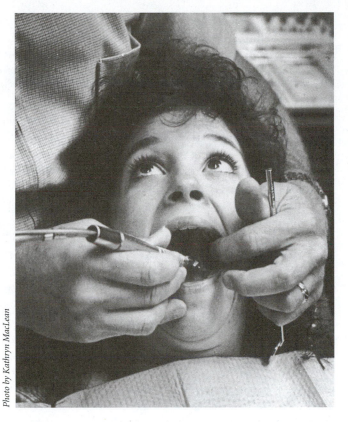

Photo by Kathryn MacLean

How do you handle the anxiety in this situation? You might try to think of something besides what the dentist is doing, or think about the value of good dental hygiene. What you probably won't do is concentrate on the potential pain.

people, find a silver lining, and pray. Women report using more coping strategies than men (Tamres, Janicki, & Helgeson, 2002), but researchers don't know if this difference is real or perhaps reflects a difference in recall or the degree to which men and women find various problems stressful (Porter et al., 2000; Tamres et al., 2002).

Investigators also find that not everyone uses the same coping strategies to reduce anxiety. After a lifetime of facing various threatening situations, each of us develops an arsenal of coping strategies that we believe work for us. Consequently, researchers can identify relatively stable patterns in the way people cope with anxiety (Holahan & Moos, 1987; Terry, 1994). Like other personality variables, our reliance on these coping strategies tends to be stable over time and across different anxiety-provoking situations. We sometimes refer to a person's general approach to dealing with stress as his or her *coping style.*

Types of Coping Strategies

I was once involved in a discussion at a local Red Cross office concerning the showing of a potentially anxiety-provoking film to expectant parents. The topic of the film was Sudden Infant Death Syndrome (SIDS), an illness that mysteriously kills thousands of infants annually. One group of parents did not want to expose themselves to anything that suggested their child could die in infancy. The other group argued that they wanted to know as much as possible about any such situation to prepare themselves in case the unfortunate event should happen to them.

The differences in opinion clearly reflected different strategies for dealing with anxiety. Early researchers in this area probably would have divided the two groups of parents along a personality dimension called *repression-sensitization* (Byrne, 1964). At one end of this dimension are people who typically respond to threatening situations by avoiding them. These *repressors* try not to think about the situation and thereby succeed in avoiding the anxiety as much or as long as possible. We see this strategy at work when people advise us, "worrying about it will do no good" and "try to think of something else to take your mind off it." If you have ever put off seeing a doctor or talking to a professor because you expected the encounter to be stressful, you have used the *repression* strategy. At the other end of the dimension are the *sensitizers*. These people typically deal with a stressful situation by finding out as much as possible, as soon as possible, and thereby put themselves in a position to take the most effective action. You may have employed this strategy if you collected information about a scheduled medical procedure or spent a great deal of time thinking about an upcoming job interview.

As psychologists have continued to study coping, several schemes have been developed to categorize the different strategies (Ayers, Sandler, West, & Roosa, 1996; Carver, Scheier, & Weintraub, 1989; Endler & Parker, 1990; Folkman & Lazarus, 1988; Stanton, Kirk, Cameron, & Danoff-Burg, 2000). However, we can identify a few basic distinctions that most researchers find useful. First, we can divide coping strategies into those in which people take an active role in dealing with the problem and those in which people try to avoid the problem. This is similar to the sensitization-repression distinction drawn by early investigators. Second, we can separate coping strategies into those that focus directly on the source of the stress and those that focus on the emotional reaction to the experience.

What strategies have you used to cope with a recent source of anxiety? This was the question asked of participants in one study (Holahan & Moos, 1987). Participants were first asked to think about the most important problem they had faced during the previous year. They then were given a list of possible coping strategies and asked which ones they had used. Consistent with past work in this area, most participants used many different strategies to deal with their problem. As shown in Table 6.1, the researchers found that they could divide the various coping tactics into active and avoidance categories. The **active coping strategies** include those in which the person took action to improve the situation. For example, if your problem last year was doing poorly in school, you may have responded by getting some tutoring, learning more effective study habits, or taking some remedial classes to better prepare for future courses. Other active strategies involved actively thinking about the situation in an effort to make things better. For example, if your biggest problem was breaking up with a boyfriend or girlfriend this past year, you may have coped with this by convincing yourself that you were better off in the

Table 6.1   List of Coping Strategies

Active-Cognitive Strategies

Prayed for guidance and/or strength

Prepared for the worst

Tried to see the positive side of the situation

Considered several alternatives for handling the problem

Drew on my past experiences

Took things a day at a time

Tried to step back from the situation and be more objective

Went over the situation in my mind to try to understand it

Told myself things that helped me feel better

Made a promise to myself that things would be different next time

Accepted it; nothing could be done

Active-Behavioral Strategies

Tried to find out more about the situation

Talked with spouse or other relative about the problem

Talked with friend about the problem

Talked with professional person (doctor, lawyer, clergy, and so on)

Got busy with other things to keep my mind off the problem

Made a plan of action and followed it

Tried not to act too hastily or follow my first hunch

Got away from things for a while

Knew what had to be done and tried harder to make things work

Let my feelings out somehow

Sought help from persons or groups with similar experiences

Bargained or compromised to get something positive from the situation

Tried to reduce tension by exercising more

Avoidance Strategies

Took it out on other people when I felt angry or depressed

Kept my feelings to myself

Avoided being with people in general

Refused to believe that it happened

Tried to reduce tension by drinking more

Tried to reduce tension by eating more

Tried to reduce tension by smoking more

Tried to reduce tension by taking more tranquilizing drugs

Source: Copyright © 1987 by the American Psychological Association. Reprinted by permission of authors and APA.

long run because of the experience or by focusing on why things went wrong and how this information can help you in your next relationship. Participants using **avoidance coping strategies** dealt with their anxiety by keeping the anxiety-provoking situation out of awareness. For example, if you discovered this past year that a loved one was suffering from a serious health problem, you may have responded by not thinking about the person or even by trying to convince yourself that the problem was not as serious as people were telling you.

Other investigators divide coping strategies into categories depending on whether the person is trying to deal with the problem or with his or her emotional reaction to the problem (Lazarus & Folkman, 1984). **Problem-focused strategies** are directed at taking care of the problem and thereby overcoming the anxiety. If the problem is financial, an appropriate course of action might be to think about ways to earn more money or reduce expenses. People employing problem-focused strategies often find that simply organizing plans to deal with the problem makes them feel better than continuing to do nothing at all. **Emotion-focused strategies** are designed to reduce the emotional distress that accompanies the problem. If not being accepted to law school is the source of anxiety, it may be helpful to think about some of the ways the turn of events can be seen in a positive light or with steps you can take to lessen the disappointment.

In one investigation, men and women between ages 45 and 64 were asked how they had coped with a series of real-life events they had experienced during the past seven months (Folkman & Lazarus, 1980). Participants indicated their coping strategies on a checklist of possible responses. This list contained some emotion-focused strategies ("I tried to look on the bright side of things") and some problem-focused strategies ("I made a plan of action and followed it"). More than 1,300 examples of stressful experiences were examined. The researchers found that participants used an emotion-focused strategy, a problem-focused strategy, or both in more than 98% of the cases. Thus, this categorization scheme seems to capture most of the strategies people use to deal with their anxiety. Other research finds that women tend to use emotion-focus strategies more than men, whereas men are more likely than women to take steps to solve problems directly (Ptacek, Smith, & Dodge, 1994). This pattern is consistent with the research findings on gender roles presented in Chapter 14.

How Effective Are Coping Strategies?

Which are the most effective coping strategies for reducing anxiety? Before addressing that question, you should note that many studies find using some coping strategy is typically more effective in reducing anxiety than using no strategy. For example, smokers in one study who used at least one coping strategy were more than four times as likely to succeed at quitting smoking than were those who failed to use any techniques to deal with their withdrawal symptoms (Shiffman, 1985). In another study, the use of coping strategies proved more effective than no strategy for reducing depression among couples experiencing stress in their marriages (Mitchell, Cronkite, & Moos, 1983). One survey asked adults about the types of coping responses they typically used and how effective they perceived each of 27 coping mechanisms to be (McCrae & Costa, 1986a). The researchers found that the more people relied on effective coping strategies, the higher they scored on measures of happiness and general life satisfaction.

But are all coping strategies equally effective? The answer is no. Is it better to face a problem head on or do what you can to avoid the source of anxiety? A large amount of research has addressed this question, and the conclusion is rather clear: In almost all cases, active strategies are more effective in helping people cope with stressors than avoidance strategies (Suls & Fletcher, 1985). For example, studies find that people who rely on avoidance strategies have a more difficult time coping with a loved one's illness (Compas, Worsham, Ey, & Howell, 1996), a physical assault (Valentiner, Foa, Riggs, & Gershuny, 1996), or being diagnosed with breast cancer (Carver et al., 1993). One team of investigators looked at coping strategies among a group of women who discovered that their efforts to conceive through in vitro fertilization had failed (Terry & Hynes, 1998). All these women found the inability to conceive very upsetting. However, the women who reacted to the news with avoidance (for example, daydreamed about being in a better time and place or hoped for a miracle) were more distressed than the women who used active coping strategies.

Are avoidance strategies ever effective? Some research suggests that on occasion avoidance strategies may help in the short run (Suls & Fletcher, 1985). For example, you might decide to ignore relationship problems for a few days while you study for finals. However, at best this strategy only delays dealing with the problem. Research indicates that whatever short-term advantages there are to avoidance strategies may be limited to stressors that are relatively mild and at least partially under the individual's control (Terry & Hynes, 1998). Moreover, extensive use of avoidance strategies can create additional problems. Because escape from anxiety sometimes includes drinking, people who typically rely on avoidance strategies may be at risk for alcohol problems (Simpson & Arroyo, 1998; Windle & Windle, 1996).

Although active strategies are almost always preferable to avoidance strategies, the decision of whether to use a problem-focused or emotion-focused strategy is more difficult. Depending on the situation, either of these approaches might prove more effective for dealing with stress. The key question is whether there is any way to correct the problem, or if the situation is one that eventually has to be accepted (Aldwin & Revenson, 1987; Folkman, 1984). Research suggests that if a means to resolve the problem is available, taking quick action to eliminate the problem might prove the most effective course of action (Vitaliano, DeWolfe, Maiuro, Russo, & Katon, 1990). For example, a student who frets over difficult material in his math class probably could do himself a favor by seeking help right away instead of hoping for a sudden insight.

One team of researchers looked at how soldiers suffering from combat stress coped with long-term emotional reactions to their combat experiences (Solomon, Avitzur, & Mikulincer, 1989). The investigators examined the coping strategies and social functioning of Israeli soldiers who had suffered excessive combat stress during the 1982 Lebanon war. They found that soldiers who used problem-solving strategies were more successful in their social relationships than soldiers who tried to deal with only their emotional reactions to the war. The soldiers who increased their use of emotion-focused strategies during the years that followed the combat experience showed the poorest ability to cope. Most likely these soldiers would have benefited more from trying to deal with their problems directly rather than trying to simply change the way they felt.

However, we often encounter situations in which we do not possess any tools to repair the problem. In these cases, trying to make the problem go away is fruitless. For example, one study found parents who reacted to their infant's death with problem-focused strategies had a more difficult time coping with the loss than parents who used other coping strategies (Murray & Terry, 1999). When a situation can't be changed, working on your emotional reaction to the experience may be more effective.

One team of psychologists demonstrated this point in a dramatic way (Strentz & Auerbach, 1988). In conjunction with the FBI and some domestic airline companies, the researchers staged a four-day hostage abduction. Pilots, copilots, and flight attendants who had volunteered to participate in the exercise experienced what it would be like to be taken hostage by terrorists. Great effort was taken to make the situation as realistic as possible. FBI agents dressed as terrorists fired automatic weapons (blanks), handcuffed the hostages, and made death threats. Measures taken throughout the study showed that, as expected, the participants experienced high levels of anxiety. How did they cope with this anxiety? Before the kidnapping, some of the participants were instructed in the use of emotion-focused coping strategies, and others were instructed to use problem-focused strategies. Remember, there was little or nothing the hostages could do change the situation they were in. But they could deal with their emotional reactions. Consequently, participants instructed to use the emotion-focused strategies experienced lower levels of anxiety than those who used the problem-focused strategies.

Different types of coping strategies seem to work in different situations. The key to effective coping might be to know when to employ which type of strategy. Researchers refer to this ability as *coping flexibility* (Cheng, 2001). That is, people who can adjust their use of coping strategies to fit the realities of a given situation are likely to deal with life's problems more effectively than those who cannot. Fortunately, most of us have a number of coping strategies in our repertoires. If one approach for dealing with an anxiety-provoking situation does not work, perhaps another one will.

Psychoanalytic Concepts and Aggression

"*Men are not gentle creatures who want to be loved. They are, on the contrary, creatures among whose instinctual endowments [is] a powerful share of aggressiveness.*"

SIGMUND FREUD

Now it's all designed to blow our minds, but our minds won't really be blown, like the blow that'll get you when you get your picture on the cover of the Rolling Stone.

DR. HOOK

Suppose you are in the library late one night trying to read an article from a professional journal for one of your classes. You wade through the big words and jargon on the first few pages, hoping to make more sense of the writing as it progresses. You come to what appears to be the main point of the article, so you read each word slowly and carefully. Still you don't get it. So you read the last few paragraphs again. But again it doesn't make any sense. You try once more, but still no luck. You're running out of time and patience. What do you feel like doing? Most people react to this kind of experience with a good amount of frustration. As a result, they might pound their fists on the table or swear under their breath at the author. If they could, they might throw the journal across the room. What this example illustrates is the commonly observed connection between frustration and aggression.

Few events in our lives command as much attention as those with an element of aggression. From playground fights to muggings to war, attempts by one human to inflict pain on another have been among the most widely researched human behaviors. Naturally, the psychoanalytic approach to personality has much to say about this topic. In fact, one of the first efforts to explain the association between frustration and aggression can be found in Freud's early writings. Freud initially proposed that aggression is the result of frustrated libido. When our pleasure-seeking impulse is blocked, we experience a "primordial reaction" to attack the obstacle. Naturally, our egos keep us from assaulting anyone and everyone who spoils our fun. Therefore, Freud argued, we often displace our aggression. Because we can't attack the police officer, who won't let us drive as fast as we want, we express the aggressive impulse by yelling at employees, friends, or family members.

Freud later changed his views on the causes of aggression. After witnessing the mass destruction of human life in World War I, he introduced the concept of a death instinct, *Thanatos*. Freud claimed that we all have an instinctual desire to destroy ourselves. But because a fully functioning ego does not allow self-destruction, the instinct is turned outward toward others. However, it was Freud's original position that later inspired researchers interested in the connection between frustration and aggression. In 1939, a team of psychologists translated and modified Freud's early work to create the **frustration-aggression hypothesis** (Dollard, Doob, Miller, Mowrer, & Sears, 1939). Although many of these psychologists identified themselves more closely with behaviorism (Chapter 13), the psychoanalytic flavor of their theorizing is unmistakable.

The frustration-aggression hypothesis states that "aggression is *always* a consequence of frustration . . . that the occurrence of aggressive behavior *always* presupposes the existence of frustration and, contrariwise, that the existence of frustration *always* leads to some form of aggression" (p. 1, italics added). One attractive feature of this hypothesis is its simplicity. Notice that the psychologists argue there is but one cause of aggression (frustration) and one response to frustration (aggression). A student frustrated in efforts to get on the honor roll, a baseball player frustrated by a batting slump, and a rat frustrated in its effort to find a piece of cheese all should respond with aggression. And anyone who acts aggressively should have experienced some earlier frustration.

The researchers adopted another psychoanalytic notion to explain when aggression will stop. They proposed that aggression ceases when we experience **catharsis,** loosely conceived of as a release of tension. Freud discussed catharsis in terms of a release of psychic energy. However, these early aggression researchers described tension in terms of arousal, energy levels, and muscle tension. The frustrated student who kicks her books across the room and the slumping batter who pounds his bat against the dugout wall should feel their tensions subside. Until the frustration builds tension levels up again, we should expect no further outbreaks from the student and the batter.

At first glance, the frustration-aggression hypothesis makes some sense. You may have felt the urge to throw a difficult to understand book across the room. We've all seen how a little shoving in a long line can lead to angry words, if not an occasional fist. But given all of the frustrating experiences in our lives, why don't we spend most of our time acting aggressively? To account for this, some of the original theorists modified their positions, again borrowing from psychoanalytic theories (Doob & Sears, 1939; Miller, 1941; Sears, 1941). They proposed that frustration sometimes leads to *indirect* expressions of aggression. Indirect aggression can be expressed in many ways. One is by *displacing* the aggression to a new target, such as taking frustrating working conditions out on your spouse. Another is to attack in an indirect manner. For example, we might not hit our bosses, but we can make their jobs a little harder or spread malicious gossip about them. We can also use **sublimation** (another concept adapted from psychoanalytic theory). For example, a frustrated person might run a few miles or play a hard game of basketball to work out tension. Thus, frustration always leads to aggression, but not always in the most obvious forms.

The frustration-aggression hypothesis and its subsequent variations have spawned a large amount of research. The following sections examine three topics addressed by that research, each of which retains a psychoanalytic flavor: frustration, displacement, and catharsis.

Frustration and Aggression

The connection between frustration and aggression can be seen in many places in society. For example, elementary school children in one study were asked which of their classmates engaged in aggressive behavior, such as pushing or shoving (Guerra, Huesmann, Tolan, Van Acker, & Eron, 1995). The investigators found that the most aggressive children tended to be those who experienced the highest levels of stress and frustration in their lives. Another study looked at violent behavior in adults who had been laid off from their jobs (Catalano, Dooley, Novaco, Wilson, & Hough, 1993). Participants who had lost their jobs were six times more

Although hitting the machine probably won't get you a soft-drink or your money back, you might feel better. In this case, the frustration of not getting the drink leads to the aggression, which may lead to a cathartic release of tension.

I never eat a pig
cause a pig is a
cop, or better yet
a terminator like
Arnold Swartzanegger.
You try to play me
out like as if my
name was Sega,
but I ain't goin'
out like no punk
bitch, you get
used to one style
you know and I
must switch. Up,
up, and around, I
came to get down,
So get out your
seat and jump
around. Jump
around.

House of Pain

likely to have engaged in an act of violence, such as striking a spouse, than those who were still employed. In a pair of investigations, researchers looked at the relation between frustrating social and political conditions in Israel and violent crime rates (Landau, 1988; Landau & Raveh, 1987). The investigators found when stressors like unemployment increased, often there was a corresponding increase in violent crimes like homicide.

Several direct tests of the frustration-aggression hypothesis find that frustrated people act more aggressively than nonfrustrated people (Berkowitz, 1989). For example, researchers in one study intentionally provoked unsuspecting people

Figure 6.1

Verbal and Non-
verbal Aggression
as a Function of
Place in Line

Source: Adapted from
Harris (1974).

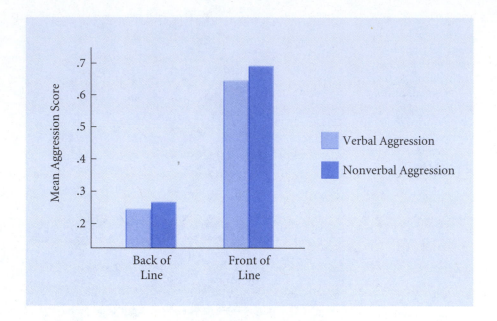

standing in lines in stores, banks, and ticket windows (Harris, 1974). Because previous studies had shown greater frustration the closer people are to their goal, researchers cut in front of either the third person in line (close to the goal) or the
twelfth person in line. The investigators glanced back to notice the person's response and, after 20 seconds, apologized and left. Responses were coded for verbal
and nonverbal aggression, such as making threatening comments or pushing and
shoving. The results are shown in Figure 6.1. As expected, frustrated people toward
the front of the line expressed more aggression than the less frustrated people toward the end.

Thus, data from a variety of sources indicate that frustration is one cause of aggression. Although this conclusion validates one aspect of the original frustration-
aggression hypothesis, current aggression researchers argue that the original
model was too narrow. That is, frustration is but one of many negative emotions
that increase the chances of aggression (Berkowitz, 1989, 1994, 1998; Lindsay &
Anderson, 2000). Things that frustrate us are unpleasant, and it is the unpleasantness that we respond to when frustrating circumstances trigger aggression. According to this analysis, any unpleasant emotion should increase aggression. For
example, researchers find uncomfortably high temperatures, at least up to a point,
increase aggression (Anderson & Anderson, 1998). Similarly, irritating cigarette
smoke and loud noise increase the amount of punishment people give to innocent
bystanders (Berkowitz, 1989). Thus, the question is not whether a particular event
is frustrating, but rather how unpleasant is the accompanying emotion.

This newer way of looking at frustration and aggression has several advantages
over the original hypothesis. First, the new model explains why frustration does
not always lead to aggression. Frustration facilitates aggression only to the extent

that it is perceived as unpleasant. Second, the model clarifies why certain thoughts increase or decrease the likelihood of acting aggressively. For example, you may be very frustrated if you do poorly on a test because your roommate drove home for the weekend with your textbooks in the back of his or her car. However, you will have a very different reaction to this frustration if you believe your roommate was unaware of the books than if you determine he or she deliberately took off with them. Thoughts that create negative feelings make the whole experience more unpleasant and thus increase the chances for aggression. Thoughts that decrease negative feelings are less likely to lead to aggression.

Displacing Aggression

Like most people, you have probably had the regrettable experience of lashing out at a friend far more than the situation called for. The outburst was most likely met with a "What's the matter with you today?" or "Someone had a bad day." After calming down, you may have recognized that the source of your anger wasn't really your friend at all, but rather a poor grade on an assignment or a boss who would not let you off work this coming weekend. Incidents like these illustrate one prediction from early versions of the frustration-aggression hypothesis. That is, we don't always attack the source of our frustration directly. Rather, we sometimes direct our frustration-induced anger toward someone who does not deserve it. Expressing aggression toward these indirect targets is usually safer than going after a frustrating teacher or employer.

Dozens of studies find support for the notion that we sometimes displace aggression from a frustrating source to an innocent target (Marcus-Newhall, Pedersen, Carlson, & Miller, 2000). Participants in one of these studies were asked to work on some anagram problems (Konecni & Doob, 1972). Some people found the task frustrating, especially because another participant (a confederate of the experimenter) persistently annoyed them while they worked on the problems. Other participants were allowed to work on the task without interruptions. Participants were then given the opportunity to grade another person on a creativity task. The means of grading was electric shock. Participants were told to give this other person painful (but not harmful) shocks whenever they heard uncreative responses. Although no actual shocks were delivered, the number of shocks participants thought they were giving was used to measure aggression.

How was displacement tested in this study? Some participants were fortunate enough to find that the person who had earlier annoyed them was the one hooked up to the shock apparatus. For other participants, the person receiving the shock was a stranger. The results from the relevant conditions are shown in Figure 6.2. Not surprisingly, participants given the chance to get even with the person who had frustrated them gave more shocks than the nonfrustrated participants. However, frustrated participants given the opportunity to shock a stranger also delivered more shocks than the nonfrustrated participants. In other words, these people *displaced* their aggressive tendencies onto the innocent bystander.

Figure 6.2

Mean Number of
Shocks Delivered

Source: Data from
Konecni and Doob
(1972).

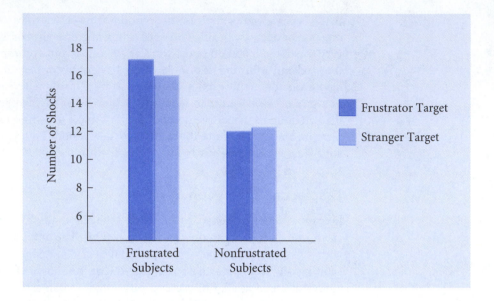

Displaced aggression is most likely to occur when we encounter a minor source of annoyance that we otherwise would easily tolerate or ignore (Pedersen, Gonzales, & Miller, 2000). We see examples of this effect when a frustrated mother overreacts to her child's messy room or a basketball player having a bad game lashes out at an opponent who happens to brush up against him too hard. In short, a number of empirical investigations support the notion that frustration can lead to displaced aggression, validating one aspect of the frustration-aggression hypothesis and, in turn, some of Freud's original thinking on the topic.

Catharsis and Aggression

Each of us has been told at one time or another that we needed to "let off a little steam" rather than do something in anger we'll later regret. We are told to punch a pillow or spend 10 minutes vigorously shooting baskets. Some therapists advise clients to strike plastic dolls or use foam-rubber bats to work off their tensions. The idea is to get the aggressive tendencies out of the client's system so therapy can continue in a violence-free atmosphere. These examples illustrate one more prediction from the frustration-aggression hypothesis: Our need to aggress is reduced after a cathartic release of tension. Conventional wisdom often agrees. The best way to deal with frustration, many people believe, is to express our feelings against some harmless target. The problem is, this widely dispensed advice appears to be wrong.

Consider the experience of participants in one investigation, who wrote essays that supposedly were graded by another participant (Bushman, 2002). The feedback from this other person was particularly harsh, ending with a handwritten comment that "This is one of the worst essays I have ever read!" Needless to say, this irritated the real participants. Some of these angry participants were then given the chance to hit a punching bag as hard and for as many times as they wished while looking at a picture and thinking about the person who had just insulted them. Other participants hit the punching bag, but were told to do so while thinking about how much exercise they were getting. Some participants had no opportunity to hit anything, and simply sat quietly for a few minutes. As shown in Figure 6.3, the conventional wisdom about letting off steam didn't work. Not only were the participants who hit the bag while thinking of their insulter the angriest, they also were the most aggressive when later given a chance to do something that would hurt the person they were mad at. Contrary to the advice we have all received, the least angry and least aggressive participants were those who calmly sat alone without punching anything.

The original frustration-aggression hypothesis maintained that allowing frustrated people to act aggressively would lead to a tension-reducing catharsis, which would reduce the need for aggression. Consistent with that notion, some studies find a sudden drop in physiological arousal after participants are allowed to attack another person (Geen, Stonner, & Shope, 1975; Hokanson & Edelman, 1966). But does this apparent catharsis lead to a decrease in aggression? In other words, should we encourage people to act aggressively when they are frustrated? Apparently not. Not only does aggression not decrease the likelihood of further aggression, but studies also find that acting aggressively often *increases* the tendency to aggress (Bushman, Baumeister, & Stack, 1999).

Participants in one study were asked to engage in three successive tasks (Geen et al., 1975). First, they gave their opinions on some controversial issues. Another participant (again, a confederate) graded the quality of the opinions by giving

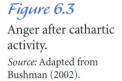

Figure 6.3

Anger after cathartic activity.

Source: Adapted from Bushman (2002).

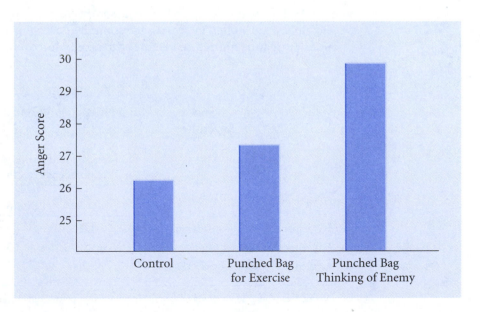

either few or many electric shocks. Thus, half the participants were made angry, and half were not. Next, the tables were turned. It was the confederate's turn to get shocked for making mistakes on a maze task. Sometimes the participants were the ones doing the shocking, sometimes they watched the experimenter do the shocking, and sometimes the confederate received no shocks. Consistent with the frustration-aggression hypothesis, when angry participants were allowed to retaliate against the confederate, they experienced a significant drop in blood pressure—a cathartic reaction.

The key to the study came in the last phase. The frustration-aggression hypothesis predicts that, because of the cathartic release of tension, participants should be less inclined to act aggressively than those not given an opportunity to attack the confederate. To test this prediction, the researcher gave all participants an opportunity to shock the confederate, this time as a means of grading his performance on a decoding task. Participants set the shock level from 1 (mild shock) to 10 (extreme shock) whenever the confederate made a mistake. As shown in Table 6.2, the participants who had experienced the release in tension after retaliating against the confederate actually showed the *highest* level of aggression when given another opportunity.

Several studies have produced similar effects. Although the opportunity to act aggressively may provide a cathartic release of tension, it also seems to produce an increase rather than the predicted decrease in aggression. Why should this be the case? Researchers have identified several reasons (Geen & Quanty, 1977). Acting aggressively may lead to a kind of disinhibition. That is, most of us have strong reservations about physically hurting other people. However, once we violate that rule, we may find it easier to attack in the future. Another reason for the aggression-breeds-aggression finding may be the presence of aggressive cues.

As described in Chapter 14, seeing something we associate with violence (for example, a gun) often increases aggression. By observing our own aggressive actions, we may be spurred on to more aggression. Moreover, these violent cues may

Table 6.2 **Mean Shock Level Set by Participants During Third Phase of Experiment**

	Treatment of Participant by Confederate in Phase I	
	Attacked	Not Attacked
Participant shocked confederate	6.65	3.92
Experimenter shocked confederate	4.13	3.62
Confederate received no shocks	5.20	3.20

Source: From Geen, Stonner, and Shope (1975); reprinted by permission of Russell G. Geen.

tap into other memories and emotions related to aggression. As described in Chapter 15, activating these aggressive thoughts and feelings is likely to lead to more aggressive action, not less. In addition, because a cathartic release of tension feels good, aggressive acts may be reinforced. Researchers find that people sometimes feel better after punching a bag or blasting another participant with loud noise (Bushman, Baumeister, & Phillips, 2001; Bushman et al., 1999). As discussed in Chapter 13, behaviors that lead to pleasant consequences are likely to be repeated. Thus, rather than reducing aggression, catharsis may do the opposite.

Attachment Style and Adult Relationships

When people are asked what brings them happiness, they usually talk about their relationships with other people (Myers, 1992). Career, personal accomplishments, and material possessions almost always come in a distant second to our loved ones when people stop to think about what they treasure most in their lives. Indeed, Erikson and Sullivan both identified the establishment of deep, meaningful relationships as one of the foremost tasks we face, particularly in late adolescence and early adulthood. Ironically, even though our relationships are our biggest source of happiness, they can also be a significant source of distress. Most adults have been in relationships that for one reason or another simply didn't work. You may have gone through the frustration of being involved with someone who remained emotionally distant. Or you may have suffered through a relationship in which your partner was so dependent and clinging that you felt smothered. If you are

According to attachment theory, infants who experience loving, secure relationships with their parents develop unconscious working models for secure, trusting relationships as adults.

lucky, you also have found a romantic partner who is confident and emotionally engaging. But what is it that allows some people to enter relationships easily, whereas for others it is such a chore? There are, of course, many reasons why relationships succeed and fail. But a recently resurrected approach to studying relationships maintains that understanding adult romantic behavior begins by looking at very early childhood experiences. The neo-Freudians who first presented these ideas maintained that how we relate to significant others as adults is a reflection of the relationship we had with our parents. Recent research finds considerable merit in this notion.

Object Relations Theory and Attachment Theory

Among the many theorists who expanded on Freud's personality theory in the middle part of the twentieth century were a group of psychologists who became known as the *object relations* theorists. Some of the most influential of these psychologists are Melanie Klein, Donald Winnicott, Margaret Mahler, and Heinz Kohut. Although these theorists often present different interpretations of object relations theory, some general principles unite most of the viewpoints. First, like other neo-Freudians, object relations theorists place great emphasis on early childhood experiences. Instead of focusing on the internal conflicts and drives that Freud described, these psychologists are interested in the infant's relationship with important people in his or her life. In most cases, this means the child's relationship with the parents, most often with the mother. Second, as the name suggests, object relations theorists postulate that the child develops an unconscious representation of significant objects in his or her environment. Moreover, the child's unconscious representation of the parents does more than provide the infant with an object to relate to in the physical absence of the mother or father. The way the child internalizes the parent's image serves as a basis for how the child thinks of others when he or she enters into future relationships. In other words, the kind of attachment children feel with their parents influences their ability to develop meaningful attachments with significant others as adults.

Object relations theory became the springboard for what has been called *attachment theory.* Perhaps the two biggest contributors to this theory are John Bowlby (1969, 1973, 1980) and Mary Ainsworth (1989; Ainsworth, Blehar, Waters, & Wall, 1978). These psychologists examined the emotional attachment between infants and their caregivers, again usually the mother. Bowlby refers to these as *attachment relationships* because they meet our human need to form attachments with a supportive and protective other. Bowlby is particularly interested in the reactions of infants who are separated from their primary caregiver. Some children deal with the separation quite well. These infants seem to understand that mother is gone for the moment but that she will return and that the love and nurturance they need will not be lost. However, Bowlby observed that other children seem to protest the separation by crying. Still other infants react to their mother's absence by falling into a type of despair, and some respond with a kind of detachment to the mother even when she returns.

Ainsworth and her colleagues made similar observations in their studies with infants and mothers. They identified three types of parent-child relationships (Ainsworth et al., 1978). First, there are *secure* infant-mother pairs. Mothers in these dyads are attentive and responsive to their child. Infants who experience such attachment understand that mother is responsive and accessible even if she is not physically present. Secure children tend to be happy and self-confident. In contrast, we sometimes find *anxious-ambivalent* relationships. Mothers in these dyads are not particularly attentive or responsive to the child's needs. The children are anxious whenever mother leaves, sometimes breaking into tears as soon as they are separated. These children are not easily calmed by other adults and may be afraid in unfamiliar situations. Additionally, there are *avoidant* relationships. Mothers in these relationships also are not very responsive to the child. However, the child reacts to this treatment by developing a type of aloofness or emotional detachment from the mother. These children do not become anxious when mother leaves and are not particularly interested in her attention when she returns.

Attachment theorists then took their observations about different attachment styles one step further. Like the object relations theorists, they argue that these different infant-parent relationships have long-term implications for the child's ability to enter into relationships later in life. Bowlby argues that the infant forms unconscious "working models" for interpersonal involvement. If the child experiences love and trust in this early relationship, the child will come to see himself or herself as lovable and trustworthy. However, if the infant's attachment needs are not met, the child will develop a less healthy self image. "An unwanted child is likely not only to feel unwanted by his parents but to believe that he is essentially . . . unwanted by anyone," Bowlby (1973) explained. "Conversely, a much-loved child may grow up to be not only confident of his parent's affection but confident that everyone else will find him lovable too" (pp. 204–205).

Thus, our earliest experiences with caretakers become the foundation upon which we approach later relationships. If our parents were caring, attentive, and responsive, we come to see relations with others as sources of love and support. If our needs for attachment and attention were not met, we become suspicious and mistrusting. Consistent with the psychoanalytic flavor of the object relations theorists, these mental models of attachment relationships are said to be largely unconscious.

Adult Attachment Styles

If the attachment theorists are correct, we should be able to identify adults who fit the descriptions of the different attachment styles found among infants. In other words, the secure, avoidant, and anxious-ambivalent styles Ainsworth and her colleagues saw in children should surface when these same children become adults and enter into adult romantic relationships. We should find secure adults, who have little difficulty getting close to others. These are people who easily trust and depend on those they become romantically involved with. On the other hand, we should also find avoidant adults, who are suspicious of those who say they love them, who fear that getting too close means making themselves vulnerable. These people may be wary of making emotional commitments for fear of being hurt by the inevitable separation. We might also find anxious-ambivalent adults, who are so insecure about the partner's love that they become demanding and sometimes overwhelming in their relationships. These people may require so much attention that they scare away potential romantic partners.

Interestingly, one of the first attempts to identify and measure these three adult attachment styles came in the form of a survey printed in the *Rocky Mountain News* (Hazan & Shaver, 1987). More than a thousand readers mailed in their responses to the "love quiz" they found in the Lifestyle section of the Colorado newspaper. One of the questions in this quiz asked respondents to indicate which of the following three descriptions most closely captured them:

_____ I find it relatively easy to get close to others and am comfortable depending on them and having them depend on me. I don't often worry about being abandoned or about someone getting too close to me.

_____ I am somewhat uncomfortable being close to others; I find it difficult to trust them completely, difficult to allow myself to depend on them. I am nervous when anyone gets too close, and often, lover partners want me to be more intimate than I feel comfortable being.

_____ I find that others are reluctant to get as close as I would like. I often worry that my partner doesn't really love me or won't want to stay with me. I want to merge completely with another person, and this desire sometimes scares people away.

The first description depicts an adult with a *secure attachment style.* The second portrays an *avoidant style,* the third an *anxious-ambivalent style.* Although the sample was far from scientific, the results were enlightening. Fifty-six percent of the respondents placed themselves in the secure category, 25% said the avoidant description fit them best, and the remaining 19% identified themselves as part of the anxious-ambivalent group. A subsequent national survey with a large stratified sample (Mickelson, Kessler, & Shaver, 1997) found a similar breakdown among Americans: 59% secure, 25% avoidant, 11% anxious (5% unclassifiable). The significance of these numbers was not lost on the investigators. They were quick to point out that the percentages of adults who fall into the three categories match quite closely those found by developmental psychologists calculating the number of secure, avoidant, and anxious-avoidant infants (Campos, Barrett, Lamb, Goldsmith, & Stenberg, 1983). Although only suggestive, the similarity in numbers is consistent with the notion that the adult attachment styles were formed in childhood.

Results of additional studies indicate that the connection between early parent-child relationships and adult attachment style is more than speculative. When asked about family members, secure adults are more likely than others to describe positive relationships with parents and a warm and trusting family environment (Brennan & Shaver, 1993; Diehl, Elnick, Bourbeau, & Labouvie-Vief, 1998; Feeney & Noller, 1990; Hazan & Shaver, 1987; Levy, Blatt, & Shaver, 1998). In contrast, anxious-ambivalent people in these studies recall little parental support, and avoidant people describe their relationships with family members as distrustful and emotionally distant. People who describe their parents' marriage as unhappy are more likely to fall into the avoidant category and less likely to develop a secure attachment style.

Alternate Models and Measurement

The introduction of adult attachment styles has resulted in an explosion of writings and research. This work includes new ideas about the number of adult attachment styles and new scales for determining how to classify individuals (Bartholomew, 1990; Bartholomew & Shaver, 1998; Carver, 1997). In recent years, attachment researchers have found it useful to divide attachment style along two dimensions (Bartholomew & Horowitz, 1991; Brennan, Clark, & Shaver, 1998). Researchers first divide people into those who are and are not fearful that their romantic partner will abandon them. Drawing from attachment theory, we can say this fear of abandonment reflects the person's internalized feelings of self-worth. Those who rarely worry about abandonment see themselves as worthwhile and capable of being treasured. On the other hand, some people are burdened with self-doubts about their value and reservations about whether anyone would find them lovable. Researchers refer to this dimension as *Anxiety*. The second dimension concerns how comfortable people are with closeness and dependency. On one side of this dimension, we find people who believe that others can be trusted and will be there to provide for their emotional needs. At the other end are those who see people as unreliable and rejecting. Researchers refer to this dimension as *Avoidance*.

When we combine these two dimensions, we get the four-category model shown in Figure 6.4. Adults who are comfortable with closeness and who don't overly concern themselves about being abandoned are classified as *secure*. Like the secure adults in the three-category model, these people tend to seek out and are comfortable with intimate relationships. However, some people who don't fear abandonment still have a deep-seated mistrust of others. These *avoidant* individuals (sometimes called *dismissing*) shy away from close relationships. They are reluctant to trust others or to become too emotionally dependent for fear of being hurt.

People classified in the other two quadrants of the model suffer from feelings that they are unlovable, which burdens them with a constant fear that their loved

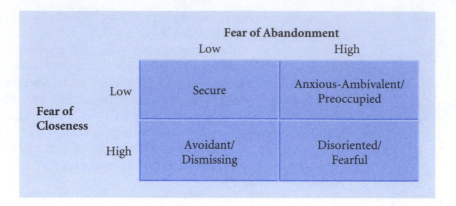

ones will abandon them. Those who are comfortable with closeness fall into the *anxious-ambivalent* category (sometimes called *preoccupied*). Because these individuals lack internal feelings of self-worth, they seek self-acceptance by becoming close and intimate with others. In a sense, they are trying to prove that they must be worthy of love if this other person finds them lovable. Unfortunately, their lack of self-worth leaves preoccupied people vulnerable to heartbreak when their partner fails to meet their strong intimacy needs. Additionally, we have *disoriented* (sometimes called *fearful*) people. These adults see themselves as unworthy of love and doubt that romantic involvement will provide the much-needed intimacy. They avoid getting close to others because they fear the pain of rejection.

Students correctly ask whether the three- or four-category model best describes the different kinds of adult attachment styles. The answer is that both models are useful, although there appears a trend in recent research toward using the four-category model. Because researchers sometimes divide participants into three categories and sometimes into four, occasionally it is difficult to compare results across studies. Nonetheless, because of the similarity between the two models, research using either scheme is valuable, and the research reviewed in the next section relies on studies using both models.

Attachment Style and Romantic Relationships

Do attachment styles really affect our romantic relationships? A good starting point for answering this question might be to ask how happy people are with their romantic relationships. As you might expect, several studies find that adults with a secure attachment style tend to be more satisfied with their relationships than people in the other categories (Brennan & Shaver, 1995; Keelan, Dion, & Dion, 1994; Pistole, 1989; Simpson, 1990; Tucker & Anders, 1999). This phenomenon also works in the other direction. That is, people are more likely to be happy with their relationship if they have a partner with a secure attachment style. And perhaps not surprisingly, adults with secure attachment styles tend to have partners with a similar attachment style (Brennan & Shaver, 1995; Collins & Read, 1990; Kirkpatrick & Davis, 1994).

One team of investigators measured attachment style in a sample of 52-year-olds (Klohnen & Bera, 1998). The researchers already had measures of relationship satisfaction from when the participants were 21, 27, and 43 years old. As expected, the secure adults in the sample had a long history of stable and satisfying romantic relationships. As shown in Figure 6.5, the secure participants were more likely to be married and to stay married than the avoidant participants. By age 52, 95% of the secure adults had been married, and only 24% had ever been divorced. In contrast, only 72% of the avoidant adults had ever been married, and 50% of them had experienced a divorce.

But why are relationships with secure adults better than relationships with people with an avoidant or anxious-ambivalent attachment style? To answer this question, researchers look at the characteristics that make up romantic relationships. They find that people with a secure attachment style are more likely than others to characterize their current romantic relationship as having a great deal of love, a strong commitment, and a large amount of trust (Keelan et al., 1994; Simpson, 1990). Moreover, these secure individuals are able to accept and support their partner despite the partner's personal faults (Hazan & Shaver, 1987). Conversations between secure partners tend to be warmer and more intimate than those with avoidant or anxious-ambivalent partners (Simpson, 1990). And compared to people with other attachment styles, secure adults are more likely to share personal information when appropriate (Mikulincer & Nachshon, 1991; Tidwell, Reis, & Shaver, 1996).

This kind of relationship is very different from one with an avoidant adult. People with an avoidant attachment style are hampered by a fear of intimacy and problems with jealousy (Hazan & Shaver, 1987). They tend to believe that real romance rarely lasts forever and that the kind of head-over-heels love depicted in

Figure 6.5

Marriage Rates as a Function of Attachment Style

Source: Adapted from Klohnen and Bera (1998).

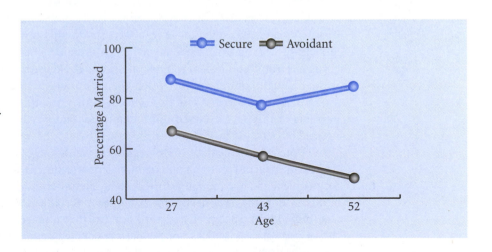

movies and romance novels doesn't really exist. Not surprisingly, 43% of the undergraduate students classified with an avoidant attachment style in one study said they had never been in love (Feeney, Noller, & Patty, 1993).

In contrast, people with an anxious-ambivalent attachment style fall in love many times but have difficulty finding the long-term happiness they desperately seek (Hazan & Shaver, 1987; Rholes, Simpson, Campbell, & Grich, 2001). These people are afraid of losing their partner and are quick to give in to the partner's wishes in an effort to keep him or her happy (Pistole, 1989). College students in one study watched their dating partners evaluate the physical attractiveness of other people (Simpson, Ickes, & Grich, 1999). The anxious-ambivalent participants were particularly likely to feel their relationship was threatened by the experience. Yet, like the newborns in the original research, both avoidant and anxious-ambivalent adults experience heightened stress when separated from their romantic partners (Feeney & Kirkpatrick, 1996). Anxious-ambivalent people are also more likely to fall in love with someone who does not love them in return (Aron, Aron, & Allen, 1998).

Attachment style also affects how adults respond to stress and separation in their relationships (Simpson, Rholes, & Phillips, 1996). Researchers in one study asked couples in airport lounges to complete an attachment style inventory (Fraley & Shaver, 1998). The investigators then watched surreptitiously and coded various behaviors (for example, hugs, eye contact, sitting close) while the couple waited for the departure. As expected, secure partners showed signs of closeness when one of them was leaving. In contrast, avoidant participants showed signs of pulling away from their partners as the departure approached. Presumably, these avoidant adults were experiencing anxiety and fear related to the impending separation from their partners.

Avoidant individuals also have difficulty giving and seeking emotional support from their partners just when they need support the most. This pattern has been found in a series of laboratory studies that look at couples' reactions to stress (Collins & Feeney, 2000; Feeney & Collins, 2001; Simpson, Rholes, Orina, & Grich, 2002). Women in one study were told they would soon be going through an anxiety-provoking experience involving an isolation chamber and some threatening electronic equipment (Simpson, Rholes, & Nelligan, 1992). Whereas secure women sought more comfort from their partners as their anxiety increased, avoidant women wanted less support when they became anxious. Secure male partners in this study offered more emotional support when their partners expressed anxiety, but avoidant men did not.

Before closing the door on this research, we should offer a bit of optimism to those with an avoidant or anxious-ambivalent attachment style. It may be possible for people to change their attachment style when they enter a secure, long-lasting adult relationship (Carnelley, Pietromonaco, & Jaffe, 1994; Davila, Karney, & Bradbury, 1999). Specifically, a loving and trusting adult relationship may provide the secure working model some people were denied as children. Thirty percent of the young women in one study changed their attachment style classification over a two-year span (Davila, Burge, & Hammen, 1997). This observation suggests that attachment style may not be as set early in life as Bowlby and others suggested. It also makes it difficult to know if relationships last because people have secure attachment styles or if people develop secure attachment styles because their relationships last so long.

Summary

1.   People do not passively accept their discomfort when faced with an anxiety-provoking situation. Instead, each of us has learned to take steps to reduce that anxiety. Researchers have divided these coping strategies into active and avoidant categories, and into those that focus on the problem and those that deal with the emotional reaction. Which of these strategies will be more effective in reducing anxiety depends on the availability of means to solve the problem.

2.   Researchers have applied many psychoanalytic concepts to understanding the causes and consequences of aggression. Studies find that frustration is a source of aggression, but not all frustrating events lead to aggression. Recent models suggest that frustration causes aggression because it is unpleasant. Other studies find that frustration-induced aggression can be displaced onto innocent targets. Additionally, the widely held belief that aggression leads to catharsis and less aggression has not been supported in empirical investigations. Allowing people to act out their aggressive impulses appears to increase, not decrease, the likelihood of further aggression.

3.   Recent research has used concepts from object relations theory and attachment theory to explain adult romantic relationships. Based on the works of John Bowlby and Mary Ainsworth, investigators can identify adult attachment styles that presumably stem from early parent-child relationships. Researchers find adults with secure, avoidant, and anxious-ambivalent attachment styles approach and participate in romantic relationships differently.

InfoTrac Key Terms

For additional readings go to http://www.infotrac-college.com/wadsworth and enter a search term related to your interest. Use the key terms suggested here to pull up several related articles. Also see the text Web site at http://psychology.wadsworth.com for more suggested readings and interactive quizzes to test your knowledge.

Aggressiveness (psychology)   Avoidance strategies
Anxiety   Coping style
Attachment relationships

Chapter 7

The Trait Approach

Theory, Application, and Assessment

Suppose for the moment that, like many college freshmen living in on-campus housing, you have been assigned a roommate you don't know. A few weeks before classes, your new roommate sends you an e-mail message. After saying hello and introducing himself or herself, your roommate asks: "What kind of person are you?" When replying, you find describing your physical features is relatively easy, and giving facts about your hometown, number of siblings, and so on takes almost no time at all. But how do you describe your personality to someone you have never met?

If you are like most people, you probably tackle this problem in one of two ways. You might start by describing the type of person you are—a quiet type, an independent type, an outgoing type. The other approach is to describe your characteristics—studious, shy, and friendly. In either case, you are describing yourself in terms of relatively stable features, either by classifying yourself as a *type* of person or by identifying the extent to which you hold certain *traits*. In essence, you would be using the trait approach to personality to answer the question. Trait researchers identify types or traits that describe a large number of people and that can be used to predict behavior.

People have tried to describe personality for probably about as long as humans have used language. Gordon Allport, one of the original trait theorists, counted more than 4,000 adjectives in the English language that can be used for this purpose (Allport, 1961). Thus, an early challenge for personality psychologists was combining all these characteristics into a usable structure. The first attempt to identify and describe these characteristics was to develop *typology* systems. The goal was to discover how many types of people there are and identify each person's type. For example, the ancient Greeks divided people into four types: sanguine (happy), melancholic (unhappy), choleric (temperamental), and phlegmatic (apathetic). Another effort identified three basic personality types based on general physique: endomorphic (obese), mesomorphic (muscular), and ectomorphic (fragile). The three types were said to differ in personality as well as physical appearance (Sheldon, 1942).

However, few researchers use this approach today because a strict type approach makes several assumptions that are not easily justified. For example, the type approach assumes that each of us fits into one personality category and that all people within a category are basically alike. Further, the approach assumes that the behavior of people in one category is distinctly different from the behavior of people in other categories. You can't be a little of category A and a little of B. You must be either A or B. These assumptions are obviously difficult to meet. Although typologies are still popular with lay audiences (zodiac signs, for instance), today the type approach has been replaced with the trait approach.

The Trait Approach

Personality as Trait Dimensions

Almost any personality characteristic you can think of—optimism, self-esteem, achievement motivation—can be illustrated with the trait continuum shown in Figure 7.1. Several important characteristics about the trait approach are illustrated in this simple diagram. First, trait psychologists identify a wide range of behaviors that can be represented along the continuum. For example, achievement motivation can range from highly driven persistence at one extreme to indifference at the other. Trait psychologists also maintain that we can take any given person and place him or her somewhere along the continuum. We are all more or less aggressive, more or less friendly, and so on. Finally, if we were to measure a large group of people and place their scores at appropriate points along the continuum, we probably would find that the scores are normally distributed. This means that relatively few people score extremely high or extremely low, and that most of us fall somewhere toward the middle of the distribution.

Figure 7.1

Trait Continuum

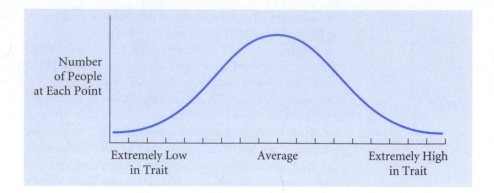

A **trait** is a dimension of personality used to categorize people according to the degree to which they manifest a particular characteristic. The trait approach to personality is built on two important assumptions. First, trait psychologists assume that personality characteristics are relatively stable over time. It would make little sense to describe someone as high in sociability if that person loved being around people one day but shied away from social settings the next. Of course, we all have times we prefer to be alone and other times we seek out friends. But if we were to examine a given individual's behavior over a long period of time, we would see a relatively stable level of sociability. Trait researchers also maintain that someone who is highly sociable today will probably be sociable next month, next year, and many years down the road. Indeed, researchers find scores from personality measures are remarkably consistent over time once we reach adulthood (Roberts & Del Vecchio, 2000).

The second assumption underlying the trait approach is that the personality characteristics are stable across situations. For example, aggressive people should exhibit higher-than-average amounts of aggression during family disagreements as well as when playing football. Again, we all act more aggressively in some situations than in others. But the trait approach assumes that over many different situations a relatively stable average degree of aggressiveness can be determined. As discussed later, these assumptions of trait stability across time and situations have not gone unchallenged.

Finally, we use the term *trait* rather broadly here. Thus, as you will see in this and the next chapter, trait theorists include people who study individual differences in needs and strategies, among other concepts. In each case, the psychologist is interested in relatively stable patterns of behavior that can be measured and categorized along a normal distribution.

Special Features of the Trait Approach

The trait approach to personality differs from the other approaches presented in this book in several important ways. Unlike psychologists from other approaches, trait researchers are usually not interested in predicting one person's behavior in a given situation. Instead, they want to predict how people who score within a certain segment of the trait continuum will typically behave. Thus, a trait researcher might compare people who score relatively high on a social anxiety scale with those who score relatively low. The investigators might find that, on average, people high in social anxiety talk less in a group situation than those low on this trait. However, they probably would not attempt to predict any one person's behavior. Surely a few high-anxiety people in the study would talk a lot, whereas a few low-anxiety participants would say very little. The goal of this kind of study is to identify differences between the typical behavior of someone who falls into one of the two groups. This contrasts with the psychoanalytic approach, in which therapists try to understand the behavior of one particular person.

Another distinguishing feature of the trait approach is that, compared to theorists from other approaches, trait theorists often place less emphasis on identifying the mechanisms' underlying behavior. Rather than explaining why people behave the way they do, many trait researchers focus on describing personality and predicting behavior. When psychologists try to explain behavior with traits alone, they often fall victim to the problem of circular reasoning. For example, if asked to explain why Bob hit Scott, we might say "because Bob is aggressive." If we are then asked how we know Bob is aggressive, we might answer "because he hit Scott." We could substitute any word for aggressive in this example, and the logic would be just as compelling.

However, it would be incorrect to conclude that trait researchers are interested only in describing traits. Identifying traits and predicting behavior are often just the first step in the explanatory process. As the examples in the next chapter illustrate, trait researchers often examine the processes behind the behaviors characteristic of people high or low on a particular trait. For example, some trait researchers look at the parenting styles that lead to a high need for Achievement, and psychologists interested in social anxiety sometimes examine the underlying concerns of shy people that cause them to avoid social encounters.

One of the major advantages of studying personality through the trait approach is that we can easily make comparisons across people. A trait description places people on a personality continuum relative to others. When we say someone is feminine, we are saying that the person is more feminine than most people. A researcher who concludes, "People high in self-consciousness have difficulty making friends," is really saying that these people have a more difficult time making friends than people who score at the lower end of this continuum.

One distinction between the trait approach and many of the other approaches to personality is that the trait approach has relatively little to say about personality change. Information collected by trait researchers can be useful to therapists making diagnoses and charting progress during therapy. In addition, many of the characteristics examined by trait researchers, such as self-esteem and social anxiety, are relevant to a client's adjustment and well-being. But research findings on personality traits typically provide only a direction for how to change people who may be too high or too low on a personality dimension. Trait psychologists are more likely to be academic researchers than practicing therapists. Thus, no major schools of psychotherapy have evolved from the trait approach to personality.

Important Trait Theorists

You will notice references to traits and trait measures scattered throughout most of the chapters in this book. This is testimony to how widely accepted the trait concept has become in personality psychology. Personality psychologists from nearly every approach, as well as psychologists from many other fields of psychology, use traits and trait measures in their work. The expansion of the trait approach from virtually nothing 80 years ago to its prominent influence today can be attributed in part to the pioneering work of some early trait theorists. These psychologists went beyond proposing and examining a few trait dimensions. They also described the nature of traits, the structure of personality, and the relationship between traits and other aspects of psychology.

Gordon Allport

The first recognized work on traits by a psychologist did not appear until 1921. That was the year Gordon Allport, along with his brother Floyd, published *Personality Traits: Their Classification and Measurement.* Gordon Allport also taught what is believed to be the first college course on personality in the United States, in 1925 (Nicholson, 1997). Although psychologists and laypeople today frequently speak of traits, much of Allport's work in the early years of his career was indeed groundbreaking. Only one year after receiving his bachelor's degree, the unconventional Allport somehow managed to arrange a meeting with Sigmund Freud. Allport wanted to talk psychology, but Freud spent much of the time inquiring about Allport's unconscious motives. As far as Allport was concerned, there were obvious, conscious reasons for his behavior. But Freud's limited orientation wouldn't allow him to see the obvious. "Psychologists would do well," Allport concluded from the visit, "to give full recognition to manifest motives before probing the unconscious" (1968, p. 384).

"*Dispositions are never wholly consistent. What a bore it would be if they were—and what chaos if they were not at all consistent.*"
GORDON ALLPORT

Unlike Freud, whom he accused of blindly adhering to psychoanalytic theory, Allport acknowledged the limitations of the trait concept from the beginning. He accepted that behavior is influenced by a variety of environmental factors and recognized that traits cannot predict what a single individual will do. Yet "in a person's stream of activity there is, besides a variable portion, likewise a constant portion," he argued. "And it is this constant portion we seek to designate with the concept of trait" (1961, p. 333). Allport also believed that our traits have physical components in our nervous systems. He maintained that scientists would one day develop technology advanced enough to identify personality traits by examining neurological structures.

Although Allport may not have invented the trait concept, he can certainly be credited with promoting its use in personality psychology. Allport introduced many other concepts that today are accepted features of the trait approach. These include the different ways researchers use traits to study personality, the relation between past and present motives, and the psychological concept of the "self." As described in the next section, Allport sometimes used different labels for these concepts than researchers use today, but his work was pioneering nonetheless.

Nomothetic Versus Idiographic Approaches to Personality. Allport identified two general strategies researchers might take when investigating personality. So far, we have described traits and trait research along the lines of what Allport called the **nomothetic approach** to personality measurement and description. Researchers using this approach assume that all people can be described along a single dimension according to their level of, for example, assertiveness or anxiety. Each person in a study using the nomothetic approach is tested to see how his or her score for the given trait compares with the scores of the other participants. Allport referred to these traits that presumably apply to everyone as *common traits.*

Allport called nomothetic research "indispensable" for understanding human personality. But he also championed another way to research personality traits that is often ignored. Rather than forcing all people into categories selected beforehand, researchers using the **idiographic approach** identify the unique combination of traits that best accounts for the personality of a single individual. To illustrate Allport's point, take a few minutes to list 5 to 10 traits you believe are the most important in describing your behavior. Have a friend do the same for herself or himself, and then compare your answers. You will most likely discover that the two of you have compiled two very different lists of traits. You might have used *independent* or *genuine* to describe yourself. Yet it may not have occurred to your friend to think of himself or herself in terms of independence or genuineness. Similarly, the traits your friend came up with might never have crossed your mind when you wrote your self-description.

Allport referred to these 5 to 10 traits that best describe an individual's personality as **central traits.** If you want to understand one particular person, Allport's recommended strategy is to first determine the central traits for this individual and then decide where he or she falls on each of these dimensions. Although the number of central traits varies from person to person, Allport proposed that occasionally a single trait will dominate a personality. These rare individuals can be described with a **cardinal trait.** Allport pointed to historical figures whose behavior was so dominated by a single trait that the behavior became synonymous with the individual. Thus, we speak of people who are *Machiavellian, Homeric,* or *Don Juans.*

The advantage of using the idiographic approach is that the person, not the researcher, determines what traits to examine. With the nomothetic approach, the traits selected by the investigator might be central for some people, but only what

Gordon Allport

1897–1967

In many ways Gordon Allport's life and career choices reflect the notion of individual differences that he championed. Allport was born in Montezuma, Indiana, to a family with three older brothers, including seven-year-old Floyd. Even as a child, Gordon did not fit in. "I was quick with words, poor at games," he wrote. "When I was ten a schoolmate said of me, 'Aw, that guy swallowed a dictionary'" (1967, p. 4). Allport was persuaded by his brother Floyd to attend Harvard. This was the beginning of an academic and professional shadow in which the younger Allport was to spend many of his early adult years. Not only did Gordon follow his brother to both undergraduate and graduate degrees at Harvard, but he also chose Floyd's field of study, psychology. Floyd was the teaching assistant for Gordon's first psychology class. Later, Gordon took a course in experimental psychology from his brother, served as a participant in some of his research, and helped him with the editing of the *Journal of Abnormal and Social Psychology.*

But Gordon soon developed a very different view of psychology. Floyd was a social psychologist and went on to achieve substantial recognition in that field. However, Gordon had different ideas about the best way to understand human behavior. In graduate school, Allport once again felt different from the other psychology students. "Unlike most of my student colleagues," he wrote, "I had no giftedness in natural science, mathematics, mechanics (laboratory manipula-

tions), nor in biological or medical specialties" (1967, p. 8). After confessing these feelings to one of his professors, he was told, "But you know, there are many branches of psychology."

"I think this casual remark saved me," Allport later reflected. "In effect he was encouraging me to find my own way in the . . . pastures of psychology" (1967, p. 8). This he did, despite much early resistance to his notion of personality traits. Perhaps the earliest of these confrontations came in graduate school, when Allport was given three minutes to present his research ideas at a seminar at Clark University in front of the famous psychologist Edward Titchener. His presentation about personality traits was followed by total silence. Later, Titchener asked Allport's advisor: "Why did you let him work on that problem?"

But Allport was not discouraged. He went on to a distinguished career, most of it at Harvard. His 1937 book, *Personality: A Psychological Interpretation,* outlined his theory of personality traits and was well received by many psychologists. Two years later Allport was elected president of the American Psychological Association. In 1964 he received the prestigious Distinguished Scientific Contribution Award from that same organization.

Allport's decision to wander off into different pastures of psychology was appropriate for the man who promoted the idea of individual differences. This decision also took him out of his brother's shadow, perhaps best symbolized when Gordon later became the editor of the *Journal of Abnormal and Social Psychology*

(continues)

Allport called *secondary traits* for others. A test score indicating a person's level of sociability is of great value when sociability is a central trait for that person, but of limited value when it is not. Allport illustrated the idiographic approach in his study of an elderly woman who used the pseudonym Jenny Masterson. In his book *Letters from Jenny,* Allport (1965) examined more than 300 letters written by Jenny over a 12-year period. Allport identified eight of the woman's central traits with this method. Although time-consuming, this idiographic research contributed to a much more enlightening portrait of Jenny than could have been attained by obtaining test scores on a few preselected dimensions.

Functional Autonomy and the Proprium. Allport also disagreed with Freud on the relationship between childhood and adult personalities. According to Freud, the seeds of adult personality are planted during childhood. Within Freud's theory, the motives that underlie your adult personality are a reflection of the motives that guided your behavior as a child. However, Allport argued that although childhood behaviors may resemble adult behaviors, they don't necessarily represent the same underlying motives. For example, many children who read frequently because their parents insist on it become avid readers as adults. But this does not mean the adults read for the same reasons they did in childhood. The behavior that was once a means to an end (pleasing the parents) has become **functionally autonomous.** That is, reading is now enjoyable for its own sake. Similarly, new employees who need their paychecks to survive might work very hard to make sure they are not fired. But many of these people continue to work hard even after attaining job security and comfortable salaries. The behavior that was once motivated by a need for money continues without that motivation. Allport agreed that we can often trace a certain adult behavior back to earlier times. But he argued that there is no reason to assume the adult behavior and the earlier behavior come from the same motive.

Allport was particularly interested in the process by which children develop a sense of themselves. We all talk about a self and recognize our identity as separate from others. But how does this notion develop? Allport suggested that at birth children have no concept of themselves as distinct from their environment. Gradually, they come to sense that their bodies are somehow different from other objects in the world. Babies soon discover that, unlike other parts of the environment, they can control the movement of their bodies and sense when a part of their body has been touched. From here the child develops a sense of self-identity

"*Personality, like every other living, changes as it grows.*"
GORDON ALLPORT

Table 7.1   Murray's Psychogenic Needs

Need	Description
Abasement	To surrender. To comply and accept punishment. To apologize, confess, atone. Self-depreciation. Masochism.
Achievement	To overcome obstacles. To exercise power. To strive to do something difficult as well and as quickly as possible.
Affiliation	To form friendships and associations. To greet, join, and live with others. To cooperate and converse sociably with others. To love. To join groups.
Aggression	To assault or injure another. To murder. To belittle, harm, blame, accuse, or maliciously ridicule a person. To punish severely. Sadism.
Autonomy	To resist influence or coercion. To defy an authority or seek freedom in a new place. To strive for independence.
Blameavoidance	To avoid blame, ostracism, or punishment by inhibiting asocial or unconventional impulses. To be well behaved and obey the law.
Counteraction	Proudly to refuse admission of defeat by restriving and retaliating. To select the hardest tasks. To defend one's honor in action.
Defendance	To defend oneself against blame or belittlement. To justify one's actions. To offer extenuations, explanations, and excuses. To resist "probing."
Deference	To admire and willingly follow a superior allied other. To cooperate with a leader. To serve gladly.
Dominance	To influence or control others. To persuade, prohibit, dictate. To lead and direct. To restrain. To organize the behavior of a group.
Exhibition	To attract attention to one's person. To excite, amuse, stir, shock, thrill others. Self-dramatization.
Harmavoidance	To avoid pain, physical injury, illness, and death. To escape from a dangerous situation. To take precautionary measures.
Infavoidance	To avoid failure, shame, humiliation, ridicule. To refrain from attempting to do something that is beyond one's powers. To conceal a disfigurement.
Nurturance	To nourish, aid, or protect a helpless other. To express sympathy. To "mother" a child.
Order	To arrange, organize, put away objects. To be tidy and clean. To be scrupulously precise.
Play	To relax, amuse oneself, seek diversion and entertainment. To "have fun," to play games. To laugh, joke, and be merry. To avoid serious tension.
Rejection	To shun, ignore, or exclude another. To remain aloof and indifferent. To be discriminating.
Sentience	To seek and enjoy sensuous impressions.
Sex	To form and further an erotic relationship. To have sexual intercourse.
Succorance	To seek aid, protection, or sympathy. To cry for help. To plead for mercy. To adhere to an affectionate, nurturant parent. To be dependent.
Understanding	To analyze experience, to abstract, to discriminate among concepts, to define relations, to synthesize ideas.

Source: From Explorations in Personality by Henry A. Murray. Copyright 1938; renewed 1966 by Henry A. Murray. Used by permission of Oxford University Press, Inc.

and self-esteem, until finally the full sense of a self has evolved. Allport agreed with the neo-Freudians, who argued that the development of personality continues long after the first few years of life. Like Erikson and Sullivan, he believed identity development continues throughout adolescence. Allport developed the term **proprium** to describe all aspects of the self united under a single concept.

Today the self plays a central role in the theories of many humanistic psychologists (Chapter 11) and more recently in the theorizing and research of cognitive psychologists (Chapters 15 and 16). By introducing and promoting concepts such as traits, central traits, and the self, Allport assured himself a prominent place in the history of personality psychology.

Henry Murray

Unlike most trait theorists, who typically disregard psychoanalytic theory, Henry Murray's approach to personality represents a blend of psychoanalytic and trait concepts. Early in his career Murray had the opportunity to interact extensively with Carl Jung. Jung's strong influence can be seen in the emphasis Murray gave to the unconscious in his writings. The psychoanalytic flavor of Murray's work also can be found in one of his principal contributions to the field of personality, the Thematic Apperception Test (TAT). As described in Chapter 3, the TAT is a projective measure designed to get at material not readily accessible to conscious thought.

Murray called his approach *personology* and identified the basic elements of personality as needs. He was not very concerned with *viscerogenic needs,* such as the need for food and water. Rather, his work focused on **psychogenic needs,** which are similar to the traits described by other theorists. A psychogenic need is a "readiness to respond in a certain way under certain given conditions" (1938, p. 124). In keeping with his psychoanalytic background, he postulated that these needs are largely unconscious. Murray eventually arrived at a list of 27 psychogenic needs, many of them shown in Table 7.1.

According to Murray, each of us can be described in terms of a personal hierarchy of needs. For example, if you have a strong need for a lot of close friends, you would be said to have a high need for Affiliation. The importance of this need is not so much how it compares with the Affiliation needs of other people, but rather how strong it is compared to your other needs. Suppose you have a big test tomorrow, but your friends are having a party tonight. If your Achievement need is higher on your personal need hierarchy than your need for Affiliation or your need for Play, you'll probably stay with your books. If your Achievement need, although high, is not quite as strong as these other needs, your grade will probably suffer.

Murray recognized that whether a need is activated depends on the situation, which he call the *press.* For example, your need for Order won't affect your behavior without an appropriate press, such as a messy room. If you have a strong need for Order, you probably make time to clean your room even when it is only slightly disheveled. If you have a relatively weak need for Order, you might wait until the

©Bettmann/CORBIS

Henry Murray

1893–1988

There is little in Henry Murray's background and early training to suggest that he not only would settle on personality psychology as a career, but would also come to be recognized as one of its most influential theorists. In his own words, "[my] record consisted of nothing but items which correlated negatively . . . with the records of the vast majority of professional psychologists" (1967, p. 286). Murray attended one psychology lecture as an undergraduate. He found it boring and walked out. Murray earned his bachelor's degree in history in 1915, followed by a medical degree from Columbia in 1919. After working a few years in embryology, Murray went to Cambridge University in England, where he earned a doctorate in biochemistry in 1927.

How does a biochemist become an important personality theorist? During the latter years of his academic training, Murray was exposed to and enthusiastically embraced the writings of Carl Jung. He was particularly impressed with Jung's description of psychological types. In 1925, while studying in England, he arranged to meet with Jung in Vienna. His conversations with Jung persuaded Murray that his real interests were in the budding field of psychology. After working at the Harvard Psychological Clinic and receiving formal psychoanalytic training, Murray accepted a position at Harvard, where he taught until his retirement in 1962. Like most turns in his career, Murray was struck by the improbability of becoming a lecturer in psychology. Not only did he have a relatively weak background in psychology, he also was a stutterer. Nonetheless, Murray's academic career was long and successful.

Murray's commitment to psychology did not end his professional diversity. He took a brief break from academia in 1943, when he was recruited by the Office of Strategic Services, a forerunner of the Central Intelligence Agency. His job was to apply his understanding of personality to the selection of undercover agents. Murray also became something of a literary scholar, although he confessed once that "in school, [I] had received [my] consistently worst marks in English." He had a particular passion for the writings of Herman Melville and became an authority on Melville's life. Murray died in 1988 at the age of 95.

room is too messy to move around in—and even then the cleaning might be motivated more by a need to please your roommates than to see things arranged neatly.

In addition to the TAT, Murray's principal legacy to the field of personality is the research his personology theory has stimulated. Several of Murray's psychogenic needs have been subjected to intense research, often by his students who went on to become important personality researchers in their own right. Among the more extensively researched are the need for Power, the need for Affiliation, and as presented in the next chapter, the need for Achievement.

Factor Analysis and the Search for the Structure of Personality

Alongside Allport and Murray, we find another pioneer of the trait approach, Raymond Cattell. Unlike other theorists, Cattell did not begin with insightful notions about the elements that make up human personality. Rather, he borrowed the approach taken by other sciences. Notably, Cattell's first college degree was in chemistry. And just as chemists did not begin by guessing what chemical elements must exist, Cattell argued, so psychologists should not begin with a preconceived list of personality traits. Instead of trying to verify our intuition about what personality must be, he suggested researchers use empirical methods to answer their questions.

The central goal directing much of Cattell's work was discovering just how many basic personality traits there are. Psychologists have identified, measured, and researched hundreds of personality traits. But certainly many of these traits are related. For example, being sociable is not entirely different from being extraverted, although we can identify some fine distinctions. Cattell reasoned that we could identify the basic structure of personality by grouping together those traits that are related and separating those that are independent.

In his quest to discover this structure, Cattell employed a sophisticated statistical technique called **factor analysis.** Although a complete understanding of the procedure is beyond the scope of this book, an example can illustrate how factor analysis is used to determine the number of basic personality traits.

Suppose you had tests to measure the following 10 traits: *aspiration, compassion, cooperativeness, determination, endurance, friendliness, kindliness, persistence, productivity,* and *tenderness.* You could give these tests to a group of people and obtain 10 scores per person. You might then use correlation coefficients (Chapter 2) to examine how scores on one test compare with scores on the other nine tests. For example, you might find that friendliness and tenderness scores are highly correlated. If a person scores high on one test, you can predict with some confidence that the person also will score high on the other test. Looking at the pattern of correlation coefficients, you might discover that the tests tend to cluster into two groups. That is, five of the tests are highly correlated with one another, but not with the other five tests. These other five tests are similarly correlated among themselves, but not with the tests in the first group. The two groups might look something like this:

Group A	*Group B*
aspiration	compassion
determination	cooperativeness
endurance	friendliness
persistence	kindliness
productivity	tenderness

Raymond B. Cattell

1905–1998

Raymond Cattell spent most of his childhood by the ocean in the resort town of Torquay in the south of England. There he developed a lifelong love for the ocean and sailing. Unfortunately, this happy childhood was interrupted when England entered World War I. Cattell suddenly found himself treating wounded and maimed soldiers in a makeshift wartime hospital. Cattell did not realize until many years later how these experiences would one day affect his choice of careers. He won a scholarship to the University of London, the only member of his family to attend college. Images of wounded soldiers returned to him a few months before his graduation with honors in chemistry. Suddenly his plans for a career in the physical sciences no longer appealed to him. Cattell also was impressed with a lecture he attended by the famous psychologist Cyril Burt, who argued that the science of psychology offered the best hope solving many of society's problems (Horn, 2001).

"My laboratory bench began to seem small and the world's problems vast," Cattell wrote. "Gradually I concluded that to get beyond human irrationalities one had to study the workings of the mind itself" (1974, p. 64).

His decision to study psychology, which "was then regarded, not without grounds, as a subject for cranks," led him to graduate work at London University. There Cattell—and psychology—stumbled into a fortunate association. Cattell was hired as a research assistant for the famous psychologist and mathematician Charles Spearman, who was studying the relationship between measures of intelligence. Spearman found evidence for a single general concept of intelligence, as compared to models arguing for many unrelated aptitudes. In the course of this research, Spearman developed the statistical procedure known as factor analysis. Cattell would later use factor analysis to understand the structure of personality.

After five years working at various clinics in England, Cattell was tempted to America by an offer to work with the learning theorist E. L. Thorndike at Columbia. He also worked at Clark University until Gordon Allport invited him to join the faculty at Harvard in 1941. It was at Harvard, while working alongside Allport and Henry Murray, that Cattell first developed the notion that factor analysis could be a useful tool for personality researchers ("Raymond B. Cattell," 1997). He put those ideas into practice after joining the faculty at the University of Illinois in 1945, where he spent most of his career. Cattell was always a hard worker, sometimes going into his office on Christmas day. The result of this diligence was 56 books and more than 500 research articles. His decision to study personality clearly was psychology's gain and physical science's loss.

Although you originally measured 10 traits, a reasonable conclusion would be that you actually measured two larger personality dimensions, one having to do with achievement and the other with interpersonal warmth. This is a simple illustration of Cattell's basic approach. By analyzing data from various sources with factor analyses, he attempted to determine how many of these basic elements exist. He called the basic traits that make up the human personality **source traits.**

Unfortunately, the data obtained from factor analysis typically are not as neat and clear-cut as this example suggests. If they were, we would have determined the number of source traits a long time ago. One serious limitation of factor analysis is that the procedure is confined by the type of data chosen for analysis. For example, what would happen if you took a few tests out of the previous example and inserted a few new ones, such as *independence, absentmindedness,* and *honesty?* Most likely, this would change the number of categories (called factors) and the traits associated with them (or, in factor analytic terms, "loaded on" them).

In response to this problem, Cattell looked at information about personality from many different sources. He examined data from records, such as report cards and ratings by employers, data about how people act when placed in lifelike situations, and data from personality questionnaires. He called these three *L-data, T-data,* and *Q-data.* Cattell identified 16 basic traits in his research and in 1949 published the first version of the Sixteen Personality Factor Questionnaire (16 PF) to measure these. The revised version of the 16 PF remains a widely used personality inventory today (H. E. P. Cattell, 2001). Cattell's 16 source traits are shown in Table 7.2.

The Big Five

Efforts to identify and describe the basic dimensions of personality did not end with Cattell's original model. Rather, personality structure has been an ongoing issue in personality research for decades. Since Cattell's early work, sophisticated statistical tests, computers to crunch the numbers, and larger, more varied sets of data have been added to the search. And although there may never be complete agreement on this issue, researchers have noticed a surprisingly consistent finding in factor analytic studies of personality. Different teams of investigators using many different kinds of personality data have repeatedly found evidence for five basic dimensions of personality (Costa & McCrae, 1988; Digman, 1990; Goldberg, 1990, 1992; McCrae & Costa, 1986b, 1987; McCrae, Costa, & Busch, 1986; Noller, Law, & Comrey, 1987; Peabody & Goldberg, 1989). Although there is still some controversy about the names and exact number of factors, researchers have frequently uncovered factors that look like the ones listed in Table 7.3.

The five factors described in the table have shown up in so many studies using a variety of methods that researchers now refer to them as the **Big Five.** Remember, these investigators did not begin with a theory about how many factors they would find or what these basic dimensions of personality would look like. Rather,

Table 7.2   Cattell's Sixteen Source Traits

Warmth	Outgoing and warmhearted versus aloof and critical
Reasoning	Bright and abstract-thinking versus less intelligent and concrete-thinking
Emotional Stability	Calm and emotionally stable versus changeable and easily upset
Dominance	Assertive and aggressive versus docile and accommodating
Liveliness	Enthusiastic and lively versus sober and serious
Rule-Consciousness	Conscientious and moralistic versus expedient and rule disregarding
Social Boldness	Uninhibited and venturesome versus shy and timid
Sensitivity	Tender-minded and sensitive versus tough-minded and self-reliant
Vigilance	Suspicious and vigilant versus trusting and accepting
Abstractedness	Imaginative and absentminded versus practical and grounded
Privateness	Polished and astute versus forthright and unpretentious
Apprehension	Insecure and worrisome versus self-assured and complacent
Openness to Change	Free-thinking and experimenting versus conservative and traditional
Self-Reliance	Self-sufficient and resourceful versus group-oriented and a joiner
Perfectionism	Controlled and compulsive versus undisciplined and lax
Tension	Driven and tense versus relaxed and composed

Source: Reprinted by permission of the Institute of Personality and Ability Testing.

Table 7.3 **The Big Five Personality Factors**

Factor	Characteristics
Neuroticism	Worried versus calm Insecure versus secure Self-pitying versus self-satisfied
Extraversion	Sociable versus retiring Fun-loving versus sober Affectionate versus reserved
Openness	Imaginative versus down-to-earth Preference for variety versus preference for routine Independent versus conforming
Agreeableness	Softhearted versus ruthless Trusting versus suspicious Helpful versus uncooperative
Conscientiousness	Well organized versus disorganized Careful versus careless Self-disciplined versus weak willed

Source: Adapted from McCrae and Costa (1986b).

they let the data do the talking. Consequently, once researchers saw which traits clustered with one another, they had to come up with descriptive terms for the five dimensions. Although different researchers sometimes use different names, the most commonly used terms are Neuroticism, Extraversion, Openness, Agreeableness, and Conscientiousness. Alert students have recognized that the beginning letters of the five labels cover the OCEAN of human personality.

The *Neuroticism* dimension places people along a continuum according to their emotional stability and personal adjustment. People who frequently experience emotional distress and wide swings in emotions will score high on measures of Neuroticism. People high in Neuroticism tend to become more upset over daily stressors than those low on this dimension (Gunthert, Cohen, & Armeli, 1999; Suls, Green, & Hillis, 1998). Although there are many different kinds of negative emotions—sadness, anger, anxiety, guilt—that may have different causes and require different treatments, research consistently shows that people prone to one kind of negative emotional state often experience others (Costa & McCrae, 1992). Individuals low in Neuroticism tend to be calm, well adjusted, and not prone to extreme and maladaptive emotional reactions.

Researchers have identified the second personality dimension as *Extraversion*, with extreme extraverts at one end and extreme introverts at the other. Extraverts are very sociable people who also tend to be energetic, optimistic, friendly, and assertive. Introverts do not typically express these characteristics, but it would be incorrect to say that they are asocial and without energy. As one team of researchers explained, "Introverts are reserved rather than unfriendly, independent rather than followers, even-paced rather than sluggish" (Costa & McCrae, 1992, p. 15). As you might imagine, studies find that extraverts have more friends and spend more time in social situations than introverts (Asendorpf & Wilpers, 1998).

The *Openness* dimension refers to openness to experience rather than openness in an interpersonal sense. The characteristics that make up this dimension include an active imagination, a willingness to consider new ideas, divergent thinking, and intellectual curiosity. People high in Openness are unconventional and independent thinkers. Those low in Openness tend to be more conventional and prefer the familiar rather than something new. Given this description, it is not surprising that innovative scientists and creative artists tend to be high in Openness (Feist, 1998). Some researchers refer to this dimension as *Intellect,* although it is certainly not the same as intelligence.

People who are high on the *Agreeableness* dimension are helpful, trusting, and sympathetic. Those on the other end tend to be antagonistic and skeptical. Agreeable people prefer cooperation over competition. Those low in Agreeableness like to fight for their interests and beliefs. Researchers find that people high in Agreeableness have more pleasant social interactions and fewer quarrelsome exchanges than those low on this dimension (Berry & Hansen, 2000; Cote & Moskowitz, 1998; Jensen-Campbell & Graziano, 2001).

The *Conscientiousness* dimension refers to how controlled and self-disciplined we are. People on the high end of this dimension are organized, plan oriented, and determined. Those on the low end are apt to be careless, easily distracted from tasks, and undependable. Little wonder that those low in Conscientiousness tend to have more automobile accidents (Arthur & Graziano, 1996). Because the characteristics that define Conscientiousness often show up in achievement or work situations, some researchers have referred to this dimension as *Will to Achieve* or simply *Work.*

Many researchers have been impressed with the pervasiveness of the Big Five regardless of how personality is measured. Of course, the five factors show up when researchers look at responses to self-report trait inventories. But researchers also find evidence for five basic factors when looking at other indicators of personality, such as the terms people use to describe their friends and acquaintances (Goldberg, 1990; Watson, Hubbard, & Wiese, 2000) and the way teachers describe their students (Digman & Inouye, 1986; Goldberg, 2001). The five factors also emerge in studies with elementary school children (Donahue, 1994; Markey, Markey, Tinsley, & Ericksen, 2002) and appear to be fairly stable over time (McCrae, 1993; McCrae & Costa, 1990; Von Dras & Siegler, 1997). One team of researchers used college student interview and questionnaire data from 1939–1944 to determine Big Five scores (Soldz & Vaillant, 1999). These scores correlated highly with Big Five test scores taken when the participants were 45 years older. In short, evidence from many different sources indicates that the many traits comprising our personalities can be organized along five basic personality dimensions.

Assessing Your Own Personality

Conscientiousness

Indicate the extent to which each of the following terms describes you. Use a 9-point scale to indicate your response, with 1 = Extremely Inaccurate and 9 = Extremely Accurate.

_____	Careful	_____	Negligent*
_____	Careless*	_____	Organized
_____	Conscientious	_____	Practical
_____	Disorganized*	_____	Prompt
_____	Efficient	_____	Sloppy*
_____	Haphazard*	_____	Steady
_____	Inconsistent*	_____	Systematic
_____	Inefficient*	_____	Thorough
_____	Impractical*	_____	Undependable*
_____	Neat	_____	Unsystematic*

This scale was developed by Goldberg (1992) to measure Conscientiousness, one of the Big Five personality dimensions. Although different scoring procedures are possible, the most straightforward procedure is as follows (Arthur & Graziano, 1996): Reverse the answer values for the ten items with an asterisk (that is, for these items only, 1 = 9, 2 = 8, 3 = 7, 4 = 6, 5 = 5, 6 = 4, 7 = 3, 8 = 2, 9 = 1). Then add all 20 answer values. Arthur and Graziano (1996) report a mean score of 123.11 for a sample of college students, with a standard deviation of 23.99.

Scale: *Big Five Factor Markers for Conscientiousness*

Source: Goldberg (1992)

Criticism and Limitations of the Big Five Model

Although research on the five-factor model has produced impressively consistent findings and an unusually high level of agreement among personality researchers, the model is not without its critics. First, there is some debate about what the five factors mean (Digman, 1989; Digman & Inouye, 1986; Westen, 1996). For example, these factors may simply represent five dimensions built into our language. That is, although personality may in reality have a very different structure, our ability to describe personality traits is limited to the adjectives available in our language, which may fall into five primary categories. It also may be the case that our cognitive ability to organize information about ourselves and others is limited to these five dimensions. Thus, although people may describe personality as if all traits can be subsumed under five factors, this model may not accurately capture the complexities and subtleties of human personality.

In response to these concerns, many researchers have looked at the structure of personality among people who speak languages other than English (Benet-Martinez & John, 1998; Church, Reyes, Katigbak, & Grimm, 1997; Digman & Shmelyov, 1996; Katigbak, Church, Guanzon-Lapena, Carlota, & del Pilar, 2002; McCrae & Costa, 1997; Paunonen, Jackson, Trzebinski, & Forsterling, 1992; Saucier & Goldberg, 2001; Somer & Goldberg, 1999; Yang & Bond, 1990). Although a few exceptions to the rule are found, the results from numerous studies indicate that the five-factor model does not merely reflect the structure of the English language but appears to be a universal pattern for describing personality.

Second, there remains some disagreement about the structure of the five-factor model of personality. For example, some factor analytic studies find patterns that do not fit well within the five-factor structure (Block, 1995; Waller & Ben-Porath, 1987). Researchers sometimes find three or four factors, and sometimes as many as seven (Church, 1994; Church & Burke, 1994; Di Blas & Forzi, 1999; Zuckerman, Kuhlman, Joireman, Teta, & Kraft, 1993). Hans Eysenck, whose work is described in Chapter 9, promoted a model of personality with three main factors. One investigation suggested the Big Five may actually reflect just two super factors (Digman, 1997). This confusion has led some psychologists to refer to "The Big Five, plus or minus two" (Briggs, 1989).

Some of the confusion about the number of personality dimensions goes back to the question of what kind of data to include in the factor analysis (McCrae & Costa, 1995). For example, most studies finding five factors do not include traits that are evaluative, such as *special* or *immoral*. When these terms are included, researchers sometimes find two additional personality factors. These investigators refer to this new factor structure as the "Big Seven" (Almagor, Tellegen, & Waller, 1995; Benet-Martinez & Waller, 1997). Beyond this, a few personality descriptors simply do not fit well within the five-factor model. These maverick traits include *religiousness, youthfulness, frugality, humor,* and *cunning* (MacDonald, 2000; Paunonen & Jackson, 2000; Piedmont, 1999; Saucier & Goldberg, 1998).

Other researchers point out that even when five factors emerge from factor analytic studies, they do not always look the same when one study is compared to another. Indeed, researchers disagree on what to call some of the factors. This has prompted some critics to ask, *Which* Big Five? In response to this criticism, proponents have argued that the similarities between the factors uncovered using different methods and different populations are really quite remarkable (John, 1990; McCrae, 2001). Indeed, one would be hard-pressed to find many examples within the field of personality research of such consistent findings.

Third, the five-factor model has been criticized for being atheoretical (Briggs, 1989; H. J. Eysenck, 1997). That is, researchers did not anticipate ahead of time how many factors they would generate from their factor analytic studies or what those factors might be. As described in Chapter 2, this lack of prediction beforehand leaves the results of the research open to any number of explanations. Some personality theorists speculate that there may be evolutionary reasons for the development of five major dimensions of personality; others have guessed that the five factors relate to some kind of neurological structure. But because these hypotheses were generated after the results of the research were seen, researchers have no evidence to explain why these particular factors emerge in their research.

Nonetheless, if personality researchers continue to find evidence for the five-dimension model of personality, would this mean that trait theorists would be better off examining only five main traits instead of the hundreds they now investigate? The answer is no. In most cases, examining a specific trait is more useful for predicting behavior than measuring a global personality dimension (Mershon & Gorsuch, 1988; Paunonen, 1998; Paunonen & Ashton, 2001a, 2001b). For example, being sociable and being adventurous may be part of the larger personality concept of Extraversion. However, if researchers want to understand how people act in social situations, it is probably more useful to examine their sociability scores than to measure only the more general dimension of Extraversion. This is exactly what researchers found when they looked at cooperative and competitive behavior (Wolfe & Kasmer, 1988). Although Extraversion scores predicted who would act cooperatively and who would act competitively, researchers obtained even better predictions when they looked at scores for sociability.

Another example makes the point even clearer. Scales designed to measure the Big Five personality dimensions usually combine subscales measuring anxiety with subscales measuring depression as part of the global dimension Neuroticism (Briggs, 1989). Although it makes sense that both anxiety and depression contribute to this larger dimension, surely psychotherapists and researchers will want to know which of these emotional difficulties their clients and participants are suffering from. This is not to say that understanding where an individual falls on the basic five dimensions is not useful. On the contrary, research suggests that the Big Five model can be valuable for diagnosing clinical disorders and working with therapy patients (Costa & Widiger, 1994; O'Connor & Dyce, 2001; Reynolds & Clark, 2001; Trull, Widiger, & Burr, 2001) and for identifying problem health behaviors (Booth-Kewley & Vickers, 1994; Marshall, Wortman, Vickers, Kusulas, & Hervig, 1994). In addition, as you will see later in this chapter, how people score on measures of the Big Five dimensions is often related to how they perform on the job.

The Situation Versus Trait Controversy

The trait concept has come a long way since Allport's early battles to gain acceptance for the theory among the psychologists of his day. Trait measures have been embraced by psychologists from nearly every perspective and used by professionals working in a wide variety of settings. Since World War II, psychologists in mental health settings have relied on trait scores as a primary basis for diagnosing psychological disorders. Patients admitted to mental health facilities often spend several hours taking tests that yield scores on a variety of traitlike measures. Educators became enchanted with achievement and aptitude measures that could be used to classify children and to identify problem cases. Anyone who has gone through the American education system in recent years can recall hours of such tests, often beginning in the first grade. And for several decades now, academic personality researchers have been busy developing trait measures and correlating scores with a number of behaviors. In short, personality trait measurement has become a widely used psychological tool.

Criticism of the Trait Approach

Unfortunately, along with the widespread use of personality measurement came the possibility of abuse. One psychologist in particular criticized the way many psychologists were using and interpreting test scores. Walter Mischel (1968) pointed out that too many psychologists relied on one or two test scores to make important decisions, such as psychiatric diagnoses and whether an individual should be imprisoned. He argued there was no empirical evidence demonstrating that personality tests could accurately predict such behaviors. "On the basis of very little behavior sampling, all sorts of behaviors were predicted," Mischel wrote. "And key decisions were made about people's fate" (1983, p. 580).

"Can personality psychologists predict behavior? Yes, of course we can—sometimes."
WALTER MISCHEL

Although critics have accused Mischel of denying the existence of personality traits, he argues that this was never his point (Mischel, 1973, 1979, 1983, 1990). Mischel maintains his complaint is with the overinterpretation of personality test scores. He argues that trait measures, as well as other types of test scores, do not predict behavior as well as many psychologists claim. For this reason, heavy reliance on these scores when predicting future behavior cannot be justified. In addition, Mischel argues there is little evidence for consistency of behavior across situations. A person who is outspoken or courageous in one situation might be meek and cowardly in another. Let's look at each of these criticisms in depth.

Trait Measures Do Not Predict Behavior Well. At the heart of this argument is the issue of whether personality or the situation determines your behavior. Do you act the way you do because of the situation you are in or the kind of person you are? Advocates on one extreme side of this debate argue that the situation determines behavior almost exclusively. Although these psychologists don't assert that everyone acts the same in a given situation, they often refer to individual differences in behavior as merely "error variance." Advocates on the other extreme claim that stable individual differences are the primary determinants of how we act.

Early in this debate, some psychologists sought an answer to the person-versus-situation question by measuring how well personality scores and how well situations predict people's behavior. Typically, this research found that both the person and the situation were related to behavior and that knowing about personality and the situation was better than having information about only one (Endler & Hunt, 1966, 1968). Unfortunately, this approach has a major weakness. The results of any such investigation are limited by the type of situation and the kind of personality variable examined. For example, we can think of situations in which nearly all people react the same. It would be absurd to try to predict whether high- or low-self-esteem people will run outside when a building catches on fire. Although the situation would account for nearly all of the variance in this case, it also would be incorrect to conclude that differences in self-esteem are therefore not related to behavior. Self-esteem simply doesn't predict behavior in this situation. However, if we look at other behaviors in other situations, such as how people react to criticism, we will probably find large differences between high- and low-self-esteem people.

Today, most psychologists agree that the person and the situation interact to determine behavior (Endler & Magnusson, 1976; Magnusson, 1990). Knowing that a person is high in aggressiveness or that a particular situation is frustrating does not help researchers predict behavior as well as knowing both of these facts. Thus, although people high in aggressiveness may be more prone to act aggressively than those scoring low on this dimension, and frustrating situations are more likely to produce aggression than are nonfrustrating situations, researchers would expect the highest amount of aggression when an aggressive person is placed in a frustrating situation. This way of looking at the relationship among traits, situations, and behaviors is called the **person-by-situation** approach.

Nonetheless, arguments remain over the validity of using personality trait scores to predict behavior. Mischel (1968) pointed out that personality trait scores rarely correlate with measures of behavior above the .30 or .40 correlation coefficient level. This "personality coefficient," as it is derogatorily called, statistically accounts for only about 10% of the variance in behavior. Although these numbers confirm that personality is related to behavior, there remains a considerable amount of behavior that single trait scores do not explain.

There Is Little Evidence for Cross-Situational Consistency. In one of the earliest studies on personality traits, a research team spent several years looking at honesty in more than 8,000 elementary school children (Hartshorne & May, 1928). They measured honesty 23 different ways (lying, cheating, stealing, and so on) and found an average intercorrelation among these measures of only .23. Because personality traits are assumed to show some consistency across situations, this finding was widely cited as a challenge to the trait approach. Knowing that a child is honest in one situation, such as telling the truth to a parent, may reveal little about whether the child will cheat on the playground or steal something from another child's desk.

Mischel also challenges the evidence for cross-situational consistency in traits (Mischel & Peake, 1982, 1983). Although people appear to show fairly strong consistency in behavior across situations, Mischel refers to this as "more apparent than real." For many reasons, we tend to see consistent behavior that, on close examination, is not really there (Nisbett & Ross, 1980). For example, people often see what they expect to see. If you expect Karen to be unfriendly, you tend to notice when she insults someone but ignore the times when she pays a compliment. In addition, we typically see people in only one type of situation or role and fail to fully realize the extent to which the situation, not the person, is responsible for the behavior. For example, students are sometimes surprised to find that their stuffy, conservative professor is a fun-loving, adventurous person outside the classroom. Sometimes the way we treat people causes them to act more consistently than they otherwise might. If you assume Ron is going to be hostile, you will probably approach him in such a confrontational way that he will react with hostility. For all of these reasons, we may see people acting more consistently across situations than they really are.

In Defense of Personality Traits

Naturally, attacks on something as central to personality theory as the use of traits have not gone unchallenged. Responses to Mischel's criticisms center around the question of how behaviors and traits are measured and the importance of the percentage of variance these traits explain.

Measuring Behavior. Proponents of the trait approach argue that, on the surface, denying the existence of personality traits is absurd (Epstein, 1980, 1983, 1986). If behavior were completely inconsistent over time and across situations, how would we know who to marry or who to hire? Without predictable behavior patterns, we might as well marry someone at random because our spouse's behavior will change from day to day depending on the situation.

Trait psychologists argue that researchers often fail to produce strong links between personality traits and behavior because they don't measure behavior correctly. The typical investigation held up by the critics uses trait scores to predict only one measure of behavior. For example, investigators might measure the number of minutes spent on an activity or ask people to indicate on a 7-point scale the likelihood that they will volunteer for a charity drive. This approach violates a basic concept in psychological testing. A behavior score based on one item or one measure is so low in reliability that it is almost impossible to find a correlation with any test score higher than the .30 to .40 "personality coefficient."

To understand this principle, think about why a final examination would never consist of just one true-false question. A student who knows the material might miss one particular item for any number of reasons. But over the course of, say, 50 items, the student who knows the material is likely to get a higher score than the student who does not. In psychometric terms, the 50-item test has a greater internal consistency (Chapter 2) and is thus a better indicator of the student's knowledge. Unfortunately, at the time Mischel launched his attack, many trait studies measured behavior with what were essentially one-item tests. A personality trait may be a good predictor of behavior, but psychologists will never know if they don't measure behavior reliably.

As an alternative to one-item measurement, researchers can **aggregate data.** For example, if you want to measure how much time students spend studying, you'll obtain a much better score by observing their behavior each night over the course of a few weeks than by observing just one night. Consider a study in which scores on an extraversion-introversion scale were used to predict social behavior (Epstein, 1979). College students in this study recorded the number of social contacts they initiated each day. Although we would expect extraverts to initiate more social contacts than introverts, the researchers found an insignificant correlation between any one day's total of social contacts and extraversion scores. However, when the researchers looked at the relation between the scale score and the student's two-week total of initiated social contacts, they found an impressive correlation of .52.

Identifying Relevant Traits. Another reason personality trait measures usually fail to break the .30 to .40 barrier is that researchers may be looking at the wrong traits. Recall Allport's distinction between central and secondary traits. A trait is more likely to predict a person's behavior if that trait is important, or central, for the person. For example, suppose you were interested in the trait *independence.* You might give an independence scale to a large number of people, and then correlate the scores with how independently people acted in some subsequent situation. But in doing this, you probably would group together those people for whom independence is an important (central) trait and those for whom it is a relatively unimportant (secondary) trait. You undoubtedly would do better predicting independent behavior by limiting your sample to people who consider independence an important personality dimension. By including people for whom the trait is only secondary, you dilute the correlation between the trait score and the behavior (Britt & Shepperd, 1999).

To illustrate this problem, researchers identified people who were either fairly consistent or relatively inconsistent in two kinds of behavior, friendliness and conscientiousness (Bem & Allen, 1974). Some personality researchers refer to these two groups as *traited* and *untraited* people because the personality trait is either an important one for them or insignificant. The goal of this study was to predict six measures of friendly behavior (for example, how friendly the participant was while waiting for the experiment to begin) and six measures of conscientiousness (for example, how well the student kept up with class readings). As Table 7.4 shows, correlation coefficients obtained for high-consistency people and low-consistency people showed a noticeably different pattern. Correlations between measures of friendliness averaged .57 for the consistent (traited) participants, but only .27 for the inconsistent (untraited) ones. Similarly, correlations for the conscientiousness data averaged .45 for the high-consistency participants and .09 for the low-consistency people.

Other studies have produced similar findings (Baumeister, 1991; Britt, 1993; Reise & Waller, 1993; Siem, 1998). For example, researchers identified traited and

Table 7.4   Mean Correlations between Trait Measures
in High- and Low-Consistency Participants

	High-Consistency Participants	Low-Consistency Participants
Friendliness Measures		
Self-report	.57	.39
Mother's report	.59	.30
Father's report	.60	.16
Peer's report	.54	.37
Group discussion	.52	.37
Spontaneous friendliness	.59	.01
All friendliness variables	*.57*	*.27*
Conscientiousness Measures		
Self-report	.41	.11
Mother's report	.56	.10
Father's report	.49	.22
Peer's report	.49	.16
Returning evaluations	.40	.06
Course readings	.32	−.12
All conscientiousness variables	*.45*	*.09*

Source: Adapted from Bem and Allen (1974); reprinted by approval of Daryl J. Bem.

untraited people on the extent to which they generally felt in control of the events in their lives (called *locus of control*—Chapter 14). Participants were then presented with a video game requiring them to maneuver an airplane through a race-course. When the investigators correlated trait scores for all participants with how many practice trials the participants took, they found a nonsignificant .09 correlation. However, when the researchers looked at just the participants for whom the trait was fairly consistent, they found a correlation of .50 (Baumeister & Tice, 1988). These findings demonstrate that personality trait measures can be strong predictors of behavior, but only if the trait is relevant or, in Allport's terms, a central trait for the individual.

The Importance of 10% of the Variance. Another argument on the side of personality traits concerns the significance of .30 to .40 correlation coefficients. Critics have attacked trait theory on the basis of the weak relationship between trait measures and behavior. But how high does a correlation have to be before it is considered important? One team of researchers answered this question by looking at several social-psychological (situation-focused) investigations often cited for their "important" findings (Funder & Ozer, 1983). The researchers converted the data from these studies into correlation coefficients and found that they ranged from .36 to .42. Similar results are obtained when researchers look at the typical correlation between, for example, attitudes and behavior (Kraus, 1995). In other words, the "important" effects of these situational variables are, statistically speaking, no more important than the effects deemed weak by critics of personality traits.

Yet another way to examine the importance of such correlations is to compare the amount of variance accounted for in personality research with the typical results from other fields. For example, one psychologist examined some highly acclaimed research in the field of medicine (Rosenthal, 1990). One large medical study he examined made headlines when researchers found that aspirin significantly reduced the risk of heart attacks. In fact, the investigators ended the experiment earlier than planned because the results were so clear. To continue to give one group of patients placebo pills instead of aspirin would have been unethical. Obviously, the researchers considered this an important finding. Yet when we examine the data, we find that the medical researchers were dealing with a correlation of around .03 that accounted for less than 1% of the variance!

The point is that importance is a subjective judgment. When dealing with medical treatments, reliably saving a relatively small number of lives is important. When trying to predict behavior from personality test scores, we must remember that most of the behaviors we are interested in are determined by a large number of causes. No one will ever discover a single cause for why people suffer from schizophrenia or why consumers buy one product over another. Rather, the goal of most studies is to account for *some* of the variance in these behaviors. When we think about all the complex influences on our behavior, we probably should be impressed that personality psychologists can explain even 10%.

Current Status of the Trait Debate

Although the fervor has declined in recent years, the appropriate use of personality trait measures remains a topic of discussion (Wiggins, 1997). The trait approach is as strong as it has ever been. Nevertheless, critics can be credited for alerting psychologists to inappropriate uses of trait scores. Many psychologists now examine information from a number of relevant sources before making diagnoses or recommending a certain type of education program.

Another positive outcome of the debate is the attention that has been drawn to the issues of data aggregation and the identification of relevant traits, although just how much these procedures will be used in future research remains to be seen. The ongoing discussion about traits should also fuel a continued search for more sophisticated and better methods for measuring individual differences.

Application: The Big Five in the Workplace

Imagine you own your own business and have to make a quick hiring decision. You have five applications on your desk, all nearly identical. You notice that each applicant's file includes some personality test scores. Specifically, you have scores for each job candidate on each of the Big Five personality dimensions. A quick glance through the applications tells you that each applicant has one score that distinguishes him or her from the rest of the pack. One applicant is high in Extraversion, another scored very low on Neuroticism, and one is notably high in Openness. Predictably, another applicant is especially high in Agreeableness, whereas the final applicant's distinguishing score is his or her high level of Conscientiousness. Time is running out, and you have to make your decision based on this information alone. Looking back at the descriptions of the Big Five factors on pages 179–180, which of these five people do you suppose you will hire? Of course, the answer to the question depends on the kind of job and many other important variables. But if you had to make a quick decision based on this limited amount of information, you might consider a growing body of research that points to the best answer.

Employers have used scores from personality tests to make hiring and promotion decisions for many years (Hogan, 1991). And for just about the same length of time, critics have complained that employers misuse and misinterpret personality test scores when making these decisions. Just as Mischel criticized clinical psychologists for relying too heavily on test scores to make diagnoses about psychological disorders, these critics point to research indicating low correlations between test scores and job performance (Reilly & Chao, 1982; Schmidt, Gooding, Noe, & Kirsch, 1984).

Although researchers have debated the value of using personality tests to predict success in the workplace for a long time, this debate changed with the development of the Big Five model (Goldberg, 1993; Landy, Shankster, & Kohler, 1994). Rather than examine a large number of personality variables that may or may not be related to how well people perform their jobs, many researchers now address the question of personality and job performance by using the five larger personality dimensions identified in the Big Five model. The findings from that research provide much stronger evidence for the relationship between personality and job performance than had been previously demonstrated (Tett, Jackson, & Rothstein, 1991).

So, which of the five applicants is likely to make the best employee? Although a case can be made for each of the five, a great deal of research indicates that, of the Big Five factors, Conscientiousness may be the best predictor of job performance (Barrick & Mount, 1991; Barrick, Mount, & Judge, 2001; Hurtz & Donovan, 2000; Salgado, 1997). To understand why, we need only look at some of the characteristics that make up this personality dimension. People who score high in Conscientiousness are said to be careful, thorough, and dependable. That is, they don't rush through a job, but rather take their time to do the job correctly and completely. Highly conscientious people tend to be organized and lay out plans before starting a big project. These individuals also are hardworking, persistent, and achievement oriented.

It's not difficult to see why people who exhibit this combination of traits make great employees. For example, researchers in one study looked at the way sales representatives for a large appliance manufacturer did their jobs (Barrick, Mount, & Strauss, 1993). As in other studies, the investigators found Conscientiousness scores were fairly good predictors of how many appliances the employees sold. But a closer examination of the work styles of these salespeople helped to explain their success. Highly conscientious workers set higher goals for themselves than did the other employees. Thus, from the beginning, they had their eyes on fairly ambitious end-of-the-year sales figures. In addition, these highly conscientious salespeople were more committed to reaching their goals than other workers. That is, they were more likely to expend extra effort to hit their targets and were more persistent when faced with the inevitable obstacles and downturns that got in their way.

In short, there are many reasons why a person high in Conscientiousness would make an excellent employee. As one team of investigators put it, "It is difficult to conceive of a job in which the traits associated with the Conscientiousness dimension would not contribute to job success" (Barrick & Mount, 1991, pp. 21–22). And these efforts do not go unnoticed. Highly conscientious employees typically receive higher evaluations from their supervisors (Barrick et al., 1993). Moreover, one study found that workers who scored high on Conscientiousness were among the least likely to lose their jobs when companies were forced to lay off some of their employees (Barrick, Mount, & Strauss, 1994). Little surprise that highly conscientious people do better in college (Paunonen & Ashton, 2001a) and in their careers (Judge, Higgins, Thoresen, & Barrick, 1999) than others.

This is not to say that Conscientiousness is the only Big Five dimension related to job performance. On the contrary, a strong case can be made for hiring people high in Agreeableness (Tett et al., 1991). These people are trusting, cooperative, and helpful. They are pleasant to have around the office and probably work especially well in jobs calling for teamwork. Others studies indicate that extraverts often have an edge in the business world over introverts and that openness to experience can be beneficial in some job settings (Barrick & Mount, 1991; Caldwell & Burger, 1998; Mount, Barrick, & Strauss, 1994; Tett et al., 1991). In short, knowing where an applicant falls on the Big Five personality dimensions may be useful information when making a hiring decision.

Nonetheless, one caveat is in order. Although the research relating Big Five personality characteristics and job performance has been encouraging, it would be an egregious oversimplification to conclude that one should always hire the person highest in Conscientiousness. Personality may account for a significant proportion of job performance variance, but it is only one of many important variables that contribute to how well an individual performs his or her job. Just as it is inappropriate to base decisions about mental health or education solely on personality test scores, making hiring and promotion decisions on test score data alone is unwise and unfair.

Assessment: Self-Report Inventories

It is unlikely you have reached college age without taking a number of self-report inventories. You may have received interest and abilities tests from a counselor, achievement and aptitude tests from a teacher, or personality and diagnostic inventories from a therapist. You may have even tried a few of those magazine quizzes for your own entertainment and curiosity. Self-report inventories are more widely used than any other form of personality assessment. Typically, these are pencil-and-paper tests that ask people to respond to questions about themselves. Relatively simple scoring procedures allow the tester to generate a score or set of scores that can be compared with others along a trait continuum. Hundreds of self-report inventories have appeared over the past 50 years, some carefully constructed with attention to reliability and validity, others not.

Self-report inventories are popular among professional psychologists for several reasons. They can be given in groups and can be administered quickly and easily by someone with relatively little training. Contrast this with the Rorschach inkblot test, which must be administered and interpreted by a trained psychologist one test at a time. Scoring a self-report inventory is also relatively easy and objective. Researchers typically count matched items or total response values. In addition, self-report measures usually have greater face validity than other instruments. That is, we can be reasonably sure from looking at the items on a self-esteem test that they actually measure self-esteem. Although face validity alone does not establish the value of a test (Chapter 2), psychologists are less likely to disagree about what the test is measuring when the intent of the items is so obvious.

Self-report inventories come in all forms and sizes. Some have fewer than 10 items, others more than 500. Some provide detailed computer analyses on a number of subscales and comparison groups, others a single score for a specific trait dimension. They are used by researchers investigating individual differences on a specific trait dimension, personnel managers making hiring decisions, and clinical psychologists getting a quick profile of their client's personality to aid in making diagnoses.

The Minnesota Multiphasic Personality Inventory

The prototypic self-report inventory used by clinical psychologists is the Minnesota Multiphasic Personality Inventory (MMPI). The original MMPI was developed in the late 1930s. A revised version of the scale, the MMPI-2, was published in 1989. A large number of clinical psychologists, counseling psychologists, personnel psychologists, and school psychologists give the MMPI-2 regularly to their patients and clients.

The MMPI-2 contains 567 true-false items. These items generate several scale scores that are combined to form an overall profile of the test taker. The original scales were designed to measure psychological disorders. Thus, psychologists obtain scores for such dimensions as *depression, hysteria, paranoia,* and *schizophrenia.* However, most psychologists look at the overall pattern of scores rather than one specific scale when making their assessments. Of particular interest are scores that are significantly higher or lower than those obtained by most test takers. A sample profile is shown in Figure 7.2.

Many additional scales have been developed since the original MMPI scales were presented. Researchers interested in a particular disorder or concept usually determine those items that separate a normal population from the group they are interested in. For example, to develop a creativity scale, you would identify those test items that highly creative people tend to answer differently from people who are not very creative.

For many years, the MMPI (and now the MMPI-2) has ranked among the most widely used clinical assessment tools (Camara, Nathan, & Puente, 2000; Piotrowski & Keller, 1989; Watkins, Campbell, Nieberding, & Hallmark, 1995). One survey found nearly universal agreement among directors of graduate programs in clinical psychology that the MMPI-2 should be part of a clinical student's training (Piotrowski & Zalewski, 1993). The scale has also been used in an enormous amount of research (Butcher & Rouse, 1996). However, this does not mean the MMPI-2 is without its critics. Psychologists continue to debate the validity of the some of the scales, the appropriateness of some of the norm data provided by the test makers, and the nature of some of the constructs the test is designed to measure, among other issues (Helmes & Reddon, 1993). As you will see in the following section, scores from self-report inventories are not as easy to interpret as the seemingly precise and objective numbers generated from these tests sometimes suggest.

Problems with Self-Report Inventories

Despite their widespread use, self-report inventories have several limitations that need to be considered when constructing a scale or interpreting test scores. Researchers who use self-report inventories still must depend on the participants' ability and willingness to provide accurate information about themselves. Sometimes these inaccuracies can be identified and test scores discarded, but more often the misinformation probably goes undetected. Clinical psychologists who rely too heavily on self-report measures run the risk of making inaccurate assessments of their clients' mental health (Shedler, Mayman, & Manis, 1993).

Faking. Sometimes test takers intentionally give misleading information on self-report inventories. For example, some people "fake good" when taking a test. This

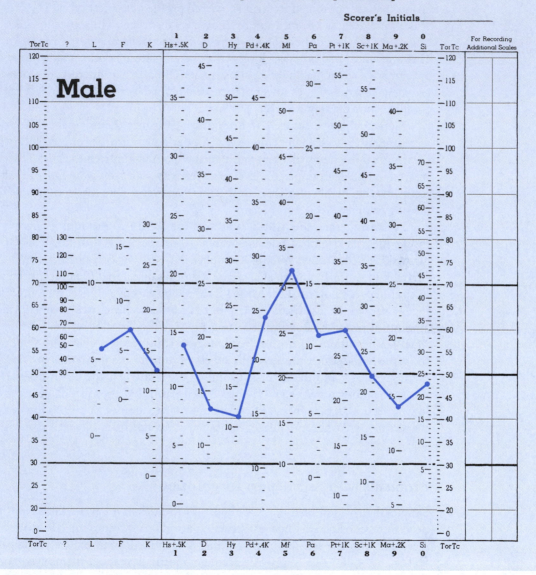

Figure 7.2

Sample MMPI Profile

The scales identified by numbers 1 through 0 are Hypochondriasis, Depression, Hysteria, Psychopathic Deviancy, Masculinity-Femininity, Paranoia, Psychasthenia (anxiety), Schizophrenia, Mania, and Social Introversion.

Reprinted by permission of the University of Minnesota Press.

means they try to present themselves as better than they really are. Such a strategy is not uncommon when scales are used to make employment decisions (Rosse, Stecher, Miller, & Levin, 1998). Why would people admit something negative about themselves if an employer is using that information to decide who to hire? On the other hand, sometimes people are motivated to "fake bad." These test takers want to make themselves look worse than they really are. For example, someone who wants to escape to a "safe" hospital environment might attempt to come across as having psychological problems.

What can a tester do in these cases? Basically, important decisions probably should not be made on test data alone. An employer would be foolish to promote a worker who scored high on a leadership measure if that person had never shown leadership qualities in five years of employment. Beyond this, test makers sometimes build safeguards into tests to reduce faking. If possible, the purpose of a test can be made less obvious, and filler items can be added to throw the test taker off track. However, these efforts are probably, at most, only partially successful. Another option is to test for faking directly (Bagby, Rogers, Nicholson, Buis, Seeman, & Rector, 1997; Nicholson, Mouton, Bagby, Buis, Peterson, & Buigas, 1997). Like many large personality inventories, the MMPI contains scales designed to detect faking. To create these scales, test makers compared responses of people instructed to fake good or fake bad with the responses of other populations. The test makers found certain items that distinguish between fakers and, for example, genuine schizophrenics. People trying to look schizophrenic tend to check these items, thinking they indicate a psychological disorder. But real schizophrenics do not. When testers detect fakers, they can either throw out the results or adjust the scores to account for the faking tendency. However, some psychologists challenge the usefulness of relying on such methods to obtain accurate scores (Piedmont, McCrae, Riemann, & Angleitner, 2000).

Carelessness and Sabotage. Although the person administering a test usually approaches the testing very seriously, this cannot always be said for the test taker. Participants in experiments and newly admitted patients can get bored with long tests and not bother to read the test items carefully. Sometimes they don't want to admit to poor reading skills or their failure to fully understand the instructions. As a result of these motivation and comprehension problems, some or all of the responses will be made at random or after only very briefly skimming the question. And these problems are not limited to poorly educated individuals. Researchers in one study allowed university students taking a standard personality test to indicate when they did not know the meaning of a word (Graziano, Jensen-Campbell, Steele, & Hair, 1998). The investigators found that some test questions were not understood by as many as 32% of the students.

Even worse, test takers sometimes report frivolous or intentionally incorrect information to sabotage the research project or diagnosis. I once found a test answer booklet that appeared normal at first, but at second glance discovered that the test taker had spent the hour-long research session filling in answer spaces to form

In the News

Using Personality to Predict Athletic Performance

Decades of research findings allow personality psychologists to draw a number of conclusions. We now know that individual differences are better thought of as traits on a continuum than as distinct types. We also know that personality scores are useful only when predicting relevant behaviors. Thus, extraversion scores predict social behavior, but are not very useful when asking how organized and planful a person is. After much debate, researchers also recognize that behavior is the result of many factors, and that personality can account for only a small percentage of the differences seen in any given behavior. We also know that personality assessment is difficult. Developing reliable and valid measures requires extensive testing and sophisticated statistical analysis.

These lessons have not been lost on many professionals who use personality tests. Most clinical psychologists and educators understand that test scores provide only a single bit of information that must be used alongside data from many other sources before making decisions about diagnosis, treatment, and classification. Business professionals have learned the same lesson when using personality scores for hiring and promotion decisions. More recently, sports psychologists have recognized that personality also plays a role in athletic performance. Decades of basic research have shown these psychologists the appropriate use of personality scores when predicting behavior. They appreciate that many factors besides personality contribute to success in sports, and that developing appropriate and psychometrically sound measures is an ongoing challenge.

But this is not always the case. Consider a recent craze among some professional athletes. It's called *brain typing,* a procedure developers claim can identify which young players will become the stars of tomorrow (Hale, 2002; "A doctor in the house," 2002). The assessment procedure was developed by Jonathan Niednagel, who calls himself "the brain doctor," although his formal education consists of a bachelor's degree in finance. Niednagel is the founder and director of the Brain Type Institute. According to brain typing advocates, there are 16 types of people. These types are, in fact, the 16 used in the Myers-Briggs Type Indicator (Chapter 5). As with other typologies, all people are said to fall into one and only one of these type categories. Moreover, Niednagel doesn't use written tests to determine which type a person is. He simply watches and sometimes talks to the person before rendering his decision. Sometimes all he needs is a few minutes of videotape or a short phone conversation (Hale, 2002). "I can watch guys run up and down the floor . . . and tell you how their minds work," Niednagel says (in Aschburner, 2001). According to the Brain Type Institute Web page, within the next few years, Niednagel expects to develop a blood test that will determine personality type from DNA.

Not surprising, people with a basic understanding of personality traits and measurement find the whole brain typing notion amusing. Professional psychol-

(continues)

Using Personality to Predict Athletic Performance (continued)

ogists who have examined Niednagel's claims are very skeptical (Carree, 2002). And, as this book went to press, not one study on brain typing had been published in any academic journal. However, few coaches, general managers, and owners have a background in psychology. Perhaps this is why Niednagel has been hired by several professional sports teams to help with drafting and personnel decisions. The list now includes teams from the National Basketball Association, the National Football League, and major league baseball as well as some college sports teams. "If I was ever a general manager in any sport," said former Phoenix Suns coach Danny Ainge, "[Niednagel] would be my first hire, because he would give me an advantage that no one else would have." Of course, the Brain Type Institute offers a number of other products and services for professional and nonprofessional athletes, for a price.

In addition, although personality researchers recognize that personality traits are useful only when predicting relevant behaviors, brain typing advocates make no such claims. According to the Brain Type Institute Web page, "much research has led to exceptional success" when applying brain typing to areas other than athletic performance. The list includes (but is not limited to) business hiring, leadership, enhancing sales, better learning in school, correcting learning disorders, weight loss, harmony within families, disciplining children, communication in relationships, showing love in romantic relationships, identifying criminals, enhanced spiritual awareness, and a better understanding of God.

Source: Lockard and Paulhus (1988).

obscene words. A similar lack of cooperation is not uncommon among those who resent medical personnel or law enforcement officials.

The best defense against this problem may be to explain instructions thoroughly, stress the importance of the test, and maintain some kind of surveillance throughout the testing session. Beyond this, tests can be constructed to detect carelessness. For example, some tests present items more than once. The tester examines the repeated items to determine if the test taker is answering consistently. A person who responds A one time and B the next when answering two identical items might not be reading the item or might be sabotaging the test.

Response Tendencies. Before reading this section, you may want to take the test presented on page 198. This test is designed to measure a response tendency called **social desirability**—the extent to which people present themselves in a favorable light. This is not the same as faking, in which people answer test items in a manner they know is inaccurate. People high in social desirability unintentionally present themselves in a way that is slightly more favorable than the truth. A look at the items on the scale illustrates the point. For example, few of us can say we have never covered up our mistakes. Yet someone who tries to meet this standard might

Assessing Your Own Personality

Response Tendencies

Indicate the extent to which you agree with each of the following statements. Use a 7-point scale to indicate your response, with 1 = Not True and 7 = Very True.

_____   1. I sometimes tell lies if I have to.*

_____   2. I never cover up my mistakes.

_____   3. There have been occasions when I have taken advantage of someone.*

_____   4. I never swear.

_____   5. I sometimes try to get even rather than forgive and forget.*

_____   6. I always obey laws, even if I'm unlikely to get caught.

_____   7. I have said something bad about a friend behind his or her back.*

_____   8. When I hear people talking privately, I avoid listening.

_____   9. I have received too much change from a salesperson without telling him or her.*

_____   10. I always declare everything at customs.

_____   11. When I was young, I sometimes stole things.*

_____   12. I have never dropped litter on the street.

_____   13. I sometimes drive faster than the speed limit.*

_____   14. I never read sexy books or magazines.

_____   15. I have done things that I don't tell other people about.*

_____   16. I never take things that don't belong to me.

_____   17. I have taken sick-leave from work or school even though I wasn't really sick.*

_____   18. I have never damaged a library book or store merchandise without reporting it.

_____   19. I have some pretty awful habits.*

_____   20. I don't gossip about other people's business.

This scale was designed to detect a social desirability response tendency. To obtain your score, give yourself one point for each 1 or 2 response to an odd-numbered item (the ones with asterisks) and one point for each 6 or 7 response to an even-numbered item. The test developer found a mean score of 4.9 and a standard deviation of 3.2 for female college students, and a mean score of 4.3 and a standard deviation of 3.1 for male college students. People who score high on this measure tend to present themselves in an overly favorable light.

Scale: *The Impression Management Scale from the Balanced Inventory of Desirable Responding*

Source: Paulhus (1984, 1991)

exaggerate the truth slightly and indicate that this is true for him or her. What can be done about this? By measuring social desirability tendencies directly, a tester can adjust the interpretation of other scores accordingly. However, some researchers have questioned whether this adjustment actually improves the validity of the scores (McCrae & Costa, 1983).

Social desirability scores are also useful when testing the discriminant validity of a new personality scale (Chapter 2). For example, suppose you developed a self-report inventory to measure the trait *friendliness*. Most of your items would be fairly straightforward, such as "Do you make a good friend?" High scores on this test might reflect an underlying trait of friendliness, but they might also reflect the test takers' desire to present themselves as nice people. For this reason, test makers often compare scores on their new inventory with scores on a social desirability measure. If the two are highly correlated, test makers have no way of knowing which of the two traits their test is measuring. However, if scores on your new friendliness inventory do not correlate highly with social desirability scores, you would have more confidence that high scorers are genuinely friendly and not just those who want to be seen that way.

But presenting oneself in a favorable light is not the only response tendency that testers have to worry about. Some people are more likely than others to agree with test questions. If you ask these people, "Do you work a little harder when given a difficult task?" they probably will say yes. If you ask them a little later, "Do you usually give up when you find a task difficult?" they probably will say yes again. This *acquiescence* (or *agreement*) *response* can translate into a problem on some self-report scales. For example, if the score for the trait is simply the number of "true" answers on a scale, someone with a strong acquiescence tendency would score high on the scale regardless of the content of the items. Moreover, people susceptible to an acquiescence response tendency tend to differ from other test takers on several personality dimensions (Knowles & Nathan, 1997). Thus, if not accounted for, the tendency for some people to agree with test items could distort the meaning of scores on the personality test. Just how seriously acquiescence response tendencies distort test scores is still a matter of debate (Nunnally, 1978; Paulhus, 1991). However, to be safe, many test makers word half the items in the opposite manner. That is, sometimes "true" is indicative of the trait, and sometimes "false" is. In this case, any tendency to agree or disagree with statements should not affect the test final score.

Strengths and Criticisms of the Trait Approach

In many ways the trait approach to personality is different from the other approaches examined in this book. Trait theorists tend to be academic researchers instead of therapists. Their focus is on describing and predicting behavior rather than on behavior change or development. In addition, trait researchers rarely try to understand the behavior of just one person. These differences give the trait approach some unique advantages, but they are also the source of criticism.

Strengths

The empirical nature of the work by Allport, Murray, and other early trait psychologists sets them apart from the founders of other personality theories. Rather than relying on intuition and subjective judgment like Freud and many of the neo-Freudians, these trait theorists used objective measures to examine their constructs. Some of these theorists, such as Cattell, specifically allowed the data to determine the theory, which was then subject to further empirical validation. This approach reduces some of the biases and subjectivity that plague other approaches.

Another strength of the trait approach is its many practical applications. Mental health workers routinely use trait measures when evaluating clients. Similarly, many educational psychologists have embraced trait measures in their work. Psychologists working in industrial and organizational settings often use personality trait measures in hiring and promotion decisions. Job counselors frequently rely on trait scores to match clients with careers. Although this widespread use of trait measures invites abuse if the scores are used incorrectly, the popularity of these measures attests to the value many psychologists place on them.

Like any important theoretical perspective, the trait approach has generated a large amount of research. Personality journals are filled with investigations about a variety of personality traits. Predicting behavior from personality trait measures has become a standard feature in research by clinical, social, industrial-organizational, educational, and developmental psychologists.

Criticisms

Criticisms of the trait approach are often based not so much on what the approach says but on what it leaves out. Trait psychologists describe people in terms of traits, but they often do not explain how these traits develop or what can be done to help people who suffer from extreme scores. For example, what do psychologists do for people who have extreme scores on measures of test anxiety, self-consciousness, and assertiveness? Knowing about these scores can help teachers and employers match people with the tasks and jobs best suited to them, but no schools of psychotherapy have originated from the trait approach. The failure of the trait approach to do more than identify potential problems limits its usefulness.

Another criticism concerns the lack of an agreed-upon framework. Although all trait theorists use empirical methods and are concerned with the identification of traits, no single theory or underlying structure ties all of the theories together. We can see the confusion this creates by asking how many basic traits there are. Murray reduced personality to 27 psychogenic needs. Cattell found somewhere between 16 and 20 basic elements of personality. And more recent investigations suggest the number is really five. Then again, other studies challenge this figure. Although research continues to determine which of these models is correct, without an agreed-upon framework, it is difficult to gain a cohesive overview of the approach or to see how research on one aspect of personality traits fits with research in other areas.

Summary

1. The trait approach assumes we can identify individual differences in behaviors that are relatively stable across situations and over time. Trait theorists are usually not concerned with any one person's behavior but rather in describing behavior typical of people at certain points along a trait continuum.

2. Gordon Allport was the first acknowledged trait theorist. Among his contributions were the notion of central and secondary traits, nomothetic versus idiographic research, functional autonomy, and the proprium. Henry Murray identified psychogenic needs as the basic elements of personality. According to Murray, a need will affect behavior depending on where it lies on a person's need hierarchy and the kind of situation the person is in.

3. Raymond Cattell was interested in identifying the basic structure of personality. He used a statistical procedure called factor analysis to determine how many basic traits make up human personality. More recent research provides fairly consistent evidence that personality is structured along five basic dimensions. Although questions remain, the evidence to date tends to support the five-factor model.

4. An enduring controversy in personality concerns the relative importance of traits compared to situational determinants of behavior. Critics charge that traits do not predict behavior well and that there is little evidence for cross-situational consistency. Trait advocates answer that if traits and behaviors are measured correctly, a significant relationship can be found. In addition, they maintain that the amount of behavior variance explained by traits is considerable and important.

5. The recent development of the five-factor model has renewed interest in the relationship between personality and job performance. Although several of the Big Five dimensions are related to performance in the business world, many studies indicate that Conscientiousness may be the best predictor of performance.

6. Trait researchers typically rely on self-report assessment procedures in their work. One of the most commonly used self-report inventories is the Minnesota Multiphasic Personality Inventory. Test users need to be aware of problems inher-

ent in self-report inventories. These include faking, carelessness and sabotage, and response tendencies.

7.   Like other approaches to personality, the trait approach has strengths and criticisms. The strengths include a strong empirical base, a host of practical applications, and the large amount of research generated. Criticisms include the limited usefulness of the approach for dealing with problem behaviors and the lack of an agreed-upon framework.

InfoTrac College Edition Key Terms

For additional readings go to http://www.infotrac-college.com/wadsworth and enter a search term related to your interest. Use the key terms suggested here to pull up several related articles. Also see the text Web site at http://psychology .wadsworth.com for more suggested readings and interactive quizzes to test your knowledge.

Acquiescence response
Agreeableness
Authoritarianism (personality trait)
Extraversion
Minnesota Multiphasic Personality
   Inventory

Neuroticism
Social desirability
Trait

Chapter 8

The Trait Approach

Relevant Research

Achievement Motivation

Type A-Type B Behavior Patterns

Social Anxiety

Emotions

Optimism and Pessimism

Summary

In preparing this chapter, I paused to conduct a brief, partially scientific survey. I examined the last three issues of the *Journal of Personality,* the *Journal of Research in Personality,* and the personality section of the *Journal of Personality and Social Psychology.* These journals are prominent outlets for current research on personality. Of the 45 articles with empirical studies I found in these journals, I counted 40 that included at least one trait measure. That is, in 88.9% of these studies, researchers measured individual differences and used these scores either to compare people who fell on different parts of a trait continuum or to predict scores on another measure. This finding supports an assertion I have made for a while—the trait approach has become so entrenched in personality research today that for many psychologists, personality research is synonymous with the measurement and examination of traits. The use of trait measures has become so widespread that it is part of the research arsenal for experimenters from all of the approaches to personality covered in this book. In addition, if you were to conduct a similar survey of research journals in developmental psychology, social psychology, clinical psychology, industrial-organizational psychology, and other fields, I suspect you would also run across a liberal use of trait measures.

Although personality researchers have studied dozens and dozens of traits in depth, we'll look at research on five trait concepts that illustrate the breadth and depth of the trait approach. We will first examine research on achievement and achievement motivation. Beginning with studies on the need for Achievement, we'll look at some of what researchers have discovered about this trait and how psychologists develop new ways to investigate a well-researched concept. We will also examine a personality concept that came to the attention of trait researchers via the medical community. The Type A behavior pattern was originally used by medical professionals to identify candidates for heart disease. This concept soon piqued the interest of personality psychologists, who subsequently found that Type A relates to a large number of behaviors. Next, we'll look at how personality research helps psychologists understand a common interpersonal problem, namely social anxiety or shyness. This research was initiated in the mid-1970s, when psychologists realized that they knew very little about the causes or remedies of this sometimes painful experience. Today, data from numerous investigations provide psychology with a much better idea of who suffers from social anxiety and why. We also will examine research on individual differences in emotions. Although our emotions vary depending on the events we encounter, personality psychologists can identify relatively stable patterns in how we experience and express our feelings. We also will look at research on optimism and pessimism. Recent work in this area suggests that how typically optimistic or pessimistic we are in our approach to life has many important implications.

Achievement Motivation

Look at the picture on page 205. What is happening? Who do you think this person might be? Think of a story that might be told about him. How is the story resolved? There are no right or wrong answers to these questions. One person might see a man deep in thought, weighing all the possible solutions to an important problem, on his way to accomplishing something of value. Another person might say the man is bored with his job, daydreaming about where he would rather be, and contemplating an excuse to leave the office early to spend the afternoon with his friends or family.

This brief exercise is similar to one of the initial procedures developed by psychologists to tackle the question of why some people work hard and achieve in the business world, whereas others do not (McClelland, 1961, 1985; McClelland, Atkinson, Clark, & Lowell, 1953; Stewart, 1982). Predicting success in achievement situations has been a focus of personality research for more than half a century. Much of the early work on this question was concerned with individual differences in one of the needs identified by Henry Murray—the need for Achievement. Murray described the **need for Achievement** as the desire "to accomplish something difficult; to master, manipulate or organize . . . to overcome

Who is this person? What is he doing? How will things turn out? Whether you see a man thinking about a difficult business problem or dreaming about going fishing may indicate your own level of need for Achievement.

obstacles and attain a high standard; to excel one's self" (1938, p. 164). To assess this need, researchers sometimes use another of Murray's contributions to psychology, the Thematic Apperception Test (TAT). As described in Chapter 3, test takers create stories about the scenes they see in the TAT cards. Investigators then use objective coding systems to obtain a need for Achievement score from the stories. For example, if you saw in the photograph a man working hard to reach an important goal, your story would probably indicate a high need for Achievement. On the other hand, if your story was about how this man was thinking about his loved ones and personal goals when he should be working, your response would probably yield a low need for Achievement score.

The TAT has been used in a large number of need for Achievement studies. However, the test is also time-consuming and has been subject to questions about how to interpret scores (McClelland, 1980; Tuerlinckx, De Boeck, & Lens, 2002). Consequently, today most investigators rely on easier to administer self-report inventories to assess achievement motivation (Spence & Helmreich, 1983; Schmalt, 1999). More than 50 years of research using both of these methods has provided a great deal of information about the relation between personality and achievement.

High Achievement Motivation Characteristics

What are people with a high achievement motivation like? The original need for Achievement researchers were not interested in all types of achievement, but rather with *entrepreneurial* behavior. That is, they wanted to understand and predict behavior in the business world rather than, for example, the arts or sciences. The investigators soon discovered that high need for Achievement people do not always fit the stereotype of the highly successful businessperson. For example, what would you guess about the need for Achievement level of a person who takes chances to get ahead, whose goal is to succeed against high odds? You may be surprised to find that such behavior is *not* indicative of a high need for Achievement. One of the prominent features of high need achievers is that they are *moderate* risk takers. They want to succeed, but they also are highly motivated to avoid failure. They take some risks, such as fairly secure business ventures with a moderate chance of failure. But they avoid large risks, such as placing most of their money on a highly speculative investment despite potentially large payoffs. People with strong achievement motivation are optimistic that their decisions are correct and they will succeed (Puca & Schmalt, 2001). However, their desire to achieve prevents them from taking a large chance on failure.

Predictably, people with a high need for Achievement tackle their work with a lot of energy. But high need-achievers don't work hard at everything. Rather, they limit their enthusiasm for tasks with the potential for personal achievement. Routine and boring jobs hold no more interest for high need achievers than they do for anyone else. But a job that requires creativity and provides an opportunity to demonstrate what they can do is very appealing to someone with a high need for Achievement.

High need achievers also prefer jobs that give them personal responsibility for outcomes. They want credit for success but also are willing to accept blame for failure. In particular, the opportunity to receive concrete feedback about their performance is appealing to high need-achievers (Fodor & Carver, 2000). They want to find out how good they are and how they compare to others. This observation helps to explain why high need for Achievement people typically choose careers in the business world. Some professionals rarely receive clear feedback on how they are doing. For example, a social worker may never see clear evidence that he or she is helping the clients who pass through a community mental health clinic. In contrast, sales, productivity, and profit figures provide members of the business world with constant barometers of their performances. This need for immediate feedback is complemented by the high need for Achievement person's desire to anticipate future possibilities and make long-range plans. These people succeed in business in part because they look ahead, anticipate many courses of action and possible pitfalls, and thereby increase their chances of obtaining the goal of personal achievement.

Predicting Achievement Behavior

Why do some people become highly successful entrepreneurs, whereas others show little interest in making their millions in the business community? Is there something parents can do to create high achievement motivation in their children? These were some of the questions asked by the original need for Achievement investigators. Although no simple answers were found, researchers did identify a few parenting practices associated with high need for Achievement in children (McClelland, 1961; McClelland & Pilon, 1983). In essence, parents can promote

When to let go and when to hold on? The mother might decide to let the boy fall a few times, but in the process allow him to develop a sense of mastery and independence. However, she might also want to protect him just a little longer so that he can retain his sense of security and confidence. McClelland argues that such decisions have an impact on the child's need for Achievement.

PrOMptihg

balance

achievement motivation by providing support and encouragement long enough to allow the child to develop a sense of personal competence, but not so long that the child is robbed of independence and initiative. The prescription for raising a high need for Achievement child thus seems to be finding that fine line between too much parental involvement and not enough. Parents should encourage achievement in young children, reward them, and show enthusiasm for their accomplishments. But too much parental involvement can stifle children's sense of independence and undermine their perception of mastery and accomplishment.

But can we use need for Achievement scores to predict who will become the business leaders of the future? To answer this question, researchers obtained need for Achievement scores for a group of male college students (McClelland, 1965). Fourteen years later, the investigators contacted these men again and compared the high and low need-achievers on their choice of occupations. As expected, 83% of the participants in entrepreneurial positions had been classified earlier as having a high need for Achievement. In contrast, 79% of the nonentrepreneurs had been in the low need for Achievement group.

Predictably, people with a high need for Achievement are more likely than others to find economic prosperity (Littig & Yeracaris, 1965). But researchers also warn that a high need for Achievement can sometimes be a two-edged sword. The same high level of achievement motivation that helps some people succeed can also interfere with effective performance. For example, success in upper management and executive positions often depends on the person's ability to delegate authority and motivate others. Someone too concerned about his or her own accomplishments might have a difficult time relinquishing control over details and effectively relying on subordinates. This may explain why one study found need for Achievement was related to success for low-level managers but not for those higher up the corporate ladder (McClelland & Boyatzis, 1982). Another example of this phenomenon comes from an intriguing study that examined need for Achievement and effectiveness among American presidents (Spangler & House, 1991). Presidents whose inaugural speeches indicate a high need for Achievement are usually rated by historians as relatively ineffective leaders.

Gender, Culture, and Achievement

You may have noticed that much of the early work on need for Achievement was conducted with men participants. There are reasons for this. When this research was initiated in the 1950s, relatively few women entered the business world and even fewer had opportunities to advance into high managerial positions. Because the investigators were concerned with entrepreneurs, it was reasonable to limit their studies to men. Obviously, things have changed quite a bit since then. As career aspirations and opportunities for women changed, researchers found a comparable increase in need for Achievement among women college students (Veroff, Depner, Kulka, & Douvan, 1980). As with men, a high need for Achievement predicts success in the business world for women. In one study, need for Achievement scores taken from female college students predicted job choice and job characteristics 14 years later (Jenkins, 1987).

Although need for Achievement predicts success in the business world for both genders, research suggests that many other variables come into play when comparing the achievement behavior of men and women. For example, some researchers find that men and women differ in the values that they assign to achievement tasks (Eccles, 1985; Eccles, Adler, & Meece, 1984). That is, because of differences in gender-role socialization (Chapter 14), men and women may differ on the kinds of achievement they value and where achievement falls among their personal goals. In some cases, women value achievement but may put the welfare of other people ahead of their own accomplishments. We see examples of this in women who sometimes make sacrifices for their family rather than pursue career goals. Thus, rather than ask why women don't always act like men in achievement settings, a better question might be why men and women sometimes make different choices in such settings (Eccles, 1985).

Other investigators find that men and women differ in the way they define success (Gaeddert, 1985). Men in our society are more likely to see success in terms of external standards, such as gaining prestige or recognition for accomplishments. In contrast, women are more likely to rely on internal definitions of success, such as whether they accomplished what they set out to do . Thus, when comparing men and women in achievement settings, psychologists must be careful that they don't automatically apply standards of success based only on traditional male achievement definitions.

culture

Similar caution should be exercised when applying research findings to non-Western cultures. Researchers find that the meaning of achievement sometimes varies as a function of culture (Hui, 1988; Salili, 1994). In individualistic countries like the United States (Chapter 1), achievement is typically defined in terms of personal accomplishments. In these cultures, individual effort is rewarded and people are singled out for their successes. However, in collectivist cultures, success is more likely to be defined in terms of cooperation and group accomplishments. Workers in a collectivist culture might have a strong sense of accomplishment when they do their part and the entire company reaches its goal. Individual recognition is not sought after and is not needed. In short, it may not be useful to use concepts like need for Achievement that focus on the individual when studying behavior in a collectivist culture. Rather, new definitions for achievement and success may be needed to fully understand achievement behavior in different societies.

Attributions and Goals

Imagine for a moment that you have just received an F on a midterm exam (remember, this is only hypothetical). How would you react? Because passing the class is important to you, you will no doubt spend part of the next few days trying to figure out why you did so poorly. You might conclude there was something peculiar about the test—the professor selected bizarre points to test on or wrote ambiguous questions. Another possibility is that personal problems kept you from studying as much as you would have liked. Then again, you might decide that you really don't have what it takes to be a college student, no matter how hard you study.

How you respond to the poor midterm grade and how well you do on the next test depend in part on which of these explanations you adopt. For example, if the problem is not enough studying, you can set aside extra time for the next exam. But if the problem is a lack of ability, there may be little reason to try next time. This example illustrates another approach researchers take when trying to understand achievement. Many psychologists are interested in cognitive variables (Chapter 15) that affect achievement behavior. These researchers examine such things as what people expect they will do on an upcoming task, what they think of their own abilities, how difficult they believe the task to be, and how much they value the anticipated outcomes versus the anticipated costs (Atkinson, 1957, 1974; Eccles, 1983; Eccles & Wigfield, 1994). In the following sections, we'll look briefly at two of the many cognitive variables examined in this research—attributions and achievement goals.

Assessing Your Own Personality

Achievement Goals

Indicate with a number from 1 to 7 the extent to which each of the following statements is true about you in the class you are currently taking. A response of 7 indicates the statement is *very true* about you; 1 indicates the statement is *not at all true* about you.

_____ 1. It is important for me to do better than other students.

_____ 2. I worry that I may not learn all that I possibly could in this class.

_____ 3. I want to learn as much as possible from this class.

_____ 4. I just want to avoid doing poorly in this class.

_____ 5. It is important for me to do well compared to others in this class.

_____ 6. Sometimes I'm afraid that I may not understand the content of this class as thoroughly as I'd like.

_____ 7. It is important for me to understand the content of this course as thoroughly as possible.

_____ 8. My goal in this class is to avoid performing poorly.

_____ 9. My goal in this class is to get a better grade than most of the other students.

_____ 10. I am often concerned that I may not learn all that there is to learn in this class.

_____ 11. I desire to completely master the material presented in this class.

_____ 12. My fear of performing poorly in this class is often what motivates me.

The scale provides a score for each of the four kinds of achievement goals. Add the following answer values to obtain your scores: Mastery-Approach goals (items 3, 7, and 11); Mastery-Avoidance goals (items 2, 6, and 10); Performance-Approach goals (items 1, 5, and 9); Performance-Avoidance goals (items 4, 8, and 12). Use the following means and standard deviations obtained from college under-graduates (Elliot & McGregor, 2001) to interpret your scores:

	Mean	Standard Deviation
Master-Approach	5.52	1.18
Master-Avoidance	3.89	1.53
Performance-Approach	4.82	1.68
Performance-Avoidance	4.49	1.67

Scale: *The Achievement Goal Questionnaire*

Source: Elliot and McGregor (2001)

Table 8.1	**Three Dimensions for Attributions**	
Stability	*Stable Attributions*	*Unstable Attributions*
	Good coordination	Good luck
	Poor math aptitude	Have a cold
Locus	*Internal Attributions*	*External Attributions*
	Extra effort	Easy test
	Poor skills	Difficult competition
Control	*Controllable Attributions*	*Uncontrollable Attributions*
	High motivation	From a wealthy family
	Not enough practice	Weak national economy

Attributions. Attribution researchers are interested in the explanations people generate for why they do well or poorly in achievement situations (Weiner, 1979, 1985, 1990). According to this approach, we often ask ourselves why we have failed or succeeded. The answer to this question—our *attribution*—determines how we feel about the performance and how we perform in similar situations in the future. There are many ways to analyze the kinds of attributions people give for their performances, but researchers typically focus on three dimensions (Table 8.1). One is the *stability* dimension. We can explain our performance by pointing to stable causes, such as intelligence, or to unstable causes, such as luck. In addition, an attribution may be either internal to us, such as the amount of effort put forth, or external, such as a difficult test. Researchers refer to this dimension as *locus*. Finally there is the dimension of *control*—whether we can control or not control the cause of the success or failure.

By examining attributions along these three dimensions, researchers can predict how people respond to successes and failures. For example, performing well on a test, being promoted in an organization, or winning a tennis match should enhance your sense of well-being, but only if you believe the reason for success is internal. If you win a tennis game because your opponent is a lousy tennis player or had the sun in her eyes (external attributions), you probably won't feel very good about the victory. How a person responds to future events often depends on the perceived stability of the cause of the performance. If you lose the tennis match because your opponent is a better player (stable), you probably will not expect to win next time you two play. However, if you attribute the loss to some unstable bad luck, you might be eager for another match. This analysis helps explain why most people continue to participate in sports, even though not everyone can be a winner. Research indicates that most of us attribute our losses to unstable sources, thus keeping alive hope of winning the next time (Grove, Hanrahan, & McInman, 1991).

The attributional analysis also suggests a relatively easy way to improve achievement motivation: Change people's attributions. One team of researchers did just that with a group of college freshmen (Wilson & Linville, 1982, 1985). Participants in this study were students who, like many freshmen, didn't do very well their first two semesters in college. The researchers explained to some of these students that the causes of low grades during one's freshman year are usually only temporary. In other words, they replaced stable attributions ("I am not a good student") with unstable ones ("Freshman year is always the most difficult"). As a result, students using unstable attributions to explain their performance not only got better grades during the next semester but also did better when they later took the Graduate Record Exam. The implications for education, sports, the business world, and other achievement domains are obvious.

Achievement Goals. Achievement is not only determined by how we account for performances after the fact, but also by the goals we set for ourselves at the outset. Researchers refer to these aspirations as *achievement goals* (Ames, 1992; Archer, 1994; Dweck, 1986; Elliot & McGregor, 2001; Urdan, 1997). Achievement goals provide targets that individuals aspire to in achievement situations. For example, one person might be motivated to win the salesperson-of-the-month award. Another person might set a goal of playing a difficult piece of music on the piano.

Although terminology and classification schemes vary, most investigators divide achievement goals into two broad categories: mastery goals and performance goals (Ames & Archer, 1988). *Mastery goals* are concerned with developing competence. Students motivated by a strong mastery goal will work hard to learn the subject matter in a course. Satisfaction comes from feeling they understand the material and a sense of proficiency. *Performance goals* are concerned with demonstrating accomplishments to others. Students motivated by strong performance goals want to obtain a high grade, possibly the highest grade in the class. Satisfaction comes from receiving the recognition that accompanies the achievement. In the typical classroom, we can usually find two students who work equally hard preparing for tests and completing assignments, and who achieve similar grades, yet who are motivated by very different goals. One achieving student wants to learn the material and relishes the sensation of overcoming challenges to obtain a sense of competence. The other determines what is needed for a good grade and arranges his or her study time to get the desired grade.

But people aren't just motivated to succeed in an achievement situation. Occasionally, they are more concerned about not failing. Thus, psychologists sometimes find it useful to draw a distinction between *approach goals* and *avoidance goals* (Elliot & McGregor, 2001). As shown in Figure 8.1, by dividing both mastery and performance into approach and avoidance categories, we create a 2 by 2 model of achievement goals. Within this framework, students trying to learn difficult material (mastery goal) can be motivated either by a desire to achieve a sense of mastery (approach) or by a wish to not feel incompetent (avoidance). Similarly,

Figure 8.1

Achievement Goal
Framework

Source: From Elliot and
McGregor (2001).

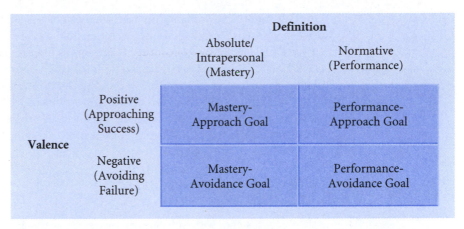

students who rely on performance goals might be motivated to gain recognition for their accomplishments or to avoid the embarrassment of a poor performance.

Because achievement motivation has important implications in education, business, and many other areas of our lives, psychologists have asked whether some achievement goals are more effective than others. Is it better for students to focus on learning the material or obtaining a good grade? Can teachers alter assignments and grading policies or should business managers change the way they evaluate and reward employees to improve learning and productivity? Although both mastery and performance goals motivate people to achieve, investigators often find differences between people who seek competence and those who focus on recognition.

Most of the research on this question has compared the effects of mastery and performance goals (Ames, 1992; Ames & Archer, 1988; Dweck & Leggett, 1988; Urdan, 1997). Psychologists find that students using mastery goals often choose more challenging tasks and are more interested in their classes than students who rely on performance goals. When given the choice between two assignments, mastery-oriented students are likely to select the one they are more curious about, whereas students relying on performance goals ask which will lead to a better grade. A student interested in learning the material is unlikely to ask, "Will this be on the test?"

People motivated by mastery goals are likely to retain the information and skills they learn longer than those driven by performance goals (Elliot & McGregor, 1999). A piano student whose goal is to master a difficult concerto is likely to remember the piece longer than the student who simply wants to sound good at the recital. Similarly, people motivated by mastery goals often continue their interest in the material after the recognition for achievement is gone (Rawsthorne & Elliot, 1999). The student who reads Charles Dickens with the goal of obtaining a deeper appreciation for fine literature is more likely to read good books during the summer than the student who reads Dickens only to do well on the exam.

This is not to say reliance on performance goals is all bad. Both mastery and performance goals can lead to achievement, and it is possible to aspire to both a sense of mastery and recognition for accomplishments (Ames & Archer, 1988; Harackiewicz, Barron, Carter, Lehto, & Elliot, 1997). Moreover, there is some evidence that a combination of mastery and performance goals can be particularly effective (Barron & Harackiewicz, 2001; Harackiewicz & Elliot, 1998). Whether mastery or performance goals are preferable probably depends on the kind of task and what the individual hopes to get out of it.

Type A–Type B Behavior Patterns

A few decades ago, some physicians and medical researchers were frustrated by their inability to identify which patients were likely to suffer from cardiovascular problems. Although they knew high blood pressure, smoking, obesity, and inactivity all contributed to the risk of heart disease, combinations of these factors were still unable to predict new cases with much accuracy (Jenkins, 1971, 1976). But these medical professionals also noticed that their heart attack patients seemed to act differently than other patients (Friedman & Rosenman, 1974). Heart attack

Type A people often have a sense of urgency and like to do more than one thing at a time.

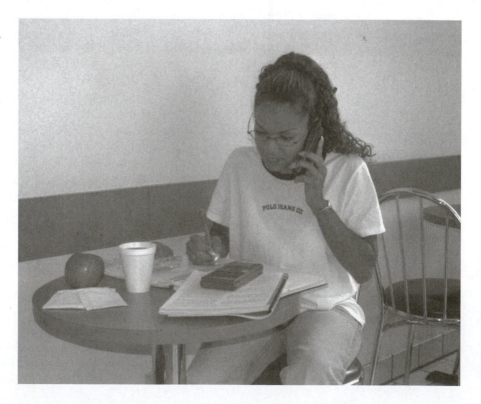

victims were more active, more energetic, and more driving than those without cardiovascular problems. In short, they seemed to have different personalities.

This personality dimension was identified as the *coronary-prone behavior pattern* because it seemed to consist of a combination of behaviors associated with coronary disease. Today, this dimension is more commonly referred to as **Type A-Type B,** or just Type A. Strictly speaking, the name is an inappropriate one, because it is not a true typology. Instead of identifying two types of people, A and B, we should think of a trait continuum with extreme Type A people at one end and extreme Type B people at the other. Typical Type A people are strongly motivated to overcome obstacles and are driven to achieve. They are attracted to competition, enjoy power and recognition, and are easily aroused to anger and action. They dislike wasting time and do things in a vigorous and efficient manner. Type A people often find more easygoing people a source of frustration. On the other hand, typical Type B people are relaxed and unhurried. They may work hard on occasion, but rarely in the driven, compulsive manner of Type A people. These people are less likely than Type A's to seek competition or to be aroused to anger or action. Naturally, not all people classified as Type A or Type B fit these profiles exactly, and there are times when Type A people behave in a Type B manner and vice versa. But, as with other traits, researchers can identify the extent to which each of us behaves, on average, like a Type A or a Type B person.

Type A as a Personality Variable

What these medical researchers were examining, of course, is a personality trait. Naturally, a trait as intriguing as Type A soon caught the attention of personality researchers. Before long, psychologists identified three major components that appear to make up the Type A trait (Glass, 1977). First, Type A people have a higher competitive achievement striving than Type B's. For example, Type A's work harder at achievement tasks regardless of outside pressure, such as deadlines. Second, Type A people show a sense of time urgency. They feel time is important and shouldn't be wasted. Whereas Type B people might procrastinate, Type A's jump right in. Studies find that Type A students volunteer for experiments earlier in the term than do Type B's, and show up earlier to participate (Gastorf, 1980; Strube, 1982). Third, Type A's are more likely to respond to frustrating situations with anger and hostility. Type A participants in one study were more likely to give what they thought were electric shocks to another participant, but only when the other person had irritated them (Glass, 1977).

Subsequent research has compared Type A and Type B people on a wide variety of behaviors, including driving habits, study habits, reactions to failure, and reactions to persuasive messages. One particularly interesting hypothesis to come out of this work explains differences in Type A and Type B behavior in terms of a motivation for control (Glass, 1977). That is, achievement striving, time urgency, and hostility reflect the Type A person's desire to exercise effective control over the

Figure 8.2

Systolic Blood
Pressure While
Working on Task

Source: Adapted from
Holmes et al. (1984); re-
printed by permission of
David Holmes.

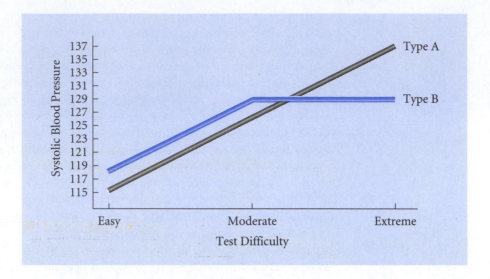

people and situations he or she encounters. Consistent with this notion, research-ers find that Type A's are more likely than Type B's to dominate a group discussion (Yarnold, Mueser, & Grimm, 1985). Type A's are less likely to give up control over a task, even if someone else might do a better job (Strube, Berry, & Moergen, 1985). Type A's are also more likely than Type B's to want something after being told they can't have it (Rhodewalt & Comer, 1982; Rhodewalt & Davison, 1983).

Other studies look at the different way Type A and Type B people respond to challenges. Researchers in one investigation measured participants' blood pressure while they worked on easy, moderately difficult, and extremely difficult tasks (Holmes, McGilley, & Houston, 1984). As shown in Figure 8.2, arousal levels gen-erally went up as people worked on more difficult tasks. However, the most difficult task, and therefore the one that posed the greatest threat to the partici-pants' perception of control, aroused Type A participants more than Type B par-ticipants. Similar results have been found when examining heart rate (Ortega & Pipal, 1984) and pulse rate (Pittner, Houston, & Spiridigliozzi, 1983). Type A's get pumped up when faced with a challenge.

Type A people also seem less aware of or perhaps are less inclined to acknowl-edge stress. Participants in one study were asked to exert themselves on a treadmill test (Carver, Coleman, & Glass, 1976). The Type A participants pushed themselves more on the test than did the Type B's, but reported less fatigue. In other studies, Type A participants deny they are having trouble when threatened with shock or loud noise (Pittner & Houston, 1980; Weidner & Matthews, 1978). Why do Type A people refuse to acknowledge fatigue and other difficulties? One possibility is that they learn to work through such problems on their way to higher levels of achievement. It also may be that Type A people particularly dislike to admit they are losing control over a challenging task.

Type A and Achievement

Who achieves more, the typical Type A individual or the typical Type B? The obvious guess is Type A. After all, these people are driven and hardworking. They're stimulated by challenges and competition, and hate to admit when they are becoming tired. However, we could also make a case that some of these Type A characteristics interfere with achievement. Due to their sense of time urgency, Type A's may not spend the time necessary to consider alternative approaches or to develop creative answers to difficult problems. Consistent with this reasoning, Type B participants in one study did better than Type A's when a delay between problem presentation and responding was required (Glass, Snyder, & Hollis, 1974).

So is Type A an asset or a liability on the job? One way to answer this question is to look at how Type A and Type B people respond when given achievement tasks in laboratory studies. These investigations find that Type A people tend to work harder on achievement tasks than Type B's, but not always. Type A's work hard when challenged, but often let their motivation wane when given an easy task (Fazio, Cooper, Dayson, & Johnson, 1981; Schwartz, Burish, O'Rourke, & Holmes, 1986). However, across numerous laboratory studies researchers find Type A participants typically outperform Type B's on achievement tasks. One reason for this difference is that Type A's tend to set higher goals for themselves (Ward & Eisler, 1987). But what really fires them up is competition. What greater threat to a Type A's sense of control than to be told there can be but one winner? Their blood pressure and heart rate go up when simply being told they are competing against another person (Lyness, 1993; Van Egeren, 1979). Not only do Type A's respond to competition, they seem to be attracted to it. Type A participants in one study were more confident in their ability to win a game when told they were competing against another participant (Gotay, 1981).

Researchers also find differences in academic performance among Type A and Type B college students. One investigation found that Type A students received more academic honors and participated in more extracurricular activities than Type B students (Glass, 1977). Further, this research revealed that Type A students participated in more sports, received more athletic awards, and participated in more social activities in high school than their Type B classmates. Type A students tend to take more credit hours of classes than Type B students and expect to do better in those classes (Ovcharchyn, Johnson, & Petzel, 1981).

But does this higher achievement carry over to actual work settings? Some research suggests that it does. One survey of 12 large companies found the majority of the managers were classified as Type A (Howard, Cunningham, & Rechnitzer, 1977). Further, Type A managers had higher salaries than their Type B counterparts. Type A is also a significant predictor of how rapidly professionals rise in their fields (Mettlin, 1976). One study found Type A research psychologists published more articles and were more widely cited (a measure of work quality) than Type B researchers (Matthews, Helmreich, Beane, & Lucker, 1980).

In short, Type A people typically put in more effort and achieve more than Type B people. Not surprisingly, Type A measures correlate with measures of achievement motivation (Matthews et al., 1980; Matthews & Saal, 1978). But before concluding that Type A is preferable, consider a few additional points. Although achieving more, Type A's work longer hours and are not as happy with their jobs as Type B's (Howard et al., 1977). It also may be the case that Type B's still do better at tasks that require some thinking and careful consideration of ideas. In addition, there is the connection between Type A and health problems. We turn to that issue next.

Type A and Health

As the medical researchers who first identified Type A anticipated, early studies found Type A was a good predictor of heart disease (Cooper, Detre, & Weiss, 1981). Type A men in one 8½-year study had more than twice the incidence of heart disease than Type B men (Rosenman et al., 1975). In another investigation, Type A was a better predictor of heart attacks than cholesterol level or cigarette smoking (Jenkins, Zyzanski, & Rosenman, 1976). Naturally, findings like these caught the attention of the medical community as well as the media. Not only could physicians do a better job of predicting heart attacks, but the findings hinted at lifestyle changes that might reduce the risk of heart disease.

However, as is often the case, results from subsequent studies found that the connection between Type A and health is more complex than the original research suggested. In the 1980s, several investigators reported low or nonexistent relationships between Type A behavior and coronary disease (Matthews & Haynes, 1986; Siegman, 1994). How can we interpret these findings? It seems unlikely that Type A behavior once caused heart disease but that suddenly it did not. It also does not seem likely that all of the earlier studies somehow identified a relationship that does not exist.

Many explanations have been offered for why measures of Type A do not always predict cardiovascular problems. Two seem particularly promising. The first concerns the way the Type A construct is measured. The second explanation examines the individual components that make up the Type A trait.

Measuring Type A: A Question of Validity. Recall from Chapter 2 that researchers using personality measures must be concerned with the question of validity. That is, does the test measure what it is supposed to measure? There are many ways to assess Type A behavior, but are all these procedures equally valid? The original medical researchers decided Type A behavior could best be assessed by observing people in a structured interview. These investigators recorded such things as how quickly people spoke and whether or not they used exaggerated hand and face gestures.

Perhaps because structured interviews are difficult and time-consuming, many researchers developed self-report measures of Type A. The most popular of these is the Jenkins Activity Survey (Glass, 1977). Items on this test ask people such questions as, How often does your job stir you to action? and Ordinarily, how rapidly do you eat? When investigators looked back over the studies on Type A behavior and heart disease, it seemed that most of the failures to uncover a significant relationship occurred when investigators used self-report inventories. Thus, it may be that whatever factor is responsible for the link between Type A behavior and cardiovascular problems is not measured to the same degree with the different assessment procedures.

This observation does not surprise advocates of the structured interview procedure (Rosenman, 1986). These investigators argue that Type A's lack insight into their own behavior necessary to answer the items on the test accurately. Subsequent research findings support the suspicion that Type A as measured in a structured interview may be different from Type A as measured with self-report tests (Contrada, 1989; Suls & Wan, 1989). Although this observation helps to explain some of the difficulty researchers have had replicating earlier studies, other research suggests this may be only part of the answer.

Identifying the Toxic Component. A second explanation for the discrepant findings between early Type A research and later investigations breaks the Type A trait into its components. As you may recall, Type A is actually a collection of several behavior tendencies that tend to go together. In essence, when we measure Type A, we are measuring more than one trait. It is possible that only one or two of these components are responsible for health problems. Because other components are measured along with these few health-related component, we might find only weak and sometimes nonsignificant associations between Type A behavior and cardiovascular disease.

This line of reasoning led some researchers to look for the "toxic component" of Type A behavior. And it appears they have been successful in that search. A large amount of evidence now points to the *anger and hostility* component as the culprit (Dembroski & Costa, 1987; Krantz & McCeney, 2002; Musante, MacDougall, Dembroski, & Costa, 1989; Ravaja, Keltikangas-Jarvinen, & Keskivaara, 1996). People high in anger and hostility aren't necessarily violent or even bossy. Rather, they tend to have a strong reaction to the daily frustrations and inconveniences we all experience. They respond to even minor annoyances with "expressions of antagonism, disagreeableness, rudeness, surliness, criticalness, and uncooperativeness" (Dembroski & Costa, 1987). For example, people high in anger and hostility might become upset when stuck in a slow-moving line at the post office or when they misplace something and can't find it right away. Most of us have learned to take these minor inconveniences in stride, but some people become highly irritated. We sometimes refer to these people as "quick-tempered" because it usually doesn't take much to send them into a fit of anger.

Several investigations find that scores on anger and hostility measures do a good job of predicting coronary artery disease (Kawachi, Sparrow, Spiro, Vokonas, & Weiss, 1996; Miller, Smith, Turner, Guijarro, & Hallet, 1996; Williams, Nieto,

Sanford, Couper, & Tyroler, 2002; Williams, Nieto, Sanford, & Tyroler, 2001). One recent investigation followed 12,986 healthy middle-age men and women over a 4½-year period (Williams et al., 2000). Compared to participants low in trait anger, participants who scored high in trait anger were more than twice as likely to suffer some form of coronary heart disease during this time. More alarming, the high-anger participants were nearly three times as likely to be hospitalized or die from heart disease during the study.

Why is anger and hostility related to cardiovascular problems? Researchers have identified several possible connections, including unhealthy lifestyles (Siegler, 1994), poor social support (Smith, Fernengel, Holcroft, Gerald, & Marien, 1994), immune system weaknesses (Uchino, Caccioppo, & Kiecolt-Glaser, 1996), and blood lipid levels (Richards, Hof, & Alvarenga, 2000). Other studies find that people high in anger and hostility frequently exhibit the kind of physiological reactions associated with cardiovascular problems, such as high blood pressure (Jorgensen, Johnson, Kolodziej, & Schreer, 1996; Martin & Watson, 1997; Powch & Houston, 1996; Raikkonen, Matthews, Flory, & Owens, 1999). Male participants in one investigation wore a blood pressure monitor for an entire day (Guyll & Contrada, 1998). The men also kept a record of their activities and their moods. As shown in Figure 8.3, participants high in hostility typically showed elevated levels of blood pressure when they interacted with other people, whereas the low hostility participants showed no such reaction. Apparently the high hostility participants found many of their conversations frustrating or annoying, and this reaction resulted in higher blood pressure. Interestingly, the high hostility women in the study did not have this reaction. Perhaps this is because women generally find social interactions more pleasant and less a source of frustration than do men.

Identifying the toxic component in Type A behavior has led to a considerable amount of research examining the relation between anger and hostility and health. As shown in Table 8.2, the results from these studies paint a consistently dangerous picture for those high on these personality dimensions (Suinn, 2001). Fortu-

Figure 8.3

Blood Pressure Response to Social Transactions

Source: Adapted from Guyll and Contrada (1998).

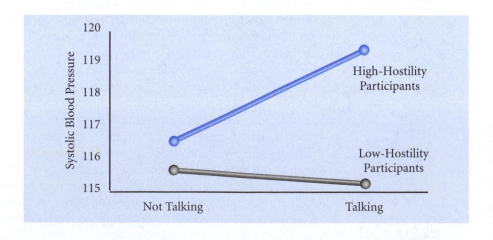

Table 8.2	**Some Health Consequences of High Anger and Hostility**
Physical Illness	High hostility scores predict increased incidence of many illnesses, including asthma, liver disease, and arthritis.
Immune System	High anger is related to weakness in the immune system, especially after conflict.
Pain	High anger scores are associated with lower pain tolerance in lab studies and with complaints of greater pain among patients experiencing pain.
Cholesterol	High trait anger is correlated with higher cholesterol levels.
Cardiovascular Disease	High hostility is related to higher incidence of many cardiovascular diseases, including atherosclerosis and coronary artery blockage.
Death	High scores on measures of anger and hostility are associated with death from cardiovascular disease as well as death from other causes.

Source: From Suinn (2001).

nately, investigators also have some encouraging findings to report. First, there is evidence that programs designed to help potential cardiovascular victims reduce their anger responses may be effective (Gidron, Davidson, & Bata, 1999; Suinn, 2001). In general, these programs train anger-prone participants to replace their initial reaction to frustrating situations with relaxation. Instructors often teach participants to think about the situation differently. That is, instead of making a small inconvenience out to be a disaster, participants are taught to keep events in perspective and recognize there are more effective solutions to the problem than anger. One team of investigators found these training procedures to be especially effective for drivers whose "road rage" had gotten so out of hand they required psychological counseling (Deffenbacher, Huff, Lynch, Oetting, & Salvatore, 2000).

A second piece of good news applies to those who are Type A but lack the anger and hostility component. Contrary to initial warnings, Type A is not necessarily bad for your health. Workaholics who push themselves to meet ever greater challenges and who prefer to work through lunch might not be headed for an early heart attack after all. If these people don't let minor setbacks and little frustrations upset them, it may be possible to be productive *and* healthy.

Social Anxiety

I took a few moments at a recent psychology conference to take note of the different ways my colleagues went about meeting and greeting other professionals. I positioned myself in the corner of a large room and watched as people entered what was designated a "social hour." The event was scheduled so that people in the field could meet one another and perhaps exchange a few ideas about each other's work. Some people seemed quite at home in this setting. One woman in particular amazed me with her ability to introduce herself to someone she obviously had never met and immediately begin what appeared to be a lively and pleasant conversation. But other people approached the social hour in a very different manner. One man stopped about two feet inside the door and examined the proceedings for a few minutes. Then he slowly worked his way around the exterior of the room, looking for someone to talk to. When people did speak to him, he appeared to smile nervously. The man looked at the floor more than at the person he was speaking to, and his conversations never seemed to last more than 30 seconds. After about 10 minutes, he left.

It would be easy to speculate that these two visitors to the social hour probably fall on opposite ends of the personality trait we call *social anxiety.* The man was very anxious in this situation and behaved in a manner most people would identify as shy. I would guess that the woman has never suffered from shyness. Although most people would probably consider the woman's behavior normal and appropriate for a social gathering, researchers find that the shy man's experience may be more common than most of us realize. In fact, shyness appears to be a widespread social problem. Researchers consistently find about 40% of the people they survey identify themselves as shy (Zimbardo, 1977, 1986). Approximately another 40 –50% say they have been shy before or are shy in certain situations. This leaves only a small percentage of people who do not know the pain of social anxiety or shyness.

Speaking in front of a group creates high levels of nervousness for someone high in social anxiety. High social-anxiety people are often concerned about negative evaluation.

Social anxiety is anxiety related specifically to social interactions or anticipated social interactions. People suffering from social anxiety experience many of the usual anxiety symptoms: increased physiological arousal, inability to concentrate, feelings of nervousness. But socially anxious people recognize that the source of their discomfort is the social encounter they are now or will soon be engaged in. Although everyone has on occasion been at least a little nervous about an upcoming interview or date, we can identify a relatively stable tendency for people to experience social anxiety. That is, each of us can be placed along a continuum for how much social anxiety we typically experience.

Social anxiety is the same as or related to many other constructs investigated by psychologists and communication researchers. The names for these concepts include shyness, dating anxiety, communication anxiety, reticence, and stage fright. Although some psychologists draw a distinction between social anxiety and some of these related concepts (Buss, 1980; Leary, 1983b), most researchers today appear to use the terms *social anxiety* and *shyness* synonymously. Concepts like dating anxiety and stage fright are often regarded as specific examples of the larger concept of social anxiety. Moreover, scales designed to measure social anxiety, shyness, and related constructs are highly correlated with one another (Anderson & Harvey, 1988). Consequently, we will use the terms *social anxiety* and *shyness* interchangeably here.

It also is important to recognize that social anxiety is not the same as introversion. Whereas introverts often choose to be by themselves, the vast majority of socially anxious people do not like their shyness. Nearly two-thirds of the socially anxious people in one study identified their shyness as "a real problem," and one-quarter of the shy participants said they would be willing to seek professional help to overcome their social anxiety (Pilkonis, 1977a).

Characteristics of Socially Anxious People

People who suffer from social anxiety have a difficult time in many social situations. Socially anxious people report feeling awkward and nervous when they have to talk to others (Cheek & Buss, 1981). They are very concerned about what others will think of them and become self-conscious when they meet new people or have to talk in front of an audience. Quite often, socially anxious people think about what they are doing wrong, how stupid they must sound, and how foolish they must look (Bruch, Hamer, & Heimberg, 1995; Ickes, Robertson, Tooke, & Teng, 1986; Ritts & Patterson, 1996). Shy people often stumble over their words, say the wrong thing, and show outward signs of nervousness, such as perspiration and shakiness. These feelings of awkwardness are not merely in the minds of socially anxious people. The people they interact with also identify shy people as more tense, inhibited, and unfriendly than nonshy people (Cheek & Buss, 1981; Papsdorf & Alden, 1998). Shy people are more likely than most people to feel ashamed or embarrassed about what they say or do in social situations. This is

Assessing Your Own Personality

Social Anxiety

Indicate the extent to which each of the following statements describes you. Indicate your answers with a 5-point scale, with 1 = Not at all characteristic to 5 = Extremely characteristic.

_____   1. I often feel nervous even in casual get-togethers.

_____   2. I usually feel uncomfortable when I am in a group of people I don't know.

_____   3. I am usually at ease when speaking to a member of the opposite sex.*

_____   4. I get nervous when I must talk to a teacher or boss.

_____   5. Parties often make me feel anxious and uncomfortable.

_____   6. I am probably less shy in social interactions than most people.*

_____   7. I sometimes feel tense talking to people of my own sex if I don't know them very well.

_____   8. I would be nervous if I were being interviewed for a job.

_____   9. I wish I had more confidence in social situations.*

_____   10. I seldom feel anxious in social situations.

_____   11. In general, I am a shy person.

_____   12. I often feel nervous when talking to an attractive member of the opposite sex.

_____   13. I often feel nervous when calling someone I don't know very well on the telephone.

_____   14. I get nervous when I speak to someone in a position of authority.

_____   15. I usually feel relaxed around other people, even people who are quite different from me.*

This scale was designed to measure social anxiety surrounding what Schlenker and Leary (1982) call contingent interactions. This is the anxiety we sometimes experience in unrehearsed social encounters, such as when meeting new people or when on a date, as compared with the kind of anxiety people experience when delivering a prepared speech before a group. Interaction anxiousness includes what we commonly refer to as shyness and dating anxiety. People who score high on the scale tend to experience social anxiety more often and more intensely than those who score low. To obtain your score, first reverse the values for your answers to items with an asterisk (that is, 1 = 5, 2 = 4, and so on). Then add all 15 answer values together. Researchers find a mean score on the scale of about 39 for undergraduate students, with a standard deviation of about 10 (Leary, 1986).

Scale: *The Interaction Anxiousness Scale*

Source: Leary (1986)

probably why shy people also are more likely than nonshys to blush (Leary & Meadows, 1991). At times, socially anxious people become so concerned about how they are coming across that it interferes with their ability to carry on a conversation. Shy people sometimes report they are so self-conscious and nervous that they cannot think of anything to say. They may allow the conversation to fall into silence, which can be extremely uncomfortable for someone already suffering from social anxiety (Pilkonis, 1977b).

As noted earlier, shy people are not introverts. Rather, most would like to have a larger network of friends than they do. In particular, shy people often say that they would like more people they could turn to when they need help. Unfortunately, their shyness often keeps them from developing more friends or asking the friends they have for help when they are in need. One study found that shy students were less likely than nonshy students to talk to a counselor about career advice (Phillips & Bruch, 1988). Researchers in another study deliberately asked people to work on a task that could not be completed without asking another participant for assistance (DePaulo, Dull, Greenberg, & Swaim, 1989). Nonetheless, the socially anxious people were more reluctant than the other participants to ask a nearby person for help. This inability to ask for assistance appears to stem from socially anxious people's fear that the other person might not respond favorably to their request.

Not only do socially anxious people fear that others will think poorly of them, they also tend to interpret whatever feedback they get in a negative light. This was demonstrated in a study in which college students were asked to work on a series of tasks with other participants (DePaulo, Kenny, Hoover, Webb, & Oliver, 1987). When later asked what they believed the other students thought of them, the socially anxious students felt they were less liked and had come across as less competent than did the nonanxious participants. Participants in another experiment carried on what they believed to be a two-way discussion via a television hook-up (Pozo, Carver, Wellens, & Scheier, 1991). In reality, all participants watched a prerecorded videotape of a confederate posing as a participant. Although the feedback was identical, socially anxious people were more likely than the nonanxious participants to interpret the other person's facial expressions as indicating disapproval.

In short, people high in social anxiety expect their social interactions to go poorly and look for evidence that the other person is rejecting them. Unfortunately, this pessimism may cause the social rejection that the socially anxious person fears in the first place. For example, people sometimes mistake shyness for a lack of interest or a lack of intelligence (Paulhus & Morgan, 1997). Moreover, because they feel the other person dislikes them, socially anxious people may cut conversations short or avoid them altogether. As a result, they may nip pleasant interactions and potential friendships in the bud before they have a chance to bloom.

Explaining Social Anxiety

Why do shy people become so anxious in certain social situations? What are they afraid of? Many researchers believe **evaluation apprehension** is the underlying cause of social anxiety. In other words, socially anxious people are afraid of what other people think of them (Baldwin & Main, 2001; Leary & Kowalski, 1995). In particular, they fear negative evaluation. Socially anxious people worry that the person they are talking with is going to find them foolish, boring, or immature. Situations that lend themselves to evaluation by others are particularly anxiety provoking. Thus, just thinking about going on a blind date, giving a speech in front of a large audience, or meeting people for the first time can be a nightmarish experience for someone high in social anxiety.

This evaluation apprehension leads socially anxious people to take steps to reduce their fear of what others think of them. Often, socially anxious people avoid the social encounter altogether. They skip parties where they might not know anyone, avoid blind dates, and opt for a term paper instead of a class presentation. When getting out of the situation is not realistic, shy people will do what they can to reduce the amount of social interaction. One way they do this is to avoid eye contact (Farabee, Holcom, Ramsey, & Cole, 1993; Garcia, Stinson, Ickes, Bissonnette, & Briggs, 1991; Pilkonis, 1977b). Making eye contact with someone signals a readiness or willingness to talk. By refusing to give this signal, shy people tell those around them that they would prefer to avoid social interaction. In this way, socially anxious people limit the opportunities for others to evaluate them.

However, when their efforts to avoid potentially awkward social situations fail, shy people do what they can to keep the conversation short and nonthreatening. Participants in one experiment were asked to tell four stories about themselves to an interviewer (DePaulo, Epstein, & LeMay, 1990). Some of the participants believed the interviewer was going to use these stories to evaluate them afterward. The socially anxious people who thought they were going to be evaluated told shorter and less revealing stories about themselves than the other participants. Apparently these shy people were worried about creating a poor impression in the mind of the interviewer.

Participants in another experiment were asked to engage in a 5-minute "get-acquainted" conversation with someone they had just met (Leary, Knight, & Johnson, 1987). When researchers examined tapes of these conversations, they found several differences in the way shy and nonshy participants acted. For example, socially anxious participants were more likely to agree with what the other person said and to merely restate or clarify their partner's remarks when it was their turn to talk. This interactive style allows socially anxious people to create an image of politeness and interest without becoming too involved in the conversation. In this way, shy people hope to minimize the amount of evaluation by their conversation partners and, in particular, to reduce the chances that this other person will find something objectionable about them. This concern about evaluation also explains why socially anxious people limit the amount of personal information they reveal to a person they've just met (Meleshko & Alden, 1993). Not surprisingly, we find higher rates of shyness in cultures that emphasize concern for what others think of you and the importance of avoiding criticism (Okazaki, 1997).

In short, the shy person's interaction style is a type of self-protective strategy. Because they are so concerned with negative evaluations, socially anxious people do what they can to control the impressions others have of them (Schlenker & Leary, 1982; Shepperd & Arkin, 1990). Thus, shy people deliberately keep conversations short and pleasant and avoid potentially controversial or embarrassing topics. In this way, they reduce the likelihood that the other person will form a negative impression of them.

Although this picture of the shy person may sound rather hopeless, one research finding suggests that socially anxious people may not be as incapable of carrying on a conversation as they seem. Researchers sometimes find that shy people do not have much difficulty interacting with others once they get started. That is, for at least some shy people, it's *initiating* a conversation that seems to be the real stumbling block (Curran, Wallander, & Fischetti, 1980; Paulhus & Martin, 1987). In one study, shy and nonshy participants were left alone to carry on a conversation with a member of the opposite sex (Pilkonis, 1977b). Although the nonshy people spoke more often and were more likely to break periods of silence than the shy participants, there was no difference in how long these two kinds of people spoke when they did say something.

Observations like these lead some researchers to speculate that what socially anxious people really lack is confidence in their ability to make a good impression (Hill, 1989; Leary & Atherton, 1986; Maddux, Norton, & Leary, 1988). Fear that they might say the wrong thing often keeps shy people from saying anything. Consequently, therapy programs designed to help people overcome problems with shyness often focus on developing the clients' belief that they are capable of saying the right thing and of making a good impression (Glass & Shea, 1986; Haemmerlie & Montgomery, 1986; Leary & Kowalski, 1995). Shy people who lack social skills can be taught how to carry on a conversation, but for many, the key may be developing confidence that social encounters will be more successful than most shy people now expect.

Emotions

At first glance, you might wonder why a topic like emotions is included in a chapter on personality traits. After all, traits are consistent characteristics, and common observation tells us that our moods fluctuate constantly. Each of us goes through good days and bad—times when we are extremely happy, tremendously sad, proud, ashamed, enthusiastic, and guilty. Common sense also suggests that how we feel depends on the situation. We're happy when good things happen to us, proud when we accomplish something, sad when unfortunate events occur. However, if I ask you to think of someone you know who always seems to be in a good mood, my guess is you will have little difficulty coming up with an example. Similarly, I find people can easily think of individuals they would describe as "gloomy," "grouchy," or "confident." In other words, after a little reflection it also is apparent that, although each of us experiences a wide range of positive and negative emotions, we can also identify relatively stable patterns in emotions that distinguish each person from the people around him or her.

What are some of these consistent patterns? Researchers identify at least three ways our emotions can be examined as relatively stable personal characteristics. First, each of us differs in the extent to which we typically experience positive and negative emotions. Second, we differ in the typical strength of the emotions we experience. Third, we differ in the way we express our emotions. Personality psychologists refer to these three aspects of emotion as *affectivity*, *intensity*, and *expressiveness*.

Emotional Affectivity

Thumb through a dictionary, and you will find dozens and dozens of words that describe human emotions. People can be happy, irritated, content, nervous, embarrassed, and disgusted. We experience shame, joy, regret, rage, anxiety, and pride. But it is reasonable to ask if these are all different emotions or, as researchers have found when examining personality traits, connected to one another along a few major dimensions. Like psychologists studying the Big Five personality dimensions, researchers use factor analysis to examine the relation among various emotions (Watson & Tellegen, 1985; Watson & Clark, 1991). These researchers look at emotions as measured by self-report inventories, use of words, facial expressions, and evaluations from others. And like Big Five researchers, they find that certain emotions indeed tend to go together. People who are happy also tend to be enthusiastic, those who are irritable are also sad.

Eventually, these investigators discovered that affect could be organized around two general dimensions. As shown in Table 8.3, researchers identified one of these dimensions simply as *positive affect*. At one extreme we find such emotions as *active, content,* and *satisfied*. At the other extreme we find *sad* and *lethargic*. The other dimension that emerged in this research was identified, perhaps predictably, as *negative affect*. At one extreme of this dimension we find *nervousness, anger,* and *distress*. At the other end we find *calm* and *serene*.

The same two dimensions can be used to identify our typical emotional experiences. As with other traits, our general tendencies to experience positive affect and negative affect are relatively stable over time. That is, if I know where to place you on the two affect dimensions today, I can predict with reasonable accuracy your general tendency to experience positive and negative affect years from now (Charles, Reynolds, & Gatz, 2001). Psychologists refer to these individual differences as **emotional affectivity.**

Table 8.3 Positive and Negative Affect Examples	
High Positive Affect	**High Negative Affect**
Active	Distressed
Elated	Fearful
Enthusiastic	Hostile
Excited	Jittery
Peppy	Nervous
Strong	Scornful
Low Positive Affect	**Low Negative Affect**
Drowsy	At rest
Dull	Calm
Sleepy	Placid
Sluggish	Relaxed

One of the key issues addressed by researchers in this area is the relationship between positive and negative affect. Initial investigations indicate that these two affect dimensions are relatively independent from one another (Diener & Emmons, 1984; Mayer & Gaschke, 1988; Meyer & Shack, 1989; Watson, Clark, & Tellegen, 1988). If this is the case, knowing your score on a test measuring positive affect would tell me nothing about how you score on a test measuring negative affect. However, later studies found support for the more intuitive notion that being high on one of these dimensions means being low on the other, and vice versa (Russell & Carroll, 1999). In other words, the more I experience positive emotions like happiness and contentment, the less likely I am to experience anger and anxiety. Currently, the relation between positive and negative affect remains an issue of great discussion and continuing investigation (Carver, 2001; Green, Salovey, & Truax, 1999; Schimmack, Oishi, Diener, & Suh, 2000; Watson, Wiese, Vaidya, & Tellegen, 1999; Yik, Russell, & Barrett, 1999; Zautra, Reich, Davis, Potter, & Nicolson, 2000). No doubt the relation between positive and negative affect is more complex than researchers initially recognized. Although common observations tell us that doing something fun helps to take away the blues, each of us also has read stories and seen movies that make us happy and sad at the same time (Larsen, McGraw, & Cacioppo, 2001).

Regardless of the outcome of this debate, psychologists find that individual differences in positive affect and negative affect predict a number of important behaviors. Researchers consistently find positive affect is related to social activity. That is, people who are high in trait positive affect tend to engage in more social activities and tend to enjoy those activities more than those who score low on this trait (Berry & Hansen, 1996; Clark & Watson, 1988; Watson, 1988). This high level of social activity also extends to romance. People high in trait positive affect are more likely to be involved in a romantic relationship and are more satisfied with their partners than are people low in positive affect (Berry & Willingham, 1997).

Why is positive affect related to social activity? One reason may be that social activity *causes* positive affect. Students in one study completed a scale measuring positive and negative mood each week for 13 consecutive weeks (Watson, Clark, McIntyre, & Hamaker, 1992). Participants also completed a questionnaire each week indicating how often they had engaged in each of 15 different social activities (for example, attending a party, having a serious discussion, or going to a movie or concert). The researchers found the more social activities the students engaged in, the higher their positive affect scores that week. A similar finding was uncovered when researchers looked at the mood and activity levels of Japanese students (Clark & Watson, 1988).

Thus, one reason positive affectivity is related to social behavior may be that social activity leads to positive affect. But it is important to note that this research is correlational (Chapter 2). In other words, it is possible that the causal arrow runs the other way as well. People may engage in social activity *because* they experience positive affect. Consistent with this interpretation, studies find that when we feel good, we are more likely to seek out friends and to act friendly toward the people we meet (Cunningham, 1988).

People high in trait positive affect also appear to act in ways that make friends, which then leads to more social activities. For example, participants in one study were asked to engage in a 6-minute conversation with a stranger. When judges examined videotapes of these conversations, they found high positive affect participants generally were more pleasant and engaging than low positive affect participants (Berry & Hansen, 1996). High positive affect people report fewer conflicts with their friends (Berry, Willingham, & Thayer, 2000) and are more likely to be accommodating when they have a disagreement with their romantic partners (Berry & Willingham, 1997). That is, they are better at resolving conflicts and thus maintaining solid, happy relationships. In short, people high in trait positive affect tend to be happy, enthusiastic, and attentive. Little wonder they develop and keep friendships and romantic relationships.

What kinds of behaviors are related to negative affect? Perhaps predictably, high scores on negative affect are generally related to psychological stress (Tarlow & Haaga, 1996; Watson, Clark, & Carey, 1988). People on the high end of this dimension suffer from a diverse list of emotional problems. Studies also find that negative affect is related to complaints about health (Leventhal, Hansell, Diefenbach, Leventhal, & Glass, 1996; Watson & Pennebaker, 1989). That is, people who score high on measures of negative affect report more health problems than people with low negative affect. Not surprisingly, we are more likely to find high negative affect people in a doctor's office than people who are low on this dimension.

But these findings raise another question: Do people high in negative affect really suffer from more health problems, or do they simply complain more? Perhaps these people report more health problems because they complain more about everything. Maybe people high in negative affect simply think about their symptoms more than most of us. To test this possibility, one group of healthy volunteers was deliberately exposed to cold and flu viruses (Cohen et al., 1995). These participants were then quarantined in a hotel for several days, where they were monitored for real symptoms as well as daily self-reports of their symptoms. The researchers found that the volunteers characteristically high in negative affect reported more cold and flu symptoms than those who scored low on this dimension. However, when the investigators looked at actual symptoms (such as mucus excretions), they found no difference between those high and low in negative affect.

But before we dismiss the higher rate of health problems among negative affect people as exaggerated complaining, consider that both of these possibilities may be true—perhaps people high in negative affect complain more, but they also may suffer more genuine symptoms. This was the conclusion of a 7-year study looking at patients suffering from rheumatoid arthritis (Smith, Wallston, & Dwyer, 1995). The patients high in negative affect did report more symptoms and more severe symptoms than those on the other end of this dimension. However, it also was the case that these patients had higher levels of physical ailments that could not be explained away simply by their tendency to focus on the negative. In short, patients high in negative affect complained more than the symptoms warranted, but they also had more legitimate reasons to complain.

This last observation leads to a final question: Why should different levels of negative affect be related to one's physical health? As of yet, no clear answers to this question are available. One possibility is that people high in negative affect have difficulty dealing with stress, which subsequently affects their health. It might also be the case that mood affects health-related behaviors. For example, high and low negative affect people might have different exercise, eating, or health habits. In addition, it's possible that people who suffer from a lot of health problems become more negative about their lives in general.

Affect Intensity

Several years ago, students participating in a psychology experiment were asked to keep daily records of their emotions for 84 consecutive days (Larsen, 1987). Each day the students completed a short scale indicating the extent to which they had experienced positive emotions, such as happiness and fun, and negative emotions, such as sadness and anger. The researchers plotted each person's emotional pattern for the length of the study.

What were these investigators looking for? Consider the data from two of the participants in that study, shown in Figure 8.4. The average amount of positive and negative emotion was about the same for each of these students over the nearly 3-month period. But here is an example in which averages tell only part of the story. Clearly, these two students have very different emotional lives. The first student has highs and lows, but these typically aren't extreme. We all know people like this. We call them steady and even-tempered. They enjoy themselves, but rarely

Figure 8.4

Examples of Daily Mood Fluctuation in Two People

Source: Adapted from Larsen (1987).

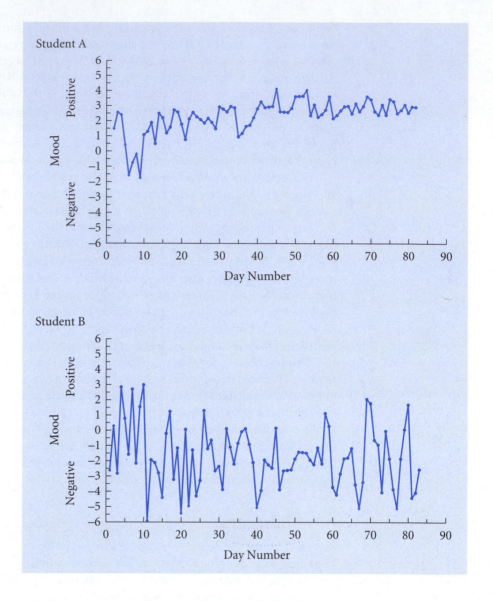

become ecstatic. They get irritated, but rarely irate. Each of us also knows someone like the second student. When he gets happy, he gets very happy. When he gets down, he gets very down. We say these people are unpredictable, they fly off the handle, they're moody. Today they might be pumped up and enthusiastic, tomorrow frustrated and hostile.

Personality researchers would say the two students differ on the dimension of affect intensity (Larsen & Diener, 1987). **Affect intensity** refers to the strength or degree to which people typically experience their emotions. At one end of the dimension we find people who respond to emotional situations with relatively mild reactions, at the other we find those with strong emotional reactions. As shown in the two students' data, high-intensity people not only experience their emotions more intensely, they also tend to be more variable. They experience higher highs and lower lows. It is important to recognize that affect intensity applies to both positive and negative emotions. A person who experiences strong positive emotions also tends to experience strong negative emotions (Schimmack & Diener, 1997). Where we find peaks, we also find valleys.

We might think that the difference between high- and low-intensity people is that the former simply have more exciting or emotionally loaded events in their lives. However, this does not seem to be the case. When researchers compare the kinds of activities high- and low-intensity people experience, they find no differences (Larsen, Diener, & Emmons, 1986). High- and low-intensity people tend to go to the same number of parties and concerts; they have the same number of hassles and setbacks. The difference lies in how they react to those events. In one study, researchers presented participants with identical hypothetical situations, such as receiving a letter from a friend or discovering a flat tire on your bicycle (Larsen et al., 1986). When asked to imagine how they would respond, high-intensity participants said they would enjoy the positive events to a greater degree and be more upset by the negative events than did the low-intensity participants. Even relatively mild situations can evoke strong reactions in high-intensity individuals. High-intensity participants in one study had stronger emotional reactions than lows to magazine ads for alcoholic beverages (Geuens & De Pelsmacker, 1999). Other studies find that high-intensity people tend to overestimate the extent to which events will affect them and are guilty of drawing unwarranted conclusions based on one good or one bad experience (Larsen, Billings, & Cutler, 1996; Larsen, Diener, & Cropanzano, 1987). To a high-intensity individual, one friendly smile suggests a blossoming relationship, one bad grade the end of the world. No doubt high-intensity people are often told they are overreacting by those from the other end of the affect intensity dimension.

These observations lead to another question: Is it better to be high on affect intensity and really experience life or low on this dimension and maintain a steady and calm approach to achievements and calamities? In other words, how does affect intensity relate to well-being? The answer is that high- and low-intensity people tend to score about the same on measures of happiness and well-being (Larsen, Diener, & Emmons, 1985). High-intensity people experience more positive affect, of course. But this seems to be offset by the fact that they also experience more negative affect (Kring, Smith, & Neale, 1994). However, there does seem to be a difference in the *way* these two kinds of people experience happiness. For high-intensity people, happiness means a lot of exhilarating and enlivening experiences. For low-intensity people, happiness takes the form of a calm, enduring sense of contentment (Larsen & Diener, 1987). In short, these people simply lead different, not necessarily better or worse, emotional lives. Moreover, both kinds of people can be productive, but again in different ways. For example, one researcher found that scientists tend to be low in affect intensity, whereas artists tend to be high (Sheldon, 1994). These findings fit the stereotypes of the pondering scientist satisfied with incremental steps toward his or her goal and the temperamental artist operating on bursts of inspiration-driven energy. Both get where they want to be, but each takes a different emotional route.

Emotional Expressiveness

If I tell you Maria is an emotional person, you probably have little difficulty imagining what she is like. The "emotional" people I know cry at sad movies, tell friends they are loved, and move about excitedly when given good news. If Maria is an emotional person, you could probably tell me what kind of mood she is in just by seeing the expression on her face. No doubt her friends share her joys as well as her disappointments. Most of us know someone like Maria, but what is it that makes these people stand out from the crowd?

By now it should be clear that the kinds of emotions we experience (affectivity) and the strength of our emotions (intensity) represent important aspects of our emotional experiences. Yet when we identify someone as an "emotional" person, we probably aren't referring exactly to either of these individual differences. Rather, I suspect what distinguishes these people from most of us is that they are high in what researchers call emotional expressiveness.

Emotional expressiveness refers to a person's outward display of emotions. Some people tend to be particularly expressive of their feelings. We say that such people "wear their emotions on their sleeves" or that we can "read them like a book." If they're feeling a little down today, it shows. They move slowly; their shoulders sag; they wear sad faces. And if these same people have just received good news or simply feel good about what they're doing, we can tell in a minute. They bounce when they walk; they grin. We hear the enthusiasm in their voices. When highly expressive women in one study were told they had answered some difficult problems correctly, they could not keep themselves from showing their pleasure by smiling (Friedman & Miller-Herringer, 1991).

As with affectivity and intensity, researchers find relatively stable differences in the extent to which we express our emotions (Friedman, Prince, Riggio, & Di-Matteo, 1980; Gohm & Clore, 2000; Kring, Smith, & Neale, 1994). Like other personality traits, we can place people along a continuum ranging from those who are highly expressive to those who show few outward signs of how they are feeling. Consistent with common observations, researchers find that women tend to be more expressive of their emotions than men (Gross & John, 1998; Kring & Gordon, 1998; Timmers, Fischer, & Manstead, 1998). Interestingly, women also tend to be better than men at reading the emotions in other people's faces (McClure, 2000).

How well we express our feelings has important implications for how we get along with others. In particular, the more people express their feelings, the fewer problems they have in their romantic relationships (Noller, 1984). Communication is aided when partners understand what the other person is feeling, and communication almost always contributes to harmony and satisfaction in relationships.

Assessing Your Own Personality

Emotional Expressiveness

Indicate the extent to which each of the following statements describes you. Indicate your response using a 6-point scale with 1 = Never true and 6 = Always true.

_____   1. I think of myself as emotionally expressive.

_____   2. People think of me as an unemotional person.*

_____   3. I keep my feelings to myself.*

_____   4. I am often considered indifferent by others.*

_____   5. People can read my emotions.

_____   6. I display my emotions to other people.

_____   7. I don't like to let other people see how I'm feeling.*

_____   8. I am able to cry in front of other people.

_____   9. Even if I am feeling very emotional, I don't let others see my feelings.*

_____ 10. Other people aren't easily able to observe what I'm feeling.*

_____ 11. I am not very emotionally expressive.*

_____ 12. Even when I'm experiencing strong feelings, I don't express them outwardly.*

_____ 13. I can't hide the way I'm feeling.

_____ 14. Other people believe me to be very emotional.

_____ 15. I don't express my emotions to other people.*

_____ 16. The way I feel is different from how others think I feel.*

_____ 17. I hold my feelings in.*

To calculate your score, first reverse the answer values for the items with asterisks. That is, for these items only, 6 = 1, 5 = 2, 4 = 3, 3 = 4, 2 = 5, 1 = 6. Then add all 17 answer values. The higher your score, the more expressive you tend to be. When the test developers gave this scale to a group of undergraduates, they came up with the following norms:

	Mean	Standard Deviation
Females	66.60	2.71
Males	61.15	12.69
Total Sample	64.67	12.97

Scale: *The Emotional Expressivity Scale*

Source: Kring, Smith, and Neale (1994)

Moreover, people who express their emotions freely tend to experience less confusion when trying to read another person's emotions (King, 1998).

Expressing emotions also seems to be good for our psychological health. Participants in one study completed a series of well-being measures and kept daily records of their moods for 21 consecutive days (King & Emmons, 1990). The participants identified as highly expressive were happier and experienced less anxiety and guilt than those who were low in expressiveness. Other researchers using similar procedures found that expressive people were less prone to depression (Katz & Campbell, 1994). Highly expressive people also tend to be higher in self-esteem than those on the other end of this trait dimension (Friedman et al., 1980). In short, emotional expressiveness is good for us. In Chapter 12, we'll return to some of the reasons for this relation between well-being and expressing one's emotions.

Optimism and Pessimism

For many years, researchers have recognized that a positive outlook is related to high achievement and a positive mood (Taylor, 1989). People who approach an upcoming event believing they will do well tend to perform better and feel better about themselves than those who enter the situation thinking things will likely turn out poorly. Similarly, when people face a specific problem, those who believe they will beat the odds tend to do better and feel better than those who think the odds will beat them. A large number of investigations find support for this idea. For example, heart transplant patients in one study were asked about their expectations prior to the surgery (Leedham, Meyerowitz, Muirhead, & Frist, 1995). Those with positive expectations did a much better job of adjusting to life after the surgery than those with a more pessimistic outlook.

But researchers also find that optimism and pessimism aren't simply tied to specific events or problems. Rather, even though each of us can be optimistic or pessimistic on occasion, psychologists can also identify a relatively consistent degree of optimism for each person that characterizes the way that person approaches most of life's challenges (Scheier & Carver, 1985). We can place people on a continuum ranging from those who tend to look at life in the most optimistic light to those who typically view the world through the most pessimistic lenses. Because people are relatively consistent in the extent to which they adopt one of these viewpoints, researchers sometimes refer to this personality variable as **dispositional optimism.**

When researchers compare people who are high in dispositional optimism with those who are not, they usually find clear advantages for the optimists. People who take an optimistic approach to life usually achieve more than those who don't (Brown & Marshall, 2001; Taylor & Brown, 1988). Optimists tend to set their goals higher and believe they can reach those goals. Just like the moral of so many stories, researchers find that having confidence in one's abilities is often the key to success. In particular, optimists are less likely to allow setbacks and temporary failures get them down (Gibbons, Blanton, Gerrard, Buunk, & Eggleston, 2000). One team of researchers looked at how new life insurance agents reacted to the inevitable rejections they face when selling insurance (Seligman & Schulman, 1986). They found the pessimists were more than twice as likely as the optimists to quit within the first year. When the going got rough, many of the pessimists decided it was never going to get any better. Meanwhile, the undiscouraged and persistent optimists sold more insurance policies than their pessimistic colleagues.

As with many other personality variables, researchers find optimism and pessimism are related to culture (Chang, 2001). Much of this research has compared people in individualistic cultures with those from collectivist cultures (Chapter 1). One study asked Canadian and Japanese students to estimate the likelihood that certain events (e.g., live a long life, develop skin cancer) would happen to them (Heine & Lehman, 1995). The Japanese students consistently expressed a more pessimistic outlook than the Canadians. Other investigators have compared scores on dispositional measures of optimism and pessimism between cultures (Chang, 1996; Lee & Seligman, 1997). These researchers also find Asian participants are more pessimistic than participants from individualistic cultures. As you will see, optimism and pessimism are related to coping with adversity, well-being, and health. Thus, these cultural differences have important implications for counselors working with people from diverse cultural backgrounds (Chang, 2001).

Dealing with Adversity

Investigators find clear differences in the way optimists and pessimists deal with unexpected, stressful events. Consider the stress experienced by Israeli citizens in a study conducted during the Persian Gulf war (Zeidner & Hammer, 1992). The researchers looked at coping and adjustment among residents of Haifa, an area repeatedly threatened with SCUD missile attacks during the time the study was conducted. The investigators found that the dispositional optimists in their sample experienced less anxiety and less depression than those identified as pessimists. Similar results are found when less acute sources of stress are examined. One team of researchers looked at adjustment levels in men and women who had spent at least one year caring for a spouse diagnosed with Alzheimer's disease (Hooker, Monahan, Shifren, & Hutchinson, 1992). The spouses who generally approached life with an optimistic outlook experienced less stress and less depression than the pessimistic caregivers.

Other investigators look at how optimists and pessimists react to health problems and medical procedures. For example, one team of researchers found optimistic women who had surgery for breast cancer reported less distress during the year following the surgery than pessimistic women going through the same experience (Carver et al., 1993). Similarly, rheumatoid arthritis patients high in dispositional optimism scored higher on measures of psychological adjustment than did pessimistic patients (Long & Sangster, 1993). In yet another study, men recovering from coronary artery bypass surgery were compared for general mood and

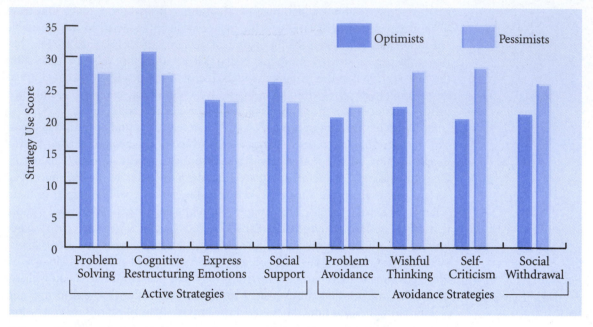

Figure 8.5

Use of Coping Strategies

Source: Adapted from Chang (1998).

quality of life 6 months after the surgery (Scheier et al., 1989). As in the other investigations, the dispositionally optimistic men looked much better after their surgery than did the pessimists.

The results of these studies clearly demonstrate that optimists deal with adverse situations better than pessimists. But the benefits of optimism are not limited to extreme situations like war and surgery. One team of investigators looked at students' adjustment to college life (Aspinwall & Taylor, 1992). Freshman students with an optimistic outlook had a significantly easier time adjusting to the demands of their first quarter of college than did pessimistic students.

Clearly, dispositional optimists do a better job of handling stressful situations than pessimists. But why is this the case? What is it about an optimistic disposition that helps some people come through life's crises and challenges so well? One answer seems to be that optimists and pessimists use different strategies to cope with their problems (Lai & Wong, 1998; Peacock & Wong, 1996; Scheier, Carver, & Bridges, 2001; Scheier, Weintraub, & Carver, 1986). Optimists are more likely to deal with their problems head-on—that is, to use active coping strategies (Chapter 6). On the other hand, pessimists are more likely to distract themselves or resort to denial when faced with a difficult problem. Consider a recent investigation that compared optimistic and pessimistic college students on the coping strategies they used when facing a big exam (Chang, 1998). As shown in Figure 8.5, the optimists dealt with the stress of the upcoming exam by using direct problem solving, such as preparing for the test and talking with other students about their experience. On the other hand, the pessimists dealt with their anxiety by relying on wishful thinking and withdrawing from others.

Researchers find a similar pattern when examining optimists and pessimists facing other types of stressors. For example, optimistic cancer patients in one study were more likely than pessimists to use active coping strategies (Friedman et al., 1992). The optimistic patients did what they could to deal with their cancer and talked to other people about their feelings. In contrast, pessimistic patients tried to avoid thinking about their situation and kept their feelings to themselves. The optimistic women in the breast cancer study mentioned earlier were more likely than the pessimists to make plans early in the course of the disease and to rely on such positive coping strategies as humor (Carver et al., 1993). The pessimistic patients were more likely to use denial. A similar pattern was found for the men recovering from bypass surgery (Scheier et al., 1989). Even the freshman students dealing with the stresses of entering college showed this different use of coping strategies. The optimistic students dealt with the stress of new classes, new friends, and new social pressures by trying to do something about these problems directly. The pessimistic students were more likely to pretend the problems did not exist or simply avoid dealing with them for as long as possible.

Optimism and Health

Researchers also find that optimism may be good for your health. Optimists are typically in better physical health than pessimists (Robinson-Whelen, Kim, Mac-Callum, & Kiecolt-Glaser, 1997; Segerstrom, Taylor, Kemeny, & Fahey, 1998; Scheier & Carver, 1987, 1992; Scheier et al., 1989). In one study, researchers used essays written years earlier to determine how optimistic or pessimistic a group of men had been when they were 25 (Peterson, Seligman, & Vaillant, 1988). The investigators found that the optimists at age 25 were in better health at ages 45 through 60 than the pessimists in their sample.

Why are optimists healthier than pessimists? The relationship between optimism and health appears to be complex, but investigators have identified several possible links (Peterson & Bossio, 2001). For example, we know that optimists are more likely to develop wide social networks and turn to friends in times of crisis (Brissette, Scheier, & Carver, 2002). Numerous studies find social support often contributes to better health. Other research identifies more direct associations between optimism and physical measures. One team of researchers found evidence of a stronger immune system for optimists (Kamen-Siegel, Rodin, Seligman, & Dwyer, 1991). On the other hand, because they more often experience negative emotions, pessimists tend to have higher blood pressure, and this can have an impact on their health (Raikkonen, Matthews, Flory, Owens, & Gump, 1999).

Perhaps the most likely reason that optimists are healthier than pessimists is that an optimistic outlook leads to the kinds of attitudes and behaviors that contribute to good health. For example, one team of researchers looked at patients in a cardiac rehabilitation program (Shepperd, Maroto, & Pbert, 1996). Each participant entered the program after suffering a heart attack or having been diagnosed with some other cardiovascular problem. Compared to the pessimists in the program, the optimistic patients were more successful in reducing saturated fat from their diet, decreasing body fat, and increasing their aerobic capacity. These optimistic patients apparently decided they could reach their rehabilitation goals and did what it took to succeed. Other studies find that optimists pay more attention to relevant health information than do pessimists (Aspinwall & Brunhart, 1996) and are less prone to health-destructive habits, such as substance abuse (Carvajal, Clair, Nash, & Evans, 1998). In addition, the fatalistic view taken by pessimists may prevent them from practicing reasonable safety and health precautions, such as wearing a seat belt or using a designated driver. One team of investigators found pessimists—particularly those who expect bad events to occur in a wide range of situations—were more likely than optimists to be involved in fatal accidents (Peterson, Seligman, Yurko, Martin, & Friedman, 1998).

Defensive Pessimism

The research discussed thus far makes it clear that an optimistic outlook is more likely to lead to happiness and success than a pessimistic approach. But then how do we account for Sparky Anderson? Sparky Anderson was one of the most successful baseball managers in the history of the game. He was a major league manager for more than a quarter of a century, led his teams to more victories than all but two managers in baseball history, and is the only person to manage a World Series champion in both the American and National Leagues. We might guess that Sparky Anderson is as confident and optimistic as anyone ever hired to manage a sports team. But we would be wrong. Something else motivated Sparky every time he put on his uniform—he was terrified of losing. Although he managed nearly 4,000 games, he still became nervous the morning of a game and stayed that way all day. He considered all the things that could go wrong, all the ways his team might lose. After all his experience and all his success, just thinking about an upcoming game could make Sparky Anderson's hands shake enough to spill his cup of coffee (Antonen, 1993).

Sparky Anderson represents another type of strategy some people use when approaching a task. Researchers refer to these people as **defensive pessimists** (Norem, 2001). Unlike pessimists who simply expect the worst, defensive pessimists generate their gloomy expectations as part of a deliberate strategy for dealing with upcoming events. Defensive pessimists think about failure. Not only do they worry and fret over what may be a worst-case outcome, they even tell themselves that they probably won't do well on the upcoming task. When researchers ask people to estimate how they will perform on an upcoming test, defensive pessimists predict they will do significantly worse than most people (Norem & Cantor, 1986a, 1986b).

But why would anyone deliberately take this pessimistic approach? It's not that defensive pessimists want to fail. On the contrary, it is the defensive pessimists' fear of failure that motivates them. Defensive pessimists appear to take a dismal outlook for two reasons. First, one way these people prepare themselves for failure is by setting low expectations in advance. The sting of defeat is lessened for the defensive pessimist if it was expected all along. And to actually succeed after such low expectations is probably all the sweeter. Second, the real possibility (for them) that they might fail may actually push defensive pessimists to try harder. In some ways, it's as if the pleasure that comes from success is not enough to motivate these people. Rather, it is the fear that they might do poorly that provides the incentive.

Are there really people who strategically expect the worst? Consider the results of a study with college honors students (Cantor, Norem, Niedenthal, Langston, & Brower, 1987). The researchers used a self-report inventory to identify the defensive pessimists as well as some dispositional optimists among freshman students. Both groups had done equally well in high school. The defensive pessimists had a mean grade point average (GPA) of 3.81, which was comparable to the optimists' GPA of 3.83. Yet when these students were asked what grades they expected their first semester, the defensive pessimists gave an average GPA estimate of 3.24, whereas the optimists guessed 3.64. Clearly, the two kinds of students had different expectations for how they would do in their classes.

How did these different expectations affect the students' actual classroom performance? On the one hand, we might expect a kind of self-fulfilling prophecy to operate here. That is, psychologists find people sometimes do poorly on a test because they expect a poor outcome (Jones, 1977). On the other hand, the defensive pessimists' strategy is not to fail but simply to prepare themselves for the worst possible outcome. In fact, the defensive pessimists and the optimists devoted an equivalent amount of time to their schoolwork. Consequently, when first-semester grades arrived, the defensive pessimists had an average GPA of 3.34, nearly identical to the optimists' 3.38. Their lowered expectations did not appear to have hurt them after all.

Other studies confirm that defensive pessimists deliberately think about the very things that make them anxious when facing a potential failure (Cantor & Norem, 1989; Norem, 1989; Showers & Ruben, 1990). But do defensive pessimists actually benefit from focusing on the negative rather than the positive? What would happen if defensive pessimists didn't engage in this worrisome thinking? To find out, one team of investigators told defensive pessimists they would soon be tested on a series of mental arithmetic problems (Norem & Illingworth, 1993). Half the participants were allowed to do what defensive pessimists typically do when facing this kind of task. They were instructed to reflect on their thoughts and feelings about the upcoming test and to list those thoughts for the experimenter. The remaining defensive pessimists were given a proofreading exercise that effectively prevented them from thinking about the upcoming arithmetic problems. The researchers measured the participants' mood just prior to taking the test and looked at how well they did on the arithmetic problems. As shown in Figure 8.6,

Figure 8.6

Anxiety Level
and Arithmetic
Test Scores

Source: Adapted from
Norem and Illingworth
(1993).

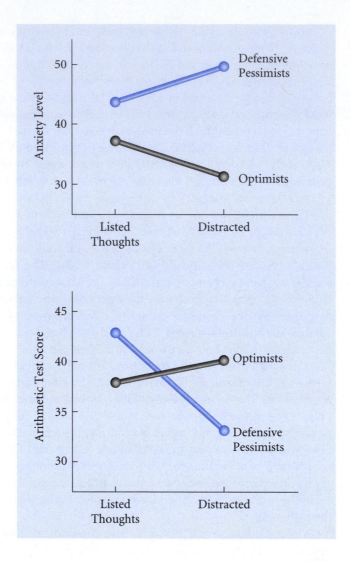

the defensive pessimists allowed to worry and fret about the upcoming test actually felt better than the participants not allowed to do this. Moreover, the defensive pessimists allowed to list their thoughts performed better on the arithmetic problems than the participants who were distracted prior to the test.

The results of this experiment suggest that thinking about all that can go wrong before a test actually helps some people. But is this true for everyone? The answer is no. In the same experiment, the researchers also looked at dispositional optimists. In contrast to the defensive pessimists, thinking about their thoughts beforehand made the optimists more anxious and caused them to perform more poorly on the arithmetic problems. If given a choice, optimists expect to succeed and prefer not to think about failure. In this way, optimists avoid the anxiety that comes from fretting over worst-case scenarios. One study found that optimists did best at a dart-throwing game when allowed to relax for 10 minutes as they waited to play (Spencer & Norem, 1996). Predictably, defensive pessimists in this study did better when given 10 minutes to think about how they might deal with all the things that might go wrong.

The benefits defensive pessimists derive from focusing on the negative are not limited to achievement situations. Defensive pessimists in one study were told they were to have a short conversation with a stranger and that this other person would evaluate them afterward (Showers, 1992). In many ways this experimental situation is similar to dates, first meetings, and other social situations in which we are concerned about making a good impression. As in the earlier experiment, half the defensive pessimists were allowed to engage in their typical strategy. These participants were instructed to think about all the things that could go wrong in the upcoming conversation (e.g., There are long, awkward silences.). The other half was told to imagine positive outcomes (e.g., It is easy to talk to each other.). The participants then spent 5 minutes talking to a student they did not know. How did the conversations go? The defensive pessimists allowed to contemplate potential negative consequences talked significantly more and were liked more by the person they spoke with than the defensive pessimists forced to think about potential positive outcomes only. Again, this pattern was not found when the researchers looked at people who generally take an optimistic approach to their social encounters. Thus, in social settings as well as achievement situations, thinking about the worst appears to help some people do their best.

 *Summary*

1.   Achievement motivation has been an important research topic for several decades. Much of the early work in this area was based on Henry Murray's description of people high in need for Achievement. More recent investigations look at the effects of attributions and goals on achievement behavior.

2.   Research on the Type A behavior pattern developed out of some atheoretical predictions about who suffers heart attacks. Among other behaviors related to this personality trait, Type A people generally perform better in achievement situations than Type B's. Although early researchers found a strong link between Type A behavior and cardiovascular problems, later studies did not always replicate these findings. Two explanations for this failure concern the way researchers measure Type A and recognizing that anger and hostility is the Type A component related to health problems.

3.   Research on socially anxious people finds a number of characteristic behaviors that interfere with the shy person's ability to interact effectively with others. Shy people tend to be self-conscious during social encounters, are reluctant to ask

others for help, and often interpret feedback from their conversation partners as rejection. Research suggests that socially anxious people suffer from evaluation apprehension. Shy people try to avoid negative evaluation from others by limiting their social interactions or by keeping these interactions short and pleasant. The socially anxious persons' lack of confidence makes initiating conversations especially difficult for them.

4.   Although emotions fluctuate considerably over time and across situations, researchers have identified three ways our emotions can be examined in terms of relatively stable individual differences. Researchers place our emotions along two major dimensions, which they identify as positive affect and negative affect. Personality researchers also look at emotional intensity and at individual differences in the extent to which people express their emotions.

5.   People can be identified along a continuum from dispositionally optimistic to dispositionally pessimistic. Researchers find optimists typically deal more effectively with adversity, probably because they use more active and direct coping strategies than pessimists. Researchers have also identified people they call defensive pessimists. These individuals deliberately focus on all the things that can go wrong in an effort to motivate themselves to do well.

InfoTrac College Edition Key Terms

For additional readings go to http://www.infotrac-college.com/wadsworth and enter a search term related to your interest. Use the key terms suggested here to pull up several related articles. Also see the text Web site at http://psychology.wadsworth.com for more suggested readings and interactive quizzes to test your knowledge.

Achievement goals	Social anxiety
Attributions	Type A personality
Hostility	Type B personality

Chapter 9

The Biological Approach

Theory, Application, and Assessment

Hans Eysenck's Theory of Personality
Temperament
Evolutionary Personality Psychology
Application: Children's Temperaments and School
Assessment: Brain Electrical Activity and Cerebral Asymmetry
Strengths and Criticisms of the Biological Approach
Summary

Have you ever been told that you look or act like one of your parents? Perhaps one of your mother's friends has said, "You're your mother's son (daughter) all right." My brother's quick temper has often been described as "inherited from his father." I know one couple who were more interested in learning about the family of their daughter's fiancé than about the fiancé. They told me that meeting the new in-laws would help them see what their future grandchildren would be like. As these examples suggest, the notion that children inherit characteristics from their parents is widely held in this society. Not only do people accept that parents pass physical characteristics, such as eye color or height, through their genes, but we often expect children's personalities to resemble their parents'.

Although conventional wisdom has for years acknowledged the role of biology in the development of personality, the same cannot be said of many psychologists. Thirty to 40 years ago, many academic psychologists looked at all healthy newborns as blank slates, perhaps limited by differences in intelligence or physical skills but otherwise equally likely to develop into any kind of adult personality.

Different adult personalities were attributed to differences in experiences, particularly in the way parents raised their children during the children's early years. However, this view has slowly changed over the past several decades. No reputable psychologist would argue that people are born with their adult personalities intact, but today few psychologists would deny that personality is at least partly the result of inherited biological differences.

This acceptance of a genetic influence on personality has coincided with a growing recognition that personality cannot be separated from other biological factors. Recent evidence tells us that not all people have identical physiological functioning. That is, we can identify differences between people in terms of brain-wave activity, hormone levels, heart-rate responsiveness, and other physiological features. More important for personality psychologists, researchers find these biological differences often translate into differences in behavior. We'll review an example of this later in this chapter when we look at individual differences in brain-wave patterns.

We also have seen in recent years a growing recognition that human personality, like other human features, is the product of many generations of evolutionary development. Just as biologists find it useful to ask about the evolutionary function of the physical characteristics of a species, some psychologists have found this same question useful in understanding certain features of personality.

This growing acceptance of a biological influence on personality is partly a reflection of behaviorism's declining influence on the thinking of academic psychologists. As described in Chapter 13, early behaviorists tended to ignore individual differences among newborns, and a few even claimed that with enough control over the child's experiences they could shape a child into whatever personality they wanted. Probably no behaviorist would argue such an extreme position today. The movement away from the "blank slate" position has also been stimulated by research demonstrating rather clearly that at least some of our personality is inherited from our parents. This research is reviewed in the next chapter.

In this chapter, we'll look at three ways psychologists have used biological concepts to explain personality. First, we'll examine Hans Eysenck's description of personality, which has been an influential model in personality research for several decades. From the beginning, Eysenck maintained that the individual differences in personality he described are based on physiological differences. Second, we will look at individual differences in general dispositions, called temperaments. A strong case can be made that temperaments are based on biological differences. Psychologists have been successful in identifying some of these differences in temperaments among very young babies. Third, we'll examine a fairly new area of personality research called evolutionary personality psychology. Psychologists using this approach borrow the concept of natural selection from biology to explain a large number of relatively stable human behaviors.

What each of these three theoretical perspectives makes clear is that a complete understanding of human personality requires us to go beyond some of the traditional boundaries of the discipline. It is no longer useful to think of our personality as somehow separate from our physiological makeup.

Hans Eysenck's Theory of Personality

More than 30 years ago, when the conventional wisdom in psychology traced an individual's personality to his or her experiences, a respected psychologist argued that personality was, in fact, determined more by biological makeup than by any actions or mistakes made by one's parents. Although Hans Eysenck's (pronounced Eye-Zinc) theory of personality has always been accorded respect within the field, his initial claims about such a large biological determinant of personality were met by many with a mix of skepticism and tolerance. But today Eysenck's emphasis on biological aspects of individual differences is increasingly compatible with the growing recognition of biology's role in personality.

The Structure of Personality

Like Raymond Cattell and other psychologists described in Chapter 7, Eysenck was concerned with discovering the underlying structure of personality traits. Also like these trait researchers, Eysenck employed factor analysis to identify the basic number of what he called types, or supertraits. However, unlike most of the trait researchers, Eysenck's conclusion after years of research was that all traits can be subsumed within *three* basic personality dimensions. He called these three dimensions extraversion-introversion, neuroticism, and psychoticism.

Eysenck's research strategy begins by dividing the elements of personality into various units that can be arranged hierarchically (Figure 9.1). The basic structure in this scheme is the *specific response level,* which consists of specific behaviors. For example, if we watch a man spend the afternoon talking and laughing with friends, we would be observing a specific response. If this man spends many afternoons each week having a good time with friends, we have evidence for the second level in Eysenck's model, a *habitual response*. But it is likely that this man doesn't limit himself to socializing just in the afternoon and just with these friends. Suppose this man also devotes a large part of his weekends and quite a few evenings to his social life. If you watch long enough, you might find that he lives for social gatherings, discussion groups, parties, and so on. You might conclude, in Eysenck's terms, that this person exhibits the *trait* of sociability. Eysenck also argued that traits such as sociability are part of a still larger dimension of personality. That is, people who are sociable also tend to be impulsive, active, lively, and excitable. All of these traits combine to form the *supertrait* Eysenck calls extraversion.

How many of these supertraits are there? Originally, Eysenck's factor analytic research yielded evidence for two basic dimensions that could subsume all other traits: *extraversion-introversion* and *neuroticism*. Because the dimensions are in-

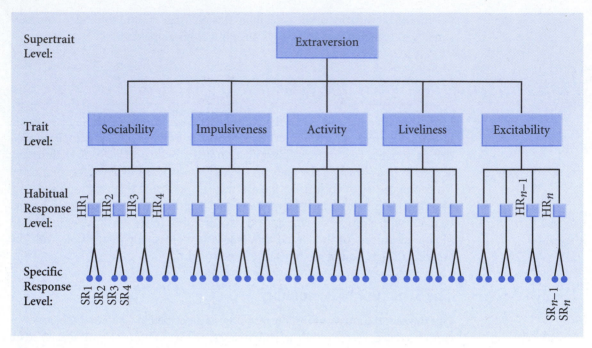

Figure 9.1

Eysenck's Hierarchical Model of Personality

dependent of one another, people who score on the extraversion end of the first dimension can score either high or low on the second dimension. Further, as shown in Figure 9.2, someone who scores high on extraversion and low on neuroticism possesses traits different from a person who scores high on both extraversion and neuroticism.

Where do you suppose you fall in this model? If you are the prototypic extravert, you are "outgoing, impulsive, and uninhibited, having many social contacts and frequently taking part in group activities. The typical extravert is sociable, likes parties, has many friends, needs to have people to talk to, and does not like reading or studying by himself" (Eysenck & Eysenck, 1968, p. 6). An introvert is "a quiet, retiring sort of person, introspective, fond of books rather than people; he is reserved and distant except to intimate friends" (p. 6). Of course, most people fall somewhere between these two extremes, but each of us is perhaps a little more of one than the other.

Eysenck argued that extraverts and introverts differ not only in terms of behavior but also in their physiological makeup. He originally maintained that extraverts and introverts have different levels of cerebral cortex arousal when in a nonstimulating, resting state (Eysenck, 1967). Although it may sound backward at first, he proposed that extraverts generally have a *lower* level of cortical arousal than do introverts. Extraverts seek out highly arousing social behavior because their cortical arousal is well below their desired level when doing nothing. In a sense, highly extraverted people are simply trying to avoid unpleasant boredom. Their problem is feeding their need for stimulation. Introverts have the opposite problem. They typically operate at an above-optimal cortical arousal level. These people select solitude and nonstimulating environments in an effort to keep their already high arousal level from becoming too aversive. For these reasons, extraverts enjoy a noisy party that introverts can't wait to leave.

Unfortunately, a great deal of research has failed to uncover the different levels of base-rate cortical arousal proposed by Eysenck. For example, introverts and extraverts show no differences in brain-wave activity when at rest or when asleep (Stelmack, 1990). But this does not mean that Eysenck's original theorizing was entirely off base. Rather, there is ample evidence that introverts are more sensitive to stimulation than extraverts (Bullock & Gilliland, 1993; Stelmack, 1990; Swickert & Gilliland, 1998). That is, introverts are more quickly and strongly aroused when exposed to external stimulation. Introverts are more likely to become aroused when they encounter loud music or the stimulation found in an active social encounter. Introverts are even more responsive than extraverts when exposed to chemical stimulants, such as caffeine or nicotine.

As a result of these research findings, many researchers now describe extraverts and introverts in terms of their different sensitivity to stimulation rather than the different base rate of cortical activity Eysenck proposed. However, the effect is

Figure 9.2

Traits Associated with Eysenck's Two Major Personality Dimensions

Source: Adapted from Eysenck and Eysenck (1968); reprinted by permission of Educational and Industrial Testing Service.

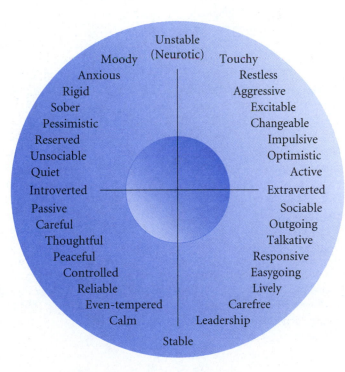

Hans J. Eysenck

1916–1997

If heredity plays a large role in determining personality, we might guess that Hans Eysenck was born to be the center of attention in whatever field he chose to enter. Eysenck was born in Germany into a family of celebrities. His father, Eduard Eysenck, was an accomplished actor and singer, something of a matinee idol in Europe. His mother, whose stage name was Helga Molander, was a silent film star. They planned a glamorous career in the entertainment field for Hans, who at age eight had a small role in a motion picture. However, like many Hollywood marriages today, Eysenck's parents divorced when he was young (only later to marry other show business people). Most of Eysenck's early years were spent with his grandmother in Berlin.

Upon graduating from public school in Berlin, the rebellious Eysenck decided not only to pursue a career in physics and astronomy, much to his family's displeasure, but to do so abroad. After a year in France, he moved to England, where he eventually completed his Ph.D. at the University of London. Like so many others at the time, Eysenck left Germany in 1934 in part to escape the rise of the Nazis. "Faced with the choice of having to join the Nazi storm troops if I wanted to go to a university," he wrote, "I knew that there was no future for me in my unhappy homeland" (Eysenck, 1982, p. 289). Because he was a German citizen, Eysenck was prohibited from joining the British military and spent World War II working in an emergency hospital. Following the war, Eysenck returned to the University of London, where his long career produced 79 books and more than 1000 journal articles (Farley, 2000).

Although he never pursued the career in show business his parents desired, he did not avoid the public's eye. Eysenck appeared to seek out and dive right into some of the biggest controversies in psychology. In 1952 he published a paper challenging the effectiveness of psychotherapy. He was especially critical of psychoanalysis, pointing out that empirical evidence at the time showed psychoanalysis to be no better than receiving no treatment at all. More controversy occurred when he stated that individual differences in intelligence are largely inherited. Although this notion is widely accepted today, Eysenck was sometimes unfairly associated with those who proposed inherent racial differences in intelligence. In 1980 Eysenck published a book arguing that the case for cigarettes as a cause of health problems was not as strong as many people claimed. Critics were particularly harsh when they discovered that some of this work had been sponsored by American tobacco companies.

This lifelong combative style caused one biographer to call Eysenck the "controversialist in the intellectual world" (Gibson, 1981, p. 253). Eysenck would no doubt have enjoyed this title. "From the days of opposition to Nazism in my early youth, through my stand against Freudianism and projective techniques, to my advocacy of behavior therapy and genetic studies, to more recent issues, I have usually been against the establishment and in favor of the rebels," he wrote. "[But] I prefer to think that on these issues the majority were wrong, and I was right" (1982, p. 298).

essentially the same. Because of physiological differences, introverts are more quickly overwhelmed by the stimulation of a crowded social gathering, whereas extraverts are likely to find the same gathering rather pleasant. Extraverts are quickly bored by slow-moving movie plots and soft music because they are less likely than introverts to become aroused by these subtle sources of stimulation.

Other researchers describe differences between extraversion and introversion in terms of a biologically based sensitivity to reinforcement (Gray, 1982, 1987). According to this explanation, extraverts are more aware of and more attracted to situations that promise rewards. When extraverts encounter an opportunity to have a good time, an activation system is triggered that causes them to approach the object of their desire. As a result, extraverts are more impulsive than introverts and are more likely to find themselves in the middle of a party or riding on a roller coaster. One implication of this description is that extraverts aren't necessarily attracted to all social situations, but only to those that are likely to be enjoyable (Lucas, Diener, Grob, Suh, & Shao, 2000). One team of researchers found that extraverts actually preferred nonsocial situations, such as going for a walk alone, more than introverts did *if* they thought the experience would be pleasant (Lucas & Diener, 2001).

The second major dimension in Eysenck's model is *neuroticism*. High scores on this dimension indicate a tendency to respond emotionally. We sometimes refer to people high in neuroticism as unstable or highly emotional. They often have strong emotional reactions to minor frustrations and problems and take longer to recover from these. They are more easily excited, angered, and depressed than most of us. Those falling on the other end of this dimension are less likely to fly off the handle and less prone to large swings in emotion.

Research findings later led Eysenck to add a third supertrait: *psychoticism*. People who score high on this dimension are described as "egocentric, aggressive, impersonal, cold, lacking in empathy, impulsive, lacking in concern for others, and generally unconcerned about the rights and welfare of other people" (Eysenck, 1982, p. 11). Needless to say, people scoring particularly high on this dimension are good candidates for some type of judicial correction or psychotherapy.

A Biological Basis for Personality

"Heritability is not a fixed number. Once you realize what's inherited, there's a lot you can do about it."

HANS EYSENCK

Eysenck (1990) pointed to three arguments when making the case that individual differences in personality are based in biology. First, he noted the consistency of extraversion-introversion over time. Several studies find that a person's level of this individual difference remains fairly stable for many years. Participants in one study showed a consistent level of extraversion-introversion over a span of 45 years (Conley, 1984, 1985). Of course, this finding alone does not establish that extraversion-introversion is determined through biology. It is possible that people remain in similar environments throughout their lives or throughout the time period in which this personality trait is developed.

How do you spend your spare time? If you're an extravert, it probably never occurs to you to take a long walk by yourself. If you're an introvert, you may rely on a long walk to reduce your arousal level after an intense and active day.

Photo by Marlene Somsak

Therefore, Eysenck also used the results of cross-cultural research to make his point. He argued that researchers find the same three dimensions of personality—extraversion-introversion, neuroticism, and psychoticism—in research conducted in many different countries with different cultural backgrounds and histories (Barrett & Eysenck, 1984; Lynn & Martin, 1995). Moreover, Eysenck argued that the three "superfactors" not only appear in his research, but also in the work of other investigators using different data gathering methods (Eysenck & Long, 1986). "Such cross-cultural unanimity would be unlikely if biological factors did not play a predominant part," Eysenck reasoned. "The great differences in culture, education, and environment generally would be expected to produce a variety of different personality dimensions" (1990, p. 246).

Third, Eysenck pointed to the results of several studies indicating that genetics plays an important role in determining a person's level on each of the three personality dimensions. As presented in detail in the next chapter, this research strongly suggests that each of us inherited a predisposition to be introverted or extraverted.

After examining the evidence from all of these sources, and no doubt adding a bit of his own intuition, Eysenck (1982) asserted that about two-thirds of the variance in personality development can be traced to biological factors. Although our current state of knowledge does not allow for such a precise estimate, data from a continuing stream of studies suggests that extraverts and introverts differ on a number of biological measures (Cox-Fuenzalida, Gilliland, & Swickert, 2001; Doucet & Stelmack, 2000; Stelmack & Pivik, 1996). This is not to say that environmental factors do not play a role, particularly in shaping how general personality orientations are expressed. Nonetheless, as the evidence reviewed in the next chapter makes clear, biology probably sets limits on how much we can change an introverted friend into a highly sociable individual or the likelihood of shaping that impulsive, outgoing child into a calmer, easygoing adult.

Temperament

If you were to spend a few minutes watching toddlers in a nursery school, one of the first observations you might make is that even before they are a year old, children seem to be different. If you were to spend a week working in the nursery, you would most likely be able to identify the active babies, the ones who cry frequently, and (hopefully) a few who are usually quiet and happy. Although it is possible these differences are the result of different treatment the children receive at home, a growing number of researchers are convinced these general behavioral styles may be present at birth. Further, they argue that these general styles are relatively stable and influence the development of personality traits throughout a person's life.

But does this mean that some people are born to be sociable and others born to be shy? Probably not. More likely we are born with broad dispositions toward certain types of behaviors. Psychologists refer to these general behavioral dispositions as **temperaments.** The concept of temperaments has been around for a long time in personality theory. Allport described temperament as "the characteristic phenomena of an individual's emotional nature" (1961, p. 34). Today researchers generally think of temperaments as general patterns of behavior and mood that can be expressed in many different ways and that, depending on one's experiences, develop into different personality traits. How these general dispositions develop into stable personality traits depends on a complex interplay of one's genetic predispositions and the environment that a person grows up in.

emotionality

Temperament and Personality

How many temperamental differences can we identify in humans? Although the number of personality traits identified by researchers is practically unlimited, the number of dimensions along which human temperaments can vary are few. This is because temperament researchers are more concerned with *how* a person responds than with *which* response is made. To these psychologists, it is not so important to know that a person frequently gives speeches in front of large groups. Rather, we can get a better idea of the person's temperament by examining whether he or she speaks quickly or slowly, with great emphasis or in a restrained manner (Buss & Plomin, 1975). Moreover, temperaments are broad personality dispositions rather than specific personality traits. How general behavioral dispositions develop into specific traits depends on how those dispositions interact with the environment the person grows up in. Individual differences in temperament can usually be seen in the first year of life and persist throughout a person's lifetime (A. H. Buss, 1991).

Although researchers agree that temperaments are general behavioral patterns that can often be seen in newborns, they do not always agree on how to identify and classify the different kinds of temperaments they observe (Caspi, 1998; Rothbart, Ahadi, & Evans, 2000; Shiner, 1998). Indeed, researchers often disagree on the number of basic temperaments. One widely accepted temperament model that applies to both children and adults identifies three temperament dimensions (Buss & Plomin, 1984, 1986). These three dispositions are emotionality, activity, and sociability. In this model, *emotionality* refers to the intensity of emotional reactions. Children who cry frequently and easily become frightened and aroused to anger are high in this temperament. Adults who easily become upset and have a "quick temper" are also high in general emotionality. *Activity* refers to the person's general level of energy output. Children high in this temperament move around a lot, prefer games that require a great deal of activity, and tend to fidget and squirm when forced to sit still for an extended period of time. Adults with a high level of activity temperament are always on the go, prefer active to quiet pastimes, and keep busy most of the time. *Sociability* relates to a person's general tendency to affiliate and interact with others. Sociable children seek out others to play with. They enjoy and are responsive to people. Adults with this temperament have a lot of friends and enjoy social encounters. You can get an idea of how you compare on these three temperaments by completing the scale on pages 256–257.

Where do temperaments come from? Because we can identify temperament differences in babies, it is reasonable to argue that temperaments are largely inherited. In contrast to the approach taken by many physicians and psychologists a few decades ago, it is now widely agreed that not all babies are born alike. Parents with difficult-to-manage babies are often troubled by descriptions of the "typical" baby who sleeps whenever put into a crib, eats meals on a regular schedule, and responds to parental attention with calm, loving sounds. Fortunately, most popular baby books today assure parents that some babies are going to be more active and more emotional than others. Research using a variety of methods (reviewed in the next chapter) has produced considerable evidence that temperaments are to a large degree inherited (Neale & Stevenson, 1989).

Can we look at temperament levels in a preschool child and determine what kind of adult personality he or she will have? To a certain degree, the answer is yes.

Consider the results of an ongoing longitudinal study conducted in Dunedin, New Zealand (Caspi, 2000). Ninety-one percent of the children born in this town between April 1, 1972 and March 31, 1973 were tested for temperament at age 3. The researchers identified three temperament types in these toddlers. The *well-adjusted* children exhibited self-control and self-confidence, and were capable of approaching new people and situations with little difficulty. The *undercontrolled* children were impulsive and restless, and easily distracted. The *inhibited* children were fearful, reluctant to get involved in social activities, and uneasy in the presence of strangers. The investigators examined personality development and behavior at several points as the children moved through childhood and adolescence and into their young adult years. Although the well-adjusted children became relatively healthy, well-adjusted adults, the undercontrolled and inhibited children's lives were different. During the elementary school years and adolescence, undercontrolled children were more likely to have problems with fighting, lying, and disobeying at both school and home. As young adults, these individuals were more likely to experience legal, employment, and relationship problems. Inhibited children showed more signs of worrying and fussing when growing up, and as adults were less socially engaged and more likely to suffer from depression. Although temperament by no means is the sole determinant of adult personality and behavior, this study and others argue that temperament plays an important role in personality development.

But the process through which general temperaments develop into personality traits is complex and influenced by a large number of factors (Caspi, 1998; Rothbart & Ahadi, 1994). Although the child's general level of emotionality or activity points the development of personality in a certain direction, that development is also influenced by the child's experiences as he or she grows up. For example, a highly emotional child has a better chance of becoming an aggressive adult than does a child low in this temperament. But parents who encourage problem-solving skills over the expression of anger may turn the highly emotional child into a cooperative, nonaggressive adult. A child low in sociability is unlikely to become an outgoing, highly gregarious adult. But that child might develop excellent social skills, be a wonderful friend, and learn to lead others with a quiet, respectful style.

One reason general dispositions set the direction for adult personality traits is that a child's disposition influences the type of environment he or she lives in (Caspi, 1998; Rothbart & Ahadi, 1994). How other people react to us, and whether they will be a part of our environment at all, is partly determined by our temperament. Thus, children high in sociability are likely to seek out situations with other people. Parents react differently to a baby who is constantly fussing and restless than to one who sleeps calmly. As a result, the restless baby experiences a different parent-child relationship than children with other temperaments. Temperament also generates expectations in other people that can affect the way they treat a child. Preschool teachers in one study expected different personalities in the children in their classes based on observations about the child's general activity level

Assessing Your Own Personality

Temperament

Rate each of the items using the following scale: 1 = Not at all characteristic of me; 2 = Somewhat uncharacteristic of me; 3 = Neither characteristic nor uncharacteristic of me; 4 = Somewhat characteristic of me; 5 = Very characteristic of me.

_____   1. I like to be with people. (S)

_____   2. I usually seem to be in a hurry. (Ac)

_____   3. I am easily frightened. (F)

_____   4. I frequently get distressed. (D)

_____   5. When displeased, I let people know it right away. (An)

_____   6. I am something of a loner. (S)

_____   7. I like to keep busy all the time. (Ac)

_____   8. I am known as hot-blooded and quick-tempered. (An)

_____   9. I often feel frustrated. (D)

_____   10. My life is fast-paced. (Ac)

_____   11. Everyday events make me troubled and fretful. (D)

_____   12. I often feel insecure. (F)

_____   13. There are many things that annoy me. (An)

_____   14. When I get scared, I panic. (F)

_____   15. I prefer working with others rather than alone. (S)

(Graziano, Jensen-Campbell, & Sullivan-Logan, 1998). It is not hard to imagine that these different expectancies lead to different treatment.

In short, adult personalities are determined by both inherited temperament and the environment. Moreover, temperament influences the environment, and the environment then influences the way temperament develops into stable personality traits. Two children born with identical temperaments can grow up to be two very different people. A child with a high activity level may become an aggressive, achieving, or athletic adult. But that child will probably not become lazy and indifferent. A child does not represent a blank slate on which parents may draw whatever personality they desire. But neither is a child's personality set at birth, leaving the parents and society to settle for whatever they get.

_____ 16. I get emotionally upset easily. (D)

_____ 17. I often feel as if I'm bursting with energy. (Ac)

_____ 18. It takes a lot to make me mad. (An)

_____ 19. I have fewer fears than most people my age. (F)

_____ 20. I find people more stimulating than anything else. (S)

To obtain your scores, first reverse the value you gave items 6, 18, and 19 (that is, $5 = 1$, $4 = 2$, $3 = 3$, $2 = 4$, $1 = 5$). Then use the letters in the parentheses following each item to identify which subscale the item belongs to. (Note that the researchers have divided the Emotionality dimension into three parts.) Sum the items for each of the scales to obtain your five scores. To get a better idea of what these scores mean, compare your scores with the averages the test developers obtained for a sample of adults:

	Women	Men
Emotionality		
Distress	10.08	9.72
Fearfulness	10.60	8.92
Anger	10.28	10.80
Activity	13.40	12.80
Sociability	15.24	14.60

Scale: *The EAS Temperament Survey for Adults*

Source: Buss and Plomin (1984)

Inhibited and Uninhibited Children

Many years ago, two developmental psychologists reported the results of an investigation on personality trait stability (Kagan & Moss, 1962). Traits had been measured when the participants were 2 or 3 years old and again when these same people were 20. Although most traits showed some change over time, one appeared remarkably stable. The researchers found that children who were passive and cautious when faced with a new situation usually grew up to be adults who showed a similar pattern of shyness around strangers. Because environmental explanations of behavior were prevalent at the time, the researchers assumed this stable trait was the result of some type of "acquired fearfulness" shaped by the parents during childhood.

Some children appear to inherit a tendency to respond to unfamiliar situations with increased arousal. When entering a new situation with new people, many of these children display what we typically call "shy" behavior.

Today, those psychologists have a different interpretation. Recent research suggests this tendency to react to unfamiliar situations with an inhibited style is an inherited disposition (Kagan, 1989; Kagan, Reznick, & Snidman, 1986, 1988; Kagan & Snidman, 1991a, 1991b). Studies indicate that approximately 10% of Caucasian American children can be classified as inhibited (Kagan & Snidman, 1991a). **Inhibited children** are controlled and gentle. When they throw a ball or knock over a tower of blocks, they do it in a manner that is "monitored, restrained, almost soft." Inhibited children are the ones who cling to their mothers or fathers when entering a new playroom or when meeting new children. They are slow to explore new toys or equipment and may go for several minutes without saying a word.

Researchers compare these inhibited children with **uninhibited children,** who show the opposite pattern. Approximately 25% of the children in their samples fall into this category (Kagan & Snidman, 1991a). These youngsters express themselves in an energetic and spontaneous manner. They typically play with new toys right away and speak within a few minutes after entering a new play area.

On the surface, the difference between the two kinds of children appears to be how they experience and express anxiety. But inhibited children are not simply more afraid of everything. Rather, they are vulnerable to a specific form of anxiety generated by unfamiliar people and situations. Psychologists refer to this as *anxiety to novelty.* Toddlers typically express their anxiety about the unfamiliar by turning away from strangers and burying their face in mother's or father's leg. As adults, they may express their discomfort in a new situation by withdrawing socially and waiting for others to speak first.

Anyone who has worked with young children can agree that some children fit the inhibited description and others fit the uninhibited description. But are these stable styles or just a passing phase? Can we predict from very early childhood behavior what kind of adult the child will become? Psychologists suggest that the answer is yes because these differences in temperament appear to be biologically based. Inhibited and uninhibited children show a number of physical differences almost from the moment of birth. They differ in terms of body build, susceptibility to allergies, and even eye color (inhibited children are more likely to have blue eyes). Inhibited children are more likely than uninhibited children to show signs of irritability, sleep disturbances, and chronic constipation during the first few months of life. Some newborns show increases in heart rate and pupil dilation when presented with unfamiliar stimuli as early as the first few days of life. These babies are often identified as inhibited children a few years later (LaGasse, Gruber, & Lipsitt, 1989).

How stable are these different tendencies in response to the unfamiliar? One study attempted to identify inhibited and uninhibited children from a group of 4-month-old infants (Kagan, 1989; Kagan & Snidman, 1991a, 1991b). Trained judges looked at the babies' motor activity—arm and leg movements, tongue protrusions, crying—to place the children into categories. The infants with the highest levels of motor activity were expected to develop into inhibited children. All the children were tested for their level of fearfulness to unfamiliar events at ages 9, 14, and 21 months. Several tests were given at each age and the amount of anxiety expressed by the child recorded. For example, at 9 months the children saw a puppet speaking in an angry tone, and at 14 months they were shown a large metal robot they could play with. The researchers recorded indications of fear, such as crying or hiding.

The children identified as candidates for an inhibited style at age 4 months indeed showed more signs of fearfulness at the later testing sessions. Forty percent of the infants classified as likely inhibited children frequently expressed fear at 14 and 21 months, but none of the children identified as uninhibited did. The findings from this study support the contention that inhibited and uninhibited styles in children are fairly stable beginning at a very early age.

Do these temperaments show up after the first few years of life? The results of another study suggest that they do (Reznick et al., 1986). These investigators measured children's fear of unfamiliar situations at 21 months of age and again when the children reached 4 years. When the children reached age 5½, they were brought back into the laboratory and examined in a number of situations. For example, experimenters coded how much the children played with unfamiliar children in the laboratory playroom, how spontaneously they allowed themselves to fall onto a mattress when playing a falling game, and how risky they were in a

Table 9.1 Correlations Between Earlier Inhibition Measures and Behaviors at Age 5½ Years

Behavior at Age 5½ Years	Inhibition Score at Age 21 Months	Inhibition Score at Age 4 Years
Play with unfamiliar children	.43	.76
Laboratory activity level	.38	.27
Look at experimenter	.22	.41
Play with new toys	.19	.35
Spontaneous falling	.40	.32
Ball-toss riskiness	.35	.25
Social interaction in school	.34	.12
Mother's rating of shyness	.55	.36

Note: The higher the score, the better the earlier inhibition score predicts the behavior at 5½.

Source: From Reznick et al. (1986), with permission.

ball-tossing game. The researchers compared the behavior of the 5½-year-olds to the earlier inhibition scores. The results are shown in Table 9.1. The children who had shown an inhibited behavior pattern at each of the two earlier testing times showed the same pattern at age 5½. In other words, the toddler who clung to mother or father in a new situation showed a similar style of behavior when examined four years later.

Studies like these suggest inhibited children are likely to exhibit anxiety when responding to unfamiliar situations throughout early childhood. But what about after that? Do inhibited children become inhibited adults? To answer this question, one study measured inhibition in a group of children between the ages of 8 and 12 (Gest, 1997). These same participants were tested again nearly 10 years later, just as they were entering young adulthood. The investigator found an impressively high correlation of .57 between the two measures, indicating that quiet, apprehensive children retain many of these characteristics when they become adults.

Do these results mean inhibited children are sentenced to become shy adults? Fortunately, the answer is *no.* Researchers point out that environment still determines the degree to which this biological tendency shapes the development of adult personality (Kagan & Snidman, 1991b). Nonetheless, one study found inhibited children were more likely than uninhibited children to become shy teenagers (Schwartz, Snidman, & Kagan, 1999). Thus, although inhibited children are more likely to become shy adults, this is far from a certainty. Parents of inhibited children can do their offspring a favor by becoming sensitive to the child's discomfort in unfamiliar settings and by teaching the child how to deal with new situations and people. Research with adults indicates that many business leaders, community workers, and entertainers have learned to overcome their shyness and lead very social lives.

Evolutionary Personality Psychology

Think for a moment about some recent experiences you have had with anxiety. That is, what happened to you the last two or three times you felt nervous, worrisome, or anxious? Although direct threats to one's well-being—such as experiencing an earthquake or a physical assault—are certainly sources of anxiety, these events fortunately are relatively rare for most of us and probably did not make your list. Instead, if you are like most people, you probably thought of something like receiving a poor grade, talking in front of a group, making a fool of yourself at a party, or having a fight with a friend. In other words, you probably thought of at least one situation that involved some sort of negative evaluation and possibly even rejection by other people. Other situations on your list may have only suggested that some sort of social rejection might be coming, such as forgetting to turn in an assignment or discovering that you forgot to use deodorant one morning. What this simple exercise illustrates is that negative evaluation by other people, either directly or potentially, is a common source of anxiety.

But why might this be the case? Is this a learned behavior? Do we fear that others will punish us or refuse to give us something we want? That's certainly possible. Or could there be a psychoanalytic basis for this anxiety? At some deep level are we reminded of a traumatic separation from our parents? Perhaps. But another explanation suggests that the roots of anxiety go back much further than this. According to this approach, we react to negative social evaluation the same way our ancestors did. We inherited this tendency to become nervous and upset in certain situations because experiencing this anxiety serves an important function that has allowed human beings to survive over many generations.

This different approach is known as *evolutionary personality theory* (D. M. Buss, 1991, 1995, 1997; Buss, Haselton, Shackelford, Bleske, & Wakefield, 1998). Proponents of this theory use the process of natural selection, borrowed from the theory of evolution, to explain universal human characteristics such as anxiety. These psychologists argue that many characteristics of "human nature" make sense if we understand the evolutionary function they serve. We'll return to the example of anxiety later to illustrate this point. But first, we need to examine some of the assumptions underlying evolutionary personality theory.

Natural Selection and Psychological Mechanisms

Evolutionary personality psychology is based on the theory of evolution, as developed in the field of biology for more than a century. According to evolution theory, physical features evolve because they help the species survive the challenges of the environment and reproduce new members of the species. The key to this process is *natural selection*. That is, some members of a species possess inherited characteristics that help them meet and survive the threats from the natural environment, such as severe climate, predators, and food shortages. These survivors are more likely than those less able to deal with the environment to reproduce and pass their inherited characteristics on to their offspring. The net result over many generations is the evolution of species-specific features. Through the process of natural selection, those species developing features that help them survive prosper, and those failing to develop these features die out. In many cases, physical features evolve because they provide solutions to a serious threat to the species' survival. For example, in humans, the problem of disease was resolved by the evolution of an immune system, and the potential problem of bleeding to death when cut or wounded led to the evolution of blood clotting (D. M. Buss, 1991). This is not to say that these features were created *because* they were needed. Rather, the theory of evolution maintains that because of these changes our species was better prepared to survive.

According to evolutionary personality theory, just as the natural selection process has led to the evolution of certain physical characteristics in humans, this process is also responsible for what are called *psychological mechanisms*. These psychological mechanisms are characteristically human functions that allow us to deal effectively with common human problems or needs. Through the process of natural selection, mechanisms that increased the chances of human survival and reproduction have been retained, and those that failed to meet the challenges to survival have not.

Psychologists have identified a large number of these mechanisms. For example, most humans have an innate fear of strangers. Evolutionary personality psychologists argue that this fear evolved to meet the problem of attack by those not belonging to the group or tribe (D. M. Buss, 1991). Anger might have assisted our ancestors in such survival behaviors as asserting authority and overcoming enemies (McGuire & Troisi, 1990). Thus, it makes sense that anger is a common human characteristic. Some psychologists argue that humans have an innate need to belong to groups and form attachments (Baumeister & Leary, 1995). It is not difficult to imagine how a species that worked together would survive better than a species that did not. But whereas the survival function of some human characteristics may be easy to explain, the advantages of other psychological mechanisms might not be so obvious. We turn next to an example of one such mechanism.

Anxiety and Social Exclusion

Evolutionary personality theory maintains that human characteristics such as anxiety evolved because they proved beneficial to the survival of our ancestors. But how can this be? Anxiety is an unpleasant emotional state, something a normally functioning person would prefer to avoid. Moreover, anxiety is almost always problematic. It interferes with our ability to learn new tasks, remember information, perform sexually, and so on. How can something as disruptive as anxiety help the species?

We can answer this question by looking at what causes anxiety. Some psychologists have argued that one of the primary causes of anxiety is social exclusion (Baumeister & Tice, 1990). These investigators propose that all humans have a strong need to belong to groups and to be in relationships. Consequently, when we experience exclusion or rejection from social groups, we suffer great distress. This distress is not just limited to those relatively rare instances when we are literally rejected from a group or tossed out of a relationship. Rather, any information that suggests we might be excluded socially or that we are no longer attractive to other people is threatening to our need to belong.

As you thought about the situations that recently caused you to feel anxious, you may have recognized that many were related to a fear of social rejection. You may also have noticed that you didn't have to experience actual exclusion from a group or relationship to feel anxious. Rather, information that even hints that someday you might be rejected by others is often enough to bring on anxiety. Thinking about anxiety as fear of social rejection helps us understand why people feel anxious when they have to give a speech in front of an audience or when they discover that first gray hair. The speaker is afraid the audience members will evaluate him or her negatively, a form of social rejection. The thirtyish adult discovering a gray hair worries about his or her attractiveness to others. Although outright social rejection is not common, fear of what others will think of us may be an everyday experience.

This social exclusion explanation of anxiety fits nicely with evolutionary personality theory. Primitive people who lived together in small groups were more likely to survive and reproduce than those living alone. An isolated person would be more susceptible to injury, illness, lack of shelter, and limited resources and would be less able to mate and raise offspring than individuals living in groups or tribes. Consequently, anything that motivates people to avoid behaviors that might lead to their exclusion from the group would help the species survive. Anxiety serves this purpose. Thus, evolutionary personality psychologists argue, anxiety evolved to meet the needs of the species.

Proponents of this view cite other pieces of evidence for the evolutionary roots of anxiety. For example, although expressed in different ways, anxiety is found in nearly all cultures (Barlow, 1988). Moreover, the kinds of behavior that lead to social exclusion are typically those that impair the survival of the species (Buss, 1990). These include adultery, aggression, and taking valuable resources away from others. In this sense, evolutionary theory crosses paths with Sigmund Freud. Freud also argued that primitive people came to live in groups and developed laws against many sexual and aggressive behaviors so that the species might survive. Although Freud was concerned with repressing unconscious impulses, his analysis is in many ways similar to that of more recent evolutionary theorists.

In short, what we call "human nature" can be thought of as a large number of psychological mechanisms that have allowed humankind to survive as long as we have. Advocates of this approach do not argue that all human characteristics are necessarily beneficial. It is possible that some of our psychological mechanisms could someday contribute to the extinction of the species. But in the meantime, evolutionary personality psychology appears to provide a fruitful approach for understanding some basic features of human personality.

Application: Children's Temperaments and School

Most of us have been exposed at one time or another to a parent's or grandparent's description of the strict and regimented way teachers used to run their classes "when I was a kid." According to these stories, all children were treated alike. Each was expected to sit quietly during reading period, to work at the pace set by the teacher, and above all, to pay full attention at all times. Any deviations from the routine were met with strict and sometimes severe punishment.

Although the accuracy of these descriptions might be challenged, the point is that teachers do not approach their job the same way they did a few generations ago. There are no doubt many differences in teaching style today and many reasons for these changes. But one important difference between teaching then and teaching now is an awareness that not all children approach learning the same way. Because children are born with different temperaments, some jump right in and begin participating in lessons, but others are slow to warm up to new tasks. Some students have difficulty focusing their attention on any one activity for very long, whereas other students become frustrated when forced to move on to a new assignment before they are ready.

In fact, the transition from a familiar home environment to an unfamiliar classroom is just the kind of event that is likely to highlight differences in temperament. This was illustrated in a study in which researchers used measures of inhibition taken at age 21 months to predict how children would react to their first day of kindergarten (Gersten, 1989). Observers watched the children during a relatively unstructured free-play period their first day of school. The children who had earlier been identified as inhibited responded to this unfamiliar situation by keeping to themselves and watching their new classmates. Compared to the other children in the class, the inhibited children were less likely to play with the other boys and girls, to touch other children, to offer a toy to one of their classmates, or even to laugh. Clearly inhibited and uninhibited children respond very differently to the first day of class, and researchers find that these differences often continue throughout the school year (Gersten, 1989).

Researchers have studied other temperamental differences that affect a child's performance in school. One team of investigators identified nine of these differences (Chess & Thomas, 1996; Thomas & Chess, 1977). As shown in Table 9.2, children's temperament can vary in terms of activity level, adaptability, approach

Table 9.2   **Thomas and Chess's Nine Temperament Dimensions**

Activity Level	General level of motor activity during such periods as eating, playing, walking, or crawling.
Rhythmicity	Predictable or unpredictable patterns of behaviors, such as sleeping and hunger. Also known as regularity.
Approach or Withdrawal	Initial response to new situations or experiences, either to approach eagerly or to pull away and wait.
Adaptability	Ability to respond to a new or altered situation (after the initial reaction).
Threshold of Responsiveness	Amount of stimulation necessary to evoke a response. Includes reactions to new sensations, objects, or people.
Intensity of Reaction	Amount of energy behind response regardless of type of response.
Quality of Mood	General mood level, either pleasant and friendly or unpleasant and unfriendly.
Distractibility	Ability to stay with ongoing behavior in the face of environmental distractors.
Attention Span and Persistence	How long child can focus his or her attention on one task; how long child persists at a task in the face of obstacles.

or withdrawal, distractibility, intensity, mood, persistence, rhythmicity, and threshold. Research with these nine temperament dimensions led to the identification of three basic patterns. First, there is the *easy child,* who approaches rather than withdraws from new situations, is adaptive, and generally experiences a positive mood. Most teachers would probably prefer an entire room full of these students. However, classrooms are likely to include some examples of the *difficult child.* These children tend to withdraw rather than approach new situations, are typically low in adaptability, and are often intense and in a negative mood. A classroom is also likely to include some children who fall in the third general pattern, the *slow-to-warm-up child.* These children are similar to the inhibited children described earlier in the chapter. They tend to withdraw from unfamiliar situations and are slow to adapt to a new academic task or a new activity.

In a 6-year study of children primarily from middle-class backgrounds, researchers found that about two-thirds of the elementary school children could be identified with one of these three styles (Thomas & Chess, 1977). Forty percent of the students in the sample fell into the easy-child category, 10% in the difficult-child group, and 15% into the slow-to-warm-up category. Thus, the typical elementary school class contains a mix of children with different temperamental patterns. Obviously, this represents a significant challenge for the teacher.

Temperament and Academic Performance

Numerous studies find that a child's temperament affects how well that child does in school (Coplan, Barber, & Lagace-Seguin, 1999; Cowen, Wyman, & Work, 1992; Keogh, 1986, 1989; Lerner, Lerner, & Zabski, 1985; Martin, 1985, 1989). As you might expect, children with either the difficult or slow-to-warm-up pattern tend to perform more poorly than students with the easy-child pattern. Children with an easy-child temperament get higher grades and better evaluations from their teachers. However, differences related to temperament are also found in standardized achievement tests.

Studies indicate that temperament is not related to intelligence (Keogh, 1986). So, how does temperament affect a child's performance in school? Researchers have identified several possibilities. First, some temperaments are probably more compatible with the requirements of the typical classroom than others. For example, in most classes, children who are attentive, adaptable, and persistent are likely to do better than those who are low on these temperament dimensions. On the other hand, children with a short attention span and children who are easily distracted may have difficulty completing assignments or paying enough attention to learn their lessons the first time. Students who take a long time to adapt to new situations often find themselves behind the rest of the class. Moreover, children's reactions to these difficulties can lead to further problems. Children who fall behind or do poorly on assignments may become discouraged or give up, thus adding to their academic problems.

Second, a student's behavior evokes responses from the teacher. The student who is attentive and seemingly eager to learn is going to draw a different reaction from the typical elementary school teacher than the student who is easily distracted and withdrawn. Working with the former student probably will be pleasant and rewarding; working with the latter may be frustrating and demanding. Perhaps quite unintentionally, teachers may pay more attention to and work more closely with some students than with others. As a result, opportunities for learning and achievement may be shaped by the child's temperament.

Third, teachers sometimes misinterpret temperamental differences in their students (Keogh, 1989). Slow-to-warm-up children may be seen as unmotivated when they fail to eagerly attack an assignment or as unintelligent when they require several tries to master a new task. A highly active student might be identified as a troublemaker. An easily distracted student might be seen as uninterested in learning. These false impressions can then color the way a teacher responds to the student. A large amount of research demonstrates that teachers' explanations for their students' behavior often affect how the teacher interacts with the student and subsequently how well the student does in school (Cooper & Good, 1983).

This indirect impact of temperament on learning is illustrated in the real-life case of an elementary school student who approached schoolwork with a high-intensity, high-persistence style (Chess & Thomas, 1986). This boy had a long attention span and preferred to spend an extensive amount of time absorbed in one lesson before moving on to the next. Unfortunately, the teacher's schedule rarely allowed for this. The boy became upset whenever the teacher interrupted his lessons. Initially, the teacher interpreted the boy's reaction as an indication of some underlying behavior disorder. Fortunately, the problem was resolved when the boy's parents transferred him to a school that encouraged the kind of persistent and intense style of involvement that had been a problem in the earlier class. The happy ending in this example illustrates the main point in the next section—that differences in temperament can help or hinder academic performance, depending on the demands of the situation.

The "Goodness of Fit" Model

We might be tempted at this point to ask, what temperament characteristics contribute to better school performance? However, this is probably not the right question. Instead, most researchers in this area prefer to ask, what *kind* of environment and procedures are most conducive to learning for *this* student, given his or her temperament? The second question reflects the thinking behind the **Goodness of Fit Model.** According to the model, how well a child does in school is partly a function of how well the demands of the learning environment match the child's "capabilities, characteristics, and style of behaving" (Thomas & Chess, 1977). In other words, not all children come to school with the same learning styles or abilities. We can't do much to change a child's temperament. But if lessons and assignments are presented in a way that matches the child's learning style, an optimal amount of learning can take place. Several investigations find support for the Goodness of Fit Model (Keogh, 1986; Lerner, 1983; Lerner et al., 1985). Students get higher grades and better evaluations from teachers when the student's temperament matches the teacher's expectations and demands.

The Goodness of Fit Model thus provides an obvious strategy for improved teaching. Classroom assignments that require extensive concentration create a problem for the easily distracted girl with a short attention span. However, this girl will probably have little difficulty mastering the assignment if the same material is presented in short, easily processed segments. A slow-to-warm-up boy will fall behind when his teacher works at a pace set for the average member of the class. But if allowed to progress at his own pace, the boy eventually will come around and do as well as his classmates.

Teachers who match teaching style with temperament not only increase the chances of academic success, they may also contribute to the child's feelings of self-worth (Chess & Thomas, 1991). Children who do poorly in school begin to blame themselves. These negative evaluations are often reinforced by parents and teachers who accuse the child of not trying or communicate to the child in various ways that he or she simply may not have the ability to keep up with classmates. Such experiences can result in low self-esteem, which may then contribute further to the child's academic difficulties.

Fortunately, today most teachers are aware of differences in temperament and take steps to adapt their teaching to meet the students' individual styles (Chess & Thomas, 1996). Although time and resources may limit teachers' abilities to meet the individual needs of all their students, recognizing temperamental differences is an important step toward better learning.

Assessment: Brain Electrical Activity and Cerebral Asymmetry

The next time you're talking to some friends, you might try this quick experiment. Ask your friends some reflective questions, such as "How do you feel when you are anxious?" or "Picture and describe the most joyous scene you have recently been in." When most people engage in a little reflective thought, they tend to look off to one side. Some people consistently, although not always, glance to the right, whereas others tend to look to the left. As described later, the significance of this difference lies in what it may tell us about your friend's tendency to experience happiness or sadness. This is because which direction people look when contemplating may be a general indicator of the brain-activity patterns psychologists associate with emotion.

The notion that we can examine personality with physiological measures has been around a long time. Freud speculated that scientists would one day discover the neurological underpinnings of personality. Similarly, Allport argued that future technological advances would identify differences in the central nervous system associated with different traits. But we don't need to wait for scientific breakthroughs. Personality researchers have used various physiological measures in their experiments for many years (Geen, 1997). For example, researchers use physiological indicators of arousal, such as heart rate and galvanic skin response, to test their ideas about anxiety and coping. Other personality studies have examined hormones, immune systems, respiration, automatic muscle reflexes, and enzymes in the blood. In this section, we look at another example of how psychologists use physiological measures in personality research. These researchers examine differences in brain-activity level.

Measuring Brain Activity

How can we measure brain activity without going into a person's skull? Fortunately, technology provides relatively nonintrusive procedures for measuring brain-activity level in normal humans. Most often, researchers use an instrument called an *electroencephalograph* (EEG) to measure electrical activity in different parts of the human brain (Davidson, 1988). This procedure has been particularly useful to personality researchers for several reasons. The procedure is relatively

Researchers measure brain-activity levels with an instrument known as an EEG. This information may tell us about the person's tendency to experience positive or negative emotions.

simple and does not harm the individual in any way. Typically, small electrodes are attached to the person's head with hair clips and elastic straps. Participants report that the procedure is not uncomfortable, although electrode paste can sometimes leave messy spots in their hair. In addition, the EEG allows researchers to record brain activity in very quick intervals. Some instruments can measure this activity within milliseconds. This sensitivity is important when looking at emotions, which often change very rapidly.

Most EEGs automatically record brain activity. The data are usually described in terms of cycles per second, or waves. One kind of wave identified through this process, known as an *alpha wave*, has proven particularly useful for research on personality and emotion. The lower the alpha-wave activity, the more activation in that region of the brain.

Cerebral Asymmetry

Although EEG data can be used to assess activity level in many different regions of the brain, recent research on alpha-wave levels in the anterior (front) regions of the cerebral hemisphere has proven particularly useful in understanding individual differences in emotion. This region has considerable connections with the parts of the brain that regulate emotions. Researchers find the anterior region of a person's right cerebral hemisphere often shows a different activity level than the anterior region of that same person's left cerebral hemisphere. Researchers refer to this difference in right and left hemisphere activity as **cerebral asymmetry.**

Recent studies suggests that different patterns of cerebral asymmetry are associated with differences in emotional experience. More specifically, higher activation in the left hemisphere has been associated with positive moods, whereas higher activation in the right hemisphere is indicative of negative moods (Wheeler, Davidson, & Tomarken, 1993). This difference was demonstrated in an experiment in which researchers showed emotion-arousing films to participants while taking EEG measures of right and left hemisphere brain activity (Davidson, Ekman, Saron, Senulis, & Friesen, 1990). When participants experienced feelings of happiness, as determined by their facial expressions, the researchers found increased activation in the left cerebral hemisphere. When the participants experienced disgust, there was more activity in the right hemisphere.

Similar patterns have been found in children less than a year old. For example, in one study with 10-month-old infants, smiling was associated with higher left hemisphere activity, whereas crying was associated with higher right hemisphere activity (Fox & Davidson, 1988). In other experiments, infants showed increases in left hemisphere activity when their mothers reached down to pick them up (Fox & Davidson, 1987), when they heard laughter (Davidson & Fox, 1982), and when they tasted something sweet (Fox & Davidson, 1986). In all cases, the children experiencing positive emotions had relatively more activity in their left hemisphere than in the right. Because these results are found in children who have not yet reached their first birthday, researchers argue that this association between cerebral asymmetry and emotion is something we are born with rather than the result of learning.

Individual Differences in Cerebral Asymmetry

More recent research has taken the association between cerebral asymmetry and emotion one step further. Investigators typically find higher activation in one hemisphere than the other, even when people are in a relatively nonemotional resting state. However, which hemisphere displays the higher activity level is not the same in all people. That is, some people tend to have a higher activity in the left hemisphere when resting, whereas others tend to have more right hemisphere activity. Moreover, like other individual differences, differences in cerebral asymmetry tend to be fairly stable over time. If you show a higher level of activity in one hemisphere over the other today, you probably will show the same pattern when taking an EEG test next week or even next year.

This observation leads to another intriguing question. Because left and right hemispheric activity is associated with positive and negative moods, can we use EEG data to predict who is more likely to experience certain kinds of moods or even mood disturbances? Some initial data on this question are promising. Participants in one study were identified as having either higher left hemisphere or higher right hemisphere activity when resting (Davidson & Tomarken, 1989).

These people then watched films designed to elicit certain emotions, such as happiness or fear. As expected, people with a higher level of left hemisphere activity were more responsive to the positive mood films, whereas the participants with the higher right hemisphere activity levels reacted more to the films that produced negative moods.

Again, similar patterns can be found in infants. Ten-month-old babies in one study were identified as having either higher left hemisphere or higher right hemisphere activity when resting (Davidson & Fox, 1989). The babies were then divided into those who cried and those who did not cry when separated from their mothers. As expected, the criers tended to have higher right hemisphere activity, whereas the noncriers were those with higher left hemisphere activity.

How can we account for these findings? Some researchers explain the results in terms of thresholds for positive and negative mood (Davidson & Tomarken, 1989). People with a higher right hemisphere activity level require a less intense negative event before they experience fear or sadness. A minor disappointment or a rude remark in a conversation might be enough to push them over the threshold into a negative emotional state. It probably requires a more severe setback to elicit negative emotions in people who do not start out with this high level of activation. On the other hand, people who generally have a higher level of left hemisphere activity may require a less intense positive experience before they experience happiness. An enjoyable conversation or a favorite song on the radio might be enough to bring out pleasant emotions.

However, other investigators argue that differences in hemispheric activity are related to differences in the tendency to either approach or withdraw from emotional events (Harmon-Jones & Allen, 1997; Harmon-Jones & Sigelman, 2001). Left hemisphere activity is associated with movement toward the source of the emotion, right hemisphere activity is related to movement away. According to this interpretation, higher right hemisphere activity is associated with sadness because depression is essentially an effort to withdraw from whatever is triggering the emotion. Consistent with this analysis, researchers find that anger is related to higher left hemisphere activity (Harmon-Jones & Allen, 1998). Although anger is a negative emotion like depression, angry people tend to approach or even attack the source of their distress.

We can also ask if this physiological difference plays a role in the development of emotional disorders. Some research findings suggest that it may. Depressed participants in these studies show more right-side activation than nondepressed participants (Davidson, Chapman, & Chapman, 1987; Heller, Etienne, & Miller, 1995). More importantly, in one study, researchers examined EEG measures of people who were currently not depressed but who had suffered from previous bouts of depression (Henriques & Davidson, 1990). These people tended to have less left hemisphere activity in the anterior region of the brain when resting than a group of participants who had never suffered from depression. In other words, these previously depressed individuals may have a physiologically based vulnerability to frequent bouts with depression. Clearly, whether we suffer from any emotional disorder depends on many factors, including the kinds of experiences we have. But it may be that some people require fewer or less intense negative experiences before succumbing to feelings of depression.

In summary, the results from several studies suggest physiological differences in the relative activity levels of the right and left anterior regions of our cerebral hemispheres may play a role in our emotional reactions to the events we encounter in life. Let's return now to the eye-drift example at the beginning of this discussion. Although not nearly as reliable as EEG data, research suggests that right-handed people who typically glance to the left when engaged in reflective thought are likely to show a higher level of right hemisphere activation when resting. Those who tend to glance to the right are more likely to be higher in left hemisphere activity (Davidson, 1991; Gur & Reivich, 1980). Of course, many other variables affect emotion. But this observation suggests that those who glance to the left may have a proclivity to experience different emotions from those who glance the other way.

Strengths and Criticisms of the Biological Approach

Strengths

One of the strengths of the biological approach is that it provides a bridge between the study of personality and the discipline of biology. For too many years, personality psychologists often ignored the biological roots of human behavior. But it has become increasingly difficult to disregard the fact that we are the product of an evolutionary history and our individual genetic makeup. Human behavior is influenced by many factors, one of which is biology. By incorporating what biologists know about such concepts as evolution and genetics, personality psychologists come closer to understanding what makes each of us the kind of person we are.

The biological approach also has succeeded in identifying some realistic parameters for psychologists interested in behavior change. The "blank slate" image of humankind can be very appealing. If the newborn personality is like clay, then with enough knowledge, resources, and effort we should be able to mold that personality any way we want. If all babies are essentially alike, then with enough research psychologists could advise parents and teachers on the "correct" way to raise all children and teach all students. Unfortunately, past acceptance of this blank slate notion created many problems. Parents with difficult-to-control babies were blamed for not knowing how to raise their child. Highly active children were punished for not sitting as still as their friends or classmates. Advocates of the biological approach argue that our inherited biological differences probably place limits on the kind of children and adults we become. Some people are born with a tendency to be more introverted than others, and there is probably little a parent, teacher, or spouse can do to turn an introvert into an extravert.

Another strength of the biological approach is that most of its advocates are academic psychologists with a strong interest in testing their ideas through research. Consequently, investigators have generated empirical support for many of the hypotheses advanced from this perspective. In addition, psychologists from the biological approach have often modified their theories as a result of research findings. For example, after Eysenck outlined a comprehensive model of personality several decades ago, he and others conducted research on many of the predictions generated from the model. Much of this work supported Eysenck's ideas, but investigators altered other ideas to better reflect the research findings.

Criticisms

Advocates of the biological approach often face inherent limits on their ability to test some of their ideas. In particular, evolutionary personality psychologists must often argue from the relatively weak position of analogy and reasonable deduction (Eagly, 1997). A reasonable case can be made that anxiety helps the species survive because it prevents social isolation. But how can we test this hypothesis directly? Direct manipulation is often out of the question, thus making demonstrations of cause-and-effect relationships difficult, if not impossible. Consider the example offered by one psychologist (Cornell, 1997). As discussed in the next chapter, psychologists use evolutionary theory to explain gender differences, such as why men are more dominant, stronger, and more sexually promiscuous than women (Archer, 1996; Gangestad & Thornhill, 1997). But imagine if just the opposite were the case—that men were more timid and physically weaker than women, and less likely to seek out multiple sex partners. One could use evolutionary theory to explain these results as well. We could speculate that because men were free to roam and did not have to protect offspring, the tendency for them to timidly run away from potential fights evolved. Women evolved to be stronger because child-care responsibilities required them to carry children, lift them into trees for safety, and fight off predators. And sexual promiscuity allowed a woman to avoid the risk of pairing up with a man who might be unable to make her pregnant and thus not allow her to pass along her genes. As this example illustrates, if a theory can explain all possible outcomes, it cannot be tested. As a result, the research support for many of the ideas postulated by evolutionary personality psychologists remains relatively weak.

Another criticism is directed at theory and research on temperament. Students and researchers may be bewildered by the lack of an agreed-upon model. One prominent model identifies three basic temperaments. Yet other models describe five, seven, and nine temperament dimensions (Bates, Wachs, & Emde, 1994). Students have a right to ask which of these is correct. More important, it is difficult to make comparisons across investigations when researchers rely on different names and descriptions for these temperaments. For example, is the "inhibited" child the same as the "slow-to-warm-up" child? We can hope that clearer answers about the number and description of basic temperaments will be forthcoming as researchers continue to work in this area.

Like the trait approach, the biological approach offers few suggestions for personality change. Although many ideas from this approach are probably useful for psychotherapists, there are no schools of psychotherapy based on this perspective. On the contrary, the message from the biological approach is that we need to be more aware of some of the limitations on how much we can change people. Therapists might do better to recognize that, because of biological differences, not all clients will respond identically to their treatments.

 # Summary

1.   Hans Eysenck was an early proponent of the biological approach to personality. He argued that personality can be divided along three primary dimensions. He called these extraversion-introversion, neuroticism, and psychoticism. Research suggests that introverts are more sensitive to stimulation than extraverts. Eysenck argued that these differences are based on inherited biological differences.

2.   Many personality researchers have identified general inherited dispositions called temperaments. One prominent temperament model identifies three temperament dimensions: emotionality, activity, and sociability. Psychologists argue that temperament is largely inherited and that these inherited dispositions interact with experiences to form adult personality traits. Children identified as inhibited show a fear of unfamiliar situations that other children do not. There is evidence that this tendency is inherited and that it remains fairly stable throughout childhood.

3.   Evolutionary personality psychology uses the concept of natural selection to explain the development and survival function of human personality characteristics. Theorists point out that anxiety often results from events related to social rejection. They argue that because social isolation decreases the chances of survival and reproducing, the evolution of anxiety has helped the species survive.

4.   Research on temperament has important implications for teaching. Studies find that children identified with a difficult temperament pattern and those identified with a slow-to-warm-up pattern perform more poorly in school than children identified with an easy temperament pattern. The Goodness of Fit Model suggests that children will learn best when the demands of the learning environment match the child's temperament.

5.   Personality researchers have often used physiological measures in their research. Recently, researchers have used EEG data to look at individual differences

in emotions. They find that differences in the activity levels of the right and left halves of the cerebral hemispheres are associated with differences in positive and negative mood. Some research indicates that people inherit different base-rate levels of brain activity in the two hemispheres and that this difference may make them more vulnerable to certain emotional experiences.

6. One strength of the biological approach is that it ties personality psychology to the discipline of biology. In addition, research in this area has identified realistic limitations on the "blank slate" model of personality development. Another strength of the biological approach is its strong emphasis on research. Criticisms of the approach include the difficulty researchers have in testing some of their ideas directly. Other criticisms are that there is no agreed-upon model for temperament researchers and that the biological approach provides little information about behavior change.

InfoTrac College Edition Key Terms

For additional readings go to http://www.infotrac-college.com/wadsworth and enter a search term related to your interest. Use the key terms suggested here to pull up several related articles. Also see the text Web site at http://psychology .wadsworth.com for more suggested readings and interactive quizzes to test your knowledge.

EEG
Hans Eysenck
Inhibited children

Personality and academic achievement
Temperament

Chapter 10

The Biological Approach

Relevant Research

Heritability of Personality Traits
Extraversion-Introversion
Evolutionary Personality Theory and Mate Selection
Summary

The theories presented in the last chapter continue to capture the attention and respect of personality researchers, and today most psychologists acknowledge that biology plays an important role in human personality. However, many psychologists have come to accept this conclusion rather reluctantly. There are many reasons for this resistance. One is that the "blank slate" view of humankind has great appeal. If we accept that personality is formed largely or exclusively by one's experiences, it is possible to shape a child into the kind of adult we want and to change personality traits that create problems. Perhaps another reason some psychologists have not eagerly embraced the biological approach is that they remain leery of inappropriate and even offensive interpretations that come from placing too much emphasis on biological determinants of personality. For example, in the past, some people have argued against social programs by maintaining that certain racial or gender differences are the result of biological rather than cultural factors.

Of course, accepting a biological component to personality does not mean that personality is fixed at birth. Those who resign themselves with, "That's the way men/women are," or "It's just my nature," are foolishly ignoring the power of experience. But it would be equally foolish to ignore the wealth of evidence indicating that biology does play a role in personality. The most persuasive case for the biological approach can be found in the growing amount of supportive research findings. We'll review some of those findings in this chapter. As with research from other approaches to personality, the studies reported here are sometimes subject to criticisms and alternate interpretations. However, taken together, the data make it difficult to ignore the biological determinants of personality we inherited from our parents and our ancestors.

We begin by looking at research on the heritability of personality characteristics. More specifically, we examine how researchers determine how much of our personality is inherited from our parents. Investigators use a variety of methods to produce consistent evidence for a strong genetic influence on personality. However, these research findings are not without their critics, and identifying the precise strength of the genetic component remains elusive.

Next we'll review research generated from Hans Eysenck's theory of personality. Specifically, we'll look at some of the differences between extraverts and introverts. This research suggests that your level of extraversion-introversion affects a wide range of behavior, including how happy you are and where you sit in the library.

We'll also examine one application of evolutionary personality theory. According to this theory, men and women should differ in what they look for in a romantic partner. Research with a variety of cultural groups finds some support for the evolutionary theory predictions.

Heritability of Personality Traits

How much of your personality is the result of your genetic makeup, and how much is the result of the environment you grew up in? This "nature-nurture" question is one of the oldest and most enduring issues in psychology. Interestingly, people with little or no exposure to personality research seem to readily accept that both genetic background and experiences are important in shaping personality. Parents often point to personality traits their children "got from me," but few would deny that the way they raise their children also plays a large role in what kind of adults the children become. Thus, the question is not which of these, genetics or environment, shapes our personalities, but rather to what extent and how our personalities are shaped by each.

So we might rephrase the question this way: To what degree was the mold for your adult personality already cast by the time you were born? Researchers now agree that relatively stable abilities and aptitudes, such as intelligence, appear to be largely inherited (Bouchard & McGue, 1981; Plomin & DeFries, 1998). This is not to say that a highly intelligent child cannot be born to relatively unintelligent parents or that a child's environment plays no role in intellectual development. But it does appear we are born with a potential for intelligence that combines with environmental influences to determine adult intelligence levels. Similarly, many psychological disorders appear to have a genetic component (Crabbe, 2002; Di-Lalla, Carey, Gottesman, & Bouchard, 1996; McGue & Christensen, 1997; Rhee &

In the News

Genetics and Intelligence

A large amount of research indicates that, as with personality traits and psychological disorders, a significant portion of intelligence is determined by our genetic inheritance. Although at first glance this conclusion hardly seems surprising, it is in fact at the heart of a controversy that flares up periodically among psychologists and those who debate social policy. More than 30 years ago, psychologist Arthur Jensen (1969) considered the research on intelligence and the finding that black Americans typically score lower on standard intelligence tests than whites. He suggested from these observations that blacks might be genetically less intelligent than whites. As you can imagine, this suggestion ignited a strong response. Richard Herrnstein and Charles Murray rekindled the debate in 1994 when they published *The Bell Curve: Intelligence and Class Structure in American Life.* These psychologists also began by pointing out that intelligence is largely inherited. Their review of research findings led them to suggest that between 40% and 80% of the variability in human intelligence can be tied to our genes. If that is correct, they reasoned, programs like Head Start, which are aimed at helping disadvantaged individuals, will be largely ineffective. The psychologists argued that any gains from educational intervention will be short-lived and that the individual's genetically determined aptitude will ultimately determine his or her success. Herrnstein and Murray touched a social and political nerve when they then tied their analysis to the question of race. They argued that if black Americans on average score lower on IQ tests than white Americans, perhaps efforts to provide educational opportunities for African Americans are a waste of time.

Reaction to these suggestions about racial differences in intelligence was again strong and swift. News analysts, political commentators, and political leaders were quick to challenge the interpretation. Reaction from many academic psychologists was equally intense. Not only do the vast majority of psychologists find the suggestion of inherent racial differences in intelligence offensive, but they point out that such a conclusion is simply inconsistent with research findings (Flynn, 1999). Although most psychologists agree that genetics plays a role in intelligence, most estimate the influence to be far less than Herrnstein and Murray assert. Moreover, it is simply incorrect to say that intelligence level is fixed by nature and unamenable to environmental influence (Kihlstrom, 1998a).

Psychologists are also quick to point out that black children often grow up in an environment that is less intellectually stimulating than that of the average white family (Zernike, 2000). Because intelligence does appear partially determined by the environment, we should only be surprised if we find no differences between blacks and whites. That would be the finding to support a fixed, inherited intelligence level. Indeed, researchers have found that black children adopted by white families of reasonable socioeconomic means develop IQ scores no different from those of adopted white children (Scarr & Weinberg, 1976).

(continues)

Genetics and Intelligence (continued)

Beyond this, critics have raised the issue of culture-bound intelligence tests. They argue that the questions asked on most intelligence tests reflect what white, middle-class Americans consider important. For example, one subtest on the widely used Wechsler intelligence tests asks about general knowledge. The assumption behind these questions is that, although all children are exposed to this information, the more intelligent ones will attend to and retain it. But clearly a child growing up in an African American culture is exposed to different information from one growing up in a white, middle-class culture. Because of this problem, many psychologists have been working to develop "culture-free" intelligence tests, and recent versions of the adult and children's Wechsler tests have been revised to account for some of these concerns.

The American Psychological Association responded to this debate by forming a task force to review research on the question of race and intelligence. The group's conclusion regarding racial differences in test scores was unequivocal: "There is certainly no . . . support for the genetic interpretation," they wrote. "At present, no one knows what causes this difference" (Neisser et al., 1996, p. 97).

Waldman, 2002). Again, this does not mean people are born to be schizophrenic or depressed, but rather that some people are born with a higher susceptibility to these disorders than are others.

What about personality traits? Are people born to be aggressive or extraverted? There is now ample evidence that genetics influences these and other personality traits. However, collecting evidence on this issue is not easy, and many questions remain about how to interpret the data that are available.

Separating Environmental from Genetic Influences

Psychologists working on the environment-genetics question have a somewhat different task facing them than those working in other areas of personality research. For technological and ethical reasons, it is not possible to manipulate people's genes and observe the kind of adults they become. Instead, researchers must rely on less direct means. Like detectives trying to piece together a picture of how we got to where we are, these researchers use innovative and sometimes clever experimental procedures to track down the roots of adult personalities. Each method has limitations and weaknesses, but data from a number of sources suggest a significant role for genetics in the development of our personalities.

The most obvious source of information on this question is the similarity of parents and children. Aggressive parents often have aggressive offspring, shy children often come from homes with shy parents. Similarly, we often see brothers who are both outgoing or sisters who both are sensitive and caring. Casual observers look at these relationships and often assume the children inherited these traits from their parents. However, there is an obvious alternative explanation for these similarities. Members of a family not only share genes, they share living environments as well. Siblings' personalities may be similar because the parents raised them in the same basic manner. Children of introverted parents might become introverted because of the calm and quiet home they grow up in.

In most cases, therefore, shared genes and shared environments seem hopelessly confounded. Can we peel one of these influences away from the other? Fortunately, there are ways. The most popular procedure for separating the role of genetics and the role of environment is the **twin-study method.** This method takes advantage of a naturally occurring phenomenon: the two types of human twins. Some twins are *monozygotic* (MZ); that is, the two babies come from the same fertilized egg. These are the twins that look alike physically, the ones we commonly call identical twins. The important point for researchers is that MZ twins have identical genes. The other type, *dizygotic* (DZ) twins, come from different eggs. These two babies, commonly called fraternal twins, are no more alike genetically than any two siblings.

The logic behind the twin-study method is illustrated in Figure 10.1. We assume that two same-sex DZ twins and two MZ twins (who are always the same sex) share very similar environments. That is, in studies using this method, twin pairs, regardless of type, are the same age and the same sex and live in the same house under the same rules. Therefore, the extent to which the environment is responsible for their personalities is going to be about the same for both types of twin

Identical twins not only share physical features but also have similar personalities. Researchers attribute this similarity in part to genetic influences, although the extent of genetic influence on personality continues to be debated.

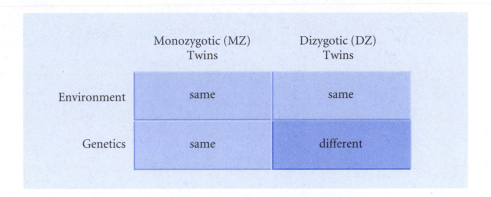

Figure 10.1

Twin-Study
Research Diagram

	Monozygotic (MZ) Twins	Dizygotic (DZ) Twins
Environment	same	same
Genetics	same	different

pairs. However, if there is also a genetic influence on personality, we would expect the MZ twins to be more like each other than are the DZ twins. This is because the MZ twins also have identical genes, but the DZ twins do not.

Researchers using the twin-study method give personality trait measures to both members of both kinds of twins. They then look at how similar the twin brothers and sisters are on the traits. If trait scores for the MZ twin pairs are more highly correlated than the scores for the DZ twin pairs, they have evidence for genetic influence on personality. Because the environmental influence is roughly the same for both kinds of twins, it is assumed that the MZ twins are more alike because they also have identical genes.

Twin-study research usually generates correlation tables similar to the one found in Table 10.1. In this example, adult MZ and DZ twin pairs were compared on the Big Five personality traits (Chapter 7). As seen in the table, the MZ twin pairs were more similar than the DZ twin pairs in each case (Riemann, Angleitner, & Strelau, 1997). The data in the table are similar to those obtained in other twin studies looking at different measures of the Big Five dimensions (Borkenau, Riemann, Angleitner, & Spinath, 2001; Jang, Livesley, & Vernon, 1996; Jang, McCrae, Angleitner, Riemann, & Livesley, 1998; Loehlin, McCrae, & Costa, 1998; McCrae, Jang, Livesley, Riemann, & Angleitner, 2001). When we combine twin studies examining many different personality traits, we find that MZ twins' scores tend to correlate on average about .50, whereas DZ twin correlations are in the .25 to .30 range (Loehlin, 1992). Behavior genetics researchers plug these numbers into formulas to estimate that about 40% of the stability in our adult personalities can be attributed to what we inherit from our parents (Loehlin, 1992; Plomin, Chipuer, & Loehlin, 1990).

Other methods for teasing apart genetic and environmental influences also find evidence for genetic influence, but usually not as strong as in the twin-study data. One example comes from research with adopted children. In situations where children are raised from birth by someone other than their biological parents, genetic and environmental influences are not confounded. For example, think of a family in which parents raise one child they adopted and one they gave

Table 10.1 Correlations from a Twin Study		
	MZ Twins	DZ Twins
Neuroticism	.53	.21
Extraversion	.56	.33
Openness	.54	.35
Agreeableness	.42	.24
Conscientiousness	.54	.23

Source: Riemann, Angleitner, and Strelau (1997).

birth to. Which child should have a personality similar to the parents'? If genes are playing a role, we would expect the biological offspring to be more like the parents because that child shares not only the environment but also some genes with the parents. In fact, this is what researchers find (Scarr, Webber, Weinberg, & Wittig, 1981). However, calculations with the data from these studies indicate the genetic influence is less than that suggested by the twin-study data. In fact, data from adoption studies suggest that the heritability of personality is about half what the twin-study data suggest (Plomin, Chipuer, & Loehlin, 1990; Plomin, Corley, Caspi, Fulker, & DeFries, 1998).

But the adoption situation provides even more opportunities to test the genetic-environmental influence question. For example, what would you expect if you compared the personalities of the adopted children with those of their biological mothers? The children have shared no environment with the mothers but are still linked by genes. When the personality scores of adopted children are compared with those of their adoptive parents and their biological mothers, the children look more like the biological mothers, whom they have never known (Loehlin, Willerman, & Horn, 1982, 1987). Although the strength of the relationship is also weaker than that suggested by the twin-study data, we have evidence from yet another source that genetics plays at least some role in the formation of adult personalities.

It is also possible to combine the twin-study and adoption situations. Although rare, some researchers have taken advantage of situations in which MZ twins are separated from their parents at birth and in addition are raised in two different households. The twins in these pairs share genes, but not environments. These twins are then compared with MZ twins raised in the same household, who share both genes and environments. A summary of the findings from studies using this method is shown in Table 10.2. As you can see, the MZ twins tend to be quite similar to each other regardless of whether they are raised with or separated from their twin brother or sister (Rowe, 1987). The obvious explanation for this similarity is that the twins' genes shaped their personalities in a similar manner regardless of the environments they grew up in.

Table 10.2   Correlations for Twins Raised Apart and Twins Raised Together

	Identical Twins Raised Apart	Identical Twins Raised Together
Extraversion	.61	.51
Neuroticism	.53	.50
Intelligence	.72	.86

Source: From Rowe (1987), with permission.

One team of researchers took this methodology a step further (Tellegen et al., 1988). They compared MZ twins reared together and reared apart with DZ twins reared together and reared apart. When the numbers from these studies are entered into formulas, researchers estimate that about 50% of differences in personality can be attributed to differences in genetic makeup.

In summary, researchers have used a variety of clever procedures to separate the influence of genetics on personality from the influence of the environment. Although the precise extent of the genetic influence is still uncertain, the consistency of the findings from so many sources suggests that adult personalities clearly are affected by heredity. However, the book is far from closed on this issue. As discussed in the next section, there are reasons to challenge some of the conclusions behavior geneticists draw from their data.

Problems with Genetics Research

The strongest and most consistent evidence in favor of genetic influence on personality comes from twin-study research. However, researchers using this method make two key assumptions. The first is that twin pairs can be accurately identified as MZ or DZ twins. Many "identical" twins may in fact be DZ twins who look very much alike. Fortunately, biological advances have made this less of a problem than it once was. Today, zygosity can be determined in almost all cases through blood tests.

The second assumption presents a bigger problem. Researchers assume that MZ and DZ twins have equally similar environments. However, there is evidence that MZ twins share more of their environment than DZ twins (Hoffman, 1991; Lytton, 1977; Scarr & Carter-Saltzman, 1979). That is, identical twins may be treated more alike than are DZ twins. Identical twins are often thought of as one unit—they are dressed alike, given identical presents, and so on. DZ twins grow up in similar environments, but they are usually allowed to dress differently, join different clubs, and have different friends. DZ twins may even experience environments that are less similar than those typical for siblings (Hoffman, 1985). This is because parents may look for and emphasize their differences (for example, "Terry is the studious one; Larry is the troublemaker").

If this is the case, we would have to modify Figure 10.1. The environmental influence on personality traits may not be as similar for DZ twins as it is for MZ twins. This possibility creates a problem when interpreting the twin-study findings. We can't be certain if the higher correlations between MZ twins are caused by greater genetic similarities or greater environmental similarities. This interpretation problem may explain why data from twin-study research suggest a larger role for genetic influences than is found with other procedures (Plomin et al., 1990).

However, some of these other procedures also rest on questionable assumptions (Hoffman, 1985, 1991; Stoolmiller, 1999). Adoptions are not random events. Families who adopt children are typically older, more affluent, more stable, and without many of the problems found in families that do not adopt. Although separated twins may be placed in different homes, the homes typically selected for placement are very similar. Perhaps more misleading is the assumption that parents treat an adopted child the same way they do their biological offspring. It is likely parents have different expectations for adopted children. Because they don't know the biological parents, adopting parents may have few preconceived ideas about how the child's personality will unfold.

There are some additional problems with genetics research. Genetics may influence only certain personality traits, and then only during certain stages of life. One study found that many differences in MZ twin and DZ twin correlations didn't show up until the twins reached adulthood (Dworkin, Burke, Maher, & Gottesman, 1976). It also is possible that the genetic influence for some traits may be different for males and females (Finkel & McGue, 1997; Rose, 1988). Further, if genetics plays such an important role, we would expect the correlations between family members' personality scores to change as biological relationships become more distant. For example, we would expect two sisters to be more alike than two cousins. However, at least one team of researchers failed to uncover any such relationship (Price, Vandenberg, Iyer, & Williams, 1982).

In short, some of the discrepancies between the results of twin studies and studies using other methods might be attributed to methodological problems. However, twin studies might produce higher estimates of heritability for another reason. It may be that personality traits aren't passed down from parents to child in a simple, direct manner. Rather, the inherited part of personality might be the result of a complex combination of more than one gene (Finkel & McGue, 1997; Plomin et al., 1998). That is, the genetic influence of some personality traits may not be seen unless a unique combination of more than one gene is inherited. Researchers refer to these complex influences as *nonadditive effects*. DZ twins share many genes, but may not share the exact combination of genes that make up a specific personality trait. However, because MZ twins have identical genes, they also share any unique combinations of genes that come together to influence personality. Thus, nonadditive effects would show up in identical twins, but not in fraternal twins. This analysis also could explain why twin studies find evidence for a larger genetic influence on personality than studies using other methods.

So where does this leave us? Exactly how or how much genes determine our adult personalities remains an open question. Some of the answers to this question may come from new methodological and technological developments. For example, researchers are beginning to identify connections between personality traits and DNA markers for specific genes (Plomin & Crabbe, 2000). But regardless of what future discoveries tell us, at this point it seems foolish to ignore the relatively strong case that genetics has an influence on personality.

Extraversion-Introversion

Few personality variables have received as much attention from researchers and theorists as extraversion and introversion. Clearly, this aspect of Hans Eysenck's personality theory has drawn more attention than any other. As described in Chapter 9, extraverts are less sensitive to stimulation than introverts. This is why extraverts can drink more coffee than introverts without being overtaken by the effects of caffeine. It also explains why it is not uncommon to find extraverts at loud social gatherings or in the middle of a crowd, whereas introverts seek out solitary activities and gravitate to a quiet corner at a party.

Space allows us to examine only three of the many topics investigated by researchers in this area. First, we'll tie individual differences in extraversion-introversion to the research covered in the previous section by looking at the evidence for the heritability of this personality variable. Second, we'll look at research examining one of the basic differences between introverts and extraverts postulated by Eysenck: preference for arousal. Third, we'll address the question: Who is happier, introverts or extraverts?

The Heritability of Extraversion

If you are an introvert, it's likely you've been given some of the following pieces of advice: "You need to get out more often," "Why can't you be more sociable?" or "Loosen up and enjoy yourself a little." Extraverts have probably heard some of these: "There's more to life than having fun all the time," "Can't you think a little before you do something?" or "Slow down and enjoy life." In short, whether you are introverted or extraverted, someone has probably asked you to become more of the other. Even the most extreme extravert can sit still for a few minutes, and the most introverted person you know occasionally cuts loose and has a good time with friends. But is it possible for an extravert to become permanently more introverted? Can you raise your child to be less introverted or less extraverted?

The answer to these questions depends on what causes a person to become an extravert or an introvert. Eysenck championed the role of genetics in answering this question. People are said to be born with a general level of cortical activity or, according to more recent descriptions, a sensitivity to stimulation. This inherited difference in physiology remains fairly constant throughout one's life and eventually develops into the adult behavior styles of extraversion or introversion. Of course, each person who inherits a predisposition toward introversion will develop a slightly different style of dealing with his or her heightened sensitivity to stimulation. But most people eventually take on many of the characteristics described by Eysenck. Eysenck (1990) pointed to data from many different sources when making the case that individual differences in extraversion-introversion are based in biology (Chapter 9). Some of the strongest evidence for this position comes from research on genetic heritability. Although little evidence for heritability was available when Eysenck first introduced his theory of personality, today an impressive body of work appears to support Eysenck on this point.

As described earlier, researchers often use the twin-study method to determine the heritability of personality variables. Consequently, much of the evidence for the heritability of extraversion-introversion comes from research comparing correlations between pairs of MZ twins with correlations between pairs of DZ twins. Studies using this procedure find consistent evidence for a genetic component of extraversion-introversion (Baker & Daniels, 1990; Eaves & Eysenck, 1975; Heath, Neale, Kessler, Eaves, & Kendler, 1992; Neale, Rushton, & Fulker, 1986; Scarr, 1969). In fact, the findings suggest such a strong genetic influence that some researchers are convinced the heritability estimates for this personality variable are somehow exaggerated (Plomin et al., 1990).

Nonetheless, two of these studies deserve special attention. One group of researchers gave a version of the Eysenck Personality Inventory to 12,898 adult twin pairs in Sweden (Floderus-Myrhed, Pedersen, & Rasmuson, 1980). This number represents virtually all of the contactable twins born in Sweden between the years 1926 and 1958. Another team of researchers tested 7,144 adult twin pairs in Finland (Rose, Koskenvuo, Kaprio, Sarna, & Langinvainio, 1988). This is nearly every living twin in that country born before 1958. Several features of these samples make them particularly important. Not only are the samples large, but they represent nearly every twin in these two countries. This means researchers don't have to worry about only a certain kind of person volunteering to participate in the study. In addition, for some unknown reason, the number of DZ twins born in these countries during the years studied was significantly higher than it was elsewhere in the world. Thus, DZ twin pairs are more proportionally represented in these samples than in other research.

When the within-pair correlations for DZ and MZ twins are compared, considerable evidence for a genetic component for extraversion-introversion is found. As shown in Table 10.3, the MZ twins were more like each other than were the DZ twins, which argues for a genetic influence. Beyond this, the researchers in the

Table 10.3 Within-Pair Extraversion Correlations for MZ and DZ Twins

	Males		Females	
	MZ Twins	*DZ Twins*	*MZ Twins*	*DZ Twins*
Swedish sample	.47	.20	.54	.21
Finnish sample	.46	.15	.48	.14

Source: From Floderus-Myrhed et al. (1980) and Rose et al. (1988).

Table 10.4 Within-Pair Correlations of Extraversion Scores for Twins Reared Apart and Together

Twins Reared Apart		Twins Reared Together	
MZ Twins	*DZ Twins*	*MZ Twins*	*DZ Twins*
.30	.04	.54	.06

Source: From Pedersen et al. (1988).

Finnish study examined the amount of social contact between the members of the twin pairs as well as the amount of social contact the twins generally engaged in. Although the researchers did find that MZ twins were more likely to stay in communication with each other, this factor alone was not sufficient to explain the differences in MZ and DZ correlations on the extraversion-introversion measure.

Another study takes the twin-study method one step further (Pedersen, Plomin, McClearn, & Friberg, 1988). As in the earlier studies, the investigators compared MZ and DZ twins who grew up together. However, these researchers also located 95 pairs of MZ twins and 220 pairs of DZ twins reared apart. Again, a positive correlation between the scores of identical twins separated at birth and reared in different environments would provide strong evidence for a genetic component. And indeed, as shown in Table 10.4, there was a relatively strong correlation between the scores of MZ twins reared in separate environments, albeit not as strong as that for MZ twins reared together.

We can conclude from this research that how introverted or extraverted you are probably is strongly influenced by the set of genes you inherited. This is not to say that you can't be more outgoing at times if you are highly introverted or learn to stop and introspect for a few minutes if you're an extravert. But how often you act in either of these styles was probably determined largely by the genetic hand you were dealt many years ago.

Is this student an introvert or an extravert? According to research his choice of study areas provides a clue. Extraverts prefer this type of open study area, where opportunities for interruptions and occasional social stimulation are possible.

Extraversion and Preferred Arousal Level

Imagine it's a few days before a big test in one of your classes. You've put off preparing for the exam long enough, so tonight you'll go to the library and spend a few hours behind the books. There are two study areas in this library. One contains a series of one-person desks where you can isolate yourself behind the quiet of the book stacks. Few people walk by these desks, and the room is relatively free of whispers, photocopy machines, and other library noises. The other study area consists of long tables, sofas, and easy chairs. You can easily scan the room to see who else is there. Many people pass by on their way to other parts of the library, and short conversations with those passing through are common. Which of these study areas will you choose?

Your choice in this situation depends in part on whether you are an extravert or an introvert. One team of researchers demonstrated this phenomenon when they asked students studying in the two kinds of library rooms just described to complete the Eysenck Personality Inventory (Campbell, 1983; Campbell & Hawley, 1982). Students in the noisy, open room were more likely to be extraverts, whereas the ones in the isolated, quiet room were more likely to be introverts. Those in the noisy room said they preferred the amount of noise and the opportunities for socializing. The others said they chose the quiet room to get away from these distractions.

These findings are entirely consistent with the theorists' descriptions of extraversion-introversion. Introverted students are more sensitive to stimulation. Thus, an introvert in a noisy room is probably so disturbed by all the activity that he or she will have a difficult time studying. On the other hand, the understimulated extravert probably finds the quiet room boring. Unless the study material is particularly exciting, the extravert will probably take a number of breaks, look around for distractors, and generally have a difficult time keeping his or her mind on the task.

This difference in preferred stimulation level also is found in more controlled laboratory experiments (Geen, 1983). For example, extraverts more quickly press a button to change slides on a visual learning task, presumably because they become bored more quickly with the pictures and designs (Brebner & Cooper, 1978). In another study, extraverts and introverts worked on a word-memory task while listening to noise through earphones (Geen, 1984). When given the opportunity, introverted participants set their earphones at considerably lower levels than did extraverts. However, some introverts in this study were forced to listen to loud noise and some extraverts were restricted to soft noise. Consistent with Eysenck's model, the introverts did worse when exposed to higher levels of stimulation, whereas the extraverts performed worse when listening to the softer noise.

This last finding helps to explain why some students can study only with the stereo and a TV blaring, whereas other students have to find a quiet library room and then stuff pieces of foam in their ears to block out any remaining noise. Too much stimulation makes it difficult to concentrate, and even extraverts can reach a point when they have to turn their radios down. But for introverts this point comes much earlier. Of course, the other side of the coin is that too little stimulation also interferes with performance. Whereas it may take hours of solitude to bring an introvert to this point, a few minutes in quiet isolation might be tough on a high extravert.

Extraversion and Happiness

Clearly, extraverts and introverts lead different lives. We are more apt to find extraverts at parties, visiting friends, going places, and generally being active. Introverts are more likely to spend time alone, engaging in quiet, low-stimulation tasks. Who do you suppose is happier? Not surprisingly, I usually find introverts guess introverts are happier people, whereas extraverts can't imagine how anyone could lead a life as boring as the introverted style.

Although introverts may have difficulty understanding this at first, researchers find that on average extraverts report higher levels of happiness and *subjective well-being* than introverts (Brebner, Donaldson, Kirby, & Ward, 1995; De-Neve, 1999; DeNeve & Cooper, 1998; Headey & Wearing, 1989; Lucas & Fujita, 2000). Extraverts and introverts in one investigation were asked to provide a daily mood report for 84 consecutive days (Larsen & Kasimatis, 1990). As shown in Figure 10.2, the researchers found an interesting pattern when they compared moods on days of the week. Perhaps not surprisingly, Monday was the students' least favorite day, with the week becoming progressively better as Saturday approached. But the figure also illustrates that no matter what the day of the week, extraverts

Figure 10.2

Happiness Ratings
of Extraverts and
Introverts

Source: Adapted from
Larsen and Kasimatis
(1990).

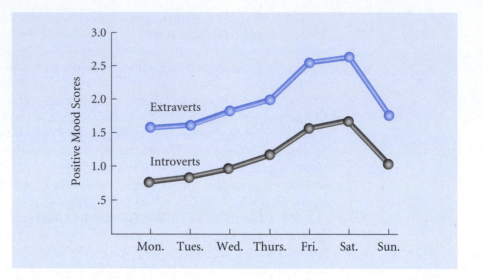

reported higher levels of positive mood than introverts. As with other personality
variables, this pattern seems to be fairly stable over time. One team of researchers
found that extraversion test scores could significantly predict levels of positive affect measured two years later (Headey & Wearing, 1989). Another investigation
used extraversion scores to predict the number of pleasant experiences people
would have over a four-year period (Magnus, Diener, Fujita, & Pavot, 1993).

If extraverts generally experience more happiness than introverts, why might
this be the case? Researchers have uncovered at least two reasons. First, extraverts
tend to socialize more than introverts. Extraverts have more friends, and they interact with those friends more often. There are several reasons why this increase
in social activity leads to happiness. Researchers have repeatedly found that social
contact is closely tied to feelings of well-being (Diener, 1984). Interacting with
friends is usually pleasant, as are other extraverted behaviors, such as going to
dances, parties, and football games. Many basic needs, such as feeling competent
and worthwhile, are also satisfied in social settings. In addition, friends often serve
as a buffer against stress (Cohen & Wills, 1985). That is, people usually cope with
their problems better with friends' help than when they try to handle the situation alone. Consistent with this observation, one study found that extraverts were
more likely to seek out friends when they had a problem than were introverts
(Amirkhan, Risinger, & Swickert, 1995).

The second explanation for extraverts' happiness is that they may be more sensitive to rewards than are introverts (Gray, 1981; Rusting & Larsen, 1998; Strelau,
1987). An extravert who receives a good grade on a test may be more pleased than
an introvert receiving the same news. In a laboratory test of this hypothesis, extraverts and introverts were given a test of "Syncretic Skill," supposedly a new type
of intelligence (Larsen & Ketelaar, 1989). Although the test was bogus, participants
received information indicating either that they had done well on the test or that

they had done poorly. Mood measures indicated that extraverts were much happier than introverts after receiving the positive feedback. Interestingly, extraverts were no more disappointed than introverts when told they had done poorly. Other studies find extraverts are more likely to find rewards in situations that introverts don't see. Participants in one investigation simply wrote down words as if taking a spelling test (Rusting, 1999). However, many of the words were homonyms (words that sound like other words). Thus, in some cases it was possible to hear a happy word (*peace* instead of *piece*) and in other cases to hear a sad word (*mourning* instead of *morning*). Although either answer was correct, extraverted participants were more likely than introverts to hear the happy words.

Does this mean extraverts are always happier than introverts? Not necessarily. This is because extraverts are not only more sociable than introverts, they also are more impulsive. Extraverts are more likely to act on the spur of the moment, to respond to what they are feeling without pausing to think. And this impulsivity can create problems (Emmons & Diener, 1986). Saying the first thing that comes to mind often is not a good idea. Doing what feels good at the moment without considering the eventual consequences is also fraught with danger. Anyone who has enjoyed a trip to the beach or an evening with friends instead of writing a term paper can appreciate the problem of acting impulsively. Thus, extraversion appears to be a two-edged sword. Extraverts are more likely than introverts to have friends and have fun. But they also are more likely to act before thinking and get themselves into trouble. Introverts may not always reap the benefits of social interactions, but they avoid the price of lapses in judgment.

Evolutionary Personality Theory and Mate Selection

Imagine that, like many people these days, you decide to look for a romantic partner through the personal want ads. You call the "lonely hearts" number to place your ad and find that you are faced with two tasks. First, you must describe yourself in a way that will make you attractive to others. Second, you must identify the kind of person you are looking for. What do you say?

Researchers examining these kinds of ads have uncovered valuable information about gender roles and the nature of romantic relationships. This research finds that how people describe themselves and the kind of person they are looking for depends largely on whether they are male or female. For example, one study revealed that women tend to identify themselves as physically attractive and say they are looking for someone who is older and can provide financial security (Harrison & Saeed, 1977). Fortunately, these requests fit rather well with what the men say about themselves. Men placing ads typically say they are looking for someone who is younger and physically attractive. The men also are likely to describe themselves as someone who can provide financial security.

Besides their practical uses for someone seeking romance, do these results tell us something about the nature of personality? According to advocates of evolutionary personality theory, the answer is yes. These psychologists think of romantic relationships in terms of male and female members of a species getting together to (eventually) reproduce. Consequently, choosing a partner is based in part on concerns for *parental investment* (Geary, 2000; Trivers, 1972). That is, as members of a species, we are concerned about reproducing and passing our genes along to the next generation. Because of this concern, we select mates who are likely to be a part of successful reproduction and effective child raising. This analysis does not suppose that we actively consider reproduction success when we select among potential dating partners, but rather that certain mate-selection preferences have been passed down to us through the evolutionary process.

According to the evolutionary analysis, men and women have different ideas about parental investment. Because they bear and in most cases raise the offspring, females are more selective about whom they choose to mate and reproduce with. In contrast, in many species males are free to attempt to reproduce with as many females as they can. Frequent mating with many different females increases the probability that one will pass along the male's genes to the next generation. In evolutionary terms, the investment in selecting a mate is larger for women than for men. She has more to lose by making a poor choice than he does. Because they have different ideas about parental investment, evolutionary personality theory predicts that men and women look for very different characteristics in their partners.

What do men look for in a woman? What do women want in a man? Complete answers to these commonly asked questions have eluded the most insightful of us. Although they cannot explain everything, evolutionary personality psychologists argue that men and women select their mates based in part on what serves the needs of the species. As described in the next section, research supports many of these speculations.

What Men Look for in Women

From an evolutionary perspective, men can best serve the needs of the species by reproducing as frequently as possible (D. M. Buss, 1991). Consequently, men should be attracted to women with "high reproductive value." In other words, a man should select a woman who is likely to give him many children. But what outward signs do we have of a woman's likely fertility? One indicator is the woman's age. A young wife has the potential to produce more offspring than an older wife. Thus, some evolutionary personality psychologists predict that men prefer younger women to older women (D. M. Buss, 1991). Moreover, physical features associated with young adult women, such as "smooth skin, good muscle tone, lustrous hair, and full lips," provide "cues to female reproductive capacity" (D. M. Buss, 1991, p. 2). Not coincidentally, these physical attributes are the ones our society associates with beauty.

Consequently, evolutionary personality psychologists predict that men prefer partners who are physically attractive and probably younger than they are. But can the same reasoning be applied to women? Probably not. If anything, as described later, a young man is probably less likely than an older man to provide a woman and her offspring with the kinds of material resources she seeks from a partner. Thus, according to the theory, men are more likely than women to use physical attractiveness to select their marriage partner. In addition, we would expect most couples to consist of an older husband and a younger wife.

Research tends to support these speculations. A national survey of unmarried American adults found that men preferred younger women as potential marriage partners, whereas women expressed a preference for older men (Sprecher, Sullivan, & Hatfield, 1994). Married couples in one study were asked about the importance they placed on various characteristics when choosing their spouse (Buss & Barnes, 1986). As expected, husbands were more likely than their wives to rate *physically attractive* and *good looking* as features they sought in a marriage partner. Another study found the more attractive their partner, the more efforts men make to retain their relationship with that woman (Buss & Shackelford, 1997). Men are more likely than women to be upset if their partner were to become less attractive (Cramer, Manning-Ryan, Johnson, & Barbo, 2000). Another study found women identified as the most desirable dates were also among the most physically attractive (Speed & Gangestad, 1997).

The importance of a woman's physical attractiveness can also be seen in the tactics women use to gain a man's attention (Buss, 1988). In evolutionary personality theory this is known as *intrasexual selection*—the competition among members of the same gender for mating access to the best members of the opposite gender. If men select partners who are youthful and beautiful, a woman can improve her chances of pairing up with the most desirable partner by emphasizing these attributes. To test this possibility, newlyweds in one study were asked to describe what they did to attract their spouse when they first began dating (Buss, 1988). As predicted, the women were more likely to report that they altered their appearance (such as with makeup and jewelry), wore stylish clothes, wore sexy clothes, and kept themselves clean and groomed. Another study found that women were more jealous of a potential rival for their partner's affections when that other woman was physically attractive (Dijkstra & Buunk, 1998). In addition, women in one study felt worse about their desirability as a marriage partner after looking at photographs of very attractive women. Men looking at photographs of physically attractive men did not have this reaction (Gutierres, Kenrick, & Partch, 1999).

In short, there is abundant evidence that men are more likely than women to look at physical attractiveness when selecting a dating or marriage partner (Feingold, 1990). However, it is important to keep in mind that it is fertility men are said to be seeking in younger women, not necessarily youthfulness. When one team of investigators interviewed teenage boys, they found a preference for slightly older women (Kenrick, Keefe, Gabrielidis, & Cornelius, 1996). In other words, the boys were more attracted to the females most likely to reproduce regardless of their age.

Nonetheless, there is one important limitation in the studies reviewed so far. That is, they tell us a lot about the preferences of American men and women, but little about romantic choices in other cultures. To make a strong case for the evolutionary personality position, we need to demonstrate that this effect is not limited to certain social or cultural groups. For example, if men were found to rely on physical attractiveness more than women only in Western cultures, a strong argument could be made that this difference reflects social learning patterns rather than an inherited human characteristic.

To solve this problem, one team of researchers conducted an elaborate cross-cultural investigation (Buss, 1989). The researchers looked at gender differences in partner preferences in 37 cultural groups. These groups were located in 33 different countries, on six continents and five islands, and included people from cultural backgrounds very different from that of Americans, such as South African Zulus, Gujarati Indians, and Santa Catarina Brazilians. Participants in each of these samples were asked about what they considered the ideal age for themselves and their partner when marrying. Participants were also asked how important each of 18 personality traits were for choosing a potential mate (for example, *intelligence, good financial prospect,* and *good looks*).

The findings provide strong support for evolutionary personality theory. As shown in Table 10.5, in each of the 37 samples men preferred partners who were younger than they were. Additional evidence for this preference was found when researchers looked at the actual age at which people first married. Information about the age of marrying couples was available in 27 of the countries studied. These data confirmed that men in all these cultures not only said they preferred younger partners but also tended to marry women younger than themselves. Although the investigators made no predictions about the womens' preferences, the women in all 37 cultures said they preferred an older partner.

More evidence for the evolutionary personality position was found when the researchers looked at the importance men and women placed on physical attractiveness when selecting a mate. In each of the 37 cultures, men were more likely than women to say that good looks are important. This difference was statistically significant in all but three of the samples. Thus, the tendency for men to prefer youthful and physically attractive women when looking for marriage partners appears to be fairly universal despite differences in cultures and social norms. Evolutionary personality psychologists interpret such findings as evidence for universal characteristics handed down from our ancestors.

What Women Look for in Men

According to evolutionary personality theory, men prefer a female partner who provides maximal opportunity for successful reproduction. But women have a different role to play in reproduction and child rearing. Consequently, they look for different features in their partners. According to the parental investment analysis,

Table 10.5   Mean Age Differences in Years Between Preferred Age of First Marriage for Spouse and for Self in 37 Cultures

Sample	Males	Females
Africa		
Nigeria	−6.45	4.90
South Africa (Whites)	−2.30	3.50
South Africa (Zulus)	−3.33	3.76
Zambia	−7.38	4.14
Asia		
China	−2.05	3.45
India	−3.06	3.29
Indonesia	−2.72	4.69
Iran	−4.02	5.10
Israel (Jewish)	−2.88	3.95
Israel (Palestinian)	−3.75	3.71
Japan	−2.37	3.05
Taiwan	−3.13	3.78
Eastern Europe		
Bulgaria	−3.13	4.18
Estonia	−2.19	2.85
Poland	−2.85	3.38
Yugoslavia	−2.47	3.61
Western Europe		
Belgium	−2.53	2.46
Finland	−0.38	2.83
France	−1.94	4.00
Germany	−2.52	3.70
Great Britain	−1.92	2.26
Greece	−3.36	4.54
Ireland	−2.07	2.78
Italy	−2.76	3.24
Netherlands	−1.01	2.72
Norway	−1.91	3.12
Spain	−1.46	2.60
Sweden	−2.34	2.91

(continues)

Table 10.5   *(continued)*

Sample	Males	Females
North America		
Canada (English)	−1.53	2.72
Canada (French)	−1.22	1.82
United States (Mainland)	−1.65	2.54
United States (Hawaiian)	−1.92	3.30
Oceania		
Australia	−1.77	2.86
New Zealand	−1.59	2.91
South America		
Brazil	−2.94	3.94
Colombia	−4.45	4.51
Venezuela	−2.99	3.62
Mean	−2.66	3.42

Note: Negative values indicate a preference for a younger mate; positive values indicate a preference for an older mate. From Buss (1989).

women prefer to mate with men who can provide for their offspring. In nonhuman species, this may simply mean a mate who can provide food and protection. In humans, this means providing the financial resources required to raise the children. Some men are better able to do this than others. Men also differ in their ability to take care of and nurture their sons and daughters as well as in their ability to transfer status or power to their children. Evolutionary personality psychologists argue that women prefer partners who possess these abilities.

Again, some research supports this speculation. When investigators asked married couples to describe what they found attractive in their spouse, women were more likely to identify such characteristics as *dependable, good earning capacity, ambitious,* and *career-oriented* (Buss & Barnes, 1986). Other investigations find women are more interested in finding a partner high in socioeconomic status and ambitiousness (Ben Hamida, Mineka, & Bailey, 1998; Feingold, 1992). However, no gender difference is found for characteristics unrelated to parental investment, such as sense of humor (Feingold, 1992). In another study, more women than men said they would be upset if their partner was unable to hold a good job (Cramer et al., 2000). Unmarried women responding to a survey said they preferred to marry a man who earned more money and had more education than they did (Sprecher et al., 1994). Undergraduate women in another study found dominant men that they observed more attractive than relatively meek men (Sadalla, Kenrick, & Vershure, 1987). According to evolutionary personality theorists, a dominant man is better able to provide needed resources for his family than a man at the bottom of the pecking order. A dominant man is also more likely to rise to the top of an organization and thereby acquire financial security and other benefits.

Other research suggests that men are aware of these preferences and, like women, compete among themselves for the most desirable partner. Newlywed husbands in one study were more likely than their spouses to say they bragged about their financial resources as a way to catch their future wives' attention (Buss, 1988). In other words, the men let it be known that they made a lot of money or went out of their way to show off a new car or condominium. Similarly, men are more likely than women to display their material resources when trying to retain a partner's affection (Buss & Shackelford, 1997). Men are also more jealous of a romantic rival when that man is a dominant individual than when he is not (Dijkstra & Buunk, 1998).

Do these findings mean that, given a choice, women prefer loud and brutish men? In other words, in the game of love, do nice guys finish last? Although the research reviewed to this point might suggest such a conclusion, additional studies indicate that this is not necessarily the case (Burger & Cosby, 1999; Graziano, Jensen-Campbell, Todd, & Finch, 1997). Returning to evolutionary personality theory, it is reasonable to ask about the survival value of mating with a man who is dominant in a competitive and selfish sense. Mating with a dominant man has its advantages, but not if he is unwilling to share resources or invest in the welfare of his children. In other words, dominance alone may not be a very attractive trait in a man. In support of this reasoning, when undergraduate women observed and evaluated interactions between men, they reported that helpful and generous men were far more appealing for both short- and long-term relationships than men who were simply dominant (Jensen-Campbell, Graziano, & West, 1995).

In summary, research finds patterns of attraction that support evolutionary theory's predictions about what women find attractive in men. But once again, we need to ask if the findings are limited to American samples. Data from the 37-sample cross-cultural study described earlier indicate that women around the world report similar preferences (Buss, 1989). As shown in Table 10.6, women in each sample were more likely than men to prefer a spouse who had good financial prospects. Only in Spain did this difference fail to reach statistical significance. Similar patterns were found when the men and women rated the importance of such characteristics as ambition and industriousness in a partner. In short, there is a nearly universal tendency for women to prefer men who can provide financial resources. These findings are entirely in line with predictions from the evolutionary personality position.

Table 10.6	Importance of "Good Financial Prospect" When Selecting a Mate	
Sample	Males	Females
Africa		
Nigeria	1.37	2.30
South Africa (Whites)	0.94	1.73
South Africa (Zulus)	0.70	1.14
Zambia	1.46	2.33
Asia		
China	1.10	1.56
India	1.60	2.00
Indonesia	1.42	2.55
Iran	1.25	2.04
Israel (Jewish)	1.31	1.82
Israel (Palestinian)	1.28	1.67
Japan	0.92	2.29
Taiwan	1.25	2.21
Eastern Europe		
Bulgaria	1.16	1.64
Estonia	1.31	1.51
Poland	1.09	1.74
Yugoslavia	1.27	1.66
Western Europe		
Belgium	0.95	1.36
Finland	0.65	1.18
France	1.22	1.68
Germany	1.14	1.81
Great Britain	0.67	1.16
Greece	1.16	1.92
Ireland	0.82	1.67
Italy	0.87	1.33
Netherlands	0.69	0.94
Norway	1.10	1.42
Spain	1.25	1.39
Sweden	1.18	1.75

(continues)

Table 10.6   (continued)

Sample	Males	Females
North America		
Canada (English)	1.02	1.91
Canada (French)	1.47	1.94
United States (Mainland)	1.08	1.96
United States (Hawaiian)	1.50	2.10
Oceania		
Australia	0.69	1.54
New Zealand	1.35	1.63
South America		
Brazil	1.24	1.91
Colombia	1.72	2.21
Venezuela	1.66	2.26

Note: Participants rated on a scale from 0 (Unimportant) to 3 (Indispensable). From Buss (1989).

Conclusions and Limitations

Research findings on what men and women look for in romantic partners tend to be consistent with the predictions from evolutionary personality psychology. Men around the world prefer younger and physically attractive women, whereas women look for a man who can provide the material resources they need to raise their children. However, as intuitive and consistent as these findings may be, there are many reasons to take them with at least a grain of salt.

As described in the previous chapter, researchers testing these hypotheses are necessarily limited in their ability to make strong tests of causal relationships. That is, because they cannot manipulate such variables as gender and physical attractiveness, these investigators are unable to rule out many alternative explanations for their findings (Eagly & Wood, 1999). For example, differences in the ages men and women marry may simply have to do with differences in maturity level, with women becoming physically and perhaps emotionally mature more quickly than men. Moreover, investigations do not always produce findings consistent with evolutionary personality theory's predictions (Costa, Terracciano, & McCrae, 2001). For example, evolutionary personality psychologists argue that men should be more upset than women when discovering their spouse's sexual infidelity, but women will be more concerned about losing their partner's emotional fidelity. These predictions stem from the men's theoretical needs to be assured the offspring they raise are their own, and from the women's desire that their partners continue to support them and the offspring after reproduction. However, studies often fail to support either of these predictions (Grice & Seely, 2000; Harris, 2000).

In addition, many learned preferences men and women have for romantic partners may overshadow instincts inherited from our ancestors. For example, in one study both men and women rated mutual love and affection the most important consideration when selecting a romantic partner (Ben Hamida et al., 1998). The basic needs of animals in the wild may be quite different from the needs of men and women in modern society. For example, many women probably prefer a partner who spends time with them rather than one devoted to an ambitious climb up the corporate ladder. This is not to say that tendencies passed down from our ancestors do not influence our choices. The research suggests that they do. But our preferences for a physically attractive woman or a wealthy man might play a relatively small role in this process. Common sense also tells us there are many exceptions to the rule. Many women no doubt prefer a man who is more sensitive than dominant. Many men prefer an older woman to a less mature partner. Evolutionary personality psychology also is limited to heterosexual mating choices. The prediction of partner choice based on parental investment says little or nothing about choices for lesbians and gay men. The analysis may also not apply to women who are past their reproductive years and older men who are interested in an intimate relationship but not in raising a family.

Summary

1.   Research examining the influence of genetics and the environment on adult personalities suggests that both sources play a role. Psychologists have used a variety of methods to pin down these roles, most notably the twin-study method. However, problems surface when interpreting these studies, particularly with some of the underlying assumptions of the methods. Nonetheless, the cumulation of evidence argues strongly for a significant heritability component in adult personality.

2.   Extraversion-introversion is probably the most widely researched aspect of Eysenck's personality theory. Evidence indicates that this personality variable has a large heritability component. Consistent with Eysenck's theory, researchers find extraverts tend to seek out stimulating environments and perform better in these environments than introverts. Research also finds that extraverts are generally happier than introverts.

3.   Evolutionary personality theory predicts that men and women look for different features when selecting a potential partner. Consistent with this hypothesis, research shows that men are more likely to consider physical attractiveness when selecting a dating partner or spouse. In addition, men are more likely to prefer a

younger partner. Research also indicates that women prefer a man who possesses the resources necessary for raising a family. Cross-cultural research suggests that these preferences may be universal.

InfoTrac College Edition Key Terms

For additional readings go to http://www.infotrac-college.com/wadsworth and enter a search term related to your interest. Use the key terms suggested here to pull up several related articles. Also see the text Web site at http://psychology .wadsworth.com for more suggested readings and interactive quizzes to test your knowledge.

Extraversion	Subjective well-being
Heritability of personality traits	Twin study method
Personality and mate selection	

Chapter 11

The Humanistic Approach

Theory, Application, and Assessment

Not long ago I was involved in a discussion about Jim Morrison, the leader of the 1960s rock group The Doors. For a few years, Morrison was a rock legend who personified counterculture thinking. But he also abused his body with drugs and alcohol and died of an apparent heart attack at age 27. One man in this discussion blamed Morrison's self-destructive behavior and death on society. He argued that Morrison's alienation from his parents, harassment by police, and pressure from record-industry executives pushed the singer to his tragic death. A woman in the group disagreed. She argued that no one forced Jim Morrison to take outrageous doses of dangerous drugs or to go on daily drinking binges. For that matter, no one kept him in the music business. If it was that much hassle, he could easily have gotten out.

Which of these views do you suppose is more "humanistic"? You may be surprised to find that the woman who blamed Morrison's problems on himself is probably more aligned with humanistic psychology's view than the man who pointed to society and the hassles Morrison faced. This is not to say humanistic psychologists are heartless or insensitive to the problems society tosses our way. But failure to take personal responsibility for how we react to those problems is completely foreign to the humanistic approach to personality and well-being.

This perspective is easier to understand if we look at the circumstances that gave birth to the humanistic view. By the middle of the twentieth century, two major views of humanity had emerged from the discipline of psychology. One was the Freudian concept. According to this perspective, we are all victims of unconscious sexual and aggressive instincts that constantly influence our behavior. The other view came from the behaviorists (discussed in Chapter 13), who, in the extreme, view humans as little more than large, complex rats. Just as a rat is conditioned to respond to laboratory stimuli, humans are said to respond to stimuli in their living environments over which they have no control. We act the way we do because of the situation we are in or the situations we have been in before—not because of some personal choice or direction.

Many psychologists had difficulty accepting either of these descriptions of human nature. In particular, important aspects of human personality such as free will and human dignity were missing from the Freudians' and behaviorists' descriptions. Behavior was said to be under the control of id impulses or learning histories rather than personal choices. In response to these concerns, a so-called "third force" was born. The humanistic approach (sometimes, perhaps incorrectly, referred to as *existential* or *phenomenological* psychology) paints a much different picture of our species.

A key distinction between the humanistic approach and other theories of personality is that people are assumed to be largely responsible for their actions. Although we sometimes respond automatically to events and may at times be motivated by unconscious impulses, we have the power to determine our own destiny and to decide our actions at almost any given moment. We have free will. Jim Morrison may have found himself under tremendous pressure and difficulties. But how he responded to that situation was his own choice. Had Morrison seen a humanistic therapist, he probably would have been encouraged to accept this responsibility and make choices about his lifestyle consistent with his individuality and personal needs.

The "third force" in American psychology caught on rapidly with a large number of psychotherapists and personality theorists. The emphasis on individuality and personal expression in the 1960s (which gave rise to the counterculture movement personified by Jim Morrison) provided fertile soil for the growth of humanistic psychology. The election of prominent humanistic psychologist Abraham Maslow to president of the American Psychological Association in 1967 symbolized the acceptance of the humanistic approach as a legitimate alternative perspective. But before exploring in depth what this alternative view is all about, let's examine where the humanistic approach came from.

The Roots of Humanistic Psychology

Although humanistic psychology evolved from many sources, its roots lie primarily in two areas: existential philosophy, which is decidedly European in flavor, and the work of some American psychologists, most notably Carl Rogers and Abraham Maslow.

Existential philosophy addresses many of the questions that later became cornerstones of the humanistic approach. Some of these include the meaning of our existence, the role of free will, and the uniqueness of each human being. Many psychologists, primarily European, align themselves so closely with existential philosophers that they have adopted the label *existential psychologists.* These psychologists rely heavily on the works of the great existential philosophers—such as Friedrich Nietzsche, Søren Kierkegaard, and Jean-Paul Sartre—in developing their theories of personality. Among the more prominent existential psychologists are Ludwig Binswanger, Medard Boss, Viktor Frankl, R. D. Laing, and Rollo May. Existential psychotherapy frequently focuses on *existential anxiety*—the feelings of dread and panic that follow the realization that there is no meaning to one's life. Therapy often emphasizes the freedom to choose and develop a lifestyle that reduces feelings of emptiness, anxiety, and boredom.

At the same time that ideas from existential philosophy were making their way into conversations among psychologists, two American psychologists were writing about their personal transitions from traditional psychology theories to a humanistic perspective. Early failures as a psychotherapist led Carl Rogers to wonder about the therapist's ability to decide for clients what their problems were and how to solve them. "It began to occur to me," Rogers reflected many years later, "that unless I had a need to demonstrate my own cleverness . . . I would do better to rely upon the client for direction" (1967, p. 359).

The turning point for Abraham Maslow came while he was watching a World War II parade. Although the parade was supposed to promote American patriotism and the war effort, it caused Maslow to question just how much psychology had contributed to the understanding of human behavior. He became determined "to prove that human beings are capable of something grander than war and prejudice and hatred" (in Hall, 1968, p. 55).

Promoting their new ideas about human behavior became a lifetime's work for Rogers and Maslow. Their writings found a receptive audience among psychologists also bothered by the limitations and deficiencies they saw in other approaches. We will review the theories of both of these men after first identifying some of the key elements of the humanistic approach.

Key Elements of the Humanistic Approach

Describing humanistic psychology is difficult because there are no agreed-upon definitions of what constitutes a humanistic personality theory. This was made obvious in the 1960s and early 1970s, when it seemed nearly everyone identified himself or herself as "humanistic" in an effort to capitalize on the popularity of the approach. As a result, humanistic psychology was associated with several faddish therapies that promised to solve problems and provide the key to happiness for the price of a paperback book. Efforts to exploit the humanistic association have faded in recent years as the public's fascination with humanistic psychology has declined. But there remain a large number of psychologists—especially psychotherapists—who identify themselves with this perspective. Although no clear criteria exist for identifying which approaches to psychotherapy fall into the humanistic category, I think it is safe to say that the following four elements are central to the general viewpoint to which we apply the "humanistic" label: (1) an emphasis on personal responsibility, (2) an emphasis on the "here and now," (3) a focus on the phenomenology of the individual, and (4) an emphasis on personal growth.

Personal Responsibility

Although we may try to deny it, we are ultimately responsible for what happens to us. This idea, borrowed from existential philosophers, is central to the humanistic approach to personality and is illustrated in the way we commonly use the phrase "I have to." We say, "I have to go to class," "I have to meet some friends," "I have to take care of my children," and so forth. But the truth is, we don't *have* to do any of these. Within limits, there is practically nothing we have to do. Humanistic psychologists argue that our behaviors represent personal choices of what we want to do at a particular moment. People *choose* to remain in relationships; they do not have to. We choose to act passively; we could decide to act forcefully. We choose to go to work, call our friends, leave a party, or send a Christmas present. We do not have to do any of these things. The price we pay for making some of these choices can be steep, but they are choices nonetheless.

Unlike the Freudian or behavioral descriptions of people at the mercy of forces they cannot control, humanistic psychologists see people as active shapers of their own lives, with freedom to change limited only by physical constraints. A typical goal of humanistic psychotherapy is for clients to accept that they have the power to do or to be whatever they desire. Of course, as Erich Fromm observed, for many this freedom is frightening.

The Here and Now

Think about the last time you walked to a class or some other appointment. Perhaps you spent the time thinking about what you did last weekend or ruminating over an embarrassing incident. Maybe you rehearsed something you wanted to say to someone or thought about how nice it would be to get through this week. A humanistic psychologist might say that what you really did was to lose 10 minutes. You failed to experience fully the 10 minutes that life handed you. You could have experienced the fresh air, appreciated the blue sky, or learned something from observing or talking with other people.

According to the humanistic perspective, we can't become fully functioning individuals until we learn to live our lives as they happen. Some reflection on the past or future can be helpful, but most people spend far too much time thinking about events that have already happened or planning those that might. Time spent on these activities is time lost, for you can live life fully only if you live it in the here and now.

A popular poster reminds us that "Today Is the First Day of the Rest of Your Life." This phrase could well have been coined by a humanistic psychologist. The humanistic view maintains that we need not be victims of our past. Certainly our past experiences shape and influence who we are and how we behave. But these experiences should not dictate what we can become. People do not need to remain shy and unassertive just because they "have always been that way." You do not have to remain in an unhappy relationship simply because you don't know what else to do. Your past has guided you to where you are today, but it is not an anchor.

The Phenomenology of the Individual

No one knows you better than yourself, according to humanistic psychologists. It is therefore absurd for therapists to listen to clients, decide what their problems are, and force them to accept the therapist's interpretation of what should be changed and how it should be changed. Instead, humanistic therapists try to understand where clients are "coming from" and provide what clients need to help themselves.

Some people find this approach to therapy a bit puzzling at first. What about disturbed people incapable of understanding their problems? And if the answers were easy and therapy the client's job anyway, why would anyone need to see a psychotherapist? The reply is that, whereas some people may not be able to understand the source of their difficulties right now, the therapist also has no access to this information. During the course of therapy, clients come to understand themselves and develop an appropriate strategy for resolving their problems. You may have had a similar experience when dealing with personal problems. Friends offer advice, but allowing someone else to decide what is best for you is unsatisfying and probably ineffective. If you are like many people, it was only when you weighed the advice of others and came to a decision on your own that you were able to resolve the problem.

Personal Growth

According to humanistic psychology, there is more to life than simply having all of your immediate needs met. Suppose tomorrow you inherited several million dollars, settled down with someone who will admire and love you always, and were promised a long and healthy life. Would you be happy? For how long? Humanistic theorists maintain that people are not content when their immediate needs have been met. Rather, they are motivated to continue their development in a positive manner. If left alone, unencumbered by life's difficulties, we eventually progress toward some ultimately satisfying state of being. Carl Rogers referred to this state as becoming a *fully functioning* individual. Abraham Maslow borrowed the term *self-actualization* to describe it. We become self-actualized as we become "more what one idiosyncratically is, to become everything that one is capable of becoming" (Maslow, 1970, p. 46).

This growth process is assumed to be the natural manner of human development. That is, we progress toward this satisfying state unless certain problems prevent us from doing so. When these obstacles block our growth, humanistic psychotherapy can be helpful. However, the therapist does not put clients back on track. Only the client can do that. Rather, the therapist allows clients to overcome their problems and continue growing. Rogers describes this ever-unfolding of one's self as a "process of becoming."

> *"Whether one calls it a growth tendency, a drive toward self-actualization, or a forward-moving of becoming. . . ."*
>
> CARL ROGERS

Carl Rogers

Humanistic psychology could ask for no better example of how to live life fully than the career of Carl Rogers. His role as a shaper of the humanistic perspective spanned several decades. He pioneered humanistic psychotherapy and was the first therapist to popularize a "person-centered" approach (Rogers, 1951). Rogers later became an important figure in the growth of encounter groups as a means of therapy (Rogers, 1970) and expanded what he learned from psychotherapy into a general theory of personality (Rogers, 1961). Later in his career, Rogers applied the humanistic approach to social issues like education and world peace (Rogers, 1969, 1977, 1982). For many people, Rogers' optimistic view of humanity and belief in each individual's potential for fulfillment and happiness provide a pleasant alternative to some of the approaches to personality covered thus far.

The Fully Functioning Person

"The good life," Rogers said, "is a process, not a state of being. It is a direction, not a destination" (1961, p. 186). Like other humanistic theorists, Rogers maintained that we naturally strive to reach an optimal sense of satisfaction with our lives. He called people who reach this goal **fully functioning.**

Carl R. Rogers

1902–1987

Like the inevitable unfolding of one's true self that he promoted, Carl Rogers' interest in science and his concern for people carried him from Midwest farm boy to leader of the humanistic revolution in psychology. Carl was a shy but very intelligent boy growing up in Illinois. He had a particular fondness for science, and by the time he was 13 had developed a reputation as the local expert on biology and agriculture. Ironically, the Rogers household was anything but warm and affectionate. Openly expressing emotions, later a key feature of Rogerian therapy, was not allowed. As a result, like two of his siblings, Carl developed an ulcer by age 15.

Rogers went to his mother and father's alma mater, the University of Wisconsin, in 1919 to study agriculture. He planned a career in farming but soon found agriculture unchallenging. He took a correspondence course in psychology one summer but found it boring. He finally settled on religious studies. When he left Wisconsin with his new wife, Helen, in 1924, he went to Union Theological Seminary in New York to prepare for a career as a minister.

Two developments in New York again changed the direction of his life. First, intensely studying theology caused him to question his own religious beliefs. "The Christian religion satisfies very different psychological needs in different men," he observed. "The important thing is not the religion but the man" (in Kirschenbaum, 1979, p. 45). The second development was a renewed introduction to psychology. While at the seminary, Rogers and several classmates took psychology courses across the street at Columbia University. These classmates included Theodore Newcomb and Ernest Hilgard, who also went on to become important figures in psychology.

A career in theology promised Rogers an opportunity to help people, but his faith continued to wane. "It would be a horrible thing to have to profess to a set of beliefs in order to remain in one's profession," he said. "I wanted to find a field in which I could be sure my freedom of thought would not be limited" (in Kirschenbaum, 1979, pp. 51-52). Much to his parents' dismay, Rogers left the church to pursue graduate study in psychology at Columbia.

After graduation, Rogers worked at a child guidance clinic in Rochester, New York. Later he joined the faculty at Ohio State University and the University of Chicago before returning to the University of Wisconsin in 1957. Throughout this time, Rogers battled with the established Freudian approach to psychotherapy and the dominant behavioral influence in academia. But in time he began to win many of these battles. When the American Psychological Association handed out its first annual award for distinguished scientific contribution in 1956, Carl Rogers was the recipient.

In 1963 Rogers moved to La Jolla, California, where he founded the Center for Studies of the Person. The thread that ties Rogers' career together is his genuine concern for people. "Rogers seemed ordinary," a colleague wrote. "He was not a sparkling conversationalist. [But] he would certainly listen to you, and with real interest" (Gendlin, 1988, p. 127). Rogers devoted the last 15 years of his life to the issues of social

(continues)

Carl R. Rogers (continued)

conflict and world peace. Even in his 80s, he led workshops and communication groups in such places as the Soviet Union and South Africa.

Rogers continued to write extensively and shape the discipline of psychology until his death in February 1987.

So what are fully functioning people like? Rogers identified several characteristics. Fully functioning people are open to their experiences. Rather than falling into familiar patterns, they look to see what life will throw their way. Related to this, fully functioning people try to live each moment as it comes. The idea is to experience life, not just pass through.

Fully functioning people learn to trust their own feelings. If something feels right, they'll probably do it. They aren't insensitive to the needs of others, but they aren't overly concerned with meeting the standards of behavior society sets for them. If a fully functioning woman wants to cut her hair or quit her job, she probably won't stop herself just because others might not approve. Fully functioning people are less prone than others to conform to the roles dictated by societal expectations. Instead, they're more likely to follow their own interests, values, and needs when making important life decisions, such as those about career and lifestyle.

Fully functioning people experience their feelings more deeply and more intensely than others. This applies to both positive and negative emotions. Thus, fully functioning people accept and express their anger. To do otherwise would be to cut themselves off from their feelings. Because of this sensitivity, fully functioning people experience a greater richness in their lives.

Anxiety and Defense

If we all have the potential to be fully functioning, constructive members of society, why is there so much unhappiness in the world? Why doesn't everyone get the maximum enjoyment out of life? Rogers was well aware that we often fall short of becoming happy, fully functioning adults. The problem begins when we experience anxiety and respond with various psychological defenses. According to Rogers, anxiety results from coming into contact with information that is inconsistent with the way we think of ourselves. You may believe that you are a good tennis player, a kind person, a good student, or a pleasant conversationalist. But occasionally you receive information that contradicts this self-concept. For example, you may think of yourself as the kind of person everybody likes. But one day you overhear someone say what a jerk he thinks you are. How do you react?

Let's first describe how a fully functioning person would react. If you were fully functioning, you would accept the information. Here is someone who does not like you. You might want to think about this new information for a while and then incorporate it into your self-concept. You might recognize now that, although you are a fine person, not everyone is going to find you pleasant and wonderful. Unfortunately, most of us are not capable of such a well-adjusted reaction. More commonly, the information leads to anxiety. You believe you are liked by everyone, and here is some evidence that not everyone likes you.

If the information is very threatening to your self-concept, the anxiety will be difficult to manage. This is where Rogers' theory takes on a slight Freudian flavor. Rogers proposed that people receive information inconsistent with their self-concepts at a level somewhere below consciousness. Rogers called this process **subception** rather than perception. If the information is not threatening, it might enter awareness. However, if the information contradicts the self-concept, it creates anxiety. To deal with the anxiety, people use defense processes to keep the information from entering consciousness.

The most common defense is *distortion.* Returning to the example, you might convince yourself that the person who called you a jerk was in a bad mood or is just a rude person. This distorted message does not contradict your self-concept and thereby avoids anxiety. In more extreme cases, you might even resort to outright *denial.* No, you might convince yourself, he wasn't really talking about me, but someone else with a name that sounds like mine.

An interesting twist on this part of Rogers' theory is that anxiety also can result from positive information, if that information is inconsistent with our self-concepts. For example, people who consider themselves socially undesirable may use defenses when they hear that someone is attracted to them. They might tell themselves the admirer is just being polite or maybe is scheming to get something from them.

A lot of anxiety-provoking information comes from self-observation. Each of us on occasion will act in ways that fall short of our personal standards. Perhaps you have cheated a friend out of money, said some hurtful things to a loved one, or lied to take advantage of someone. Even fully functioning individuals sometimes disappoint themselves. But in most cases these people acknowledged their shortcomings and try to correct the situation, if possible, and learn from their mistakes. Unfortunately, more commonly, people distort the information ("She really shouldn't get that upset by what I said") or deny the facts ("I didn't know the money was his").

Distortion and denial often succeed in the short run in that they effectively reduce anxiety. But each use takes us further and further away from experiencing life fully. In severe cases, people replace reality with fantasy. A man may think of himself as the world's most desirable bachelor when in fact there are no objective reasons to draw this conclusion. A student with poor grades might convince herself that she is a genius whose thoughts are simply too sophisticated for her instructors to understand. When the incongruence between the self-concept and reality is so large that the defense processes cannot operate adequately, the person experiences what Rogers calls a state of *disorganization*. When this happens, protection against inconsistent information collapses. The result is extreme anxiety.

Conditions of Worth and Unconditional Positive Regard

Why is it so difficult to accept and incorporate inconsistent information into our self-concepts? Rogers' answer is that most of us have grown up in an atmosphere of **conditional positive regard.** As children, our parents and caregivers provide love and support. However, they rarely do this unconditionally. Rather, most parents love their children as long as the children do what is expected of them. When parents disapprove of children's behavior, they withhold their love. The children get the message they are loved, but only when they do what their parents want. The positive regard the children need and want is conditional upon their behavior.

As a result of this conditional positive regard, children learn to abandon their true feelings and desires and to accept only the parts of themselves their parents deem appropriate. In short, they deny their weaknesses and faults. Ultimately, children become less and less aware of themselves and less able to become fully functioning in the future. As adults, we continue this process of incorporating into our self-concepts only those aspects that are likely to win the approval, and thus the

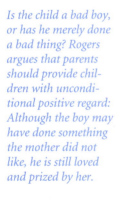

Is the child a bad boy, or has he merely done a bad thing? Rogers argues that parents should provide children with unconditional positive regard: Although the boy may have done something the mother did not like, he is still loved and prized by her.

love and support, of significant people in our lives. Certainly each of us has characteristics that, if revealed to loved ones, might cause disapproval and possibly rejection. So instead of acknowledging and perhaps expressing these thoughts and desires, we deny or distort them. We keep them out of awareness. As a result, we lose touch with our feelings and become less fully functioning.

The question then becomes this: How can we come to accept our faults and weaknesses, when we know they may not be accepted by others? According to Rogers, we need **unconditional positive regard.** When we experience unconditional positive regard, we know we will be accepted and loved no matter what we do. Parents should communicate to their children that although they don't approve of a specific behavior, they will always love and accept them. Under these conditions, children no longer feel a need to deny thoughts and feelings that might otherwise have led to a withdrawal of positive regard. They are free to experience all of themselves, free to incorporate faults and weaknesses into their self-concepts, free to experience all of life.

Parents are not the only source of unconditional positive regard, and growing up in a family without this acceptance does not condemn a person to a less-than-full life. Therapists can create an atmosphere of unconditional positive regard during psychotherapy. Rogers maintained that such an environment is necessary to help adults become fully in touch with all their thoughts and feelings. We'll examine some more of Rogers' ideas about psychotherapy later in this chapter.

Abraham Maslow

> *"I'm someone who likes plowing new ground then walking away from it. I get bored. I like discovery, not proving."*
> ABRAHAM MASLOW

Abraham Maslow spent most of his career filling in the gaps he found in other approaches to understanding human personality. For example, when most psychotherapists were directing their attention to why people develop psychological disorders, Maslow wondered how psychology might aid the happy, healthy side of personality. "Freud supplied to us the sick half of psychology," he wrote, "and we must now fill it out with the healthy half" (1968, p. 5). He replaced Freud's pessimistic and dismal view of human nature with an optimistic and uplifting portrayal. Maslow acknowledged the existence of unconscious motives, but focused his attention on the conscious aspects of personality.

Motivation and the Hierarchy of Needs

For a moment, contrast the concerns of the average middle-class American today with those of the typical blue-collar worker during the Great Depression of the 1930s. Today's financially secure professionals fret over their personal relationships and their standing in the social community. Many seem to be concerned about where their lives are going; others find satisfaction working in community service projects and charitable organizations. They read novels, get involved with social

Abraham H. Maslow

1908–1970

©Bettmann /CORBIS

The changes and developments in Abraham Maslow's personal and professional life resemble in many ways the personal growth he described in his theory of personality. Although generally regarded as a warm and gregarious adult, Maslow had a cold and lonely childhood. "I was the little Jewish boy in the non-Jewish neighborhood," he recalled. "I was isolated and unhappy. I grew up in libraries and among books, without friends" (in Hall, 1968, p. 37).

His professional career also started on a path far from his eventual position as the father of humanistic psychology. His parents, uneducated Russian immigrants, encouraged Maslow to go to law school. He went to City College of New York in this pursuit but found it uninteresting and dropped out during the first year. Maslow went to Cornell and then to the University of Wisconsin to study psychology. Ironically, what initially attracted him to psychology was behaviorism, particularly the works of John B. Watson. "I was so excited about Watson's program," he said. "I was confident that here was a real road to travel, solving one problem after another and changing the world" (in Hall, 1968, p. 37). Although his enthusiasm for behaviorism would eventually wane, Maslow's desire to solve the world's problems through psychology never diminished.

Maslow stayed at Wisconsin to finish his Ph.D. in 1934. He remained a loyal behaviorist throughout this period, working closely with Harry Harlow in his animal lab. After graduation, Maslow went to Columbia University to work with the famous learning theorist E. L. Thorndike. But with the birth of his first daughter, Maslow went through a mystical experience similar to the peak experiences he later studied. Looking at his newborn child, Maslow realized that behaviorism was incapable of providing the understanding of human behavior that he now needed. "I looked at this tiny, mysterious thing and felt so stupid," he said. "I was stunned by the mystery and by the sense of not really being in control. . . . Anyone who had a baby couldn't be a behaviorist" (in Hall, 1968, p. 56).

After Columbia, Maslow taught at Brooklyn College for 14 years, where he came into contact with Karen Horney, Erich Fromm, and Alfred Adler. Most important, he met Max Wertheimer, one of the founders of Gestalt psychology, and Ruth Benedict, a cultural anthropologist. It was his desire to better understand these two people, whom he called "the most remarkable human beings," that led him to his exploration of self-actualized people (Maslow, 1970). Maslow moved to Brandeis University in 1951 and remained there until shortly before his death in 1970. He hoped to leave a new movement in psychology and personality as his legacy. "I like to be the first runner in the relay race," he once said. "Then I like to pass on the baton to the next man" (in Hall, 1968, p. 56).

causes, and take classes to develop their writing skills or appreciation for the arts. But things were very different when nearly a third of the workforce lost their jobs in the 1930s. Feeding oneself and one's family became the dominant concern of many Americans. A job, any job, was of primary importance. Spending time contemplating the direction of one's life and experimenting with various avenues to express one's potential were luxuries reserved for those who did not have to worry about day-to-day existence.

The contrasting motives of Depression-era workers and many middle-class citizens today fit nicely within Maslow's theory of personality. Maslow identified two basic types of motives. One is a **deficiency motive,** which results from a lack of some needed object. Basic needs such as hunger and thirst fall into this category. Deficiency motives are satisfied once the needed object has been obtained. These are often the only needs considered in other approaches to personality. For example, Freud described human motivation in terms of tension reduction, with the return to a tensionless state the ultimate aim of the motivating system.

But Maslow also talked about another set of needs he called **growth needs.** These include the unselfish giving of love to others and the development of one's unique potential. Unlike deficiency needs, growth needs are not satisfied once the object of the need is found. Rather, satisfaction comes from expressing the motive. Satisfying growth needs can be quite enjoyable and may even lead to an increase in rather than a satiation of the need.

Maslow identified five basic categories of needs—both deficiency and growth—and arranged them in his well-known **hierarchy of needs.** As shown in Figure 11.1, he placed the five kinds of needs into a hierarchy of prominence. That is, some needs demand satisfaction before others. Although there are exceptions, we typically satisfy the needs at the lower levels before concerning ourselves with needs at higher levels. For example, if you are hungry, your behavior will center

Figure 11.1

Maslow's Hierarchy of Needs

around obtaining food. Until this need is met, you will not be very concerned about making new friends or developing a romantic relationship. Of course, once satisfied, the lower need may return, causing you to divert your attention again. But over the course of a lifetime, most of us progress up the hierarchy, until satisfying our need for self-actualization dominates our actions. According to Maslow, only a fraction of a percentage of us ultimately attain the state of self-actualization. Let's go through the hierarchy one step at a time.

Physiological Needs. Physiological needs, including hunger, thirst, air, and sleep, are the most demanding in that they must be satisfied before we can move to higher-level needs. Throughout history—and, unfortunately, in many places today—many people's lives have centered around meeting these basic needs. Finding enough food and water for survival takes priority over concerns about gaining the respect of peers or developing potential as an artist.

Safety Needs. When physiological needs are met, we become increasingly motivated by our safety needs. These include the need for security, stability, protection, structure, and order, and freedom from fear or chaos. These needs are most evident when the future is unpredictable or when stability of the political or social order is threatened. People who perceive threats to their safety may build large savings accounts or settle for a job with a lot of security rather than pursue a better but riskier position. Sometimes they seek out the predictable orderliness of organized religion or the military. People stuck at the safety-need level in their personal development may put up with an unhappy marriage or a military dictatorship if these situations provide stability or a sense of security.

Belongingness and Love Needs. For most middle-class American adults, the need for food and water and the need for security and stability are fairly well satisfied. Most of us have jobs, homes, and food on the table. But satisfaction of these lower-level needs does not guarantee happiness. The need for friendship and love soon emerges. "Now the person will feel keenly, as never before, the absence of friends, or a sweetheart, or a wife, or children," Maslow wrote. "He will hunger for affectionate relations with people . . . for a place in his group or family" (1970, p. 43). Although some adults remain slaves to their safety needs and devote most of their energy to their careers, most people eventually find work unsatisfying if it means sacrificing time spent with friends and loved ones.

Maslow identified two kinds of love. *D-love,* like hunger, is based on a deficiency. We need this love to satisfy the emptiness we experience without it. It is a selfish love, concerned with taking, not giving. But it is a necessary step in the development of the second type of love, B-love. *B-love* is a nonpossessive, unselfish love based on a growth need rather than a deficiency. We can never satisfy our need for B-love simply with the presence of a loved one. Rather, B-love is experienced and enjoyed and grows with this other person. It is a "love for the Being of another person."

Assessing Your Own Personality

Self-Actualization

Indicate the extent to which each of the following statements applies to you, using this 4-point scale:
1 = Disagree, 2 = Disagree somewhat, 3 = Agree somewhat, 4 = Agree.

_____   1. I do not feel ashamed of any of my emotions.

_____   2. I feel I must do what others expect of me.

_____   3. I believe that people are essentially good and can be trusted.

_____   4. I feel free to be angry at those I love.

_____   5. It is always necessary that others approve of what I do.

_____   6. I don't accept my own weaknesses.

_____   7. I can like people without having to approve of them.

_____   8. I fear failure.

_____   9. I avoid attempts to analyze and simplify complex domains.

_____   10. It is better to be yourself than to be popular.

_____   11. I have no mission in life to which I feel especially dedicated.

Esteem Needs. Although poets and songwriters might disagree, there is more to life than love. Satisfaction of our belongingness and love needs will direct attention to our esteem needs. Maslow divided these into two basic types: the need to perceive oneself as competent and achieving, and the need for admiration and respect. He cautioned that this respect must be deserved. We cannot lie or cheat our way into positions of respect and authority. Even with money, spouse, and friends, failing to satisfy our need for self-respect and admiration will result in feelings of inferiority and discouragement.

Need for Self-Actualization. Nearly every culture has a story of someone who, by virtue of a magic lamp or contact with a supernatural being, receives everything he or she wishes. Inevitably, granting wishes of wealth, love, and power isn't enough to make these characters happy. For, as Maslow explained, when all of these lower-level needs are satisfied, a new discontent and restlessness develops. People who obtain all the obvious sources of happiness and contentment in our society soon turn their attention to developing themselves. "A musician must make music, an artist must paint, a poet must write, if he is to be ultimately at peace with himself," Maslow wrote. "What a man can be, he must be. He must be true to his own nature" (1970, p. 46).

_____ 12. I can express my feelings even when they may result in undesirable consequences.

_____ 13. I do not feel responsible to help anybody.

_____ 14. I am bothered by fears of being inadequate.

_____ 15. I am loved because I give love.

To calculate your score, first reverse the values for items 2, 5, 6, 8, 9, 11, 13, and 14 (1 = 4, 2 = 3, 3 = 2, 4 = 1). Then add the values for all 15 items. The higher the score, the more self-actualized you are said to be at this point in your life. You can compare your score with the norms for college students reported by the test developers:

	Mean	Standard Deviation
Men	45.02	4.95
Women	46.07	4.79

Scale: *Index of Self-Actualization*

Source: Jones and Crandall (1986)

When all our lower-level needs are satisfied, we begin to ask ourselves what we want out of life, where our lives are headed, what we want to accomplish. The answers to these questions are different for each of us. Maslow believed very few adults ever reach this state of self-actualization, the point at which their potential is fully developed. But we all have the need to move toward that potential. Most of us will eventually direct some attention toward that goal, perhaps in ways we may not now be able to imagine.

Misconceptions About Maslow's Need Hierarchy

Maslow was quick to point out that his initial five-level need hierarchy oversimplifies the relationship between needs and behavior. Although the order of the needs makes sense for most of us, there are some notable exceptions. For example, some people may need to satisfy their needs for self-esteem and respect before they can enter a love relationship. Some artists are so intent on expressing their creative desires that they sacrifice satisfaction of some lower-level needs. Painting or writing may be more important than a steady income or a dependable source of food. And occasionally we hear about martyrs who sacrifice life itself for a value or an ideal.

Another common misconception about the need hierarchy is the assumption that our lower needs must be satisfied 100% before we can turn to higher needs. More accurately, Maslow said that our needs are only partially satisfied at any given moment. He estimated that for the average American, 85% of our physiological needs, 70% of our safety needs, 50% of our belongingness and love needs, 40% of our self-esteem needs, and 10% of our self-actualization needs are satisfied. Of course, how well our lower needs are satisfied determines how much those needs influence our behavior.

Although Maslow described the need hierarchy as universal, he acknowledged that the means of satisfying a particular need vary across cultures. A person can earn respect from others in our society by becoming a doctor or community leader. But in other societies this esteem is awarded for good hunting or farming skills. Maslow argued that these differences are somewhat superficial. The basic needs themselves, not the manner in which they are satisfied, remain the same across cultures.

Another oversimplification of Maslow's theory is that any given behavior is motivated by a single need. Maslow argued that behavior is the result of multiple motivations. He gave the example of sexual behavior. Someone might say this is motivated by a physiological need for sexual release. But Maslow argued the same behavior can also be motivated by a need to win or express affection, or to express a sense of conquest or mastery, or a desire to feel masculine or feminine. People engage in sexual activity to satisfy any one of these needs or to satisfy all of them.

The Study of Psychologically Healthy People

Psychologists have long studied people who suffer from psychological problems. But what do you do if you are Abraham Maslow and want to study psychologically healthy people? Maslow began by selecting people who appeared to have made great progress in satisfying their need for self-actualization. Some of these individuals were contemporaries of Maslow. But others were historical figures who seemed to have lived a self-actualized lifestyle. Maslow interviewed the living examples on his list and used historical documents to gather information about such seemingly self-actualized people as Thomas Jefferson, Albert Einstein, Eleanor Roosevelt, and Albert Schweitzer. By his own admission, Maslow's methods were far from scientifically rigorous. Rather than statistical or other quantitative analyses, Maslow provided "holistic analysis." That is, he arrived at his own general impressions of his selected participants. Through this process he developed a list of characteristics that seemed to typify the personalities of psychologically healthy people.

> *"Self-actualizing individuals have more free will than average people."*
> ABRAHAM MASLOW

What are self-actualized people like? You may notice as we go through the list that these individuals sound a lot like the fully functioning people described by Rogers. To begin, psychologically healthy people tend to accept themselves for what they are. They admit to their weaknesses, although they still work to improve themselves where they can. Because of this self-acceptance, self-actualized people don't spend a lot of time worrying or feeling guilty about the bad things they have done. Self-actualized people aren't perfect, but they respect and feel good about themselves for what they are.

Psychologically healthy people are also less restricted by cultural norms and customs than the average person. Whereas most of us are concerned about doing the "proper" thing, self-actualized people feel free to express their desires, even when those desires run counter to society's wishes. It is not that these people are insensitive to social pressures. On the contrary, Maslow described them as very perceptive. They are simply less inhibited and more spontaneous than most of us. Society provides a long list of rules about how our lives should progress: go to school, get a job, make some money, buy a house and car, raise a family, and on and on. There are also rules about how to act in public, how to spend leisure time, how to dress, how to eat, and so on. However, psychologically healthy people are less likely than the rest of us to conform to society's mandates unless they feel their own goals and desires would be met in the process.

Maslow described every psychologically healthy person he studied as creative. However, he distinguished between the traditional definition of creativity, which is based on producing something traditionally associated with talent (for example, a poem), and what he called *self-actualizing creativity*. Self-actualizing creativity is revealed when people approach routine tasks in an unconventional manner. A self-actualized teacher develops innovative ways to communicate ideas to students. A self-actualized businessperson thinks of clever ways to improve business and devises new solutions to old problems. Moreover, a well-known painter is not necessarily self-actualized. The paintings might spring more from innate talent than from a healthy personality.

In essence, self-actualizing creativity is a way of approaching life. Maslow compared it with the spontaneous way a child examines and discovers the world, ever in awe and admiration of the little things that make it such an interesting place. According to Maslow, most adults would express self-actualizing creativity if we didn't succumb to *enculturalization,* which inhibits our spontaneity. Somehow, psychologically healthy people retain or rediscover the fresh and naive way of looking at life they knew as children.

Maslow discovered several other characteristics common to psychologically healthy people. It may surprise you to find that these people have relatively few friends. But the friendships they have are deep and rewarding. They have a "philosophical, unhostile" sense of humor. They poke fun at the human condition, including themselves, rather than at any particular person or group. Self-actualized people also have a strong need for solitude, as we'll explore in depth in the next chapter. And, like Rogers' fully functioning people, self-actualized people express a continued appreciation for life's experiences.

Another feature Maslow discovered in psychologically healthy people is what he called *peak experiences*. A peak experience is one in which time and place are transcended, in which people lose their anxieties and experience a unity of self with the universe and a momentary feeling of power and wonder. However, consistent with the humanistic notion of individuality, peak experiences are different for each person. Maslow likened them to "a visit to a personally defined Heaven." Peak experiences are growth experiences, for afterward people report feeling more spontaneous, more appreciative of life, and less concerned with whatever problems they may have had.

Psychologically healthy people are not the only ones who have these experiences. After all, most of us on occasion experience emotional growth and wrestle with higher-level concerns. But peak experiences for self-actualized people tend to be more intense and occur more often. However, even in the self-actualized group, Maslow found there were "peakers" and "nonpeakers." Each of these types of psychologically healthy people serves a different function in society. The nonpeaking self-actualizers are "the social world improvers, the politicians, the workers of society, the reformers, the crusaders." They have their feet planted firmly on the ground and have a clear direction in life. On the other hand, the peakers "are more likely to write the poetry, the music, the philosophies, and the religions" (1970, p. 165). The two types of self-actualizers play different roles in society, but both are on the way to fulfilling their potentials, each marching to a slightly different drummer.

The Psychology of Optimal Experience

What makes people happy? This question threads its way through much of the writings of the humanistic personality theorists. Of course, these theorists are concerned with more than the relatively superficial signs of happiness, such as a good job, a nice car, or an attractive family. And, as Maslow argued, people are not content simply because they have no pressing problems.

Rather, much of humanistic personality theory focuses on the individual's quest to attain a sense of meaning and personal satisfaction in his or her life. Humanistic psychotherapy may help clients work toward a sense of contentment and self-actualization. But what about finding happiness in the everyday, routine activities in life? Can people structure the events in their daily lives in a way that promotes a sense of personal fulfillment and self-worth?

Optimal Experience

One starting point for answering these questions is simply to ask people to describe the activities that make them happy. This is one of the strategies for understanding happiness employed by psychologist Mihaly Csikszentmihalyi (pronounced Chick-*Sent*-Me-High). Try it yourself. Think of a time when you felt alive and totally engaged in an activity, when what you were doing was more than pleasurable, but truly enjoyable. What were you doing? When Csikszentmihalyi (1990, 1999; Csikszentmihalyi & Csikszentmihalyi, 1988) asked people to identify these experiences, he found a great variety of answers. Some people talked about mountain climbing, others about playing tennis, others about performing surgery. But when he asked these people to describe the experience, he found they used surprisingly similar terms.

Csikszentmihalyi's participants talked about becoming so involved in what they were doing that nothing else seemed to matter. Climbing the mountain or performing the surgery demanded all their attention. Although each step seemed to flow almost automatically to the next, the task was almost always challenging and demanded the person's full concentration. Reaching the goal provided a sense of mastery, but the real pleasure came from the process rather than the achievement.

Csikszentmihalyi refers to these moments as **optimal experience.** Because people typically say these experiences feel as if they are caught in a natural, almost effortless movement from one step in the process to the next, Csikszentmihalyi has come to refer to this experience as *flow.* Optimal experiences are intensely enjoyable, but they are usually not restful, relaxing moments. On the contrary, most often flow experiences are quite demanding. "The best moments usually occur when a person's body or mind is stretched to its limits in a voluntary effort to accomplish something difficult and worthwhile," Csikszentmihalyi explains. "Optimal experience is thus something that we make happen" (1990, p. 3).

Interestingly, the flow experience is described in fairly identical terms by people of all ages, in all cultures. After examining thousands of descriptions of people's most satisfying and enjoyable moments, Csikszentmihalyi (1990) identified eight characteristics of the flow experience. These are listed in Table 11.1. Not every flow experience contains each of these eight. But any flow experience you might be thinking about probably includes many of these components. The flow experience that comes to mind for me happens when I become lost in my writing. I sometimes find myself writing for hours, almost totally unaware of anything around me. I become so absorbed in what I'm doing that I've written through ringing telephones and important meetings. When I finally stop after 3 or 4 hours, it always seems as if I had been working only 10 minutes.

Optimal Experience and Happiness in Everyday Activities

If flow experiences make us happy, then understanding how to incorporate these experiences in our daily lives may provide an avenue for increasing happiness. Like other humanistic theorists, Csikszentmihalyi recognizes that many people suffer from a sense that their lives have no meaning. Society provides many sources of relief from this feeling. Some people seek happiness by acquiring material possessions. Some turn to fitness centers and plastic surgery in an effort to hang on to youth. Others try out new and seemingly mystical religions. But Csikszentmihalyi (1999) argues that none of these diversions brings permanent happiness. True happiness comes when we take personal responsibility for finding meaning and

Table 11.1   Eight Components of Optimal Experience

1. *The Activity Is Challenging and Requires Skill.*

   The task is sufficiently challenging to demand full attention, but not so difficult that it denies a sense of accomplishment.

2. *One's Attention Is Completely Absorbed by the Activity.*

   People stop being aware of themselves as separate from their actions, which seem spontaneous and automatic.

3. *The Activity Has Clear Goals.*

   There is a direction, a logical point to work toward.

4. *There Is Clear Feedback.*

   We need to know if we have succeeded at reaching our goal, even if this is only self-confirmation.

5. *One Can Concentrate Only on the Task at Hand.*

   During flow we pay no attention to the unpleasant parts of life.

6. *One Achieves a Sense of Personal Control.*

   People in flow enjoy the experience of exercising control over their environments.

7. *One Loses Self-Consciousness.*

   With attention focused on the activity and the goals, there is little opportunity to think about one's self.

8. *One Loses a Sense of Time.*

   Usually hours pass by in what seems like minutes, but the opposite can also occur.

enjoyment in our ongoing experiences. That is, we can enjoy life to its fullest by discovering what it is that makes us feel alive and then doing it.

Of course, in a perfect world we could all do what we wanted when we wanted. But reality does not allow us the luxury of such simple solutions. The common lament these days seems to be that we face so many demands, yet have so little free time. This brings us to an important question: When are people more likely to experience flow—at work or during leisure hours? Most of us answer quickly that we are happier during time away from work. In fact, people often point to their long working hours as a cause of their unhappiness. However, researchers find this is not the case. Although people often experience flowlike experiences when engaging in sports and other recreational activities (Stein, Kimiecik, Daniels, & Jackson, 1995), these experiences are far more likely to happen when people are at work than during their off hours (Csikszentmihalyi & LeFevre, 1989). Csikszentmihalyi argues that most of us simply buy into the conventional wisdom that says work is work and play is play. Consequently, we fail to recognize the frequency with which our jobs provide us with a sense of mastery, accomplishment, and enrichment.

Fortunately, this is not true of all people. A woman I know, a writer, keeps her computer near her bed so that she can turn to her work even before her first cup of coffee in the morning. Friends say she often has to be pried away from her writing at night. She doesn't understand the fuss. She loves what she does for a living. Time spent writing is time spent learning and growing. Each day her work produces more challenges and more opportunities for personal development. Movie maker Woody Allen is another example. Friends and colleagues are constantly amazed at the energy and attention he gives to his movies. "I love to work," he once said. "I'd work seven days a week. I don't care about hours. When we solve this problem, whether it's five o'clock or ten at night, we move on to something else. Hours or days mean nothing" (in Lax, 1991, p. 337). Woody Allen clearly experiences flow when he's working. That his movies also provide money and fame seems to be secondary.

Of course, not everyone can be a writer or a movie maker. What about the average person who puts in 40 hours a week at a less glamorous profession? Csikszentmihalyi argues that nearly any job can become a flow experience if we approach it the right way. Even mowing the lawn or making dinner can be a source of happiness if we look at these chores as challenges and take pride and satisfaction in a job well done. Rather than thinking of such jobs as something we have to do or something others expect us to do, we can approach these daily tasks by searching for what we can get out of them.

This advice also applies to students. High school students are most content when they face academic challenges that are within their power to overcome (Moneta & Csikszentmihalyi, 1996). Researchers in one study identified high school students who studied and participated in their classes not because they wanted good grades, but because they found the learning process fascinating and satisfying (Wong & Csikszentmihalyi, 1991). Interestingly, these students' grades were not particularly high. But they did take more advanced courses than the grade-driven students, probably because they wanted to learn more about the subjects they found most interesting. Intrinsically-motivated undergraduates in another study were more likely to lose track of time and to report that time passed quickly than students who were less interested in the learning experience (Conti, 2001).

In summary, Csikszentmihalyi's prescription for happiness contains many of the elements traditionally embraced by humanistic personality psychology. Flow experiences require people to live in the present and to get the most out of their lives in the "here and now." Achieving the goal is not the point. Rather, it is the struggle and experience along the way that provide the enjoyment. Happiness comes from taking control of your life rather than caving in to conventional standards or demands from others. In the flow state, people are intensely in touch with themselves and their experiences. They feel a sense of mastery and an awareness of finding themselves. Like the peak experiences described by Maslow, flow experiences are occasions for personal growth.

Application: Person-Centered Therapy and Job Satisfaction

Obviously, the works of Rogers and Maslow have had a great impact on psychology and personality theory. In this section we examine two applications of humanistic personality theory. We first look at Rogers' contribution to psychotherapy practices. Then we explore some of the ways Maslow's theory of motivation and the hierarchy of needs have been applied to working environments and the issue of job satisfaction.

Person-Centered Therapy

"When I accept myself as I am, then I change."
CARL ROGERS

Carl Rogers' personality theory presents an interesting challenge for humanistic psychotherapists. According to Rogers, a therapist cannot possibly understand clients as well as clients understand themselves. He also maintained that clients, rather than the therapist, are responsible for changing themselves. So what is left for therapists to do with clients who come to them for help?

Rogers' answer was that a therapist's job is not to change the client, but rather to provide an atmosphere within which clients are able to help themselves. He called his approach to treatment **person-centered therapy.** Rogers believed each of us grows and develops in a positive, self-actualizing fashion unless our progress is in some way impeded. The therapist simply allows the client to get back on that positive growth track. After successful Rogerian therapy, clients should be more open to personal experience, more able to accept all aspects of themselves, and therefore less likely to use distortion and denial when faced with information incongruent with their self-concepts. By the end of the therapy sessions, clients should be more fully functioning and happier people.

How is this accomplished? Therapists must first create the proper relationship with their clients. The most important rule here is to be open and genuine with clients. Therapists have to be themselves rather than play the role of therapist they were taught in graduate school. This means being honest with clients, even if that includes being very frank (but not cruel) at times. Entering a genuine relationship with another person is necessary for clients to explore their feelings openly and thereby come to understand and overcome their problems. Rogers believed clients can always tell when a therapist isn't being genuine with them.

The proper therapeutic relationship also requires unconditional positive regard. Therapists must accept and "prize" their clients for what they are. Clients must feel free to express and accept all their thoughts and feelings during therapy without fear of rejection from the therapist. Clients can overcome defenses and come to grips with experiences that have been denied or distorted only when they feel the freedom to identify and express all their feelings, not just those that are socially acceptable.

Unconditional positive regard does not mean therapists must approve of everything clients say and do, especially acts that may hurt the client or someone else. Indeed, in the safe atmosphere provided by the therapist, clients may disclose some disturbing information about themselves. But because therapists accept clients with positive regard despite these faults and weaknesses, clients learn to acknowledge these aspects of themselves, too. They can't begin to change these things until they've acknowledged their existence.

In addition to providing an accepting relationship, therapists can help clients understand themselves better through a process of *reflection*. Rather than interpret what clients really mean, as a Freudian therapist might, a Rogerian therapist helps clients listen to what they are saying. Part of this comes about when clients are given the opportunity to put their feelings into words. By translating vague feelings into precise words, clients come to understand their feelings. Clients listen to their words and examine their thoughts, perhaps for the first time. One technique a therapist can use to further this process is to restate the client's statements. Some people mistakenly think this means the therapist must repeat the client's words back to him or her verbatim. But as the following excerpt demonstrates, the goal is to help clients explore their thoughts and feelings by directing their attention to what they are saying. In this example, Rogers is working with a woman who is struggling with her sense of personal identity:

> *Client:* I suppose I want to know just what to do, but then maybe nobody could give me that.
>
> *Therapist:* You realize that you are probably looking for immediate answers that nobody could give you.
>
> *C:* I just don't know. I don't know what I'm looking for. It's just that I wonder if I'm insane sometimes. I think I'm nuts.
>
> *T:* It just gives you concern that you're as far from normal as you feel you are.
>
> *C:* That's right. It's silly to tell me not to worry because I do worry. It's my life. . . . Well, I don't know how I can change my concept of myself—because that's the way I feel.
>
> *T:* You feel very different from others and you don't see how you can fix that.
>
> *C:* I realize, of course, that it all began a long time ago—because everything begins somewhere. I wasn't just—somehow or other something failed somewhere along the line. And I guess we sort of have to get at it, a sort of reeducation. But I don't feel as though I can do it myself.
>
> *T:* You realize that the roots must go a long way back, and that at some point you will have to start in reworking it, but you're not sure whether you can do it.
>
> *C:* That's right. It's just the idea that I can see myself going through life this way, 50-, 60-, and 70-years-old—still thinking these horrible thoughts. And it just doesn't seem worthwhile—I mean, it's so ridiculous. While everybody else is going their way and living life, I'm sort of at the edge, and looking on. It just isn't right.
>
> *T:* The future doesn't look very bright when you look at it that way.
>
> *C:* No. I know I'm lacking in courage, that's the big thing I'm lacking. That must be it, 'cause other people aren't swayed so easily. . . . It's a hard thing to explain these things. It's just as though—it's—true but I laugh at it in a way. . . . It's a very confused feeling.

T: Logically, you realize that courage is one of your deficiencies, but inside yourself you find yourself laughing at that notion and feeling that it doesn't really have anything to do with you. Is that it?

C: That's right. I always sort of make myself different. That's it. (1947, pp. 138–140)

The therapist never tells clients what they really mean to say. Instead, therapists offer restatements of what they believe they are hearing, but these are only suggestions for the client to agree with or reject. If the process is effective, clients come to see themselves as others do and eventually accept or modify what they see. Clients may come to understand that they have been distorting or denying parts of their experiences. For example, a man may realize he has been trying to live up to his father's impossibly high expectations, or a woman may come to understand she is afraid to commit herself to a serious relationship. In the freedom provided by the therapist's unconditional support, clients peel away their defenses, accept who they are, and begin to appreciate all of life's experiences.

Today a large number of psychotherapists identify their approach as humanistic (Mayne, Norcross, & Sayette, 1994). Many other therapists and counselors have expanded or modified aspects of person-centered therapy in their work with clients (Cain & Seeman, 2002). A recent review of studies found considerable evidence for the effectiveness of humanistic psychotherapy (Elliott, 2002). Not only do many clients benefit from the person-centered approach, but the effects of the treatment can be seen many months after the end of the therapy sessions.

Job Satisfaction and the Hierarchy of Needs

Think for a moment of two or three careers you would like to have someday (maybe you already work at one of these). Now ask yourself what it is about each of these jobs that makes it appealing. That is, what do you hope to gain from it that you can't get from just any job? Now, take the answers to this last question and apply them to Maslow's hierarchy of needs. Which of the five levels of needs will your chosen occupation satisfy? If you find a job attractive because it pays a lot of money or provides good job security, the job probably will satisfy your safety needs. On the other hand, a job may appeal to you because it brings respect and admiration or allows you to express yourself artistically. Such a job might go a long way in satisfying your need for esteem or your need for self-actualization.

The point of this exercise is that your occupation provides an important source of need satisfaction. Besides sleeping, there is no single activity that will take up more of your adult life than your job. Maslow argued that to spend 40 hours a week at a job that pays well but doesn't allow for development of personal potential is a tragic waste. "Finding one's lifework is a little like finding one's mate," he wrote. "If you are unhappy with your work, you have lost one of the most important means of self-fulfillment" (1971, p. 185). Research confirms that the amount of satisfaction we get from our job is related to the amount of satisfaction we have with our life (Judge & Watanabe, 1993).

Is the job a chore that must be endured 8 hours a day, or does this man get more out of work than just a paycheck? According to Maslow, occupations should provide opportunities for personal growth and the satisfaction of higher-order needs. Besides money, a job can satisfy our needs for belongingness, self-esteem, and respect from others.

Maslow was critical of job counselors who direct young people into careers simply because they pay well or fit the needs of the job market. A better approach would be to match a person's unique talents and potential to a job that allows the expression and development of that potential. Maslow promoted what he called *Eupsychian management*—rearranging an organization to help employees satisfy higher-level needs. For example, an employer might structure jobs so that people have the opportunity to develop feelings of self-worth about what they do for a living. Workers move toward satisfying their esteem needs when they take pride in their job performance. In addition, workers might be given opportunities to suggest creative solutions to some of the problems they see. An employer might also foster a sense of belongingness and feelings of camaraderie among workers. In short, a career can provide an avenue for personal growth as well as a means for paying the bills.

Assessment: The Q-Sort Technique

A persistent challenge for psychotherapists of all stripes is to demonstrate the effectiveness of their treatment. Carl Rogers was very aware of this challenge and strongly encouraged research on the effectiveness of person-centered psychotherapy. Rogers recognized that therapy sessions are often declared a success after the therapist and client agree the client has shown improvement. But without empirical evidence of therapeutic change, psychologists are in danger of fooling themselves. Further, Rogers believed that research into *how* people change during psychotherapy would help therapists better understand the process and thereby improve their ability to work with clients.

But how does a therapist establish that a client is more fully functioning or closer to self-actualization after a few months of person-centered therapy? One tool that has proven useful in this task is an assessment procedure called the **Q-Sort.** The Q-Sort technique was developed by Stephenson (1953). The basic procedure has been used to assess a wide variety of psychological concepts, including parent-child attachment (DeMulder, Denham, Schmidt, & Mitchell, 2000), defense mechanisms (Davidson & MacGregor, 1996), group dynamics (Peterson, Owens, & Martorana, 1999), and strength of romantic relationships (Bengston & Grotevant, 1999). Carl Rogers also saw that the procedure fit nicely with the humanistic model of personality and quickly adopted it.

Psychologists often create their own Q-Sort materials to fit their needs, but Block's (1961) California Q-Sort is a good example of the technique used by many humanistic therapists. The materials for this test are not very elaborate. They consist of a deck of 100 cards. A self-descriptive phrase is printed on each card, such as "is a talkative individual," "seeks reassurance from others," or "has high aspiration level for self."

If you were a client about to begin a series of sessions with a Rogerian therapist, you might be instructed to read the cards and sort them into categories. On the first sort, you would be asked to place the cards into nine categories according to how much you believe the description on the card applies to you. The nine categories represent points on a normal distribution (Figure 11.2), with the categories on the extreme ends representing those characteristics most descriptive of you (Category 9) and least descriptive of you (Category 1).

For example, let's suppose the description on the first card is "is a talkative individual." If this phrase describes you very well, you would place the card in Category 9 or 8. If this phrase describes you only slightly, you might place it in Category 6. If you think you are a very quiet person, you might put the card in Category 1 or 2. There is a limit to how many cards can be placed in each category so that indecisive test takers are forced to select cards that are most descriptive of them. In this manner, you provide the therapist and yourself with a profile of your self-concept.

After recording the positions of the cards, you would be asked to shuffle the deck and take the test again. However, this time you would distribute the cards according to your "ideal" self. For example, if "is a talkative individual" does not describe you very well, but you want to become more talkative, you would move this card to a higher category when you sort your ideal self. When you have laid out descriptions of your "real" and "ideal" selves, you and the therapist can compare the two profiles. By assigning each card a number from 1 to 9 according to the category you placed it in, you can compute a correlation coefficient between your real self and your ideal self.

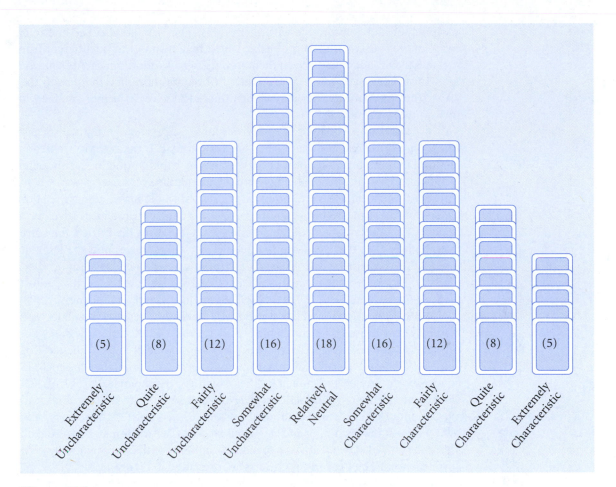

Figure 11.2
Distribution of Cards in Block's Q-Sort

The Q-Sort technique fits very nicely with Rogers' theory for several reasons. Consistent with Rogers' assumption that clients know themselves best, clients are allowed to describe themselves however they please. A therapist will not always agree with a client's placement of the Q-Sort cards. For example, a client might describe herself as socially aware, polite, and sensitive to the needs of others when a perceptive therapist sees right away that her crude insensitivity may be part of her problem. But humanistic therapists maintain that in the appropriate therapeutic atmosphere clients come to see themselves in a more realistic manner and eventually adjust their Q-Sorts accordingly.

As clients free themselves from distortion and denial of their experiences, they should obtain a more accurate understanding of who they are and become more accepting of and comfortable with themselves. They should also become more aware of the sources of their problems, which may turn out to be different from the ones they thought had driven them into therapy. In addition, clients can work to change themselves where appropriate, to become more like the person they want to be. Alternatively, they may modify their ideal selves to be more in line with the way they really are.

In a correlational analysis of Q-Sort responses, a psychologically healthy person is one whose real and ideal selves are very similar. If the category values are identical for both profiles, a perfect 1.0 correlation would be obtained, although it is difficult to imagine people being just like their ideal selves in every way. Clients whose real and ideal selves are completely unrelated would have a zero correlation. Clients' profiles can also be negatively correlated if their real and ideal selves are at opposite extremes on many of the descriptions. Obviously, the further the correlation is from 1.0, the less accepting people are of themselves and the less fully functioning. Consistent with Rogers' descriptions, researchers have found that a high correlation between a person's real and ideal self is related to positive adjustment (Gough, Fioravanti, & Lazzari, 1983; Gough, Lazzari, & Fioravanti, 1978).

Other studies find that the real-ideal self correlation increases as clients move through client-centered psychotherapy (Butler, 1968). To illustrate how the Q-Sort can be used to track therapeutic progress, let's look at one of Rogers' clients (Rogers, 1961). This 40-year-old woman came to Rogers with problems that included an unhappy marriage and guilt about her daughter's psychological problems. The woman attended 40 therapy sessions over the course of 5½ months and returned a few months later for some additional sessions. She completed the real and ideal self Q-Sorts at the beginning and at various stages of her treatment. She also completed the Q-Sort at two follow-up sessions, 7 and 12 months after her therapy. The correlations among the various Q-Sorts are presented in Figure 11.3.

Several important changes in the way the woman viewed her real self and her ideal self occurred during her treatment. There was a significant increase in the congruence between her real and ideal selves over the course of the therapy sessions that continued to grow after she discontinued therapy. At the beginning of her treatment, her real and ideal self Q-Sorts were quite discrepant, correlating at only .21. In other words, when she first entered Carl Rogers' door, she did not see herself at all as the kind of person she wanted to be. However, as therapy progressed, the two descriptions became more and more similar. In particular, this client changed the way she viewed herself. We can tell this from the low correlation (.30) between the way she described herself at the beginning of the therapy and the way she described herself at the end. Thus, by exploring her feelings in these person-centered sessions, the client came to see herself in very different and presumably more accurate terms.

There also were some noticeable but less dramatic changes in the way the woman described her ideal self. She may have come to realize through therapy that the goals she set for herself were far too ideal. It is not uncommon for clients to

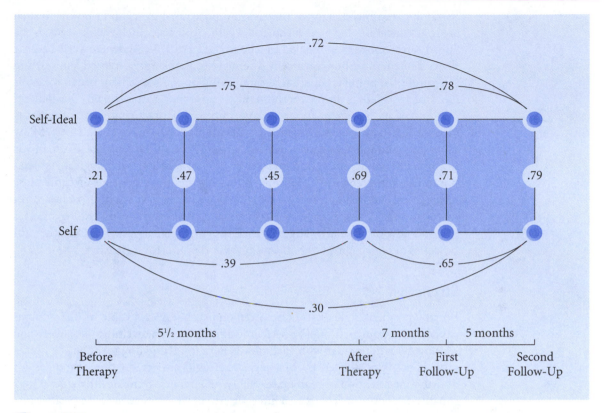

Figure 11.3
Changing Real and Ideal Self Q-Sorts for a 40-Year-Old Female Client
Source: From Rogers (1954), with permission.

enter therapy expecting near perfection of themselves and to consider themselves failures when they fall short of these impossible goals. It is clear from this example that Rogers' therapy was successful in bringing the client's real and ideal selves closer together. No doubt, she was better able to experience life as a fully functioning person than she was before entering therapy.

Strengths and Criticisms of the Humanistic Approach

The humanistic movement hit psychology like a storm in the 1960s. Therapists from every perspective were converted to the person-centered approach. Humanistically oriented encounter groups and workshops sprang up everywhere.

Psychologists applied many of the ideas proposed by Rogers and Maslow to such areas as education and the workplace. Then, almost as quickly as it arrived, the "third force" movement seemed to fade in the late 1970s. Many converts became disenchanted, some humanistically oriented programs were declared failures, and the number of popular paperbacks capitalizing on the movement began to dwindle. But, also like a storm, the humanistic approach to personality has left reminders of its presence. Today a large number of practicing psychotherapists identify themselves as humanistic in their orientation (Mayne et al., 1994). Many others have adopted various Rogerian techniques in their practice. Humanistic psychologists enjoy an active division in the American Psychological Association and publish their own journal. Although the movement never came close to replacing the well-entrenched psychoanalytic or behavioral approaches, it remains an appealing alternative view of human nature for many psychologists. This ebb and flow of popularity suggests that the humanistic approach, like other approaches to personality, has both strengths and points for criticism.

Strengths

Because personality theorists often dwell on psychological problems, the humanists' positive approach offers a welcome alternative. The writings of Rogers and Maslow remain popular with each new generation struggling through the higher growth needs postulated by Maslow. We should also credit these theorists for drawing the attention of many personality researchers to the healthy side of personality. Recently, we have seen a huge interest in what has been called *positive psychology* (Seligman & Csikszentmihalyi, 2000). An increasing number of researchers are turning their attention to such topics as creativity, happiness, and sense of well-being.

Not surprisingly, humanistic psychology has had a huge impact on the way psychologists and counselors approach therapy. Many therapists identify themselves as "humanistic." More important, several aspects of the humanistic approach to therapy have been adopted or modified in some form by a large number of therapists from other theoretical perspectives (Cain & Seeman, 2002). Many therapists like Rogers' emphasis on making the client the center of therapy. In addition, many therapists include in their practices such Rogerian techniques as therapist empathy, positive regard for clients, giving clients responsibility for change, and self-disclosure by client and therapist. The humanistic approach also sparked the growth of encounter groups in the 1960s. Variations of encounter groups remain today in the form of group therapy and other self-improvement and personal-growth therapies.

Humanistic psychology's influence has not been limited to psychology and psychotherapy. Students in such disciplines as education, communication, and business are often introduced to Rogers and Maslow. Many employers and organizational psychologists are concerned about promoting job satisfaction by taking care of employees' higher needs. And many teachers and parents have adopted or modified some of Rogers' suggestions for education and child rearing. Because they focus on issues that many of us address in our lives—fulfilling personal potential, living in the here and now, finding happiness and meaning—books by Maslow, Rogers, and other humanistic psychologists continue to sell in popular bookstores.

Criticisms

Like all influential personality theories, humanistic psychology has its critics. One area of controversy centers around humanistic psychology's reliance on the concept of free will to explain human behavior. Some psychologists argue that this reliance renders the humanistic approach unfit for scientific study. Science relies on the notion that events are determined by other events. Thus, the science of behavior relies on the assumption that behavior is determined and therefore predictable. However, if we accept the idea that behavior is sometimes caused by free will, which is not subject to these laws of determination, these assumptions fall apart. How can we scientifically test whether free will exists or not? Because we can explain any behavior as caused by "free will," no investigation will ever fail to support a free will interpretation. Free will by definition is not under the control of any observable or predictable force. These observations do not mean free will does not exist—only that it cannot be explored through scientific inquiry. Maslow was aware of this problem, but pointed out that there are more avenues for understanding human personality than the scientific method.

Another criticism of the humanistic approach is that many key concepts are poorly defined. What exactly is "self-actualization," "fully functioning," or "becoming"? How do we know if we're having a "peak experience" or just a particularly pleasant time? Maslow responded that we simply don't know enough about self-actualization and personal growth to provide clear definitions. But this defense is far from satisfying for most researchers. Such vagueness prevents psychologists from adequately studying many humanistic concepts. How can we investigate self-actualization if we can't decide who's got it and who hasn't? Because most psychologists are trained as careful researchers, the inability to pin down humanistic concepts causes many to challenge the usefulness of the approach.

Rogers, Maslow, and other humanistic psychologists provide research findings to support their views. However, the data on which many of these studies are based have been challenged by more experimentally oriented psychologists. Although Rogers is to be commended for his efforts to assess the effectiveness of person-centered therapy, he still relied too heavily on his intuition to satisfy many hard-nosed researchers. Similarly, Maslow selected people for his list of "self-actualized" individuals based on his own subjective impressions. Because of these weak data, much of what humanistic theorists say must be taken more as a matter of faith than scientific fact. Most likely, psychologists and lay readers embrace the humanistic approach because it is consistent with their own observations and values, not because they are persuaded by the evidence.

Other problems people have with the humanistic approach concern the limited applicability of humanistic psychotherapy techniques. Some critics argue that humanistic psychotherapy may be limited to a narrow band of problems. Creating the proper atmosphere for personal growth might be of value for many of Rogers' clients, but may provide little help to someone with an extreme psychological disorder. Similarly, reflecting on one's values and direction in life might prove beneficial for well-educated, middle-class clients. But these questions might be irrelevant to someone from a different background. Person-centered therapy may be useful for working through certain kinds of adjustment problems, but not for dealing with the myriad of serious psychological disturbances that cause people to seek therapy.

Humanistic psychologists have also been criticized for making some overly naive assumptions about human nature. For example, most humanists assume that all people are basically good. Although this is more a theological than an empirical question, many people find the premise difficult to accept. Another assumption many find difficult to swallow is that each of us has a desire to fulfill some hidden potential. Maslow's description of self-actualization implies that each individual is somehow destined to become, for example, a painter, a poet, or a carpenter. For Maslow the key is discovering which of these true selves lies bottled up inside waiting to develop. This predeterministic tone seems to contradict the general free will emphasis of the humanistic approach.

 ## *Summary*

1.   The humanistic approach to personality grew out of discontent with the psychoanalytic and behavioral descriptions of human nature prominent in the 1950s and 1960s. Humanistic psychology has its roots in European existential philosophy and the works of some American psychologists, most notably Carl Rogers and Abraham Maslow.

2.   Although many approaches to psychotherapy have been described as humanistic, four criteria seem important for classifying a theory under this label. These criteria are an emphasis on personal responsibility, an emphasis on the here and now, focusing on the phenomenology of the individual, and emphasizing personal growth.

3.   Carl Rogers introduced the notion of a fully functioning person. According to his theory, we all progress toward a state of fulfillment and happiness unless derailed by life's obstacles. People who encounter evidence that contradicts their self-

concepts often rely on distortion and denial to avoid the anxiety this might create. People who grow up in families that give only conditional positive regard may come to deny certain aspects of themselves. Rogers advocated the use of unconditional positive regard by parents and therapists to overcome this denial.

4. Abraham Maslow introduced a hierarchy of human needs. According to this concept, people progress up the hierarchy as lower needs are satisfied. Maslow also examined psychologically healthy people. He found several characteristics typical of these self-actualized individuals, including the tendency by some to have frequent peak experiences.

5. One recent outgrowth of the humanistic approach to personality is presented by Mihaly Csikszentmihalyi. He finds people describe the happiest and most rewarding moments in their lives in terms of a "flow" experience. Csikszentmihalyi argues that turning one's life into a series of challenging and absorbing tasks, what he calls optimal experiences, is the key to happiness and personal fulfillment.

6. One of Rogers' contributions to psychology is the person-centered approach to psychotherapy. Rogers said the therapist's job is to create the proper atmosphere for clients' growth. This is accomplished by entering a genuine relationship with clients, providing unconditional positive regard, and helping clients hear what they are saying. Maslow's hierarchy of needs concept has been applied to the problem of job satisfaction. He argued that one's career provides an opportunity for personal growth and that employers should arrange working situations to better meet employees' higher-order needs.

7. Many person-centered therapists have adopted the Q-Sort assessment procedure. This procedure allows therapists and clients to see discrepancies between clients' images of themselves and the person they would like to be. Therapists can administer the Q-Sort at various points during treatment to measure therapy progress. Improvement is seen when clients close the gap between their real and ideal selves.

8. Among the strengths found in the humanistic approach to personality are the attention given to the positive side of personality and the influence this approach has had on psychotherapy and job satisfaction. Criticisms include the unscientific reliance on free will to explain behavior and the difficulty in dealing with many of the poorly defined constructs used by humanistic theorists. Some therapists have challenged the usefulness of person-centered therapy for many types of clients and psychological problems. The humanistic approach has also been criticized for making many naive assumptions about human nature.

InfoTrac College Edition Key Terms

For additional readings go to http://www.infotrac-college.com/wadsworth and enter a search term related to your interest. Use the key terms suggested here to pull up several related articles. Also see the text Web site at http://psychology .wadsworth.com for more suggested readings and interactive quizzes to test your knowledge.

Abraham Maslow

Carl Rogers

Hierarchy of needs

Humanistic psychology

Ideal self

Need (psychology)

Self-actualization (psychology)

Chapter 12

The Humanistic Approach

Relevant Research

Self-Disclosure

Loneliness

Self-Esteem

Solitude

Summary

The rapid growth of humanistic psychology a few decades ago was in part a reaction against the research-oriented approaches to understanding human behavior that had come to dominate American universities. Humanistic psychologists argued that people cannot be reduced to a set of numbers. Scores on a battery of personality tests don't capture a person's inner strength, feelings, and character. Most important, finding a person's place along a trait continuum erases that person's uniqueness and individuality. As the name implies, the third force in psychology was developed to attend to the "human" element lost in number-crunching approaches.

Ironically, this strength also proves to be one of humanistic psychology's weaknesses. Critics sometimes refer to the approach as "soft" psychology. Flowery descriptions of one's unique character are fine, but they are of little value when trying to find empirical support for the theory. Clinical observations and intuitive feelings by humanistic therapists may provide insights into personality and the therapy process, but they cannot replace reliable assessment procedures. This is not to say that humanistic psychologists don't conduct research. On the contrary, Carl Rogers continually evaluated the effectiveness of person-centered therapy, as have many humanistic therapists to follow (Cain & Seeman, 2002). But on the whole, advocates of the humanistic perspective have probably generated less empirical research than psychologists from the other approaches covered in this book.

Nonetheless, Rogers, Maslow, and other humanistic psychologists have introduced a number of intriguing concepts and hypotheses about human personality, and many of these have generated or promoted a great deal of empirical research. Although some of the original research on these topics was conducted by humanistic psychologists, in most cases the better empirical work was done by investigators outside the humanistic circle. A good example of this is research on self-disclosure, the first topic we'll explore in this chapter. Rogers and other therapists argued that the act of revealing personal information has important psychological consequences. This theorizing stimulated more decades of research on self-disclosure. Most of this work has been conducted by psychologists who probably would shun the "humanistic" label. Nonetheless, the findings from this research have important implications for humanistic theory and therapy.

Similarly, research on the other three topics we'll examine in this chapter—loneliness, self-esteem, and solitude—was inspired in part by humanistic writers but largely conducted by more empirically oriented academic psychologists. Of course, there is some irony in this situation. The cold, empirical approach to understanding personality, once rejected by many humanistic types, has popularized many of the concepts central to the humanistic perspective.

Self-Disclosure

Imagine you are with someone you don't know very well but who seems to be a pleasant person. You both have time to kill, so you begin to talk. The conversation starts casually with a discussion about the classes you're taking. However, soon this person mentions some difficulties she's having with her parents. You find yourself talking about similar experiences you have had. Before the conversation is over, you learn quite a lot about this individual—problems with her family, with dating, with her self-confidence. You reveal that you, too, sometimes have difficulty relating with members of the opposite sex. Perhaps you tell this person about an embarrassing dating situation you've been in. When the conversation ends, you feel good about her and maybe even about yourself.

Most of us have participated in this kind of conversation. If you think back to your own experience, you may recall that the conversation began with relatively impersonal topics and gradually worked toward more private information. Most likely, the conversation was anything but one-sided. You and this individual probably took turns sharing information about yourselves. And it's quite possible you left the conversation feeling good about your new acquaintance and perceiving that he or she also felt good about you. This may well have been the first step toward a long-lasting friendship. The whole encounter may also have put you in a pleasant mood and kept you in good spirits for the rest of the day.

According to self-disclosure theory and research, these experiences are typical when two people share personal information. People engage in **self-disclosure** when they reveal intimate information about themselves to another person. The discloser considers the information personal, and the choice of who to disclose to is fairly selective. Many humanistic psychologists argue that self-disclosure is an important step in our personal growth and happiness. For example, Rogers (1961) suggested that disclosing openly within a trusting relationship is a necessary step for understanding oneself. However, the person most responsible for promoting self-disclosure as a key concept in humanistic psychology was Sidney Jourard.

According to Jourard (1971), the causal arrow between self-disclosure and well-being runs both ways. People freely reveal information about themselves to others because they are psychologically healthy, and our psychological health increases because we disclose personal information to friends and loved ones. The key to becoming a fully functioning person is, in Jourard's words, to make ourselves *transparent*. We should be willing and able to disclose fully about ourselves to all the significant people in our lives. Of course, this is far from the way most people act. We often go to great lengths to keep others from finding out about bad habits and parts of our character they might not like. We're afraid of embarrassing ourselves or perhaps losing the respect of the people we love and admire. But the result of all this deception is simply more to worry about and the ever-present fear that the real you might be revealed. More important, Jourard argued, it is only through self-disclosure that we can truly come to know ourselves. Putting feelings into words allows us to understand those feelings in a way that simply thinking about emotions cannot. Until we are open and transparent to others, we can never be open and transparent to ourselves. And if we are not aware of all aspects of ourselves, we cannot grow and become fully self-actualized.

Naturally, Jourard and others have applied the concept of the transparent self to psychotherapy. They argue that clients benefit most when they engage in an open exchange of thoughts and feelings with the therapist. When clients feel free to explore their true feelings, they move closer to becoming their true selves. Today, therapists from many approaches acknowledge the important role self-disclosure plays in the psychotherapeutic process (Derlega, Margulis, & Winstead, 1987). Moreover, as you will see, a growing body of evidence finds the act of expressing important feelings and thoughts often has significant therapeutic value.

But a therapeutic relationship is not one-sided. Rogers, Jourard, and other humanistic psychologists propose that appropriate self-disclosure by the therapist is also beneficial. They argue that disclosing therapists create an atmosphere of trust and elicit more disclosure from clients (Derlega, Hendrick, Winstead, & Berg, 1991). Consistent with this position, some studies find a positive relationship between therapist disclosure and client progress (Hill, Helms, Tichenor, Spiegel, O'Grady, & Perry, 1988; Hill, Mahalik, & Thompson, 1989). One team of investigators instructed counselors to either increase or decrease the amount of personal information they disclosed to clients during therapy sessions (Barrett & Berman,

Self-disclosure plays a key role in the development of personal relationships. However, researchers find that this is rarely one-sided. Instead, relationships develop as each person reveals intimate information about himself or herself at roughly the same level of intimacy.

2001). After four weeks, clients receiving the increased disclosure reported fewer symptoms of distress than clients who experienced a decrease in disclosure. However, other psychologists are concerned about potential harm to the therapeutic process when therapists talk about themselves, and the appropriate level of self-disclosure for therapists remains an open question (Bridges, 2001).

Of course, self-disclosure is not limited to psychotherapy. We face decisions about how much to conceal and how much to reveal daily. We'll look briefly at what researchers have discovered about the rules for self-disclosure, differences in the way men and women self-disclose, and how self-disclosure can affect your psychological well-being and physical health.

Disclosure Reciprocity

If you are like me, you have had the unfortunate experience of being stuck on a plane or a bus sitting next to a stranger who wanted to tell you all about his or her life. During a recent plane trip, the woman next to me described her relationship with her husband, problems in raising her child, her opinions on drugs, sex education, and abortion—all without a single bit of encouragement or comparable disclosure from me.

What is notable about this "stranger on the bus" phenomenon is that it violates society's rules for the way social interaction is supposed to progress. Like many social behaviors, the way we reveal information about ourselves is governed by a set of unstated but understood rules. Occasionally, parents teach us these rules directly ("Don't stare at people"), but more often we are not aware of how we learned what is expected and what is inappropriate when interacting with others. One of these rules is reflected in what Jourard called the *dyadic effect.* Jourard observed that conversation partners tend to match each other's intimacy level. That is, when one person discloses personal information, the other person almost always reciprocates. Later investigators identified this as the rule of *disclosure reciprocity.* According to this social rule, people involved in a get-acquainted conversation reveal information about themselves at roughly the same level of intimacy. I reveal personal information to you as long as you continue to match that level of intimacy with personal information about yourself.

Investigators have demonstrated the rule of disclosure reciprocity in laboratory research (Davis, 1977; Taylor & Belgrave, 1986). Undergraduate students in one study were randomly paired with a member of the same gender whom they did not know (Davis, 1976). Students took turns getting to know one another by volunteering information about themselves. They were given a list of 72 discussion topics, previously ranked for level of intimacy, ranging from fairly trivial to extremely revealing. The winner of a coin toss began by talking for 1 minute on any one of the topics. The partner then talked for 1 minute on any one of the remaining topics. This procedure continued until both partners had spoken 12 times. As shown in Figure 12.1, the students selected increasingly intimate topics as the interaction progressed. They typically began with something safe, per-

Figure 12.1

Progression of Intimacy During Dyad Conversion

Source: Adapted from Davis (1976); reprinted by permission of the author.

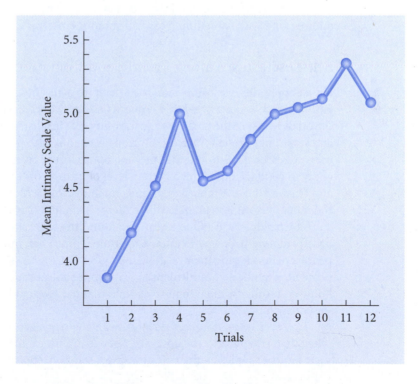

haps discussing their favorite movies or foods. But they soon moved to more personal areas, such as problems with their parents or ways in which they felt personally inadequate. Moreover, participants tended to match their partners' intimacy levels. That is, if one person chose an intimate topic, the partner usually responded by selecting a similarly intimate topic. In other words, the students in this experiment followed the rule of disclosure reciprocity. Other studies show that children as young as eight years old seem to understand and follow the disclosure reciprocity rule (Cohn & Strassberg, 1983).

Why do we reciprocate disclosure intimacy? Jourard (1971) believed self-disclosure follows feelings of attraction and trust. When people disclose information about themselves to us, we are attracted to them, and a feeling of trust develops. We respond to these feelings by disclosing personal information back to that person, thus creating the reciprocity effect. Consistent with this explanation, studies find that we disclose to people we like and we like those who disclose to us (Collins & Miller, 1994).

However, liking the other person appears to be only part of the story. Another reason we reciprocate self-disclosure is because our partner's intimacy level tells us something about how we are supposed to act in that particular situation. Consistent with this explanation, participants in disclosure experiments sometimes match their partner's level of intimacy when they don't particularly like the person (Derlega, Harris, & Chaikin, 1973; Ehrlich & Graeven, 1971; Lynn, 1978). Even when their partners reveal something unpleasant about themselves, the participants in these studies apparently conclude that intimate disclosure is appropriate and respond with something personal about themselves.

Self-Disclosure Among Friends and Romantic Partners

If you apply the disclosure reciprocity rule to a recent conversation you've had with a friend, you may find that it doesn't always work. It's quite possible that one of you did most of the talking while the other one just listened. When a friend calls and says "I need to talk," we usually don't interrupt with personal examples of our own. Researchers also find that the rule of disclosure reciprocity does not always apply to good friends. After a certain level of intimacy is reached in a relationship and trust has been established, friends often disclose with the understanding that the other person's acceptance will be there (Altman & Taylor, 1973; Derlega, Wilson, & Chaikin, 1976). One researcher found the highest level of disclosure reciprocity among people who knew each other somewhat, but who were still in the process of developing their relationship (Won-Doornink, 1985). Apparently these people had made a commitment to learn more about each other, but they didn't know each other well enough to assume that trust would be there without some sign of assurance.

However, these findings do not mean that strangers disclose more to each other than friends. On the contrary, friends are much more likely to talk about such intimate topics as their relationships, self-concepts, and sexual experiences

(Rubin & Shenker, 1978). In one demonstration of this difference, researchers recorded (with permission) the telephone conversations of female college students (Hornstein & Truesdell, 1988). The students talked about significantly more intimate information when they interacted with their friends than when they spoke on the phone with someone they identified as only an acquaintance. Conversations among good friends also include many noticeable signs of intimacy that are lacking in conversations with strangers (Hornstein, 1985). These signs include the use of familiar terms, laughing at similar points, and understanding when to speak and when the conversation is coming to an end.

Studies with couples in long-term romantic relationships find similar patterns. The amount of self-disclosure in a marriage is a strong predictor of marital satisfaction (Harvey & Omarzu, 1997; Hendrick, 1981). The more couples talk to one another about what's personal and important to them, the better each of them feels about the marriage. Of course, it also may be that couples disclose because they feel good about each other. However, it is not the case that people who disclose a lot have more success at romance. Rather, researchers find that couples in good relationships usually have selectively chosen one another to disclose to rather than being high disclosers generally (Prager, 1986). And, as with good friends, married couples do not feel the need to reciprocate their partner's disclosure level during a conversation (Morton, 1978).

Disclosing Men and Disclosing Women

Not long ago, my wife made an interesting observation about one of my male friends. "He interacts with people like a woman," she said. I immediately understood her point. My friend's voice is deep and masculine, and he doesn't use feminine hand gestures. But he often fills our conversations with fairly revealing information about his thoughts and feelings. This behavior would be appropriate, my wife continued, if my friend were a woman. But high levels of self-disclosure seem inappropriate for a man.

Consistent with these observations, investigators typically find that women disclose more intimately and to more people than men (Dindia & Allen, 1992). Why should this be so? According to Jourard (1971), men learn as they grow up that it is inappropriate to be as expressive and disclosing as females. They fear being ridiculed or rejected if they express too many of their true feelings. Some research supports these observations. Participants in one study read about someone who was either highly disclosing or not very disclosing about personal problems (Derlega & Chaikin, 1976). Half the participants thought they were reading about a man, and half thought the person was a woman. The participants who thought they were reading about a female rated that person better adjusted when she was disclosing. However, when they thought the discloser was a male, personal disclosure was seen as a sign of poor psychological adjustment.

Other studies suggest at least a few exceptions to this rule. The freedom women feel to disclose may be limited by the nature of what they are talking about.

Highly disclosing women in one study were liked more when they talked about their parents or about their sexual attitudes. However, women who disclosed about their personal aggressiveness were liked less (Kleinke & Kahn, 1980). Similarly, self-disclosing men were seen as well adjusted as long as they talked about masculine topics (Cunningham, Strassberg, & Haan, 1986). In other words, men and women are more likely to be accepted when they disclose within the appropriate societal roles for their gender. For men, this usually means withholding information; for women, it means being open and disclosing, but only on topics society deems appropriate. The result is an unfortunate limitation on personal expression. American men have learned to be friendly but avoid intimacy. Women feel freer expressing themselves with their friends, but within limits. Perhaps as traditional gender roles continue to erode, men and women will feel free to interact with friends at whatever level of intimacy they choose.

Disclosing Traumatic Experiences

"No man can come to know himself except as an outcome of disclosing himself to another person."
SIDNEY JOURARD

Students participating in an experiment several years ago were asked to write anonymously about an upsetting or traumatic experience they once had, something they may have kept inside for years and told to no one (Pennebaker, 1989). One of the interesting findings from this and other studies like it is that nearly every participant is able to identify a secret trauma. People write about personal failures and humiliations, illegal activities, drug and alcohol problems, and experiences with sexual abuse. They often express guilt over regrettable actions or great sadness about a personal loss. About a quarter of the participants cry.

What advice does psychology have for people carrying around these emotional secrets? Should they bare their souls to someone or keep things under wraps? Results from studies like the one previously described suggests that holding these secrets inside may be hazardous to our health (Pennebaker, 1989). Because it is customary to not burden others with our problems and because it might be too embarrassing to discuss them, most of us have not talked to many people—perhaps not to anyone—about our most traumatic experiences. But not talking about these experiences does not mean we are unaffected by them.

Researchers in one study contacted people who had suffered the tragedy of losing a spouse either through an accidental death or because of suicide (Pennebaker & O'Heeron, 1984). The investigators asked how often the participants had discussed the experience with friends and about the participants' health since the death. They found the more people had talked about the tragedy, the fewer health problems they had. Put another way, not talking to others about the disturbing experience was associated with increased health problems.

What about those of us who hide less painful memories? Would we also benefit from seeking out a close friend and talking about our secrets? To answer this question, researchers asked a group of healthy undergraduates to write about themselves for 15 minutes each night for four consecutive November nights (Pennebaker & Beall, 1986). Some of these students were instructed to write about rel-

Assessing Your Own Personality

Disclosure and Concealment

Indicate the extent to which you agree with each of the following statements. Use a 5-point scale to indicate your response, with 1 = Strongly disagree and 5 = Strongly agree.

_____ 1. When I feel upset, I usually confide in my friends.

_____ 2. I prefer not to talk about my problems.

_____ 3. When something unpleasant happens to me, I often look for someone to talk to.

_____ 4. I typically don't discuss things that upset me.

_____ 5. When I feel depressed or sad, I tend to keep those feelings to myself.

_____ 6. I try to find people to talk with about my problems.

_____ 7. When I am in a bad mood, I talk about it with my friends.

_____ 8. If I have a bad day, the last thing I want to do is talk about it.

_____ 9. I rarely look for people to talk with when I am having a problem.

_____ 10. When I'm distressed, I don't tell anyone.

_____ 11. I usually seek out someone to talk to when I am in a bad mood.

_____ 12. I am willing to tell others my distressing thoughts.

To score, reverse the answer values for items 2, 4, 5, 8, 9, and 10 (that is, 1 = 5, 2 = 4, etc.). Then add all 12 answer values together. High scores indicate a tendency to disclose distressing experiences to others, whereas low scores indicate a tendency to conceal information about distressing events. You can compare your score with norms from an undergraduate student sample (Kahn & Hessling, 2001). Men in this sample had a mean score of 36.33 (standard deviation = 8.98), and women had a mean score of 42.21 (standard deviation = 9.16).

Scale: *The Distress Disclosure Index*

Source: Kahn and Hessling (2001)

atively trivial topics (for example, a description of their living room). However, others were asked to write about an experience they found personally upsetting.

What impact did this exercise have on the students? Measures of blood pressure and self-reported mood indicated that writing about a traumatic experience led to more stress and more negative moods immediately after the disclosure. However, the investigators recontacted the students in May, six months after they had written about their experiences. Students were asked about their health during the six months and about how many days they had been restricted because of an illness during this period. In addition, the number of visits each student had made to the campus health center was recorded.

Figure 12.2

Mean Number of
Visits to the Health
Center as a Function
of Experimental
Condition

Source: From Pennebaker
and Beall (1986).

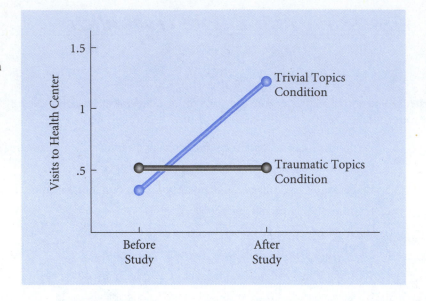

Some of the differences between the two groups are shown in Figure 12.2. Students in the trivial-topic group showed a significant increase in the number of days they were restricted by illness and the number of visits they made to the health center. But this was not the case for the students who had written about their traumatic secrets. Similarly, only the disclosing students showed a decrease in the number of illnesses. In other words, although writing about their problems created some mild, short-term discomfort, it appears that the act of disclosing, even in the relatively mild form used in this study, improved the health of the already healthy college students. Similar results were obtained when researchers asked freshmen to write about the problems and emotions they encountered leaving home and adjusting to college (Pennebaker, Colder, & Sharp, 1990). Participants who wrote about these thoughts and feelings for three consecutive nights made fewer visits to the health center over the next several months than those who wrote about trivial topics.

The health benefits of disclosing traumatic experiences have been found in numerous investigations with many kinds of participants (Cameron & Nicholls, 1998; Cole, Kemeny, Taylor, & Visscher, 1996; Greenberg, Wortman, & Stone, 1996; Kelly & McKillop, 1996). But the value of disclosure is not limited to physical health. People who typically conceal unpleasant information about themselves also experience more distress and a lower sense of well-being (Kahn & Hessling, 2001; Larson & Chastain, 1990). College students in one study were less emotionally upset about taking graduate school entrance exams when they wrote about their feelings concerning the upcoming exam (Lepore, 1997). Freshmen in another study who wrote about the problems they faced adjusting to college had higher grade point averages their first semester than students who wrote about trivial topics (Cameron & Nicholls, 1998).

In the News

Keeping Secrets

From the outside, Tom Paciorek seemed to have a life almost anyone would envy. Paciorek is a former all-star outfielder who played major league baseball for 18 years. He stands 6 foot 4 inches and was once voted the second most handsome man in baseball. Upon retiring from the game, he became a television broadcaster. He and his wife of many years raised six healthy children.

Yet at age 55, Paciorek was not a happy man. In fact, he had spent most of his life hiding a dark, humiliating secret. When Paciorek was a boy growing up in Detroit, he was molested repeatedly over a period of several years by a teacher at his Catholic high school. That teacher later became a priest. Like many children who are the victims of sexual abuse, Paciorek told no one. The abuse did not stop until he went away to college. Yet the emotional pain Paciorek carried with him as a result of the molestation never ended.

"You try to deny it ever happened, to bury it in your mind," Paciorek said, "but you live with horrible emotions, with the loss of self-esteem, with a loss of trust for others" (in Berkow, 2002).

As researchers have demonstrated in numerous studies, traumatic experiences like the one Paciorek went through often take their toll emotionally and physically. The memories haunted Paciorek throughout his adult life. He described his life as "chaos." More than 20 years after the abuse ended, Paciorek sought out psychotherapy. For 15 years he tried to work through his emotional pain with his counselor. But when Paciorek read that the priest who had once molested him had been assigned to work with students, he knew the time had come to disclose his secret. Paciorek joined hundreds of other victims who came forward during the wave of sexual abuse scandals that rocked the Catholic Church in 2002. He was 55 years old, and had held onto his secret for nearly 40 years.

Paciorek didn't sleep the night before his story appeared in the *Detroit Free Press.* But he soon discovered, as have other trauma victims, that talking about the experience is often better than holding emotions inside. Paciorek received a flood of supportive phone calls and e-mail messages. In an important way, disclosing his secret had set him free. On the day his story was reported in the media, Paciorek went jogging. Sometime during his run, while his thoughts were filled with the events from so many years before, Paciorek heard a voice that caused him to burst into tears (Whitley, 2002).

"It's over," the voice said. "It took 40 years, but it's over."

But why does disclosure, even when written anonymously, result in better physical and psychological health? One reason is that actively inhibiting thoughts and feelings about traumatic experiences requires a great deal of psychological and physiological work (Pennebaker, 1989). The impact of this stress is both immediate and long term. One study found an increase in immune system strength immediately after participants wrote about traumatic experiences (Petrie, Booth, & Pennebaker, 1998). The cumulative effect of withholding secrets over time takes its toll in the form of increased illnesses and other stress-related problems.

But expressing thoughts and feelings about traumatic events also allows people to gain insight into their feelings and what they can do to move beyond the experience (Kelly, Klusas, von Weiss, & Kenny, 2001; King, 2001; King & Miner, 2000; Smyth, True, & Souto, 2001). As Rogers and other humanistic theorists suggested, expressing feelings into words allows people to "see" their emotions and thereby deal with them more effectively. Participants in one study watched a disturbing 14-minute video and slide presentation about the Nazi Holocaust (Lepore, Ragan, & Jones, 2000). Afterwards, some participants were allowed to talk about their feelings and reactions for two minutes. Other participants were not given this opportunity. Over the next two days, the participants who discussed their feelings had fewer intrusive thoughts about the Holocaust presentation than the nondisclosing participants. That is, these individuals were less likely to have sudden, unsettling images about the Holocaust jump into their awareness. Because they were allowed to put their feelings into words, the disclosing participants were better able to understand their reactions to the disturbing images and to deal with them.

The findings from this research clearly have implications for psychotherapy (Cepeda-Benito & Short, 1998; Kelly, 1998; Kelly & Archer, 1995). Talking or writing about traumatic events may be an important step in working through trauma (Janoff-Bulman, 1992). Turning vague emotional images into coherent explanations often produces insight (Clark, 1993). Providing clients with an opportunity to openly discuss emotions is probably one reason why psychotherapy works for some people (Donnelly & Murray, 1991; Murray, Lamnin, & Carver, 1989; Segal & Murray, 1993).

Loneliness

From time to time, we have all felt the pain of loneliness. Each of us has suffered through a period when there was no one to talk to, when everyone else appeared to be with someone while we were alone, when all our relationships seemed superficial. Loneliness is a widespread problem in American society. Ironically, loneliness has become epidemic on college campuses. Despite the presence of people seemingly everywhere, 75% of the freshmen contacted at a large university two weeks into the school year said they had experienced loneliness since school began (Cutrona, 1982). More than 40% said their loneliness had been either moderate or severe.

Humanistic psychologists are concerned with loneliness for a number of reasons. Some have argued that humanistic psychology's rise in popularity in the 1960s can be attributed to feelings of alienation and loneliness that had begun to creep into many American lives (Buhler & Allen, 1972). People faced with an increasingly dehumanized, mechanistic society welcomed the humanists' emphasis

Loneliness is a common problem on college campuses, but some people are more prone to bouts of loneliness than others.

on the individual with his or her unique potential. Some psychologists believe feelings of loneliness reflect existential anxiety and a need to find meaning in one's life (Sadler & Johnson, 1980). Humanistic therapists often help clients develop meaningful encounters to overcome loneliness (Moustakas, 1961, 1968). Perhaps the most notable development in this area was the growth of encounter groups in the late 1960s and early 1970s. Within the safe confines of the group, humanistic therapists helped members discover the richness of intimate interpersonal encounters with others and thereby learn something about themselves (Rogers, 1970).

However, it would be incorrect to say that only humanistic psychologists have shown an interest in understanding loneliness. Psychoanalytic psychologists such as Frieda Fromm-Reichman (1959), Harry Stack Sullivan (1953), and Erich Fromm (1956/1974) have also written about the causes and effects of loneliness. In truth, most of the empirical research on loneliness has been conducted by investigators interested in interpersonal relationships rather than humanistic psychology per se. Nonetheless, the research reviewed in this section has implications for many of the humanistic psychologists' concerns, particularly for therapists working with clients suffering from loneliness.

Defining and Measuring Loneliness

Loneliness is not the same as isolation. Some of the loneliest individuals are surrounded by people most of the day. Rather, loneliness concerns our perception of how much social interaction we have and the quality of that interaction. As one team of investigators explained, "Loneliness occurs when a person's network of social relationships is *smaller* or *less satisfying* than the person desires" (Peplau, Russell, & Heim, 1979, p. 55, italics added). You can have very little contact with people, but if you are satisfied with that contact, you won't feel lonely. On the other hand, you may have many friends, yet still feel a need for more or deeper friendships and thus become lonely.

Thinking of loneliness in terms of personal satisfaction with one's social relationships helps explain why some people who live in virtual isolation find the solitude enjoyable, whereas other individuals surrounded by people feel lonely. I commonly hear college students complain that, although they have a lot of acquaintances and people to hang around with, they don't have many real friends. For these students, the unmet need to interact with that special person in an intimate and honest way can create intense feelings of being alone.

Loneliness is often caused by the circumstances people find themselves in, such as moving to a new city or attending a new school. Moreover, the kinds of relationships we desire change as we pass through the life cycle (Green, Richardson, Lago, & Schatten-Jones, 2001; Pinquart & Sorensen, 2001). Young adults often require a larger number of friends to fend off loneliness, whereas older adults prefer fewer but closer friends. The causes and consequences of loneliness also vary as a function of culture (Anderson, 1999). The absence of an intimate friend or romantic partner often contributes to loneliness in Western societies. In fact, when people in individualistic cultures think of loneliness, they often imagine someone without a spouse or romantic partner. However, this source of loneliness is less common in Asian cultures, which emphasize instead associations with family members and the community (Rokach, 1998). Because collectivist cultures emphasize one's place in a larger social network, feeling alone in these cultures is more likely to lower a person's sense of well-being (Goodwin, Cook, & Yung, 2001).

Although feelings of loneliness come and go as circumstances change, researchers also find loneliness can be conceived of as a fairly stable personality trait. That is, although everyone feels lonely on occasion, each of us also maintains a fairly stable susceptibility to these experiences. Some people are highly vulnerable to feelings of loneliness and seem to chronically suffer from not having enough close friends. Other people are relatively immune from loneliness. Although they may experience loneliness in certain situations, they rarely feel as if they have too few friends. Several personality inventories have been developed to assess individual differences in our tendency to feel lonely (Cramer, Ofosu, & Barry, 2000; Rubenstein & Shaver, 1980; Russell, Peplau, & Cutrona, 1980; Schmidt & Sermat, 1983). Like other personality variables, our vulnerability to loneliness is relatively stable over time (Segrin, 1999; Weeks, Michela, Peplau, & Bragg, 1980).

The Causes of Loneliness

No doubt you've met people you seemed to like right away and others who took a long time to understand and appreciate. We are naturally drawn to someone who comes across as friendly and self-confident. Chances are good you'll want to get together with this person again and possibly develop a more personal relationship. However, you are much less likely to become friends with someone who is aloof and self-conscious and who seems to show no interest in you. Yet investigators find that lonely people, who need friends the most, often come across like the latter person.

Correlations between measures of loneliness and other personality variables paint a drab and sullen picture of lonely people. High scores on loneliness scales are related to high scores on social anxiety and self-consciousness and low levels of self-esteem and assertiveness (Bruch, Kaflowitz, & Pearl, 1988; Jones, Freemon, & Goswick, 1981; Solano & Koester, 1989). Lonely people also are more likely to be introverted, anxious, and sensitive to rejection (Russell et al., 1980) and more likely to suffer from depression (Joiner, Catanzaro, Rudd, & Rajab, 1999; Koenig, Isaacs, & Schwartz, 1994). They have difficulty trusting others (Rotenberg, 1994) and are often uncomfortable when others open up to them (Rotenberg, 1997). Lonely people spend less time with friends, date less frequently, attend fewer parties, and have fewer close friends than do nonlonely people (Archibald, Bartholomew, & Marx, 1995). They report difficulties making friends, initiating social activity, and participating in groups (Horowitz & de Sales French, 1979). Acquaintances of lonely people confirm the accuracy of these assessments. College students say their relationships with lonely people are noticeably less intimate than they are with nonlonely people (Williams & Solano, 1983).

What is it about lonely people that continually frustrates their need for meaningful social contact? Researchers have identified two characteristics that seem to contribute to this loneliness. Lonely people tend to approach social interactions with overly pessimistic expectations for how the encounter will go. In addition, many lonely people lack basic social skills, which may keep them from developing lasting friendships with others.

Negative Expectations. Lonely people often enter a social situation with the expectation that this encounter, like so many before, will not go well (Goswick & Jones, 1981; Hanley-Dunn, Maxwell, & Santos, 1985; Jones et al., 1981; Jones, Sansone, & Helm, 1983; Levin & Stokes, 1986). Consider a study in which lonely and nonlonely college students were asked to participate in a series of group activities with three other students (Christensen & Kashy, 1998). The students discussed and solved problems together for 30 minutes. The participants were then separated and asked to rate the other members of the group in terms of their intelligence, friendliness, and so on. The participants also rated themselves on these dimensions and guessed what kind of ratings they would receive from the other group members. The researchers found that lonely participants evaluated themselves less favorably than they evaluated the other group members. The nonlonely students did not do this. Moreover, the lonely participants expected the other three members of the group also would rate them poorly. However, they were wrong. Despite their low expectations for how the other students would see them, the lonely students were evaluated no differently than anyone else—with one

Assessing Your Own Personality

Loneliness

Indicate T (true) or F (false) for each of the following statements, depending on whether it accurately describes you or your situation. If an item is not applicable because you are not currently involved in the situation, score it F.

_____	1. I feel close to members of my family.
_____	2. I have a lover or spouse (boyfriend, girlfriend, husband, or wife) with whom I can discuss my important problems and worries.
_____	3. I feel I really do not have much in common with the larger community in which I live.
_____	4. I have little contact with members of my family.
_____	5. I do not get along very well with my family.
_____	6. I am now involved in a romantic or marital relationship where both of us are making a genuine effort at cooperation.
_____	7. I have a good relationship with most members of my immediate family.
_____	8. I do not feel that I can turn to my friends living around me for help when I need it.
_____	9. No one in the community where I live seems to care much about me.
_____	10. I allow myself to become close to friends.
_____	11. I seldom get the emotional security I need from a good romantic or sexual relationship.
_____	12. I feel that I have "roots" (a sense of belonging) in the larger community or neighborhood I live in.

exception. The lonely students were actually perceived as being friendlier than most of the people in the group. In short, the lonely students thought the others would not like them, yet as it turned out they were greatly mistaken.

These low expectations can be poisonous when trying to develop a friendship or romantic relationship. Lonely people doubt a new acquaintance will enjoy talking with them and suspect the person will find them boring or stupid by the end of the conversation. Consequently, lonely people often show little interest in getting to know other people and are quick to end the conversation and move on to something else. These negative expectations may also lead lonely people to interpret any small sign as rejection. Participants in one experiment spent 5 minutes talking with a stranger (Frankel & Prentice-Dunn, 1990). Later, participants saw a videotape of their partner's evaluation of them. The videotape contained positive and negative comments. As expected, the lonely people paid attention to and re-

_____ 13. I do not have many friends in the city where I live.

_____ 14. I do not have any neighbors who would help me out in a time of need.

_____ 15. I get plenty of help and support from my friends.

_____ 16. My family seldom really listens to what I say.

_____ 17. Few of my friends understand me the way I want to be understood.

_____ 18. My lover or spouse senses when I am troubled and encourages me to talk about it.

_____ 19. I feel valued and respected in my current romantic or marital relationship.

_____ 20. I know people in my community who understand and share my views and beliefs.

This scale was designed to measure loneliness in four types of situations: friendships, relationships with families, romantic-sexual relationships, and relationships with larger groups. To obtain your score, give yourself 1 point every time your answer matches the following:

> Friendship subscale: 8-T, 10-F, 13-T, 15-F, 17-T.
> Family Relationships subscale: 1-F, 4-T, 5-T, 7-F, 16-T.
> Romantic-Sexual Relationships subscale: 2-F, 6-F, 11-T, 18-F, 19-F.
> Larger Groups Relationships subscale: 3-T, 9-T, 12-F, 14-T, 20-F.

Mean scores for college students on the total scale are usually between 5 and 6, with a higher score indicating more loneliness. By examining your score within each of the four subscales, you can discover in which parts of your life you experience the most difficulty with loneliness.

Scale: *The Differential Loneliness Scale* (student version)

Source: From Schmidt and Sermat (1983); reprinted with permission.

called the negative feedback better than the nonlonely participants. Because they believe their interactions have gone worse than they probably have, lonely people may be less likely than nonlonely people to pursue a friendship with someone they've met or to seek out others to do things with.

Given this negative approach to social interactions, it is not surprising that lonely people have such a difficult time making friends. This research also helps explain why loneliness is a problem for many students on crowded college campuses. With so many potential friends around, there is little reason to seek out and nurture the friendship of someone who appears to be unfriendly.

Loneliness and Social Skills. Perhaps you are one of those lucky people for whom conversation comes easily. You enjoy meeting people, effortlessly finding out about them, and occasionally talking about yourself. If this is you, then you may be puzzled by people who have difficulty interacting with others. Even for people who are not shy and who would like to meet new friends, engaging in more than a short and trivial conversation can be a chore. What these people may lack are basic social skills, the knowledge of how to carry on a conversation that both you and the other person find valuable and enjoyable.

Several studies implicate just such a lack of social skills as part of what keeps lonely people in their cycle of loneliness (Segrin, 1999; Segrin & Flora, 2000). The best way to develop social skills is to talk with others. Yet people without social skills may have such a difficult time developing relationships that they have little opportunity to develop these skills. They never learn how to initiate an interaction or how to keep the conversation lively, so their difficulty making friends continues. Consider the interaction styles one team of researchers found when they examined conversations with lonely and nonlonely people (Jones, Hobbs, & Hockenbury, 1982). Participants who scored high on loneliness measures showed relatively little interest in their partners. They asked fewer questions about their partners, often failed to comment on what the partner said, and made fewer references to the partner. Instead, these lonely people were more likely to talk about themselves and introduce new topics unrelated to their partner's interests. Another study found lonely people were more likely to give advice to strangers and, when talking with their roommates, less likely to acknowledge what the other person said (Sloan & Solano, 1984). In addition, lonely people tend to take on a "passive interpersonal role" (Vitkus & Horowitz, 1987). That is, they don't make much of an effort to get involved in a conversation. Little wonder, then, that we often fail to enjoy conversations with lonely people. It's not that lonely people are intentionally rude, but rather that they don't understand how their interaction style turns away potential friends. Fortunately, some efforts to combat loneliness with social skills training have been promising (Rook & Peplau, 1982; Young, 1982).

Other researchers have examined the way lonely and nonlonely people use self-disclosure. Studies find that lonely people generally reveal less about themselves than their partners (Berg & Peplau, 1982; Sloan & Solano, 1984). Lack of self-disclosure may be a particular problem for lonely people interacting with members of the opposite sex. In one study, lonely people selected relatively nonintimate topics to talk about in a mixed-sex conversation (Solano, Batten, & Parish, 1982). Not surprisingly, the lonely participants' partners reciprocated with nonintimate topics as well. Other studies find lonely people are often not aware of social rules about when and how much to disclose (Chelune, Sultan, & Williams, 1980; Solano & Koester, 1989; Wittenberg & Reis, 1986). Because of this, they may disclose too much or fail to reveal enough about themselves when the other person expects it. Consequently, others may see them as either weird or aloof, and respond accordingly.

Self-Esteem

If there is a single concept that threads its way through the writings of the humanistic psychologists, it may be how people feel about themselves. A central goal of Rogerian psychotherapy is to get clients to accept and appreciate themselves for what they are. Maslow wrote about the need for self-respect and the need to feel content about who we are and what we do with our lives. In short, humanistic personality theory is concerned with the individual's self-esteem. Most researchers draw a distinction between self-esteem and self-concept. Your *self-concept* is the cumulation of what you see as your personal characteristics—that is, the kind of person you believe yourself to be. **Self-esteem** refers to your evaluation of your self-concept. In essence, do you like this person you believe yourself to be?

Although we often speak of self-esteem in our everyday conversations, researchers face several challenges when trying to identify and measure this concept. One problem is that the way we feel about ourselves can change from one situation to the next. Most people get a little down on themselves when they act in ways they know they shouldn't, and most of us can't help but think well of ourselves when someone heaps praise on us for a job well done (Heatherton & Polivy, 1991). However, these fluctuations in feelings probably should not be confused with self-esteem. Rather, some psychologists refer to these ups and downs as *feelings of self-worth* (Brown & Dutton, 1995). In contrast, self-esteem has to do with relatively stable self-evaluations. As with other personality variables, researchers find some people are prone to more positive self-evaluations than others. These individuals may have bad days and disappoint themselves on occasion, but in general they like themselves and feel good about who they are and what they do. These people score high on measures of self-esteem. Of course, we also can identify people who frequently experience negative self-evaluations. Although these low self-esteem people also have good days and feel good about much of what they do, compared to others they seem to lack a basic confidence in themselves or an appreciation for who they are.

Another issue facing personality researchers concerns *global* versus *domain-specific* self-esteem. Very few people feel entirely good or bad about themselves. All of us can point to deficiencies and weaknesses, areas where we feel less confident than others. Thus, researchers sometimes find it useful to examine self-esteem within specific domains. For example, investigators might ask participants how they feel about themselves in terms of friends, work, morality, or physical appearance. However, global self-esteem is not simply the sum or average of how we feel about ourselves in each of these domains. Rather, how much your academic performance or social competence affects your overall evaluation of yourself depends on the importance you place on these aspects of your life (Crocker & Wolfe, 2001). You may be terrible at sports or math, but if you don't base your sense of self on how you do in these areas, they probably will not affect your overall self-esteem. The research reviewed in the remaining part of this section is concerned with global self-esteem.

Self-Esteem and Reaction to Failure

Although many people dislike it, evaluation is unavoidable part of most of our lives. After only a few years of elementary school, most students become accustomed to having their schoolwork graded by teachers. Evaluation by a superior is commonplace in the business world, if not overtly in the form of an annual review, then implicitly in the size of one's raise. Any type of competition, from sports to chess to gardening, brings with it the possibility of both victory and defeat as we compare our abilities and accomplishments against those of others. All of this evaluation means that each of us has experienced our share of successes and failures. However, not all people react the same way to these evaluations. In particular, research suggests that your self-esteem level plays an important role in how you respond to this information.

Low Self-Esteem and Failure. Several laboratory experiments have looked at how high and low self-esteem people react to being told they have done well or poorly on a test (Brockner, 1979; Brown & Dutton, 1995; Shrauger & Rosenberg, 1970; Shrauger & Sorman, 1977; Stake, Huff, & Zand, 1995; Tafarodi & Vu, 1997). Participants in these studies usually take a test supposedly measuring some intellectual aptitude or work on a task calling for some specific ability. Researchers then give bogus feedback to participants, indicating they have done either very well or rather poorly. How do high and low self-esteem people react when told they have failed in this situation? Low self-esteem people typically don't try as hard, perform more poorly, and are more likely to give up on a second test when they think they have failed the first test. In contrast, high self-esteem people work just as hard regardless of how they think they performed.

The importance of such findings to the lives of college students was illustrated in a study examining students' reactions to their midterm exam grades (Brockner, Derr, & Laing, 1987). Students took a self-esteem test at the beginning of the semester, but the experimenters did not inform the students about the results or purpose of the test at that time. The students took their first exam for the class five weeks into the term and received their grade one week later. The researchers found that high and low self-esteem students performed almost identically on this test. The investigators then divided the students into those who had done well on the test (received an A or a B) and those who had not done as well (received a C or lower). The researchers wanted to know if the low self-esteem students would react to their low score on the test with the same decrease in motivation low self-esteem laboratory participants show when told they have done poorly. That is, would they more or less "give up" on the class and perform poorly on the next test?

As shown in Figure 12.3, the answer is yes. Low self-esteem students who did well on the first test continued to perform well. However, low self-esteem students who had not done well on the first test performed significantly worse on the second exam. Another investigation found that low self-esteem students, unlike their high self-esteem classmates, experienced strong negative emotions (for example,

Figure 12.3

Performance on
Second Test as a
Function of Self-
Esteem and Perfor-
mance on First Test

Source: Adapted from
Brockner et al. (1987).

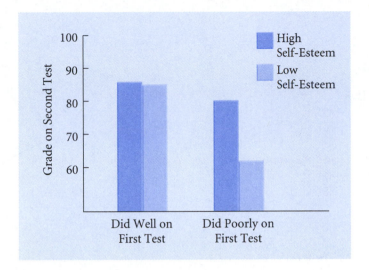

sadness) and reported low motivation to try on the next test when they did poorly on a midterm exam (Kernis, Brockner, & Frankel, 1989).

Yet another study found that low self-esteem people do not have to actually experience failure to show these negative effects, but rather only have to imagine that they have failed (Campbell & Fairey, 1985). Participants in this investigation were asked to imagine they had done well or poorly on a 25-item anagram test. Low self-esteem people who imagined failing said they expected to do poorly on a subsequent test, and indeed performed more poorly on the test compared to low self-esteem people who first imagined they had done well.

Explaining the Different Reactions. A substantial amount of research demonstrates that people low in self-esteem become discouraged and unmotivated when they receive negative feedback about a performance. However, high self-esteem people seem relatively unfazed when told they have done poorly on a test or when they discover they can't do well on a challenging task. How can we explain this difference?

One possibility is that people are more likely to accept feedback consistent with their self-concepts (McFarlin & Blascovich, 1981; Story, 1998). People with low self-esteem probably accept the fact that they fail more than others. Consequently, it is easier for them to believe feedback confirming their negative self-images than information that violates their expectations. Another way to look at this is to say that the negative feedback reminds low self-esteem people of the low evaluations they have of themselves (Dutton & Brown, 1997; Tafarodi & Vu, 1997). The feedback triggers associations with other negative thoughts, reminding the low self-esteem person of other faults and weaknesses. According to this explanation, people low in self-esteem become generally discouraged and unmotivated after receiving information about failing on a specific task. This interpretation helps

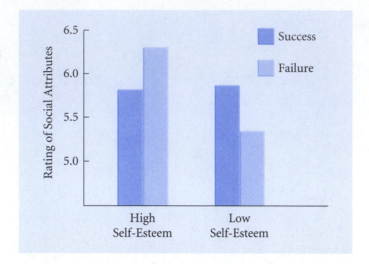

Figure 12.4

Ratings of Social Attributes Following Success and Failure

Source: Adapted from Brown and Smart (1991).

us understand why low self-esteem people perform more poorly on a task even when they have just imagined what it would be like to fail.

But we also can turn this question around. What is it about high self-esteem people that prevents them from becoming discouraged after failure? Why don't they give up when they fail a test or do poorly at work? Recent research indicates that high self-esteem people develop personal strategies for blunting the effects of negative feedback (Heimpel, Wood, Marshall, & Brown, 2002). Included in this arsenal is a tendency to respond to failure by focusing attention on their good qualities rather than on what they have done wrong. Thus, whereas negative feedback causes the people low in self-esteem to think about their faults and failures, this same feedback causes high self-esteem people to think about their abilities and achievements.

The high self-esteem strategy for blunting the effects of failure has been demonstrated in several investigations (Brown & Gallagher, 1992; Brown & Smart, 1991; Dodgson & Wood, 1998; Schlenker, Weigold, & Hallam, 1990). As in earlier studies, participants in one experiment received feedback indicating they had performed either well or poorly on an achievement test (Brown & Smart, 1991). Participants were then asked how well a series of adjectives described them. Some adjectives were related to achievement situations (for example, *competent, intelligent*), and others were relevant for social situations (for example, *sincere, kind*). The results for the social-attribute ratings are shown in Figure 12.4. As expected, low self-esteem participants rated themselves poorly after discovering they had failed the test. However, high self-esteem participants actually rated themselves higher on their social attributes after failing than when they thought they had done well on the test.

These results demonstrate one tactic high self-esteem people use to maintain their feelings of high self-worth even in the face of negative feedback. When told they did not do well in one area, they simply reminded themselves of how well they do in other areas. It is important to recognize that these high self-esteem participants did not simply ignore the test feedback and enhance their feelings of self-worth in achievement areas. Instead, they appeared to think about what they were good at rather than where they occasionally fall down. If they mess up at work, high self-esteem people might remind themselves that they have a lot of friends. If they lose badly at handball, they might recall how well they play chess. This strategy keeps high self-esteem people feeling good about themselves even when faced with life's inevitable downturns.

Self-Enhancement and Self-Protection Motives

I recently encountered a situation that illustrates another important difference between high and low self-esteem people. As a Little League manager watching the members of my new team playing catch, I became particularly impressed with one player. This boy clearly was able to throw the ball faster, farther, and more accurately than most players his age. As a rule, nearly every Little Leaguer wants to be a pitcher. And so I was a little surprised to find this boy quickly turned me down when I asked if he wanted to try pitching. He clearly had the talent but was adamant in his decision not to pitch. As I learned more about this player during the season, I came to understand his decision. Although the pitcher is the center of attention during the game and provides the greatest opportunity to show off what one can do, it was this very spotlight the boy wanted to avoid. Despite his abilities, the boy suffered from low self-esteem. The possibility that he might not do well in front of everyone was far too threatening for him to take advantage of the possibility that he might perform quite well.

As this example illustrates, high self-esteem and low self-esteem people may be motivated by very different concerns. More specifically, people high in self-esteem are motivated by a concern for *self-enhancement* (Baumeister, Tice, & Hutton, 1989; Rudich & Vallacher, 1999; Tice, 1993). That is, high self-esteem people are interested in enhancing their prestige and public image. They want others to think well of them, to admire them, and to praise them when they do something well. But certainly people low in self-esteem want this admiration as well. We all enjoy hearing others say nice things about us and knowing that other people respect and admire us. Nonetheless, researchers find low self-esteem people are less likely to take advantage of opportunities to show off. Why is this? The answer is that people low in self-esteem are motivated by a concern for *self-protection*. In other words, they are concerned about protecting themselves from public humiliation and embarrassment. Opportunities to be in the public spotlight create the possibility of drawing praise and admiration from others. But these same opportunities carry the risk that we will fail or look foolish, thus leading to public disapproval or ridicule. When push comes to shove, the low self-esteem person's need for self-protection is likely to win out over his or her need to look good.

This need for self-protection often causes low self-esteem people to simply avoid comparisons with others they think they might lose. Students in one study were given a choice of tasks on which they could compare their performance with the performance of other students (Wood, Giordano-Beech, Taylor, Michela, & Gaus, 1994). The participants were led to believe they would look good by comparison on some tasks, but poor by comparison on others. Consistent with the self-protection notion, low self-esteem participants wanted to know how they did compared to this other person only when it was safe. When they knew they would look good, they wanted the information. When they knew they would look bad, they did not. Low self-esteem people may experience this fear of unfavorable comparison even before they are evaluated. University students in one study rated their confidence in doing well on an upcoming exam three weeks before the test and the day of the test (Sanna & Meier, 2000). Although the high self-esteem students' confidence stayed high throughout this period, the students low in self-esteem felt less confident and were in a worse mood as the test day approached.

Sometimes low self-esteem people go to great lengths to avoid information suggesting they are not good at something. For example, imagine a low self-esteem tennis player anticipating an upcoming match he or she is likely to lose. That player could practice all week and give it his or her best shot. But if this person is truly motivated to self-protect, another strategy is available. Sometimes low self-esteem people resort to *self-handicapping* (Harris & Snyder, 1986; Rhodewalt, Morf, Hazlett, & Fairfield, 1991; Tice, 1991; Tice & Baumeister, 1990). People self-handicap when they deliberately hurt their chances of performing well on a task, such as by not studying for a test or by turning up distracting music while working on a task requiring concentration. These actions obviously reduce the person's chances for success, but they also provide a reasonable excuse in case of failure. In the tennis example, the low self-esteem player might avoid practicing the entire week before the match. The player will surely lose, but at least he or she can say the poor showing reflects a lack of practice rather than a lack of ability. It's not as good as winning, but it's better than losing without an excuse.

Self-Esteem Stability

Recently, researchers have found that knowing an individual's general self-esteem level provides only part of the picture when trying to understand how that person feels about himself or herself. Consider the case of two women, both of whom score high on measures of global self-esteem. One woman seems to feel good about herself every time you see her. She never gets carried away with her self-importance and never gets too down on herself. The second woman feels good about herself more often than not, but there are times when she feels absolutely grandiose and times when her self-confidence takes a beating. Most days she likes herself, but some days she is filled with self-doubt.

These two women differ on what researchers call **self-esteem stability.** That is, in addition to differences in level of self-esteem, we can also identify differences in how frequently and to what degree a person's feelings of self-worth fluctuate. Actually, the term *self-esteem stability* might be confusing. It is not the person's self-esteem that goes up and down from day to day, but rather temporary feelings about his or her self-worth. We might think of self-esteem as the relatively stable level around which these feelings of self-worth fluctuate.

To measure a person's self-esteem stability, researchers sometimes ask participants to report on their feelings of self-worth at several points during the day for several days at a time (Greenier, Kernis, & Waschull, 1995). One of the surprising findings in this work is that self-esteem stability tends to be unrelated to self-esteem level (Kernis & Waschull, 1995). That is, a person with a high level of self-esteem can have feelings of self-worth that fluctuate wildly or that stay at a relatively predictable level. Knowing someone's self-esteem score tells us very little about how stable that person's feelings of self-worth are.

Why do some people have feelings about themselves that fluctuate widely, whereas others have relatively stable feelings of self-worth? Researchers find that people with low self-esteem stability are very concerned with outside evaluations (Greenier et al., 1999; Kernis, Cornell, Sun, Berry, & Harlow, 1993). In particular, low-stability people are sensitive to how others respond to them. They feel bad about themselves when criticized by friends and acquaintances, but feel good about themselves when the feedback is positive. Whereas high-stability people typically make decisions based on what they want to do, people low in self-esteem stability are more likely to act in a way they hope will please others (Kernis, Paradise, Whitaker, Wheatman, & Goldman, 2000). In a sense, people low in self-esteem stability continually put their self-worth on the line (Greenier et al., 1995). A bad grade, a rude remark or a broken date can trigger self-doubt, whereas a good grade, a compliment or a pleasant conversation will lead to pride and self-liking.

Unfortunately, this rapid fluctuation in feelings of self-worth carries a price. Because no one lives in a world limited to successes and wonderful social interactions, people low in self-esteem stability are more vulnerable to negative emotions, such as anger and depression. For many years, researchers have found that self-esteem is related to depression, with low self-esteem associated with higher levels of depression. However, researchers also find self-esteem stability is related to depression, and in some cases may be more important than self-esteem level for determining reactions to stressful events (Butler, Hokanson, & Flynn, 1994; Kernis, Grannemann, & Mathis, 1991; Oosterwegel, Field, Hart, & Anderson, 2001). One team of investigators looked at students' reactions to an important exam (Roberts & Monroe, 1992). The researchers found self-esteem stability was a better predictor of how the students reacted to a poor grade than the students' typical self-esteem level. Students high in self-esteem stability had relatively little reaction to the bad news. However, the students with unstable self-esteems were more likely to become depressed after receiving a poor grade.

But it's not just major disappointments that affect people low in self-esteem stability. They are also sensitive to the minor setbacks and little problems that plague each of us daily. Participants in one study were asked how often they experienced such annoyances as time pressures, disagreements with friends, and so on over a three-week time span (Kernis et al., 1998). Researchers measured the par-

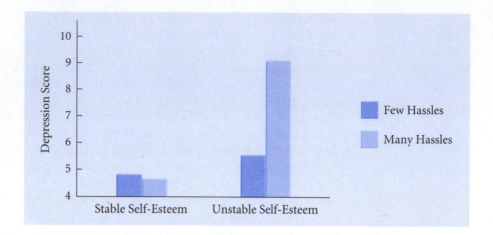

ticipants' depression level at the beginning and end of this period. As shown in Figure 12.5, participants with a stable self-esteem were relatively unfazed by these daily hassles. However, those with unstable self-esteems were okay only when their lives were relatively problem-free. When hassles piled up, these participants became increasingly depressed.

Self-Esteem and Culture

People growing up in Western culture often assume that everyone wants to excel, to stand out from the crowd, to be recognized for personal accomplishments. Teachers and parents foster high self-esteem in children by identifying the child's unique strengths and helping the child develop and excel in these areas. Adolescents who say they are "no better than average" at anything might be readily labeled as poorly adjusted. Indeed, youth from disadvantaged backgrounds are encouraged to believe in themselves, to believe they can achieve whatever they set their minds to. In short, in most Western societies, the recipe for high self-esteem is feeling good about who you are and what you do to distinguish yourself.

However, some researchers have challenged the universality of these notions (Heine, 2001; Kitayama & Markus, 1994; Markus & Kitayama, 1991, 1994; Triandis, 1989, 2001). Recall from Chapter 1 that Western conceptions of the self are not shared by all cultures. People in collectivist cultures are more concerned with interdependence than with independence. Whereas individualistic countries like the United States emphasize the uniqueness of the individual, people in collectivist countries see themselves as a part of the larger cultural unit.

One implication of these different views is that we may need to rethink the way we conceptualize self-esteem when working with people from different cultures. Self-esteem scales developed primarily for American research participants often ask test takers about feelings of competence and about how much they value their unique attributes. Such items make little sense to people who see their value in terms of belongingness and cooperation. Researchers sometimes illustrate the difference between an individualistic country like the United States and a collectivist country like Japan by pointing to a pair of expressions from these cultures. In the United States we sometimes say, "The squeaky wheel gets greased," meaning that one has to stand up and assert oneself to get ahead. In Japan one often hears, "The nail that stands up is the one that gets hammered," meaning that asserting one's individuality is unacceptable and is likely to result in negative consequences.

This different perspective on the self also means that people from the two types of cultures have different ideas about what leads to self-satisfaction and feeling good. People in individualistic cultures typically feel good about themselves when they think about their unique value and personal accomplishments. In contrast, people from collectivist cultures derive self-satisfaction from their perceived relationships with others. People from collectivist cultures feel good when they obtain a sense of belonging within the culture, of occupying their appropriate place. Fitting in and doing one's duty are sources of pride in collectivist cultures. Personal achievements and independence are valued in individualistic cultures.

Consistent with these observations, research with American students finds a nearly universal tendency to see oneself in a better light than objective data might suggest. When American college students are asked to compare themselves to their peers on a variety of skills and aptitudes, they almost always report their superiority over those around them (Taylor, 1989). In this country, it seems, we are all better than average. However, when researchers present these same questions to students from collectivist cultures, they find relatively little evidence for such a bias (Heine & Lehman, 1997; Kitayama, Markus, Matsumoto, & Norasakkunkit, 1997; Yik, Bond, & Paulhus, 1998). The typical citizen in a collectivist culture simply does not see himself or herself as any better than the other members of society. In America, these feelings of averageness might be taken as evidence of a poor self-esteem. However, in other countries such a self-evaluation is considered quite healthy. In a collectivist culture, it is the person full of self-importance who is the cause of concern, the nail that gets hammered down. Needless to say, this cultural difference can be a source of conflict for people who move from one culture to another. American baseball players, known for their elevated sense of self, often have a very difficult time playing for Japanese clubs, which emphasize the team above the individual (Whiting, 1989).

In an interesting demonstration of the relation between culture and self-esteem, one group of researchers compared average self-esteem scores for Asians as a function of their exposure to North American culture (Heine, Lehman, Markus, & Kitayama, 1999). Remember, the self-esteem scales were designed so that high scores reflect Western notions of individual accomplishment and pride in personal achievements. As shown in Figure 12.6, the participants' self-esteem scores changed with their amount of contact with individualistic cultures. Three generations after the participants' family had immigrated to Canada, the Asian-Canadian self-esteem scores were no different than those of the European-Canadians.

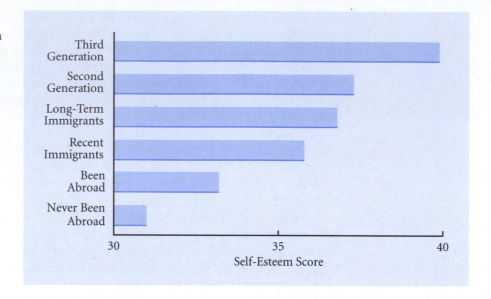

Figure 12.6

Average Self-Esteem Score of Asians and Asian-Canadians as a Function of Exposure to Western Culture

Source: Adapted from Heine et al. (1999).

Culture also affects the standards people use to decide if they are satisfied with their lives. Most Americans assume that happiness is the key to life satisfaction. That is, I will be satisfied with my life to the extent that I feel good about myself and experience positive emotions, such as happiness. Indeed, studies find this to be the case in individualistic cultures (Diener & Diener, 1995; Oishi & Diener, 2001; Suh, Diener, Oishi, & Triandis, 1998). However, this path to life satisfaction does not apply in collectivist cultures. Instead, how well people meet the culturally defined standard of proper behavior predicts life satisfaction in collectivist nations. Thus, whereas feeling good is the key to a good life in individualistic cultures, fitting into the role prescribed by society is the key in collectivist cultures.

In short, the theory and research on self-esteem presented in this chapter is probably applicable only to people living in individualistic cultures. However, we should not take this to mean that people in collectivist cultures do not have a self-esteem. Rather, we should recognize that concepts like the self and self-esteem have different meanings in different cultures. Personality researchers have only recently begun to appreciate these differences and are in the early stages of conducting research on these questions.

Solitude

In many ways, Naomi is different from most people. Although she could easily join her coworkers in the company cafeteria, Naomi often chooses to have lunch alone. She'll eat a sandwich in the nearby park or sometimes spend the lunch hour taking a solitary walk around the neighborhood. When friends ask her to drop by on the weekend or to join them after work, she frequently declines even when she has no other plans. Last Saturday, she decided she didn't want to attend an afternoon party her friend was giving and instead spent the time quietly gardening. Surprisingly, most people who know her describe Naomi as a warm and engaging person. And Naomi very much enjoys her friends and coworkers. Still, compared to most people, Naomi spends a significant amount of time by herself.

What might a personality psychologist say about Naomi? Research indicates that our interpersonal relationships are among our most important sources of happiness (Diener & Seligman, 2002; Myers, 1992). So why would someone frequently turn down opportunities to socialize? Several possible explanations can be found in earlier sections of this book. Perhaps Naomi is introverted (Chapter 10). It may simply be her nature to spend time by herself because of her sensitivity to the stimulation in social situations. On the other hand, Naomi might avoid people because she suffers from social anxiety (Chapter 8). Perhaps she is afraid that others will evaluate her negatively, so she reduces her anxiety by simply avoiding social interactions whenever possible. In some ways this description is similar to what Karen Horney called the neurotic style of "moving away from people" (Chapter 5). According to this analysis, Naomi may have adopted her avoidance style as a way to protect herself from anxiety when she was a child. Today she uses this same coping strategy in her adult relationships. Yet another possibility is that Naomi suffers from loneliness. As described earlier in this chapter, she may lack some basic social skills and spends time alone because she has difficulty interacting with people and developing relationships.

Although each of these explanations can account for a person's desire to spend time alone, there is at least one more interpretation, one that casts Naomi's quest for solitude in a different light. When Abraham Maslow studied his psychologically healthy people, he found a curious similarity among members of this select group. Although these self-actualized people possessed characteristics that made them the warmest of friends, they also spent a surprisingly large amount of time by themselves. "For all my subjects it is true that they can be solitary without harm to themselves and without discomfort," Maslow (1970) observed. "Furthermore, it is true for almost all that they positively like solitude and privacy to a definitely greater degree than the average person" (p. 160).

Maslow's observations thus provide another explanation for Naomi's preference for solitude. It is possible that she is not introverted, socially anxious or lonely. Perhaps Naomi's desire to spend time by herself is something positive. Her preference for solitude may be both a reflection of and a contributor to her personal growth and development. Maslow was quick to point out that psychologically healthy people also tend to express a great deal of interpersonal warmth and have especially close relationships with their closest friends. Thus, people with a high desire for solitude are not necessarily trying to escape from relationships. Rather, some people who spend a great deal of time by themselves have come to recognize the benefits of solitude.

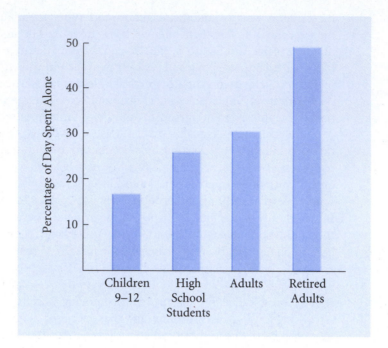

Figure 12.7

Percentage of Day Spent Alone as a Function of Age

Source: Adapted from Larson (1990).

Time Alone

Although most of us live in social worlds, in truth we also spend a good deal of our day alone. To determine how often we spend time by ourselves, one team of investigators employed a procedure known as the *Experience Sampling Method* (Larson & Csikszentmihalyi, 1980; Larson, Csikszentmihalyi, & Graef, 1982; Larson & Richards, 1991; Larson, Zuzanek, & Mannell, 1985). Participants in these studies carry electronic pagers or handheld computers with them 24 hours a day for about a week. At random intervals throughout each day, the researchers signal participants that it is time to fill out a quick report on what they are doing and how they feel at that moment. The results of this research, shown in Figure 12.7, confirm that Americans spend a significant amount of their waking hours alone. Moreover, the researchers discovered that solitude becomes a more common experience as we age.

How do people react to time alone? As suggested by conventional wisdom, most people find time by themselves less pleasant than time spent with others (Larson, 1990). People typically complain of loneliness and boredom when they are by themselves. After spending a long period of time by themselves, most people eagerly seek out social interaction (O'Connor & Rosenblood, 1996). Emotional difficulties are often made worse when there is no one around. People prone to depression may find they are more likely to become depressed when alone. One study found that bulimics had a particularly negative reaction to solitude (Larson

& Johnson, 1985). The researchers speculate that the loneliness and confusion experienced by bulimics when alone contributes to their eating disorder.

Clearly, time by oneself can be unpleasant and unsatisfying for many people. But consider the results of one national survey (Crossen, 1996). Only 6% of American adults in that survey said they wanted less time by themselves. In contrast, 31% wished they had *more* time alone in their lives. These numbers are consistent with observations of several researchers who argue that isolation from other people also has benefits (Bates, 1964; Buchholz & Helbraun, 1999; Burger, 1995; Larson, 1990; Storr, 1988; Suedfeld, 1982). To better understand the advantages of time alone, investigators sometimes divide solitude into three kinds of experiences (Burger, 1998). We can look at the effects of short periods of solitude during the day, usually measured in minutes. We also can study the effects of longer, planned time by oneself, typically measured in hours. Or we can examine the impact of extended periods of solitude, such as those measured in days. Each of these kinds of solitude has the potential to contribute to our well-being.

Even short periods of solitude spaced throughout the day can make a rough day go better. Sometimes we just need a break from constant social activity to organize our thoughts and psychologically prepare for future activities. Some writers have referred to this as a kind of "self-restoration" process in which we reestablish a sense of self separate from the "social" self we present to others (Altman, 1975). Other psychologists describe these moments of solitude as a kind of emotional renewal. For example, adults and adolescents in the pager studies said they felt more cheerful and more alert after spending short periods of time by themselves (Larson et al., 1982). Not surprisingly, a common complaint among people experiencing high levels of stress is that they have too little time to themselves (Webb, 1978).

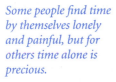

Some people find time by themselves lonely and painful, but for others time alone is precious.

But sometimes people need more than a few minutes alone. Occasionally, we need a more extended amount of time by ourselves to work through personal problems and make important decisions. Although consulting with others can be useful, many times people need extended time alone to think things through. Time for contemplation may be especially valuable for adolescents as they address personal questions about religion, values, personal identity, and life goals. To test this possibility, adolescents in one study were followed for one week through the Experience Sampling Procedure to determine how much time they spent by themselves (Larson, 1997). The investigator found that teenagers who spent a moderate amount of time by themselves, roughly between 25% and 45% of their nonclass hours, tended to be better adjusted and less depressed than either those who spent very little time in solitude or those who spent a great deal of their time alone. The teenagers who spent a moderate amount of time alone also had better grades than the other students. Thus, although some time alone has positive benefits, more solitude is not necessarily better. Teenagers who spend an excessive amount of time away from others may fail to accrue some of the benefits that come from social contact.

For some, the benefits of solitude may be found in extended periods of isolation. Long periods of solitude—days or perhaps even weeks alone—can provide the opportunity to develop oneself spiritually, intellectually, and creatively. One psychologist found examples of several influential people whose contributions could be traced back to an extended period of isolation and introspection (Storr, 1988). The works of several famous writers, such as Beatrix Potter and Rudyard Kipling, are the result of inspiration that evolved during extended solitude. Similarly, many religious leaders, including Jesus and Buddha, are said to have come to their insights during extended periods alone (Storr, 1988). Even psychologists have been known to take advantage of extended solitude. You may recall from Chapter 5 that Carl Jung deliberately isolated himself for the better part of seven years while he explored the contents of his own unconscious. Isolation from others can also be used during psychotherapy (Suedfeld, 1980, 1982). Volunteers who go through extended periods of social isolation and sensory restriction often describe the experience as pleasant and rewarding.

Individual Differences in Preference for Solitude

It seems clear that spending time alone can have both positive and negative consequences. Solitude can be boring and lonely, or it can bring insight and a sense of restoration. Whether people dislike or enjoy their time alone may be a function of their **preference for solitude.** As with other personality variables, researchers find that people exhibit relatively stable patterns in the extent to which they seek out and enjoy time by themselves (Burger, 1995; Cramer & Lake, 1998; Larson & Lee, 1996; Pedersen, 1999). On one end of this individual difference dimension, we have people who avoid solitude whenever possible and get eaten up by loneliness

Table 12.1 Free Time Spent by Students with High and Low Preference for Solitude

	Preference for Solitude	
	High	Low
Percentage of time spent alone	19.80	11.00
Percentage of time alone rated as pleasant	74.50	55.80
Percentage of time with others rated as pleasant	87.30	92.90

Source: From Burger (1995).

and sadness when forced to spend even a few free hours by themselves. People on the other end of this dimension are more likely to resemble the self-actualized people Maslow described. They have learned to appreciate the benefits that come from solitude and probably arrange their days so they have at least a little time to themselves to collect their thoughts and reflect on matters that concern them.

In one demonstration of these individual differences, college students were asked to complete daily reports of their activities for seven consecutive days (Burger, 1995). Students filled out a 24-hour report sheet indicating what they had done each hour of the day, whether they had been alone or with others, and whether they had found the experience enjoyable. The researcher also measured the students' preference for solitude. After eliminating time spent in class, at work, and sleeping, students with a high and low preference for solitude were compared for how they spent their free time. As shown in Table 12.1, virtually all the students spent most of their free time with other people. Thus, it is not the case that people who enjoy solitude are hermits who avoid contact with others. However, the students with a high preference for solitude did manage to find more time for solitude in their days than the typical student. Moreover, whereas almost all the students said their time with others was pleasant, the students with a high preference for solitude were significantly more likely to report that their time alone was enjoyable. Interestingly, even the students with a high preference for solitude said their time with others was more often pleasant than their time spent alone. However, considering the kinds of activities college students often engage in alone (writing papers, studying), this is probably not surprising. One conclusion that seems clear is that people with a high preference for solitude do not avoid social encounters and, in fact, enjoy their time with others quite a lot. These findings are entirely consistent with Maslow's observations of psychologically healthy people. Thus, not only are a preference for solitude and good interpersonal relations compatible, they may actually go hand in hand.

Summary

1.   Although humanistic psychologists sometimes shun empirical research, research on topics introduced or promoted by these psychologists has provided insight into some important aspects of humanistic personality theory.

2.   Research on self-disclosure finds that people follow social rules concerning when and how to reveal information about themselves. Foremost among these is the rule of disclosure reciprocity. People in a get-acquainted situation tend to match the intimacy level of the person they are talking to. However, friends who have already shared intimate information in a reciprocal manner need not always return to this pattern. Other studies find men and women are restricted in what they disclose by what society deems appropriate. Holding traumatic secrets inside may take its toll on a person's health.

3.   Loneliness is not the same as isolation. Researchers define loneliness as a discrepancy between the amount and quality of social contact we desire and the amount and quality we receive. Although loneliness is influenced by social situations, people tend to suffer from loneliness at a fairly stable level. Research on chronically lonely people indicates they approach conversations with negative expectations and lack some basic social skills. Because of this tendency, they inadvertently stifle social interactions and discourage potential friends.

4.   High and low self-esteem people react differently to failure. Low self-esteem people become discouraged and unmotivated when they receive negative feedback, whereas high self-esteem people employ tactics to blunt the effects of failure. Researchers also find that high self-esteem people are often motivated by a concern for self-enhancement, and low self-esteem people are often more concerned about self-protection. People also differ in the extent to which their feeling of self-worth fluctuates. Researchers refer to this individual difference as self-esteem stability. Recent research indicates that notions about the self and self-esteem taken from individualistic cultures may not apply to collectivist cultures.

5.   Maslow observed that virtually all of his psychologically healthy people reported a high preference for solitude. Subsequent research finds that most people spend a large percentage of their time in solitude. Although people typically find this time unpleasant, others seek out and enjoy their time alone. Researchers find that people differ in the extent to which they prefer solitude. People with a high preference for solitude enjoy their time alone but also enjoy time spent with others.

InfoTrac College Edition Key Terms

For additional readings go to http://www.infotrac-college.com/wadsworth and enter a search term related to your interest. Use the key terms suggested here to pull up several related articles. Also see the text Web site at http://psychology.wadsworth.com for more suggested readings and interactive quizzes to test your knowledge.

Loneliness
Self-concept
Self-disclosure

Self-esteem
Self-handicapping

Chapter 13

The Behaviorial/Social Learning Approach

Theory, Application, and Assessment

Behaviorism
Basic Principles of Conditioning
Social Learning Theory
Social-Cognitive Theory
Application: Behavior Modification and Self-Efficacy Therapy
Assessment: Behavior Observation Methods
Strengths and Criticisms of the Behavioral /Social Learning Approach
Summary

What do the following scenes have in common? A hospital patient suffering from depression makes her bed in the morning, dresses herself, and shows up to breakfast on time. A staff member hands the patient three tickets for completing these three acts. A middle-aged man attends a workshop to overcome a fear of snakes. He watches another middle-aged man, who shows no outward signs of fear, pick up a snake. A college student declines her friends' request to join them at a cocktail lounge after dinner. She knows people will be smoking there and is trying to break her habit.

In each of these scenes, someone is attempting to modify behavior by applying basic principles of learning. Psychologists have studied how people and animals learn for almost as long as there have been psychologists. The list of psychology topics examined from the *behaviorist's* perspective includes attitude change, language acquisition, psychotherapy, student-teacher interactions, problem solving, gender roles, and job satisfaction. Naturally, such a far-reaching approach to the understanding of human behavior also provides a model for explaining why people engage in consistent behavior patterns—that is, a model for personality.

Behavioral accounts of personality have gone through a slow but steady transition over the years. Early behaviorists limited their descriptions to observable behaviors. Later, social learning theorists expanded this position to include more cognitive and social features. These theories considered such nonobservable concepts as thoughts, values, expectancies, and individual perceptions. These psychologists also emphasize the importance of learning merely by watching or even hearing about someone else's behavior. Recent years have seen a noticeable shift among many social learning theorists toward more cognitive explanations of human personality. Thus, we can see a clear bridge between traditional behaviorism—presented next—and the cognitive approaches to personality described in later chapters. However, as you will see, traditional behavioral accounts still have a lot to tell us about the causes of personality and avenues for behavior change.

Behaviorism

In 1913 a young and brash psychologist named John B. Watson published an article titled "Psychology as the Behaviorist Views It." This article signaled the beginning of a new movement in psychology: *behaviorism.* By 1924, with the publication of his book *Behaviorism,* Watson had made significant progress in his effort to redefine the discipline. He argued that if psychology were to be a science, psychologists must stop examining mental states. Researchers who concerned themselves with consciousness, the mind, and thoughts were not engaging in legitimate scientific study. Only the observable was reasonable subject matter for a science. Because our subjective inner feelings cannot be observed or measured in an agreed-upon, accurate manner, they have no place in an objective science. The sooner psychology abandons these topics, Watson maintained, the sooner it can become a respectable member of the scientific community.

What, then, was the appropriate subject matter for psychology? Watson's answer was *overt* behavior—that which can be observed, predicted, and eventually controlled by scientists. We should recognize just how much of psychology Watson was ready to jettison in his quest. Emotions, thoughts, expectancies, values, reasoning, insight, the unconscious, and the like were of interest to behaviorists only if they could be defined in terms of observable behaviors. Thus, according to Watson, thinking was simply a variant of verbal behavior, a "subvocal speech," as evidenced by the small vocal-cord movements he claimed accompanied it.

At about this same time, other researchers were beginning to study the basic processes of conditioning, or learning. Watson embraced these principles as the key to understanding human behavior. Like Watson, these researchers focused their efforts on predicting overt behaviors without introducing inner mental states

John B. Watson

1878–1958

As a child growing up in Greenville, South Carolina, John Broadus Watson exhibited two characteristics that would later come to shape his career—he was a fighter, and he was a builder. He once wrote that his favorite activity in elementary school was fighting with classmates "until one or the other drew blood." But by age 12 he had also become something of a master carpenter. Later, during his first few years as a psychology professor, he built his own 10-room house virtually by himself.

Watson's lack of enthusiasm for contemporary standards also surfaced early. In grammar school, "I was lazy, somewhat insubordinate, and, so far as I know, I never made above a passing grade." He also found that "little of my college life interested me . . . I was unsocial and had few close friends" (1936, p. 271). Watson bragged about being the only student to pass the Greek exam his senior year at Furman University. His secret was to cram the entire day before the test, powered only by a quart of Coca-Cola. "Today," he reported years later, ". . . I couldn't to save my life write the Greek alphabet or conjugate a verb" (1936, p. 272).

Watson began his doctoral work in philosophy at the University of Chicago (in part because Princeton required a reading knowledge of Greek). He soon switched to psychology, where, unlike his classmates, he preferred working with rats instead of humans. "Can't I find out by watching their behavior," he asked, "everything the other students are finding out?" (1936, p. 276).

Watson joined the faculty at Johns Hopkins University in 1908, where he began his quest to replace the psychology of the day with his new behavioral approach. His views received a surprisingly warm welcome from many scholars and academics, and in 1912 he was invited to give a series of public lectures on his theory at Columbia University. He published an influential paper, "Psychology as the Behaviorist Views It," in 1913 and his first book in 1914. Within a few years, behaviorism swept over the discipline. Watson was elected president of the American Psychological Association in 1915. Watson the fighter had taken on contemporary psychology and won, whereas Watson the builder had constructed an approach to understanding of human behavior that would change the discipline of psychology for many decades to come.

But his academic career was cut short in 1920. Watson suddenly divorced his wife of 17 years and married Rosalie Rayner, with whom he had conducted the Little Albert experiments. The scandal that surrounded these actions forced Watson out of an intolerant Johns Hopkins and into the business world, where he eventually settled into a successful career in advertising. After writing a few popular articles and a book in 1925, Watson severed his ties with psychology while still in his late forties. But several decades later, the foundation he built for the behavioral approach to personality still stands.

to explain their findings. The famous Russian physiologist Ivan Pavlov demonstrated that animals could be made to respond to stimuli in their environment by pairing these stimuli with events that already elicited a response. This process soon became known as *classical conditioning.* At the same time, other psychologists were exploring what today is known as *operant conditioning.* For example, Edward Thorndike found that animals were less likely to repeat behaviors that met with negative consequences than were animals given no punishments.

This work convinced Watson that a few key conditioning principles would suffice to explain almost any human behavior. Personality, according to Watson, was "the end product of our habit systems." In other words, over the course of our lives we are conditioned to respond to certain stimuli in more or less predictable ways. You might have been conditioned by parents and teachers to respond to challenges with increased effort. Someone else might have learned to give up or try something new. Because each of us has a unique history of experiences that shaped our characteristic responses to stimuli, each adult has a slightly different personality.

Watson had tremendous faith in the power of conditioning. His most outrageous claim, which he admitted went "beyond my facts," was that given enough control over the environment, psychologists could mold a child into whatever kind of adult they wanted. "Give me a dozen healthy infants, well formed, and my own specified world to bring them up in," he wrote. "I'll guarantee to take any one at random and train him to become any type of specialist I might select—doctor, lawyer, artist, merchant-chief, and yes, even beggarman and thief" (1924/1970, p. 104). This he promised regardless of the child's inherited abilities, intelligence, or ancestry. Although somewhat frightening in its implications for controlling human behavior, this type of thinking found a receptive audience among Americans who believed in the tradition of equal opportunity for all regardless of background or social class.

Watson's legacy was extended by the career of another influential psychologist, B. F. Skinner. Skinner, who identified his particular brand of behaviorism as **radical behaviorism,** took a small step away from the more extreme position Watson advocated. He did not deny the existence of thoughts and inner experiences. Rather, Skinner challenged the extent to which we are able to observe the inner causes of our own behavior. For example, suppose you are typically uncomfortable at social events. As you prepare for a party one evening, you begin to feel nervous. It's going to be a big party, and you don't think you will know very many people. At the last minute, your anxiety becomes intense and you decide to stay home. Why did you skip the party? Most people would answer that they avoided the party because they felt anxious. But Skinner (1974) argued that behavior does not change *because* you feel anxious. Rather, in this example, the decision to skip the party and the anxiety are both conditioned reactions to the situation.

In other words, when we introduce an inner cause for behavior, such as anxiety, we may think we have identified the cause of the behavior, but we are mistaken.

B. F. Skinner

1904–1990

When Burrhus Frederick Skinner was born in Susquehanna, Pennsylvania, his father, a lawyer, announced the birth in the local paper: "The town has a new law firm: Wm. A. Skinner & Son." But all of the father's efforts to shape his son into the legal profession failed. After growing up in a "warm and stable" home, Skinner went to Hamilton College to study English. He planned a career as a professional writer, not a lawyer. This ambition was reinforced the summer before his senior year when an instructor introduced Skinner to the poet Robert Frost. Frost asked to see some of Skinner's work. Skinner sent three short stories, and several months later received a letter from Frost encouraging him to continue writing.

Skinner devoted the two years after his graduation to writing, first at home and later in Greenwich Village in New York. At the end of this time, he realized he had produced nothing and was not likely to become a great novelist. "I was to remain interested in human behavior, but the literary method had failed me," he wrote. "I would turn to the scientific. The relevant science appeared to be psychology, though I had only the vaguest idea of what that meant" (1967, p. 395).

So Skinner went to Harvard to study psychology. He immersed himself in his studies, rising at six each morning to hit the books. After teaching at the University of Minnesota and Indiana University, Skinner returned to Harvard in 1948, where he remained the rest of his career. Literature's loss was psychology's gain. A survey of psychology historians taken at about the time of his death ranked Skinner as the most influential of all contemporary psychologists (Korn, Davis, & Davis, 1991).

Although his work in psychology earned him numerous professional awards and recognitions, Skinner never relinquished his interest in literature. In the 1940s, he returned to fiction, writing a novel, *Walden Two,* about a utopian society based on the principles of reinforcement he had found in his laboratory experiments. "It was pretty obviously a venture in self-therapy," Skinner wrote, sounding more psychoanalytic than behavioristic. "I was struggling to reconcile two aspects of my own behavior represented by [the characters] Burris and Frazier" (1967, p. 403).

Nonetheless, Skinner remained an adamant believer in the power of the environment and an unwavering critic of those who introduce nonobservable concepts to explain human behavior. "I do not believe that my life shows a type of personality à la Freud, an archetypal pattern à la Jung, or a schedule of development à la Erikson," Skinner wrote nearly eight decades after his birth. "There have been a few abiding themes, but they can be traced to environmental sources rather than to traits of character. They became part of my life as I lived it; they were not there at the beginning to determine its course" (1983, p. 401).

When you say you began eating because you were hungry, you have only put a label on your behavior—you have not explained why you are eating. Similarly, saying that people behave the way they do because they are friendly or aggressive or introverted does not explain where these behaviors come from. Although radically different in many ways, Skinner's view is much like Freud's in one respect. Both maintained that people simply do not know the reason for many of their behaviors, although we often think we do.

Naturally, Skinner's theory and some of the implications derived from it are highly controversial. For example, Skinner described happiness as "a by-product of operant reinforcement." The things that bring happiness are the ones that reinforce us. In his most controversial work, *Beyond Freedom and Dignity* (1971), Skinner argued that it is time we moved beyond the illusion of personal freedom and the so-called dignity we award ourselves for our actions. We don't freely choose to do something as the result of inner moral decisions, but rather as a response to environmental demands. We attribute dignity to people for admirable behavior, but because behavior is under the control of external contingencies, dignity is also an illusion. If you rush into a burning building to save people, it is not because you are heroic or foolish, but because you have a history of reinforcements and contingencies in similar situations.

Basic Principles of Conditioning

Traditional behaviorists explain the causes of behavior in terms of learning experiences, or conditioning. They do not deny the influence of genetics but downplay its importance relative to the power of conditioning. According to behaviorists, if we are to understand the processes that shape our personalities as well as develop procedures for changing problem behaviors, we must examine basic conditioning principles. It is convenient to divide conditioning into two categories: classical (or Pavlovian) conditioning and operant (or instrumental) conditioning.

Classical Conditioning

Classical conditioning begins with an existing stimulus-response (S-R) association. For example, some people jump (response) whenever they see a spider (stimulus). Although you may not be aware of them, your behavior repertoire contains a large number of S-R associations. For example, you might feel faint when you see blood, want to eat whenever you smell chocolate, or become nervous when you find yourself more than a few feet off the ground.

In his classic demonstration of conditioning, Pavlov used the S-R association of food and salivation. He presented hungry dogs in his laboratory with meat powder (stimulus), to which they would always salivate (response). Because this S-R association existed without any conditioning from Pavlov, we call the meat

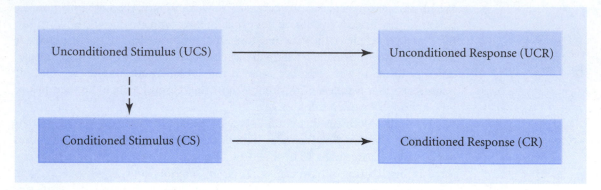

Figure 13.1
Classical Conditioning Diagram

powder the *unconditioned stimulus* (UCS) and the salivation the *unconditioned response* (UCR). Then Pavlov paired the old, unconditioned stimulus with a new, *conditioned stimulus* (CS). Whenever he presented the meat powder to the dogs, he also sounded a bell. After several trials of presenting the meat powder and the bell together, Pavlov simply sounded the bell without the powder. What happened? As nearly every psychology student knows, the dogs began to salivate at the sound of the bell, even though no meat powder had been presented. The salivation had become the *conditioned response* (CR), part of a new S-R association (bell tone and salivation) in the dogs' behavioral repertoire.

The classical conditioning procedure is diagramed in Figure 13.1. Once the new S-R association is established, it can be used to condition still another S-R association. For example, if you paired a green light with Pavlov's bell tone, after a while the dogs would start to salivate when the green light came on. This process of building one conditioned S-R association on another is called *second-order conditioning*.

Because the stimuli and events you experience are often inadvertently paired with other aspects of the environment, you are probably not aware of the many S-R associations that influence your behavior. Research suggests that our preferences in food, clothing, and even friends can be determined through this process. A friend of mine guesses that he enjoys country and western music because his father used to play it on Saturday, his favorite day of the week. Anxious participants in one study sat in a waiting room with a stranger (Riordan & Tedeschi, 1983). Although the two did not interact, participants reported unpleasant impressions of this other person. The researchers reasoned that the incidental pairing of the anxiety with the stranger created a negative association with that person.

However, researchers have also uncovered several limitations of classical conditioning. For a new S-R association to persist, the unconditioned and conditioned stimuli must be paired occasionally or otherwise reinforced (as explained in the next section). When Pavlov presented his conditioned dogs with just the bell tone, the dogs salivated less and less until finally the dogs failed to salivate to the tone at all. This gradual disappearance of the conditioned S-R association is called *extinction.* Moreover, two events presented together will not always produce an association (Rescorla, 1988). Certain stimuli are easily associable, but it may be impossible to create some S-R bonds through classical conditioning.

Operant Conditioning

At about the time Pavlov was demonstrating classical conditioning in Russia, American psychologists were investigating another type of learning through association. Edward Thorndike put some stray cats into "puzzle boxes." To escape from the box and thereby obtain a piece of fish, hungry cats had to engage in a particular combination of actions. Before long, the cats learned what they had to do to receive their reward. These observations helped Thorndike (1911) formulate the *law of effect:* that behaviors are more likely to be repeated if they lead to satisfying consequences and less likely to be repeated if they lead to unsatisfying consequences. Thorndike's cats repeated the required behaviors because they led to the satisfying consequences of escape and food.

At first glance, Thorndike's observations hardly seem insightful. Do you know any parents who don't occasionally try rewards and punishments to mold their children's behavior? Teachers, judges, and employers also regularly rely on the connection between actions and consequences to shape behavior. But vague feelings that such a connection exists are not the same as understanding how this learning

Much of what we know about the basic principles of conditioning was first demonstrated with laboratory animals. Here a researcher uses operant conditioning to teach a rat to press a bar. The rat receives positive reinforcement (a pellet of food) whenever it presses the bar.

works or the most efficient and productive way to use it. Ask a group of parents the best way to deal with a problem child, and you will soon understand how little agreement there is among nonscientists on how to use rewards and punishments.

This poor understanding of basic learning principles is unfortunate, given the power of conditioning processes. It is especially tragic because several decades of research have provided psychologists with a relatively good understanding of how reinforcement and punishment shape and control behavior. Unlike classical conditioning, which begins with an existing S-R bond, operant conditioning begins with behaviors the organism (human or lower animal) emits spontaneously. We can observe these operant behaviors when a laboratory rat is placed in a new cage. The animal moves about, scratches, sniffs, and claws in a haphazard manner, for none of these responses have been reinforced or punished. However, if one of these behaviors is always followed by a pellet of food, its frequency will increase.

Operant conditioning concerns the effect certain kinds of consequences have on the frequency of behavior. A consequence that increases the frequency of a behavior that precedes it is called a *reinforcement,* one that decreases it is called a *punishment.* Whether a consequence is reinforcing or punishing varies according to the person and the situation. If you are hungry, strawberry ice cream is probably a reinforcement. But if you don't like strawberry ice cream or if you are cold, the ice cream may serve as a punishment.

Psychologists have discovered two basic reinforcement strategies for increasing the frequency of a behavior (Table 13.1). With *positive reinforcement,* the behavior increases because it is followed by the presentation of a reward. Hungry rats that receive a pellet of food every time they press a bar will begin to press the bar frequently. Students who receive an A after dedicated studying for a test are likely to study hard for subsequent tests. We can also increase the frequency of a behavior by using *negative reinforcement,* the removal or lessening of an unpleasant stimulus when the behavior occurs. Rats that can turn off an electric shock by pulling a string will quickly learn to pull the string. People whose headaches go away when they take a few minutes to relax will soon learn to relax.

Table 13.1   **Operant Conditioning Procedures**

Procedure	Purpose	Application
Positive reinforcement	Increase behavior	Give reward following behavior
Negative reinforcement	Increase behavior	Remove aversive stimulus following behavior
Extinction	Decrease behavior	Do not reward behavior
Punishment	Decrease behavior	Give aversive stimulus following behavior or take away positive stimulus

The other side of operant conditioning is the reduction of unwanted behaviors. Teachers and parents are keenly aware of the need to reduce the frequency with which students and children do certain things. They are quick to turn to operant conditioning when children cause problems and get into trouble. Unfortunately, a poor understanding of how operant conditioning reduces unwanted behavior probably leaves most teachers and parents frustrated.

As with the task of increasing desired behaviors, operant conditioning provides two methods for decreasing undesired behaviors. The most efficient method is to cease reinforcement and thereby allow the behavior to extinguish. Although this concept is simple enough, people often reinforce problem behaviors without realizing what they are doing. For example, a teacher may react to a child who acts up in class by criticizing the child in front of the other students. The teacher may not realize that the attention the child gains from other students in the form of laughter and classroom status has turned the intended punishment into a reinforcement. An observant teacher might take disruptive children out into the hall for discipline, thereby removing the reinforcer.

Alternatively, we can use *punishment* to eliminate unwanted behaviors. In theory, the frequency of a behavior is reduced when it is followed by an aversive stimulus, such as an electric shock, or the removal of a positive stimulus, such as taking away toys. The effects of punishment can be demonstrated in laboratory animals, and therapists have had some success applying this technique in special cases. But research shows the effectiveness of punishment is limited for several reasons.

First, punishment does not teach appropriate behaviors, it can only decrease the frequency of undesired ones. Rather than simply punish a child for hitting another student, it's better to help the child learn alternative ways to deal with frustrating situations. Second, to be effective, punishment must be delivered immediately and consistently. A parent needs to punish the problem behavior as soon as possible, not "when your father gets home." The punishment must also be fairly intense and should be administered after every instance of the undesired behavior. Parents who sometimes let their children use bad language, but other times decide to punish such talk, will probably have little success in changing their children's vocabulary. Third, punishment can have negative side effects. Although parents or therapists intend to suppress a certain response, a child might associate other behaviors with the punishment. For example, a child who is punished for hitting a toy against a window may stop playing with toys altogether. In addition, through classical conditioning, aversive feelings that accompany the punishment may be associated with the person doing the punishing. Children who are spanked by their parents may associate the parent with the pain of the spanking. Another side effect is that undesirable behaviors may be learned through modeling. For example, children who are spanked may learn that physical aggression is okay as long as you are bigger and stronger. Punishment can also create negative emotions, such as fear and anxiety, strong enough to interfere with learning appropriate responses. Taken together, these factors make punishment one of the least desirable choices for behavior therapists seeking to change problem behaviors. At most, punishment can temporarily suppress an undesirable response long enough for the therapist to begin reinforcing a desired, hopefully incompatible behavior.

Shaping. Suppose you are hired to work with patients in a psychiatric hospital. Your job is to get reluctant patients more involved in some of the activities on the ward. You start with one patient who has never participated in any of the ward activities. Your goal is to get him into daily art therapy sessions. Positive reinforcement seems the right tool. Every time the patient joins in one of the voluntary art sessions, you will reward him with coupons for free items in the hospital store. The patient skips art therapy the first day. So no reward. He skips art therapy the rest of the week. Still no reward. You wait two months, and still the patient has not attended one of the sessions. By now, one of the problems encountered when using operant conditioning is apparent to you: A behavior can be reinforced only after it is emitted.

Does this mean operant conditioning is useless in this situation? Fortunately, the answer is no. A behavior therapist working with the reluctant patient might use a technique known as *shaping,* in which successive approximations of the desired behavior are reinforced. For example, you might reward the withdrawn patient for getting out of bed and sitting among the other patients. Once this behavior is established, you might reinforce him only when he is near or in the art therapy room. From here, rewards might be limited to time spent in the room during the sessions and later to time spent attending to and participating in the sessions. Shaping is particularly useful when teaching complex behaviors. Children will learn to enjoy reading if each step along the way is reinforced. If learning the alphabet, letter sounds, and short words is difficult and unpleasant, it is unlikely the child will move on to reading sentences and stories.

Generalization and Discrimination. Operant conditioning would be rather limited if every different situation required learning a new response. Fortunately, because of **generalization,** this is not the case. For example, pigeons trained to peck at large red circles to receive food will also peck at small orange circles, although not as frequently. This process, called *stimulus generalization,* helps explain why personality characteristics generalize across situations. A child rewarded for acting politely around relatives will probably act politely around new acquaintances. The polite response has been generalized from the stimulus of the relative to the new stimulus, the stranger. When we observe polite behavior consistently across situations, we say this pattern is part of the child's personality.

As long as the generalized response is met with reinforcement, the behavior is likely to continue. But if the pigeon is not rewarded for pecking at orange circles, it will soon learn to **discriminate** between rewarded and nonrewarded stimuli and will peck only at the red ones. Similarly, the polite child may come in contact with adults who punish friendly behavior with harshness. Soon the child will learn to discriminate between people who are friendly and people who aren't. The difference between a good and a great tennis player or between a second-string baseball player and a star may be the ability to make fine discriminations between those actions that lead to a reinforcement (a winning shot or a home run) and those that do not.

In summary, the behaviorist description of personality is different from that provided by the other approaches in several ways. Traditional behaviorists focus on observable behaviors and consider consistent behavior patterns the result of conditioning experiences. Moreover, they argue that classical conditioning and operant conditioning are the processes responsible for these behavior patterns. If this explanation seems too simple to you, you are not alone. Many adherents of the behavioral approach also find traditional behaviorism too limited. Their elaborations of the approach are described in the following section.

Social Learning Theory

It is difficult to overstate the impact traditional behaviorism had on psychology and subsequently the field of personality. Watson and his followers provided a scientific, easily testable account of human behavior that complemented the growing empirical flavor of psychology in American universities. The basic principles of learning were so universal they could be tested on lower animals. The image many people have of the lab-coated psychologist, pencil in hand, watching rats running through mazes comes from this era. But somewhere in the 1950s or 1960s some of the enthusiasm for traditional behaviorism began to wane. Many psychologists who still accepted the basic principles of behaviorism began to question the assertion that all human learning takes place as a result of classical or operant conditioning. "The prospects for survival would be slim indeed if one could learn only from the consequences of trial and error," one psychologist wrote. "One does not teach children to swim, adolescents to drive automobiles, and novice medical students to perform surgery by having them discover the requisite behavior from the consequences of their successes and failures" (Bandura, 1986, p. 20).

These psychologists also began to question whether behaviorism was too limited in the scope of its subject matter. For example, why couldn't "internal" events like thoughts and attitudes be conditioned in the same way as overt behaviors? Paranoid people who believe evil agents are out to get them might have been reinforced in the past for these beliefs. If this were the case, behavioral models of psychotherapy could also be applied to treating these patients. Thus began the transition from traditional behaviorism to a group of theories known collectively as *social learning theory.*

One of the concepts introduced by social learning theorists is the notion of *behavior-environment-behavior interactions* (Staats, 1975, 1981, 1996). That is, not only does the environment influence our behavior, but that behavior then determines the kind of environment we find ourselves in, which can then influence behavior, and so on. The way people treat you (environment) is partly the result of how you act (behavior). And, of course, how you act is partly a result of how people treat you. Moreover, people often provide their own reinforcers in the absence of visible external rewards. It is reinforcing to meet internals standards or reach personal goals even if no one else knows about it. Many social learning theorists also incorporate internal concepts into their descriptions of conditioning and personality. They argue that beliefs and self-concept—foreign words to strict behaviorists—can be developed and changed through the same conditioning principles used to develop and change overt behaviors.

Julian Rotter's Social Learning Theory

Julian Rotter (1954, 1982; Rotter, Chance, & Phares, 1972) is one of the personality theorists who found the behaviorist approach useful but questioned the narrowness of the traditional behaviorist position. Rotter argues that the causes of human behaviors are far more complex than those of lower animals. To predict how people will respond in a certain situation, we have to take into account such variables as perceptions, expectancies, and values. In particular, Rotter uses the concepts of behavior potential, expectancy, and reinforcement value to account for human personality.

Behavior Potential. Imagine someone has just insulted you at a party. How do you respond? You have several courses of action to choose from. You might attempt to top the remark with something clever and witty. You could calmly say the behavior was out of line and ask for an apology. You could get angry and yell an equally rude insult at the offender, or you could simply leave the scene. The key to predicting what you will do in this situation lies in understanding what Rotter refers to as the *behavior potential* for each option. The behavior potential is the likelihood of a given behavior occurring in a particular situation. Each possible response to the insult has a different behavior potential. If you decide to scream out an insult, it means the behavior potential for that response was stronger than for any of the other possible responses.

The question then becomes this: What determines the strength of the behavior potential? According to Rotter, two variables need to be considered: *expectancy* and *reinforcement value* (Figure 13.2). In short, when deciding whether to engage

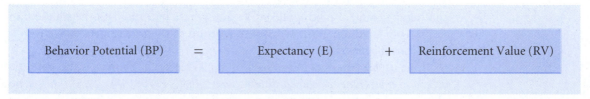

| Behavior Potential (BP) | = | Expectancy (E) | + | Reinforcement Value (RV) |

Figure 13.2

Rotter's Basic Formula for Predicting Behavior

Julian B. Rotter

1916–

Julian Rotter first learned about psychology in the Avenue J Library in Brooklyn, where he spent a great deal of his grade school and high school years. One day, after exhausting most of the books in other sections of the library, he wandered over to the Philosophy and Psychology shelf. Among the first books he encountered were Alfred Adler's *Understanding Human Nature* and Sigmund Freud's *Psychopathology of Everyday Life*. From that point on, he was hooked. But for a time his love of psychology took a backseat to the realities of the world. He decided to major in chemistry at Brooklyn College because "there was no profession of psychology that I knew of. And in 1933, in the depths of the Great Depression, one majored in a subject one could use to make a living" (1982, p. 343).

But circumstances soon changed things. One day during his junior year Rotter discovered that Alfred Adler was teaching at the Long Island School of Medicine. Rotter began attending the nearby lectures. Eventually, Adler invited Rotter to attend the monthly meetings of the Society of Individual Psychology held in Adler's home. Unfortunately, Adler died the next year. Nonetheless, by then Rotter's enthusiasm for psychology dictated that he go to graduate school. He chose the University of Iowa so that he could study with the famous Gestalt psychologist Kurt Lewin. He went to the University of Indiana for his Ph.D. because it was one of the few schools at the time to offer a degree in clinical psychology. He wanted an academic position, but few were available when Rotter graduated in 1941. After working in a hospital for a year, Rotter served as a psychologist in the Army and later the Air Force during World War II.

Circumstances intervened into Rotter's career path again following the war. The need for clinical psychologists was suddenly high, but their numbers were few. Rotter took a position at Ohio State University, finally fulfilling his ambition to be a professional academic psychologist. He stayed there until 1963, when he moved to the University of Connecticut.

in a particular action, we calculate the probability that the action will result in a given reinforcer and the value that reinforcer has for us. If the odds of being reinforced for a certain course of action are slim or if the possible reinforcement to be gained is not particularly prized, the behavior potential is weak. However, if we expect to receive something of value for a behavior, we'll probably perform it.

Expectancy. Before you decide to stay up all night studying for an exam, you probably ask yourself what the likelihood is that the all-nighter will help you do better on the test. Similarly, when debating whether to attend a dance, you probably try to figure out the probability that you will have a good time. Rotter refers to these estimations as *expectancies*. Obviously, we base our expectancies largely on how things turned out other times we were in this situation. If you always do well after studying all night, you will probably have a high expectancy of receiving the reward again. If you never seem to enjoy yourself at a dance, the expectancy of being rewarded for going to the dance is slim.

Of course, traditional behaviorists would also make these predictions. People are more likely to engage in a behavior when it has been reinforced. But where Rotter and the behaviorists disagree is on how to explain the behavior. Behaviorists say that an operant conditioning association or habit has been strengthened by the earlier experience. However, Rotter argues that the more often people are reinforced for a certain behavior (for example, studying all night and receiving an A), the stronger their expectancy that the behavior will be reinforced in the future. On the other hand, when behaviors are not reinforced (studying all night and receiving a low grade), the expectancy of reward is decreased. Of course, expectancies are not necessarily accurate. For example, you may expect that studying for your SAT will result in a higher score, even if in reality the studying has little effect. In this case, your expectancy will probably predict your behavior better than the actual contingencies.

After being reinforced in the same situation many times, you develop a great deal of confidence in your expectancies for rewards. If you always have a great time at parties, you expect that going to a party will be rewarded again this weekend. But how can expectancies account for behavior in situations we encounter for the first time? Rotter explains that the expectancy in this case is based on experiences we have had in similar situations. The recent graduate who was rewarded for staying up all night to write papers in college probably expects that staying up all night to finish a report for the boss will lead to similar rewards. This example illustrates how expectancies lead to stable behavior patterns (that is, personality). We might call this person a procrastinator or perhaps say he is diligent because we see the same style of behavior over time and across situations. According to Rotter, the consistency in this person's behavior is the result of well-defined and stable expectancies.

Beyond this, Rotter (1966) proposes that in new situations we rely on *generalized expectancies*. These are beliefs we hold about how often our actions *typically* lead to reinforcements and punishments. Subsequent research on this concept, reviewed in the next chapter, indicates that people can be placed along a continuum of what has been called **locus of control.** At one end of this dimension we find people with an extreme *internal* orientation—those who generally believe that what happens to them is the result of their own actions or attributes. On the other end we find people who hold an extreme *external* orientation—those who generally maintain that what happens to them is the result of forces outside their control, such as chance or powerful others. Of course, most of us fall somewhere between the two extremes.

In novel or ambiguous situations, we use these generalized expectancies to calculate behavior potentials. If you are the kind of person who typically says, "I think

I can do it," in a new situation, Rotter would say you are relying on your generalized belief that you have the ability to make things happen. If you more often have doubts in new situations, you probably fall on the other end of the locus of control dimension.

Reinforcement Value. Suppose Chuck is trying to decide whom to ask out this Friday. He believes there is a high probability that Alice will say yes if he asks her out and a low probability that Barbara will go out with him. Nonetheless, he still decides to ask Barbara. Why? Rotter would explain this choice by looking at the reinforcement value for each option. Chuck might ask Barbara out because a date with her is much more valuable to him than a date with Alice.

Rotter defines *reinforcement value* as the degree to which we prefer one reinforcer over another. Naturally, the reinforcement value we assign a certain outcome can vary from situation to situation and across time. When we are lonely, social contact holds a higher reinforcement value than when we aren't. Yet there are relatively stable individual differences in how much we value one reinforcer over another. Some people always take free baseball tickets over free ballet tickets. Hence, consistent behavior patterns can also be traced to relatively stable feelings about what certain rewards are worth. Some people consistently work hard, placing work ahead of family and recreation. We might call these people obsessive or driven. But using Rotter's model, their personalities can be explained in terms of the consistently high value they put on achievement.

Rotter maintains that reinforcement value is independent of expectancy. That is, whether something holds a high or a low reinforcement value for you tells us nothing about your expectancy for obtaining that reinforcer. Thus, to predict behavior, we have to know both the expectancy and the reinforcement value for each behavior option. Returning to the insult situation, we would need to understand what you expect will happen following each possible response and how much you valued that reaction. Some hypothetical possibilities are diagramed in Table 13.2. In this case, asking for an apology is the likely behavior because the person expects to receive an apology back and that apology is highly valued.

Table 13.2   **Calculating Behavior Potential Example**

Option	Possible Outcome	Expectancy	Value	Behavior Potential
Ask for apology	Apology	High	High	High
Insult back	Laughter	Low	High	Average
Yell at insulter	Ugly scene	High	Low	Average
Leave the party	Feel foolish	Average	Low	Low

Social-Cognitive Theory

The evolution from traditional behavioristic views of personality to more cognitive approaches is probably best illustrated by the work of Albert Bandura (1977a, 1986, 1997, 2001). Bandura rejects the radical behaviorist view of human beings as passive recipients of whatever stimuli life throws their way. Certainly people respond to environmental events, and certainly they often learn characteristic behaviors as the result of rewards and punishments. But people possess other capacities that are distinctly human. By reducing the process by which people grow and change to the way a rat learns to press a bar for a pellet of food, strict behaviorists overlook some of the most important causes of human behavior and sources of human personality. Because these overlooked causes generally involve thinking and symbolic processing of information, Bandura refers to his approach as a *social-cognitive theory.*

Reciprocal Determinism

Bandura introduces a new twist to the question of whether behavior is determined by internal or by external forces. He argues that there are both internal and external determinants of behavior, but behavior is not determined exclusively by either or by a simple combination. Bandura introduces instead the concept **reciprocal determinism.** That is, external determinants of behavior, such as rewards and punishments, and internal determinants, such as beliefs, thoughts, and expectations, are part of a system of interacting influences that affect not only behavior but the various parts of the system as well. Put more simply, each part of the system—behaviors, external factors, and internal factors—influences each of the other parts.

Some examples will help clarify what Bandura means. Like Rotter, Bandura maintains that internal factors, such as our expectancies, affect our behavior. Suppose someone you don't like much asks you to play racquetball. You can just imagine what a dismal afternoon you would have with this person. Thus, your internal expectation will probably cause you to reject the invitation. But what would happen if this person offered to buy you that new, expensive racket you've been eyeing if you play with him? Suddenly the external inducement is powerful enough to determine your behavior, and you say, "Let's play." Now imagine further that you have one of the most enjoyable sets of racquetball ever. You're evenly matched with this person, and he even cracks a few jokes to make the afternoon fun. You actually look forward to playing with him again. The behavior in this case has changed your expectations, which will affect future behavior and so on.

The reciprocal determinism process is diagrammed in Figure 13.3. You may notice that the arrows point in both directions, indicating that each of the three variables in the model is capable of influencing each of the other variables. This situation is very different from traditional behaviorism, which limits explanations of

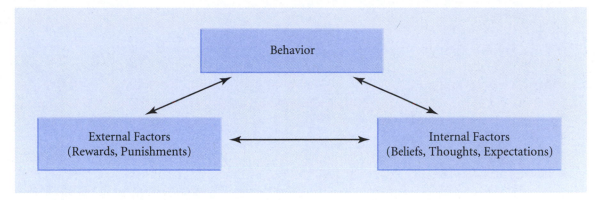

Figure 13.3

Bandura's Reciprocal Determinism Model

human behavior to a two-factor, one-way model, in which external events cause behavior. Not only can the environment affect behavior in Bandura's model, but the opposite effect is also possible. A rude person's behavior at a party can lead those around her to create an environment with punishments and few rewards. In this case, the behavior has changed the environment. Bandura draws a distinction between the *potential environment,* which is the same for everyone in a situation, and the *actual environment,* the one we create with our behaviors. A friendly person at the same party might create an environment of many rewards and few punishments. Bandura would agree with those who claim we create our own opportunities. He might add that we also create our own defeating circumstances.

How can we predict which of the three parts in the reciprocal determinism model is going to influence which other part? This depends on the strength of each of the variables. At times, environmental forces are most powerful; at other times, internal forces dominate. The example used in an earlier chapter of both high and low self-esteem people fleeing a burning building illustrates how environmental factors can override internal individual factors on occasion. Though at times we mold our environment to meet our needs, at other times we are faced with environmental factors we cannot control. We often create our own opportunities and defeats, but they can also be created for us.

Cognitive Influences on Behavior

A major difference between Bandura's theory and the traditional behaviorist approach is Bandura's emphasis on cognitive (internal) aspects of human personality. Bandura identifies several features unique to human functioning that must be considered in understanding personality. Unlike lower animals, people use symbols and forethought as guides for future action. Instead of working our way

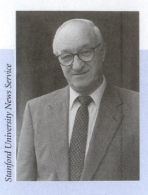

Albert Bandura

1925–

Albert Bandura was born in a small farming community located among the wheat fields of Alberta, Canada. He attended the only school in the area, a combined elementary and high school with a total of about 20 students and two teachers. Summer jobs included filling in holes in the highways of the Yukon. Bandura stayed in Canada for his undergraduate education, receiving a bachelor's degree from the University of British Columbia in 1949.

Bandura chose the University of Iowa for graduate work, in part because of its strong tradition in learning theory. Among the Iowa faculty members who influenced Bandura was the learning theorist Kenneth Spence. The faculty at Iowa also emphasized the need for empirical research. This training left Bandura with the conviction that psychologists should "conceptualize clinical phenomena in ways that would make them amenable to experimental tests" (Bandura, in Evans, 1976, p. 243). Bandura received his Ph.D. in 1952.

After a year of clinical internship in Wichita, Bandura accepted a position at Stanford University in 1953 and has remained there ever since. While at Stanford, he has continued to build bridges between traditional learning theory and cognitive personality theories, between clinical psychology and empirically oriented approaches to understanding personality. Bandura has received numerous professional honors, including election to the presidency of the American Psychological Association in 1974.

through rewards and punishments in a trial-and-error fashion every time we face a new problem, we imagine possible outcomes, calculate probabilities, set goals, and develop strategies. We do all of this in our mind without engaging in random actions and waiting to see which will be rewarded or punished. Of course, past experiences with reinforcements or punishments affect these judgments. But think about the way you prepare for a vacation. Most likely you think about several options of where and when to go, how to get there, who to go with, what to bring, what to do when you arrive, and so on. By imagining what a vacation will be like at various locations and with various people, you don't have to literally try out each option to see if the experience will be reinforcing or punishing.

Bandura also argues that most behavior is performed in the absence of external reinforcements and punishments. Except for extreme situations, such as in a prisoner-of-war camp, most of our daily actions are controlled by what Bandura calls **self-regulation.** He challenges the radical behaviorist assertion that we can be swayed into performing just about any action if the environmental contingencies are altered appropriately. You've probably seen people hold to their beliefs in spite of external pressure to change. "Anyone who attempted to change a pacifist into an aggressor or a devout religionist into an atheist," Bandura wrote, "would quickly come to appreciate the existence of personal sources of behavioral control" (1977a, pp. 128–129).

Although people often strive to obtain external rewards, Bandura argues that we also work toward self-imposed goals with internal rewards. For example, many amateur runners push themselves in races, even though few expect to win. The reward comes from the feelings of accomplishment and self-worth they get from reaching a personal goal or perhaps for just finishing the race. Self-regulation also includes self-punishment. When we fail to maintain personal standards, we often degrade and feel bad about ourselves. For example, you may have chastised yourself for being rude to a stranger or not sticking to your diet, even when no one else seemed to notice.

Observational Learning

Perhaps social-cognitive theory's most important contribution to the understanding of human behavior and personality is the concept of vicarious or observational learning. Bandura argues that learning is not limited to classical and operant conditioning. We can also learn by observing or reading or hearing about other people's actions. Many behaviors are too complex to be learned through the slow process of reinforcement and punishment. For example, we don't teach pilots to fly by putting them in the cockpit and reinforcing correct behaviors and punishing incorrect ones. Bandura maintains that children would never learn to talk during their preschool years if they had to be reinforced for every correct utterance. Instead, the pilots and the toddlers watch others fly and talk, noting which behaviors lead to rewards.

Bandura draws an important distinction between *learning* and *performance*. Behaviors learned through observational methods need not be performed. This idea again clashes with traditional behaviorists, who maintain that we cannot learn something until we have actually engaged in that behavior. But think for a moment of some of the behaviors you could perform if you wanted to, even though you never have. For example, although you have probably never picked up a pistol and shot another human being, you've observed this behavior in movies often enough for it to be part of your behavioral repertoire. You might even know to stand with your feet apart and to hold the weapon at eye level with both hands in front of you, just like the actors portraying police do. Fortunately, most of us will never perform this behavior, but it is one we have probably learned through observation.

Why do we perform some of the behaviors we have learned through observation but not others? The answer lies in our expectations about the consequences of the performance. That is, do you believe the action will be rewarded or punished? In the case of shooting another person, most of us expect this behavior to lead to punishment—if not in a legal sense, then through self-punishment in the form of guilt and lowered feelings of worth.

But if we have never performed the behavior, where do we get our expectations about its consequences? Again, from observing others. Your perception of what will happen to you is based on whether your model was rewarded or punished after engaging in the behavior. For example, a high school boy may watch an older friend ask someone for a date. He pays close attention to how the friend engages the potential date in conversation, what is said, and so on. If the friend's behavior is rewarded (a date is made), the boy may believe that he, too, will be rewarded if he acts just like his friend. Most likely, he'll soon get his courage up and ask a girl he's interested in for a date. But what if the boy watches his friend get turned down? It's unlikely he will imitate the punished behavior. In both cases the boy paid close enough attention to learn how his friend went about asking for a date. But whether he will perform the behavior depends on whether he thinks he'll be rewarded or punished, which he also learned from his friend's example.

In a classic experiment with important social implications, Bandura (1965) demonstrated this learning-performance distinction. Nursery school children watched a television program in which an adult model performed four novel aggressive acts on an adult-size plastic Bobo doll:

> First, the model laid the Bobo doll on its side, sat on it, and punched it in the nose while remarking, "Pow, right in the nose, boom, boom." The model then raised the doll and pommeled it on the head with a mallet. Each response was accompanied by the verbalization, "Sockeroo . . . stay down." Following the mallet aggression, the model kicked the doll about the room, and these responses were interspersed with the comment, "Fly away." Finally, the model threw rubber balls at the Bobo doll, each strike punctuated with "Bang." (pp. 590-591)

The children saw one of three endings to the film. Some saw a second adult reward the aggressive model with soft drinks, candy, and lots of praise. Others saw the model spanked with a rolled-up magazine and warned not to act aggressively again. A third group was given no information about the consequences of the aggressive behavior. Next, each child was left alone for 10 minutes of free playing time. Among the many toys in the room were a Bobo doll and all the materials needed to perform the aggressive acts they had seen (for example, a mallet). An experimenter watched through a one-way window to see how many of the four acts of aggression the children would perform spontaneously. Each child was then offered fruit juice and small toys for each of the four aggressive acts he or she could perform for the experimenter. This was done to see if the children could perform the behavior if they wanted to—that is, had they learned the responses from watching the model?

The results are shown in Figure 13.4. Nearly all the children in all three groups could perform the behaviors when asked. However, as Bandura predicted, whether they chose to perform the behavior when left alone depended on the consequences they expected. Although all of them had learned how to act aggressively, the children who had seen the model rewarded were significantly more likely to perform the behaviors than those who had seen the model punished.

Figure 13.4

Mean Number
of Aggressive
Responses
Performed

Source: Adapted from
Bandura (1965); reprinted
by permission of the
author.

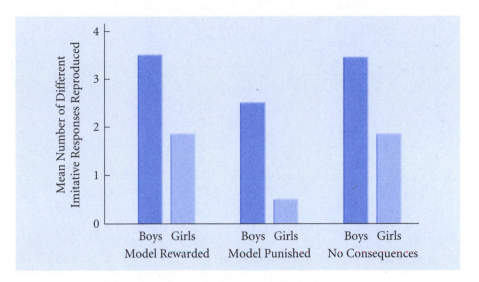

We learn more than aggressive behavior by watching the numerous models in our lives. Much of what we learn about acting friendly, seductively, or professionally comes from the many people we have seen act this way. Bandura explains that this is why siblings exposed to the same parents often develop very different personalities. The children draw from the behavior modeled by many different people—parents, siblings, friends, television characters—and each develops a unique pattern of behavioral responses and expectancies.

Application: Behavior Modification and Self-Efficacy Therapy

One of the appeals of traditional behaviorism is its presentation of a simple, rational model of human nature. Looking at the world through behaviorism glasses, everything makes sense. Employees work hard when they are reinforced properly. Children stop fighting when aggressive behavior is punished and working together is reinforced. But what about some of the seemingly irrational behaviors enacted by people suffering from psychological disorders? How can basic conditioning principles explain a fear of stairs or a belief that people are out to get you? As you will see, not only can behaviorists account for these and other abnormal behaviors, but many psychotherapy techniques are based on basic conditioning principles.

Explaining Psychological Disorders

John B. Watson was the first to demonstrate how seemingly "abnormal" behaviors are created through normal conditioning procedures. Watson used classical conditioning to create a fear of white rats in an 11-month-old baby known as Little

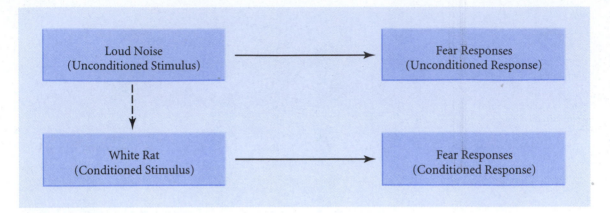

Figure 13.5

Diagram of Little Albert's Classical Conditioning

Albert (Watson & Rayner, 1920). As shown in Figure 13.5, Watson began with the stimulus-response association between a loud noise and fear present in most infants. That is, whenever Watson would make the loud noise, Albert would cry and show other signs of fear. Next, Watson showed Albert a white rat, each time accompanied by the loud noise. Soon Albert was responding to the white rat with fear responses (crying, crawling away) similar to those he had made to the loud noise, even when the noise was not sounded. Watson demonstrated that what appeared to be an abnormal fear of white rats in an infant could be explained by knowing the past conditioning of the child.

Behaviorists argue that many of our seemingly irrational fears may have been developed in a similar manner. For example, we may not recall when bridges or snakes were ever associated with an existing fear. But such associations could have taken place a long time ago or even without our awareness. However, there is a problem with this explanation. As Pavlov discovered, new associations formed through classical conditioning extinguish once the pairing is removed. Why, then, do phobias not just become extinct on their own without psychological intervention? The answer is that operant conditioning may take over to keep the phobia operating. Let's take the example of a three-year-old girl who falls off a tall slide. The pain and fear she experiences are paired with the sight of the slide, and those feelings reemerge the next time she approaches a slide. Her fear and anxiety increase as she gets closer and closer to it. Quite likely, she'll decide to turn away and try the slide some other time, thereby reducing the fear and anxiety. What has happened in this situation is that the act of avoiding the slide has been reinforced through negative reinforcement. Running away was followed by a reduction in the aversive stimulus, the feelings of fear and anxiety. If this avoidance behavior is reinforced a few more times, the girl could develop a strong fear of slides. This fear might then be generalized to a fear of all high places, and years later the woman may seek therapy for this debilitating phobia.

Behaviorists view other problem behaviors as the result of a learning history that somehow reinforced the wrong behavior. For example, a very socially anxious boy may have found the only escape from criticism and ridicule he received at home was to avoid social contact as much as possible (negative reinforcement), a behavior he then generalized to other people. An aggressive girl might have been reinforced for her aggressive behavior by earning the "respect" of other children who allowed her to have her own way most of the time. A man suffering from paranoid delusions may believe he has thwarted a plan to capture him by staying in his house all day, thereby rewarding the behavior. Behavior theorists also explain a lack of appropriate behaviors as the result of too little reinforcement. For example, if a woman's efforts to initiate conversations with others are never rewarded, she'll probably stop trying.

Behavior Modification

If we accept that a problem behavior is the result of unusual conditioning experiences, then another principle of behaviorism should follow: Problem behaviors can be changed through similar conditioning experiences. Several therapy procedures, generally grouped under the label **behavior modification,** have been developed from behaviorist theory and research. These procedures differ from more traditional therapies in several respects. The treatment usually lasts for several weeks, as compared to perhaps years. The focus is on changing a few well-defined behaviors rather than changing the entire personality of the client. And behavior therapists are often unconcerned with discovering where the problem behavior originated. Their goal is simply to remove it or replace it with a more appropriate set of responses. These features have made behavior modification techniques popular among therapists from a variety of theoretical orientations.

Classical Conditioning Applications. Pairing one stimulus with another is a powerful tool for creating new stimulus-response associations. Therapists often use classical conditioning to eliminate or replace stimulus-response associations that cause a client problems. Although these techniques traditionally use physical pairing of objects and reactions, psychologists also find that mental images can be classically conditioned (Dadds, Bovbjerg, Redd, & Cutmore, 1997). Thus, in the safety of a behavior therapist's office clients can imagine themselves facing the situations they fear without actually visiting those places.

One example of a treatment for phobias based on classical conditioning pairs images of the feared object with a relaxation response. Through *systematic desensitization* the old association between the feared stimulus and the fear response is replaced with a new association between the stimulus and relaxation. Clients and therapists begin the treatment by creating a list of imagined scenes ranging from mildly arousing to highly anxiety-provoking. For example, people afraid of heights might begin their list with a scene of them standing on a 2-foot-high footstool. The next scene might be walking up a flight of stairs, followed by a scene of them standing on an 8-foot ladder. Last on the hierarchy come the highly anxiety-provoking scenes, such as looking out from the top floor of a skyscraper or flying in a small airplane.

After clients complete relaxation training, they imagine the scenes while practicing relaxing. One step at a time, they slowly move through the list until they can imagine the scene without feeling anxious. In theory, the fear response is being replaced with a new, incompatible response—relaxation. If this therapy works, clients who used to be mildly anxious when thinking about standing on a 2-foot-high stool can imagine (and eventually perform) looking out over the city from the top of a tall building without experiencing fear.

Aversion therapy is another example of classical conditioning used to alter problem behaviors. Here therapists try to rid clients of undesirable behaviors by pairing aversive images with the behavior. For example, for a client trying to quit smoking, the image of a cigarette might be paired with images of them becoming nauseated and vomiting.

Operant Conditioning Applications. Sometimes therapy can be as basic as reinforcing desired behaviors and punishing undesirable ones. However, this is more difficult than it may sound. Behavior modification therapists begin this treatment by identifying the target behavior and defining it in specific operational terms. For example, what would you reinforce or punish when a child's problem is "acting too immature"? A behavior therapist would probably interview parents and teachers to determine which specific immature behaviors they wanted to reduce. Next, the therapist would want to determine a baseline of behavior frequency. How do you know if you're reducing the frequency of a behavior if you don't know how often it occurs now? For example, through observation or interviews, the therapist might find that a child throws an average of two and a half tantrums per week.

Once we know how often the behavior occurs under the current system of rewards and punishments, we change the contingencies. If it is a desired behavior, the environment is altered so the client is rewarded for it. If it is an undesired behavior, punishment or a reduction of reinforcement is introduced. Ideally, appropriate responses are reinforced at the same time undesired behavior is extinguished or punished. In the case of the child throwing tantrums, parents might be told to stop rewarding the action with their attention and concern. In addition, punishments might be introduced, such as not allowing the child to watch television for one day after a tantrum. At the same time, the child should be reinforced for handling frustrating situations in an appropriate way, such as seeking help instead of throwing a tantrum. The frequency of the target behavior is monitored throughout the therapy. After a few weeks, the therapist can see if the treatment is working or if adjustments need to be made. If the child is down to one tantrum a week, the treatment will probably continue for a few more weeks until the tantrums disappear entirely. If they are still occurring two and a half times a week, a new therapy program may have to be developed.

A therapist who wants to change a large number of behaviors for a large number of people at once might use another treatment system based on operant conditioning called a *token economy*. People in a well-defined institutional unit, such as a psychiatric ward or a class, are given the opportunity to earn tokens (for example, poker chips) worth a certain number of points. They can exchange these tokens for more tangible rewards, such as snack food or extra privileges. Psychiatric ward patients might be given two tokens for making their beds in the morning, five for attending therapy sessions on time, 10 for doing their assigned work on the ward, and so on. When clients show inappropriate behaviors, they might be punished by having tokens taken away.

Biofeedback is another type of operant conditioning used to treat psychological problems. Biofeedback requires special equipment that provides information about somatic processes. This information is not readily perceivable without the equipment and is therefore difficult to control. For example, a woman suffering from anxiety might use a machine that tells her when she is tightening and relaxing certain facial and back muscles, an action she is otherwise not aware of. After several muscle relaxation sessions with the immediate feedback of the machine, she may learn to reduce tension on her own and thereby overcome her anxiety. In operant conditioning terms, she was reinforced for producing the response that lowered her muscle tension, as indicated by the machine. As with other reinforced behaviors, she soon learned to make the relaxation response. Other bodily indicators that may be controlled through biofeedback include blood pressure, heart rate, and brain waves.

Self-Efficacy

Every year millions of Americans seek professional help to stop smoking or lose weight. Although many of these people go several weeks without cigarettes or succeed in dropping a few pounds, only a small percentage permanently end their habit or keep the lost pounds off. What is it about these few successful cases that separates them from the others? The answer may lie in what Bandura calls **self-efficacy.** People stop smoking and lose weight when they convince themselves they can do it. Smokers frequently explain that they have tried to quit but just can't. From a social-cognitive analysis, one reason these smokers are unable to quit their habit is precisely because they believe they cannot.

According to Bandura (1977b, 1997), people aren't likely to alter their behavior until they make a clear decision to change and expend the necessary effort. Bandura draws a distinction between outcome expectations and efficacy expectations. An *outcome expectation* is the extent to which people believe their actions will lead to a certain outcome. An *efficacy expectation* is the extent to which they believe they can bring about the particular outcome. Simply put, it is the difference between believing that something can happen and believing that you can make it happen. For example, you may hold the outcome expectation that if you devote several hours to studying each night and abandon social life on weekends, you will get good grades—possibly straight A's—this term. However, you may also hold the efficacy expectation that you are incapable of such devoted work and sacrifice.

Bandura argues that efficacy expectations are better predictors of behavior than outcome expectations. Whether people make an effort to cope with problems and how long they persist in their efforts to change are determined by whether they believe they are capable of such change. Students are unlikely to work hard for good grades if they don't think it possible. Therapy clients are unlikely to stop smoking, lose weight, or overcome a fear of flying if they don't believe they are capable of doing so.

Where do efficacy expectations come from, and how can therapists change their clients' beliefs about their abilities? Bandura describes four sources. The most important of these is *enactive mastery experiences.* These are successful attempts to achieve the outcome in the past. Sky divers suddenly struck with fear before a jump may tell themselves that they've done this many times before without incident and therefore can do it again. However, a history of failures often leads to low efficacy expectations. People with a fear of heights who have never been able to climb a ladder without coming back down in a fit of anxiety will probably conclude they can't perform this behavior.

Although not as powerful as actual performances, *vicarious experiences* also alter efficacy expectations. Seeing other people perform a behavior without adverse effects can lead us to believe that we can do it too. People who are afraid to speak in front of an audience may change their efficacy expectation from "I can't do that" to "maybe I can" after seeing other members of a public speaking class give their speeches without disastrous results. When you tell yourself something like "If she can do it, so can I," you are changing your efficacy expectation through vicarious experience.

A less effective way to alter efficacy expectations is through *verbal persuasion.* Telling someone who is reluctant to stand up to the boss "you can do it" might convince the person to assert his or her rights. However, this expectation will be easily eliminated if the actual performance isn't met with the expected result.

Physiological and affective states can also be a source of efficacy expectations. A woman who has difficulty approaching men may find her heart beats rapidly and her palms perspire as she picks up the phone to call a man to ask for a date. If she interprets these physiological responses as signs of anxiety, she may decide she is too nervous to go through with it. However, if she notices how calm she is just before dialing, she may decide she is more courageous than she realized.

The key to successful treatment programs is changing a client's efficacy expectation through one or more of these means. For example, therapists helped snake-phobic people in one study overcome their fear of the reptiles by taking them through the process of touching and picking up snakes (enactive mastery experience) and/or watching someone else go through this procedure (vicarious experience). In nearly every case, whether the people believed they could approach and touch the snakes was the best predictor of whether they would actually do it (Bandura, Adams, & Beyer, 1977).

But if successful experiences are the most effective method for altering a client's efficacy expectations, this creates a bit of a problem. How can a therapist provide the client with a mastery experience of overcoming a fear of heights if the client is afraid to leave the first floor of a building? One answer is a procedure known as *guided mastery* (Bandura, 1997). Using this procedure, the therapist arranges the situation so that the client is almost guaranteed a successful experience. The treatment is broken down into small steps that can be accomplished with only a slight increase in the client's effort. For example, the client with a fear of driving might begin by driving a short distance on a secluded street (Bandura, 1997). This step is followed with gradually longer drives on busier streets. With each successful experience, the client strengthens the belief that he or she is capable of driving an automobile. You may have noticed that this procedure sounds similar to systematic desensitization. Indeed, in many cases the distinction between the two therapy procedures may lie only in how they are interpreted. The behavior modification therapist explains successful systematic desensitization in terms of replacing old stimulus-response bonds with new ones. Social-cognitive therapists maintain that the mastery experiences change efficacy expectations, leading to the change in behavior.

The other side of this process is that failure to instill a sense of efficacy in a client might very well doom therapeutic efforts. People battling alcohol abuse typically do not succeed in treatment programs when they doubt their ability to overcome the problem (Sitharthan & Kavanaugh, 1990). Similarly, one investigation found that smokers who were not confident they could stop smoking were the most likely to fall back into their habit within four weeks after quitting (Shiffman et al., 2000).

Researchers find self-efficacy beliefs can play a role in overcoming a wide variety of psychological problems. These include childhood depression (Bandura, Pastorelli, Babaranelli, & Caprara, 1999), post-traumatic stress disorder (Solomon, Weisenberg, Schwarzwald, & Mikulincer, 1988), test anxiety (Smith, 1989), substance abuse (DiClemente, Fairhurst, & Piotrowski, 1995), phobias (Williams, 1995), and bereavement (Bauer & Bonanno, 2001). Moreover, self-efficacy has been found to mediate behavior change in many other areas of interest to psychologists. Efficacy expectations affect job performance (Stajkovic & Luthans, 1998), academic achievement (Bandura, Barbaranelli, Caprara, & Pastorelli, 1996), and health-related behaviors (Maddux, Brawley, & Boykin, 1995), among others. Clearly, believing that one is capable of making changes and moving forward is an important component for dealing with many of the challenges and problems we face in our lives.

Assessment: Behavior Observation Methods

Let's begin this section by thinking about one of your bad habits. Unless you are quite different from the rest of us, you probably chew your nails, eat junk food, lose your temper, use harsh language, smoke, talk too much, or engage in some other behavior you probably would like to change. Now imagine that you seek out a behavior therapist for help with this problem. The therapist asks you a simple question: How often do you perform the behavior? If you have been keeping track, you may be able to say exactly how many cigarettes you smoke per day or how often you chew your nails each week. But most likely your answer will be far from precise. Behavior therapists can't tell if a treatment program is effective unless they know how often the behavior occurs before treatment. Yet too often clients say they perform the unwanted behavior "every once in a while," "not too often," or "all the time."

Unlike those who practice other approaches to psychotherapy, behavior therapists typically do not spend much time trying to discover the true cause of a client's problem. Instead, they focus on observable behaviors. Other therapists may see the behavior as a sign of some underlying conflict, but for behavior therapists, the behavior *is* the problem. Therefore, objective and reliable assessment of behavior is critical. Behavior therapists use assessment procedures for a variety of purposes. Obviously, they want to determine how often a problem behavior occurs. But they may also want to know about the events surrounding the behavior. Does the client smoke alone or with other people? Do the tantrums occur at a certain time of day or after a certain kind of experience, such as a scolding? These data can be very helpful in designing treatment programs. Therapists probably also want to monitor the therapy's progress and make some judgment about its success. They base this judgment on how often the target behavior occurs before and after the introduction of the treatment.

So how do behavior therapists obtain accurate information about the frequency of target behaviors? When one team of researchers surveyed members of a behavior therapist organization, they found the therapists had developed a variety of procedures (Elliott, Miltenberger, Kaster-Bundgaard, & Lumley, 1996). Some of the most common methods of assessment mentioned by the therapists are shown in Table 13.3. Let's look at a few of these in depth.

Direct Observation

The most obvious way to find out how often a behavior occurs is to observe the person directly. Although a therapist usually can't watch a client all day long, it is often possible to observe a representative sample of the client's behavior. For example, if you wanted to know how much time a girl spends interacting with children her own age, you might watch the child playing on the playground for several recesses. However, the therapist probably is not going to be around when a socially

Table 13.3 Behavior Therapists' Assessment Methods	
Method	**Percentage of Cases Using**
Interview with client	94.1
Direct observation	52.3
Client self-monitoring	44.1
Behavioral rating scales	43.7
Interview with client's significant others	42.0
Information from other professionals	38.0
Role playing	19.4

Source: Adapted from Eliott et al. (1996).

phobic person goes on a job interview or a married couple has an argument. In these cases, the psychologist might rely on *analogue behavioral observation* (Haynes, 2001). That is, the therapist creates a situation that resembles the real-world setting in which the problem behavior is likely to occur. For example, a therapist might stage a dance for clients suffering from acute shyness or ask a couple to enter into a discussion that recently sparked a disagreement. Occasionally therapists ask clients to *role-play.* A therapist helping a man to be more assertive might ask the client to imagine that someone just cut in front of him in line. The client then acts out what he would do in that situation. In this case, the way the client acts in the role-playing exercise is probably similar to the way he acts when confronting such situations in real life.

However, good behavioral assessment requires more than simply observing a person. If the information is to be useful, the therapist should follow certain procedures. The behaviors to be observed must first be defined as precisely as possible. This is fairly simple when talking about the number of cigarettes smoked. But what if the target behavior is "appropriate classroom responses"? In this case, the therapist might define appropriate responses as those relevant to the topic being discussed or those in which the child waits for teacher recognition before speaking. But even these definitions leave considerable room for observer interpretation. A good definition includes examples of behaviors to be counted and rules for dealing with borderline cases.

One way to improve the accuracy of behavior observation is to have two or more observers independently code the same behaviors. For example, two judges can watch the same child during the same set of recesses. If the two are largely in agreement on how often they count the target behavior, they can be confident that the count is fairly accurate. However, if one coder sees few behaviors and a second coder sees many, we have little indication about how often the target behavior actually occurs. One solution may be to videotape the behavior so that many differ-

Psychologists working with children often use direct observation. This procedure allows them to assess how a child plays alone, how parents interact with their child, or how well a child interacts with other children. Many psychologists have also discovered the value of videotaping behavior samples for more extensive observation and coding later.

ent judges can observe the same behavior. Videotapes also allow the therapist to analyze the person's actions more precisely at a later, more convenient time.

Behavior therapists must also be concerned about bias. Although they strive for objective data based on observable events, therapists can unintentionally see what they want or what they expect to see. To guard against this problem, therapists should define behaviors in a manner that minimizes subjective judgment. If possible, they can use observers who don't know what the therapist expects to find.

Self-Monitoring

Although direct observation provides a relatively accurate assessment of behavior frequency, it is often too costly and time-consuming to be useful. An alternative is *self-monitoring*—clients observing themselves. However, simply asking clients how often they engage in a certain act may be of little help. Clients often have a distorted idea about how often a behavior occurs. In addition, it is usually important to understand the circumstances surrounding the behavior. Are there places the client is particularly likely to smoke, such as in a restaurant or at a party? Is the smoking associated with a certain time of day, a certain type of activity, or a certain mood? With accurate information, a therapist can develop a treatment that includes, for example, not going to cocktail lounges where everyone seems to be smoking or an alternative activity when the client feels stressed at work.

Unfortunately, few clients can provide accurate information about these variables from memory. Therefore, therapists often ask clients to observe and record their behaviors for a period of time. Clients are sometimes surprised by what they find. For example, people trying to watch their weight may not have realized that they eat more when they're alone, when watching television, or after they've had a drink. An interesting benefit of the self-monitoring method is that watching your own behavior can be therapeutic in itself. For example, clients forced to pay attention to their eating or smoking sometimes show improvement during the first few weeks of the process, before the treatment has even begun (Mahoney & Arnkoff, 1979). Naturally, self-monitoring is also used to assess progress throughout the treatment period to determine the success of the therapy. One problem that sometimes surfaces is the client's honesty. Clients may not want to admit to their therapists that they increased their smoking or lost their temper several times in one week. Therapists who suspect a problem may want to use other assessment methods, such as the one discussed next.

Observation by Others

Some clients are unwilling or just unable to provide accurate information about themselves. For example, self-monitoring is probably inappropriate with children or those with severe psychological disorders. In these cases, it may be possible to rely on other people to make the observations. For example, parents and teachers can often record the frequency of a child's problem behaviors. It is best if these people actually observe for a period of time rather than rely on their memories. Thus, a teacher might be asked to record each time she punishes a child for inappropriate classroom behavior. Therapists in mental health settings can ask nurses and aides to record the occurrence of patients' behaviors. Although this process can introduce bias, it provides the most accurate assessment of a client's behavior in some situations.

Many psychologists use these reports to complement data obtained through other methods. For example, children sometimes act differently in the presence of a therapist than they do at home. A client may be able to role-play the appropriate behaviors when confronting a make-believe belligerent boss but may become timid when facing the real boss at work. Getting family members involved in the process can have other advantages, such as making them aware of the client's problem and how their reactions might affect his or her behavior.

Strengths and Criticisms of the Behavioral/Social Learning Approach

Behaviorism roared onto the psychology scene in the 1920s and put a grip on the discipline that didn't loosen for several decades. Although not as influential as it once was, behaviorism in various forms remains alive and well today. Explanations of behavior that evolved from behaviorism, such as social-cognitive theory, remain popular today. Obviously, the behavioral/social learning approach to personality could not have withstood this test of time without some unique strengths. Of course, no theory as influential as this can hope to escape criticism, either.

Assessing Your Own Personality

Assertiveness

Indicate how characteristic or descriptive each of the following statements is of you by using this code: +3 = very characteristic; +2 = rather characteristic; +1 = somewhat characteristic; −1 = somewhat uncharacteristic; −2 = rather uncharacteristic; −3 = very uncharacteristic.

_____ 1. Most people seem to be more aggressive and assertive than I am.*

_____ 2. I have hesitated to make or accept dates because of "shyness."*

_____ 3. When the food served at a restaurant is not done to my satisfaction, I complain about it to the waiter or waitress.

_____ 4. I am careful to avoid hurting other people's feelings, even when I feel that I have been injured.*

_____ 5. If a salesman has gone to considerable trouble to show me merchandise that is not quite suitable, I have a difficult time saying "No."*

_____ 6. When I am asked to do something, I insist upon knowing why.

_____ 7. There are times when I look for a good, vigorous argument.

_____ 8. I strive to get ahead as well as most people in my position.

_____ 9. To be honest, people often take advantage of me.*

_____ 10. I enjoy starting conversations with new acquaintances and strangers.

_____ 11. I often don't know what to say to attractive persons of the opposite sex.*

_____ 12. I will hesitate to make phone calls to business establishments and institutions.*

_____ 13. I would rather apply for a job or for admission to a college by writing letters than by going through with personal interviews.*

_____ 14. I find it embarrassing to return merchandise.*

_____ 15. If a close and respected relative were annoying me, I would smother my feelings rather than express my annoyance.*

_____ 16. I have avoided asking questions for fear of sounding stupid.*

_____ 17. During an argument I am sometimes afraid that I will get so upset that I will shake all over.*

Strengths

One reason for the endurance of the behavioral/social learning approach is its solid foundation in empirical research. This contrasts with other approaches to personality, which are sometimes based on intuition or data gathered from biased samples. Most of the theorists covered in this chapter based their descriptions of

_____ 18. If a famed and respected lecturer makes a statement that I think is incorrect, I will have the audience hear my point of view as well.

_____ 19. I avoid arguing over prices with clerks and salesmen.*

_____ 20. When I have done something important or worthwhile, I manage to let others know about it.

_____ 21. I am open and frank about my feelings.

_____ 22. If someone has been spreading false and bad stories about me, I see him or her as soon as possible to "have a talk" about it.

_____ 23. I often have a hard time saying "No."*

_____ 24. I tend to bottle up my emotions rather than make a scene.*

_____ 25. I complain about poor service in a restaurant and elsewhere.

_____ 26. When I am given a compliment, I sometimes just don't know what to say.*

_____ 27. If a couple near me in a theater or at a lecture were conversing rather loudly, I would ask them to be quiet or take their conversation elsewhere.

_____ 28. Anyone attempting to push ahead of me in a line is in for a good battle.

_____ 29. I am quick to express an opinion.

_____ 30. There are times when I just can't say anything.*

Many people have difficulty asserting their rights. In behavioral terms, these people need to increase the frequency of their assertive behaviors in appropriate situations. A behavior modification treatment called *assertiveness training* allows participants to watch models asserting themselves appropriately, role-play their own assertive responses, and receive immediate reinforcement for appropriate assertive actions. To obtain your assertiveness score, first reverse the sign for your answer on each of the items with an asterisk (that is, a plus becomes a minus, and vice versa). Then add all 30 answer values together. A positive score indicates high assertiveness; a negative score reflects low assertiveness. The average score is around 8 for college women and 10 for college men (Nevid & Spencer, 1978). Two-thirds of all college females score between 31 and −17, and two-thirds of college males have scores that fall between 33 and −11.

Scale: *Rathus Assertiveness Inventory*

Source: Rathus (1973)

human personality on empirical research findings and relied on empirical data in the development and refinement of their theories. Critics often challenge the existence of Freud's Oedipus complex, but it would be difficult to deny that behaviors sometimes change through operant and classical conditioning.

Another strength of the behavioral/social learning approach lies in the development of some useful therapeutic procedures. Behavior modification procedures have several advantages over other therapy approaches. One advantage is their use of baseline data and objective criteria for determining success or failure. Other approaches often begin treatment without first determining the level of the problem; the therapy is declared a success when the therapist or the client decides there has been some improvement. In addition, behavior modification may be the most useful approach when working with certain populations, such as children or severely emotionally disturbed patients. These people might have a difficult time discussing abstract psychoanalytic concepts or dealing with some of the existential questions posed by humanistic therapists. Behavior modification is also relatively quick and easy to administer. Treatment often lasts a matter of weeks, compared with months or years with other approaches. The basic methods can be taught to parents, teachers, and hospital personnel, who can carry out the therapy without the therapist present. This means that more people can benefit from therapy procedures at a lower cost than is possible with most other types of psychotherapy.

The social learning theories and Bandura's social-cognitive theory added cognitive variables to the behavioral approach and thereby expanded the range of phenomena explained by this perspective. These theories have helped to fill in the gaps many psychologists see in traditional behaviorism. Social learning models of personality allow us to understand thoughts, expectancies, and values along with basic behavior conditioning principles within one consistent framework. In addition, the introduction of these cognitive elements has helped to link behavioral personality theory with some of the more recent cognitive approaches to personality. These approaches, covered in Chapter 15, have been strongly influenced by the work of the social learning theorists.

Criticisms

A persistent criticism of the behavioral/social learning approach is that it is too narrow in its description of human personality. Many psychologists feel that, although the approach touches on several crucial aspects of human experience such as thinking, emotion, and levels of consciousness, it does so in a limited way. Critics are particularly concerned with the Skinnerian brand of behaviorism, which rejects the usefulness of examining inner feelings and intuition. Others criticize the behavioral/social learning approach for giving inadequate attention to the role of heredity. In addition, research points to limits on how easily certain behaviors can be conditioned. For example, it is more difficult to create a fear of food in animals by pairing the food with electric shocks than it is to create an avoidance of the food by pairing it with nausea (Garcia & Koelling, 1966; Seligman & Hager, 1972). Thus, behaviorists may need to recognize the limits of the conditioning principles they promote.

Another criticism, directed primarily at traditional behaviorism, is that human beings are more complex than the laboratory animals used in behavioral research. Critics challenge the way behaviorists use laboratory rat data to explain human behavior. As Bandura and some of the social learning theorists recognize, people are capable of considering alternative courses of action, of weighing the probabilities and values of different reinforcers, of looking at long-term goals, and so forth. These critics do not deny that we often respond to stimuli in an automatic fashion or that some of our behaviors are conditioned. But they maintain that these are the least important and least interesting human behaviors. An example of the difficulty in generalizing from animal data to human behavior is seen in research on the effects of extrinsic reinforcers on intrinsically motivated behavior. Although this remains an area of controversy (Eisenberger & Cameron, 1996; Sansone & Harackiewicz, 1998), researchers often find that paying people to engage in a behavior they already enjoy results in a reduction in the frequency of the behavior. People seem to redefine the behavior as work instead of play ("I play the piano because I am paid") and therefore lose interest unless rewarded.

Despite the success of behavior therapists in dealing with many problem behaviors, some critics argue that too often these therapists distort the real therapy issues when they reduce everything to observable behaviors. For example, a client who complains that he has no meaning in his life might be asked to define this abstract issue in terms of measurable behaviors. A behavior therapist might count the number of times the person engages in pleasant activities and set up a treatment program that rewards the client for going to parties, talking with friends, reading good books, and so on. These activities might make the person feel better. However, critics might argue that the therapy has not addressed the client's real problem, but instead has temporarily diverted his attention from his concern for finding meaning in life.

 *Summary*

1. Behaviorism was introduced by John B. Watson in the 1920s. In its most extreme form, behaviorism limits psychology to the study of observable behaviors. Classical conditioning and operant conditioning are used by behaviorists to explain the development and maintenance of behaviors. Personality is described as the end result of one's history of conditioning. B. F. Skinner later became the spokesperson for what he called radical behaviorism. He rejected the use of inner states, such as anxiety, as explanations of behavior in favor of observable external events.

2. Traditional behaviorism identifies two basic kinds of conditioning. Classical conditioning occurs when a new stimulus is paired with an existing stimulus-response bond. Operant conditioning results when a behavior is followed by either reinforcement or punishment.

3.   Later social learning theorists expanded on the basic behaviorist position. Rotter argues that the probability of engaging in a behavior changes after rewards and punishments because our expectancies change. He uses these expectancies and the values given to particular reinforcers to predict which of many behavior options will be enacted.

4.   Bandura proposes that internal states, the environment, and behavior all affect one another. He maintains that people often regulate their own behavior and that we engage in purposeful, future-oriented thinking. Bandura has added to classical and operant conditioning the notion that we learn through observing others, although whether we perform the behaviors we learn depends on our expectancies for rewards or punishments.

5.   Behavior modification therapists apply basic conditioning principles when dealing with their clients. Some of these, such as systematic desensitization, are based on classical conditioning. Others, such as token economies, are based on operant conditioning. Bandura has identified clients' self-efficacy beliefs as crucial in the psychotherapy progress. Whether clients expect to succeed is an important determinant of therapy success. These expectancies come from a variety of sources, including past performance accomplishments and vicarious learning.

6.   Behavioral assessment includes a variety of techniques, including direct observation, self-monitoring, and observation by others. Each of these techniques can provide useful data for determining baseline frequencies, the conditions under which the target behavior occurs, and the success of the treatment procedure.

7.   The behavioral/social learning approach has its strengths and its criticisms. Among the strengths are its empirical base and the useful therapeutic procedures it has generated. The criticisms include the inappropriate attention given to heredity. People have also criticized the way behavior therapists interpret problems into observable behaviors.

InfoTrac College Edition Key Terms

For additional readings go to http://www.infotrac-college.com/wadsworth and enter a search term related to your interest. Use the key terms suggested here to pull up several related articles. Also see the text Web site at http://psychology.wadsworth.com for more suggested readings and interactive quizzes to test your knowledge.

Aversion therapy   Operant conditioning
Biofeedback   Reinforcement
Classical conditioning   Role playing
Observational learning   Self-efficacy

Chapter 14

The Behavioral/Social Learning Approach

Relevant Research

Individual Differences in Gender-Role Behavior
Observational Learning of Aggression
Learned Helplessness
Locus of Control
Summary

Research psychologists are sometimes portrayed as aloof, data-oriented scientists more concerned with how many times a rat presses a bar than with the people in their lives. Although it's true these researchers often attend to minute experimental details and precise theoretical issues that seem overly esoteric to an outside observer, it is unfair to say they have lost sight of the human element or their goal of improving the human condition. Even B. F. Skinner, who conducted most of his research on rats, wrote extensively on how we can use the information coming out of animal laboratories to overcome many of the problems facing society today. This concern for application can be seen in each of the four research topics reviewed in this chapter. Each has something to say about pressing social problems or personal lifestyle issues.

First, many men and women today are concerned about how gender roles shape and restrict their behavior. In increasing numbers, women are abandoning traditional gender roles to take important positions in business and government. Some men are experimenting with nontraditional male roles, such assuming child-rearing responsibilities. But understanding why we make some of the gender-related choices we do requires an examination of how operant conditioning and observational learning shape those choices. We'll look at these processes and at how individual differences in masculinity and femininity are related to psychological adjustment and the way we interact with others.

Second, in response to the ever-present issue of violence in our society, many psychologists have focused their attention on the impact aggressive models have on aggressive behavior. Bandura's observational learning model helps explain some of this process. We'll look at relevant research and the question of how mass media violence affects the behavior of those who consume it.

Third, applying animal research findings to human beings is a standard feature of the behavioral approach to personality. A particularly fruitful example of this application is the work on learned helplessness. From some surprising observations of dogs in a classical conditioning experiment, researchers have developed a theory with implications for depression and adjustment among the elderly.

Fourth, we'll look at one aspect of Rotter's social learning theory. Individual differences in locus of control have been the focus of an enormous amount of personality research. Some of these findings provide important information about how our expectancies are related to our well-being and health.

Individual Differences in Gender-Role Behavior

I would like to describe two friends of mine. The first is a very caring and loving person. This friend never forgets my birthday, is sensitive to my needs and moods, and is the person I seek first when I need someone to talk to. This friend also confides in me and is not afraid to share intimate feelings. My other friend is on the way to becoming a leader in the business world. This friend knows how to be assertive when necessary, how to express opinions directly, and how to get others to do what is needed for the company. Unlike the first person I described, this one sometimes has difficulty being intimate with others or sharing feelings. I've never seen this friend cry.

Unless you've already caught on to my point here, you probably imagined that the first person is a woman and the second is a man, even though I never identified the gender of either. This doesn't mean you're gullible or sexist, but rather that you are aware of the gender-role stereotypes that affect the way men and women behave in this culture. Traditional stereotypes portray men as aggressive, independent, and unemotional, and women as passive, dependent, and affectionate. Much has been written recently about changes in these gender roles, with men being told it is all right to show emotion and women being encouraged to be assertive and businesslike. However, although some gender restrictions may have loosened in the past few decades, gender roles remain a part of our culture and, although different in each case, probably a part of every culture (Williams & Best, 1982).

Most little girls occasionally play "dress up." Girls put on their mother's clothes, jewelry, and makeup after identifying that this is something females, but not males, do. We would not expect to find little boys imitating this behavior.

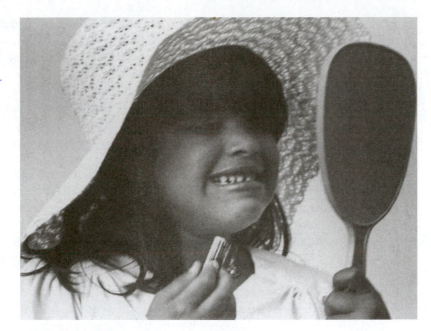

Why do women tend to behave in certain ways and men in others? Although biological differences between the sexes play some role, behaviorists and social learning theorists point to a lifelong process of gender-role socialization. Children and adults acquire and maintain gender-appropriate behaviors largely through operant conditioning and observational learning. You can see the effects of operant conditioning whenever young children act in gender-inappropriate ways. For example, boys often tease one another for crying, playing with dolls, or showing an interest in cooking or sewing. Similarly, playmates make fun of girls when they act like tomboys. At the same time, boys are rewarded with camaraderie and parental nods for playing football and standing up to those who try to push them around. And girls win approval for showing an interest in caring for babies and for acting sweet and cute. This pattern of rewards and punishments soon shapes the amount of time children spend engaging in traditionally masculine and feminine behaviors.

You can appreciate the difficulty in changing these behavior patterns when you realize how early this operant conditioning starts. Consider what one team of researchers found when interviewing parents of sons and daughters within 24 hours after the birth of their first child (Rubin, Provenzano, & Luria, 1974). Parents rated daughters as softer, finer featured, smaller, and less attentive than sons. In addition, parents of daughters described their child as beautiful, pretty, or cute, and often said the child resembled the mother. In reality, the newborns did not differ in terms of weight, length, or measures of general health. Another group of experimenters looked at the toys and clothing of boys and girls from ages 5 months to 25 months (Pomerleau, Bolduc, Malcuit, & Cossette, 1990). The researchers found that the girls were more likely to have dolls and toy furniture. The boys were more likely to have sports equipment, toy tools, and toy cars and trucks. Perhaps not surprisingly, the girls were more likely to have pink clothing, and the boys blue. Clearly, boys and girls are treated differently beginning at a very early age.

Within a few years, impressions of what is appropriate for boys and girls are communicated to the child. By the time children enter kindergarten, they are well aware of gender-role expectations (O'Brien et al., 2000; Vogel, Lake, Evans, & Karraker, 1991). Preschool boys and girls in one study were given a choice between traditional "boy" toys (tools) and "girl" toys (dishes) during a free-play period (Raag & Rackliff, 1998). Not only did the children typically select the toys traditionally associated with their gender, but most of the boys also explained that their fathers would not approve of them playing with the girls' toys. Because parents and peers share these same expectancies, preschool children are surrounded by people ready to reward gender-appropriate behaviors and punish inappropriate ones.

Gender-role behaviors are also acquired through observational learning. There is certainly no shortage of models exhibiting gender-appropriate behaviors. Children have the opportunity to learn which behaviors are expected of men and which are expected of women by watching parents, neighbors, siblings, playmates, and television characters. When children are very young, parents are probably the most influential models, which may explain why people's gender-role behavior tends to resemble that of their mother or father (Jackson, Ialongo, & Stollak, 1986). Later, children are more likely to take their cues about appropriate and inappropriate behavior from their friends.

This finding does not mean, however, that boys imitate only male models and girls only female models. Instead, the child must first notice that a certain behavior is performed more often by one gender than the other (Bussey & Bandura, 1984; Perry & Bussey, 1979). Boys and girls may notice that men, but rarely women, work on mechanical things. When an appliance needs fixing, father is the one to do it. All the garage mechanics seem to be men, and if someone on television uses a screwdriver or a wrench, it is almost always a male. Children are likely to conclude that men are rewarded for mechanical behavior but women are not. Thus, boys are more likely to get involved with mechanical things, anticipating rewards, whereas girls tend to seek out other activities. At this point, operant conditioning may also come into play, such as when a father rewards his son for showing an interest in cars and laughing when his daughter asks to help with an oil change.

Masculinity-Femininity

After a lifetime of socialization through operant conditioning and observational learning, we should not be surprised that most adult men and women act in gender-appropriate ways. But even a casual observation of the people you meet in the next few hours will confirm there are large individual differences in the extent to which people act in a masculine or feminine manner. Although men are gener-

Figure 14.1

Traditional Masculinity-Femininity Model

ally more aggressive and independent than women, there are many exceptions. Similarly, finding women who do not fit the stereotypic affectionate, emotional, and sensitive pattern is not difficult.

As with other individual differences, personality psychologists are interested in identifying, measuring, and describing the way people differ in terms of their masculinity and femininity. Early scales developed to measure the masculinity-femininity construct were based on two assumptions. First, masculinity and femininity were assumed to represent two extreme positions on a continuum of gender-role behavior. As shown in Figure 14.1, masculinity and femininity were considered opposites. The more a person was of one, the less he or she was of the other. Each of us can be placed on this continuum, with very masculine and very feminine people on the extremes and those who are both, but not much of either, toward the middle.

The second assumption was that the more people's gender-role behavior matched the stereotype for their gender, the more psychologically healthy they were. Masculine men and feminine women were considered well adjusted. But a man who acted too much the way society said a woman was supposed to act or a woman who acted too much like a stereotypic man were said to have adjustment problems. One of the original scales on the Minnesota Multiphasic Personality Inventory (MMPI) is the Mf (Masculinity-Femininity) Scale. Researchers originally maintained that scoring too high or too low for one's gender on this scale was indicative of psychological disturbances.

Androgyny

Researchers soon uncovered several problems with the masculinity-femininity model (Constantinople, 1973). In response, psychologists developed a new approach for measuring and identifying gender-role behaviors called the **androgyny** model (Bem, 1974, 1976, 1977). Coupled with society's rising concern for women's issues during these years, the androgyny model stimulated an immense amount of interest in gender-role research and an accompanying degree of disagreement and controversy. The model begins by rejecting the notion that masculinity and femininity are opposites on a single continuum. Instead, masculinity and femininity are seen as independent traits. People can be high on both traits, on only one trait, or on neither. Further, because these traits are independent, knowing that someone is high in masculinity tells us nothing about how feminine that person is.

The androgyny model also challenges the assumption that the most well-adjusted people are those whose gender matches their sex-type. Instead, the new model maintains that the most well-adjusted person is one who is both masculine and feminine, that is, *androgynous*. According to this perspective, people who are only masculine or only feminine often lack the ability to engage in adaptive behavior. For example, masculine people do well as long as the situation calls for a masculine response, such as asserting one's rights or taking over the leadership of a group. But when masculine people are called on to act in a traditionally feminine manner, such as showing compassion or sensitivity, they falter. A well-adjusted person must have the flexibility to engage in masculine behaviors when the situation demands, as well as feminine behaviors when those are the most appropriate.

Gender-Role Research

The androgyny model helped to renew interest in gender-role research. The number of investigations on individual differences in masculinity and femininity ballooned during subsequent decades. Scales were developed to measure the traits of masculinity and femininity separately (Bem, 1974; Lenney, 1991; Spence, Helmreich, & Stapp, 1974). Although some changes in gender-role expectations have occurred since the development of these inventories, recent studies suggest the scales are still valid measures of masculinity and femininity (Holt & Ellis, 1998; Twenge, 1997).

Some psychologists have argued that we should replace *masculinity* and *femininity* with more specific and less emotionally loaded labels. In particular, many researchers prefer the terms *agency* and *communion* (Helgeson, 1994; Spence, 1993). Agency refers to independence, assertiveness, and control, and is roughly similar to masculinity. Communion refers to attachment, cooperation, and interpersonal connection, and is similar to femininity. Nonetheless, because most researchers continue to rely on the masculinity and femininity labels, we will also use these terms.

Today, most gender-role inventories allow researchers to classify test takers as high or low on both a masculinity scale and a femininity scale. By using the median score as a cutoff point on each scale, researchers can place people into one of four sex-type categories, as shown in Figure 14.2. Those who score high in both masculinity and femininity are classified as *androgynous*. Those scoring high on one scale but not the other fall into either the *masculine* or *feminine* category. Those who score low on both scales are classified as *undifferentiated*.

Which of the four categories people fall into has been tied to a large number of relevant behaviors. Two of these behaviors will be briefly reviewed next. We begin by examining the issue responsible for instigating the androgyny model in the first place: the relationship between individual differences in gender-role behavior

Figure 14.2

Androgyny Model

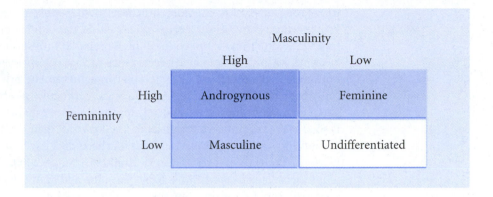

and psychological adjustment. Then we look at research concerned with how your gender-type affects the quality of your personal relationships.

Gender-Type and Psychological Adjustment. How does your gender-type affect psychological adjustment and well-being? Despite numerous investigations into this question, no clear answer has emerged. Instead, there are at least three logical answers to how being masculine, feminine, or androgynous relates to personal adjustment.

The first, and probably least supported, description is the traditional *congruence model.* According to this model, masculine men and feminine women are the most well adjusted. Although this approach reflects old-fashioned attitudes and may even border on sexism, a case can be made. Think about all the pressure society puts on men and women to act in gender-appropriate ways. What can we conclude about people who emerge from this socialization without developing the gender-type dictated by society? Perhaps they are merely liberated from the restraints society places on most of us. But remember that the rewards and punishments for gender-appropriate behavior begin in childhood and continue throughout adult life. For example, one study looked at the long-term adjustment of 12-year-old boys who tended to act in feminine ways (Aube & Koestner, 1992). These boys had more adjustment problems than other men when they became adults. Masculine women and feminine men probably face continual social rejection and ridicule, albeit more subtle than that imposed in the school playground. Society is geared to give masculine men and feminine women most of the rewards in life. Thus, we might expect these people to be the happiest and most content.

Although this reasoning makes some sense, reviews of relevant research rarely find support for the congruence model (Taylor & Hall, 1982; Whitley, 1983). Masculine men and feminine women are not the most well adjusted. There may have been a time many years ago when this was the case, but we can probably safely conclude that those days are past.

The second explanation is based on the *androgyny model.* According to this view, androgynous people are the most well adjusted because they have the ability to respond effectively in more situations than people in the other categories. People whose behavioral repertoires lack either masculine or feminine behaviors find many situations in which they are ill prepared to respond appropriately. For example, without masculine characteristics such as decisiveness and assertiveness, both men and women are likely to falter in achievement situations. At the same time, people unable to express emotions have difficulty establishing good interpersonal relationships. Only androgynous people are capable of getting ahead on the job while relating well with friends and lovers in their leisure time.

Several investigations find support for the androgyny model (Bem, 1975; Bem & Lenney, 1976; Bem, Martyna, & Watson, 1976; Stake, 2000; Shaw, 1982). For example, when confronted with a baby, feminine and androgynous—but not masculine—people show appropriate nurturant behavior. Also, feminine people are easily swayed by the opinions of others, whereas masculine and androgynous people better resist conformity pressures.

However, overall support for the androgyny model is mixed. Whereas many studies show the superior adaptability of androgynous people, others do not (Taylor & Hall, 1982; Worell, 1978). In particular, although androgynous people may be well prepared to deal with many different situations, this often does not translate into a sense of well-being or high self-esteem.

A third approach, the *masculinity model,* maintains that being masculine is the key to mental health. Before rejecting this view as masculine propaganda, consider that in many ways our society is still geared toward admiring and rewarding the traits traditionally associated with men and masculinity. Stereotypically, men are independent, and women are dependent. Men are achieving and powerful; women are unassertive and conforming. Men are leaders, whereas women are followers. Given these descriptions, it makes sense that those who fit the masculine role might accomplish more and feel better about themselves than those who do not. Women do not have to abandon their femininity to get ahead in the traditionally male business world. But they may need some traditionally masculine attributes to be successful.

Several investigations find support for the masculinity model (Cheng, 1999; Marsh, Antill, & Cunningham, 1987; O'Heron & Orlofsky, 1990; Orlofsky & O'Heron, 1987; Roos & Cohen, 1987). For example, because masculine people are more likely to use direct, problem-focused strategies for dealing with stress, they seem better able to deal with stressors than do people low in masculinity. Masculine prostate cancer patients in one study adjusted better to their situation and had fewer cancer-related difficulties than those low in masculinity (Helgeson & Lepore, 1997). Masculine widowed men in another study coped better with the loss of their spouse and subsequent changes in their lives than widowers in any of the other gender-role categories (Bowers, 1999). Masculine women are good at influencing others and getting what they want, thus avoiding feelings of helplessness and depression (Sayers, Baucom, & Tierney, 1993). Support for the masculinity model is particularly consistent when looking at the relationship between gender-type and self-esteem (Whitley, 1983). People who possess traditionally masculine attributes (such as achieving, athletic, powerful) also feel good about themselves.

So what are we to make of all this? Although the picture is far from clear, a few conclusions seem appropriate. First, very little research supports the congruence model. Second, some of the inconsistent findings may reflect the way masculinity and femininity are measured. For example, the most widely used measure in this research, the Bem Sex Role Inventory, asks people the extent to which 20 masculine and 20 feminine items describe them. Unfortunately, the masculine items in the scale tend to be more desirable than the feminine items (Pedhazur & Tetenbaum, 1979). It makes sense that people who describe themselves with the more flattering and positive masculine items (for example, self-reliant, ambitious) have higher self-esteem than those who describe themselves with the feminine items (for example, gullible, shy). Third, it seems quite possible that some aspects of a healthy personality, such as dealing with stress and personal achievement, are related to masculinity, whereas other aspects, such as developing good interpersonal relationships, are not (Marsh & Byrne, 1991). Individual differences in gender-role behavior are clearly tied to well-being in some way. However, just how these two are related remains the fuel for continued research.

Gender-Type and Interpersonal Relations. Who would you turn to if you needed to talk to someone about a personal problem—a masculine, feminine, androgynous, or undifferentiated person? Who would you prefer for a friend? For a romantic partner? Advertisements and TV shows often portray masculine men and feminine women as the most desirable partners for romantic encounters. Americans spend a considerable amount of money on makeup, body-building equipment, and the like to make themselves appear more feminine or masculine. But is this the road to a perfect relationship? Some research suggests it may not be.

A simple way to examine how people react to different gender types is to ask participants about hypothetical character sketches of masculine, feminine, androgynous, and undifferentiated individuals. In general, researchers using this procedure find the androgynous character is liked more than the other three (Brooks-Gunn & Fisch, 1980; Gilbert, Deutsch, & Strahan, 1978; Jackson, 1983; Korabik, 1982; Kulick & Harackiewicz, 1979; Slavkin & Stright, 2000). For example, college students in one study said the androgynous person was more popular, more interesting, better adjusted, more competent, more intelligent, and more successful than people described in masculine, feminine, or undifferentiated terms (Major, Carnevale, & Deaux, 1981). Moreover, when researchers asked college students to estimate the desirability of various hypothetical people as romantic partners, both the men and the women showed a preference for the androgynous person (Green & Kenrick, 1994). Thus, in terms of first impressions, androgynous people come across quite well.

But do these impressions of hypothetical people translate into actual behaviors? To examine this question, one team of researchers created four types of male-female pairs: a masculine man and a feminine woman, an androgynous woman

Figure 14.3

Mean Liking Rating
Between Couples
During Five-Minute
Interaction

Source: From Ickes and
Barnes (1978).

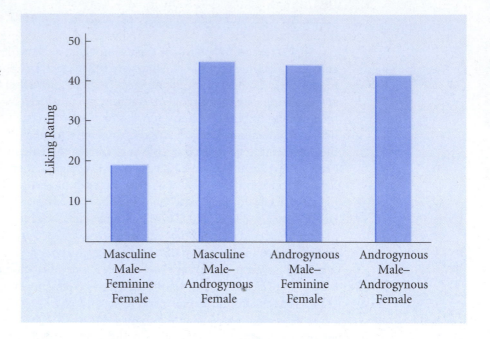

and a masculine man, a feminine woman and an androgynous man, and two androgynous people (Ickes & Barnes, 1978). The couples who did not know each other before the study were left alone in a room for five minutes. The participants were free to carry on a conversation or simply sit quietly and wait.

The participants' behavior was recorded with a hidden video camera for later evaluation. When the experimenter returned, participants were asked to rate how much they had enjoyed the interaction. As shown in Figure 14.3, members of the masculine man-feminine woman dyads enjoyed their interactions the least. Analyses of the videotapes revealed that these couples talked to each other less, looked at each other less, used fewer expressive gestures, and smiled and laughed less than the people in the other combinations.

These results argue against the masculine man-feminine woman combination as the ideal couple. When we examine the different ways masculine and feminine people approach an interpersonal encounter, some of the reasons for this become clear. The masculine style emphasizes control, self-monitoring, and self-restraint, whereas feminine people look for an active expression of feelings and warmth in their interactions. Little wonder, then, that this combination didn't work out well in this or other experiments (Ickes, 1993; Ickes, Schermer, & Steeno, 1979; Lamke & Bell, 1982).

But what about long-term relationships? After the initial awkwardness, it's possible a masculine man and a feminine woman will get along well once they get to know one another. However, this notion is also not supported by the evidence. One study examined combinations of gender-types among married couples and how happy the couples were with their marriages (Antill, 1983). The findings suggest that happiness comes from marrying a partner with feminine characteristics. That is, when a participant's spouse was either feminine or androgynous, that person was satisfied with the relationship. Being married to a partner who lacks feminine characteristics (masculine or undifferentiated) was indicative of an unhappy marriage. Another study not only found this pattern among married couples but discovered that it also held in relationships among cohabiting heterosexuals, gay couples, and lesbian couples (Kurdek & Schmitt, 1986).

What is it that makes feminine and androgynous people preferable partners? Research suggests at least three reasons. First, look at the characteristics that make up the feminine trait. People scoring high on this scale are affectionate, compassionate, and sensitive to others' needs. Feminine people are better able to express their feelings and understand the feelings of others. It only makes sense that we turn to them when we want to talk. Second, androgynous people are more aware of and better able to express romantic feelings (Coleman & Ganong, 1985). This is because they have both the sensitivity and the understanding needed for intimacy, as well as the assertiveness and willingness to take the risk needed to make things happen. People married to someone who is high in both expressiveness as well as sensitivity report the highest level of satisfaction with their relationships (Bradbury, Campbell, & Fincham, 1995; Zammichieli, Gilroy, & Sherman, 1988). Consequently, androgynous people may make the best romantic partners. Third, because they communicate well, feminine and androgynous people are better able to resolve problems and avoid unnecessary disputes (Voelz, 1985). These people are more sensitive to their partners' feelings and needs, are better able to express their own feelings, and are thus more likely to live harmoniously than people who lack these qualities (Aube, Norcliffe, Craig, & Koestner, 1995).

Looking back on nearly three decades of research, what can we say about masculinity and femininity? In particular, is it better to be masculine, feminine, or both? At this point, there is ample evidence that masculinity is related to measures of well-being, such as self-esteem, whereas femininity is related to indices of relationship satisfaction (Helgeson, 1994). Clearly, both personal well-being and social relationships are important parts of our lives. It may be that people who fall short in either domain will find their lives less satisfying. Some researchers refer to this lack of either set of skills as *unmitigated agency* or *unmitigated communion* (Helgeson, 1994). Consistent with research on masculinity and femininity, investigators find that people who lack either independence and assertiveness (agency) or attachment and cooperation (communion) characteristics are vulnerable to a host of adjustment and personal problems (Helgeson & Fritz, 1999, 2000; Saragovi, Koestner, Di Dio, & Aube, 1997). What is clear is that the androgyny model has stimulated a great deal of research that has furthered our understanding of individual differences in gender-role behavior.

Observational Learning of Aggression

In December 1997, a 14-year-old boy entered his Kentucky high school carrying five guns. The boy opened fire on classmates who had gathered for a prayer meeting. Three students were killed. Later the boy said he was acting out a scene from a movie called *The Basketball Diaries.* In July 1991, the motion picture *Boyz 'n the Hood* began showing at theaters around the country. Although calm was the norm at most of the theaters, many became the setting for real-life violence, including several shootings. Thirty-five people were reported wounded or injured the first night the movie was shown. A man in Chicago was killed. In May 1981, John Hinckley tried to assassinate President Ronald Reagan. Investigators soon discovered that Hinckley had viewed the motion picture *Taxi Driver* several times before the shooting. The film portrays the life of a man who falls in love with a young prostitute, played by Jodie Foster, and who later attempts to shoot a presidential candidate. The subsequent investigation uncovered that Hinckley also had a strong attraction to Jodie Foster.

These tragic incidents are examples of one of the most widely researched aspects of Bandura's social-cognitive theory, the relationship between modeled aggression and performance of aggression. Research in this area not only demonstrates how people often learn behaviors through observing models, but also raises some important questions about the portrayal of aggression in the mass media.

Bandura's Four-Step Model

As you will see, decades of research demonstrate that people exposed to aggressive models sometimes imitate the aggressive behavior. But before reviewing some of that research, an observation is in order. Anyone who watches television or goes to an occasional movie (which is just about all of us) undoubtedly has seen some murders, beatings, shootings, and the like. Yet rarely do we step away from our TV set or leave the theater in search of victims. Obviously, simple exposure to an aggressive model is not enough to turn us into violent people. Why, then, do people sometimes imitate aggression when most of the time they do not?

Bandura (1973, 1986) has an answer to this question. He explains that observational learning and performance consist of four interrelated processes. People must go through each of these steps before exposure to aggression leads them to act aggressively. They must *attend* to the aggressive action, *remember* the information, *enact* what they have seen, and *expect* that rewards will be forthcoming. Fortunately, most of the time circumstances prevent people from moving through the entire process. Unfortunately, sometimes they do. Let's look at each of the four steps in the process more closely.

For observational learning to take place, people must first *attend* to the significant features of the model's behavior. We can sit in front of violent TV programs all day long, but the aggressive models will have little or no impact unless we

Research indicates that children learn aggression by imitating aggressive models. Rehearsing aggression, as when children play with toy guns, is one step in this process.

pay attention to them. Children who watch a lot of television have probably seen so many TV characters punched in the face or shot that only the most graphic and spectacular action grabs their attention. Children in one study imitated aggressive models only when the acts were carried out quite vigorously (Parton & Geshuri, 1971). Less intense action apparently failed to hold the children's attention. A viewer's mental state can also make him or her more attentive to the aggression. Frustrated children in one study were more likely to attend to an aggressive model (Parker & Rogers, 1981). The frustration seemed to make them more receptive to images of attacking whoever got in their way (recall the connection between frustration and aggression described in Chapter 6).

But attending to an aggressive act is only the first step in the observational learning process. People must also *remember* information about the model's behavior. You are unlikely to recall any one aggressive behavior you saw on television a few weeks ago unless the behavior was quite gripping. And if you can't recall the action, you are not likely to imitate the model. Unfortunately, although most aggressive acts we witness soon fade from our memories, not all do. Practice and mental rehearsal can keep the action fresh in our minds. For example, children who play with toy guns and plastic combat equipment may embed the actions of their aggressive heroes permanently into their memories.

The importance of selective recall was demonstrated in a study with first- and second-grade children (Slife & Rychlak, 1982). The researchers asked the children how much they liked each of the aggressive acts they saw on a videotape. They also determined which toys used by the aggressive model each child liked. Then, as in Bandura's classic study, the children were watched for five minutes while they

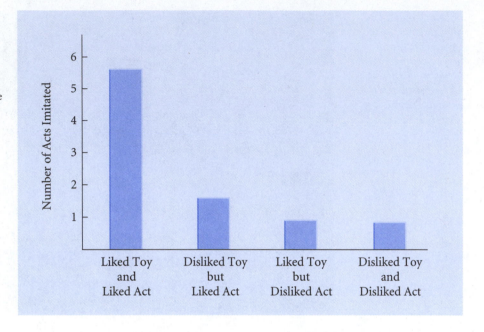

Figure 14.4

Mean Number of Aggressive Acts Imitated

Source: Adapted from Slife and Rychlak (1982).

played in a room containing all the equipment necessary to imitate the aggressive acts they had just seen. As shown in Figure 14.4, the children were most likely to imitate the aggression when it was an act they liked and when it was performed with a toy they liked. The researchers argue that these are the acts the children re-member. This interpretation helps to explain why the boys in the study were more aggressive than the girls: They liked and recalled the aggressive behavior more.

The third step in the observational learning process is that people must *enact* what they have seen. Remember that Bandura draws a distinction between learn-ing and performance. One reason we don't carry out every aggressive act we notice and recall is that we may lack the ability to do so. For example, few of us can imi-tate the behavior of a martial arts champion, even after watching a dozen Jackie Chan movies. We must also have the opportunity to carry out the act. I may re-member from repeated exposure in movies how to hold and fire a gun. But because I don't have access to a gun and because I hope I am never in a situation where a gun would be useful, shooting someone with a handgun is one learned behavior I will probably never enact.

The final step in the process requires individuals to *expect* that the aggres-sive act will lead to rewards, not punishment. One study of elementary school chil-dren found that aggressive boys were particularly attracted to what they saw as the positive consequences of aggression, such as controlling other children (Boldi-zar, Perry, & Perry, 1989). These same boys were not very concerned about poten-tially negative consequences, such as causing suffering or being rejected by their classmates.

Where do aggressive children develop these expectancies? As described in the previous chapter, we not only learn what to do from aggressive models, we also learn what is likely to happen to us as a result of acting aggressively. If our model is declared a hero and praised, we may expect that we, too, would be rewarded. If the model is arrested or hurt by someone even more aggressive, we will probably anticipate punishment. Researchers find that aggressive children learn the kinds of consequences to expect from watching children their age or slightly older (Huesmann, 1988; Huesmann & Guerra, 1997). If an older child who pushes and punches gets his choice of toys or gets to bat first, there is a good chance the behavior will be imitated. Information about rewards and punishments is communicated in other ways as well. Parents who physically punish children for fighting may communicate that bigger and stronger people can do what they want, which may be why corporal punishment is related to more aggression in children, not less (Gershoff, 2002).

People are also more likely to imitate aggressive behavior that is portrayed as justified (Paik & Comstock, 1994). Children are more likely to imitate a superhero who smacks around a bad guy for the good of society than a supervillain who acts violently only for his own good. Children see that the villain is punished, but they also see the good guy's aggressive behavior rewarded. Unfortunately, most people believe *their* side in a conflict is the correct and just one. Therefore, like the superhero, aggression may seem an appropriate solution to their problems (Smith & Donnerstein, 1998). This observation leads us to the next issue—the impact of mass media violence.

Mass Media Aggression and Aggressive Behavior

If you watch even a small amount of television, you are surely aware that the average American receives a heavy dose of modeled aggression almost daily. For several decades, many people have been concerned about how this constant exposure to stabbings, shootings, beatings, and so on affects children. Although today the action may consist of a space monster's being killed by a superhero's laser beam instead of a bank robber felled by a bullet from a sheriff's gun, more aggression is shown on Saturday morning "children's" entertainment than on prime-time television (National Institute of Mental Health, 1982). One estimate claimed the average American child will view about 8,000 murders and more than 100,000 other acts of violence on television *before* leaving elementary school (Smith & Donnerstein, 1998).

As the examples at the beginning of this section suggest, there are some very convincing instances of people witnessing and then imitating media violence. The problem is we can't conclusively determine that viewing the aggressive act actually caused the person to behave violently. For example, it is possible that John Hinckley would have committed some other violent act if he hadn't watched *Taxi Driver*. After all, millions of people saw the movie without reacting aggressively. Although most of us find it difficult not to see a link between viewing aggression and

In the News

Television Violence

In 1951, when television was in its infancy, Senator Estes Kefauver raised questions about the impact the new medium might have on impressionable children. The debate over appropriate subject matter for television programming has continued throughout the half century that television has been a part of American life. In the middle of this debate is the question of violence. Psychologists have produced strong evidence suggesting exposure to violent scenes and themes increases the likelihood of violence by viewers. Because of its prevalence in American homes and its easy access by children, violence on television may pose a particular problem.

Although objections to television violence have been around for decades, the issue has drawn increased attention in recent years (Garvey, 2002). Concern about violence in society and the rapid expansion of relatively unregulated cable channels in most viewing areas has raised questions about whether the content of television programs should be regulated. A 3-year study commissioned by the National Cable Television Association confirmed the concern about television violence (Brown, 1998; Murray, 1998). The $3.5-million study found 61% of all television programs contained some form of violence. Moreover, the incidence was on the rise. Prime-time violence increased 10% between 1994 and 1997 on cable stations and 14% on the major networks. Psychologists were also disturbed by the finding that nearly 40% of the violence was performed by "good" characters and that more than 70% of the aggressors showed no remorse for their actions. Thus, viewers are often exposed to the kind of violence most likely to be imitated—violence performed by desirable role models with apparently positive consequences.

Professional organizations, the television industry, and political leaders have entered into the ongoing discussion about television violence. The American Academy of Pediatrics has called on the entertainment industry to reduce the amount of violence children are exposed to. Congress passed a law requiring all new television sets to come equipped with an electronic blocking device known as a V-chip (the V stands for violence). The device allows parents to block their children's access to programs identified as too violent for young viewers. More recently, U.S. Surgeon General David Satcher released a report declaring that violent television programs were an important cause of aggressive behavior in children (Leeds, 2001).

Despite widespread agreement that there is a lot of violence on television, there is little consensus on what to do about it. Even the harshest critics are often reluctant to interfere with the broadcasters' freedom of speech. Television representatives argue that parents should take the lead in regulating what their children watch. Others fear that the rating system will lead to even more graphic violence in programs identified as unfit for children, similar to what has happened in motion pictures. What seems certain is that the debate over televised violence will continue.

performing aggression in these examples, they supply only weak evidence for this relationship.

Fortunately, we don't have to rely on this circumstantial evidence. Researchers have provided us with a wealth of experimental data concerning the impact of viewing aggression on performing aggression. The vast majority finds the causal link irrefutable: Viewing aggression increases the likelihood of acting aggressively, especially over a short time span (Anderson & Bushman, 2002; Bushman & Huesmann, 2001; Friedrich-Cofer & Huston, 1986; Geen, 1998; Paik & Comstock, 1994; Smith & Donnerstein, 1998; Wood, Wong, & Chachere, 1991). Today researchers concentrate on understanding the theoretical reasons for this relationship and on identifying variables that increase or decrease the effect.

Most of the evidence suggesting that watching aggression increases aggression comes from controlled laboratory research. Typically, participants watch a segment from either a violent or an arousing but nonviolent program. Then they are given the opportunity to act aggressively against another person, usually by administering electric shocks they believe are hurting the other person. In almost all cases, researchers find the participants who watched the violent program act more aggressively than those who saw the nonviolent program. As impressive as this body of research is, it contains some serious limitations. The effects are short-lived, and the opportunity to hurt another person provided by the experimenter is unique. Therefore, it is reasonable to wonder how much these studies tell us about the impact of aggressive movies and television shows in real-life situations.

In response to this problem, several investigators have conducted long-term field studies to gauge the impact of exposure to violence and aggressive behavior outside the laboratory (Eron, 1987; McCarthy, Langner, Gersten, Eisenberg, & Orzeck, 1975; Singer & Singer, 1981). In each case, the researchers used the amount and kind of television that children watched at one point in their lives to predict how aggressive the children would be later in life. Investigators uncovered significant evidence in each study indicating that watching a lot of aggressive television leads to more aggression in children and adults.

Consider the impressive study conducted by one team of researchers (Eron, 1987; Huesmann, Eron, Dubow, & Seebauer, 1987; Lefkowitz, Eron, Walder, & Huesmann, 1977). The investigators first measured how much television a group of 8-year-old children watched. They then examined aggressive behavior in these same people 22 years later, at age 30. The researchers found a significant relationship between the amount of television the people watched as children and the likelihood that they would have been convicted for criminal behavior by age 30. As shown in Figure 14.5, the seriousness of the criminal act was directly related to the amount of television watched. The more TV the 8-year-old had watched, the more serious the adult crime.

Another investigation measured the amount of television boys and girls watched at age 14 and incidences of aggression over the next eight years (Johnson, Cohen, Smailes, Kasen, & Brook, 2002). As shown in Figure 14.6, the percentages of men and women who engaged in some act of aggression (assault, physical fights

Figure 14.5

Seriousness of
Criminal Act at
Age 30 as a Function
of Frequency of TV
Viewing at Age 8

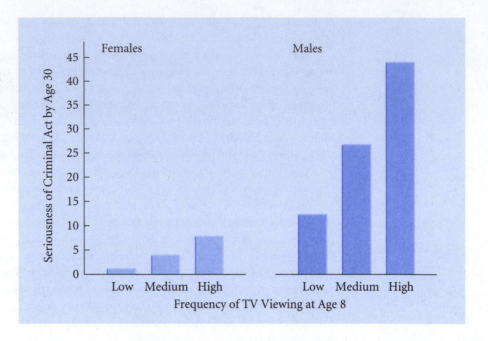

Figure 14.6

Violence as a Func-
tion of Television
Viewing

Source: Adapted from
Johnson et al. (2002).

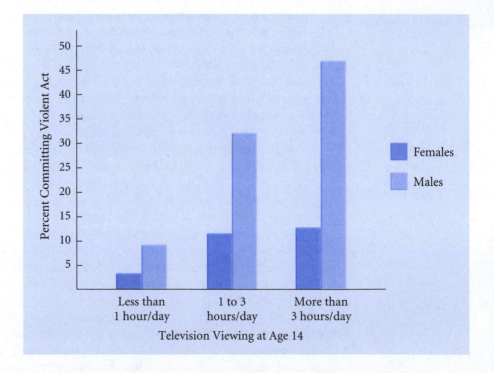

resulting in injury, robbery, crime committed with a weapon) increased dramatically with an increase in television viewing.

One potential difficulty in interpreting this research concerns the possibility that the children watched television *because* they were aggressive, not the other way around. Research shows that aggressive people prefer aggressive television programs (Bushman, 1995; Fenigstein, 1979). However, when researchers control for the child's initial aggressiveness level statistically, the findings still suggest that watching television causes the later aggressive behavior. Moreover, when researchers account for other possible influences on aggressive behavior, such as neighborhood violence, childhood neglect, and family income, they still find the association between television viewing and aggression (Johnson et al., 2002).

In short, frequent exposure to aggressive models on television appears to increase aggressive behavior over the short run and many years later. Some of this relationship can be explained through Bandura's observational learning model. However, closer examination of the model suggests imitation may be only part of the picture. In many studies, the aggressive acts displayed by participants are different from the acts modeled in the films participants are shown (Geen & Thomas, 1986). That is, exposure to an aggressive motion picture increases aggressive acts, but not necessarily the acts shown in the movie. To account for this observation, some researchers suggest that aggressive memories are primed by the presentation of violent cues in aggressive programs (Berkowitz, 1984, 1986; Bushman & Geen, 1990; Huesmann, 1986). The violent images found in mass media presentations activate other violent images and feelings in the viewer's memory. Because these violent memories and emotions are then highly accessible, the likelihood that the viewer will act aggressively increases.

A large number of studies support this reasoning (Carlson, Marcus-Newhall, & Miller, 1990). Second- and third-grade boys were shown either violent or nonviolent films in one study (Josephson, 1987). Some of the boys were later shown a cue from the violent film (a walkie-talkie like the one used by snipers in the film) just before playing hockey. The boys who had seen the violent film and saw the walkie-talkie engaged in more aggression during the game (tripping opponents, hitting with their stick) than the other boys. Other studies find that playing violent video games increases aggressive thoughts (Anderson & Bushman, 2001). Not surprisingly, this research also finds a connection between playing such games and aggression.

One interesting investigation examined the relationship between homicide rates and the highly publicized violence associated with championship boxing matches (Phillips, 1983). Anyone who has sat through 15 (or fewer) rounds of a heavyweight championship fight will agree that aggression is being modeled. In addition, the prefight publicity, with its verbal attacks and aggressive language ("I'm gonna knock his head off"), and the postfight highlights add to the climate of aggression and provide numerous aggressive cues. The researcher compared the expected homicide rate (for the time of year, day of week, and so on) and the actual homicide rate in the United States following the 18 heavyweight championship fights held over a 6-year period. The number of murders increased by an average of 12.46% over the expected rate 3 days after the fight. The largest increases came after the most widely publicized and most widely seen fights, with the famous bout between Muhammad Ali and Joe Frazier associated with an increase of more than 26 murders.

Learned Helplessness

Consider the following three cases: A woman is fired from her job because her employer believes the position is too demanding for her abilities. After a few frustrating weeks of job-hunting, she decides to just stay home. She stops going out with friends and shuts down other parts of her life she once enjoyed—dancing, movies, jogging. She becomes more and more depressed, develops lower and lower self-esteem, and has little faith in her ability to get another job. An elderly man is moved to a senior residential community and is told the staff will take care of all the chores he used to do. He no longer has to cook for himself or clean his room or even do the shopping. Shortly after the move, he becomes less active. He is less talkative and less cheerful. His health begins to fail. A fourth-grade boy fails a math test. He becomes frustrated and distressed on his next few math assignments and eventually refuses to even try. He begins to do poorly in other subjects and soon loses interest in school altogether.

What these three hypothetical people have in common is that they are all examples of what researchers refer to as learned helplessness. Psychology's interest in learned helplessness began with the curious behavior of some dogs in a classical conditioning study and evolved into a widely applied concept.

Learning to Be Helpless

Like so many of the topics to come out of the behaviorist tradition, research on learned helplessness began with studies on laboratory animals. In the original learned helplessness experiments, harnessed dogs were subjected to a series of electric shocks from which they could not escape (Overmier & Seligman, 1967; Seligman & Maier, 1967). After several trials of inescapable electric shock, the animals were placed in an avoidance learning situation. Whenever a signal sounded, the dogs could avoid electric shocks by jumping over a small partition to the other side of a shuttle-box (Figure 14.7). Naturally, dogs that had not gone through the earlier shock experience scurried about frantically when the electric shock came on and quickly learned to leap over the barrier to safety whenever they heard the signal. But the researchers were totally surprised by the response of the dogs that had first gone through the inescapable shock experience. These dogs also ran around for a few seconds after the shock came on. But then the dogs stopped moving. "To our surprise, it lay down and quietly whined," a researcher explained, describing

Figure 14.7

Shuttle-Box for Learned Helpless-ness Experiments

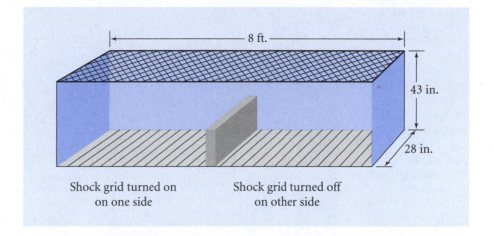

8 ft.

43 in.

28 in.

Shock grid turned on on one side

Shock grid turned off on other side

one of the dogs. "After one minute of this we turned the shock off; the dog had failed to cross the barrier and had not escaped from the shock" (Seligman, 1975, p. 22).

What had happened to these dogs? According to the researchers, the animals had learned that they were helpless. During the inescapable shock trials, the dogs tried various moves to avoid the shock and found that none were rewarded. The animals eventually learned there was nothing they could do to turn off the shock and became resigned to their helplessness. Of course, this reaction was no surprise. It's probably the most reasonable response to inescapable shock. The problem became apparent when the dogs experienced shock in the shuttle-box situation— shock from which they *could* escape. In behavioral terms, the dogs inappropriately *generalized* what they had learned in the first situation to the second situation. Although the dogs could easily have escaped the shock in the shuttle-box, they responded with the helplessness they had learned earlier. In fact, before the animals could learn the simple response, researchers had to physically move the dogs into the other side of the shuttle-box to show them the shock was escapable.

Learned Helplessness in Humans

Soon after the first demonstrations of learned helplessness in animals, psychologists wondered if learned helplessness could also be found in people. Ethically, we can't put human volunteers in a harness and subject them to inescapable shock. But with a few modifications in the basic procedure, researchers figured out a way to test whether humans were also susceptible to this effect (Hiroto, 1974; Hiroto & Seligman, 1975). Instead of inescapable shock, irritating (but not painful) loud noise was used. Participants were told they could turn off the noise by solving a problem (for example, pressing some buttons in the correct sequence). Some participants quickly worked through dozens of these problems, turning off each noise

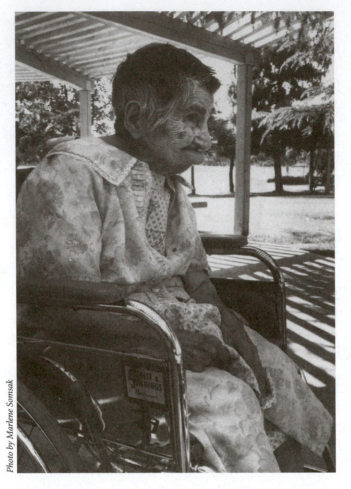

Photo by Marlene Somsak

blast by figuring out the answer. However, other participants were given problems for which there were no solutions. Like the dogs in the earlier studies, these people soon learned there was no way to escape the aversive stimulus.

Would these people generalize their feelings of helplessness to other situa-tions? Participants were taken out of the noise situation and given a different kind of problem to work on. The ones who had found the earlier problems solvable had little difficulty with the new problems. In fact, they did no worse than a compari-son group of participants who received no noise. However, participants who had felt helpless to turn off the noise performed significantly worse on the second set of problems. Like the dogs in the shuttle-box, they appeared to have inappropri-ately generalized their perception of helplessness in one situation to a new, con-trollable situation.

Numerous replications of this experiment confirm that humans are as sus-ceptible as other animals to learned helplessness (Peterson, Maier, & Seligman,

1993). People learn they are helpless in the initial uncontrollable setting and can't break out of that association in subsequent situations. Later, researchers demonstrated that the initial uncontrollable experience might not even be necessary to generate learned helplessness. People can simply be told they are helpless to overcome a serious obstacle (Maier & Seligman, 1976) or can learn through observation that they are helpless (Brown & Inouye, 1978; DeVellis, DeVellis, & McCauley, 1978). Imagine your reaction when you see several people with ability similar to yours trying yet failing to pass an important test. You might conclude that you also can't pass the test, even though you have yet to try ("There's no use in trying; nobody ever passes"). These feelings of helplessness might then be generalized to a new situation, and you could suffer from learned helplessness without ever experiencing failure yourself.

Some Applications of Learned Helplessness

Since it was first demonstrated in humans, learned helplessness has been studied in hundreds of investigations and used to explain a wide variety of human problems. One reason for the popularity of the learned helplessness theory is that it provides psychologists with useful insight into many important human problems. We'll look at two of those problems in the following sections: well-being among older individuals and psychological disorders.

Learned Helplessness in the Elderly. We commonly assume in Western society that elderly people deserve to rest after a lifetime of hard work. Retirement is structured to relieve older individuals of their daily concerns and responsibilities. Retirement communities are often designed to take care of the cooking and cleaning and structuring of daily activities. But is this approach really in the best interests of the retired person? If we apply a learned helplessness analysis to the situation, we see that these living situations may be taking away the older persons' control over their daily experiences. For formerly active people used to exercising a great deal of control, living under such conditions may be similar to the experience that research participants presented with uncontrollable noise or the dogs with their inescapable shock. And, like the research participants, the elderly may generalize this perception of uncontrollability to other areas of their lives. In short, the lack of motivation and activity seen in many retired people may be a form of highly generalized learned helplessness.

One team of investigators tested this possibility in a classic study that involved residents on two floors of a retirement residence (Langer & Rodin, 1976). With the administrators' cooperation, they altered the usual treatment given to one of these groups. The researchers increased the amount of responsibility and control usually exercised by these residents in several ways. Administrators gave a presentation urging the residents to take control of their lives. Here is an excerpt from that talk:

> You have the responsibility of caring for yourselves, of deciding whether or not you want to make this a home you can be proud of and happy in. You should be deciding

how you want your rooms to be arranged—whether you want the staff to help you re-arrange the furniture. You should be deciding how you want to spend your time, for example, whether you want to be visiting friends or whether you want to be watching television, listening to the radio, writing, reading, or planning social events. In other words, it's your life and you can make of it whatever you want. (Langer & Rodin, 1976, p. 194)

In addition, participants were offered a small plant as a gift. They decided whether they wanted a plant and which plant they wanted, and were told they were re-sponsible for taking care of it.

Residents on the other floor served as the comparison group. They listened to a talk about allowing the staff to take care of things for them. They were given a plant (chosen by the staff) and were told the staff would take care of the plant for them. The differences between the two floors were soon evident. Within a few weeks, the residents in the responsibility-induced condition reported feeling hap-pier. Staff members noted they were visiting more and sitting around less. Nurses, who did not know a study was going on, reported 93% of these residents showed improved adjustment. Only 21% of the residents in the comparison group showed improvement. But the effects of the treatment did not stop there. The researchers returned to the home 18 months later to find that many of these differences in hap-piness and activity level remained (Rodin & Langer, 1977). Most dramatically, only 15% of the responsibility-induced residents had died during the 18-month period, compared to 30% of the comparison group.

Several subsequent investigations have discovered similar advantages when el-derly people are allowed to retain control over their lives (Baltes & Baltes, 1986; Schulz & Heckhausen, 1999). This does not mean we should abandon those who genuinely need assistance, but sometimes letting people take care of themselves is in everyone's best interest.

Learned Helplessness and Psychological Disorders. Soon after the demonstra-tions of learned helplessness in humans, psychologists noticed some striking par-allels between helpless research participants and people suffering from depression (Seligman, 1976). Clinical psychologists have long observed that depressed pa-tients often act as if they are helpless to control what happens to them (Beck, 1972). Severely depressed people sometimes lack the motivation even to get out of bed in the morning. Little interests them, and they often believe that nothing they do will turn out well. Like the dogs that lie whimpering in the shuttle-box, they seem to have given up on their ability to do anything about their problems.

These observations led some psychologists to suggest that depression some-times develops in a manner similar to the way research participants acquire learned helplessness (Seligman, 1975). That is, people perceive a lack of control over one important part of their lives and inappropriately generalize that percep-tion to other situations. For example, a college student might have difficulty in a particular class. No matter how hard she tries, she can't improve her test scores. At first she studies harder and gets advice from others in the class, but it doesn't seem to help. If it's important to her to do well in school, she may continue her efforts to change her grade. However, at some point she may decide that no matter what she does, she can't avoid the bad grade that is bound to come at the end of the term. In other words, she has learned she is helpless in this class. And as a result, she may become mildly depressed.

Unless other information is forthcoming to counteract these feelings, this student may soon conclude there is no sense trying in other classes or in other parts of her life, such as sports or friendships. She may decide she lacks control over most of life's outcomes and may eventually lose the motivation to try. In learned helplessness terms, she has inappropriately generalized her feelings of helplessness in one situation she can't control to others that she might be able to control.

Consistent with this interpretation of depression, people who find they cannot control relatively simple laboratory tasks, such as escaping the irritating noise, show significant increases in depressed feelings (Bodner & Mikulincer, 1998; Burger & Arkin, 1980; Gatchel, Paulus, & Maples, 1975). Other support for a learned helplessness–depression connection comes from research with animals. Investigators find the changes in neurotransmitters and receptors in animals exposed to inescapable shock are similar to what we see in the neurotransmitters and receptors of depressed individuals (Besson, Privat, Eschalier, & Fialip, 1999; Ferguson, Brodkin, Lloyd & Menzaghi, 2000; Grahn et al., 1999; Kram, Kramer, Steciuk, Ronan, & Petty, 2000; Wu et al., 1999). In particular, the neurotransmitter *serotonin* appears to play a role in the development of both learned helplessness and depression. Other investigators have examined the role of hormones in the development of learned helplessness. For example, female rats are more prone to developing learned helplessness during the menstrual cycle phase in which estrogen levels begin to rise (Jenkins, Williams, Kramer, Davis, & Petty, 2001).

Thus, data from many different sources suggest exposure to uncontrollable events can be a cause of depression. But one difference between laboratory-induced learned helplessness and genuine depression needs to be addressed. Learned helplessness in laboratory animals is short, typically lasting no more than a few days in rats and dogs (Maier, 2001). But clinical depression often lasts considerably longer, in some cases for years. One explanation for this discrepancy is that there are many different causes of depression, only one of which is learned helplessness. Another possibility is that, in a sense, people suffering from depression continually relive the initial helplessness induction. Depressed patients typically ruminate about the causes of their depression (Nolen-Hoeksema, 2000). By frequently thinking about the circumstances leading up to their depression, these individuals may continually reexperience the helplessness-inducing events. Recall that even imagining oneself in an uncontrollable situation sometimes is sufficient to generate learned helplessness. Even exposure to cues from the initial helplessness event may be sufficient to trigger depression. Consistent with this line of reasoning, when rats in one study were exposed periodically to the location in which their initial learned helplessness experience had occurred, researchers found no decline in learned helplessness over time (Maier, 2001).

In short, learned helplessness has become an important model for understanding some kinds of depression. For some people, experiences with uncontrollable aversive events can be the first step into a downward spiral of helplessness. Fortunately, research also suggests a treatment. People who experience success at controlling outcomes soon overcome feelings of helplessness (Klein & Seligman, 1976). Thus, all the failing student may need is a good grade in another class to appreciate that she still has the ability to succeed in school and make friends.

Learned helplessness remains an important model for understanding depression. However, like many topics in personality, the original theory has evolved in recent years to include many more cognitive features. As you'll discover in Chapter 16, whether people fall into learned helplessness and depression may depend not only on a perception of uncontrollability, but also on how they explain that lack of control.

Locus of Control

If you're in good health, is it because you take care of yourself or because you're lucky? Are lonely people without friends because they don't try to meet people or because they don't have many opportunities? When you win in a sporting contest, is it because you did your best or because you got some lucky breaks? These are the kinds of questions researchers ask when they investigate individual differences in **locus of control.** The key is not whether a person's health habits actually contribute to his or her good health, but rather whether the person believes this to be true.

Research on locus of control developed out of Julian Rotter's concept of *generalized expectancies,* described in the last chapter. In a new situation, we have no information upon which to draw an expectancy of what might happen. In these cases, Rotter argued, we rely on general beliefs about our ability to influence events. If you answered that good health comes from taking care of yourself, that loneliness is caused by not trying, and that winning a sporting contest is the result of effort, you probably maintain an *internal* locus of control orientation. Your generalized expectancy is that people can affect what happens to them and that good and bad experiences are generally of our own making. However, if you feel that health is a matter of luck, that people are lonely because of the circumstances they find themselves in, and that winning means you got some lucky breaks, you probably fall on the *external* end of the locus of control dimension. More than most people, you believe that what happens to you and others is outside of your control.

Neither an internal nor an external orientation is necessarily accurate. Rather, where people fall along this dimension allows locus of control researchers to predict a large number of behaviors, including how they'll do in school, whether they'll vote in the next election, and how soon they'll recover from an illness. Thinking back to Rotter's model, the extensive application of this individual difference makes sense. According to Rotter, the likelihood of engaging in a particu-

Assessing Your Own Personality

Locus of Control

Indicate the extent to which each of the following statements applies to you. Use the following scale:
1 = Disagree strongly, 2 = Disagree, 3 = Disagree slightly, 4 = Neither agree nor disagree, 5 = Agree slightly, 6 = Agree, 7 = Agree strongly.

_____ 1. When I get what I want, it's usually because I worked hard for it.

_____ 2. When I make plans, I am almost certain to make them work.

_____ 3. I prefer games involving some luck over games requiring pure skill.

_____ 4. I can learn almost anything if I set my mind to it.

_____ 5. My major accomplishments are entirely due to my hard work and ability.

_____ 6. I usually don't set goals because I have a hard time following through on them.

_____ 7. Competition discourages excellence.

_____ 8. Often people get ahead just by being lucky.

_____ 9. On any sort of exam or competition I like to know how well I do relative to everyone else.

_____ 10. It's pointless to keep working on something that's too difficult for me.

To determine your score, reverse the point values for items 3, 6, 7, 8, and 10 (1 = 7; 2 = 6; 3 = 5; 5 = 3; 6 = 2; 7 = 1). Then add the point values for each of the 10 items together. A recent sample of college students found a mean of 51.8 for males and 52.2 for females, with a standard deviation of about 6 for each. The higher your score, the more you tend to believe that you are generally responsible for what happens to you in personal achievement situations.

Scale: *Personal Efficacy Scale*

Source: Paulhus (1983)

lar behavior is largely determined by our perception of whether that action will have an effect. Therefore, we should not be surprised to find that people who believe they can control most situations act differently from those who believe they can't. No surprise, either, that psychologists working in education, psychotherapy, industrial settings, and other applied areas have found the locus of control concept so useful.

Like other personality traits, scores from locus of control scales are fairly stable over time. However, these scores are not immune to change. For example, people tend to become more internal after attending college (Wolfe & Robertshaw, 1982). One study found that women who get divorced become more external for a time, but after a few years, return to a locus of control level similar to that of married women (Doherty, 1983). Because of the tremendous amount of research on locus of control, even a brief introduction to each of the areas researched would be impossible to cover in this chapter. Instead, we'll look at two examples of how individual differences in locus of control affect behavior. We first examine the relationship between locus of control and well-being. Then we look at how this personality variable affects your physical health.

Locus of Control and Well-Being

Who is happier—internals who believe they can control most things or externals who recognize the limits that outside forces place on them? Which person is more productive, better liked, and better adjusted? A case can be made for either position. On one hand, internals probably work harder and thus achieve more because they feel they control outcomes. On the other hand, just because people believe they are in control does not mean they actually exercise control. Highly internal people may invest their efforts inefficiently chasing rainbows or making plans on a set of beliefs inconsistent with reality. Perhaps externals understand their limits and work to achieve only what is reasonably attainable. However, people who give up in the face of setbacks, who quickly conclude there is nothing they can do to correct a problem, are unlikely to get far in a world filled with obstacles and challenges.

Of course, happiness is determined by many factors, and we can point to happy and unhappy people on any point of the locus of control spectrum. Nonetheless, in general researchers find that, with a few exceptions, internals tend to be happier than externals (DeNeve & Cooper, 1998). To better understand this conclusion, let's look at the connection between locus of control and a few markers of well-being: psychological disorders, achievement, and psychotherapy results.

Psychological Disorders. In general, people suffering from psychological disorders tend to be more external than internal (Lefcourt, 1982; Phares, 1976; Strickland, 1978). For example, external locus of control scores are associated with higher levels of anxiety. However, many researchers are particularly interested in the relationship between locus of control and depression. One recent study found that HIV-positive men with an external locus of control were more depressed about their condition than those with an internal locus of control (Evans, Ferrando, Rabkin, & Fishman, 2000). One team of reviewers found an average correlation of .31 between locus of control scores and measures of depression, indicating that external scores are associated with higher levels of depression (Benassi, Sweeney, & Dufour, 1988). As discussed in Chapter 7, this is an impressively significant correlation.

You may have noticed that this association between locus of control and depression is consistent with the findings in learned helplessness studies. In both cases, a perceived inability to control events is associated with higher depression levels. It may be that externals often find themselves in situations similar to that of

Of the millions who try to lose weight each year, only a small number of people succeed in taking it off and keeping it off. One variable that may affect a diet's success or failure is the extent to which the dieter believes he or she is capable of losing the weight.

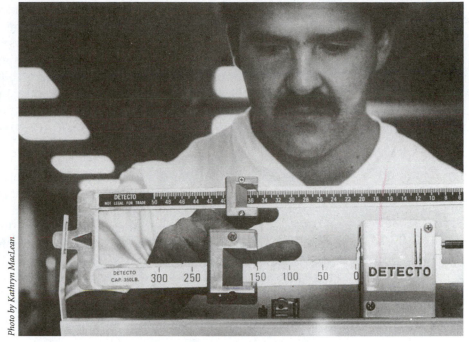

Photo by Kathryn MacLean

learned helplessness participants who cannot control important outcomes. Consider the findings of a study in which recently diagnosed cancer patients were tested for level of depression (Marks, Richardson, Graham, & Levine, 1986). For external patients, the more severe the diagnosis, the more depressed they became. However, the severity of the disease had no impact on the depression experienced by internal patients. These patients believed they could still control the course of the disease, and this belief shielded them from giving up and becoming depressed about their situation.

A dramatic example of how locus of control is related to depression was demonstrated in a study of suicidal patients (Melges & Weisz, 1971). Patients who had recently attempted suicide were asked to relive the events that took place immediately before the attempt. Patients were left alone with a tape recorder and asked to describe in the present tense what had happened to them during this time. Analysis of the recordings revealed that patients described themselves in more external terms as they became more suicidal. Other studies find suicide attempters often experience an increase in events outside their personal control prior to the attempt (Slater & Depue, 1981) and that external college students report more suicidal thoughts than internals (Burger, 1984). One investigator found that the rate of suicide in a country correlates .68 with the average locus of control score for that country's citizens, again with external scores indicating a higher rate of suicide (Boor, 1976).

Taken together, these studies suggest that locus of control is related to some forms of psychological disturbance, particularly depression. But we need to add two notes of caution when interpreting these findings. First, the vast majority of people scoring on the external end of locus of control scales are happy and well adjusted. Locus of control may be related to some disorders, but there are obviously many other variables to consider. Second, because the relationship is correlational, it is difficult to make strong statements about external locus of control *causing* the disorder. It may be that externals are susceptible to depression, but it is also possible that depressed people become more external.

Achievement. One indicator of well-being in Western society is how much we achieve in school and in our careers. Although high achievers are by no means shielded from psychological problems, we often point to a deteriorating job performance as a reason for concern. Similarly, improved performance in school or work is often seen as evidence that a therapy client is getting better. When researchers use locus of control scores to predict achievement, they consistently find that internal students receive higher grades and better teacher evaluations than externals (Findley & Cooper, 1983; Kalechstein & Nowicki, 1997). This finding is true of elementary, high school, and college students, but the relationship is especially strong among adolescents.

Why do internals do better in school? One reason may be that they see themselves as responsible for their achievements. Internal students believe studying for tests pays off, whereas externals are less likely to feel that their efforts affect their grades. Internals and externals also respond differently to feedback (Gilmor & Reid, 1978, 1979; Martinez, 1994). Internal students are likely to attribute high test scores to their abilities or to studying hard, whereas externals who do well might say they were lucky or that the test was easy. Internals also are better at adjusting their expectancies following feedback, which means they have a better idea of how to prepare for the next exam. Externals are more likely to make excuses following a poor performance (Basgall & Snyder, 1988). An external student who decides the teacher is an unfair grader probably will not study for the next test. Because they believe academic success is up to them, internal students also pay attention to information that will help them reach their goals. One investigator found internal undergraduates were more likely than externals to know about test dates, grading policies, and other relevant information that would help them do well in their classes (Dollinger, 2000).

Higher achievement by internals is not limited to the classroom. Studies in career settings also find higher levels of performance for internal workers than externals (Judge & Bono, 2001). People who believe making a sale, inspiring employees, or completing a job on time is largely up to them are more likely to reach those goals than workers who fail to see their role in achieving work objectives (Judge, Erez, & Bono, 1998; Spector, 1982). Internal workers also tend to seek out positions that provide the opportunities and rewards they prefer (Spector, 1982).

Not surprisingly, researchers find internals score higher than externals on measures of job satisfaction (Judge & Bono, 2001). One team of investigators examined locus of control and job satisfaction among managers in large corporations in 24 countries (Spector et al., 2001). Across different cultures, managers who experienced a great deal of control over their work environment reported consistently higher levels of satisfaction with their jobs than managers who felt they had little control.

Psychotherapy. Because external locus of control scores are associated with psychological disorders, we should not be surprised to find that clients tend to become more internal as they pass through successful psychotherapy (Strickland, 1978). Consider the case of Israeli soldiers suffering from post-traumatic stress disorder following their experiences with intense combat (Solomon, Mikulincer, & Avitzur, 1988). These men suffered from a variety of symptoms often found after a profoundly stressful experience. When tested shortly after combat, the soldiers scored fairly external on locus of control measures. However, as they recovered from the stress over the next three years, they became increasingly internal. Part of the soldiers' difficulties appeared to be related to their perception of losing control. But as they came to appreciate the control they could exercise over important parts of their lives, they took a step toward recovery.

Does this mean that therapists should focus on giving clients more control over therapy? Not necessarily. Although internals perform better when they see themselves in control, externals may do better when they perceive someone else is in charge. For example, one team of investigators looked at depression levels in patients with rheumatoid arthritis (Reich & Zautra, 1997). The external patients became less depressed when their spouses provided them with a lot of support and assistance. However, internal patients showed an increase in depression when their spouse gave this same amount of assistance. Researchers speculate that the spouse's care was seen as helpful by the externals, but as an indication of helplessness and dependence by the internals.

This finding suggests that the most effective therapy procedures may be those that match the client's locus of control orientation. Internals may respond well when given control over their treatment, but externals might be uncomfortable with this control. Externals may do better when treatment is in the therapist's hands. Consistent with this reasoning, internals in one assertiveness training group showed little improvement (Schwartz & Higgins, 1979). However, the externals in this same group showed significant improvement. The therapists realized that they had structured their group in such a way that the internals felt control over their treatment had been taken away. Therapies designed to help clients stop smoking also seem to work better with a good locus of control fit (Best, 1975; Best & Steffy, 1975). Internals showed the most improvement when they could administer their own rewards and punishments, whereas externals did best when the therapist was in control.

In summary, information from a number of sources indicates that locus of control is related to well-being. Although there are many exceptions, internals tend to do better than externals on most indicators of well-being. This finding does not mean that holding an external locus of control orientation causes psychological problems. But it does suggest that perception of control is a piece in the mental health puzzle.

Locus of Control and Health

One of the most frustrating problems health-care professionals face is lack of patient cooperation. Many patients simply do not take their medicine or discontinue their therapy programs. On the other hand, other patients do an excellent job of watching their diets, taking medication, attending therapy, and keeping appointments. Observations like these lead some psychologists to consider the role locus of control might play in health behaviors (Strickland, 1989; Wallston & Wallston, 1981).

How might internals and externals differ in their approach to physical health? Studies suggest that people who take an external orientation toward their health believe there is little they can do to improve their physical condition or avoid disease. Whether they become ill is out of their control, and when they become ill they depend on health professionals to make them well again. On the other hand, people with an internal locus of control believe they have a significant role in maintaining good health. Because they see a relationship between what they do and how they feel, internals are more likely than externals to eat well and participate in health-maintaining exercise programs, such as aerobics or jogging.

Consistent with these descriptions, several studies find that internals are healthier and practice better health habits than externals (Johansson et al., 2001; Klonowicz, 2001; Marshall, 1991; Perrig-Chiello, Perrig, & Staehelin, 1999; Simoni & Ng, 2002). One study found college students who held an external locus of control toward their health were more likely to smoke, drink alcohol regularly, skip breakfast, eat fatty foods, and consume less fruit and fiber than internals (Steptoe & Wardle, 2001). Internal college students made aware of the dangers of hypertension in another study sought out more information about the disease than did externals (Wallston, Maides, & Wallston, 1976). Internals tend to have more success with weight-reduction programs, particularly those oriented toward self-control of eating (Balch & Ross, 1975; Wallston et al., 1976). A study of business executives in high-stress positions found that those who remained healthy were more internal than were those who suffered from illnesses (Kobasa, 1979).

Clearly, researchers often find a connection between locus of control and health. However, this is not always the case. Some investigations fail to find health differences between internals and externals or find only weak effects (Norman & Bennett, 1996; Wallston & Smith, 1994). Why might this be so? To answer this question, we need to return to Rotter's original description of locus of control and its role within his theory. Recall that Rotter said behavior was a function of both expectancy *and* reinforcement value. That is, I might expect that studying for a test will result in a good grade. However, if I don't value that grade, I am still unlikely to make the effort.

Psychologists make similar predictions when they apply Rotter's model to health behaviors (Wallston, 1992; Wallston & Smith, 1994). That is, believing that your actions can affect your health is not enough. You also need to place a great value on good health. Of course, everyone wants good health. But if you think about some of the people you know, you probably can identify those who place health at the top of their concerns and those who don't. According to Rotter's theory, people who place a high value on their health *and* who believe there is something they can do to control their health are the ones who watch what they eat, exercise, and get regular check-ups. You might believe that daily exercise leaves you feeling fit and full of energy. But if you don't particularly value these effects (especially if you value less-exhausting activities more), it's unlikely you'll enroll in a fitness program.

Several studies find evidence for this interaction between locus of control and health value when predicting health and related behaviors (Norman & Bennett, 1996; Wallston & Smith, 1994). Internal participants in one study who placed a high value on health were found to eat more fruits and vegetables and fewer fatty foods and snacks than either external participants or internals who did not value physical health (Bennett, Moore, Smith, Murphy, & Smith, 1994). Similar results have been found in studies looking at breast self-examination (Lau, Hartman, & Ware, 1986) and efforts to stop smoking (Kaplan & Cowles, 1978). In short, health professionals face two tasks when trying to get patients to take better care of themselves. Patients must place their health high on their list of things they value, and they must believe that they can influence the extent to which they are healthy.

 *Summary*

1. One of the striking similarities of the four topics covered in this chapter is the extent to which they touch on important social and lifestyle issues. This research tells us a great deal about gender roles, aggression, depression, treatment of the elderly, and personal health. The research reminds us that psychology ultimately has a lot to say about how to improve the human condition.

2. From the day we are born, most of us face tremendous socialization pressures to take on the gender roles deemed appropriate by society. Through a combination of operant conditioning and observational learning, boys tend to act like other boys, and girls like other girls. Research on individual differences in gender-role behavior was originally stifled by a model that viewed masculinity and femininity as polar opposites. The androgyny model sees these as two independent traits and argues that the most well-adjusted people are those who are androgynous—that is, high in both masculinity and femininity.

3.   Researchers agree that exposure to aggressive models increases a person's likelihood of acting aggressively. Bandura's four-step model helps explain why people sometimes imitate aggressive acts they see and sometimes do not. Before people imitate aggression, they must attend to the act, recall it, have the opportunity to engage in the behavior, and believe the aggression will lead to rewards. Research from laboratory and long-term field studies indicates that exposure to mass media violence increases aggressive behavior. Bandura's model cannot account for all of these findings, and recent researchers have pointed to the priming effect of violent cues found in violent television programs.

4.   Like much behavioral research, work on learned helplessness began with experiments on laboratory animals. Researchers observed that dogs that learned they were helpless to escape shock in one situation inappropriately generalized this perception of helplessness to a new situation. Subsequent research found that humans are also susceptible to this effect. Research suggests elderly people may adjust better to retirement communities when they are allowed to retain some control over their situation. Depression may develop when people perceive a lack of control over an important event and inappropriately generalize that perception to other aspects of their lives.

5.   The most widely researched aspect of Rotter's social learning theory is the notion of individual differences in generalized expectancies, or locus of control. At one end of this dimension we find internals, who generally believe they control what happens to them. On the other end are externals, who generally hold that what happens to them is under the control of outside forces. Internals generally do better than externals on measures of well-being and health.

InfoTrac College Edition Key Terms

For additional readings go to http://www.infotrac-college.com/wadsworth and enter a search term related to your interest. Use the key terms suggested here to pull up several related articles. Also see the text Web site at http://psychology .wadsworth.com for more suggested readings and interactive quizzes to test your knowledge.

Androgyny
Gender role
Generalized expectancies

Learned helplessness
Locus of control

Chapter 15

The Cognitive Approach

Theory, Application, and Assessment

George Kelly's Personal Construct Theory
Cognitive Personality Variables
Cognitive Representations of the Self
Application: Cognitive Psychotherapy
Assessment: The Repertory Grid Technique
Strengths and Criticisms of the Cognitive Approach
Summary

I went to a social gathering with a friend of mine recently. We talked with old friends, met some new people, and mingled about, sampling conversations, music, food, and drink. As is our custom, we immediately shared our perceptions after leaving the party. "Did you notice how casually some people were dressed?" my friend asked. Actually, I hadn't. I asked him what he thought of a man we had both met. "Wasn't he the most arrogant person?" I asked. My friend hadn't seen anything to indicate so. As we continued to exchange impressions, I began to wonder if my friend had been at the same party interacting with the same people I had. I couldn't believe he hadn't noticed how weird the music was or realized how ill at ease the hostess seemed. My friend didn't understand how I had failed to recognize the architecture of the house or even the furniture I sat on. "I guess we learned one lesson," I said. "Never go to a party at their house again." My friend stared at me in disbelief. "Are you kidding?" he said. "I had a great time!"

How can two people participate in the same situation yet leave with very different impressions of what happened? The answer from the cognitive approach to personality is that my friend and I have very different ways of processing informa-

443

tion. Whereas I was attending to and processing information about the weirdness of the music and the arrogance of the guests, my friend entered the party prepared to notice clothing styles and furniture. Because we attended to different features of the party, we had very different perceptions of it and very different experiences. These different perceptions no doubt affected how we acted that night and how we will respond to future invitations.

The cognitive approach explains differences in personality as differences in the way people process information. Because I have developed relatively stable ways of processing information in social settings, I probably respond to parties and other social gatherings in a similar way most of the time. Other people respond differently than I do because they consistently see something different from what I see.

Although cognitive models of personality have become popular in recent years, they are not entirely new. For example, an early predecessor is found in Kurt Lewin's (1938) field theory of behavior. Lewin described the mental representations we form of the important elements in our lives and how we organize those cognitive elements within our "life space." A more recent and, for the purposes of this book, more important cognitive personality theory was developed by George Kelly. Since the publication of his book *The Psychology of Personal Constructs* in 1955, Kelly's work has evolved into a rich source of ideas and concepts for cognitive personality researchers and psychotherapists (Jankowicz, 1987; Landfield, 1984; Mischel, 1980). It is interesting that Kelly did not think of himself as a cognitive psychologist. "I have been so puzzled over the early labeling of [my] theory as cognitive," he wrote, "that several years ago I set out to write another short book to make it clear that I wanted no part of cognitive theory" (1969, p. 216). Despite his protests, Kelly's writings have become the starting point for many of the approaches to personality we now identify as "cognitive."

George Kelly's Personal Construct Theory

George Kelly's approach to personality begins with a unique conception of humankind. He called it a *man-the-scientist* perspective. Kelly said that, like scientists, people constantly generate and test hypotheses about their worlds. Just as scientists try to predict and control the things they study, we all want to predict and control as many events in our lives as possible. Not knowing why things happen or how the people around us might act can be unsettling. To satisfy our need for predictability, we engage in a process Kelly compared to template matching. That is, our ideas about the world are similar to transparent templates. We place these templates over the events we encounter. If they match, we retain the templates. If not, we modify them for a better prediction next time. For example, based on past observations, you may have generated a few hypotheses about one of your instructors.

George Kelly

1905–1967

George Alexander Kelly was born in a farming community near Wichita, Kansas, in 1905. He attended Friends University in Wichita for three years before graduating from Park College in Missouri in 1926. He was an active member of the intercollegiate debate team during these years and developed a keen ability to challenge arguments and conventional positions. Although these skills would eventually become an asset, they may have kept him away from the field of psychology for many years. Kelly described his first psychology course as boring and unconvincing. The instructor spent considerable time discussing learning theories, but Kelly was unimpressed. "The most I could make of it was that the S was what you had to have in order to account for the R, and the R was put there so the S would have something to account for," he wrote. "I never did find out what that arrow stood for" (1969, pp. 46–47). He was also skeptical when he first read Freud. "I don't remember which one of Freud's books I was trying to read," he recalled, "but I do remember the mounting feeling of incredulity that anyone could write such nonsense, much less publish it" (1969, p. 47).

After graduating with a degree in physics and mathematics, Kelly went to the University of Kansas to study educational sociology. After a series of odd jobs, including teaching speech and working as an aeronautical engineer, he went to the University of Edinburgh to study education in 1929. While there, he developed a growing interest in psychology and received his Ph.D. in psychology from the University of Iowa a few years later.

Kelly spent the next 10 years at Fort Hays Kansas State College. During this time he set up a network of clinics to provide psychological services to the poor and destitute Dustbowl victims of the 1930s. "I listened to people in trouble," he wrote, "and tried to help them figure out what they could do about it" (1969, p. 50). He soon came to see that what these people needed most was an explanation for what had happened to them and the ability to predict what would happen to them in the future. Personal construct theory evolved from this insight. After serving in the Navy in World War II, Kelly spent a year at the University of Maryland and then 20 years at Ohio State University. He moved to Brandeis University in 1965 and died there soon after.

One is that you believe this man is stuffy and arrogant. Whenever you see this instructor, you collect more information and compare it to your hypothesis. If it is verified (the instructor acts the way arrogant people act), you continue using it. If not (outside of the classroom he is warm and charming), you discard the hypothesis and replace it with a new one. The process resembles that used by scientists who retain and reject hypotheses based on empirical findings.

Kelly called the cognitive structures we use to interpret and predict events **personal constructs.** No two people use identical personal constructs, and no two people organize their constructs in an identical manner. What do these constructs look like? Kelly described personal constructs as bipolar. That is, we classify relevant objects in an either/or fashion within our constructs. For example, when I meet someone for the first time, I might apply the personal constructs *friendly-unfriendly, tall-short, intelligent-unintelligent,* and *masculine-feminine* in constructing an image of this person. I might decide, for example, that this person is friendly, tall, intelligent, and feminine. But this does not mean that we see the world as black and white with no shades of gray. Rather, after applying the original black-or-white construct, we can use other bipolar constructs to determine the extent of the blackness or whiteness. For example, after determining that this new acquaintance is intelligent, I might then apply an *academically intelligent–common sense intelligent* construct to get an even clearer picture of what this person is like.

How can personal constructs be used to explain personality? Kelly maintained that differences in personality result largely from differences in the way people "construe the world." For example, if you and I interact with Jacob, I might use *friendly-unfriendly, fun-boring,* and *outgoing-shy* constructs in forming my impression. But you might interpret Jacob in terms of *refined-gross, sensitive-insensitive,* and *intelligent-unintelligent* constructs. After we both talk to Jacob for a while, I might act as if I'm interacting with a friendly, fun, and outgoing person. You might respond to Jacob as if dealing with a gross, insensitive, and unintelligent person. We're both in the same situation, but because we interpret that situation very differently, we respond in very different ways. In addition, because I tend to use these same constructs when meeting other people, I probably have a characteristic way I interact with people that is different from yours. In other words, the relatively stable patterns in our behavior are the result of the relatively stable way we construe the world.

Kelly (1955) presented his theory of personality in a highly organized and structured manner rarely seen in the social sciences. He began with one basic postulate, upon which his entire theory is based. The *Fundamental Postulate*, as he called it, states that "a person's processes are psychologically channelized by the ways in which he anticipates events" (1955, p. 46). Kelly then added the 11 corollaries listed in Table 15.1 to elaborate the theory. Although Kelly can be criticized for the confusing way he phrased many of his key concepts, his model of personality was groundbreaking in many ways.

Personal Construct Systems

To get a rough idea of your own personal constructs, ask yourself what you tend to notice about people when you first meet them. The first few thoughts that come to mind are probably some of the constructs you typically use to make sense of other people and their behavior. For example, you might use the constructs *athletic–not athletic, good sense of humor–humorless,* and *independent-dependent* when you meet someone new. Another person might use the constructs *studious-*

Table 15.1 George Kelly's Fundamental Postulate and Eleven Corollaries	
Fundamental Postulate	A person's processes are psychologically channelized by the ways in which he anticipates events.
Construction Corollary	A person anticipates events by construing their replications.
Individuality Corollary	Persons differ from each other in their construction of events.
Organization Corollary	Each person characteristically evolves, for his convenience in anticipating events, a construction system embracing ordinal relationships between constructs.
Dichotomy Corollary	A person's construction system is composed of a finite number of dichotomous constructs.
Choice Corollary	A person chooses for himself that alternative in a dichotomous construct through which he anticipates the greater possibility for extension and definition of his system.
Range Corollary	A construct is convenient for the anticipation of a finite range of events only.
Experience Corollary	A person's construction system varies as he successively construes the replications of events.
Modulation Corollary	The variation in a person's construction system is limited by the permeability of the constructs within whose range of convenience the variants lie.
Fragmentation Corollary	A person may successively employ a variety of construction subsystems which are inferentially incompatible with each other.
Commonality Corollary	To the extent that one person employs a construction of experience which is similar to that employed by another, his psychological processes are similar to those of the other person.
Sociality Corollary	To the extent that one person construes the construction processes of another, he may play a role in a social process involving the other person.

Source: From Kelly (1955).

lazy, *charming-obnoxious,* and *neat-sloppy.* It is also possible that two people use the same constructs but construe the world differently. That is, I might think someone intelligent, and you might see the same person as unintelligent. Further, two people's constructs might be similar on one pole but not the other. For example, I might use an *outgoing-reserved* construct, whereas you use an *outgoing-melancholy* construct. If that were the case, what I see as reserved behavior you would probably see as melancholy.

Thus, one reason you and I act differently from each other is that we all use different constructs. Another reason is that we organize our constructs differently. According to Kelly, we rely on some constructs more often than others. For example, it may be important to me to know if someone is friendly or unfriendly. After I have determined that a new acquaintance appears friendly, I might then apply less important constructs to learn even more about this person. For example,

I might want to know if the person is outgoing or quiet. We could diagram the relation between these constructs this way:

Friendly-Unfriendly

Outgoing-Quiet

Note that within this construct system, I could not see an unfriendly person as either outgoing or quiet, just unfriendly. On the other hand, you might use the same constructs but organize them this way:

Friendly-Unfriendly

Outgoing-Quiet   Outgoing-Quiet

In this case, whether you judge someone as friendly or unfriendly, you can further judge that person as either outgoing or quiet. Of course, it also is possible to organize these same two constructs this way:

Outgoing-Quiet

Friendly-Unfriendly   Friendly-Unfriendly

In this case, after deciding someone is a quiet person, you might want to know if she is a quiet-friendly person or a quiet-unfriendly one. It is even possible for the same person to use different construct organizations at different times. In short, not only are there a limitless number of constructs we can use to make sense of our worlds, but the ways we organize and use these constructs also are practically endless.

Personal construct theory also helps us understand why two people can be very compatible even when they seem so different on the surface. We all know romantic couples or best friends who don't appear to have anything in common yet seem to have a strong attachment to each other. Kelly explained these kinds of relationships in terms of construct systems. According to Kelly, the better I understand your construct system, the better you and I will get along. Although researchers find that people with similar construct systems often make good friends and romantic partners (Duck, 1979; Neimeyer, 1984), it is not necessary that two people have similar constructs to have harmonious relations. If we are to get along, I need—in Kelly's words—to anticipate the way you construe the world. That is, I need to understand why you say the things you say and act the way you do. Kelly saw a similar process operating in psychotherapy. He argued that therapists are best able to help their clients when they understand the clients' construct system.

Psychological Problems

Like many personality theorists, Kelly was a practicing psychotherapist who applied his ideas about personality to understanding and treating psychological problems. However, unlike many theorists, Kelly rejected the notion that psychological disorders are caused by past traumatic experiences. Rather, he argued, people suffer from psychological problems because of defects in their construct systems. Past experiences with an unloving parent or a tragic incident may explain *why* people construe the world as they do, but they are not the *cause* of the person's problems. Kelly also had little interest in developing complex diagnostic schemes for classifying various disorders. He described all disorders in terms of faulty construct systems.

Kelly argued that anxiety was at the heart of most psychological problems. Within personal construct theory, anxiety occurs when we can't predict future events. In other words, we become anxious when our personal constructs fail to make sense of the events in our lives. We have all had this experience on occasion. An upcoming interview will cause more anxiety if you have no idea who you will meet or what kind of questions you will be asked. Similarly, when you can't understand why certain people treat you the way they do or you don't know how to behave in certain situations, you probably feel confused, disoriented, and anxious.

The problem is that construct systems are never perfect. For a variety of reasons, our constructs occasionally fail us as we try to predict events. In healthy people, new constructs are constantly generated to replace old, inadequate ones. For example, if you anticipate that a conversation with Anna is going to be boring but then find it interesting, you will probably alter your expectations for future encounters with Anna. Failure to consider this new information lessens your ability to predict what will happen the next time you do something with Anna. You may have experienced this frustration when you said to someone, "I just don't understand you anymore."

Why do our constructs sometimes fail us? In some cases our construct systems are too small or incomplete. Often construct systems are inadequate simply from lack of experience. Most of us have gone through the transition problems associated with starting a new job, attending a new school, or moving to a new city. Some of the difficulties we have during these first days may be attributed to a lack of appropriate constructs to deal with the new situations and new people we encounter. Most of us eventually modify our constructs and interact in the new situations effectively. However, occasionally people can't seem to develop appropriate constructs and may eventually turn to psychotherapy to make sense of their world again. We'll look at some of the ways cognitive psychologists approach psychotherapy later in this chapter.

Cognitive Personality Variables

During the past few decades, the field of psychology has witnessed a remarkable surge in the use of cognitive variables to explain human behavior (Robins, Gosling, & Craik, 1999). In keeping with this trend, personality psychologists have introduced a large number of cognitive personality variables to account for individual differences and intrapersonal processes. One of the most ambitious efforts to explain personality with cognitive variables was introduced by Walter Mischel (1973, 1979; Mischel & Shoda, 1995; Shoda & Mischel, 1996). You may recall from Chapter 7 that Mischel has long been a critic of the trait approach to personality. In its place he offers a model of personality that borrows heavily from cognitive psychology, social learning theory, and social-cognitive theory. Mischel argues that the events we encounter interact with a complex system of *cognitive-affective units* to determine our behavior. In this model, cognitive-affective units are all the mental representations that constitute the essential elements of our personalities. These mental representations can be placed in the five categories shown in Table 15.2.

According to this cognitive model of personality, the units in our personality system interact with the situation and with one another to produce behavior. An oversimplified illustration of this process is shown in Figure 15.1. In some ways the diagram resembles the classic "black box" model described by traditional behaviorists (Chapter 13). These behaviorists argue that the situation triggers behavior, with the unknown and unknowable black box representing what happens between stimulus and response. Cognitive personality theorists acknowledge that the situation often initiates our behavior. But it is exactly the elements between situation and response that are of greatest interest to these psychologists. Note further that, as in some of the social learning models, Mischel recognizes that a person's behavior can also affect the situation.

How do we explain individual differences in behavior within this cognitive model? The answer is that each of us possesses a different set of mental representations. Because these mental representations play a role in our behavior, two people often react to the same situation differently. Most important, cognitive-affective units differ in their accessibility. That is, we all differ in how easy or difficult it is for us to access certain kinds of information stored in our memories. Consequently, how we interpret a given situation and how we respond to that interpretation depend on which of the many cognitive categories is activated. What

Table 15.2   **Cognitive-Affective Units in Mischel's Personality System**

Encodings	Categories (constructs) for encoding information about one's self, other people, events, and situations
Expectations and Beliefs	Expectations for what will happen in certain situations, for outcomes for certain behaviors, and for one's personal efficacy
Affects	Feelings, emotions, and emotional responses
Goals and Values	Individual goals, values, and life projects
Competencies and Self-Regulatory Plans	Perceived abilities, plans, and strategies for changing and maintaining one's behavior and internal states

Source: From Mischel and Shoda (1995).

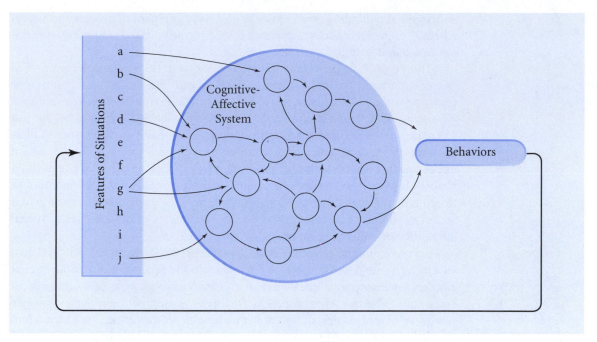

Figure 15.1

Cognitive Model of Personality

Source: Adapted from Mischel and Shoda (1995).

one person hears as a clever retort someone else might take as an insult. A Christmas tree will remind one person of religious values, another of family and seasonal joy, and a third of sad memories from childhood.

Schemas

Let's now return to the scene at the beginning of this chapter—the one in which my friend and I came away from the party with completely different impressions. Although we were exposed to essentially the same people and events, our experiences were quite different. One explanation for our different reactions is that my friend and I were using different schemas.

Schemas are hypothetical cognitive structures that help us perceive, organize, process, and use information. Because there are so many stimuli to attend to in most situations, we need some way to make sense of the mass confusion around us. Imagine what the world must look like to a baby—what psychologist William James once referred to as a "buzzing, blooming confusion." The baby has not yet developed ways to know what in all this confusion to pay attention to and what to ignore. Of course, the mass of stimuli doesn't go away. Think about all the sounds and sights bombarding your senses at this very moment. Through the use of schemas, each of us has developed systems for identifying and attending to what is important and ignoring the rest.

Thus, one of the main functions of schemas is to help us perceive features in our environment. Naturally, when something extremely important happens or someone possesses an attention-grabbing feature, everyone notices. For example, if a seven-foot-tall man attends a party, everyone probably notices his height. But less conspicuous features of an environment will probably not be noticed unless we enter the situation with a readiness to process that information. Thus, I seldom notice how tall most people are. However, a friend of mine is very aware of other people's heights (she is short). In schema terms, the reason she pays attention to height is that she has a well-developed schema for processing this information. Because I use different schemas to process information about others, she and I often have different impressions of people.

Beyond helping to perceive certain features in our environment, schemas provide us with a structure within which to organize and process information. For example, I can incorporate a new piece of information about my mother into my existing knowledge about her because I have a well-defined *mother* schema. I can give you a well-organized description of her because the information is organized into one well-formed cognitive structure rather than scattered about as bits of information in various unrelated schemas. I also should be able to process information about my mother more readily than information about a woman I have never met. For example, when asked if my mother is sociable, I should be able to answer more readily than if asked whether the queen of England is sociable. Without a strong schema for the queen, it will take me longer to process information about her. Moreover, because my *mother* schema provides me with a framework within which to process and organize information, it is easier for me to use this information. I should be able to recall information about my mother more readily than information stored loosely in my memory.

Cognitive Representations of the Self

Of all the cognitive structures that organize and store your memories, perhaps the most important mental representation is the one that is most unique to you. Beginning at a very early age, each of us develops a cognitive representation of who we are. Psychologists sometimes refer to this representation as our self-concept. As with other personality constructs, researchers find our self-concepts are relatively stable over time (Markus & Kunda, 1986). Moreover, research indicates that cognitive representations of the self play a central role in the way we process information and thus in how we interact with the world around us. We'll look next at some of the cognitive representations of *self* proposed by psychologists.

Figure 15.2

Example of a Self-Schema Diagram

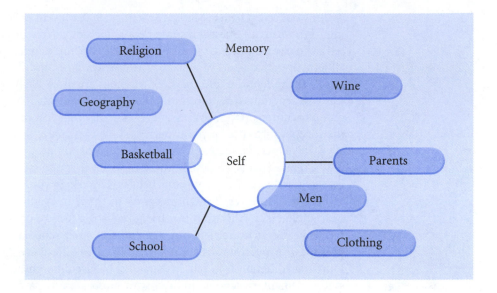

Self-Schemas

Surveys indicate most Americans are convinced that exercise is good for their physical and mental health. The majority of adults periodically take up jogging, swimming, aerobic dancing, or some other type of exercise program. However, a large number of people rarely, if ever, exercise. And about half of those who begin an exercise program quit within the first year. Why do some people succeed in making exercise a part of their lives, whereas others fail? One explanation has to do with whether the would-be exerciser incorporates exercise into his or her self-schema.

Self-schemas are cognitive representations of ourselves that we use to organize and process self-relevant information (Markus, 1977, 1983). Your self-schema consists of those aspects of your behavior that are the most important to you. Because each part of your life is not equally important, not everything you do becomes part of your self-schema. For example, if both you and I occasionally play baseball and write poetry, we can't assume that these two activities play an equally important role in our self-schemas. Baseball might be an important part of my self-schema, but not poetry, whereas the opposite might be the case for you.

If you could see your self-schema, what would it look like? An example of how a self-schema might fit in with other schemas is shown in Figure 15.2. Basic information about you makes up the core of your self-schema. This includes your name, information about your physical appearance, and information about your relationships with significant people, such as your spouse and parents. Although different for each of us, these basic elements are found in nearly everyone's self-schema. More interesting to personality psychologists are the unique features within your self-schema (Markus & Sentis, 1982; Markus & Smith, 1981). Returning to the exercise question, some people include *athlete* or *physically fit* in their self-schemas. Another way of saying this is that these individuals consider their athletic activities a part of who they are. Researchers find that people who incorporate such identities into their self-schemas are more likely to stick with regular exercise programs than those who do not (Kendzierski, 1988, 1990). When exercising becomes a part of who you are, you are much less likely to give it up when the weather turns bad or you experience a few aches and pains.

Trait concepts, such as independence or friendliness, can also be part of your self-schema. That is, you might think of yourself as a friendly person. If that is the case, you frequently evaluate your behavior by asking yourself: *Was that a friendly thing to do?* However, it might never occur to me to evaluate my actions in terms of friendliness. In this example, friendliness is a feature of your self-schema, but not mine. Because the elements that constitute self-schemas vary from person to person, we process information about ourselves differently. And because of these individual differences in self-schemas, we behave differently. For example, in one study, elementary school children with *prosocial* as a part of their self-schemas were more likely to give valuable tokens to others than did children who did not include *prosocial* as part of their self-concepts (Froming, Nasby, & McManus, 1998). In another investigation, men and women whose self-schemas included *sexuality* reported higher levels of sexual desire and stronger romantic attachments than those whose self-schemas did not include *sexuality* (Andersen, Cyranowski, & Espindle, 1999; Cyranowski & Andersen, 2000).

At this point, you may be asking *how* psychologists determine what a person's self-schema looks like. Although examining something as abstract as self-schemas presents a challenge, cognitive personality researchers have developed some creative procedures to test their hypotheses. Essentially, these psychologists look at how people perceive and use information presented to them. For example, answer the following question yes or no: Are you a competitive person? When faced with this question on a personality inventory, some people answer immediately and decisively, whereas others have to pause to think about what it means to be competitive and whether they possess those qualities. In taking the various personality tests in this book, you probably found some items that were easy to answer and some on which you simply couldn't make up your mind. According to a self-schema analysis, the items that were easy to answer are those for which you have a well-defined schema. People who say yes immediately when asked if they are competitive have a strong *competitive* schema that is part of their self-schema. The schema enables them to understand the question and respond immediately. People without a strong *competitive* schema lack the ability to process the information as quickly.

Much of the early research on self-schemas was based on this reasoning. Participants in one study were classified as possessing either a strong *independence* schema or a strong *dependence* schema or as aschematic (Markus, 1977). Later, these participants were presented with a series of adjectives on a computer screen.

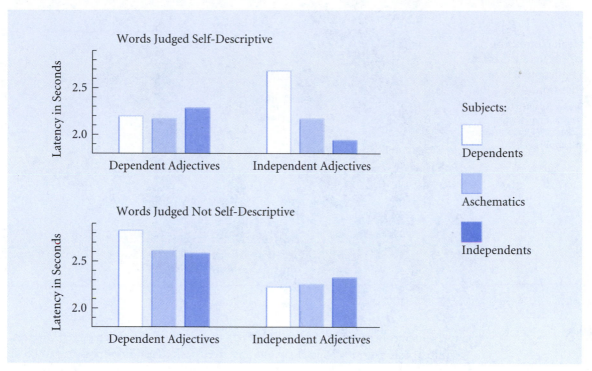

Figure 15.3

Mean Response Latencies for Adjectives

Source: Adapted from Markus (1977); reprinted by permission.

Their task was to press either a ME or a NOT ME button to indicate whether the adjective described them. Fifteen of the adjectives were related to independence (for example, *individualistic, outspoken*) and 15 to dependence (for example, *conforming, submissive*). The researchers wanted to see how quickly people in each of the three schema groups would respond to these 30 adjectives. As Figure 15.3 shows, people with strong *independence* schemas pressed the ME button quickly on the independence-related adjectives but took longer to respond on the dependence-related adjectives. Participants with strong *dependence* schemas responded in the opposite pattern. Aschematics showed no difference in making these judgments for any of the words. Researchers find similar results when they divide participants along other personality dimensions and examine how quickly they react to self-descriptive terms (Shah & Higgins, 2001).

In addition to allowing for rapid processing of schema-relevant information, self-schemas provide a framework for organizing and storing relevant information. Consequently, we would expect people to retrieve information from memory more readily when they have a strong schema for the topic than when the information is stored in a less organized manner. To test this hypothesis, researchers

Figure 15.4

Mean Number of
Words Recalled as
a Function of Cue
Question

Source: Adapted from
Rogers, Kuiper, and
Kirker (1977); reprinted
by permission.

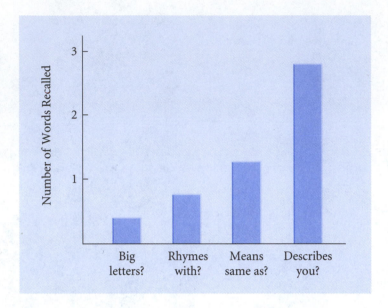

presented college students with a series of 40 questions on a video screen (Rogers, Kuiper, & Kirker, 1977). Participants answered each question by pressing a YES or a NO button as quickly as possible. Thirty of the questions were selected so that people could answer easily without using their self-schemas to process the information. For these questions, participants simply answered whether a word was printed in big letters, whether it rhymed with another word, or whether it meant the same thing as another word. However, for 10 questions participants had to decide whether a word described them. That is, they had to process the information through their self-schemas.

What the participants were not told was that afterward they would be asked to recall as many of the 40 words as possible. As shown in Figure 15.4, when participants answered questions about themselves, they were more likely to remember the information than when the question was processed in other ways. The researchers point to this finding as evidence for a self-schema. When asked whether a word describes them, participants processed the question through their self-schemas. Because information in our self-schemas is easy to access, the self-referent words were easier to remember than those not processed through self-schemas.

But might this finding be explained in other ways? Could it be that the self-referent question was simply harder than the other questions, thus causing participants to think about it more? Apparently not. When people were asked in subsequent studies if a word described the experimenter (Kuiper & Rogers, 1979) or a celebrity (Lord, 1980), they didn't recall the words as well as when they were asked about themselves. Nor can the results be explained simply in terms of the word's ability to generate emotion. Participants in another study recalled self-referent words better than equally emotional words processed another way (McCaul & Maki, 1984). In short, the accessibility and superior organization of information about ourselves seem to make information processed through the self-schema more accessible than information processed in other ways (Karylowski, 1990; Klein & Loftus, 1988; Klein, Loftus, & Burton, 1989).

Possible Selves

Suppose two college students, Denise and Carlos, receive an identical poor grade in a course on deductive logic and argumentation. Neither person is pleased with the grade, but Denise quickly dismisses it as a bad semester, whereas Carlos frets about the grade for weeks. Denise turns her attention to the next term, but Carlos looks over his final exam several times and thinks about taking another course in this area. Although many explanations can be suggested to account for the two students' different reactions, a key piece of information may be that Carlos is thinking about going to law school and becoming a trial attorney someday, but Denise is not. A negative evaluation of his deductive logic and argumentation skills means something quite different to Carlos than it does to Denise. Further, his aspiration to become an attorney leads Carlos to a different course of action than that taken by Denise.

What this example illustrates is that our behavior is directed not only by cognitive representations of the way we think of ourselves at the moment, but also by our cognitive representations of what we might become someday. You might think about a future self with a lot of friends, with a medical degree, or with a physically fit body. However, sometimes we also think about the selves we fear we might become, such as a self that is unemployed, physically ill, or lonely and depressed. Psychologists refer to these images as our possible selves (Cantor, Markus, Niedenthal, & Nurius, 1986; Markus & Nurius, 1986; Ruvolo & Markus, 1992).

Possible selves are cognitive representations of the kinds of people we think we might become someday. These include roles and occupations we aspire to, such as police officer or community leader, as well as the roles we fear we might fall into, such as alcoholic or divorced parent. Possible selves also include the attributes we think we might possess in the future, such as being a warm and loving person, an overworked and underappreciated person, or a contributor to society. In a sense, possible selves represent our dreams and aspirations as well as our fears and anxieties. Like other personality constructs, possible selves are fairly stable over time (Frazier, Hooker, Johnson, & Kaus, 2000; Morfei, Hooker, Fiese, & Cordeiro, 2001).

Possible selves serve two important functions (Markus & Nurius, 1986). First, possible selves provide incentives for future behavior. When making decisions, we ask ourselves whether a choice will take us closer to or further away from one of our future selves. For example, a woman might enter an MBA program because this decision moves her closer to becoming her *powerful business executive* possible self. A man might stop seeing old friends if he thinks the association could lead him to the *criminal* self he fears he might become.

The second function of possible selves is to help us interpret the meaning of our behavior and the events in our lives. For example, a man with a *professional baseball player* possible self will attach a very different meaning to hitting a home run than someone who does not think of himself or herself this way. A woman with a possible self of *cancer patient* will react differently to small changes in her health than someone without this cognitive representation. In other words, we pay more attention to and have a stronger emotional reaction to events that move us toward one of our possible selves than events not relevant to our possible selves.

The connection between possible selves and potential problem behaviors has been demonstrated in research with juvenile delinquents (Oyserman & Markus, 1990; Oyserman & Saltz, 1993). Thinking about the kind of person we want to become is an important part of adolescence. Significantly, more than one-third of the juvenile delinquents in one study had developed a *criminal* possible self (Oyserman & Markus, 1990). In addition, relatively few of these adolescents possessed possible selves for such conventional goals as having a job or getting along in school. If these possible selves are indicative of the goals, fears, and aspirations of these juvenile delinquents, it is perhaps not surprising that youthful offenders often become adult criminals.

Self Discrepancies

While reading the previous section, you may have been struck by the similarities between possible selves and some of the psychological concepts described in earlier parts of this book. For example, in Chapter 5 you read about Sullivan's psychoanalytic notion of *personifications.* These are the mental images we have of ourselves, which Sullivan identified as the *good-me,* the *bad-me,* and the *not-me.* Later you encountered Rogers' descriptions of the *real-self* and *ideal-self.* Within Rogers' humanistic theory, people approach a sense of self-acceptance and psychological health when the way they see themselves is similar to the person they would like to be.

Cognitive personality psychologists have also explored the relation between different self concepts. One approach, called *self-discrepancy theory,* proposes three different cognitive representations of self (Higgins, 1987, 1989). First, each of us possesses an *actual self.* The actual self contains all the information you have about the kind of person you are (or believe you are), similar to the notion of self-concept used by other personality psychologists. Second, we also possess an *ideal self,* which is your mental image of the kind of person you would like to be. The ideal self includes your dreams and aspirations and the goals you have set for yourself in life. Just as no two people have identical actual selves, no two ideal selves are alike. You may desire to play the piano well and become active in local politics. Your friend's goal might be to own his or her own business. Third, there is the *ought self.*

This is the self you believe you should be, the kind of person who fulfills all the duties and obligations various sources (parents, religion) have defined for you. Your ought self might be someone who gets involved in community activities, a devoted parent, or a patriotic citizen.

The ideal self and ought self draw our attention to relevant information and provide reference points when making important decisions. In particular, we often compare the way we act (our actual self) with the way we want to be (ideal self) or the way we should be (ought self). If we fall short in these comparisons, certain negative emotions will follow. According to the theory, discrepancies between our actual self and ideal self result in emotions related to disappointment and depression. This would be the reaction of a would-be honors student who becomes lax in his or her study habits and receives low grades. On the other hand, discrepancies between the actual self and the ought self lead to emotions associated with nervousness, anxiety, and guilt. These are the emotions we might expect when we act selfishly or take advantage of someone, in contrast with the generous and kind person we think we ought to be. As with other cognitive processes, this comparison is said to take place outside of conscious awareness. Thus, according to the theory, you can experience depression or guilt without being aware of the underlying causes.

Researchers find support for many of the predictions generated from self-discrepancy theory. In particular, people made aware of a gap between their actual and ideal self often experience depression, whereas those with discrepant actual and ought selves suffer from anxiety (Boldero & Francis, 2000; Higgins, 1999; Higgins, Bond, Klein, & Strauman, 1986; Strauman & Higgins, 1987). Researchers also find that, like other personality variables, measures of an adult's ideal-self and ought-self are fairly consistent over time (Strauman, 1996). Although little is known about how self-discrepancies affect emotions in other cultures, one study found Japanese undergraduates had larger discrepancies between their actual and ideal selves than Canadian students (Heine & Lehman, 1999). Interestingly, this increase in self-criticism by the Japanese students did not translate into higher levels of depression. This finding suggests again the need to consider culture when examining the way people construe and evaluate themselves (Chapter 12).

Application: Cognitive Psychotherapy

The increased attention given to cognitive structures by personality researchers in recent years has been paralleled by the growing popularity of cognitive approaches to psychotherapy. As the name implies, the focus of cognitive psychotherapy is the client's thoughts. Although many different therapies fall under this heading, each identifies inappropriate thoughts as a cause of debilitating mood disorders and self-defeating behavior. Within this approach, people become anxious and depressed because they harbor anxiety-provoking and depressing thoughts. Consequently, the goal of most cognitive therapies is to help clients recognize these self-defeating thoughts and replace them with more appropriate ones. Sometimes this process is referred to as *cognitive restructuring*. A cognitive therapist's role usually falls somewhere between that of the intrusive Freudian therapist and the Rogerian therapist, who relies on the client for clinical progress. Although clients must come to see how their cognitions affect their emotions and behaviors, the therapist plays an active role in the process.

As with cognitive personality theory, George Kelly (1955, 1969) was an early pioneer in the cognitive approach to treating psychological disorders. Kelly's goal as a psychotherapist was to help clients develop new constructs, reshape construct hierarchies, and modify old constructs so they were better able to predict events. He used a variety of methods to meet this goal. For example, if clients' constructs seemed particularly vague, Kelly might ask them to define the constructs more clearly and provide examples of elements that did and did not fit the categories. In this manner, clients were forced to attend to their process of construing the world and to test its accuracy for predicting events. Kelly also developed a procedure called **fixed-role therapy.** Here a team of therapists creates an imaginary person for clients to role-play. By pretending to be this other person and perceiving the world the way this person might, clients "try on" new constructs. If these constructs are helpful, clients may continue to use them after the role-playing.

Albert Ellis's Rational Emotive Therapy

One of the earliest advocates of cognitive therapy was Albert Ellis, who developed **rational emotive therapy** (Ellis & Harper, 1975). According to Ellis, people become depressed, anxious, upset, and the like because of faulty reasoning and a reliance on irrational beliefs. Ellis describes this as an A-B-C process. For example, suppose your boyfriend/girlfriend calls tonight and tells you the relationship is over. This is the A, which Ellis calls the **A**ctivating experience. However, when clients seek out psychotherapy they usually identify the reason as the C, the *emotional* **C**onsequence. In this case, you are probably depressed, guilty, or angry. But how did you logically get from A to C? Why should a personal setback or loss cause such strong negative emotions? The answer is that you have used a middle step in this sequence, B—the *irrational* **B**elief. The only way you could logically conclude from breaking up with your partner that you should be depressed is that you are also saying to yourself something like "It is necessary for me to be loved and approved by virtually every person in my life." Of course, when isolated like this, the belief is obviously irrational. But these irrational beliefs are so entrenched in our thoughts that it often takes professional help to see the flaws in our thinking.

Ellis maintains that each of us harbors and relies on a large number of these irrational beliefs. Imagine that you fail an important class (A). If you then fall back on the irrational belief "I need to do well at everything to be considered worthwhile" (B), you'll lead yourself to the conclusion that this is a catastrophe and therefore become excessively anxious (C). A rational emotive therapist would argue that, whereas failing is certainly an unfortunate event—and something you'd

"The best scientist is one who approaches his subject [as] intimately as a clinician . . . and the best clinician is one who invites his client to join him in a controlled investigation of life."
GEORGE KELLY

Table 15.3	Some Common Irrational Beliefs

Obvious Irrational Beliefs

Because I strongly desire to perform important tasks competently and successfully, I absolutely must perform them well at all times.

Because I strongly desire to be approved by people I find significant, I absolutely must always have their approval.

Because I strongly desire people to treat me considerately and fairly, they absolutely must at all times and under all conditions do so.

Because I strongly desire to have a safe, comfortable, and satisfying life, the conditions under which I live absolutely must at all times be easy, convenient, and gratifying.

Subtle and Tricky Irrational Beliefs

Because I strongly desire to perform important tasks competently and successfully, and because I want to succeed at them only some of the time, I absolutely must perform these tasks well.

Because I strongly desire to be approved by people I find significant, and because I only want a little approval from them, I absolutely must have it.

Because I strongly desire people to treat me considerately and fairly, and because I am almost always considerate and fair to others, they absolutely must treat me well.

Because I strongly desire to have a safe, comfortable, and satisfying life, and because I am a nice person who tries to help others lead this kind of life, the conditions under which I live absolutely must be easy, convenient, and gratifying.

Source: From Ellis (1987), with permission.

prefer didn't happen—it does not warrant extreme anxiety. Expecting everything to work out well all the time will only lead to disappointment and frustration. Some of the more commonly used irrational beliefs are listed in Table 15.3. Ellis (1987) points out that some of these beliefs are blatantly irrational and therefore more easily identified and corrected during therapy. However, other beliefs are more subtle or trickier and therefore more resistant to change.

The goal of rational emotive therapy is twofold. First, clients must see how they rely on irrational beliefs and thereby identify the fault in their reasoning. Second, the therapist works with the client to replace irrational beliefs with rational ones. For example, instead of deciding that your romantic breakup is a reason to be depressed, you might tell yourself that, although you enjoy a stable romantic relationship and wish this one could have continued, you know that not all relationships work out. You also know that this doesn't mean no one else can love you or that you are never going to have a good relationship again. Thus, whereas the A statement is the same—"I broke up with my partner"—the B statement is different. Because the situation is identified as unpleasant but not catastrophic, there is no need to become overly depressed, the old C.

In the following sample, taken from one of Ellis's therapy sessions with a young woman (Ellis, 1971), you can see how rational emotive therapy tries to change faulty thoughts:

> *Client:* Well, this is all a part of something that's bothered me for a long time. I'm always afraid of making a mistake.
> *Ellis:* Why? What's the horror?
> *C:* I don't know.
> *E:* You're saying that you're a bitch, you're a louse when you make a mistake.
> *C:* But this is the way I've always been. Every time I make a mistake, I die a thousand deaths over it.
> *E:* You blame yourself. But why? What's the horror? Is it going to make you better next time? Is it going to make you make fewer mistakes?
> *C:* No.
> *E:* Then why blame yourself? Why are you a louse for making a mistake? Who said so?
> *C:* I guess it's one of those feelings I have.
> *E:* One of those beliefs. The belief is: "I am a louse!" And then you get the feeling: "Oh, how awful! How shameful!" But the feeling follows the belief. And again, you're saying, "I should be different; I shouldn't make mistakes!" instead of, "Oh, look: I made a mistake. It's undesirable to make mistakes. Now, how am I going to stop making one next time?" . . .
> *C:* It might all go back to, as you said, the need for approval. If I don't make mistakes, then people will look up to me. If I do it all perfectly—
> *E:* Yes, that's part of it. That is the erroneous belief: that if you never make mistakes everybody will love you and that it is necessary that they do. . . . But is it true? Suppose you never did make mistakes—would people love you? They'd sometimes hate your guts, wouldn't they?

Rational emotive therapists challenge clients to identify their irrational beliefs and see how these beliefs lead them to their faulty conclusions. Of course, this is not easy. Most of us can readily identify what's wrong with our friends' thinking, but it's quite another matter when we're the ones with an emotional problem. Nonetheless, the success of rational emotive therapy with a large number of clients has contributed to the increased popularity of cognitive approaches to psychotherapy in recent years.

Self-Instructional Training

As with other approaches, one goal of cognitive psychotherapy is to help clients overcome the problems that caused them to seek professional help. But this typically is not the only purpose of cognitive therapy. It's important to help clients recognize they are not worthless because they failed a class. But how long until these clients run into another personal setback, another failure? Because we can never avoid potentially distressing situations, cognitive psychologists often teach clients how to prepare for and deal with potential problem situations in the future. If people learn how to avoid self-defeating thoughts, they can also avoid some of the emotional problems that may have plagued them throughout their lives.

Self-instructional training is a good example of such an approach. Self-instructional training is typically part of a larger cognitive therapy program (Meichenbaum, 1977, 1985; Meichenbaum & Cameron, 1983). As in rational emotive therapy, psychologists using this procedure identify the thoughts that drive clients' disturbing emotions and help them recognize and replace these with more adaptive thinking. But clients also develop specific cognitive strategies for dealing with the kinds of situations that frequently cause them problems.

One reason for recurrent problems is that some people typically engage in *self-defeating thinking.* For example, a man who suffers from shyness probably approaches a dance telling himself something like "I don't know why I'm going to this stupid dance. No one ever wants to dance with me. When they do, I usually look so awkward on the dance floor I'm sure people are staring at me. And when the dance is over, I never know what to say." This man has set himself up to fail. At the first awkward moment he will conclude that things are going as poorly as anticipated. All the nervousness and embarrassment he dreaded are likely to follow.

What can be done for this man? Therapists using self-instructional training try to replace these self-defeating thoughts with more appropriate, positive ones. This is not to say the man should unrealistically expect that everything will go well. Rather, he should be prepared for some disappointments and failures and learn to interpret these in appropriate ways. Some psychologists compare this process to inoculation. Like a medical vaccine that prevents a patient from becoming ill, self-instructional training is designed to keep negative thoughts from creating undue psychological distress.

Therapists using self-instructional training help clients prepare *internal monologues* for each step of the stressful experience. For example, a woman who suffers from stage fright will learn to say to herself before a performance, "Think about what you can do, not about getting nervous." As she is about to walk out on stage, she may think, "A little nervousness is normal in this situation." During the performance she may remind herself, "You're doing fine." Finally, she rewards herself afterward with, "You're getting better every time," or, "Better, but you still have a few things to work on for next time."

Once clients see the effectiveness of self-instructional training for one problem, they often develop appropriate internal monologues for other problems that arise. The college actress who overcame her stage fright with this procedure may adopt a similar strategy when she faces job interviews in a few years. Researchers find considerable evidence for the effectiveness of self-instructional training for clients suffering from a variety of problems (Kiselica, Baker, Thomas, & Reedy, 1994; Meichenbaum & Deffenbacher, 1988).

Like any approach to treatment, cognitive psychotherapy does not work for everyone and may be limited to psychological problems that are based in irrational and self-defeating thinking. Nonetheless, the success many therapists have had with this approach has been encouraging. A review of studies comparing cognitive therapy for depression with other types of therapy concluded that the cognitive approach was more successful than behavior therapy, drug treatments, and of course, no treatment (Dobson, 1989). Other studies indicate that cognitive therapies are also effective for treating clients suffering from anxiety and panic disorders (Beck, 1991).

Assessment: The Repertory Grid Technique

George Kelly made personal constructs the key concept in his theory of personality as well as the focus of his approach to psychotherapy. But this emphasis created a bit of a problem for him. Specifically, how does one go about measuring a person's personal constructs? Of course, a therapist might obtain some idea of a client's construct system during the course of therapy interviews. But Kelly and his colleagues needed a more efficient way to examine construct systems that could then be communicated fairly easily to the client. Kelly's response to this problem was to develop the *Repertory Grid Technique.* Kelly and his followers developed several variations of this technique, but the essential procedure consists of two steps (Bell, 1990). First, the test-taker creates a list of *elements.* The items on this list can be anything the individual encounters in life, but most often the list consists of specific people the test-taker knows. Second, the test-taker's personal constructs are elicited by comparing and contrasting various elements on the list.

The most common version of the grid technique is the *Role Construct Repertory Test,* or more commonly, the **Rep Test.** A shortened version of the basic Rep Test procedure is presented on pages 466–467. Therapists begin the procedure by asking clients to provide a list of 24 people from various personal experiences—for example, a teacher they liked, the most interesting person they know, and so on. The therapist then presents clients with three of the names from this list and asks, "In what important way are two of these people alike but different from the third?" A client might say, for example, that two of them are *warm* people and that the third person is *cold.* In Kelly's terms, this client has used a *warm-cold* construct to categorize the three people. The process is repeated with three different names from the list. Perhaps this time the client will divide the people along *outgoing-shy* or *generous-miserly* constructs. Kelly concluded that about 20 trials or "sorts" provides the therapist with a useful sample of the client's principal constructs.

In one variation of the Rep Test, the therapist takes away one of the three names and replaces it with a new one. This procedure can be useful in identifying clients' difficulties in applying new constructs to new situations. To examine self-concepts, therapists sometimes present the client's name along with two names from the list. Again, clients are asked how two of the three are alike and one is different. Many therapists take the list of constructs generated from the client's initial Rep Test and ask the client to evaluate each person on the list according to the construct. This step creates a grid similar to the one shown in Table 15.4 and allows the therapist and client to look for patterns across a broad set of information.

The Repertory Grid Technique has been widely used by therapists and clinical psychologists to obtain a visual map of how clients and those suffering from vari-

Table 15.4 Sample Grid

	Mom	Dad	Sister	Brother	Boss	Neighbor	Friend	Coworker	
Pleasant	P	U	U	U	U	U	P	U	Unpleasant
Trustworthy	U	U	U	U	U	U	?	U	Untrustworthy
Competitive	N	N	C	C	?	N	C	C	Not Competitive
Warm	W	C	C	C	C	C	?	C	Cold
Intelligent	N	I	I	I	I	?	N	I	Not Intelligent
Fun	D	D	D	D	D	D	F	D	Dull

ous psychological disorders construe the world (Landfield & Epting, 1987). But the grid technique has also been used by researchers when studying such diverse topics as communication within a large organization (Coopman, 1997), how we form impressions of other people (Adams-Webber, 1998), profiles of specific criminal types (Horley, 1996), and career counseling (Savickas, 1997). One reviewer recently counted more than 3,000 studies using variations of the Repertory Grid Technique (Neimeyer, 2001).

Like other assessment procedures, the grid technique also has its limitations. One concern is that, unlike other personality measures, the Repertory Grid Technique does not generate a simple test score (Horley, 1996). Although various number-generating systems have been developed, the procedure still allows for a large element of interpretation on the part of the therapist. Another limitation concerns the many assumptions underlying the test. Kelly acknowledged several assumptions therapists must make when using the Rep Test to measure personal constructs. One is that the constructs clients provide are not limited to the people on the list, but also would apply to new people in new situations. Another assumption is that the constructs elicited during the test have some degree of permanence. That is, we assume clients are not using these constructs for the first time in the testing session and never again. A related assumption is that the people on the list are representative of the kind of people clients are likely to deal with in their daily lives. Constructs used only for unique people that clients rarely encounter are of little use in understanding how clients deal with the majority of people they interact with.

But the most precarious assumption made by test givers, according to Kelly, is that people are *able* to describe the constructs they use. Unfortunately, the grid technique is subject to the inherent limits of our language. Although clients may supply words that come close to what they mean, these words may be inadequate. Kelly did not assume that words necessarily exist for describing all constructs. In fact, he identified "preverbal" constructs, those developed before we learn to speak. And even when clients do use appropriate words, therapists may interpret those words differently. For example, a client's definition of *aggressive* may be quite

Assessing Your Own Personality

Personal Constructs

To begin, write down the names of the following 12 people. Although a person may fit more than one category, you need to compile a list of 12 different people. If there is no one who fits a category, name someone who is similar to the category description. For example, if you do not have a brother, select someone who is like a brother to you.

_____   1. A teacher you liked

_____   2. A teacher you disliked

_____   3. Your wife (husband) or boyfriend (girlfriend)

_____   4. An employer, supervisor, or officer you found hard to get along with

_____   5. An employer, supervisor, or officer you liked

_____   6. Your mother

_____   7. Your father

_____   8. Brother nearest your age

_____   9. Sister nearest your age

_____   10. A person with whom you have worked who was easy to get along with

_____   11. A person with whom you have worked who was hard to understand

_____   12. A neighbor with whom you get along well

Next, take three of these people at a time, as indicated by the numbers in the following list. Then describe in what important way two of these people are alike but different from the third. Put a word or

different from a therapist's. In this case the therapist may still end up with false impressions of how the client views the world.

Strengths and Criticisms of the Cognitive Approach

Strengths

One strength of the cognitive approach to personality is that many of the ideas evolved out of and were developed through empirical research findings. For example, most of the cognitive structures used to account for individual differences phrase describing the two alike people in the *Construct* list and a description of the remaining person in the *Contrast* list.

Names	Construct	Contrast
3, 6, 7	_____	_____
1, 4, 10	_____	_____
4, 7, 8	_____	_____
1, 6, 9	_____	_____
4, 5, 8	_____	_____
2, 11, 12	_____	_____
8, 9, 10	_____	_____
2, 3, 5	_____	_____
5, 7, 11	_____	_____
1, 10, 12	_____	_____

This is an abbreviated version of Kelly's Rep Test (the Minimum Context Form). The test provides a quick idea of the constructs you use to organize information about the people you know and meet. You may want to compare your responses with those of other test takers. No doubt you will find a few overlapping constructs, but also many you hadn't thought of. Of course, these differences in personal constructs represent differences in personality that should translate into individual differences in your behavior.

Scale: *The Role Construct Repertory (REP) Test*

Source: Kelly (1955)

have been subjected to extensive investigation in controlled laboratory experiments. In many cases personality psychologists have borrowed ideas and research procedures from social and cognitive psychologists investigating similar phenomena. Moreover, cognitive models of personality have been modified as investigators learn more about cognitive structures and processes through their ongoing research.

Another strength of the cognitive approach is that it fits well with the current mood, or Zeitgeist, of psychology. The number of journal articles and doctoral dissertations examining cognitive concepts has risen dramatically over the past three decades (Robins et al., 1999). Researchers in other areas of psychology, such as developmental and social psychologists, are working on related lines of cognitive research that often complement and extend what is known from the personality perspective.

Related to the preceding point, cognitive approaches to psychotherapy have become particularly popular in recent years. Even therapists who identify with other approaches to personality sometimes incorporate aspects of cognitive therapy in their practice. A recent survey of practitioners in the Association for the Advancement of Behavior Therapy, a group originally composed of behavior therapists, found that 67% now describe their therapy orientation as "cognitive behavioral" (Elliott, Miltenberger, Kaster-Bundgaard, & Lumley, 1996). Nearly half said they occasionally use rational emotive therapy with their clients.

Criticisms

A frequent criticism of the cognitive approach is that the concepts are sometimes too abstract for empirical research. What exactly is a "personal construct" or a "possible self"? How do we know if a schema is being used? How many schemas are there, and how are they related? More important, how can we study their influence on behavior if we can't agree on clear operational definitions? Some of the answers may come with more research, but the nature of cognitions probably renders them more nebulous than many constructs used by personality theorists.

A related question is whether we need to introduce these concepts to account for individual differences in behavior. For example, behaviorists might argue that they can explain the same phenomena with fewer constructs. Introducing schemas or possible selves may be unnecessary at best and perhaps even an obstacle to understanding personality. Applying the law of parsimony, it is incumbent upon cognitive theorists to demonstrate how their approach can explain personality better than other, less complicated approaches.

Perhaps because the cognitive approach to personality is still evolving, there is no single model to organize and guide theory and research. Basic questions about how various cognitive structures relate to one another and to other aspects of information processing, such as memory, remain unanswered. A related problem concerns the relationship between the various cognitive structures different theorists have introduced. Is a personal construct different from a schema? A comprehensive model would help researchers understand precisely what these terms mean and how they are related.

Summary

1.   The cognitive approach to personality describes consistent behavior patterns in terms of the way people process information. George Kelly was an early pioneer in this approach with his personal construct theory. Kelly maintained that we are motivated to make sense out of our worlds. He compared people to scientists, always striving for better predictions about what will happen to them. Kelly

described the cognitive structures we use in this regard as personal constructs. He maintained that psychological problems stem from anxiety, which results from a person's inability to predict events.

2. Psychologists have described a number of cognitive structures to help explain individual differences and intrapersonal processes. Schemas are cognitive structures that help us perceive, organize, and store information.

3. Perhaps the most important cognitive structures for personality psychologists are the cognitive representations we have for our selves. Much research in this area is concerned with self-schemas. Studies demonstrate that we perceive information more readily and recall it better when it is relevant to our self-schemas. Researchers also find that cognitive representations of future selves guide our behavior, but that discrepancies between different self-concepts can result in negative emotions.

4. Cognitive approaches to psychotherapy have become increasingly popular in the last few decades. These therapies focus on changing the clients' thoughts. Albert Ellis, an early advocate of this approach, argues that people have emotional problems when they use irrational beliefs. Rational emotive therapy helps clients see how they use these beliefs and how to replace them with more rational ones. In self-instructional training, clients learn to replace negative internal statements with more appropriate, positive statements.

5. Kelly introduced the Repertory Grid Technique to measure individual differences in personal constructs. In one example, test takers typically develop a list of people in their lives and then divide these people into various categories. This procedure helps therapists see the constructs clients use to make sense of the world. Kelly acknowledged several assumptions behind this approach, including that people can adequately communicate the constructs they use.

6. Among the strengths of the cognitive approach is its strong empirical background. The cognitive approach also fits nicely with the current trend in psychology toward cognitive explanations of behavior. Some critics of the cognitive approach have complained that many of the concepts used by cognitive theorists are too abstract. Others have questioned whether it is always necessary to introduce cognitions to explain behavior. The cognitive approach also suffers from the lack of a general model to organize all of the work that falls under this approach.

InfoTrac College Edition Key Terms

For additional readings go to http://www.infotrac-college.com/wadsworth and enter a search term related to your interest. Use the key terms suggested here to pull up several related articles. Also see the text Web site at http://psychology .wadsworth.com for more suggested readings and interactive quizzes to test your knowledge.

Albert Ellis
Cognitive styles
George Kelly

Rational emotive therapy
Schemas

Chapter 16

The Cognitive Approach

Relevant Research

Freudian Concepts Revisited: Transference and Repression
Gender Type and Gender Differences
Cognitions and Depression
Summary

If you think back to the first chapter, you may recall the story about the blind men trying to describe an elephant. The point was that obtaining a complete understanding of human personality requires that we examine personality from several different perspectives. Although each perspective offers useful information, each also provides only a limited view of this complex topic. This lesson is clearly illustrated in the research covered in this chapter. Each program of research examines a topic introduced earlier in the book. We start by going back to Freud. Many of the concepts introduced by Freud have caught the attention of cognitive personality researchers. By looking at these concepts through the framework of contemporary cognitive psychology, investigators have renewed interest in such psychoanalytic concepts as transference and repression. Next, we return to questions about gender. The androgyny model advanced our understanding of masculinity and femininity. Subsequent research built on that progress by examining the cognitive structures responsible for gender type differences. Other studies identify differences in the way men and women store information about their selves. We'll also look at the cognitive explanations for one of the topics that has surfaced in several places throughout the book. Cognitive approaches to understanding depression have yielded a number of useful insights into this common emotional problem.

471

Freudian Concepts Revisited: Transference and Repression

More than six decades after his death, Sigmund Freud still casts a shadow on the field of personality psychology. Although some psychologists denounce Freud's theory as antiquated and irrelevant to current research questions, others recognize that we can appreciate part of Freud's work without embracing the entire package. As one observer noted, "to reject psychodynamic thinking because Freud's instinct theory or his view of women is dated is like rejecting modern physics because Newton did not understand relativity" (Westen, 1998, p. 334).

As you will see in this section, many researchers find some of Freud's concepts quite relevant and rather intriguing when looked at through the lenses of contemporary cognitive psychology. A case in point is Freud's description of *projection*—the tendency to see in others undesirable characteristics you fear you may possess. For example, through projection an untrustworthy businessman may suspect that his business partner is out to cheat him. Freud explained projection as an unconscious process used by the ego to defend against unacceptable anxiety. By projecting the characteristic onto the partner, the businessman is able to avoid the anxiety that comes with acknowledging his own lack of trustworthiness. However, one also could explain projection in terms of cognitive processes (Newman, Duff, & Baumeister, 1997). According to this analysis, when people actively avoid thinking about threatening information, they make thoughts related to that information highly accessible in memory. One might say the suspicious businessman has activated an "untrustworthy behavior" schema. Because thoughts about lack of trust are easily accessible, it's not surprising the businessman readily attends to and interprets information suggesting that his partner's actions are untrustworthy.

Psychologists find that several other Freudian concepts can be understood within a cognitive framework (Baumeister, Dale, & Sommer, 1998). We'll look at two examples in this section. Recent research on transference and repression demonstrates that Freudian psychology is not dead, although it may sometimes appear in new wrappings.

Transference

Most of us have had the strange experience of instantly feeling that we like or do not like someone we have just met, perhaps even someone we have only seen and never spoken to. A woman recently told me about a new employee in her office to whom she took an immediate dislike. My friend had never spoken with this other woman, nor did she know much about her. Nonetheless, she was sure the woman was conceited and selfish. She maintained these beliefs even when her colleagues described the other woman as warm, friendly, and generous. What was going on here? My friend is not particularly judgmental or difficult to get along with. Why would she have such strong opinions about someone she had never met?

The answer, my friend eventually realized, was that the new worker resembled her older sister. The worker not only had similar facial characteristics to the sister, but also walked and dressed like her. As you may have guessed by now, my friend has a strained relationship with her sister. She thinks her sister is conceited and selfish. In short, my friend was guilty of transferring her feelings about a significant person in her life to a person she had yet to really meet.

As you may recall from Chapter 3, Freud described a similar phenomenon many years ago. He called it *transference.* During psychoanalysis, some of Freud's patients would transfer their feelings about significant people in their lives to the therapist. By talking to Freud as if he were a deceased parent or former lover, patients were said to release previously repressed thoughts and feelings about that individual. Of course, Freud's description of transference was embedded within psychoanalytic theory. But in recent years some psychologists have turned their attention back to transference, albeit without the psychoanalytic trappings (Andersen & Berk, 1998; Singer, 1988; Wachtel, 1981; Westen, 1988, 1998). In place of Freudian concepts, these investigators use insights and research findings from cognitive psychology to account for this interesting phenomenon.

How can we explain transference from a cognitive perspective? Returning to the woman who developed instant feelings about the new worker, we could begin by saying that my friend naturally had a strong cognitive representation of her sister. The new woman resembling the sister activated this cognitive representation, which then triggered emotions and other associations. In a sense, the old cognitive representation was used to process information about the new person. Consequently, we would expect my friend to see many of the sister's characteristics in the other woman and to have many of the same feelings about the new worker as she has for her sister. Although cognitive psychologists do not describe this process as unconscious in the Freudian sense, they suggest that transference typically happens at a level that is just out of awareness.

This description explains why we sometimes have "a feeling" about someone we meet, yet can't quite say why we have it. But how can we test this interpretation experimentally? One procedure begins by asking participants to provide information about two people they know well (Andersen & Cole, 1990; Andersen, Reznik, & Manzella, 1996; Chen, Andersen, & Hinkley, 1999; Hinkley & Andersen, 1996). A few weeks later the same participants are recruited for a supposedly unrelated study. Participants are told they will meet someone sitting in the next room, but first they will learn something about that person. Participants then read a "trained interviewer's" evaluation of the person. In some conditions the evaluation resembles one of the people the participant described earlier. That is, some participants are led to believe this person they are about to meet resembles someone they know.

Researchers using this procedure find evidence for transference consistent with the cognitive formulation. For example, when trying to recall what they had

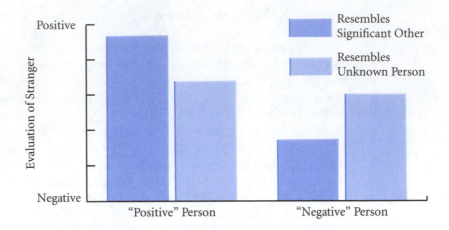

Figure 16.1

Feelings Toward
Stranger in Next
Room

Source: From Anderson
& Baum (1994); with
permission.

been told about the person in the other room, participants in one study tended to "remember" characteristics that were not on the interviewer's evaluation. Consistent with the notion of transference, what these participants remembered were in fact characteristics of the significant individual this person supposedly resembled (Andersen & Baum, 1994). Participants in this study also transferred their emotional feelings about the significant other. As shown in Figure 16.1, participants liked the stranger more when that person resembled someone they liked and less when he or she resembled a person they didn't like. Participants in another study were videotaped while they read about the person in the other room (Andersen et al., 1996). The participants' faces expressed more pleasantness when participants transferred feelings about someone they liked and more unpleasantness when the transference involved someone they did not like. Other studies suggest this transference of feelings occurs without our awareness (Glassman & Andersen, 1999b) and is not just a fleeting sensation, but can last at least several weeks (Glassman & Andersen, 1999a).

However, transference does more than alter the way we feel about people we have never met. Investigators find we also alter the way we act around people who resemble someone we know (Berk & Andersen, 2000; Hinkley & Andersen, 1996). That is, some aspects of our self-concepts are linked to the way we think about other people. For example, you might always feel incompetent around a smarter, more accomplished cousin. From a cognitive perspective, we would say these thoughts about your incompetence are connected in memory to the cognitive representation of your cousin. Consequently, if someone resembling your cousin activates that cognitive representation, you most likely will feel incompetent around this new person. This analysis helps us understand why some people seem to fall into old—sometimes self-destructive—habits every time they become romantically involved. We might say these people are relying on the cognitive representation of an old romantic partner when dealing with each new partner.

Repression

Life can be difficult. This is one of the few observations upon which almost everyone agrees. Not that life isn't also beautiful. But sprinkled throughout our daily experiences we inevitably find traffic jams, disagreeable neighbors, broken televisions, spilled drinks, lost purses, missing library journals, broken dates, poor grades, and unresponsive computers. What fascinates many psychologists about this situation is that some people appear relatively unaffected by these events, whereas others dwell on them. Personality psychologists can account for different responses to stress and failure in a number of ways. For example, we saw in earlier chapters how individual differences in Neuroticism and self-esteem play a role in these reactions. But other psychologists explain the apparent ease with which some people respond to stressors in terms of *repression*.

You may recall from Chapter 3 that Freud called repression the "cornerstone" of psychoanalysis. Of course, he was referring to an unconscious process in which the ego keeps unacceptable thoughts out of awareness. When personality researchers use the term *repression* today, they usually refer to one way people respond to unpleasant information. For example, a student who seems unconcerned with his grades even though he is on the verge of failing several classes might be identified as using repression. However, like the Freudian concept from which it takes its name, this newer version of repression also appears to take place outside of the repressor's awareness.

Although researchers have used a number of techniques to investigate repression and related phenomena, one of the most fruitful approaches looks at individual differences. Specifically, investigators can identify people who typically respond to stressful situations with relatively few signs of anxiety or worry. You may recall from Chapter 6 that early research on coping strategies placed people along a dimension called "repression-sensitization" (Byrne, 1964). At one end of this continuum we find repressors, people who typically avoid paying attention to unpleasant information. Subsequent investigators have developed more complex models of repression (Weinberger, 1998; Weinberger & Schwartz, 1990; Weinberger, Schwartz, & Davidson, 1979). Today, researchers describe repressors as people with high levels of distress and dissatisfaction with themselves, coupled with a strong tendency to keep their emotions under control. A typical repressor wrestles with many threatening conflicts and concerns but somehow manages to keep all these stressors from turning into anxiety.

Consistent with this description, repressors typically report to investigators that they experience less anxiety than nonrepressors. Repressors told they will be given an electric shock or that they must describe an embarrassing situation to a group of strangers usually say they are not particularly worried or disturbed about the situation. But are they? The most intriguing piece of the puzzle surfaces when investigators measure the participant's *actual* response. That is, when we look at the repressors' physiological response to stressful situations, we find a very strong reaction (Barger, Kircher, & Croyle, 1997; Newton & Contrada, 1992; Weinberger

& Davidson, 1994). Repressors' heart rate and blood pressure rise dramatically when faced with threatening events. Does this mean repressors simply lie about their anxiety level? Not really, at least not consciously. Although their bodies respond to threat, repressors successfully push unpleasant emotional reactions out of awareness.

Consider an experiment in which participants were asked to give a 3-minute speech about "the most undesirable aspect" of their personality (Newton & Contrada, 1992). In the crucial conditions, participants delivered the speech into a video camera, with several people supposedly watching the speech on a monitor in a nearby room. How anxious were the participants? The answer depends on how we measure anxiety. When asked to report their reactions on a self-report scale, repressors indicated lower levels of negative emotion than nonrepressors. However, the investigators also monitored the participants' blood pressure throughout the study. When the researchers looked at these data, they found the repressors actually had a *stronger* reaction to the situation than the nonrepressors. Interestingly, this pattern was not found when participants were led to believe that no one would be watching the speech.

Investigators find other telltale signs that repressors push unpleasant feelings out of awareness. Participants in one study were videotaped while discussing situations in which they behaved "particularly unsuccessfully" (Derakshan & Eysenck, 1997). When trained judges watched the videotapes for nonverbal signs like fidgeting and anxious facial expressions, they rated the repressors higher in anxiety than the nonrepressors. Interestingly, when the participants watched themselves in the videotapes, the repressors rated themselves as *less* anxious than the nonrepressors. Judges in another study analyzed the way participants spoke when nervous (Harrigan, Suarez, & Hartman, 1994). They found repressors had more speech disturbances (for example, repeated what they said, stuttered) than nonrepressors, another indication of anxiety.

These studies demonstrate that repressors characteristically have a strong reaction to unpleasant thoughts and emotions, yet somehow succeed in pushing this information out of awareness. Freud explained repression in terms of unconscious ego processes. More recently, psychologists have turned to cognitive processes to account for the repressors' ability to blunt the emotional impact of stressful events (M. W. Eysenck, 1997; Hansen & Hansen, 1988). Participants in one study were asked to describe experiences from their childhood (Davis & Schwartz, 1987). Although they were instructed to report any event that came to mind, repressors recalled fewer unpleasant experiences than nonrepressors. In a related study, participants were asked to think back to their childhood and recall a time when they experienced a specific emotion (Davis, 1987). They were given 4 minutes each to list experiences in which they felt happy, sad, angry, and afraid. Other participants were asked about similar experiences that had happened to someone else. As shown in Figure 16.2, repressors recalled fewer emotional experiences than nonrepressors when asked about their own childhood. Interestingly, the repressors did a better job of remembering sad and fearful experiences for other people. Thus, it's

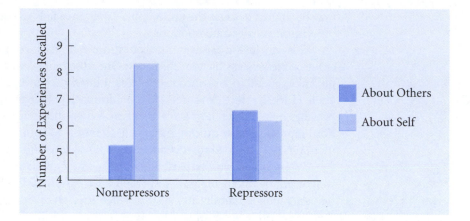

Figure 16.2

Recall of Emotional Experiences

Source: Adapted from Davis (1987).

not that repressors can't remember unpleasant events; rather, they have difficulty recalling unpleasant events that happened to them.

How can we explain the repressors' difficulty in accessing certain emotional thoughts? Some psychologists describe repression in terms of memory associations (Hansen & Hansen, 1988; Hansen, Hansen, & Shantz, 1992). That is, our memories are embedded within a network of related memories (Bower, 1981). When you think of a frightening Halloween experience from your past, you are often reminded of other frightening experiences you've had, or perhaps other memorable Halloweens. Thus, it may be that repressors simply have weaker or less developed networks of memory associations than nonrepressors. Repressors may be spared from excessive negative emotion because unpleasant experiences are less likely to trigger memories of similar experiences.

To test this possibility, one team of researchers asked participants to think about emotional experiences from their past and the emotions the experience generated for them (Hansen & Hansen, 1988). The investigators found that when repressors describe an experience they had with anger, they recalled only anger. When the nonrepressors described an experience with anger, they also recalled shame, disgust, fear, and other negative emotions along with their anger. The researchers explain these results in terms of memory associations. Nonrepressors have stronger ties between memories for negative emotions. Recalling an angry event is likely to also bring up a sad or embarrassing event. However, the repressors' weaker memory network limits associations to other unpleasant memories.

Similar results are found when participants are asked to read emotions in human faces (Hansen, Hansen, & Shantz, 1992). When nonrepressors look at sad faces, they also see signs of anger and fear. When repressors look at sad faces, they tend to see only sadness. Participants in another study were led to believe they had done poorly on a verbal ability task (Egloff & Krohne, 1996). Nonrepressors reacted to the news with a wide variety of negative emotions. But repressors limited their response only to guilt. In short, repressors' reactions to unpleasant events may be limited because the undesirable experience fails to connect with other unpleasant memories and emotions.

This conclusion raises another question: Why are these negative thoughts and emotions less accessible for repressors? One possibility is that repressors may simply fail to attend to and encode unpleasant information (Cutler, Larsen, & Bunce, 1996; Hock, Krohne, & Kaiser, 1996; Schimmack & Hartmann, 1997). That is, repressors may engage in *selective attention*. When they sense threatening information, repressors may quickly turn their attention to something else. If the information is not attended to, it is not encoded into memory and thus is inaccessible.

To test this possibility, participants in one study were told they had either done well or poorly on an anagram test (Mendolia, Moore, & Tesser, 1996). Next, participants took a "familiarity" test in which they were simply asked how familiar they were with a series of words. Many of the words in the list described positive emotions, and many referred to negative emotions. A little later the participants were asked to recall as many of the words from the familiarity test as possible. As predicted, repressors who had failed the anagram test had difficulty recalling words such as *disturbed, sorry,* and *anxious.* However, when told they had done well on the anagram test, the repressors actually did better than the nonrepressors at recalling the emotional words. Apparently, the repressors reacted to their failure on the first test by not encoding the negative emotional words on the familiarity test into memory.

Other research suggests repressors are especially threatened by information that challenges their self-concept (Mendolia, 1999). This effect was demonstrated in a study in which participants were asked simply to identify colors (Newman & McKinney, 2002). Forty words in varying colors were flashed on a computer screen, and the participant's task was to name the color. Of course, the words were not chosen at random. A few of the words had been specifically selected for the participant. That is, earlier testing had identified particular words each participant found threatening. Thus, someone especially concerned about being called self-centered saw the words *selfish* and *conceited* come on the screen. The question was how long it would take the participant to identify the color of the letters the word was written in.

As shown in Figure 16.3, nonrepressors took longer to respond when the word on the screen was personally threatening to them. This is the typical "automatic vigilance" response (Pratto & John, 1991). For most people, attention is automatically drawn toward potentially threatening information. In this case, the split-second distraction caused a noticeable delay when nonrepressors answered the question. But the repressors showed no such effect. Their ability to deflect attention away from personally threatening words was so quick, even measurements in milliseconds could not pick it up. Other studies suggest that repressors not only push unpleasant thoughts away, they sometimes prevent their return by filling their awareness with images and memories that make them happy (Boden & Baumeister, 1997).

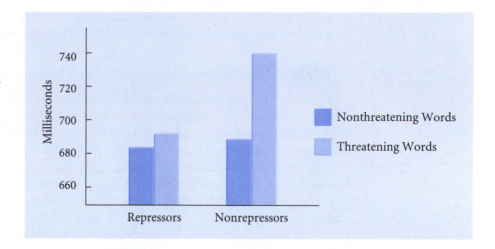

Although life is difficult, it is clear that repressors are more successful than most at keeping the emotions that accompany life's setbacks to a minimum. Does this mean we should all strive to be like repressors? Or does this avoidance come with a cost? Remember, it's not that repressors don't experience anxiety. Measures of heart rate and blood pressure suggest repressors have strong reactions to threat. As described in Chapter 12, not dealing with disturbing events can take a toll on one's health, and some studies suggests this might be the case for repressors (Myers, 2000). For example, researchers find repressors have higher levels of cholesterol and weaker immune systems than nonrepressors (Barger, Marsland, Bachen, & Manuck, 2000; Niaura, Herbert, McMahon, & Sommerville, 1992). Although it is too early to draw conclusions, such findings suggest the price repressors pay for their reduced awareness may be quite high.

Gender Type and Gender Differences

Even if they wanted to (and few do), personality psychologists could not ignore gender. When we consider variables that explain consistent behavior patterns, inevitably personality researchers find gender near the top of the list. Throughout this book we've seen that men and women differ in the kind of characters they dream about (Chapter 4), the way they approach achievement tasks (Chapter 8), how they express emotions (Chapter 8), what they look for in a romantic partner (Chapter 10), and how much they self-disclose (Chapter 12). Two chapters ago, we looked at individual differences in masculinity and femininity and their relation to well-being and interpersonal relationships. Obviously, a complete understanding of personality requires us to ask why men and women differ on so many of the topics we study. One answer comes from the cognitive perspective. That is, the differences we see in men and women's behavior may reflect different styles of processing information. We'll look at two programs of research that address this issue.

Androgyny Revisited: Gender Schema Theory

The androgyny model described in Chapter 14 moved psychologists past the notion that people could be either masculine or feminine, but not both. Instead, researchers recognized that masculinity and femininity could be thought of as independent personality dimensions and that people could be divided into androgynous, masculine, feminine, and undifferentiated categories. Although research using this model has contributed a great deal to our understanding of gender-role behavior, another question soon surfaced: *Why* do people in the four gender-type categories act differently?

One answer to this question comes from *gender schema theory* (Bem, 1979, 1981, 1985, 1987). According to the theory, people who are either highly masculine or highly feminine are *sex-typed*. That is, these people are likely to perceive, evaluate, and organize information in terms of gender. Sex-typed people are more likely to notice if that new guy is masculine or if that blouse is feminine. Sex-typed people are more likely to identify certain kinds of cars as masculine or ask if a particular toy is appropriate for a little girl. In short, these individuals have a strong **gender schema.** In contrast, androgynous and undifferentiated people typically do not process information along gender-related lines. They occasionally classify people or objects as masculine or feminine, but they do not consider this a useful way to sort information. Because sex-typed people tend to see the world in masculine-feminine terms, their behavior is often affected by gender-related information. Whereas an androgynous man might see no reason why he can't enjoy ballet, a sex-typed man identifies ballet as something women enjoy, but not men.

When examining differences in gender schemas, researchers sometimes use a technique called *clustering*. To get an idea of how clustering works, pause for two minutes to write down the names of as many kinds of birds as you can think of. If you are like most people, you probably began with a list of common birds, such as sparrows, robins, and blue jays. But soon you reached a blank. At this point, you might have expected the list to grow slowly, one name at a time, until time expired. But instead you probably found names of birds arriving in groups. Perhaps you remembered chicken, then suddenly duck, goose, and turkey. You may have thought of parrot, then suddenly parakeet, cockatiel, and toucan. The reason these groups of birds "clustered" together on your list is that you organize information about birds in these clusters in memory.

Returning to gender schema theory, if sex-typed people organize information in terms of gender, they should cluster this information on a free-recall task according to gender-related categories. To test this hypothesis, participants in one study were presented with a list of words in random order (Bem, 1981). The words consisted of proper names (*Henry, Debra*), animal names (*gorilla, butterfly*), verbs (*hurling, blushing*), and articles of clothing (*trousers, bikini*). Some of the words

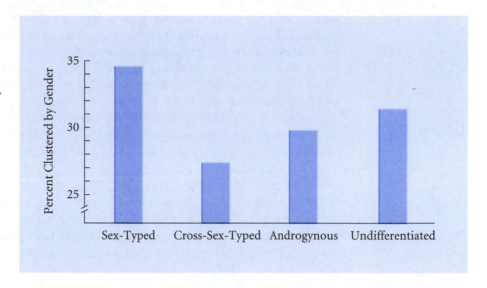

Figure 16.4

Mean Percentage of Clustered-Word Pairs

Source: From Bem (1981).

within each category could be associated with masculinity (for example, *gorilla, trousers*) and some with femininity (for example, *butterfly, bikini*). Participants were then given 8 minutes to write down as many words as they could remember in any order. As shown in Figure 16.4, sex-typed people (masculine males and feminine females) were considerably more likely than the other participants to cluster the words according to gender. Consistent with gender schema theory, when sex-typed people recall *trousers,* they also tend to recall other masculine words. Sex-typed people in another investigation tended to cluster statements into masculine and feminine categories when asked to describe themselves (Larsen & Seidman, 1986).

Other studies look at how quickly sex-typed people process gender-related information. In one study researchers projected the 60 adjectives from the Bem Sex Role Inventory onto a screen one at a time (Bem, 1981). Participants responded by pressing a ME or NOT ME button, depending on how well the adjective described them. As expected, sex-typed people were quicker than others when deciding if a schema-consistent adjective described them, but slower when deciding about a schema-inconsistent adjective. That is, masculine men could decide right away if they were *assertive* or *self-sufficient* but had a more difficult time deciding if they were *affectionate* or *compassionate*. In gender schema terms, the masculine men had a readily available schema for processing the masculine words, but not the other words.

Researchers find evidence of gender schemas using a number of other procedures. For example, sex-typed women use feminine constructs more frequently than androgynous women when placing people into categories on Kelly's Rep Test (Tunnell, 1981). When sex-typed people want to know how they have done on a task, they prefer to compare their scores with members of their own sex, even when gender has nothing to do with the task (Miller, 1984). Sex-typed people are also more likely to identify someone they read about as being either a man or a woman, even when this information is not relevant (Frable, 1989).

As with any important area of personality research, several questions remain about how and when gender schemas work. For example, some investigators suggest both masculine men and feminine women use gender categories when processing information (Bem, 1981). However, other researchers argue that masculine men process information only along masculine-related lines and feminine women only along feminine-related lines (Markus, Crane, Bernstein, & Siladi, 1982; Payne, Connor, & Colletti, 1987). Another issue concerns replication. Although researchers sometimes replicate the findings described here (Mills, 1983), other investigators do not (Deaux, Kite, & Lewis, 1985; Edwards & Spence, 1987; Ruble & Stangor, 1986). This problem suggests that the use of gender schemas is a complex process and that some as-yet-unknown variables may affect when people process information along gender lines and when they do not.

Cognitive Representations of Self

The next time you want to stir things up at a dull social gathering, raise this question: Do men or women have better memories? Inevitably, I find men and women come to the defense of their own gender. Men complain about times their spouses forgot to pay bills or fill the gas tank, and women point out the way their husbands overlook anniversaries and the names of in-laws. Although these responses reflect more than an ounce of stereotype, they also highlight the observations psychologists make about gender and memory. Research suggests men and women do not differ in their general ability to memorize and recall information. However, investigators often find differences in *what* men and women remember.

Consider a study in which men and women were asked to recall several different kinds of information (Seidlitz & Diener, 1998). Participants first were given 3 minutes to list as many positive and negative events as they could recall from the previous 3 years of their lives. Later the participants were asked to recall, among other things, emotional events from the previous year and from a randomly selected 1-hour interval the previous week. Participants were also given a limited amount of time to recall events from American history.

Who had the better recall? As shown in Figure 16.5, the answer depends on what kind of information the participants were asked to remember. The women recalled significantly more personal events than the men. This was true for both negative events and positive events. On the other hand, men did better recalling the impersonal information about American history. In short, women were better able to remember happy occasions with friends and times they embarrassed themselves, whereas men recalled better the facts they had learned in school or read about.

Psychologists explain these differences in memory by pointing to the way people process self-relevant information. Specifically, investigators identify two

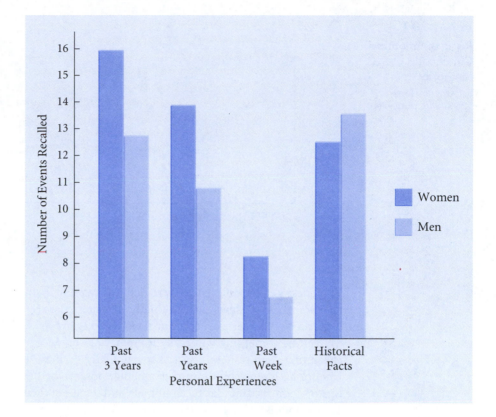

Figure 16.5

Number of Events
Recalled

Source: Adapted from
Seidlitz and Diener
(1998).

differences in the way men and women organize information in memory. First, the genders differ in the extent to which self-relevant information is associated with emotions. Second, men and women differ in the extent to which information about themselves is connected in memory with information about personal relationships.

Emotional Memories. Women are more likely to attend to and process information about emotions than are men (Kuebli, Butler, & Fivush, 1995). From an early age, women learn to pay attention to their emotions and the emotions of others. Consequently, women are more likely than men to encode information about themselves in terms of emotions (Feldman Barrett, Lane, Sechrest, & Schwartz, 2000). If women organize their memories around emotions, we should not be surprised to find that they are better able to recall both positive and negative emotional experiences (Fujita, Diener, & Sandvik, 1991). Memories for both happy and sad experiences should be more accessible for women, and the cognitive link between one emotional memory and another should be stronger for women than men. Thus, recalling one sad experience is likely to trigger another sad memory for women, but perhaps not for men.

Figure 16.6

Recall of Emotional
Childhood
Memories

Source: From Davis
(1999); with permission.

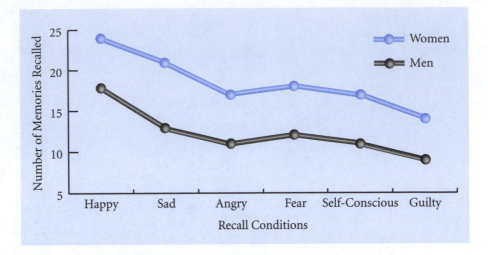

These gender differences were demonstrated in a study in which adult men and women were asked to recall childhood experiences (Davis, 1999). Participants were cued with a series of emotional words and phrases, such as "feeling rejected" or "getting something you really wanted." As shown in Figure 16.6, women recalled more emotional memories from childhood than men. Moreover, this was true for each emotion examined, whether positive or negative. When the investigator compared similar recall in male and female students in grades 3, 5, 8, and 11, she found a similar pattern. That is, regardless of age, females are better able to recall emotional memories than males. Interestingly, the researcher found no gender differences when men and women were asked to recall nonemotional memories. This tendency for women to recall more emotional memories could help explain why women suffer from depression more often than men (Nolen-Hoeksema, 1987). Not only do women remember sad experiences more often than men, but recalling one unhappy incident is also likely to activate memories about other sad events.

Memories About Relationships. Another line of research looks at the extent to which men and women consider relationships when they organize self-relevant information. Drawing from the work on individualist and collectivist cultures (Chapter 1), some psychologists argue that the way men and women are raised in our society causes them to form different cognitive representations of themselves (Cross & Madson, 1997). Men are said to develop *independent self-construals*. That is, men's self-concepts are relatively unrelated to the cognitive representations they have for other people. On the other hand, women in our society tend to develop *interdependent self-construals*. Their self-concepts are highly related to the cognitive representations they have of others and their relationships with those people. In particular, these cognitive representations are tied to those with whom women feel close and personal relations (Gabriel & Gardner, 1999).

Assessing Your Own Personality

Self-Construal

Indicate the extent to which you agree with of the following statements. Use a 7-point scale to indicate your response, with 1 = Strongly disagree and 7 = Strongly agree.

_____ 1. My close relationships are an important reflection of who I am.

_____ 2. When I feel very close to someone, it often feels to me like that person is an important part of who I am.

_____ 3. I usually feel a strong sense of pride when someone close to me has an important accomplishment.

_____ 4. I think one of the most important parts of who I am can be captured by looking at my close friends and understanding who they are.

_____ 5. When I think of myself, I often think of my close friends or family also.

_____ 6. If a person hurts someone close to me, I feel personally hurt as well.

_____ 7. In general, my close relationships are an important part of my self-image.

_____ 8. Overall, my close relationships have very little to do with how I feel about myself.

_____ 9. My close relationships are unimportant to my sense of what kind of person I am.

_____ 10. My sense of pride comes from knowing who I have as close friends.

_____ 11. When I establish a close friendship with someone, I usually develop a strong sense of identification with that person.

To obtain your score, reverse the answer values for items 8 and 9 (that is, 1 = 7, 2 = 6, etc.). Then add all 11 answer values together. High scores indicate a tendency to think of oneself in terms of your relationships with close others. That is, those scoring high on the scale have self-concepts closely tied to the cognitive representations they have of the people they feel emotionally closest to (Cross, Morris, & Gore, 2002). You can compare your score with those obtained from a sample of American undergraduates (Cross, Bacon, & Morris, 2000):

	Men	Women	Total
Mean	52.89	55.11	54.10
Standard Deviation	8.07	10.03	9.29

Scale: *The Relational-Interdependent Self-Construal Scale*

Source: Cross, Bacon, and Morris (2000)

Put another way, relationships with friends and loved ones are an important part of how women think of themselves. It's not just that they enjoy their relationships more than men, but rather that women are more likely to define themselves in terms of the relationships they share with others. Returning to the memory data, perhaps one reason women recall certain kinds of experiences more readily than men is that these events may have involved other people. Because of their interdependent self-construal, information involving relationships is more accessible for women than for men.

Consistent with this analysis, several studies find women are more likely than men to define themselves in terms of their relationships. Participants in one investigation were asked simply to list as many statements as they could in response to the question "Who am I?" (Mackie, 1983). The women in the study included more statements than the men about their roles as parents and family members. Similar findings were uncovered when elementary and high school students were asked to "tell us about yourself" (McGuire & McGuire, 1982). Another group of researchers gave participants a camera with 12-exposure film and asked them to take (or have someone else take) photographs that "describe who you are as you see yourself" (Clancy & Dollinger, 1993). In other words, the photographs provided a rough indication of the cognitive representations the men and women held of themselves. As shown in Figure 16.7, the women's photographs were more likely to include other people. When the women portrayed the way they thought of themselves, they chose to include pictures with best friends and loved ones. In contrast, the men more often portrayed their self-concept with images of themselves alone.

Other research finds gender differences in the way men and women perceive and recall information about significant people in their lives. Participants in one

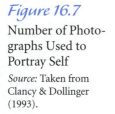

Figure 16.7
Number of Photographs Used to Portray Self
Source: Taken from Clancy & Dollinger (1993).

study were asked if certain words described them, their best friend, a group they belong to, or Ronald Reagan (Josephs, Markus, & Tafarodi, 1992). As described in the previous chapter, researchers assume information processed through a strong schema will be more accessible than information processed through weaker schemas. When participants were later asked to recall as many of the words as possible, the women remembered words processed through their *best friend* and *group* schemas better than the men. Married couples in another study were asked to talk about their first date together, their last vacation together, and a recent argument between the two of them (Ross & Holmberg, 1992). The stories told by the wives were more vivid and contained more detail than those described by the husbands. Taken together, evidence from many sources makes a strong case that men and women differ in they way they store and recall information about relationships.

Cognitions and Depression

For a moment, try to think of a time when you felt depressed. One of the first things you may notice is that this is relatively easy if you already feel a little down today and relatively difficult if you feel pretty good. Depressed people not only remember sad experiences more easily but may also have difficulty keeping themselves from generating one depressing thought after another. Sad people easily recall times when they felt lonely and unloved. They tend to dwell on their problems and worry about all the things that might go wrong. They recall embarrassing mishaps, things they wished they had never said, and experiences they wish they could erase. Even when good things happen, depressed people look for the gray cloud to go with the silver lining. Just got accepted into a good school? Think of all that pressure and what happens if you fail. You've been invited to a party? What if you don't know anyone or you embarrass yourself there? In short, when you're depressed, your mind fills with depressing thoughts.

These observations make it clear that depressing thoughts are tied to depressing feelings. This is why psychologists increasingly are turning to cognitive approaches to understand depression. Although some psychologists maintain that negative thoughts are a symptom of depression, the cognitive perspective argues that these thoughts can also *cause* people to become depressed (Beck, 1972; Clark, Beck, & Alford, 1999). The thoughts of depressed people can be described within a *depressive cognitive triad* (Beck, 1972). That is, depressed people typically have negative thoughts about themselves, are pessimistic about the future, and tend to interpret ongoing experiences in a negative manner.

Many psychologists look for clues about the causes and treatment of depression by examining the way people perceive, organize, and recall emotionally laden information (Rusting, 1998). Among other questions, these psychologists want to know if some people are more prone to depression than others because of the way they process information. We'll look at two areas of research that illustrate how differences in the way people interpret and recall information affect their experiences with depression. We'll examine research on depressive schemas and the attributions people make for uncontrollable experiences.

Depressive Schemas

Each day we encounter some good events, a few bad events, and an occasional incident with ambiguous emotional meaning. Which ones will you think about today and which will you ignore? According to a cognitive analysis, the happiest people are those who pay attention to the positive information, dismiss the negative information, and interpret the ambiguous information as positively as possible. In fact, most of us have an unrealistically positive outlook on life (Taylor & Brown, 1988). We are better than most at almost everything we do, certain that good things will happen to us, and convinced unfortunate events happen to other people. Because most of us look at life through rose-colored glasses, we remain content and in good mental health (Alloy & Abramson, 1988).

Unfortunately, many people look at life through glasses that are tinted blue. Psychologists from a cognitive perspective say that depressed people process information through an active depressive schema (Clark et al., 1999; Kuiper & Derry, 1981; Kuiper, MacDonald, & Derry, 1983). A **depressive schema** is a cognitive structure containing memories about and associations with depressing events and thoughts. People processing information through this schema attend to negative information, ignore positive information, and interpret ambiguous information in a depressing way. They also recall depressing memories easily and often associate current sad experiences with sad incidents from their past. In short, depressed people are set to process information in a way that keeps negative thoughts prominent and positive thoughts away. Little wonder, then, that these people remain depressed.

Researchers have developed a number of procedures to study depressive schemas. Along with clinical observations about how depressed people think and act, these experiments provide an impressive body of evidence pointing to the role of cognitive structures in the development and maintenance of depression. Much of the evidence for depressive schemas comes from studies employing the self-schema research techniques described in the previous chapter. For example, researchers sometimes ask depressed and nondepressed people to answer questions about a series of words. In one study, depressed patients responded to a list of adjectives by pressing a YES or a NO button to indicate if the word described them (Derry & Kuiper, 1981). Half the words were related to depression (for example, *bleak, dismal, helpless*), and half were not. The researchers then surprised the participants by giving them 3 minutes to recall as many of the words as they could.

The results of the study are shown in Figure 16.8. As predicted, depressed patients remembered the depression-associated words better, whereas two groups of nondepressed participants recalled the other words better. This finding has

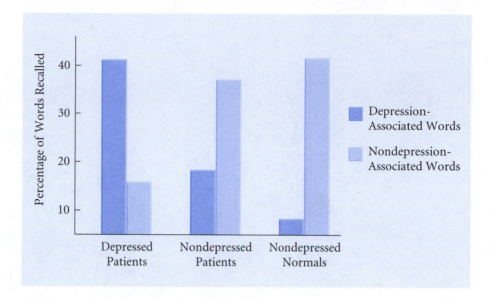

Figure 16.8

Proportion of Self-Descriptive Words Recalled with Self-Referent Processing

Source: From Derry and Kuiper (1981).

been replicated with clinically depressed patients (McDowall, 1984) and mildly depressed college students (Moilanen, 1993). Depressed people recall words like *dismal* and *helpless* better because they process these words through a depressive schema. They are more likely to attend to the depression-related words, associate them with aspects of themselves, and recall them more readily later on.

One team of investigators compared the tendency to recall negative words before and after participants received cognitive therapy for their depression (Pace & Dixon, 1993). As shown in Figure 16.9, the treatment resulted in a reduced tendency to recall depressing words. Moreover, this evidence for a reduced depressive schema was found when the clients were tested one month after completing their treatment.

If depressed people process information through a depressive schema, we would also expect them to recall sad memories more readily than people who are not depressed. For example, if I ask you to quickly think of something that happened to you in high school, most likely you will think of a pleasant time. You might recall a star performance in a play or perhaps just the fun you had hanging out with friends. But if you are depressed today, you might instead recall a test you failed or a time you were rejected by friends. This is because people processing information through a depressive schema have greater access to the depressing memories stored there. When you are depressed, it should not take long to recall times when you were sad, lonely, or embarrassed, because using a depressive schema makes these memories readily accessible.

This easy access to sad memories was demonstrated in an experiment with depressed clients (Clark & Teasdale, 1982). Clients were given a series of words (such as *train, ice*) and asked to recall a real-life experience each word brought to mind.

Figure 16.9

Percentage of
Depression-Related
Words Recalled by
Therapy Clients

Source: From Pace and
Dixon (1993).

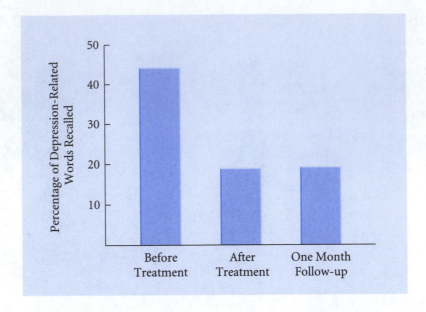

Figure 16.10

Percentages of
Happy and Unhappy
Experiences Recalled

Source: Adapted from
Clark and Teasdale
(1982).

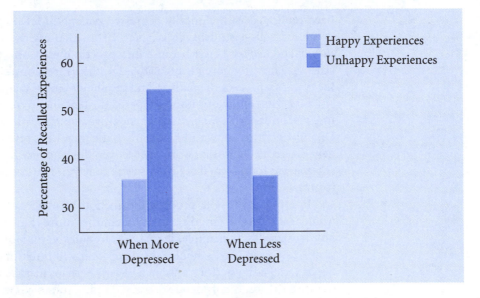

For example, a client might describe a train ride to visit her favorite aunt or a time
she missed a train. Clients were tested twice, once when they were feeling particularly depressed and once when they were less depressed. As shown in Figure 16.10,
most of the memories recalled during the depressed period were unhappy ones.
However, when clients were less depressed, they recalled happier experiences. Presumably the depressive schemas were activated more when the clients' depression
levels were higher.

More evidence that depressed individuals readily recall and process negative information comes from a variety of sources. Depressed patients in one study quickly responded to items asking them if they held negative thoughts, whereas nondepressed individuals took longer to answer these items (Sheppard & Teasdale, 2000). Other researchers find depressed patients take less time to recall unpleasant memories than pleasant ones (Lloyd & Lishman, 1975). Similarly, depressed patients have difficulty remembering positive themes in stories (Breslow, Kocsis, & Belkin, 1981) but do recall negative feedback about their performances (DeMonbreun & Craighead, 1977). Depressed people also have a difficult time not thinking about negative experiences, even when given specific instructions to repress these thoughts (Wenzlaff, Wegner, & Roper, 1988).

Because depressed people filter information through a depressive schema, they also tend to interpret ambiguous information in the most negative light possible. When depressed people consider their performances, they tend to dwell on what they did wrong and fail to give themselves enough credit for what they did right (Crowson & Cromwell, 1995; Gotlib, 1983; Moretti et al., 1996). Participants in one study were given the choice of looking at either the favorable or unfavorable scores from a battery of tests they had taken (Giesler, Josephs, & Swann, 1996). Eighty-two percent of the depressed participants chose the unfavorable feedback, significantly more than the nondepressed participants. Thus, if an instructor tells a depressed student he did well on five essay answers but was a little weak on one, the student will most likely focus his attention on the one weak answer and conclude that his performance was poor.

Not surprisingly, depressive thoughts go hand-in-hand with other depression symptoms, such as sad mood and decreased activity. Cognitive theorists see the causal arrow between depressive cognitions and these other symptoms running both ways (Clark et al., 1999). That is, depressing thoughts can cause depression, and depression can lead to an increase in depressing thoughts. However, several studies suggest that although negative thoughts decline as people recover from an episode of depression, the underlying cognitive network often remains in place (Dozois & Dobson, 2001; Hedlund & Rude, 1995; Ilardi & Craighead, 1999; Ingram & Ritter, 2000; Segal, Gemar, & Williams, 1999). If a strong depressive schema stays intact, the individual may be vulnerable to future bouts of depression (Lewinsohn, Joiner, & Rohde, 2001). In fact, people with strong depressive schemas probably face a daily battle to fend off depression. Formerly depressed patients in one study showed an increase in negative thoughts simply after listening to a sad piece of music (Gemar, Segal, Sagrati, & Kennedy, 2001).

Learned Helplessness Revisited: Attributional Model and Explanatory Style

Two chapters ago we looked at research on learned helplessness. As you recall, psychologists first demonstrated this effect in dogs that failed to escape from electric shocks after first experiencing inescapable shocks. The dogs learned they were helpless in one situation and inappropriately generalized that perception to the new situation. Not long after the demonstrations with animals, researchers found that people also sometimes generalize helpless feelings to controllable situations. Similarities between learned helplessness participants and depressed patients led some psychologists to propose learned helplessness as a model for understanding depression.

However, investigators soon found the simple model used to explain animal behavior was insufficient for understanding learned helplessness in people. Human research participants reacted to some uncontrollable situations with helplessness, but not others. Feelings of helplessness generalized to some tasks, but not every task. People exposed to inescapable noise sometimes became less motivated, but occasionally motivation increased (Costello, 1978; Depue & Monroe, 1978; Roth, 1980; Wortman & Brehm, 1975).

The limitations of the original model led some investigators to reexamine learned helplessness. Many of these psychologists turned to cognitive variables to explain human reactions to uncontrollable events. Specifically, when you encounter something you can't control, most likely you analyze the situation and generate new expectancies for your behavior. Why can't you control this situation? Can you control similar situations? Is the situation unique, or does this lack of control say something about your abilities? Examining these kinds of thoughts led researchers to a new model of learned helplessness.

The Attributional Model of Learned Helplessness. The revised account was named the *attributional model of learned helplessness* (Abramson, Seligman, & Teasdale, 1978; Miller & Norman, 1979). According to this model, learned helplessness in humans begins with a perception of uncontrollability. For example, a man may find he has no control over an employer's decision not to hire him for a job he really wanted. This perceived lack of control is followed by people asking themselves *why* they can't control the situation. The man who failed to get the job ponders the reasons his efforts were unsuccessful. Was it because the employer did not like him? Did he lack experience or skills?

The explanations people give for their lack of control, referred to as *attributions,* determine whether learned helplessness develops. If the man decides the employer is a jerk and that he really does possess what it takes to get a good job, he will probably continue his job quest elsewhere with no ill effects. However, if he concludes that he lacks the skills to ever get the kind of position he desires, feelings of helplessness and depression may result.

Which attributions lead to helplessness, and which do not? According to the model, we can examine these attributions along three dimensions (Table 16.1). First, we can classify attributions as either *internal* or *external.* You can attribute your lack of control to something personal, such as poor skills or low motivation, or to an external cause, such as an unfair test. The more internal the attribution, the more likely you will experience learned helplessness. Second, attributions can be either *stable* or *unstable.* Attributions to relatively stable causes, such as lack of

Table 16.1	Examples of Attributions by a Failing Student			
	Internal		**External**	
	Stable	Unstable	Stable	Unstable
Global	Lack of intelligence	Exhaustion	ETS gives unfair tests.	Today is Friday the 13th.
	Laziness	I have a cold, which makes me stupid.	People are usually unlucky on the GRE.	ETS gave experimental tests this time which were too hard for everyone.
Specific	Lack of mathematical ability	I'm fed up with math problems.	ETS gives unfair math tests.	The math test was from No. 13.
	Math always bores me.	I have a cold, which ruins my arithmetic.	People are usually unlucky on math tests.	Everyone's copy of the math test was blurred.

Source: From Abramson, Seligman, and Teasdale (1978); reprinted by permission of Lyn Y. Abramson.

ability, should lead to more depression than attributions to unstable causes, such as lack of effort. Third, attributions can be classified as either *global* or *specific*. Global attributions apply to many different situations, whereas specific attributions apply to very few. Global attributions are more likely to lead to helplessness.

According to the attributional model, the more people rely on internal, stable, and global attributions to explain unfortunate events in their lives, the more likely they are to experience depression. For example, if you attribute the loss of a job to a general lack of skills and aptitude that will keep you from getting a good job anywhere else, you may be headed for depression. However, if you fail an algebra class and conclude it's because this particular instructor used a strange and unfair grading system, it is unlikely you'll generalize feelings of helplessness to other math classes or other subjects. Interestingly, this depression-promoting attributional pattern seems to be limited to explanations for personal experiences. When depressed participants in one study were asked to explain the causes of events for other people, they showed no tendency to make helplessness-related attributions (Schlenker & Britt, 1996).

Explanatory Style. You have probably used each of the attributions listed in Table 16.1 on occasion. There are times when I can't do something and I know it's my fault. Other times I am certain my failure is due to some bad luck or maybe some temporary problem I can work out. However, psychologists soon observed that people tend to rely on certain attributions more than others. That is, we can identify stable individual differences in the way people explain the events they encounter. For example, you may know people who always seem to blame themselves when things go wrong. If it rains at a picnic, they apologize for picking the wrong date. Other people hold fast to a belief that things will never change. If they don't succeed on the first try, they see no use in trying again. Still others seem intent on generalizing their performance in one situation to new situations. It's as if they are saying, "If I can't do this, I can't do anything."

What these examples illustrate is what learned helplessness researchers call *explanatory style*. Investigators have developed procedures to measure the extent to which people rely on internal or external, stable or unstable, and global or specific attributions for the events in their lives (Houston, McKee, & Wilson, 2000; Peterson et al., 1982; Peterson & Villanova, 1988). As with other individual differences, this does not mean people with an internal attributional style always claim responsibility for what happens. But they have a tendency to do this more than most people and more than they tend to make external attributions. Some psychologists have compared individual differences in explanatory style to dispositional optimism and pessimism (Chapter 8). That is, people who tend to make internal, stable, and global attributions for the setbacks they encounter in life are pessimists. Those who respond to similar situations with external, unstable, and specific explanations are optimists (Gillham, Shatte, Reivich, & Seligman, 2001; Seligman, 1991).

Like other personality variables, explanatory style tends to be stable over time. Researchers in one study compared the attributions elderly participants used to explain why bad things happened to them with the attributions they had made for similar events in letters and diaries from their youth (Burns & Seligman, 1989). The investigators found a correlation of .54 between the kinds of attributions the elderly people made and the attributions they had used an average of 52 years earlier.

Not surprisingly, much of the research on explanatory style has been used to explain why some people are more prone to depression than others. If we habitually see downturns as insurmountable, permanent, and indicative of how things are in other areas of our lives, we may be highly vulnerable to episodes of depression. The connection between explanatory style and depression was demonstrated in a study looking at college students' reactions to their midterm grades (Metalsky, Halberstadt, & Abramson, 1987). Two days after receiving a grade lower than they wanted, students with a depressive attributional style were still a little depressed about their performance. Students without this attributional style shook off the bad grade and recognized it as just one test in one class. Similar results were found when researchers examined reactions among fifth and sixth graders to a bad report card (Hilsman & Garber, 1995).

Numerous investigations have examined the relationship among attributions, explanatory style, and depression. Unfortunately, not all these studies find the same results, and not all support the attributional model (Brewin, 1985; Lewinsohn et al., 2001; Peterson & Seligman, 1984; Peterson, Villanova, & Raps, 1985; Ralph & Mineka, 1998; Robins, 1988; Sweeney, Anderson, & Bailey, 1986; Swendsen, 1998). The overall pattern uncovered in this research suggests that, consistent with the attributional model, stable and global attributions are related to increased depression. However, the evidence for a link between internal attributions and depression is considerably weaker (Peterson, Villanova, & Raps, 1985; Robins, 1988).

Researchers also find that explanatory style may be related to our health (Dykema, Bergbower, & Peterson, 1995; Peterson & Seligman, 1987). In one investigation, researchers determined explanatory style by looking at personal statements written by college graduates more than 35 years earlier (Peterson, Seligman, & Vaillant, 1988). The explanatory style of the 25-year-olds was significantly related to their health at ages 45 through 60. Those who explained unpleasant events in terms of internal, stable, and global causes were the least healthy a generation or two later.

We should also note that the link between attributions and helplessness may be affected by culture. Recall from earlier chapters that people in collectivist cultures tend to emphasize their role in the community, whereas people in individualistic cultures focus on their individual aspirations and accomplishments. One team of researchers found college students in China (a collectivist culture) had a more pessimistic explanatory style than American students (Lee & Seligman, 1997). Consistent with their individualistic emphasis, the Americans were more likely to attribute their successes to themselves and their failures to other people or unfortunate circumstances. However, another investigation comparing American and Chinese students found that the kinds of attributions that predict depression in the United States are also associated with depression in China (Anderson, 1999). Thus, although the way people in two cultures explain events may be different, the kinds of attributions that lead to depression are the same.

 ## *Summary*

1. In recent years, psychologists have used concepts and procedures from cognitive psychology to examine concepts and ideas from Freud's theory. One example of this is research on transference. Researchers find evidence that we sometimes use cognitive representations of familiar people to process information about new acquaintances. The result is transference of memories and emotions from the first person to the second. Other research interprets individual differences in repression in terms of differences in the way people organize information in memory.

2. Some psychologists examine individual differences in sex-type in terms of gender schemas. Sex-typed people, those high in only masculinity or femininity, are said to process information through a strong gender schema. Studies suggest that sex-typed people are more likely to perceive and process information according to gender. Other investigators have looked at differences in men's and women's

abilities to recall certain kinds of information. These researchers find evidence that women are more likely than men to organize self-relevant information around emotions and their relationships with other people.

3. The cognitive approach assumes that depressing thoughts are an important cause of depression. Depressed people are said to process information through a depressive schema. Depressed people recall depressing information and remember depressing events more readily than nondepressed people. Although the original learned helplessness model explained the behavior of laboratory animals, it could not always account for findings in research with humans. An attributional model was proposed to deal with these problems. According to the model, the more people make internal, stable, and global attributions for uncontrollable aversive events, the more likely they are to suffer from depression.

InfoTrac College Edition Key Terms

For additional readings go to http://www.infotrac-college.com/wadsworth and enter a search term related to your interest. Use the key terms suggested here to pull up several related articles. Also see the text Web site at http://psychology .wadsworth.com for more suggested readings and interactive quizzes to test your knowledge.

Depression	Selective attention
Explanatory style	Transference
Gender schema	

Chapter 17

Some Concluding Observations

Not long ago, as I was searching through the stations on my car radio, I chanced upon an interview with a man who was introduced as an expert on pets. After the guest explained that pets have existed in nearly all societies throughout recorded history, the interviewer asked the obvious question: Why do people keep pets? As the expert rattled off his favorite theories and several listeners called in with their own, I found myself sliding into a type of game quite popular among personality psychologists.

Why do people keep pets? The first explanation that came to mind sounded humanistic. People have an inherent need to express and receive love and affection, I thought. Although a warm puppy can never completely satisfy this need, sometimes the affection we receive from our pets goes a long way toward making us feel loved and lovable. I suspect Abraham Maslow would have said something like that. At that point, the expert on the radio said something about pets touching a hidden inner part of our psyches (his word). Possible, I thought. Perhaps pets exist in some sort of Jungian archetype tucked away in our collective unconscious. This would explain why people have kept pets in all cultures throughout history.

At that point I was hooked. The theories came fast and furiously. Maybe there is something symbolic about pets—mother's love, father's affection—that we crave. I'm sure Freud would have said so. Could attraction to pets be learned? Most of the adult pet owners I know had pets as children. Their parents and older siblings probably modeled pet-loving behaviors. And certainly few things are more rewarding than cuddling a warm and furry dog or cat. Of course, I never did come to a single satisfying answer. But the point is that I enjoyed the process.

Personality Theories as Tools

Although explaining human behavior through different theoretical lenses can be fun and even addicting at times, the process is more than a game. In essence, this is part of what psychotherapists do when working with clients. For example, suppose you are a therapist, and a client comes to you for help with her stage fright. How you choose to treat this problem will depend largely on your explanation for why it developed in the first place. Is her anxiety a symptom of some underlying conflict? Perhaps the stage or the audience is a symbol of significant people or events in her past. If this is your explanation, you would probably try a psychoanalytic approach to treatment.

> *"Much of our lives is spent in trying to understand others and in wishing others understood us better than they do."*
> GORDON ALLPORT

But you might also conclude that the client's stage fright is the result of past learning. Perhaps the fear was classically conditioned during some negative childhood experiences and reinforced whenever the client declines an offer to get up on a stage. In this case, perhaps simple relaxation and desensitization therapy would be appropriate. Is the problem a lack of self-efficacy? Or perhaps the kind of internal dialogue she uses in these situations? Maybe the problem is a lack of self-esteem. These explanations suggest other kinds of treatment.

The conclusion you should draw from this discussion is that psychologists rarely find one agreed-upon answer to the question of why people act the way they do. This lesson sometimes frustrates students who expect to find the "correct" theory of personality after taking an entire course on the subject. But the purpose of this book was not to provide you with *the* theory. Rather, it was designed to give you the tools with which to derive your own answers about human personality and behavior.

Of course, this does not mean you should have found each of the theories equally credible and useful. I have never met a personality psychologist who did not favor one or more of the approaches over the others. However, I also know very few psychologists who do not find at least some value in more than one approach. Remember the story of the blind men and the elephant with which we began the book. The point of the story was that, although each perspective provided relevant information for describing an elephant, no one perspective gave the complete picture. Similarly, although most personality psychologists identify themselves with one of the major approaches, most also acknowledge their openness to other perspectives. In fact, I commonly find that psychotherapists identify themselves as "eclectic," meaning they have constructed their personal understanding of human behavior from several different schools of psychology. Thus, the question for students of personality is not "Which theory is correct?" but rather "How can each of these perspectives help me to better understand human behavior?"

Personality Theory

General Trends

In one way, the presentation of the various approaches to personality in this book reads like a historical account of the field. We began with Freud and his groundbreaking work, followed by the neo-Freudian offshoots, on through to the recent emphasis on cognitive elements. As with any history, when looking back, we can identify some general trends. We can see how approaches rise and sometimes fall in popularity, and we can recognize how ideas from one approach influenced the development of others.

When Sigmund Freud died more than 60 years ago, psychoanalysis and the many neo-Freudian versions of it dominated the field of psychotherapy. Since that time, and perhaps even before, the psychoanalytic approach has been the giant in the field that all newcomers feel a need to take aim at. Although many of the newer approaches to personality and psychotherapy have made inroads, declarations of the death of psychoanalysis have proved to be highly exaggerated. A large number of therapists still identify themselves as psychoanalytic, and many others accept and use parts of the approach. The Rorschach inkblot test and other projective measures remain immensely popular. Nonetheless, psychologists who take a strict Freudian approach to explaining personality are rare. Today, research on Freudian concepts is likely to have a cognitive or social learning flavor. Still, Freud's legacy remains intact. When at the end of the century *Time* magazine named the most influential scientists and thinkers of the previous 100 years, whose picture was on the cover? None other than Sigmund himself.

If any trend in the psychoanalytic approach is apparent in the past few decades, it is the slow decline in popularity of some of the neo-Freudian theories. At one point, studying personality meant comparing and contrasting the theories of Freud, Jung, Adler, Horney, and so on, perhaps with some attention to Allport, Murray, and a few others outside the psychodynamic realm. Today, with the increasing acceptance of other approaches, the relative importance of the neo-Freudians appears to have declined. This is not to say that these theorists lack adherents and enthusiastic advocates. On the contrary, each of the neo-Freudian theorists covered in this book continues to have a strong following. In addition, many current personality psychologists have been influenced by these theories. But relative to other approaches, the neo-Freudians' place in the larger scheme of personality theories appears to be waning.

A quick glance through any recent personality journal will confirm that the trait approach to personality is alive and well. The number of traits identified by researchers and tests developed to measure them continues to grow. Trait researchers have responded well to some of the attacks launched at them during the "trait debate" a few decades ago. Moreover, the approach appears to have been bolstered by the development of the Big Five model of personality structure. The model has provided a structure for a large number of research findings.

The ballooning interest in biological influences on personality witnessed in the past few decades shows no signs of abating. There no longer appears any debate about whether part of our personality is determined by genetics. Rather, as described in the next section, the questions now seem to be how and how much. Moreover, interest in such topics as temperament and evolutionary personality theory remain strong. It is possible that some of the lines of research spawned by the current interest in biological influences will prove to be short-lived and faddish. However, it is difficult to imagine that personality psychologists will ever return to anything approaching the "blank slate" conception of newborns advocated by Watson and others many years ago.

Thirty years ago, proponents declared the humanistic approach psychology's "third force" that would rival and eventually replace the behavioral and psychoanalytic models of human nature. I recall browsing through the psychology section at a bookstore during this time and noticing how many authors identified their approach as "humanistic," apparently cashing in on the trend. When I recently checked out the psychology section at another bookstore, I couldn't find the word *humanistic* in even one title. Although the humanistic approach never overthrew the more established approaches to personality, the once upstart perspective now seems to have established its own niche among psychotherapists and personality psychologists. Many psychotherapists identify their therapy style as humanistic, and many others borrow from the procedures outlined by Carl Rogers and other humanistic writers. In addition, I commonly find the works of Carl Rogers and Abraham Maslow taught in communication, sociology, religious studies, management, philosophy, and education classes. Nonetheless, humanistic psychology's place within the larger field of personality psychology continues to shrink, and I would not be surprised to see that role continue its decline in the coming years.

Since John B. Watson defiantly established his extreme behavioral view more than 70 years ago, behaviorism has been in a slow but steady state of transformation. Beginning in the 1950s, many behaviorists drifted to social learning and cognitive positions. The number of psychologists who identify themselves as traditional behaviorists is declining, and today the line between behavioral psychologists and cognitive psychologists is often difficult to distinguish. More than two decades ago, Bandura identified his position as "a social cognitive theory." This label seems to reflect a growing acknowledgment that traditional learning theories, social learning theories, and cognitive approaches all have something to say about personality and that limiting our focus to any one approach reduces our ability to understand human behavior.

The current popularity of the cognitive approach to understanding personality reflects a larger trend in psychology. Students come across this same theme in developmental psychology, social psychology, and abnormal psychology classes. During the past few decades, cognitive psychology has been a growing subfield within the discipline of psychology. Much of what researchers in this area have discovered about the way people process information has implications for personality. All signs point to continued popularity of the cognitive approach in the near future.

Signs of Growing Consensus

The theme of this chapter thus far is that no one approach to understanding personality provides a complete picture of the beast. Yet this does not mean the field is not progressing toward answers to some of the questions we address. Spurred on by research findings and persuasive advocates, several general ideas about the nature of human personality seem to be experiencing a growing acceptance among theorists from nearly all perspectives. One of these areas of agreement is the acknowledgment of genetic influences on personality. Personality theories have come a long way since Watson declared he could turn any infant into whatever adult he wanted, if only given enough control over the environment in which the child was raised. Seventy years ago, behaviorists promoted the idea that environmental influences could overcome whatever genetic differences people were dealt at birth. Today, researchers have made a persuasive case that genetic influences cannot easily be ignored by personality theorists. The nature and extent of that influence remains a source of debate, but few psychologists deny that at least part of adult personality is influenced by genetic predispositions.

"The world we live in is largely man-made ... but it is not well-made."

B. F. SKINNER

Yet despite the growing evidence for genetic influences on personality, some psychologists have accepted this conclusion with caution. One reason for this reluctance may be a fear that people will place too much emphasis on genetic influences, particularly when dealing with important social issues. Fortunately, most personality psychologists recognize that plenty of room is left for environmental variables after genetic predispositions and limits are accounted for. For example, even if women are genetically predisposed to be more nurturant than men, this does not mean men cannot become more nurturant than they currently are. Similarly, even if some people are born with a greater susceptibility to depression than others, much can be done to help these people avoid or overcome problems with depression. Acknowledging the role of genetic influences on personality not only helps us better understand behavior but also gives us a more realistic picture on which to base our intervention programs.

A second area of growing consensus concerns the interaction of person and situation to determine behavior. A few decades ago, shortly after Mischel launched his criticisms of personality traits, many psychologists aligned themselves with one of the extreme positions in the person-situation debate. I commonly heard psychologists declare that trait theory is dead, that consistent behavior patterns are largely an illusion, and that what consistency there is in behavior results from placing the person in similar situations. One prominent social psychologist told me in 1977 that he "didn't believe in personality."

Although discussion continues, advocates from both sides seem increasingly willing to acknowledge the importance of both the person and the situation in determining behavior. How or how much each element does so remains a source of argument and a spur for continued research. Most trait theorists acknowledge the limits of using traits to predict behavior, and critics of the trait approach no longer seem to argue that situational variables affect all people the same way. I was struck by how much psychologists have moderated their positions on this issue during a recent conversation with the social psychologist who earlier did not believe in personality. Today he identifies himself as a "social hyphen personality" psychologist.

The third area of growing consensus has to do with thoughts outside our awareness. Although their descriptions and explanations vary a great deal, personality theorists from nearly all the approaches covered in this book acknowledge that thoughts outside our awareness play an important role in determining behavior. Obviously, Freudian psychologists, who emphasize the importance of unconscious thoughts, advocate the most extreme position here. Although most psychologists do not go this far, there seems to be a growing consensus that at least some behaviors are influenced by thoughts not easily accessible to our immediate awareness.

That our behavior is sometimes influenced by thoughts outside of awareness seems to be implicitly assumed by most psychotherapists. If it were possible to easily pinpoint the thoughts that drive our unwanted behaviors or fuel our painful emotions, why would anyone need to talk to a therapist in the first place? Common experiences support this observation. For example, many of us have experienced a sudden "insight" into a personal problem that had been troubling us for some time. Where were these thoughts that suddenly came together, and where did this processing take place? We commonly speak of experiences not quite in our awareness, such as "Something about her makes me nervous" or "I can't put my finger on it, but I just don't feel right about this." Psychoanalytic, humanistic, and cognitive therapists generally work to help clients discover (that is, bring to awareness) their troubling thoughts. Sigmund Freud described elaborate processes to bring deeply buried unconscious material into awareness. Carl Rogers talked about guiding clients through a process of discovery. Albert Ellis helps clients to understand the steps in their information processing that lead them to irrational conclusions. In each case, the therapist is concerned with bringing thoughts now outside of awareness into awareness, where they can be worked on.

Personality Research

Although in some ways I have only scratched the surface in presenting the many areas currently being investigated by personality researchers, by now I hope you have come to see that, as one observer put it, "personality psychologists study some pretty interesting things" (Larsen, 1995). These interesting things include such varied topics as humor, hypnosis, loneliness, and aggression. But you also may have noticed a few research questions that surfaced repeatedly as you made your way through the book. By way of summary, I have selected four general topics that appear in several different places—achievement, relationships, well-being, and health. The point I hope emerges from this quick review is that none of these four topics, nor most of the other topics of interest to personality psychologists, can be fully understood by examining one or two personality constructs. Rather, both behavior and personality are complex, and discovering the relationship between the two is an ongoing process.

Achievement

Researchers have been interested in achievement behavior for almost as long as personality psychologists have conducted studies. The desire to predict who will rise to the top of the business ladder spawned an enormous amount of research on *need for Achievement* back in the 1950s. Decades of subsequent research demonstrate that some people clearly have a higher need to succeed in achievement situations than others. More recent investigations have looked at the explanations people give for successes and failures and the goals we set for ourselves in achievement situations.

Interest in achievement behavior was also given a boost with the development of the Type A construct, although this time coming with health warnings. *Type A* people are driven to master achievement tasks, particularly when the tasks are challenging or when they find themselves competing with someone else. Similarly, research on the Big Five and job performance finds that people high in *Conscientiousness* typically make excellent employees. These people are careful, thorough, and dependable. They are organized and persist at difficult tasks. Little wonder they do well in the business world. *Optimists* generally do better in achievement situations than pessimists. This is because they have confidence in their abilities. They set high goals for themselves and believe they can reach those goals. However, some people achieve through the use of a *defensive pessimism* strategy. These people do best when allowed to think about all that might go wrong, thereby motivating themselves to do as well as they can.

Many investigators have examined achievement behavior by looking at how people react to failure. People with a high *self-esteem* are less likely to give up in the face of negative evaluation than those with low self-esteem. Whereas low self-esteem people react to failure by thinking about their faults and failures, the same feedback causes high self-esteem people to think about their abilities and achievements. Similarly, researchers explain the connection between academic achievement and *locus of control* partly in terms of how people react to feedback. Studies typically find that internals perform better in school than externals. Internals are more likely to make appropriate adjustments after failures, whereas externals often make excuses for a poor performance.

Relationships

Several personality variables predict interest in social behavior. Most obviously, personality psychologists have looked at social activities as a function of *extraversion-introversion*. Whether we describe this personality variable in terms of Jung's theory, the Big Five model, or Eysenck's model, extraverts are far more attracted to social gatherings and interacting with other people than are introverts. Whereas the typical extravert attends parties and has meals with a table full of friends, the typical introvert is more likely to take a walk in a secluded part of campus or read a book in a quiet corner somewhere.

But there are personality traits beyond introversion that lead people to spend time by themselves. People high in *social anxiety* often avoid social situations because they fear others will think poorly of them. Unlike introverts, who often prefer solitude to social gatherings, socially anxious people wish they could be more social. Similarly, people who suffer from *loneliness* want more social contact but often lack the skills necessary to establish satisfying relationships. On the other hand, some people have a high *preference for solitude.* These individuals spend time alone not because they want to escape the excessive stimulation or feared evaluation that comes from interacting with others; rather, they have come to understand the benefits of solitude and actively pursue time to be by themselves.

The kind of person you seek out for a romantic partner may be a function of both your personality and the personality of the person you select. *Evolutionary personality theory* predicts that men prefer mates who are physically attractive and younger than they are. On the other hand, women are said to select partners who are older than themselves and who can provide the resources needed to raise a family. Research on *gender type* suggests that feminine and androgynous people may make the best romantic partners. These partners are sensitive to others' needs and able to provide the interpersonal warmth and nurturance that help a relationship grow. Although many people believe that a masculine man and a feminine woman make the ideal pair, researchers find this may be the least likely combination for a successful relationship.

Personality researchers also have examined how we approach relationships with others. Recent work on *attachment styles* suggests that early experiences with a primary caregiver result in different ways of looking at adult relationships. Although different models have been proposed, generally people identified with a secure attachment style are likely to have the most satisfying romantic relationships. Relationships with these people tend to be characterized by love, commitment, trust, and acceptance. Research on *self-disclosure* finds that how and how much we disclose personal information to others plays an important role in whether a relationship will develop into a warm and satisfying partnership. Those who disclose appropriately and in a reciprocal manner are likely to foster a good relationship. Failure to reveal intimate information about oneself is likely to limit the development of the relationship.

Well-Being

Although virtually all the topics examined by personality researchers can be tied to well-being in one way or another, several investigators have looked specifically at the connection between personality variables and happiness. Others have looked at the link between personality and negative emotional states that detract from our well-being, such as anxiety and depression. Research on *emotional affectivity* identifies stable individual differences in the extent to which people experience positive and negative emotions. People who are high in positive affect are active, content, and satisfied with their lives. Those high in negative affect frequently experience anger, guilt, and sadness. Several personality variables have been tied to happiness. In Western cultures, how life satisfaction is a function of *self-esteem,* with high self-esteem individuals feeling happier about themselves and their lives than low self-esteem people. Studies on *gender type* find that masculine and androgynous people often score higher on measures of self-esteem and other indicators of personal adjustment than people who don't fall into these groups. *Extraversion* also predicts happiness, with extraverts generally reporting higher levels of happiness than introverts. *Repressors* also typically don't pay attention to unpleasant information. However, this information does not mean they are unaffected by it.

How people deal with anxiety and potential anxiety-provoking situations is related to several personality variables. Research on *coping strategies* finds that those who rely on active strategies are better able to deal with their problems than those who use avoidant strategies. Similarly, problem-focused strategies are usually the most effective, but in some situations strategies designed to deal with our emotions may be preferable. Researchers find that *optimists* use more effective coping strategies than pessimists. *Self-disclosure* also can be an effective tool for dealing with anxiety. In particular, studies show that people who talk or write about traumatic experiences are better off than those who keep these experiences secret.

Another emotion frequently examined by personality researchers is depression. People who experience a lack of control may fall into a state of *learned helplessness* and depression. Studies find that how depressed these people become, if at all, is a function of the *attributions* they give for why they lack control. Those who explain their lack of control with stable and global causes are most likely to experience depression. Other studies find *locus of control* is related to depression. These investigations reveal that externals are more likely to experience depression than internals. People who frequently suffer from depression have also been found to process information through a *depressive schema.* These individuals tend to interpret information in a negative way, pay more attention to negative than positive feedback, and easily recall depressing memories. Consequently, they are prone to bouts of depression.

Health

The first connection between personality and health was established in the pioneering work on *Type A* behavior. Initial studies found people classified as Type A were more vulnerable to cardiovascular problems than people classified as Type B. More recent investigations find the *anger and hostility* component of Type A is the real culprit and a strong predictor of many health problems. *Negative affect* is also related to health. People who score high on measures of negative affect are more likely to complain about health problems than those low on this dimension.

Other research examines health-related behaviors. Studies with *locus of control* indicate that internals and externals typically have different ideas about their role in maintaining physical health. Internals are more likely than externals to take action to keep themselves from getting sick. Moreover, internals are more likely to learn what they can about their illnesses and take an active role in their recovery. However, these locus of control differences show up only in people who place a high value on their health. Research on *self-disclosure* reveals that talking about traumatic events can be good for one's health. Investigators find that even writing about such experiences can improve health over the following months and years.

Conclusion

The 17 chapters in this book are devoted to describing what psychologists have discovered about personality after a century of scientific inquiry. Although they differ in emphasis and style, each theory and research program is an attempt to understand what it is that makes you different from the next person. I hope you found some answers for why you and the people around you act the way you do. But the larger goal has been to give you the tools to join numerous theorists and researchers seeking a better understanding of human personality. In Chapter 1, I introduced the personality psychologists' viewpoint with the old axiom "There are few differences between people, but what differences there are really matter." I can't imagine this won't still be the case even after another century of scientific investigation. The differences between people have fascinated poets and storytellers throughout recorded history. Like the personality psychologists whose work we have explored, they (and I) continue to find personality the stuff that really matters.

 ## Summary

1.   Exploring the various approaches to personality does not identify for students the correct theory. Instead, exposure to each of these approaches provides students with the tools with which to examine questions about personality and human behavior. However, most psychologists find one or more of the approaches more useful for understanding behavior than others.

2.   Looking back at the history of personality psychology, we can identify several general trends. The psychoanalytic approach has a strong but changing following, although many of the neo-Freudian theorists probably get less attention than they did a few decades ago. The trait approach remains an important part of

personality psychology, and the popularity of the biological approach seems too strong. The humanistic approach is perhaps less popular than it once was but still retains an important place among the theories. Behaviorism has undergone a slow transformation over the past several decades. Behaviorists are steadily moving toward the social learning theories and cognitive approaches. The cognitive approach remains popular, reflecting a general emphasis on cognition in psychology.

3. We can identify at least three areas of growing consensus among personality psychologists. Most psychologists today acknowledge that genetics has some influence on personality. In addition, there is a growing acceptance that both the person and the situation are important in determining behavior. Also, although descriptions and explanations differ, most personality psychologists acknowledge the importance of thoughts that lie outside our immediate awareness.

4. Four general topics that have surfaced in many different places throughout this book are achievement, relationships, well-being, and health. Understanding these or other behaviors studied by personality psychologists requires us to look at many different personality variables.

InfoTrac College Edition Key Terms

For additional readings go to http://www.infotrac-college.com/wadsworth and enter a search term related to your interest. Use the key terms suggested here to pull up several related articles. Also see the text Web site at http://psychology.wadsworth.com for more suggested readings and interactive quizzes to test your knowledge.

Interpersonal attraction
Psychotherapy
Third-force psychology

Glossary

absorption The ability to become highly involved in sensory and imaginative experiences.

affect intensity The strength or degree to which people typically experience their emotions.

aggregate data Combining scores from more than one measure of the same concept to obtain a more reliable assessment of a variable.

anal stage The psychosexual stage of development in which the anal region is the primary erogenous zone.

androgyny A personality trait consisting of masculine as well as feminine characteristics.

anima/animus The archetype that is the feminine side of the male (anima) or the masculine side of the female (animus).

anxiety An aversive emotional state experienced as feelings of nervousness, worry, agitation, and panic.

anxious-ambivalent attachment style A style of relating to significant others characterized by a strong desire to get close coupled with a reluctance to become emotionally involved for fear of abandonment.

archetypes Primordial images that predispose us to comprehend the world in a particular manner.

attributional model of learned helplessness A model for understanding depression that examines the reasons people give for their perceived lack of control.

authoritarianism A mechanism to escape the perception of freedom, characterized by striving for submission and domination.

avoidant attachment style A style of relating to significant others characterized by difficulty with emotional closeness and establishing trust.

behavior modification Therapy procedures based on operant conditioning and classical conditioning principles.

behavior potential The likelihood that a given behavior will be performed.

behavioral validation A method for establishing a test's validity by predicting behavior from test scores.

Big Five The five basic dimensions of personality found in many factor analytic studies.

birth order Where people are placed among siblings according to the order of their birth.

cardinal trait A single trait that dominates a person's personality.

case study method An in-depth examination of one person or one group.

castration anxiety The fear a boy experiences during the phallic stage of development that his father will cut off his genitals.

catharsis A release of tension or anxiety.

central traits The five to ten traits that best describe a person's personality.

cerebral asymmetry Higher levels of brain activity in one cerebral hemisphere than the other.

classical conditioning Learning resulting from pairing a conditioned stimulus with a new, unconditioned stimulus.

cognitive restructuring Psychotherapy procedures designed to alter the thoughts people use and the way they process information.

collective unconscious The part of the unconscious mind containing thoughts, images, and psychic characteristics common to all members of a culture.

collectivist culture Culture that emphasizes the importance of belonging to a larger group, such as a family, tribe, or nation.

comparison group An experimental condition, usually a no-treatment group, that differs from other conditions in a specific way and helps to rule out alternative hypotheses.

conditional/unconditional positive regard Acceptance and respect for people either only when they act as we desire (conditional) or regardless of their behavior (unconditional).

congruent validity A method for establishing a test's validity by correlating the test scores with other measures of the same construct.

conscious In Freud's topographic model, the part of personality that contains the thoughts we are currently aware of.

construct validity The extent to which a test measures the hypothetical construct it is designed to measure.

coping strategies Conscious efforts to reduce anxiety in the face of a perceived threat.

correlation coefficient A statistic that indicates the strength and direction of a relationship between two variables.

defense mechanisms Devices the ego uses to keep threatening material out of awareness and thereby reduce or avoid anxiety.

defensive pessimism The tendency to attend to and worry about failure on upcoming tasks in a strategic effort to motivate oneself to do well.

deficiency motive A need that is reduced when the object of the need is attained.

denial A defense mechanism in which a person denies the existence of a fact.

dependent variable The experimental variable measured by the experimenter and used to compare groups.

depressive cognitive triad Three elements that describe a depressed person's cognitions: negative views of the self, pessimism, and interpreting events in a negative manner.

depressive schema A cognitive structure that allows people to readily make negative associations.

developmental epochs The seven stages of personality development in Sullivan's theory.

disclosure reciprocity Matching a conversation partner's self-disclosing intimacy level.

discriminant validity A method for establishing a test's validity by demonstrating that its scores do not correlate with the scores of theoretically unrelated measures.

discrimination A learned tendency to respond only to stimuli that result in reinforcement and not to similar, but unrewarded, stimuli.

displacement A defense mechanism in which a response is directed at a nonthreatening target instead of the unconsciously preferred one.

dispositional optimism The extent to which a person typically adopts an optimistic or pessimistic approach to dealing with life's challenges.

dizygotic twins Twins conceived from two different fertilized eggs, commonly referred to as fraternal twins.

ego In Freud's structural model, the part of personality that considers external reality while mediating between the demands of the id and the superego.

emotional affectivity The extent to which people typically experience positive and negative emotions.

emotional expressiveness The extent to which people outwardly express their emotions.

emotion-focused strategies Coping strategies designed to reduce emotional distress.

evaluation apprehension A strong concern about receiving negative evaluation from others.

experimental confound A variable that is inadvertently manipulated or allowed to vary along with the independent variable.

explanatory style Relatively stable tendency to make certain kinds of attributions for events, particularly those related to depression.

extraversion A dimension of personality concerned with a person's general level of activity and sociability.

face validity A method for establishing a test's validity, in which test items appear to measure what the test was designed to measure.

factor analysis A statistical procedure used to determine the number of dimensions in a data set.

fixation The tying up of psychic energy at one psychosexual stage, which results in adult behaviors characteristic of that stage.

fixed-role therapy A psychotherapy procedure introduced by Kelly, in which clients act out a role suggested by therapists.

free association A procedure used in psychoanalysis in which patients say whatever comes into their mind.

Freudian slip A seemingly innocent misstatement that reveals unconscious associations.

frustration-aggression hypothesis A theory that maintains that frustration always causes aggression and that all aggression is caused by frustration.

fully functioning person A psychologically healthy individual who is able to enjoy life as completely as possible.

functional autonomy The maintenance of a behavior pattern for reasons other than those that originally caused the behavior.

gender schema A cognitive structure used to process information in terms of gender-relatedness.

generalization The tendency to respond to stimuli similar to the one used in the initial conditioning.

genital stage The final psychosexual stage, in which the ability to engage in adult sexual behavior is developed.

Goodness of Fit Model A model proposing that a child performs best when the demands of the environment match with his or her temperament.

growth need A need that leads to personal growth and that persists after the need object is attained.

hierarchy of needs In Maslow's theory, the order in which human needs demand attention.

hostility The component of the Type A pattern concerned with the tendency to express anger and irritability over minor frustrations.

Human Figure Drawing test A projective test in which test takers are asked simply to draw a person.

hypothesis A formal prediction about the relationship between two or more variables that is logically derived from a theory.

hypothetical construct Imagined entity created by scientists to aid in explanation and investigation.

id In Freud's structural model, the part of personality concerned with immediate gratification of needs.

identity crisis A period in one's development characterized by a strong concern for developing a sense of self.

idiographic approach A method of studying personality through in-depth analysis of one individual and the dimensions relevant to that person's personality.

independent variable The experimental variable used to divide participants into groups.

individualistic culture Culture that places great emphasis on individual needs and accomplishments.

inferiority complex Feelings of being vastly inferior and helpless compared to others.

inhibited/uninhibited children Inhibited children show a strong anxiety about novel and unfamiliar situations; uninhibited children show very little of this anxiety.

intellectualization A defense mechanism in which the emotional content of threatening material is removed before it is brought into awareness.

interaction An experimental outcome in which the effect of one independent variable on the dependent variable depends on the level of another independent variable.

internal consistency The extent to which test items are interrelated and thus appear to measure the same construct.

latency stage The psychosexual stage of development that follows resolution of the Oedipus complex and in which sexual desires are weak.

learned helplessness The cognitive, motivational, and emotional deficits that follow a perceived lack of control over important aversive events.

libido The limited amount of psychic energy that powers mental activity.

locus of control A personality trait that divides people along a continuum according to the extent to which they believe what happens to them and others is controllable.

loneliness Unpleasant feelings brought about by a perceived discrepancy between desired and achieved social interaction.

manipulated independent variable An independent variable for which participants have been randomly assigned to an experimental group.

masculinity-femininity A personality trait indicating the extent to which a person possesses sex-typed characteristics, with masculine characteristics at one end of the trait continuum and feminine characteristics at the other end.

monozygotic twins Twins conceived from the same fertilized egg, commonly referred to as identical twins.

need for achievement The motive to engage in and succeed at entrepreneurial achievement behavior.

neodissociation theory Ernest Hilgard's theory, which maintains that consciousness is divided into aware and unaware parts during hypnosis.

neuroticism A dimension of personality concerned with a person's general level of emotional stability.

nomothetic approach A method of understanding personality that compares many people along the same personality dimensions.

nonmanipulated independent variable An independent variable for which condition assignment is determined by a characteristic of the participant.

observational learning Learning that results from watching or hearing about a person modeling the behavior.

Oedipus complex A child's sexual attraction at about age five for the opposite-sex parent and the consequent conflicts.

operant conditioning Learning resulting from the response an organism receives following a behavior.

optimal experience A state of happiness and satisfaction characterized by absorption in a challenging and personally rewarding task.

oral stage The psychosexual stage of development in which the mouth, lips, and tongue are the primary erogenous zones.

penis envy A girl's desire to have a penis and be like a male.

personal constructs In Kelly's theory, the bipolar cognitive structures through which people process information.

personality Consistent behavior patterns and intrapersonal processes originating within the individual.

person-by-situation approach An approach to understanding behavior that maintains behavior is a function of the person as well as the situation.

person-centered therapy Carl Rogers's approach to psychotherapy, in which the phenomenology of the client is the focus of the therapy.

personification A mental image of oneself or of another person.

phallic stage The psychosexual stage of development in which the genital region is the primary erogenous zone and in which the Oedipus complex develops.

possible selves Cognitive representations of the kind of people we think we might become some day.

posthypnotic amnesia Hypnotic participants' inability to recall what occurred during hypnosis after the hypnotist tells them they will not remember.

preconscious In Freud's topographic model, the part of personality that contains thoughts that can be brought into awareness with little difficulty.

preference for solitude The extent to which people seek out and enjoy time alone.

press An environmental feature that interacts with psychogenic needs to determine behavior.

primordial images The images that make up the collective unconscious.

problem-focused strategies Coping strategies directed at taking care of the problem causing the anxiety.

projection A defense mechanism in which one's own unconscious thoughts and impulses are attributed to other people.

projective tests Tests designed to assess unconscious material by asking test takers to respond to ambiguous stimuli.

proprium In Allport's theory, the aspect of personality containing all the features of the self.

psychoanalysis The system of psychotherapy developed by Freud that focuses on uncovering the unconscious material responsible for a patient's disorder.

psychogenic need In Murray's theory, a relatively stable predisposition toward a type of action.

psychosexual stages of development The innate sequence of development made up of stages characterized by primary erogenous zones and sexual desires.

psychoticism A dimension of personality concerned with a person's general level of egocentric and impersonal behavior.

Q-Sort An assessment procedure in which test takers distribute personal descriptions along a continuum.

radical behaviorism An extreme form of the behaviorist view that argues against using inner states as explanations for behaviors.

rational emotive therapy A psychotherapy procedure introduced by Ellis that examines the irrational reasoning causing emotional problems.

reaction formation A defense mechanism in which people act in a manner opposite to their unconscious desires.

reciprocal determinism The notion that external determinants of behavior, internal determinants of behavior, and behavior all influence one another.

reliability The extent to which a test measures consistently.

replication An investigation that finds results similar to those found in an earlier investigation.

repression A defense mechanism in which the ego pushes threatening material out of awareness and into the unconscious.

Rep Test The Role Construct Repertory Test, designed by Kelly to assess personal constructs.

Rorschach inkblot test A projective test in which test takers are asked to describe what they see in a series of inkblots.

schema A hypothetical cognitive structure used to process information.

secondary traits Traits besides the central traits that describe a person's personality.

secure attachment style A style of relating to significant others characterized by closeness without a fear of being abandoned.

self-actualization A state of personal growth in which people fulfill their true potential.

self-disclosure The act of revealing intimate information about oneself to another person.

self-efficacy A person's expectancy that he or she can successfully perform a given behavior.

self-esteem Evaluation of one's self-concept, usually measured in terms of a relatively stable and global assessment of how a person feels about himself or herself.

self-esteem stability The extent to which an individual's feelings of self-worth fluctuate.

self-regulation The ability to develop and apply rewards and punishments for internal standards of behavior.

self-schema A schema consisting of aspects of a person's life most important to him or her.

shadow The archetype that contains the evil side of humanity.

shaping The use of operant conditioning to obtain a response by reinforcing successive approximations of the desired behavior.

social anxiety A trait dimension indicating the extent to which people experience anxiety during social encounters or when anticipating social encounters.

social desirability The extent to which test takers tend to respond to items in a manner that presents them in a positive light.

source traits The basic dimensions of personality in Cattell's theory.

statistical significance The likelihood that a research finding represents a genuine effect rather than a chance fluctuation of measurement.

striving for superiority The primary motivational force in Adler's theory, which is the person's effort to overcome feelings of inferiority.

structural model Freud's model of personality that divides personality into the id, the ego, and the superego.

subception The perception of information at a less-than-conscious level.

sublimation A defense mechanism in which threatening unconscious impulses are channeled into socially acceptable behaviors.

superego In Freud's structural model, the part of personality that represents society's values.

temperaments General behavioral predispositions present in infancy and assumed to be inherited.

test-retest reliability A measure of a test's reliability, as indicated by the correlation between scores on the same test given to the same people at different times.

Thanatos The self-destructive (death) instinct, which is often turned outward in the form of aggression.

Thematic Apperception Test (TAT) A projective test in which test takers are asked to tell stories about a series of ambiguous pictures.

theory A general statement about the relationship between constructs or events.

topographic model Freud's original model of personality structure, in which personality is divided into three different levels of awareness.

trait A dimension of personality used to categorize people according to the degree to which they manifest a particular characteristic.

transference A stage in psychoanalysis in which the patient transfers unconscious feelings about another individual to the therapist.

twin-study method A procedure for examining the role of genetics on personality, in which pairs of monozygotic and dizygotic twins are compared.

Type A–Type B A trait dimension indicating the extent to which a person typically acts in a driving, time-urgent manner.

unconscious In Freud's topographic model, the part of personality that contains material that cannot easily be brought into awareness.

validity The extent to which a test measures what it is designed to measure.

References

Abramson, L. Y., Seligman, M. E. P., & Teasdale, J. D. (1978). Learned helplessness in humans: Critique and re-formulation. *Journal of Abnormal Psychology, 87,* 49–74.

Adams-Webber, J. R. (1998). Differentiation and sociality in terms of elicited and provided constructs. *Psychological Science, 9,* 499–501.

Ainsworth, M. D. S. (1989). Attachments beyond infancy. *American Psychologist, 44,* 709–716.

Ainsworth, M. D. S., Blehar, M. C., Waters, E., & Wall, S. (1978). *Patterns of attachment.* Hillsdale, NJ: Erlbaum.

Aldwin, C. M., & Revenson, T. A. (1987). Does coping help? A reexamination of the relation between coping and mental health. *Journal of Personality and Social Psychology, 53,* 337–348.

Alloy, L. B., & Abramson, L. Y. (1988). Depressive realism: Four theoretical perspectives. In L. B. Alloy (Ed.), *Cognitive processes in depression* (pp. 223–265). New York: Guilford.

Allport, G. W. (1961). *Pattern and growth in personality.* New York: Holt, Rinehart & Winston.

Allport, G. W. (1965). *Letters from Jenny.* New York: Harcourt, Brace & World.

Allport, G. W. (1967). Gordon W. Allport. In E. G. Boring & G. Lindzey (Eds.), *A history of psychology in autobiography* (Vol. 5, pp. 3–25). New York: Appleton-Century-Crofts.

Allport, G. W. (1968). *The person in psychology: Selected essays.* Boston: Beacon.

Almagor, M., Tellegen, A., & Waller, N. G. (1995). The Big Seven model: A cross-cultural replication and further ex-ploration of the basic dimensions of natural language trait descriptors. *Journal of Personality and Social Psychology, 69,* 300–307.

Altman, I. (1975). *The environment and social behavior.* Monterey, CA: Brooks/Cole.

Altman, I., & Taylor, D. A. (1973). *Social penetration: The development of interpersonal relationships.* New York: Holt, Rinehart & Winston.

Ames, C. (1992). Classrooms: Goals, structures, and student motivation. *Journal of Educational Psychology, 84,* 261–271.

Ames, C., & Archer, J. (1988). Achievement goals in the classroom: Students' learning strategies and motivation processes. *Journal of Educational Psychology, 80,* 260–267.

Amirkhan, J. H., Risinger, R. T., & Swickert, R. J. (1995). Extraversion: A "hidden" personality factor in coping? *Journal of Personality, 63,* 189–212.

Andersen, B. L., Cyranowski, J. M., & Espindle, D. (1999). Men's sexual self-schema. *Journal of Personality and Social Psychology, 76,* 645–661.

Andersen, S. M., & Baum, A. (1994). Transference in interpersonal relations: Inferences and affect based on significant-other representations. *Journal of Personality, 62,* 459–497.

Andersen, S. M., & Berk, M. S. (1998). Transference in everyday experience: Implications of experimental re-search for relevant clinical phenomena. *Review of General Psychology, 2,* 81–120.

Andersen, S. M., & Cole, S. W. (1990). "Do I know you?": The role of significant others in general social perception. *Journal of Personality and Social Psychology, 59,* 384–399.

Andersen, S. M., Reznik, I., & Manzella, L. M. (1996). Eliciting facial affect, motivation, and expectancies in transference: Significant-other representations in social relations. *Journal of Personality and Social Psychology, 71,* 1108–1129.

Anderson, C. A. (1999). Attributional style, depression, and loneliness: A cross-cultural comparison of American and Chinese students. *Personality and Social Psychology Bulletin, 15,* 482–499.

Anderson, C. A., & Anderson, K. B. (1998). Temperature and aggression: Paradox, controversy, and a (fairly) clear picture. In R. Geen & E. Donnerstein (Eds.), *Human aggression: Theories, research, and implications for public policy* (pp. 247–298). New York: Academic Press.

Anderson, C. A., & Bushman, B. J. (2001). Effects of violent video games on aggressive behavior, aggressive cognition, aggressive affect, physiological arousal, and prosocial behavior: A meta-analytic review of the scientific literature. *Psychological Science, 12,* 353–359.

Anderson, C. A., & Bushman, B. J. (2002). The effects of media violence on society. *Science, 295,* 2377–2378.

Anderson, C. A., & Harvey, R. J. (1988). Discriminating between problems in living: An examination of measures of depression, loneliness, shyness, and social anxiety. *Journal of Social and Clinical Psychology, 6,* 482–491.

Ansbacher, H. L., & Ansbacher, R. R. (Eds.). (1956). *The individual psychology of Alfred Adler.* New York: Basic Books.

Antill, J. K. (1983). Sex role complementarity versus similarity in married couples. *Journal of Personality and Social Psychology, 45,* 145–155.

Antonen, M. (1993, June 25). Sparky thrives on high anxiety. *USA Today,* p. 3C.

Archer, J. (1994). Achievement goals as a measure of motivation in university students. *Contemporary Educational Psychology, 19,* 430–446.

Archer, J. (1996). Sex differences in social behavior: Are the social role and evolutionary explanations compatible? *American Psychologist, 51,* 909–917.

Archibald, F. S., Bartholomew, K., & Marx, R. (1995). Loneliness in early adolescence: A test of the cognitive discrepancy model of loneliness. *Personality and Social Psychology Bulletin, 21,* 296–301.

Arkin, A. M., Antrobus, J. S., & Ellman, S. J. (1978). *The mind in sleep: Psychology and psychophysiology.* Hillsdale, NJ: Erlbaum.

Aron, A., Aron, E. N., & Allen, J. (1998). Motivations for unreciprocated love. *Personality and Social Psychology Bulletin, 24,* 787–796.

Arthur, W., & Graziano, W. G. (1996). The five-factor model, Conscientiousness, and driving accident involvement. *Journal of Personality, 64,* 593–618.

Aschburner, S. (2001, October 2). Playing mind games. *Minneapolis Star Tribune,* p. 2C.

Asendorpf, J. B., & Wilpers, S. (1998). Personality effects on social relationships. *Journal of Personality and Social Psychology, 74,* 1531–1544.

Aserinsky, E., & Kleitman, N. (1953). Regularly occurring periods of eye motility and concomitant phenomena during sleep. *Science, 118,* 273–274.

Aspinwall, L. G., & Brunhart, S. M. (1996). Distinguishing optimism from denial: Optimistic beliefs predict attention to health threats. *Personality and Social Psychology Bulletin, 22,* 993–1003.

Aspinwall, L. G., & Taylor, S. E. (1992). Modeling cognitive adaptation: A longitudinal investigation of the impact of individual differences and coping on college adjustment and performance. *Journal of Personality and Social Psychology, 63,* 989–1003.

Atkinson, J. W. (1957). Motivational determinants of risk-taking behavior. *Psychological Review, 64,* 359-372.

Atkinson, J. W. (1974). The mainspring of achievement oriented activity. In J. W. Atkinson & J. O. Raynor (Eds.), *Motivation and achievement* (pp. 13–14). Washington, DC: Winston.

Aube, J., & Koestner, R. (1992). Gender characteristics and adjustment: A longitudinal study. *Journal of Personality and Social Psychology, 63,* 485–493.

Aube, J., Norcliffe, H., Craig, J., & Koestner, R. (1995). Gender characteristics and adjustment-related outcomes: Questioning the masculinity model. *Personality and Social Psychology Bulletin, 21,* 284–295.

Aversa, J. (1998, April 16). Violence still saturates television, study reports. *San Jose Mercury News,* p. A8.

Ayers, T. S., Sandler, I. N., West, S. G., & Roosa, M. W. (1996). A dispositional and situational assessment of children's coping: Testing alternative models of coping. *Journal of Personality, 64,* 923–958.

Bagby, R. M., Rogers, R., Nicholson, R. A., Buis, T., Seeman, M. V., & Rector, N. A. (1997). Effectiveness of the MMPI-2 validity indicators in the detection of defensive responding in clinical and nonclinical samples. *Psychological Assessment, 9,* 406–413.

Baker, L. A., & Daniels, D. (1990). Nonshared environmental influences and personality differences in adult twins. *Journal of Personality and Social Psychology, 58,* 103–110.

Balch, P., & Ross, A. W. (1975). Predicting success in weight reduction as a function of locus of control: A uni-dimensional and multidimensional approach. *Journal of Consulting and Clinical Psychology, 43,* 119.

Baldwin, M. W., & Main, K. J. (2001). Social anxiety and the cued activation of relational knowledge. *Personality and Social Psychology Bulletin, 27,* 1637–1647.

Baltes, M. M., & Baltes, P. B. (1986). *The psychology of control and aging.* Hillsdale, NJ: Erlbaum.

Bandura, A. (1965). Influences of models' reinforcement contingencies on the acquisition of imitative responses. *Journal of Personality and Social Psychology, 1,* 589–595.

Bandura, A. (1973). *Aggression: A social learning analysis.* Englewood Cliffs, NJ: Prentice-Hall.

Bandura, A. (1977a). *Social learning theory.* Englewood Cliffs, NJ: Prentice-Hall.

Bandura, A. (1977b). Self-efficacy: Toward a unifying theory of behavioral change. *Psychological Review, 84,* 191–215.

Bandura, A. (1986). *Social foundations of thought and action: A social cognitive theory.* Englewood Cliffs, NJ: Prentice-Hall.

Bandura, A. (1997). *Self-efficacy: The exercise of control.* New York: Freeman.

Bandura, A. (2001). Social cognitive theory: An agentic perspective. *Annual Review of Psychology, 52,* 1–26.

Bandura, A., Adams, N. E., & Beyer, J. (1977). Cognitive processes mediating behavioral change. *Journal of Personality and Social Psychology, 35,* 125–139.

Bandura, A., Barbaranelli, C., Caprara, G. V., & Pastorelli, C. (1996). Multifaceted impact of self-efficacy beliefs on academic functioning. *Child Development, 67,* 1206–1222.

Bandura, A., Pastorelli, C., Barbaranelli, C., & Caprara, G. V. (1999). Self-efficacy pathways to childhood depression. *Journal of Personality and Social Psychology, 76,* 258–269.

Barber, T. S., & Calverley, D. S. (1964). Toward a theory of hypnotic behavior: Effects on suggestibility of defining the situation as hypnosis and defining responses to suggestion as easy. *Journal of Abnormal and Social Psychology, 68,* 585–592.

Barber, T. X. (1969). *Hypnosis: A scientific approach.* New York: Van Nostrand Reinhold.

Barber, T. X. (1999). A comprehensive three-dimensional theory of hypnosis. In I. Kirsch, A. Capafons, E. Cardena-Buelna & S. Amigo (Eds.), *Clinical hypnosis and self-regulation: cognitive-behavioral perspectives* (pp. 21–48). Washington, DC: American Psychological Association.

Barber, T. X. (1976). *Pitfalls in human research: Ten pivotal points.* New York: Pergamon.

Bardos, A. N., & Powell, S. (2001). Human figure drawings and the Draw-A-Person: Screening procedures for emotional disturbances. In W. I. Dorfman & M. Hersen (Eds.), *Understanding psychological assessment* (pp. 275–294). New York: Plenum.

Barger, S. D., Kircher, J. C., & Croyle, R. T. (1997). The effects of social context and defensiveness on the physiological responses of repressive copers. *Journal of Personality and Social Psychology, 73,* 1118–1128.

Barger, S. D., Marsland, A. L., Bachen, E. A., & Manuck, S. B. (2000). Repressive coping and blood measures of disease risk: Lipids and endocrine and immunological responses to a laboratory stressor. *Journal of Applied Social Psychology, 30,* 1619–1638.

Barlow, D. H. (1988). *Anxiety and its disorders.* New York: Guilford.

Baron, R. A. (1978a). The influence of hostile and non-hostile humor upon physical aggression. *Personality and Social Psychology Bulletin, 4,* 77–80.

Baron, R. A. (1978b). Aggression-inhibiting influence of sexual behavior. *Journal of Personality and Social Psychology, 36,* 189–197.

Barrett, M. S., & Berman, J. S. (2001). Is psychotherapy more effective when therapists disclose information about themselves? *Journal of Consulting and Clinical Psychology, 69,* 597–603.

Barrett, P., & Eysenck, S. B. G. (1984). The assessment of personality factors across 25 countries. *Personality and Individual Differences, 5,* 615–632.

Barrick, M. R., & Mount, M. K. (1991). The Big Five personality dimensions and job performance: A meta-analysis. *Personnel Psychology, 44,* 1–26.

Barrick, M. R., Mount, M. K., & Judge, T. A. (2001). Personality and performance at the beginning of the new millennium: What do we know and where to we go next? *International Journal of Selection and Assessment, 91,* 9–30.

Barrick, M. R., Mount, M. K., & Strauss, J. P. (1993). Conscientiousness and performance of sales representatives: Test of the mediating effects of goal setting. *Journal of Applied Psychology, 78,* 715–722.

Barrick, M. R., Mount, M. K., & Strauss, J. P. (1994). Antecedents of involuntary turnover due to a reduction in force. *Personnel Psychology, 47,* 515–535.

Barron, K. E., & Harackiewicz, J. M. (2001). Achievement goals and optimal motivation: Testing multiple goal models. *Journal of Personality and Social Psychology, 80,* 706–722.

Bartholomew, K. (1990). Avoidance of intimacy: An attachment perspective. *Journal of Social and Personal Relationships, 7,* 147–178.

Bartholomew, K., & Horowitz, L. M. (1991). Attachment styles among young adults: A test of a four-category model. *Journal of Personality and Social Psychology, 61,* 226–244.

Bartholomew, K., & Shaver, P. R. (1998). Methods of assessing adult attachment. In J. A. Simpson & W. S. Rholes (Eds.)., *Attachment theory and close relationships* (pp. 25–45). New York: Guilford.

Basgall, J. A., & Snyder, C. R. (1988). Excuses in waiting: External locus of control and reactions to success-failure feedback. *Journal of Personality and Social Psychology, 54,* 656–662.

Bates, A. P. (1964). Privacy—A useful concept? *Social Forces, 42,* 429–434.

Bates, J. E., Wachs, T. D., & Emde, R. N. (1994). Toward practical uses for biological concepts of temperament. In J. E. Bates & T. D. Wachs (Eds.), *Temperament: Individual differences at the interface of biology and behavior* (pp. 275–306). Washington, DC: American Psychological Association.

Bauer, J. J., & Bonanno, G. A. (2001). I can, I do, I am: The narrative differentiation of self-efficacy and other self-evaluations while adapting to bereavement. *Journal of Research in Personality, 35,* 424–448.

Baumeister, R. F. (1991). On the stability of variability: Retest reliability of metatraits. *Personality and Social Psychology Bulletin, 17,* 633–639.

Baumeister, R. F., Dale, K., & Sommer, K. L. (1998). Freudian defense mechanisms and empirical findings in modern social psychology: Reaction formation, projection, displacement, undoing, isolation, sublimation, and denial. *Journal of Personality, 66,* 1081–1124.

Baumeister, R. F., & Leary, M. R. (1995). The need to belong: Desire for interpersonal attachments as a fundamental human motivation. *Psychological Bulletin, 117,* 497–529.

Baumeister, R. F., & Tice, D. M. (1988). Metatraits. *Journal of Personality, 56,* 571–598.

Baumeister, R. F., & Tice, D. M. (1990). Anxiety and social exclusion. *Journal of Social and Clinical Psychology, 9,* 165–195.

Baumeister, R. F., Tice, D. M., & Hutton, D. G. (1989). Self-presentational motivations and personality differences in self-esteem. *Journal of Personality, 57,* 547–579.

Bechtle, R. (1984). C. G. Jung and the religion of the unconscious. In J. Heaney (Ed.), *Psyche and spirit* (pp. 138–163). New York: Paulist.

Beck, A. T. (1972). *Depression: Causes and treatments.* Philadelphia: University of Pennsylvania Press.

Beck, A. T. (1991). Cognitive therapy: A 30-year retrospective. *American Psychologist, 46,* 368–375.

Bell, R. C. (1990). Analytic issues in the use of Repertory Grid Technique. In G. J. Neimeyer & R. A. Neimeyer (Eds.), *Advances in personal construct psychology* (Vol. 1, pp. 25–48). Greenwich, CN: JAI Press.

Belle, D., Doucet, J., Harris, J., Miller, J., & Tan, E. (2000). Who is rich? Who is happy? *American Psychologist, 55,* 1160–1161.

Bem, D. J., & Allen, A. (1974). On predicting some of the people some of the time: The search for cross-situational consistencies in behavior. *Psychological Review, 81,* 506–520.

Bem, S. L. (1974). The measurement of psychological androgyny. *Journal of Consulting and Clinical Psychology, 42,* 155–162.

Bem, S. L. (1975). Sex role adaptability: One consequence of psychological androgyny. *Journal of Personality and Social Psychology, 31,* 634–643.

Bem, S. L. (1976). Probing the promise of androgyny. In A. G. Kaplan & J. P. Bean (Eds.), *Beyond sex-role stereotypes* (pp. 48–62). Boston: Little, Brown.

Bem, S. L. (1977). On the utility of alternative procedures for assessing psychological androgyny. *Journal of Consulting and Clinical Psychology, 45,* 196–205.

Bem, S. L. (1979). Theory and measurement of androgyny: A reply to the Pedhazur-Tetenbaum and Locksley-Colten critiques. *Journal of Personality and Social Psychology, 37,* 1047–1054.

Bem, S. L. (1981). Gender schema theory: A cognitive account of sex-typing. *Psychological Review, 88,* 354–364.

Bem, S. L. (1985). Androgyny and gender schema theory: A conceptual and empirical integration. In T. B. Sonderegger (Ed.), *1984 Nebraska Symposium on Motivation: Psychology and gender.* Lincoln: University of Nebraska Press.

Bem, S. L. (1987). Gender schema theory and the romantic tradition. In P. Shaver & C. Hendrick (Eds.), *Sex and gender* (pp. 251–271). Beverly Hills, CA: Sage.

Bem, S. L., & Lenney, E. (1976). Sex-typing and the avoidance of cross-sex behavior. *Journal of Personality and Social Psychology, 33*, 48–54.

Bem, S. L., Martyna, W., & Watson, C. (1976). Sex typing and androgyny: Further explorations of the expressive domain. *Journal of Personality and Social Psychology, 34*, 1016–1023.

Benassi, V. A., Sweeney, P. D., & Dufour, C. L. (1988). Is there a relationship between locus of control orientation and depression? *Journal of Abnormal Psychology, 97*, 357–367.

Benet-Martinez, V., & John, O. P. (1998). Los Cinco Grandes across cultures and ethnic groups: Multitrait multimethod analyses of the Big Five in Spanish and English. *Journal of Personality and Social Psychology, 75*, 729–750.

Benet-Martinez, V., & Waller, N. G. (1997). Further evidence for the cross-cultural generality of the Big Seven factor model: Indigenous and imported Spanish personality constructs. *Journal of Personality, 65*, 567–598.

Bengston, P. L., & Grotevant, H. D. (1999). The individuality and connectedness Q-sort: A measure for assessing individuality and connectedness in dyadic relationships. *Personal Relationships, 6*, 213–225.

Ben Hamida, S., Mineka, S., & Bailey, J. M. (1998). Sex differences in perceived controllability of mate value: An evolutionary perspective. *Journal of Personality and Social Psychology, 75*, 953–966.

Bennett, P., Moore, L., Smith, A., Murphy, S., & Smith, C. (1994). Health locus of control and value for health as predictors of dietary behaviour. *Psychology and Health, 10*, 41–54.

Berg, J. H., & Peplau, L. A. (1982). Loneliness: The relationship of self-disclosure and androgyny. *Personality and Social Psychology Bulletin, 8*, 624–630.

Berk, M. S., & Andersen, S. M. (2000). The impact of past relationships on interpersonal behavior: Behavioral confirmation in the social-cognitive process of transference. *Journal of Personality and Social Psychology, 79*, 546–562.

Berkow, I. (2002, March 27). True heroism outside the lines. *New York Times*, p. C–15.

Berkowitz, L. (1970). Aggressive humor as a stimulus to aggressive responses. *Journal of Personality and Social Psychology, 16*, 710–717.

Berkowitz, L. (1984). Some effects of thoughts on anti- and prosocial influences of media events: A cognitive-neoassociationist analysis. *Psychological Bulletin, 95*, 410–427.

Berkowitz, L. (1986). Situational influences on reactions to observed violence. *Journal of Social Issues, 42*, 93–106.

Berkowitz, L. (1989). The frustration-aggression hypothesis: An examination and reformulation. *Psychological Bulletin, 106*, 59–73.

Berkowitz, L. (1994). Is something missing? Some observations prompted by the cognitive-neoassociationist view of anger and emotional aggression. In L. R. Huesmann (Ed.), *Aggressive behavior: Current perspectives* (pp. 35–57). New York: Plenum.

Berkowitz, L. (1998). Affective aggression: The role of stress, pain, and negative affect. In R. G. Geen & E. Donnerstein (Eds.), *Human aggression: Theories, research, and implications for social policy* (pp. 49–72). San Diego: Academic Press.

Berry, D. S., & Hansen, J. S. (1996). Positive affect, negative affect, and social interaction. *Journal of Personality and Social Psychology, 71*, 796–809.

Berry, D. S., & Hansen, J. S. (2000). Personality, nonverbal behavior, and interaction quality in female dyads. *Personality and Social Psychology Bulletin, 26*, 278–292.

Berry, D. S., & Willingham, J. K. (1997). Affective traits, responses to conflict, and satisfaction in romantic relationships. *Journal of Research in Personality, 31*, 564–576.

Berry, D. S., Willingham, J. K., & Thayer, C. A. (2000). Affect and personality as predictors of conflict and closeness in young adults' friendships. *Journal of Research in Personality, 34*, 84–107.

Bess, T. L., & Harvey, R. J. (2002). Bimodal score distributions and the Myers-Briggs Type Indicator: Fact or artifact? *Journal of Personality Assessment, 78*, 176–186.

Besson, A., Privat, A. M., Eschalier, A., & Fialip, J. (1999). Dopaminergic and opioidergic mediations of tricyclic antidepressants in the learned helplessness paradigm. *Pharmacology, Biochemistry and Behavior, 64*, 541–548.

Best, J. A. (1975). Tailoring smoking withdrawal procedures to personality and motivational differences. *Journal of Consulting and Clinical Psychology, 43*, 1–8.

Best, J. A., & Steffy, R. A. (1975). Smoking modification procedures for internal and external locus of control clients. *Canadian Journal of Behavioural Science, 7*, 155–165.

Bianchi, E. C. (1988). Jungian psychology and religious experience. In R. L. Moore (Ed.), *Carl Jung and Christian spirituality* (pp. 16–37). New York: Paulist.

Block, J. (1961). *The Q-Sort method in personality assessment and psychiatric research.* Springfield, IL: Charles C. Thomas.

Block, J. (1995). A contrarian view of the five-factor approach to personality description. *Psychological Bulletin, 117,* 187–215.

Block, J. H., Gjerde, P. F., & Block, J. H. (1991). Personality antecedents of depressive tendencies in 18-year-olds: A prospective study. *Journal of Personality and Social Psychology, 60,* 726–738.

Boden, J. M., & Baumeister, R. F. (1997). Repressive coping: Distraction using pleasant thoughts and memories. *Journal of Personality and Social Psychology, 73,* 45–62.

Bodner, E., & Mikulincer, M. (1998). Learned helplessness and the occurrence of depressive-like and paranoid-like responses: The role of attentional focus. *Journal of Personality and Social Psychology, 74,* 1010–1023.

Boldero, J., & Francis, J. (2000). The relation between self-discrepancies and emotion: The moderating roles of self-guide importance, location relevance, and social self-domain centrality. *Journal of Personality and Social Psychology, 78,* 38–52.

Boldizar, J. P., Perry, D. G., & Perry, L. C. (1989). Outcome values and aggression. *Child Development, 60,* 571–579.

Bond, M. (1992). An empirical study of defensive style: The Defense Style Questionnaire. In G. Vaillant (Ed.), *Ego mechanisms of defense: A guide for clinicians and researchers* (pp. 127–158). Washington, DC: American Psychiatric Press.

Boor, M. (1976). Relationship of internal-external control and national suicide rates. *Journal of Social Psychology, 100,* 143–144. (A publication of the Helen Dwight Reid Educational Foundation.)

Booth-Kewley, S., & Vickers, R. R. (1994). Associations between major domains of personality and health behavior. *Journal of Personality, 62,* 281–298.

Borkenau, P., Riemann, R., Angleitner, A., & Spinath, F. M. (2001). Genetic and environmental influences on observed personality: Evidence from the German observational study of adult twins. *Journal of Personality and Social Psychology, 80,* 655–668.

Bouchard, T. J., & McGue, M. (1981). Familial studies of intelligence: A review. *Science, 212,* 1055–1059.

Bower, G. H. (1981). Mood and memory. *American Psychologist, 36,* 129–148.

Bowers, S. P. (1999). Gender role identity and the caregiving experience of widowed men. *Sex Roles, 41,* 645–655.

Bowlby, J. (1969). *Attachment and loss: Vol. 1. Attachment.* New York: Basic Books.

Bowlby, J. (1973). *Attachment and loss: Vol. 2. Separation: Anger and anxiety.* New York: Basic Books.

Bowlby, J. (1980). *Attachment and loss: Vol. 3. Loss, sadness, and depression.* New York: Basic Books.

Boyd, R. S. (1994, October 23). Race-IQ book treads on mine field. *San Jose Mercury News,* pp. 1A, 12A.

Bradburn, N. (1969). *The structure of psychological well-being.* Chicago: Aldine.

Bradbury, T. N., Campbell, S. M., & Fincham, F. D. (1995). Longitudinal and behavioral analysis of masculinity and femininity in marriage. *Journal of Personality and Social Psychology, 68,* 328–341.

Braffman, W., & Kirsch, I. (1999). Imaginative suggestibility and hypnotizability: An empirical analysis. *Journal of Personality and Social Psychology, 77,* 578–587.

Brebner, J., & Cooper, C. (1978). Stimulus- or response-induced excitation: A comparison of behavior in introverts and extraverts. *Journal of Research in Personality, 12,* 306–311.

Brebner, J., Donaldson, J., Kirby, N., & Ward, L. (1995). Relationships between happiness and personality. *Personality and Individual Differences, 19,* 251–258.

Brennan, K. A., Clark, C. L., & Shaver, P. R. (1998). Self-report measurement of adult attachment. In J. A. Simpson & W. S. Rholes (Eds.), *Attachment theory and close relationships* (pp. 46–76). New York: Guilford.

Brennan, K. A., & Shaver, P. R. (1993). Attachment styles and parental divorce. *Journal of Divorce and Remarriage, 21,* 161–175.

Brennan, K. A., & Shaver, P. R. (1995). Dimensions of adult attachment, affect regulation, and romantic relationship functioning. *Personality and Social Psychology Bulletin, 21,* 267–283.

Breslow, R., Kocsis, J., & Belkin, B. (1981). Contribution of the depressive perspective to memory function in depression. *American Journal of Psychiatry, 138,* 227–230.

Brewin, C. R. (1985). Depression and causal attributions: What is their relation? *Psychological Bulletin, 98,* 297–309.

Bridges, N. A. (2001). Therapist's self-disclosure: Expanding the comfort zone. *Psychotherapy, 38,* 21–30.

Briggs, S. R. (1989). The optimal level of measurement of personality constructs. In D. M. Buss & N. Cantor (Eds.), *Personality psychology: Recent trends and emerging directions* (pp. 246–260). New York: Springer-Verlag.

Brissette, I., Scheier, M. F., & Carver, C. S. (2002). The role of optimism in social network development, coping, and psychological adjustment during a life transition. *Journal of Personality and Social Psychology, 82,* 102–111.

Britt, T. W. (1993). Metatraits: Evidence relevant to the validity of the construct and its implications. *Journal of Personality and Social Psychology, 65,* 544–562.

Britt, T. W., & Shepperd, J. A. (1999). Trait relevance and trait assessment. *Personality and Social Psychology Review, 3,* 108–122.

Brockner, J. (1979). The effects of self-esteem, success-failure, and self-consciousness on task performance. *Journal of Personality and Social Psychology, 37,* 1732–1741.

Brockner, J., Derr, W. R., & Laing, W. N. (1987). Self-esteem and reactions to negative feedback: Toward greater generalizability. *Journal of Research in Personality, 21,* 318–333.

Brody, J. E. (2000, April 25). Memories of things that never were. *New York Times,* p. D–8.

Brody, L. R., Rozek, M. K., & Muten, E. O. (1985). Age, sex, and individual differences in children's defensive styles. *Journal of Clinical Child Psychology, 14,* 132–138.

Brooks-Gunn, J., & Fisch, M. (1980). Psychological androgyny and college students' judgments of mental health. *Sex Roles, 6,* 575–580.

Brown, J., & Inouye, D. K. (1978). Learned helplessness through modeling: The role of perceived similarity in competence. *Journal of Personality and Social Psychology, 36,* 900–908.

Brown, J. D., & Dutton, K. A. (1995). The thrill of victory, the complexity of defeat: Self-esteem and people's emotional reactions to success and failure. *Journal of Personality and Social Psychology, 68,* 712–722.

Brown, J. D., & Gallagher, F. M. (1992). Coming to terms with failure: Private self-enhancement and public self-effacement. *Journal of Experimental Social Psychology, 28,* 3–22.

Brown, J. D., & Marshall, M. A. (2001). Great expectations: Optimism and pessimism in achievement settings. In E. C. Chang (Ed.), *Optimism and pessimism: Implications for theory, research, and practice* (pp. 239–255). Washington, DC: American Psychological Association.

Brown, J. D., & Smart, S. A. (1991). The self and social conduct: Linking self-representations to prosocial behavior. *Journal of Personality and Social Psychology, 60,* 368–375.

Brown, R. J., & Donderi, D. C. (1986). Dream content and self-reported well-being among recurrent dreamers, past-recurrent dreamers, and nonrecurrent dreamers. *Journal of Personality and Social Psychology, 50,* 612–623.

Brown, S. (1998, April 20). Television violence stays constant. *Broadcasting and Cable, 128,* 20.

Bruch, M. A., Hamer, R. J., & Heimberg, R. G. (1995). Shyness and public self-consciousness: Additive or interactive relation with social interaction? *Journal of Personality, 63,* 47–63.

Bruch, M. A., Kaflowitz, N. G., & Pearl, L. (1988). Mediated and nonmediated relationships of personality components to loneliness. *Journal of Social and Clinical Psychology, 6,* 346–355.

Buchholz, E. S., & Helbraun, E. (1999). A psychobiological developmental model for an "alonetime" need in infancy. *Bulletin of the Menninger Clinic, 63,* 143–158.

Buhler, C., & Allen, M. (1972). *Introduction to humanistic psychology.* Monterey, CA: Brooks/Cole.

Bulkeley, K. (1997). *An introduction to the psychology of dreaming.* Westport, CT: Praeger.

Bullock, W. A., & Gilliland, K. (1993). Eysenck's arousal theory of introversion-extraversion: A converging measures investigation. *Journal of Personality and Social Psychology, 64,* 113–123.

Burger, J. M. (1984). Desire for control, locus of control, and proneness to depression. *Journal of Personality, 52,* 71–89.

Burger, J. M. (1995). Individual differences in preference for solitude. *Journal of Research in Personality, 29,* 85–108.

Burger, J. M. (1998). Solitude. In H. S. Friedman (Ed.), *The encyclopedia of mental health* (pp. 563–569). San Diego, CA: Academic Press.

Burger, J. M., & Arkin, R. M. (1980). Prediction, control and learned helplessness. *Journal of Personality and Social Psychology, 38,* 482–491.

Burger, J. M., & Cosby, M. (1999). Do women prefer dominant men? The case of the missing control condition. *Journal of Research in Personality, 33,* 358–368.

Burns, M. O., & Seligman, M. E. P. (1989). Explanatory style across the life span: Evidence for stability over 52 years. *Journal of Personality and Social Psychology, 56,* 471–477.

Bushman, B. J. (1995). Moderating role of trait aggressiveness in the effects of violent media on aggression. *Journal of Personality and Social Psychology, 69,* 950–960.

Bushman, B. J. (2002). Does venting anger feed or extinguish the flame? Catharsis, rumination, distraction, anger, and aggressive responding. *Personality and Social Psychology Bulletin, 28,* 724–731.

Bushman, B. J., Baumeister, R. F., & Phillips, C. M. (2001). Do people aggress to improve their mood? Catharsis beliefs, affect regulation opportunity, and aggressive responding. *Journal of Personality and Social Psychology, 81,* 17–32.

Bushman, B. J., Baumeister, R. F., & Stack, A. D. (1999). Catharsis, aggression, and persuasive influence: Self-fulfilling or self-defeating prophecies? *Journal of Personality and Social Psychology, 76,* 367–376.

Bushman, B. J., & Geen, R. G. (1990). Role of cognitive-emotional mediators and individual differences in the effects of media violence on aggression. *Journal of Personality and Social Psychology, 58,* 156–163.

Bushman, B. J., & Huesmann, L. R. (2001). Effects of televised violence on aggression. In D. G. Singer & J. L. Singer (Eds.), *Handbook of children and the media* (pp. 223–254). Thousand Oaks, CA: Sage.

Buss, A. H. (1980). *Self-consciousness and social anxiety.* San Francisco: W. H. Freeman.

Buss, A. H. (1991). The EAS theory of temperament. In J. Strelau & A. Angleitner (Eds.), *Explorations in temperament* (pp. 43–60). London: Plenum.

Buss, A. H., & Plomin, R. (1975). *A temperament theory of personality development.* New York: Wiley.

Buss, A. H., & Plomin, R. (1984). *Temperament: Early developing personality traits.* Hillsdale, NJ: Erlbaum.

Buss, A. H., & Plomin, R. (1986). The EAS approach to temperament. In R. Plomin & J. Dunn (Eds.), *The study of temperament: Changes, continuities and challenges* (pp. 67–79). Hillsdale, NJ: Erlbaum.

Buss, D. M. (1988). The evolution of human intrasexual competition: Tactics of mate attraction. *Journal of Personality and Social Psychology, 54,* 616–628.

Buss, D. M. (1989). Sex differences in human mate preferences: Evolutionary hypotheses tested in 37 cultures. *Behavioral and Brain Sciences, 12,* 1–49.

Buss, D. M. (1990). The evolution of anxiety and social exclusion. *Journal of Social and Clinical Psychology, 9,* 196–201.

Buss, D. M. (1991). Evolutionary personality psychology. *Annual Review of Psychology, 42,* 459–491.

Buss, D. M. (1995). Evolutionary psychology: A new paradigm for psychological science. *Psychological Inquiry, 6,* 1–30.

Buss, D. M. (1997). Evolutionary foundations of personality. In R. Hogan, J. Johnson, & S. Briggs (Eds.), *Handbook of personality psychology* (pp. 317–344). San Diego, CA: Academic Press.

Buss, D. M., & Barnes, M. (1986). Preferences in human mate selection. *Journal of Personality and Social Psychology, 50,* 559–570.

Buss, D. M., Haselton, M. G., Shackelford, T. K., Bleske, A. L., & Wakefield, J. C. (1998). Adaptations, exaptations, and spandrels. *American Psychologist, 53,* 533–548.

Buss, D. M., & Shackelford, T. K. (1997). From vigilance to violence: Mate retention tactics in married couples. *Journal of Personality and Social Psychology, 72,* 346–361.

Bussey, K., & Bandura, A. (1984). Influence of gender constancy and social power on sex-linked modeling. *Journal of Personality and Social Psychology, 47,* 1292–1302.

Butcher, J. N., & Rouse, S. V. (1996). Personality: Individual differences and clinical assessment. *Annual Review of Psychology, 47,* 87–111.

Butler, A. C., Hokanson, J. E., & Flynn, H. A. (1994). A comparison of self-esteem lability and low trait self-esteem as vulnerability factors for depression. *Journal of Personality and Social Psychology, 66,* 166–177.

Butler, J. M. (1968). Self-ideal congruence in psychotherapy. *Psychotherapy: Theory, Research and Practice, 5,* 13–17.

Byrne, D. (1964). Repression-sensitization as a dimension of personality. In B. A. Maher (Ed.), *Progress in experimental personality research* (Vol. 1, pp. 169–220). New York: Academic Press.

Cain, D. J., & Seeman, J. (2002). *Humanistic psychotherapies: Handbook of research and practice.* Washington, DC: American Psychological Association.

Cairns, R. B. (1986). An evolutionary and developmental perspective on aggressive patterns. In C. Zahn-Waxler, E. M. Cummings, & R. Iannotti (Eds.), *Altruism and aggression: Biological and social origins* (pp. 58–87). Cambridge: Cambridge University Press.

Caldwell, D. F., & Burger, J. M. (1998). Personality characteristics of job applicants and success in screening interviews. *Personnel Psychology, 51,* 119–136.

Camara, W. J., Nathan, J. S., & Puente, A. E. (2000). Psychological test usage: Implications in professional psychology. *Professional Psychology: Research and Practice, 31,* 141–154.

Cameron, L. D., & Nicholls, G. (1998). Expression of stressful experiences through writing: Effects of a self-regulation manipulation for pessimists and optimists. *Health Psychology, 17,* 84–92.

Campbell, J. B. (1983). Differential relationships of extraversion, impulsivity, and sociability to study habits. *Journal of Research in Personality, 17,* 308–314.

Campbell, J. B., & Hawley, C. W. (1982). Study habits and Eysenck's theory of extraversion-introversion. *Journal of Research in Personality, 16,* 139–146.

Campbell, J. D., & Fairey, P. J. (1985). Effects of self-esteem, hypothetical explanations, and verbalization of expectancies on future performance. *Journal of Personality and Social Psychology, 48,* 1097–1111.

Campos, J. J., Barrett, K. C., Lamb, M. E., Goldsmith, H. H., & Stenberg, C. (1983). Socioemotional development. In M. M. Haith & J. J. Campos (Eds.), *Handbook of child psychology: Vol. 2. Infancy and psychobiology* (pp. 783–915). New York: Wiley.

Cantor, N., Markus, H., Niedenthal, P., & Nurius, P. (1986). On motivation and the self-concept. In R. M. Sorrentino & E. T. Higgins (Eds.), *Handbook of motivation and cognition: Foundations of social behavior* (pp. 96–121). New York: Guilford.

Cantor, N., & Norem, J. K. (1989). Defensive pessimism and stress and coping. *Social Cognition, 7,* 92–112.

Cantor, N., Norem, J. K., Niedenthal, P. M., Langston, C. A., & Brower, A. M. (1987). Life tasks, self-concept ideals, and cognitive strategies in a life transition. *Journal of Personality and Social Psychology, 53,* 1178–1191.

Carlson, M., Marcus-Newhall, A., & Miller, N. (1990). Effects of situational aggression cues: A quantitative review. *Journal of Personality and Social Psychology, 58,* 622–633.

Carlson, R., & Levy, N. (1973). Studies in Jungian typology: I. Memory, social perception and social action. *Journal of Personality, 41,* 559–576.

Carnelley, K. B., Pietromonaco, P. R., & Jaffe, K. (1994). Depression, working models of others, and relationship functioning. *Journal of Personality and Social Psychology, 66,* 127–140.

Carree, C. (2002, July 25). Does success in sports come from brains, not brawn? *Wilmington Morning Star,* p. 1C.

Carvajal, S. C., Clair, S. D., Nash, S. G., & Evans, R. I. (1998). Relating optimism, hope, and self-esteem to social influences in deterring substance use in adolescents. *Journal of Social and Clinical Psychology, 17,* 443–465.

Carver, C. S. (1997). Adult attachment and personality: Converging evidence and a new measure. *Personality and Social Psychology Bulletin, 23,* 865–883.

Carver, C. S. (2001). Affect and the functional bases of behavior: On the dimensional structure of affective experience. *Personality and Social Psychology Review, 5,* 345–356.

Carver, C. S., Coleman, E. A., & Glass, D. C. (1976). The coronary-prone behavior pattern and the suppression of fatigue on a treadmill test. *Journal of Personality and Social Psychology, 33,* 460–466.

Carver, C. S., Pozo, C., Harris, S. D., Noriega, V., Scheier, M. F., Robinson, D. S., Ketcham, A. S., Moffat, F. L., &

Clark, K. C. (1993). How coping mediates the effect of optimism on distress: A study of women with early stage breast cancer. *Journal of Personality and Social Psychology, 65,* 375–390.

Carver, C. S., Scheier, M. F., & Weintraub, J. K. (1989). Assessing coping strategies: A theoretically based approach. *Journal of Personality and Social Psychology, 56,* 267–283.

Caspi, A. (1998). Personality development across the life course. In N. Eisenberg (Ed.), *Handbook of child psychology: Vol. 3, Social, emotional and personality development* (5th ed., pp. 311–388). New York: Wiley.

Caspi, A. (2000). The child is father of the man: Personality continuities from childhood to adulthood. *Journal of Personality and Social Psychology, 78,* 158–172.

Catalano, R., Dooley, D., Novaco, R. W., Wilson, G., & Hough, R. (1993). Using ECA survey data to examine the effect of job layoffs on violent behavior. *Hospital and Community Psychiatry, 44,* 874–879.

Cattell, H. E. P. (2001). The Sixteen Personality Factor (16PF) Questionnaire. In W. I. Dorfman & M. Hersen (Eds.), *Understanding psychological assessment* (pp. 187–215). New York: Plenum.

Cattell, R. B. (1974). Raymond B. Cattell. In G. Lindzey (Ed.), *A history of psychology in autobiography* (Vol. 6, pp. 61–100). Englewood Cliffs, NJ: Prentice-Hall.

Cepeda-Benito, A., & Short, P. (1998). Self-concealment, avoidance of psychological services, and perceived likelihood of seeking professional help. *Journal of Counseling Psychology, 45,* 58–64.

Chang, E. C. (1996). Cultural differences in optimism, pessimism and coping: Predictors of subsequent adjustment in Asian American and Caucasian American college students. *Journal of Counseling Psychology, 43,* 113–123.

Chang, E. C. (1998). Dispositional optimism and primary and secondary appraisal of a stressor: Controlling for confounding influences and relations to coping and psychological and physical adjustment. *Journal of Personality and Social Psychology, 74,* 1109–1120.

Chang, E. C. (2001). Cultural influences on optimism and pessimism: Differences in Western and Eastern construals of the self. In E. C. Chang (Ed.), *Optimism and pessimism: Implications for theory, research, and practice* (pp. 257–280). Washington, DC: American Psychological Association.

Chapman, A. H. (1976). *Harry Stack Sullivan: The man and his work.* New York: Putnam.

Charles, S. T., Reynolds, C. A., & Gatz, M. (2001). Age-related differences and change in positive and negative affect over 23 years. *Journal of Personality and Social Psychology, 80,* 136–151.

Cheek, J. M., & Buss, A. H. (1981). Shyness and sociability. *Journal of Personality and Social Psychology, 41,* 330–339.

Chelune, G. J., Sultan, F. E., & Williams, C. L. (1980). Loneliness, self-disclosure, and interpersonal effectiveness. *Journal of Counseling Psychology, 27,* 462–468.

Chen, S., Andersen, S. M., & Hinkley, K. (1999). Triggering transference: Examining the role of applicability in the activation and use of significant-other representations in social perception. *Social Cognition, 17,* 332–365.

Cheng, C. (1999). Gender-role differences in susceptibility to the influence of support availability and depression. *Journal of Personality, 67,* 439–467.

Cheng, C. (2001). Assessing coping flexibility in real-life and laboratory settings: A multimethod approach. *Journal of Personality and Social Psychology, 80,* 814–833.

Chess, S., & Thomas, A. (1986). *Temperament in clinical practice.* New York: Guilford.

Chess, S., & Thomas, A. (1991). Temperament and the concept of goodness of fit. In J. Strelau & A. Angleitner (Eds.), *Explorations in temperament* (pp. 15–28). London: Plenum.

Chess, S., & Thomas, A. (1996). Temperament: Theory and practice. New York: Brunner/Mazel.

Christensen, P. N., & Kashy, D. A. (1998). Perceptions of and by lonely people in initial social interaction. *Personality and Social Psychology Bulletin, 24,* 322–329.

Church, A. T. (1994). Relating the Tellegen and five-factor models of personality structure. *Journal of Personality and Social Psychology, 67,* 898–909.

Church, A. T. (Ed.). (2001). Culture and personality [Special issue]. *Journal of Personality, 69*(6).

Church, A. T., & Burke, P. J. (1994). Exploratory and confirmatory tests of the Big Five and Tellegen's three- and four-dimensional models. *Journal of Personality and Social Psychology, 66,* 93–114.

Church, A. T., Reyes, J. A. S., Katigbak, M. S., & Grimm, S. D. (1997). Filipino personality structure and the Big Five model: A lexical approach. *Journal of Personality, 65,* 477–528.

Clancy, S. M., & Dollinger, S. J. (1993). Photographic depictions of the self: Gender and age differences in social connectedness. *Sex Roles, 29,* 477–495.

Clark, D. A., Beck, A. T., & Alford, B. A. (1999). *Scientific foundations of cognitive theory and therapy for depression.* New York: Wiley.

Clark, D. M., & Teasdale, J. D. (1982). Diurnal variations in clinical depression and accessibility of memories of positive and negative experiences. *Journal of Abnormal Psychology, 91,* 87–95.

Clark, L. A., & Watson, D. (1988). Mood and the mundane: Relations between daily life events and self-reported mood. *Journal of Personality and Social Psychology, 54,* 296–308.

Clark, L. F. (1993). Stress and the cognitive-conversational benefits of social interaction. *Journal of Social and Clinical Psychology, 12,* 25–55.

Coe, W. C. (1989). Posthypnotic amnesia: Theory and research. In N. P. Spanos & J. F. Chaves (Eds.), *Hypnosis: The cognitive-behavioral perspective* (pp. 110–148). Buffalo, NY: Prometheus.

Coe, W. C., & Sarbin, T. R. (1991). Role theory: Hypnosis from a dramaturgical and narrational perspective. In S. J. Lynn & J. W. Rhue (Eds.), *Theories of hypnosis: Current models and perspectives* (pp. 303–323). New York: Guilford.

Coe, W. C., & Sluis, A. S. E. (1989). Increasing contextual pressures to breach posthypnotic amnesia. *Journal of Personality and Social Psychology, 57,* 885–894.

Cohen, D. B. (1979). *Sleep and dreaming: Origins, nature and function.* New York: Pergamon.

Cohen, D. B., & Cox, C. (1975). Neuroticism in the sleep laboratory: Implications for representational and adaptive properties of dreaming. *Journal of Abnormal Psychology, 84,* 91–108.

Cohen, S., Doyle, W. J., Skoner, D. P., Fireman, P., Gwaltney, J. M., Jr., & Newsom, J. T. (1995). State and trait affect as predictors of objective and subjective symptoms of respiratory viral infections. *Journal of Personality and Social Psychology, 68,* 159–169.

Cohen, S., & Wills, T. A. (1985). Stress, social support, and the buffering hypothesis. *Psychological Bulletin, 98,* 310–357.

Cohn, N. B., & Strassberg, D. S. (1983). Self-disclosure reciprocity among preadolescents. *Personality and Social Psychology Bulletin, 9,* 97–102.

Cole, S. W., Kemeny, M. E., Taylor, S. E., & Visscher, B. R. (1996). Elevated physical health risk among gay men who conceal their homosexual identity. *Health Psychology, 15,* 243–251.

Coleman, M., & Ganong, L. H. (1985). Love and sex-role stereotypes: Do "macho" men and "feminine" women make better lovers? *Journal of Personality and Social Psychology, 49,* 170–176.

Collins, N. L., & Feeney, B. C. (2000). A safe haven: An attachment theory perspective on support seeking and caregiving in intimate relationships. *Journal of Personality and Social Psychology, 78,* 1053–1073.

Collins, N. L., & Miller, L. C. (1994). Self-disclosure and liking: A meta-analytic review. *Psychological Bulletin, 116,* 457–475.

Collins, N. L., & Read, S. J. (1990). Adult attachment, working models, and relationship quality in dating couples. *Journal of Personality and Social Psychology, 58,* 644–663.

Compas, B. E., Worsham, N. L., Ey, S., & Howell, D. C. (1996). When Mom or Dad has cancer: II. Coping, cognitive appraisals, and psychological distress in children of cancer patients. *Health Psychology, 15,* 167–175.

Conley, J. J. (1984). Longitudinal consistency of adult personality: Self-reported psychological characteristics across 45 years. *Journal of Personality and Social Psychology, 47,* 1325–1333.

Conley, J. J. (1985). Longitudinal stability of personality traits: A multitrait-multimethod-multioccasion analysis. *Journal of Personality and Social Psychology, 49,* 1266–1282.

Constantinople, A. (1973). Masculinity-femininity: An exception to a famous dictum. *Psychological Bulletin, 80,* 389–407.

Conti, R. (2001). Time flies: Investigating the connection between intrinsic motivation and the experience of time. *Journal of Personality, 69,* 1–26.

Contrada, R. J. (1989). Type A behavior, personality hardiness, and cardiovascular responses to stress. *Journal of Personality and Social Psychology, 57,* 895–903.

Cooper, H. M., & Good, T. E. (1983). *Pygmalion grows up: Studies in the expectation communication process.* New York: Longman.

Cooper, T., Detre, T., & Weiss, S. M. (1981). Coronary-prone behavior and coronary heart disease: A critical review. *Circulation, 63,* 1199–1215.

Coopman, S. J. (1997). Personal constructs and communication in interpersonal and organizational contexts. In G. J. Neimeyer & R. A. Neimeyer (Eds.), *Advances in personal construct psychology* (Vol. 4, pp. 101–147). Greenwich, CN: JAI Press.

Coplan, R. J., Barber, A. M., & Lagace-Seguin, D. G. (1999). The role of child temperament as a predictor of early literacy and numeracy skills in preschoolers. *Early Childhood Research Quarterly, 14,* 537–553.

Cornell, D. G. (1997). Post hoc explanation is not prediction. *American Psychologist, 52,* 1380.

Costa, P. T., & McCrae, R. R. (1988). Personality in adulthood: A six-year longitudinal study of self-reports and spouse ratings on the NEO Personality Inventory. *Journal of Personality and Social Psychology, 54,* 853–863.

Costa, P. T., & McCrae, R. R. (1992). *Professional manual for the NEO PI-R.* Odessa, FL: Psychological Assessment Resources.

Costa, P. T., & McCrae, R. R. (1995). Primary traits of Eysenck's P-E-N system: Three- and five-factor solutions. *Journal of Personality and Social Psychology, 69,* 308–317.

Costa, P. T., Terracciano, A., & McCrae, R. R. (2001). Gender differences in personality traits across cultures: Robust and surprising findings. *Journal of Personality and Social Psychology, 81,* 322–331.

Costa, P. T., & Widiger, T. A. (Eds.). (1994). *Personality disorders and the five factor model of personality.* Washington, DC: American Psychological Association.

Costello, C. G. (1978). A critical review of Seligman's laboratory experiments on learned helplessness and depression in humans. *Journal of Abnormal Psychology, 87,* 21–31.

Cote, S., & Moskowitz, D. S. (1998). On the dynamic covariation between interpersonal behavior and affect: Prediction from Neuroticism, Extraversion, and Agreeableness. *Journal of Personality and Social Psychology, 75,* 1032–1046.

Cowen, E. I., Wyman, P. A., & Work, W. C. (1992). The relationship between retrospective reports of early child temperament and adjustment at ages 10–12. *Journal of Abnormal Child Psychology, 20,* 39–50.

Cox-Fuenzalida, L., Gilliland, K., & Swickert, R. J. (2001). Congruency of the relationship between extraversion and the brainstem auditory evoked response based on the EPI versus the EPQ. *Journal of Research in Personality, 35,* 117–126.

Crabbe, J. C. (2002). Genetic contributions to addiction. *Annual Review of Psychology, 53,* 435–462.

Craik, K. H. (1986). Personality research methods: An historical perspective. *Journal of Personality, 54,* 18–51.

Cramer, K. M., & Lake, R. P. (1998). The Preference for Solitude Scale: Psychometric properties and factor structure. *Personality and Individual Differences, 24,* 193–199.

Cramer, K. M., Ofosu, H. B., & Barry, J. E. (2000). An abbreviated form of the social and emotional loneliness scale for adults (SELSA). *Personality and Individual Differences, 28,* 1125–1131.

Cramer, P. (1991). *The development of defense mechanisms: Theory, research, and assessment.* New York: Springer-Verlag.

Cramer, P. (1997a). Identity, personality, and defense mechanisms: An observer-based study. *Journal of Research in Personality, 31,* 58–77.

Cramer, P. (1997b). Evidence for change in children's use of defense mechanisms. *Journal of Personality, 65,* 233–247.

Cramer, P. (1998a). Freshman to senior year: A follow-up study of identity, narcissism, and defense mechanisms. *Journal of Research in Personality, 32,* 156–172.

Cramer, P. (1998b). Threat to gender representation: Identity and identification. *Journal of Personality, 66,* 335–357.

Cramer, P. (1999). Personality, personality disorders, and defense mechanisms. *Journal of Personality, 67,* 535–554.

Cramer, P. (2000). Defense mechanisms in psychology today: Further processes for adaptation. *American Psychologist, 55,* 637–646.

Cramer, P. (2002). Defense mechanisms, behavior, and affect in young adulthood. *Journal of Personality, 70,* 103–126.

Cramer, P., & Blatt, S. J. (1990). Use of the TAT to measure change in defense mechanisms following intensive psychotherapy. *Journal of Personality Assessment, 54,* 236–251.

Cramer, P., Blatt, S. J., & Ford, R. Q. (1988). Defense mechanisms in the anaclitic and introjective personality configuration. *Journal of Consulting and Clinical Psychology, 56,* 610–616.

Cramer, P., & Block, J. (1998). Preschool antecedents of defense mechanism use in young adults: A longitudinal study. *Journal of Personality and Social Psychology, 74,* 159–169.

Cramer, P., & Brilliant, M. A. (2001). Defense use and defense understanding in children. *Journal of Personality, 69,* 297–322.

Cramer, P., & Gaul, R. (1988). The effects of success and failure on children's use of defense mechanisms. *Journal of Personality, 56,* 729–742.

Cramer, R. E., Manning-Ryan, B., Johnson, L. M, & Barbo, E. (2000). Sex differences in subjective distress to violations of trust: Extending an evolutionary perspective. *Basic and Applied Social Psychology, 22,* 101–109.

Crick, F., & Mitchison, G. (1983). The function of dream sleep. *Nature, 304,* 111–114.

Crocker, J., & Wolfe, C. T. (2001). Contingencies of self-worth. *Psychological Review, 108,* 593–623.

Cross, S. E., Bacon, P. L., & Morris, M. L. (2000). The relational-interdependent self-construal and relationships. *Journal of Personality and Social Psychology, 78,* 791–808.

Cross, S. E., & Madson, L. (1997). Models of the self: Self-construals and gender. *Psychological Bulletin, 122,* 5–37.

Cross, S. E., Morris, M. L., & Gore, J. S. (2002). Thinking about oneself and others: The relational-interdependent self-construal and social cognition. *Journal of Personality and Social Psychology, 82,* 399–418.

Crossen, C. (1996, March 8). Solitude is a casualty of the war with time. *Wall Street Journal,* p. R4.

Crowson, J. J., & Cromwell, R. L. (1995). Depressed and normal individuals differ both in selection and in perceived tonal quality of positive-negative messages. *Journal of Abnormal Psychology, 104,* 305–311.

Csikszentmihalyi, M. (1990). Flow: *The psychology of optimal experience.* New York: Harper & Row.

Csikszentmihalyi, M. (1999). If we are so rich, why aren't we happy? *American Psychologist, 54,* 821–827.

Csikszentmihalyi, M., & Csikszentmihalyi, I. S. (1988). *Optimal experience: Psychological studies of flow in consciousness.* New York: Cambridge.

Csikszentmihalyi, M., & LeFevre, J. (1989). Optimal experience in work and leisure. *Journal of Personality and Social Psychology, 56,* 815–822.

Cunningham, J. A., Strassberg, D. S., & Haan, B. (1986). Effects of intimacy and sex-role congruency of self-disclosure. *Journal of Social and Clinical Psychology, 4,* 393–401.

Cunningham, M. R. (1988). Does happiness mean friendliness? Induced mood and heterosexual self-disclosure. *Personality and Social Psychology Bulletin, 14,* 283–297.

Curran, J. P., Wallander, J. L., & Fischetti, M. (1980). The importance of behavioral and cognitive factors in heterosexual-social anxiety. *Journal of Personality, 48,* 285–292.

Cutler, S. E., Larsen, R. J., & Bunce, S. C. (1996). Repressive coping style and the experience and recall of emotion: A naturalistic study of daily affect. *Journal of Personality, 64,* 379–405.

Cutrona, C. E. (1982). Transition to college: Loneliness and the process of social adjustment. In L. A. Peplau & D. Perlman (Eds.), *Loneliness* (pp. 291–309). New York: Wiley.

Cyranowski, J. M., & Andersen, B. L. (2000). Evidence of self-schematic cognitive processing of women with differing sexual self-views. *Journal of Social and Clinical Psychology, 19,* 519–543.

Dadds, M. R., Bovbjerg, D. H., Redd, W. H., & Cutmore, T. R. H. (1997). Imagery in human classical conditioning. *Psychological Bulletin, 122,* 89–103.

Davidson, K., & MacGregor, M. W. (1996). Reliability of an idiographic Q-sort measure of defense mechanisms. *Journal of Personality Assessment, 66,* 624–639.

Davidson, K., & MacGregor, M. W. (1998). A critical appraisal of self-report defense mechanism measures. *Journal of Personality, 66,* 965–992.

Davidson, R. J. (1988). EEG measures of cerebral asymmetry: Conceptual and methodological issues. *International Journal of Neuroscience, 39,* 71–89.

Davidson, R. J. (1991). Biological approaches to the study of personality. In V. J. Derlega, B. A. Winstead, & W. H. Jones (Eds.), *Personality: Contemporary theory and research* (pp. 87–112). Chicago: Nelson-Hall.

Davidson, R. J., Chapman, J. P., & Chapman, L. J. (1987). Task-dependent EEG asymmetry discriminates between depressed and nondepressed subjects. *Psychophysiology, 24,* 585.

Davidson, R. J., Ekman, P., Saron, C. D., Senulis, J. A., & Friesen, W. V. (1990). Approach-withdrawal and cerebral asymmetry: Emotional expression and brain physiology I. *Journal of Personality and Social Psychology, 58,* 330–341.

Davidson, R. J., & Fox, N. A. (1982). Asymmetrical brain activity discriminates between positive versus negative affective stimuli in human infants. *Science, 218,* 1235–1237.

Davidson, R. J., & Fox, N. A. (1989). Frontal brain asymmetry predicts infants' response to maternal separation. *Journal of Abnormal Psychology, 98,* 127–131.

Davidson, R. J., & Tomarken, A. J. (1989). Laterality and emotion: An electrophysiological approach. In F. Boller & J. Grafman (Eds.), *Handbook of neuropsychology* (Vol. 3, pp. 419–441). New York: Elsevier Science.

Davila, J., Burge, D., & Hammen, C. (1997). Why does attachment style change? *Journal of Personality and Social Psychology, 73,* 826–838.

Davila, J., Karney, B. R., & Bradbury, T. N. (1999). Attachment change processes in the early years of marriage. *Journal of Personality and Social Psychology, 76,* 783–802.

Davis, J. D. (1976). Self-disclosure in an acquaintance exercise: Responsibility for level of intimacy. *Journal of Personality and Social Psychology, 33,* 787–792.

Davis, J. D. (1977). Effects of communication about interpersonal process on the evolution of self-disclosure in dyads. *Journal of Personality and Social Psychology, 35,* 31–37.

Davis, P. J. (1987). Repression and the inaccessibility of affective memories. *Journal of Personality and Social Psychology, 53,* 585–593.

Davis, P. J. (1999). Gender differences in autobiographical memory for childhood emotional experiences. *Journal of Personality and Social Psychology, 76,* 498–510.

Davis, P. J., & Schwartz, G. E. (1987). Repression and the inaccessibility of affective memories. *Journal of Personality and Social Psychology, 52,* 155–162.

Dawes, R. M. (1994). *House of cards: Psychology and psychotherapy built on myth.* New York: Free Press.

Deaux, K., Kite, M. E., & Lewis, L. L. (1985). Clustering and gender schemata: An uncertain link. *Personality and Social Psychology Bulletin, 11,* 387–397.

Deckers, L., & Carr, D. E. (1986). Cartoons varying in low-level pain ratings, not aggression ratings, correlate positively with funniness ratings. *Motivation and Emotion, 10,* 207–216.

Deffenbacher, J., Huff, M., Lynch, R., Oetting, E., & Salvatore, N. (2000). Characteristics and treatments of high-anger drivers. *Journal of Counseling Psychology, 47,* 5–17.

Dembroski, T. M., & Costa, P. T. (1987). Coronary-prone behavior: Components of the Type A pattern and hostility. *Journal of Personality, 55,* 211–235.

DeMonbreun, B. G., & Craighead, W. E. (1977). Distortion of perception and recall of positive and neutral feedback in depression. *Cognitive Research and Therapy, 1,* 311–329.

DeMulder, E. K., Denham, S., Schmidt, M., & Mitchell, J. (2000). Q-sort assessment of attachment security during the preschool years: Links from home to school. *Developmental Psychology, 36,* 274–282.

DeNeve, K. M. (1999). Happy as an extraverted clam? The role of personality for subjective well-being. *Current Directions in Psychological Science, 8,* 141–144.

DeNeve, K. M., & Cooper, H. (1998). The happy personality: A meta-analysis of 137 personality traits and subjective well-being. *Psychological Bulletin, 124,* 197–229.

DePaulo, B. M., Dull, W. R., Greenberg, J. M., & Swaim, G. W. (1989). Are shy people reluctant to ask for help? *Journal of Personality and Social Psychology, 56,* 834–844.

DePaulo, B. M., Epstein, J. A., & LeMay, C. S. (1990). Responses of the socially anxious to the prospect of interpersonal evaluation. *Journal of Personality, 58,* 623–640.

DePaulo, B. M., Kenny, D. A., Hoover, C. W., Webb, W., & Oliver, P. V. (1987). Accuracy of person perception: Do people know what kinds of impressions they convey? *Journal of Personality and Social Psychology, 52,* 303–315.

Depue, R. A., & Monroe, S. M. (1978). Learned helplessness in the perspective of the depressive disorders: Conceptual and definitional issues. *Journal of Abnormal Psychology, 87,* 3–20.

Derakshan, N., & Eysenck, M. W. (1997). Interpretive biases for one's own behavior and physiology in high-trait-anxious individuals and repressors. *Journal of Personality and Social Psychology, 73,* 816–825.

de Riviera (1997). The construction of false memory syndrome: The experience of retractors. *Psychological Inquiry, 8,* 271–292.

Derlega, V. J., & Chaikin, A. L. (1976). Norms affecting self-disclosure in men and women. *Journal of Consulting and Clinical Psychology, 44,* 376–380.

Derlega, V. J., Harris, M. S., & Chaikin, A. L. (1973). Self-disclosure reciprocity, liking and the deviant. *Journal of Experimental Social Psychology, 9,* 277–284.

Derlega, V. J., Hendrick, S. S., Winstead, B. A., & Berg, J. H. (1991). *Psychotherapy as a personal relationship.* New York: Guilford.

Derlega, V. J., Margulis, S. T., & Winstead, B. A. (1987). A social-psychological analysis of self-disclosure in psychotherapy. *Journal of Social and Clinical Psychology, 5,* 205–215.

Derlega, V. J., Wilson, M., & Chaikin, A. L. (1976). Friendship and disclosure reciprocity. *Journal of Personality and Social Psychology, 34,* 578–582.

Derry, P. A., & Kuiper, N. A. (1981). Schematic processing and self-reference in clinical depression. *Journal of Abnormal Psychology, 90,* 286–297.

DeVellis, R. F., DeVellis, B. M., & McCauley, C. (1978). Vicarious acquisition of learned helplessness. *Journal of Personality and Social Psychology, 36,* 894–899.

DeVito, A. J. (1985). Review of Myers-Briggs Type Indicator. In J. V. Mitchell (Ed.), *The ninth mental measurements yearbook* (pp. 1029–1032). Lincoln, NE: Buros Institute of Mental Measurements.

Di Blas, L., & Forzi, M. (1999). Refining a descriptive structure of personality attributes in the Italian language: The abridged Big Three circumplex structure. *Journal of Personality and Social Psychology, 76,* 451–481.

DiClemente, C. C., Fairhurst, S. K., & Piotrowski, N. A. (1995). Self-efficacy and addictive behaviors. In J. E. Maddux (Ed.), *Self-efficacy, adaptation and adjustment: Theory, research and application* (pp. 109–141). New York: Plenum.

Diehl, M., Elnick, A. B., Bourbeau, L. S., & Labouvie-Vief, G. (1998). Adult attachment styles: Their relations to family context and personality. *Journal of Personality and Social Psychology, 74,* 1656–1669.

Diener, E. (1984). Subjective well-being. *Psychological Bulletin, 95,* 542–575.

Diener, E., & Diener, M. (1995). Cross-cultural correlates of life satisfaction and self-esteem. *Journal of Personality and Social Psychology, 68,* 653–663.

Diener, E., & Emmons, R. A. (1984). The independence of positive and negative affect. *Journal of Personality and Social Psychology, 47,* 1105–1117.

Diener, E., & Seligman, M. E. P. (2002). Very happy people. *Psychological Science, 13,* 81–84.

Digman, J. M. (1989). Five robust trait dimensions: Development, stability, and utility. *Journal of Personality, 57,* 195–214.

Digman, J. M. (1990). Personality structure: Emergence of the five-factor model. *Annual Review of Psychology, 41,* 417–440.

Digman, J. M. (1997). Higher-order factors of the Big Five. *Journal of Personality and Social Psychology, 73,* 1246–1256.

Digman, J. M., & Inouye, J. (1986). Further specification of the five robust factors of personality. *Journal of Personality and Social Psychology, 50,* 116–123.

Digman, J. M., & Shmelyov, A. G. (1996). The structure of temperament and personality in Russian children. *Journal of Personality and Social Psychology, 71,* 341–351.

Dijkstra, P., & Buunk, B. P. (1998). Jealousy as a function of rival characteristics: An evolutionary perspective. *Personality and Social Psychology Bulletin, 24,* 1158–1166.

DiLalla, D. L., Carey, G., Gottesman, I. I., & Bouchard, T. J. (1996). Heritability of MMPI personality indicators of psychopathology in twins reared apart. *Journal of Abnormal Psychology, 105,* 491–499.

DiLalla, L. F., & Gottesman, I. I. (1991). Biological and genetic contributors to violence: Widom's untold tale. *Psychological Bulletin, 109,* 125–129.

Dill, K. E., Anderson, C. A., & Anderson, K. B. (1997). Effects of aggressive personality on social expectations and social perceptions. *Journal of Research in Personality, 31,* 272–292.

Dindia, K., & Allen, M. (1992). Sex differences in self-disclosure: A meta-analysis. *Psychological Bulletin, 112,* 106–124.

Dobson, K. S. (1989). A meta-analysis of the efficacy of cognitive therapy for depression. *Journal of Consulting and Clinical Psychology, 57,* 414–419.

A doctor in the house? T-Wolves playing with their heads (2002, June 24). *Sports Illustrated,* p. 46.

Dodge, K. A., & Crick, N. R. (1990). Social information-processing bases of aggressive behavior in children. *Personality and Social Psychology Bulletin, 16,* 8–22.

Dodge, K. A., & Somberg, D. R. (1987). Hostile attributional biases among aggressive boys are exacerbated under conditions of threats to the self. *Child Development, 58,* 213–224.

Dodgson, P. G., & Wood, J. V. (1998). Self-esteem and the cognitive accessibility of strengths and weaknesses after failure. *Journal of Personality and Social Psychology, 75,* 178–197.

Doherty, W. J. (1983). Impact of divorce on locus of control orientation in adult women: A longitudinal study. *Journal of Personality and Social Psychology, 44,* 834–840.

Dollard, J., Doob, L., Miller, N. E., Mowrer, O. H., & Sears, R. R. (1939). *Frustration and aggression.* New Haven, CT: Yale University Press.

Dollinger, S. J. (2000). Locus of control and incidental learning: An application to college student success. *College Student Journal, 34,* 537–540.

Domhoff, G. W. (1996). *Finding meaning in dreams: A quantitative approach.* New York: Plenum.

Domhoff, G. W. (1999). New directions in the study of dream content using the Hall and Van de Castle coding system. *Dreaming, 9,* 115–137.

Domhoff, G. W. (2001). A new neurocognitive theory of dreams. *Dreaming, 11,* 13–33.

Donahue, E. M. (1994). Do children use the Big Five, too? Content and structural form in personality description. *Journal of Personality, 62,* 45–66.

Donnelly, D. A., & Murray, E. J. (1991). Cognitive and emotional changes in written essays and therapy interviews. *Journal of Social and Clinical Psychology, 10,* 334–350.

Doob, L. W., & Sears, R. R. (1939). Factors determining substitute behavior and the overt expression of aggression. *Journal of Abnormal and Social Psychology, 34,* 293–313.

Doucet, C., & Stelmack, R. M. (2000). An event-related potential analysis of extraversion and individual differences in cognitive processing speed and response execution. *Journal of Personality and Social Psychology, 78,* 956–964.

Dozois, D. J. A., & Dobson, K. S. (2001). A longitudinal investigation of information processing and cognitive organization in clinical depression: Stability of schematic interconnectedness. *Journal of Consulting and Clinical Psychology, 69,* 914–925.

Duck, S. W. (1979). The personal and interpersonal in construct theory: Social and individual aspects of relationships. In P. Stringer & D. Bannister (Eds.), *Constructs of sociality and individuality* (pp. 279–297). London: Academic Press.

Dutton, K. A., & Brown, J. D. (1997). Global self-esteem and specific self-views as determinants of people's reactions to success and failure. *Journal of Personality and Social Psychology, 73,* 139–148.

Dweck, C. S. (1986). Motivational processes affecting learning. *American Psychologist, 41,* 1040–1048.

Dweck, C. S., & Leggett, E. L. (1988). A social-cognitive approach to motivation and personality. *Psychological Review, 95,* 256–273.

Dworkin, R. H., Burke, B. W., Maher, B. A., & Gottesman, I. I. (1976). A longitudinal study of the genetics of personality. *Journal of Personality and Social Psychology, 34,* 510–518.

Dykema, J., Bergbower, K., & Peterson, C. (1995). Pessimistic explanatory style, stress, and illness. *Journal of Social and Clinical Psychology, 14,* 357–371.

Eagly, A. H. (1997). Sex differences in social behavior: Comparing social role theory and evolutionary psychology. *American Psychologist, 52,* 1380–1382.

Eagly, A. H., & Wood, W. (1999). The origins of sex differences in human behavior: Evolved dispositions versus social roles. *American Psychologist, 54,* 408–423.

Eaves, L., & Eysenck, H. (1975). Utilization of self-schemas as a mechanism of interpretational bias in children. *Social Cognition, 5,* 280–300.

Eccles, J. (1983). Expectancies, values, and academic behaviors. In J. T. Spence (Ed.), *Achievement and achievement motives: Psychological and sociological approaches* (pp. 75–146). San Francisco: Freeman.

Eccles, J. (1985). Sex differences in achievement patterns. In T. B. Sonderegger (Ed.), *Nebraska Symposium on Motivation* (Vol. 32, pp. 97–132). Lincoln: University of Nebraska Press.

Eccles, J., Adler, T., & Meece, J. L. (1984). Sex differences in achievement: A test of alternate theories. *Journal of Personality and Social Psychology, 46,* 26–43.

Eccles, J. S., & Wigfield, A. (1994). In the mind of the actor: The structure of adolescents' achievement task values and expectancy-related beliefs. *Personality and Social Psychology Bulletin, 21,* 215–225.

Edwards, V. J., & Spence, J. T. (1987). Gender-related traits, stereotypes, and schemata. *Journal of Personality and Social Psychology, 53,* 146–154.

Egloff, B., & Krohne, H. W. (1996). Repressive emotional discreteness after failure. *Journal of Personality and Social Psychology, 70,* 1318–1326.

Ehrlich, H. J., & Graeven, D. B. (1971). Reciprocal self-disclosure in a dyad. *Journal of Experimental Social Psychology, 7,* 389–400.

Eisenberger, R., & Cameron, J. (1996). Detrimental effects of reward: Reality or myth? *American Psychologist, 51,* 1153–1166.

Elliot, A. J., & McGregor, H. A. (1999). Test anxiety and the hierarchical model of approach and avoidance achievement motivation. *Journal of Personality and Social Psychology, 76,* 628–644.

Elliot, A. J., & McGregor, H. A. (2001). A 2 × 2 achievement goal framework. *Journal of Personality and Social Psychology, 80,* 501–519.

Elliott, A. J., Miltenberger, R. G., Kaster-Bundgaard, J., & Lumley, V. (1996). A national survey of assessment and therapy techniques used by behavior therapists. *Cognitive and Behavioral Practice, 3,* 107–125.

Elliott, R. (2002). The effectiveness of humanistic therapies: A meta-analysis. In D. J. Cain & J. Seeman (Eds.), *Humanistic psychotherapies: Handbook of research and practice* (pp. 57–81). Washington, DC: American Psychological Association.

Ellis, A., & Harper, R. A. (1975). *A new guide to rational living.* North Hollywood, CA: Wilshire.

Ellis, A. E. (1971). *Growth through reason: Verbatim cases in rational-emotive therapy.* North Hollywood, CA: Wilshire.

Ellis, A. E. (1987). The impossibility of achieving consistently good mental health. *American Psychologist, 42,* 364–375.

Emmons, R. A., & Diener, E. (1986). Influence of impulsivity and sociability on subjective well-being. *Journal of Personality and Social Psychology, 50,* 1211–1215.

Endler, N. S., & Hunt, J. M. (1966). Sources of behavioral variance as measured by the S-R inventory of anxiousness. *Psychological Bulletin, 65,* 336–346.

Endler, N. S., & Hunt, J. M. (1968). S-R inventories of hostility and comparisons of the proportions of variance from persons, responses, and situations for hostility and anxiousness. *Journal of Personality and Social Psychology, 9,* 309–315.

Endler, N. S., & Magnusson, D. (1976). Toward an interactional psychology of personality. *Psychological Bulletin, 83,* 956–974.

Endler, N. S., & Parker, J. D. A. (1990). Multidimensional assessment of coping: A critical evaluation. *Journal of Personality and Social Psychology, 58,* 844–854.

Endler, N. S., & Speer, R. L. (1998). Personality psychology: Research trends for 1993–1995. *Journal of Personality, 66,* 621–669.

Epstein, S. (1979). The stability of behavior: I. On predicting most of the people much of the time. *Journal of Personality and Social Psychology, 37,* 1097–1126.

Epstein, S. (1980). The stability of behavior: II. Implications for psychological research. *American Psychologist, 35,* 790–806.

Epstein, S. (1983). Aggregation and beyond: Some basic issues on the prediction of behavior. *Journal of Personality, 51,* 360–392.

Epstein, S. (1986). Does aggregation produce spuriously high estimates of behavior stability? *Journal of Personality and Social Psychology, 50,* 1199–1210.

Erickson, M. H. (1967). *Advanced techniques of hypnosis and therapy: Selected papers of Milton H. Erickson.* New York: Grune & Stratton.

Erikson, E. H. (1950/1963). *Childhood and society* (2nd ed.). New York: Norton.

Erikson, E. H. (1968). *Identity: Youth and crisis.* New York: Norton.

Erikson, E. H. (1975). *Life history and the historical moment.* New York: Norton.

Eron, L. D. (1987). The development of aggressive behavior from the perspective of a developing behaviorism. *American Psychologist, 42,* 435–442.

Evans, K. K., & Singer, J. A. (1995). Studying intimacy through dream narratives: The relationship of dreams to self-report and projective measures of personality. *Imagination, Cognition and Personality, 14,* 211–226.

Evans, R. I. (1976). *The making of psychology.* New York: Knopf.

Evans, S., Ferrando, S. J., Rabkin, J. G., & Fishman, B. (2000). Health locus of control, distress, and utilization of protease inhibitors among HIV-positive men. *Journal of Psychosomatic Research, 49,* 157–162.

Eysenck, H. J. (1967). *The biological basis of personality.* Springfield, IL: Charles C. Thomas.

Eysenck, H. J. (1982). Development of a theory. In C. D. Spielberger (Ed.), *Personality, genetics and behavior: Selected papers* (pp. 1–38). New York: Praeger.

Eysenck, H. J. (1990). Biological dimensions of personality. In L. Pervin (Ed.), *Handbook of personality theory and research* (pp. 244–276). New York: Guilford.

Eysenck, H. J. (1997). Personality and experimental psychology: The unification of psychology and the possibility of a paradigm. *Journal of Personality and Social Psychology, 73,* 1224–1237.

Eysenck, H. J., & Eysenck, S. B. G. (1968). *Manual for the Eysenck Personality Inventory.* San Diego, CA: Educational and Industrial Testing Service.

Eysenck, M. W. (1997). *Anxiety and cognition: A unified theory.* Hove, England: Erlbaum.

Eysenck, S. B. G., & Long, F. Y. (1986). A cross-cultural comparison of personality in adults and children: Singapore and England. *Journal of Personality and Social Psychology, 50,* 124–130.

Fancher, R. E. (2000). Snapshots of Freud in America, 1899–1999. *American Psychologist, 55,* 1025–1028.

Farabee, D. J., Holcom, M. L., Ramsey, S. L., & Cole, S. G. (1993). Social anxiety and speaker gaze in a persuasive atmosphere. *Journal of Research in Personality, 27,* 365–376.

Farley, F. (2000). Hans J. Eysenck (1916–1997). *American Psychologist, 55,* 674–675.

Fazio, R. H., Cooper, M., Dayson, K., & Johnson, M. (1981). Control and the coronary-prone behavior pattern: Responses to multiple situational demands. *Personality and Social Psychology Bulletin, 7,* 97–102.

Feeney, B. C., & Collins, N. L. (2001). Predictors of caregiving in adult intimate relationships: An attachment theoretical perspective. *Journal of Personality and Social Psychology, 80,* 972–994.

Feeney, B. C., & Kirkpatrick, L. A. (1996). Effects of adult attachment and presence of romantic partners on physiological responses to stress. *Journal of Personality and Social Psychology, 70,* 255–270.

Feeney, J. A., & Noller, P. (1990). Attachment style as a predictor of adult romantic relationships. *Journal of Personality and Social Psychology, 58,* 281–291.

Feeney, J. A., Noller, P., & Patty, J. (1993). Adolescents' interactions with the opposite sex: Influence of attachment style and gender. *Journal of Adolescence, 16,* 169–186.

Feingold, A. (1990). Gender differences in effects of physical attractiveness on romantic attraction: A comparison across five research paradigms. *Journal of Personality and Social Psychology, 59,* 981–993.

Feingold, A. (1992). Gender differences in mate selection preferences: A test of the parental investment model. *Psychological Bulletin, 112,* 125–139.

Feist, G. J. (1998). A meta-analysis of personality in scientific and artistic creativity. *Personality and Social Psychology Review, 2,* 290–309.

Feldman Barrett, L., Lane, R. D., Sechrest, L., Schwartz, G. E. (2000). Sex differences in emotional awareness. *Personality and Social Psychology Bulletin, 26,* 1027–1035.

Fenichel, O. (1945). *The psychoanalytic theory of neurosis.* New York: Norton.

Fenigstein, A. (1979). Does aggression cause a preference for viewing media violence? *Journal of Personality and Social Psychology, 37,* 2307–2317.

Ferguson, S. M., Brodkin, J. D., Lloyd, G. K., & Menzaghi, F. (2000). Antidepressant-like effects of the subtype-selective nicotinic acetylcholine receptor agonist, SIB-1508Y, in the learned helplessness rat model of depression. *Psychopharmacology, 152,* 295–303.

Findley, M. J., & Cooper, H. M. (1983). Locus of control and academic achievement: A literature review. *Journal of Personality and Social Psychology, 44,* 419–427.

Finkel, D., & McGue, M. (1997). Sex differences and non-additivity in heritability of the multidimensional personality questionnaire scales. *Journal of Personality and Social Psychology, 72,* 929–938.

Fischer, A. R., Jome, L. M., & Atkinson, D. R. (1998). Reconceptualizing multicultural counseling: Universal healing conditions in a culturally specific context. *Counseling Psychologist, 26,* 525–588.

Fisher, M. (1995, December 6). Freudian slip. *San Jose Mercury News,* p. 25A.

Fleenor, J. W. (2001). Myers-Briggs Type Indicator, Form M. In B. S. Plake, & J. C. Impara (Eds.), *The fourteenth mental measurements yearbook* (pp. 816–818). Lincoln, NE: University of Nebraska Press.

Floderus-Myrhed, B., Pedersen, N., & Rasmuson, I. (1980). Assessment of heritability for personality, based on a short-form of the Eysenck Personality Inventory: A study of 12,898 twin pairs. *Behavior Genetics, 10,* 153–162.

Flynn, J. R. (1999). Searching for justice: The discovery of IQ gains over time. *American Psychologist, 54,* 5–20.

Fodor, E. M., & Carver, R. A. (2000). Achievement and power motives, performance feedback, and creativity. *Journal of Research in Personality, 34,* 380–396.

Folkman, S. (1984). Personal control and stress and coping processes: A theoretical analysis. *Journal of Personality and Social Psychology, 46,* 839–852.

Folkman, S., & Lazarus, R. S. (1980). An analysis of coping in a middle-aged community sample. *Journal of Health and Social Behavior, 21,* 219–239.

Folkman, S., & Lazarus, R. S. (1988). *Manual for the Ways of Coping Questionnaire.* Palo Alto, CA: Consulting Psychologists Press.

Foulkes, D., & Cavallero, C. (1993). *Dreaming as cognition.* New York: Harvester Wheatsheaf.

Fox, N. A., & Davidson, R. J. (1986). Taste-elicited changes in facial signs of emotion and the asymmetry of brain electrical activity in human newborns. *Neuropsychologia, 24,* 417–422.

Fox, N. A., & Davidson, R. J. (1987). Electroencephalogram asymmetry in response to the approach of a stranger and maternal separation of 10-month-old infants. *Developmental Psychology, 23,* 233–240.

Fox, N. A., & Davidson, R. J. (1988). Patterns of electrical activity during facial signs of emotion in 10-month-old infants. *Developmental Psychology, 24,* 230–236.

Frable, D. E. S. (1989). Sex typing and gender ideology: Two facets of the individual's gender psychology that go together. *Journal of Personality and Social Psychology, 56,* 95–108.

Fraley, R. C., & Shaver, P. R. (1998). Airport separation: A naturalistic study of adult attachment dynamics in separating couples. *Journal of Personality and Social Psychology, 75,* 1198–1212.

Frankel, A., & Prentice-Dunn, S. (1990). Loneliness and the processing of self-relevant information. *Journal of Social and Clinical Psychology, 9,* 303–315.

Frankl, V. E. (1959). *Man's search for meaning: An introduction to logotherapy.* New York: Beacon.

Frazier, L. D., Hooker, K., Johnson, P. M., & Kaus, C. R. (2000). Continuity and change in possible selves in later life: A 5-year longitudinal study. *Basic and Applied Social Psychology, 22,* 237–243.

Freud, A. (1965). *Normality and pathology in childhood.* New York: International Universities Press.

Freud, S. (1886–1936/1964). *The complete psychological works of Sigmund Freud* (Vols. 1–24). London: Hogarth.

Friedman, H. S., & Miller-Herringer, T. (1991). Nonverbal display of emotion in public and private: Self-monitoring, personality, and expressive cues. *Journal of Personality and Social Psychology, 61,* 766–775.

Friedman, H. S., Prince, L. M., Riggio, R. E., & DiMatteo, M. R. (1980). Understanding and assessing nonverbal expressiveness: The Affective Communication Test. *Journal of Personality and Social Psychology, 39,* 333–351.

Friedman, L. C., Nelson, D. V., Baer, P. E., Lane, M., Smith, F. E., & Dworkin, R. J. (1992). The relationship of dispositional optimism, daily life stress, and domestic environment to coping methods used by cancer patients. *Journal of Behavioral Medicine, 15,* 127–141.

Friedman, M., & Rosenman, R. (1974). *Type A behavior and your heart.* New York: Knopf.

Friedrich-Cofer, L., & Huston, A. C. (1986). Television violence and aggression: The debate continues. *Psychological Bulletin, 100,* 364–371.

Froming, W. J., Nasby, W., & McManus, J. (1998). Prosocial self-schemas, self-awareness, and children's prosocial behavior. *Journal of Personality and Social Psychology, 75,* 766–777.

Fromm, E. (1950). *Psychoanalysis and religion.* New Haven, CT: Yale University Press.

Fromm, E. (1962). *Beyond the chains of illusion: My encounter with Marx and Freud.* New York: Touchstone.

Fromm, E. (1941/1965). *Escape from freedom.* New York: Avon.

Fromm, E. (1966). *You shall be as gods.* Greenwich, CT: Fawcett.

Fromm, E. (1956/1974). *The art of loving.* New York: Harper & Row.

Fromm, E., & Nash, M. R. (1997). *Psychoanalysis and hypnosis.* Madison, CT: International Universities Press.

Fromm-Reichman, F. (1959). Loneliness. *Psychiatry, 22,* 1–15.

Fujita, F., Diener, E., & Sandvik, E. (1991). Gender differences in negative affect and well-being: The case for emotional intensity. *Journal of Personality and Social Psychology, 61,* 427–434.

Funder, D. C., & Ozer, D. J. (1983). Behavior as a function of the situation. *Journal of Personality and Social Psychology, 44,* 107–112.

Gabriel, S., & Gardner, W. L. (1999). Are there "his" and "her" types of interdependence? The implications of gender differences in collective versus relational interdependence for affect, behavior, and cognition. *Journal of Personality and Social Psychology, 77,* 642–655.

Gaeddert, W. P. (1985). Sex and sex role effects on achievement strivings: Dimensions of similarity and difference. *Journal of Personality, 53,* 286–305.

Gangestad, S. W., & Thornhill, R. (1997). Human sexual selection and developmental stability. In J. A. Simpson & D. T. Kenrick (Eds.), *Evolutionary social psychology* (pp. 169–195). Mahwah, NJ: Erlbaum.

Garcia, J., & Koelling, R. A. (1966). Relation of cue to consequence in avoidance learning. *Psychometric Science, 4,* 123–124.

Garcia, S., Stinson, L., Ickes, W., Bissonnette, V., & Briggs, S. R. (1991). Shyness and physical attractiveness in mixed-sex dyads. *Journal of Personality and Social Psychology, 61,* 35–49.

Garvey, M. (2002, March 21). The nation: Sex and violence on TV. *Los Angeles Times,* p. A-26.

Gastorf, J. W. (1980). Time urgency of the Type A behavior pattern. *Journal of Consulting and Clinical Psychology, 48,* 299.

Gatchel, R. J., Paulus, P. B., & Maples, C. W. (1975). Learned helplessness and self-reported affect. *Journal of Abnormal Psychology, 84,* 732–734.

Geary, D. C. (2000). Evolution and proximate expression of human paternal investment. *Psychological Bulletin, 126,* 55–77.

Geen, R. G. (1983). The psychophysiology of extraversion-introversion. In J. T. Cacioppo & R. E. Petty (Eds.), *Social psychophysiology: A sourcebook* (pp. 391–416). New York: Guilford.

Geen, R. G. (1984). Preferred stimulation levels in introverts and extraverts: Effects on arousal and performance. *Journal of Personality and Social Psychology, 46,* 1303–1312.

Geen, R. G. (1997). Psychophysiological approaches to personality. In R. Hogan, J. Johnson, & S. Briggs (Eds.), *Handbook of personality psychology* (pp. 387–414). San Diego, CA: Academic Press.

Geen, R. G. (1998). Aggression and antisocial behavior. In D. T. Gilbert, S. T. Fiske, & G. Lindzey (Eds.), *The handbook of social psychology* (Vol. 2, 4th ed., pp. 317–356). Boston: McGraw-Hill.

Geen, R. G., & Quanty, M. B. (1977). The catharsis of aggression: An evaluation of a hypothesis. In L. Berkowitz (Ed.), *Advances in experimental social psychology* (Vol. 10, pp. 1–37). New York: Academic Press.

Geen, R. G., Stonner, D., & Shope, G. L. (1975). The facilitation of aggression by aggression: Evidence against the catharsis hypothesis. *Journal of Personality and Social Psychology, 31,* 721–726.

Geen, R. G., & Thomas, S. L. (1986). The immediate effects of media violence on behavior. *Journal of Social Issues, 42,* 7–27.

Gemar, M. C., Segal, Z. V., Sagrati, S., & Kennedy, S. J. (2001). Mood-induced changes on the implicit association test in recovered depressed patients. *Journal of Abnormal Psychology, 110,* 282–289.

Gendlin, E. T. (1988). Carl Rogers (1902–1987). *American Psychologist, 43,* 127–128.

Gergen, K. J., Gulerce, A., Lock, A., & Misra, G. (1996). Psychological science in cultural context. *American Psychologist, 51,* 496–503.

Gershoff, E. T. (2002). Corporal punishment by parents and associated child behaviors and experiences: A meta-analytic and theoretical review. *Psychological Bulletin, 128,* 539–579.

Gersten, M. (1989). Behavioral inhibition in the classroom. In J. S. Reznick (Ed.), *Perspectives on behavioral inhibition* (pp. 71–91). Chicago: University of Chicago Press.

Gest, S. D. (1997). Behavioral inhibition: Stability and associations with adaptation from childhood to early adulthood. *Journal of Personality and Social Psychology, 72,* 467–475.

Geuens, M., & De Pelsmacker, P. (1999). Affect intensity revisited: Individual differences and the communication effects of emotional stimuli. *Psychology and Marketing, 16,* 195–209.

Gfeller, J. D., Lynn, S. J., & Pribble, W. E. (1987). Enhancing hypnotic susceptibility: Interpersonal and rapport factors. *Journal of Personality and Social Psychology, 52,* 586–595.

Gibbons, F. X., Blanton, H., Gerrard, M., Buunk, B., & Eggleston, T. (2000). Does social comparison make a difference? Optimism as a moderator of the relation between comparison level and academic performance. *Personality and Social Psychology Bulletin, 26,* 637–648.

Gibson, H. B. (1981). *Hans Eysenck: The man and his work.* London: Peter Owen.

Gidron, Y., Davidson, K., & Bata, I. (1999). The short-term effects of a hostility-reduction intervention on male coronary heart disease patients. *Health Psychology, 18,* 416–420.

Giesler, R. B., Josephs, R. A., & Swann, W. B. (1996). Self-verification in clinical depression: The desire for negative evaluation. *Journal of Abnormal Psychology, 105,* 358–368.

Gilbert, L., Deutsch, C. L., & Strahan, R. F. (1978). Feminine and masculine dimensions of the typical, desirable and ideal woman and man. *Sex Roles, 4,* 767–778.

Gill, M. M., & Brenman, M. (1967). The metapsychology of regression and hypnosis. In J. E. Gordon (Ed.), *The handbook of clinical and experimental hypnosis* (pp. 281–318). New York: Macmillan.

Gillham, J. E., Shatte, A. J., Reivich, K. J., & Seligman, M. E. P. (2001). Optimism, pessimism, and explanatory style. In E. C. Chang (Ed.), *Optimism and pessimism: Im-*

plications for theory, research, and practice (pp. 53–75). Washington, DC: American Psychological Association.

Gilmor, T. M., & Reid, D. W. (1978). Locus of control, prediction, and performance on university examinations. *Journal of Consulting and Clinical Psychology, 46,* 565–566.

Gilmor, T. M., & Reid, D. W. (1979). Locus of control and causal attribution for positive and negative outcomes on university examinations. *Journal of Research in Personality, 13,* 154–160.

Glasberg, R., & Aboud, F. (1982). Keeping one's distance from sadness: Children's self-reports of emotional experience. *Developmental Psychology, 18,* 287–293.

Glass, C. R., & Shea, C. A. (1986). Cognitive therapy for shyness and social anxiety. In W. H. Jones, J. M. Cheek, & S. R. Briggs (Eds.), *Shyness: Perspectives on research and treatment* (pp. 315–327). New York: Plenum.

Glass, D. C. (1977). *Behavior patterns, stress, and coronary disease.* Hillsdale, NJ: Erlbaum.

Glass, D. C., Snyder, M. L., & Hollis, J. (1974). Time urgency and the Type A coronary-prone behavior pattern. *Journal of Applied Social Psychology, 4,* 125–140.

Glassman, N. S., & Andersen, S. M. (1999a). Transference in social cognition: Persistence and exacerbation of significant-other-based inferences over time. *Cognitive Therapy and Research, 23,* 75–91.

Glassman, N. S., & Andersen, S. M. (1999b). Activating transference without consciousness: Using significant-other representations to go beyond what is subliminally given. *Journal of Personality and Social Psychology, 77,* 1146–1162.

Glisky, M. L., Tataryn, D. J., Tobias, B. A., Kihlstrom, J. F., & McConkey, K. M. (1991). Absorption, openness to experience, and hypnotizability. *Journal of Personality and Social Psychology, 60,* 263–272.

Gohm, C. L., & Clore, G. L. (2000). Individual differences in emotional experience: Mapping available scales to processes. *Personality and Social Psychology Bulletin, 26,* 679–697.

Goldberg, L. R. (1990). An alternative "description of personality": The Big-Five factor structure. *Journal of Personality and Social Psychology, 59,* 1216–1229.

Goldberg, L. R. (1992). The development of markers for the Big-Five factor structure. *Psychological Assessment, 4,* 26–42.

Goldberg, L. R. (1993). The structure of phenotypic personality traits. *American Psychologist, 48,* 26–34.

Goldberg, L. R. (2001). Analyses of Digman's child-personality data: Derivation of Big-Five factor scores from each of six samples. *Journal of Personality, 69,* 709–743.

Goode, E. (1999, April 23). Homosexuality-gene study released: Research fails to support report of chromosomal link. *San Jose Mercury News,* p. 8A.

Goodwin, R., Cook, O., & Yung, Y. (2001). Loneliness and life satisfaction among three cultural groups. *Personal Relationships, 8,* 225–230.

Gorassini, D. R., Sowerby, D., Creighton, A., & Fry, G. (1991). Hypnotic susceptibility enhancement through brief cognitive skill training. *Journal of Personality and Social Psychology, 61,* 289–297.

Gorassini, D. R., & Spanos, N. P. (1986). A social-cognitive skills approach to the successful modification of hypnotic susceptibility. *Journal of Personality and Social Psychology, 50,* 1004–1012.

Goswick, R. A., & Jones, W. H. (1981). Loneliness, self-concept, and adjustment. *Journal of Psychology, 88,* 258–261.

Gotay, C. C. (1981). Cooperation and competition as a function of Type A behavior. *Personality and Social Psychology Bulletin, 7,* 386–392.

Gotlib, I. H. (1983). Perception and recall of interpersonal feedback: Negative bias in depression. *Cognitive Therapy and Research, 7,* 399–412.

Gough, H. G., Fioravanti, M., & Lazzari, R. (1983). Some implications of self versus ideal-self congruence on the Revised Adjective Check List. *Journal of Personality and Social Psychology, 44,* 1214–1220.

Gough, H. G., Lazzari, R., & Fioravanti, M. (1978). Self versus ideal self: A comparison of five adjective check list indices. *Journal of Consulting and Clinical Psychology, 46,* 1085–1091.

Grahn, R. E., Will, M. J., Hammack, S. E., Maswood, M. B., McQueen, L. R., Watkins, L. R., & Maier, S. F. (1999). Activation of serotonin-immunoreactive cells in the dorsal raphe nucleus in rats exposed to an uncontrollable stressor. *Brain Research, 826,* 35–43.

Gray, J. A. (1981). A critique of Eysenck's theory of personality. In H. J. Eysenck (Ed.), *A model for personality* (pp. 246–276). New York: Springer.

Gray, J. A. (1982). *The neuropsychology of anxiety: An inquiry of the septo-hippocampal system.* Oxford, England: Oxford University Press.

Gray, J. A. (1987). Perspectives on anxiety and impulsivity: A commentary. *Journal of Research in Personality, 21,* 493–509.

Graziano, W. G., Jensen-Campbell, L. A., Steele, R. G., & Hair, E. C. (1998). Unknown words in self-reported personality: Lethargic and provincial in Texas. *Personality and Social Psychology Bulletin, 24,* 893–905.

Graziano, W. G., Jensen-Campbell, L. A., & Sullivan-Logan, G. M. (1998). Temperament, activity, and expectations for later personality development. *Journal of Personality and Social Psychology, 74,* 1266–1277.

Graziano, W. G., Jensen-Campbell, L. A., Todd, M., & Finch, J. F. (1997). Interpersonal attraction from an evolutionary psychology perspective: Women's reactions to dominant and prosocial men. In J. A. Simpson & D. T. Kenrick (Eds.), *Evolutionary social psychology* (pp. 141–167). Mahwah, NJ: Erlbaum.

Green, B. L., & Kenrick, D. T. (1994). The attractiveness of gender-typed traits at different relationship levels: Androgynous characteristics may be desirable after all. *Personality and Social Psychology Bulletin, 20,* 244–253.

Green, D. P., Salovey, P., & Truax, K. M. (1999). Static, dynamic, and causative bipolarity of affect. *Journal of Personality and Social Psychology, 76,* 856–867.

Green, L. R., Richardson, D. S., Lago, T., & Schatten-Jones, E. C. (2001). Network correlates of social and emotional loneliness in young and older adults. *Personality and Social Psychology Bulletin, 27,* 281–288.

Greenberg, M. A., Wortman, C. B., & Stone, A. A. (1996). Emotional expression and physical health: Revising traumatic memories or fostering self-regulation? *Journal of Personality and Social Psychology, 71,* 588–602.

Greenberg, R., Pillard, R., & Pearlman, C. (1978). The effect of dream (stage REM) deprivation on adaptation to stress. In S. Fisher & R. P. Greenberg (Eds.), *The scientific evaluation of Freud's theories and therapy* (pp. 40–48). New York: Basic Books.

Greenier, K. D., Kernis, M. H., McNamara, C. W., Waschull, S. B., Berry, A. J., Herlocker, C. E., & Abend, T. A. (1999). Individual differences in reactivity to daily events: Examining the roles of stability and level of self-esteem. *Journal of Personality, 67,* 185–208.

Greenier, K. D., Kernis, M. H., & Waschull, S. B. (1995). Not all high (or low) self-esteem people are the same: Theory and research on stability of self-esteem. In M. H. Kernis (Ed.), *Efficacy, agency and self-esteem* (pp. 51–71). New York: Plenum.

Grice, J. W., & Seely, E. (2000). The evolution of sex differences in jealousy: Failure to replicate previous results. *Journal of Research in Personality, 34,* 348–356.

Gross, J. J., & John, O. P. (1998). Mapping the domain of expressivity: Multimethod evidence for a hierarchical model. *Journal of Personality and Social Psychology, 74,* 170–191.

Grove, J. R., Hanrahan, S. J., & McInman, A. (1991). Success/failure bias in attributions across involvement categories in sport. *Personality and Social Psychology Bulletin, 17,* 93–97.

Guerra, N. G., Huesmann, L. R., Tolan, P. H., Van Acker, R., & Eron, L. D. (1995). Stressful events and individual beliefs as correlates of economic disadvantage and aggression among urban children. *Journal of Consulting and Clinical Psychology, 63,* 518–528.

Gunthert, K. C., Cohen, L. H., & Armeli, S. (1999). The role of Neuroticism in daily stress and coping. *Journal of Personality and Social Psychology, 77,* 1087–1100.

Gur, R. C., & Reivich, M. (1980). Cognitive task effects on hemispheric blood flow in humans: Evidence for individual differences in hemispheric activation. *Brain and Language, 9,* 78–92.

Gutierres, S. E., Kenrick, D. T., & Partch, J. J. (1999). Beauty, dominance, and the mating game: Contrast effects in self-assessment reflect gender differences in mate selection. *Personality and Social Psychology Bulletin, 25,* 1126–1134.

Guyll, M., & Contrada, R. J. (1998). Trait hostility and ambulatory cardiovascular activity: Responses to social interaction. *Health Psychology, 17,* 30–39.

Haber, R. A. (1980). Different strokes for different folks: Jung's typology and structured experience. *Group and Organizational Studies, 5,* 113–119.

Haemmerlie, F. M., & Montgomery, R. L. (1986). Self-perception theory and the treatment of shyness. In W. H. Jones, J. M. Cheek, & S. R. Briggs (Eds.), *Shyness: Perspectives on research and treatment* (pp. 329–342). New York: Plenum.

Hale, M. (2002, June 30). Mind games: 'Brain doctor' goes inside NBA's greatest heads. *New York Post,* p. 93.

Hall, C. S. (1953). A cognitive theory of dream symbols. *Journal of General Psychology, 48,* 169–186.

Hall, C. S. (1984). "A ubiquitous sex difference in dreams" revisited. *Journal of Personality and Social Psychology, 46,* 1109–1117.

Hall, C. S., & Domhoff, B. (1963). A ubiquitous sex difference in dreams. *Journal of Abnormal and Social Psychology, 66,* 278–280.

Hall, M. H. (1968, August). A conversation with the president of the American Psychological Association: The psychology of universality. *Psychology Today,* pp. 35–37, 54–57.

Handler, L. (1996). The clinical use of drawings: Draw-a-person, house-tree-person, and kinetic family drawings. In C. S. Newmark (Ed.), *Major psychological assessment instruments* (2nd ed., pp. 206–293). Needham Heights, MA: Allyn & Bacon.

Hanley-Dunn, P., Maxwell, S. E., & Santos, J. F. (1985). Interpretation of interpersonal interaction: The influence of loneliness. *Personality and Social Psychology Bulletin, 11,* 445–456.

Hansen, C. H., Hansen, R. D., & Shantz, D. W. (1992). Repression at encoding: Discrete appraisals of emotional stimuli. *Journal of Personality and Social Psychology, 63,* 1026–1035.

Hansen, R. D., & Hansen, C. H. (1988). Repression and emotionally tagged memories: The architecture of less complex emotions. *Journal of Personality and Social Psychology, 55,* 811–818.

Harackiewicz, J. M., Barron, K. E., Carter, S. M., Lehto, A. T., & Elliot, A. J. (1997). Predictors and consequences of achievement goals in the college classroom: Maintaining interest and making the grade. *Journal of Personality and Social Psychology, 73,* 1284–1295.

Harackiewicz, J. M., & Elliot, A. J. (1998). The joint effects of target and purpose goals on intrinsic motivation: A mediational analysis. *Personality and Social Psychology Bulletin, 24,* 675–689.

Harmon-Jones, E., & Allen, J. J. B. (1997). Behavioral activation sensitivity and resting frontal EEG asymmetry: Covariation of putative indicators related to risk for mood disorders. *Journal of Abnormal Psychology, 106,* 159–163.

Harmon-Jones, E., & Allen, J. J. B. (1998). Anger and frontal brain activity: EEG asymmetry consistent with approach motivation despite negative affective valence. *Journal of Personality and Social Psychology, 74,* 1310–1316.

Harmon-Jones, E., & Sigelman, J. (2001). State anger and prefrontal brain activity: Evidence that insult-related relative left-prefrontal activation is associated with experienced anger and ggression. *Journal of Personality and Social Psychology, 80,* 797–803.

Harrigan, J. A., Suarez, I., & Hartman, J. S. (1994). Effect of speech errors on observers' judgments of anxious and defensive individuals. *Journal of Research in Personality, 28,* 505–529.

Harris, C. R. (2000). Psychophysiological responses to imagined infidelity: The specific innate modular view of jealousy reconsidered. *Journal of Personality and Social Psychology, 78,* 1082–1091.

Harris, M. B. (1974). Mediators between frustration and aggression in a field experiment. *Journal of Experimental Social Psychology, 10,* 561–571.

Harris, R. N., & Snyder, C. R. (1986). The role of uncertain self-esteem in self-handicapping. *Journal of Personality and Social Psychology, 51,* 451–458.

Harrison, A. A., & Saeed, L. (1977). Let's make a deal: An analysis of revelations and stipulations in lonely hearts advertisements. *Journal of Personality and Social Psychology, 35,* 257–264.

Hartshorne, H., & May, M. A. (1928). *Studies in the nature of character: Studies in deceit.* New York: Macmillan.

Harvey, J. H., & Omarzu, J. (1997). Minding the close relationship. *Personality and Social Psychology Review, 1,* 224–240.

Haynes, S. N. (2001). Introduction to the special section on clinical applications of analogue behavioral observation. *Psychological Assessment, 13,* 3–4.

Hazan, C., & Shaver, P. (1987). Romantic love conceptualized as an attachment process. *Journal of Personality and Social Psychology, 52,* 511–524.

Headey, B., & Wearing, A. (1989). Personality, life events, and subjective well-being: Toward a dynamic equilibrium model. *Journal of Personality and Social Psychology, 57,* 731–739.

Heath, A. C., Neale, M. C., Kessler, R. C., Eaves, L. J., & Kendler, K. S. (1992). Evidence for genetic influences on personality from self-reports and informant ratings. *Journal of Personality and Social Psychology, 63,* 85–96.

Heatherton, T. F., & Polivy, J. (1991). Development and validation of a scale for measuring state self-esteem. *Journal of Personality and Social Psychology, 60,* 895–910.

Hedlund, S., & Rude, S. S. (1995). Evidence of latent depressive schemas in formerly depressed individuals. *Journal of Abnormal Psychology, 104,* 517–525.

Heimpel, S. A., Wood, J. V., Marshall, M. A., & Brown, J. D. (2002). Do people with low self-esteem really want to feel better? Self-esteem differences in motivation to repair negative moods. *Journal of Personality and Social Psychology, 82,* 128–147.

Heine, S. J. (2001). Self as cultural product: An examination of East Asian and North American selves. *Journal of Personality, 69,* 881–906.

Heine, S. J., & Lehman, D. R. (1995). Cultural variation in unrealistic optimism: Does the West feel more invulnerable than the East? *Journal of Personality and Social Psychology, 68,* 595–607.

Heine, S. J., & Lehman, D. R. (1997). The cultural construction of self-enhancement: An examination of group-serving biases. *Journal of Personality and Social Psychology, 72,* 1268–1283.

Heine, S. J., & Lehman, D. R. (1999). Culture, self-discrepancies, and self-satisfaction. *Personality and Social Psychology Bulletin, 25,* 915–925.

Heine, S. J., Lehman, D. R., Markus, H. R., & Kitayama, S. (1999). Is there a universal need for positive self-regard? *Psychological Review, 106,* 766–794.

Helgeson, V. S. (1994). Relation of agency and communion to well-being: Evidence and potential explanations. *Psychological Bulletin, 116,* 412–428.

Helgeson, V. S., & Fritz, H. L. (1999). Unmitigated agency and unmitigated communion: Distinctions from agency and communion. *Journal of Research in Personality, 33,* 131–158.

Helgeson, V. S., & Fritz, H. L. (2000). The implications of unmitigated agency and unmitigated communion for domains of problem behavior. *Journal of Personality, 68,* 1031–1057.

Helgeson, V. S., & Lepore, S. J. (1997). Men's adjustment to prostate cancer: The role of agency and unmitigated agency. *Sex Roles, 37,* 251–267.

Heller, W., Etienne, M. A., & Miller, G. A. (1995). Patterns of perceptual asymmetry in depression and anxiety: Implications for neuropsychological models of emotion and psychopathology. *Journal of Personality and Social Psychology, 104,* 327–333.

Helmes, E., & Reddon, J. R. (1993). A perspective on developments in assessing psychopathology: A critical review of the MMPI and MMPI-2. *Psychological Bulletin, 113,* 453–471.

Hendrick, S. S. (1981). Self-disclosure and marital satisfaction. *Journal of Personality and Social Psychology, 40,* 1150–1159.

Henriques, J. B., & Davidson, R. J. (1990). Regional brain electrical asymmetries discriminate between previously depressed and healthy control subjects. *Journal of Abnormal Psychology, 99,* 22–31.

Herrnstein, R. J., & Murray, C. (1994). *The bell curve: Intelligence and class structure in American life.* New York: Free Press.

Hibbard, S., Farmer, L., Wells, C., Difillipo, E., Barry, W., Korman, R., & Sloan, P. (1994). Validation of Cramer's Defense Mechanism Manual for the TAT. *Journal of Personality Assessment, 63,* 197–210.

Higgins, E. T. (1987). Self-discrepancy: A theory relating self and affect. *Psychological Review, 94,* 319–340.

Higgins, E. T. (1989). Self-discrepancy theory: What patterns of self-beliefs cause people to suffer? In L. Berkowitz (Ed.), *Advances in experimental social psychology* (Vol. 22, pp. 93–136). San Diego: Academic Press.

Higgins, E. T. (1999). When do self-discrepancies have specific relations to emotions? The second-generation question of Tangney, Niedenthal, Covert, and Barlow (1998). (1999). *Journal of Personality and Social Psychology, 77,* 1313–1317.

Higgins, E. T., Bond, R. N., Klein, R., & Strauman, T. (1986). Self-discrepancies and emotional vulnerability: How magnitude, accessibility, and type of discrepancy influence affect. *Journal of Personality and Social Psychology, 51,* 5–15.

Hilgard, E. R. (1973). A neodissociation interpretation of pain reduction in hypnosis. *Psychological Review, 80,* 396–411.

Hilgard, E. R. (1977). *Divided consciousness: Multiple controls in human thought and action.* New York: Wiley.

Hilgard, E. R. (1992). Dissociation and theories of hypnosis. In E. Fromm & M. R. Nash (Eds.), *Contemporary hypnosis research* (pp. 69–101). New York: Guilford.

Hilgard, E. R. (1994). Neodissociation theory. In S. J. Lynn & J. W. Rhue (Eds.), *Dissociation: Clinical, theoretical and research perspectives* (pp. 32–51). New York: Guilford.

Hill, C. E. (1996). *Working with dreams in psychotherapy.* New York: Guilford.

Hill, E. H., Helms, J. E., Tichenor, V., Spiegel, S. B., O'Grady, K. E., & Perry, E. S. (1988). Effects of therapist response modes in brief psychotherapy. *Journal of Counseling Psychology, 35,* 222–233.

Hill, E. H., Mahalik, J. R., & Thompson, B. J. (1989). Therapist self-disclosure. *Psychotherapy, 26,* 290–295.

Hill, G. J. (1989). An unwillingness to act: Behavioral appropriateness, situational constraint, and self-efficacy in shyness. *Journal of Personality, 57,* 871–890.

Hilsman, R., & Garber, J. (1995). A test of the cognitive diathesis-stress model of depression in children: Academic stressors, attributional style, perceived competence, and control. *Journal of Personality and Social Psychology, 69,* 370–380.

Hinkley, K., & Andersen, S. M. (1996). The working self-concept in transference: Significant-other activation and self change. *Journal of Personality and Social Psychology, 71,* 1279–1295.

Hiroto, D. S. (1974). Locus of control and learned helplessness. *Journal of Experimental Psychology, 102,* 187–193.

Hiroto, D. S., & Seligman, M. E. P. (1975). Generality of learned helplessness in man. *Journal of Personality and Social Psychology, 31,* 311–327.

Hock, M., Krohne, H. W., & Kaiser, J. (1996). Coping dispositions and the processing of ambiguous stimuli. *Journal of Personality and Social Psychology, 70,* 1052–1066.

Hoffman, L. W. (1985). The changing genetics/socialization balance. *Journal of Social Issues, 41,* 127–148.

Hoffman, L. W. (1991). The influence of the family environment on personality: Accounting for sibling differences. *Psychological Bulletin, 110,* 187–203.

Hogan, R. (1991). Personality and personality measurement. In M. D. Dunnette & L. M. Hough (Eds.), *Handbook of industrial and organizational psychology* (2nd ed., Vol. 2, pp. 873–919). Palo Alto, CA: Consulting Psychologists Press.

Hokanson, J. E., & Edelman, R. (1966). Effects of three social responses on vascular processes. *Journal of Personality and Social Psychology, 3,* 442–447.

Holahan, C. J., & Moos, R. H. (1987). Personal and contextual determinants of coping strategies. *Journal of Personality and Social Psychology, 52,* 946–955.

Holmes, D. S., McGilley, B. M., & Houston, B. K. (1984). Task-related arousal of Type A and Type B persons: Level of challenge and response specificity. *Journal of Personality and Social Psychology, 46,* 1322–1327.

Holt, C. L., & Ellis, J. B. (1998). Assessing the current validity of the Bem Sex-Role Inventory. *Sex Roles, 39,* 929–941.

Hooker, K., Monahan, D., Shifren, K., & Hutchinson, C. (1992). Mental and physical health of spouse caregivers: The role of personality. *Psychology and Aging, 7,* 367–375.

Hoover, S., Skuja, A., & Cosper, J. (1979). Correlates of college students' loneliness. *Psychological Reports, 44,* 1116.

Hopkins, J. R. (1995). Erik Homburger Erikson (1902–1994). *American Psychologist, 50,* 796–797.

Horley, J. (1996). Content stability in the repertory grid: An examination using a forensic sample. *International Journal of Offender Therapy and Comparative Criminology, 40,* 26–31.

Horn, J. (2001). Raymond Bernard Cattell (1905–1998). *American Psychologist, 56,* 71–72.

Horney, K. (1937). *The neurotic personality of our time.* New York: Norton.

Horney, K. (1945/1966). *Our inner conflicts: A constructive theory of neurosis.* New York: Norton.

Horney, K. (1967). *Feminine psychology.* New York: Norton.

Hornstein, G. A. (1985). Intimacy in conversational style as a function of the degree of closeness between members of a dyad. *Journal of Personality and Social Psychology, 49,* 671–681.

Hornstein, G. A., & Truesdell, S. E. (1988). Development of intimate conversation in close relationships. *Journal of Social and Clinical Psychology, 7,* 49–64.

Horowitz, L. M., & de Sales French, R. (1979). Interpersonal problems of people who describe themselves as lonely. *Journal of Consulting and Clinical Psychology, 47,* 762–764.

Houston, D. M., McKee, K. J., & Wilson, J. (2000). Attributional style, efficacy, and the enhancement of well-being among housebound older people. *Basic and Applied Social Psychology, 22,* 309–317.

Howard, J. H., Cunningham, D. A., & Rechnitzer, P. A. (1977). Work patterns associated with Type A behavior: A managerial population. *Human Relations, 30,* 825–836.

Howard, M. L., & Coe, W. C. (1980). The effects of context and subjects' perceived control in breaching posthypnotic amnesia. *Journal of Personality, 48,* 342–359.

Hoyt, M. F., & Singer, J. L. (1978). Psychological effects of REM ("dream") deprivation upon waking mentation. In A. M. Arkin, J. S. Antrobus, & S. J. Ellman (Eds.), *The mind in sleep: Psychology and psychophysiology* (pp. 487–510). Hillsdale, NJ: Erlbaum.

Hubbard, J. A., Dodge, K. A., Cillessen, A. H. N., Coie, J. D., & Schwartz, D. (2001). The dyadic nature of social information processing in boys' reactive and proactive aggression. *Journal of Personality and Social Psychology, 80,* 268–280.

Huesmann, L. R. (1986). Psychological processes promoting the relation between exposure to media violence and aggressive behavior by the viewer. *Journal of Social Issues, 42,* 125–139.

Huesmann, L. R. (1988). An information-processing model for the development of aggression. *Aggressive Behavior, 14,* 13–24.

Huesmann, L. R., Eron, L. D., Dubow, E. F., & Seebauer, E. (1987). Television viewing habits in childhood and adult aggression. *Child Development, 58,* 357–367.

Huesmann, L. R., Eron, L. D., & Yarmel, P. W. (1987). Intellectual functioning and aggression. *Journal of Personality and Social Psychology, 52,* 232–240.

Huesmann, L. R., & Guerra, N. G. (1997). Children's normative beliefs about aggression and aggressive behavior. *Journal of Personality and Social Psychology, 72,* 408–419.

Hui, C. H. (1988). Measurement of individualism-collectivism. *Journal of Research in Personality, 22,* 17–36.

Hunsley, J., & Bailey, J. M. (1999). The clinical utility of the Rorschach: Unfulfilled promises and an uncertain future. *Psychological Assessment, 11,* 266–277.

Hurtz, G. M., & Donovan, J. J. (2000). Personality and job performance: The Big Five revisted. *Journal of Applied Psychology, 85,* 869–879.

Ickes, W. (1993). Traditional gender roles: Do they make, and then break, our relationships? *Journal of Social Issues, 49,* 71–85.

Ickes, W., & Barnes, R. D. (1978). Boys and girls together–and alienated: On enacting stereotyped sex roles in mixed-sex dyads. *Journal of Personality and Social Psychology, 36,* 669–683.

Ickes, W., Robertson, E., Tooke, W., & Teng, G. (1986). Naturalistic social cognition: Methodology, assessment, and validation. *Journal of Personality and Social Psychology, 51,* 66–82.

Ickes, W., Schermer, B., & Steeno, J. (1979). Sex and sex-role influence in same-sex dyads. *Social Psychology Quarterly, 42,* 373–385.

Ihilevich, D., & Gleser, G. C. (1993). *Defense mechanisms: Their classification, correlates, and measurement with the Defense Mechanism Inventory.* Odessa, FL: Psychological Assessment Resources.

Ilardi, S. S., & Craighead, W. E. (1999). The relationship between personality pathology and dysfunctional cognitions in previously depressed adults. *Journal of Abnormal Psychology, 108,* 51–57.

Ingram, R. E., & Ritter, J. (2000). Vulnerability to depression: Cognitive reactivity and parental bonding in high-risk individuals. *Journal of Abnormal Psychology, 109,* 588–596.

Jackson, L. A. (1983). The perception of androgyny and physical attractiveness: Two is better than one. *Personality and Social Psychology Bulletin, 9,* 405–413.

Jackson, L. A., Ialongo, N., & Stollak, G. E. (1986). Parental correlates of gender role: The relations between parents' masculinity, femininity, and child-rearing behaviors and their children's gender roles. *Journal of Social and Clinical Psychology, 4,* 204–224.

Jacobs, S. (1995, June 9). Pediatricians declare war on entertainment violence. *San Jose Mercury News,* p. 21A.

Jahoda, M. (1977). *Freud and the dilemmas of psychology.* New York: Basic Books.

Jang, K. L., Livesley, W. J., & Vernon, P. A. (1996). Heritability of the Big Five personality dimensions and their facets: A twin study. *Journal of Personality, 64,* 577–591.

Jang, K. L., McCrae, R. R., Angleitner, A., Riemann, R., & Livesley, W. J. (1998). Heritability of facet-level traits in a cross-cultural twin sample: Support for a hierarchical model of personality. *Journal of Personality and Social Psychology, 74,* 1556–1565.

Jankowicz, A. D. (1987). Whatever became of George Kelly? Applications and implications. *American Psychologist, 42,* 481–487.

Janoff-Bulman, R. (1992). *Shattered assumptions: Towards a new psychology of trauma.* New York: Free Press.

Jefferson, T., Herbst, J. H., & McCrae, R. R. (1998). Associations between birth order and personality traits: Evidence from self-reports and observer ratings. *Journal of Research in Personality, 32,* 498–509.

Jenkins, C. D. (1971). Psychologic and social precursors of coronary disease. *New England Journal of Medicine, 284,* 244–255, 307–317.

Jenkins, C. D. (1976). Recent evidence supporting psychologic and social risk factors for coronary disease. *New England Journal of Medicine, 294,* 987–994, 1033–1038.

Jenkins, C. D., Zyzanski, S. J., & Rosenman, R. H. (1976). Risk of new myocardial infarction in middle-age men with manifest coronary heart disease. *Circulation, 53,* 342–347.

Jenkins, J. A., Williams, P., Kramer, G. L., Davis, L. L., & Petty, F. (2001). The influence of gender and the estrous cycle on learned helplessness in the rat. *Biological Psychology, 58,* 147–158.

Jenkins, S. R. (1987). Need for achievement and women's careers over 14 years: Evidence for occupational structure effects. *Journal of Personality and Social Psychology, 53,* 922–932.

Jensen, A. R. (1969). How much can we boost IQ and scholastic achievement? *Harvard Educational Review, 39,* 1–123.

Jensen-Campbell, L. A., & Graziano, W. G. (2001). Agreeableness as a moderator of interpersonal conflict. *Journal of Personality, 69,* 323–362.

Jensen-Campbell, L. A., Graziano, W. G., & West, S. G. (1995). Dominance, prosocial orientation, and female preferences: Do nice guys really finish last? *Journal of Personality and Social Psychology, 68,* 427–440.

Johansson, B., Grant, J. D., Plomin, R., Pedersen, N. L., Ahern, F., Berg, S. et al. (2001). Health locus of control in late life: A study of genetic and environmental influences in twins aged 80 years and older. *Health Psychology, 20,* 33–40.

John, O. P. (1990). The "Big Five" factor taxonomy: Dimensions of personality in the natural language and in questionnaires. In L. A. Pervin (Ed.), *Handbook of personality: Theory and research* (pp. 66–100). New York: Guilford.

Johnson, J. G., Cohen, P., Smailes, E. M., Kasen, S., & Brook, J. S. (2002). Television viewing and aggressive behavior during adolescence and adulthood. *Science, 295,* 2468–2471.

Joiner, T. E., Catanzaro, S. J., Rudd, M. D., & Rajab, M. H. (1999). The case for a hierarchical, oblique, and bidimensional structure of loneliness. *Journal of Social and Clinical Psychology, 18,* 47–75.

Jones, A., & Crandall, R. (1986). Validation of a short index of self-actualization. *Personality and Social Psychology Bulletin, 12,* 63–73.

Jones, E. (1953–1957). *The life and work of Sigmund Freud* (Vols. 1–3). New York: Basic Books.

Jones, R. A. (1977). *Self-fulfilling prophecies: Social, psychological, and physiological effects of expectancies.* Hillsdale, NJ: Erlbaum.

Jones, W. H., Freemon, J. E., & Goswick, R. A. (1981). The persistence of loneliness: Self and other determinants. *Journal of Personality, 49,* 27–48.

Jones, W. H., Hobbs, S. A., & Hockenbury, D. (1982). Loneliness and social skill deficits. *Journal of Personality and Social Psychology, 42,* 682–689.

Jones, W. H., Sansone, C., & Helm, B. (1983). Loneliness and interpersonal judgments. *Personality and Social Psychology Bulletin, 9,* 437–441.

Jorgensen, R. S., Johnson, B. T., Kolodziej, M. E., & Schreer, G. E. (1996). Elevated blood pressure and personality: A meta-analytic review. *Psychological Bulletin, 120,* 293–320.

Josephs, R. A., Markus, H. R., & Tafarodi, R. W. (1992). Gender and self-esteem. *Journal of Personality and Social Psychology, 63,* 391–402.

Josephson, W. L. (1987). Television violence and children's aggression: Testing the priming social script, and disinhibition predictions. *Journal of Personality and Social Psychology, 53,* 882–890.

Jourard, S. M. (1971). *The transparent self* (2nd ed.). New York: Van Nostrand.

Judge, T. A., & Bono, J. E. (2001). Relationship of core self-evaluations traits—self-esteem, generalized self-efficacy, locus of control, and emotional stability—with job satisfaction and job performance: A meta-analysis. *Journal of Applied Psychology, 86,* 80–92.

Judge, T. A., Erez, A., & Bono, J. E. (1998). The power of being positive: The relationship between positive self-concept and job performance. *Human Performance, 11,* 167–187.

Judge, T. A., Higgins, C. A., Thoresen, C. J., & Barrick, M. R. (1999). The Big Five personality traits, general mental ability, and career success across the life span. *Personnel Psychology, 52,* 621–652.

Judge, T. A., & Watanabe, S. (1993). Another look at the job satisfaction-life satisfaction relationship. *Journal of Applied Psychology, 78,* 939–948.

Judge throws out suit by 'recovered memory' defendant. (2000, July 20). *San Jose Mercury News,* p. 3-B.

Jung, C. G. (1933). *Modern man in search of a soul.* New York: Harcourt.

Jung, C. G. (1902–1961/1961). *The collected works of Carl Jung* (Vols. 1–17). Princeton, NJ: Princeton University Press.

Jung, C. G. (1961). *Memories, dreams, reflections.* New York: Pantheon.

Jung, C. G. (1964). Approaching the unconscious. In C. G. Jung (Ed.), *Man and his symbols* (pp. 3–94). New York: Dell.

Kagan, J. (1989). Temperamental contributions to social behavior. *American Psychologist, 44,* 668–674.

Kagan, J., & Moss, H. A. (1962). *Birth to maturity.* New York: Wiley.

Kagan, J., Reznick, J. S., & Snidman, N. (1986). Temperamental inhibition in early childhood. In R. Plomin & J. Dunn (Eds.), *The study of temperament: Changes, continuities and challenges* (pp. 53–65). Hillsdale, NJ: Erlbaum.

Kagan, J., Reznick, J. S., & Snidman, N. (1988). Biological bases of childhood shyness. *Science, 240,* 167–171.

Kagan, J., & Snidman, N. (1991a). Infant predictors of inhibited and uninhibited profiles. *Psychological Science, 2,* 40–44.

Kagan, J., & Snidman, N. (1991b). Temperamental factors in human development. *American Psychologist, 46,* 856–862.

Kahn, J. H., & Hessling, R. M. (2001). Measuring the tendency to conceal versus disclose psychological distress. *Journal of Social and Clinical Psychology, 20,* 41–65.

Kalechstein, A. D., & Nowicki, S. (1997). A meta-analytic examination of the relationship between control expectancies and academic achievement: An 11-yr. follow-up to Findley and Cooper. *Genetic, Social and General Psychology Monographs, 123,* 27–56.

Kamen-Siegel, L., Rodin, J., Seligman, M. E. P., & Dwyer, J. (1991). Explanatory style and cell-mediated immunity in elderly men and women. *Health Psychology, 10,* 229–235.

Kanagawa, C., Cross, S. E., & Markus, H. R. (2001). "Who am I?" The cultural psychology of the conceptual self. *Personality and Social Psychology Bulletin, 27,* 90–103.

Kaplan, G. D., & Cowles, A. (1978). Health locus of control and health value in the prediction of smoking cessation. *Health Education Monographs, 6,* 129–137.

Karylowski, J. J. (1990). Social reference points and accessibility of trait-related information in self-other similarity judgments. *Journal of Personality and Social Psychology, 58,* 975–983.

Katigbak, M. S., Church, A. T., Guanzon-Lepena, M. A., Carlota, A. J., & del Pilar, G. H. (2002). Are indigenous personality dimensions culture specific? Philippine inventories and the five-factor model. *Journal of Personality and Social Psychology, 82,* 89–101.

Katz, I. M., & Campbell, J. D. (1994). Ambivalence over emotional expression and well-being: Nomothetic and idiographic tests of the stress-buffering hypothesis. *Journal of Personality and Social Psychology, 67,* 513–524.

Kawachi, I., Sparrow, D., Spiro, A., Vokonas, P., & Weiss, S. T. (1996). A prospective study of anger and coronary heart disease: The Normative Aging Study. *Circulation, 94,* 2090–2095.

Keelan, J. P. R., Dion, K. L., & Dion, K. K. (1994). Attachment style and heterosexual relationships among young adults: A short-term panel study. *Journal of Social and Personal Relationships, 11,* 201–214.

Kelly, A. E. (1998). Clients' secret keeping in outpatient therapy. *Journal of Counseling Psychology, 45,* 50–57.

Kelly, A. E., & Archer, J. A. (1995). Self-concealment and attitudes toward counseling in university students. *Journal of Counseling Psychology, 42,* 40–46.

Kelly, A. E., Klusas, J. A., von Weiss, R. T., & Kenny, C. (2001). What is it about revealing secrets that is beneficial? *Personality and Social Psychology Bulletin, 27,* 651–665.

Kelly, A. E., & McKillop, K. J. (1996). Consequences of revealing personal secrets. *Psychological Bulletin, 120,* 450–465.

Kelly, G. A. (1955). *The psychology of personal constructs.* New York: Norton.

Kelly, G. A. (1969). *Clinical psychology and personality: The selected papers of George Kelly.* New York: Wiley.

Kendzierski, D. (1988). Self-schemata and exercise. *Basic and Applied Social Psychology, 9,* 45–61.

Kendzierski, D. (1990). Exercise self-schemata: Cognitive and behavioral correlates. *Health Psychology, 9,* 69–82.

Kenrick, D. T., Keefe, R. C., Gabrielidis, C., & Cornelius, J. S. (1996). Adolescents' age preferences for dating partners: Support for an evolutionary model of life-history strategies. *Child Development, 67,* 1499–1511.

Keogh, B. K. (1986). Temperament and schooling: Meaning of "Goodness of Fit"? In J. V. Lerner & R. M. Lerner (Eds.), *Temperament and social interaction during infancy and childhood* (pp. 89–108). San Francisco: Jossey-Bass.

Keogh, B. K. (1989). Applying temperament research to schools. In G. A. Kohnstamm, J. E. Bates, & M. K. Rothbart (Eds.), *Temperament in childhood* (pp. 437–450). New York: Wiley.

Kernis, M. H., Brockner, J., & Frankel, B. S. (1989). Self-esteem and reactions to failure: The mediating role of overgeneralization. *Journal of Personality and Social Psychology, 57,* 707–714.

Kernis, M. H., Cornell, D. P., Sun, C-R, Berry, A., & Harlow, T. (1993). There's more to self-esteem than whether it is high or low: The importance of stability of self-esteem. *Journal of Personality and Social Psychology, 65,* 1190–1204.

Kernis, M. H., Grannemann, B. D., & Mathis, L. C. (1991). Stability of self-esteem as a moderator of the relation between level of self-esteem and depression. *Journal of Personality and Social Psychology, 61,* 80–84.

Kernis, M. H., Paradise, A. W., Whitaker, D. J., Wheatman, S. R., & Goldman, B. N. (2000). Master of one's psychological domain? Not likely if one's self-esteem is unstable. *Personality and Social Psychology Bulletin, 26,* 1297–1305.

Kernis, M. H., & Waschull, S. B. (1995). The interactive roles of stability and level of self-esteem: Research and theory. In M. P. Zanna (Ed.), *Advances in experimental social psychology* (Vol. 27, pp. 93–141). San Diego, CA: Academic Press.

Kernis, M. H., Whisenhunt, C. R., Waschull, S. B., Greenier, K. D., Berry, A. J., Herlocker, C. E., & Anderson, C. A. (1998). Multiple facets of self-esteem and their relations to depressive symptoms. *Personality and Social Psychology Bulletin, 24,* 657–668.

Kihlstrom, J. F. (1985). Hypnosis. *Annual Review of Psychology, 36,* 385–418.

Kihlstrom, J. F. (1998a, September 21). Bell curve, no bell, no curve, no. . . . *Nation,* p. 2.

Kihlstrom, J. F. (1998b). Dissociations and dissociation theory in hypnosis: Comment on Kirsch and Lynn (1998). *Psychological Bulletin, 123,* 186–191.

King, L. A. (1998). Ambivalence over emotional expression and reading emotions in situations and faces. *Journal of Personality and Social Psychology, 74,* 753–762.

King, L. A. (2001). The health benefits of writing about life goals. *Personality and Social Psychology Bulletin, 27,* 798–807.

King, L. A., & Emmons, R. A. (1990). Conflict over emotional expression: Psychological and physical correlates. *Journal of Personality and Social Psychology, 58,* 864–877.

King, L. A., & Miner, K. N. (2000). Writing about the perceived benefits of traumatic events: Implications for physical health. *Personality and Social Psychology Bulletin, 26,* 220–230.

Kirkpatrick, L. A., & Davis, K. E. (1994). Attachment style, gender, and relationship stability: A longitudinal analysis. *Journal of Personality and Social Psychology, 66,* 502–512.

Kirsch, I. (2000). The response set theory of hypnosis. *American Journal of Clinical Hypnosis, 42,* 274–292.

Kirsch, I., & Council, J. R. (1992). Situational and personality correlates of hypnotic responsiveness. In E. Fromm & M. R. Nash (Eds.), *Contemporary hypnosis research* (pp. 267–291). New York: Guilford.

Kirsch, I., & Lynn, J. L. (1998). Dissociation theories of hypnosis. *Psychological Bulletin, 123,* 100–115.

Kirsch, I., & Lynn, S. J. (1995). The altered state of hypnosis: Changes in the theoretical landscape. *American Psychologist, 50,* 846–858.

Kirsch, I., Silva, C. E., Comey, G., & Reed, S. (1995). A spectral analysis of cognitive and personality variables in hypnosis: Empirical disconfirmation of the two-factor model of hypnotic responding. *Journal of Personality and Social Psychology, 69,* 167–175.

Kirschenbaum, H. (1979). *On becoming Carl Rogers.* New York: Delacorte.

Kiselica, M. S., Baker, S. B., Thomas, R. N., & Reedy, S. (1994). Effects of stress inoculation training on anxiety, stress, and academic performance among adolescents. *Journal of Counseling Psychology, 41,* 335–342.

Kitayama, S., & Markus, H. R. (Eds.). (1994). *Emotion and culture: Empirical studies of mutual influence.* Washington, DC: American Psychological Association.

Kitayama, S., Markus, H. R., Matsumoto, H., & Norasakkunkit, V. (1997). Individual and collective processes in the construction of the self: Self-enhancement in the United States and self-criticism in Japan. *Journal of Personality and Social Psychology, 72,* 1245–1267.

Klein, D. C., & Seligman, M. E. P. (1976). Reversal of performance deficits and perceptual deficits in learned helplessness and depression. *Journal of Abnormal Psychology, 85,* 11–26.

Klein, S. B., & Loftus, J. (1988). The nature of self-referent encoding: The contributions of elaborative and organizational processes. *Journal of Personality and Social Psychology, 55,* 5–11.

Klein, S. B., Loftus, J., & Burton, H. A. (1989). Two self-reference effects: The importance of distinguishing between self-descriptiveness judgments and autobiographical retrieval in self-referent encoding. *Journal of Personality and Social Psychology, 56,* 853–865.

Kleinke, C. L., & Kahn, M. L. (1980). Perceptions of self-disclosers: Effects of sex and physical attractiveness. *Journal of Personality, 48,* 190–205.

Klinger, B. I. (1970). Effect of peer model responsiveness and length of induction procedure on hypnotic responsiveness. *Journal of Abnormal Psychology, 75,* 15–18.

Klohnen, E. C., & Bera, S. (1998). Behavioral and experiential patterns of avoidantly and securely attached women across adulthood: A 31-year longitudinal perspective. *Journal of Personality and Social Psychology, 74,* 211–223.

Klonowicz, T. (2001). Discontented people: Reactivity and locus of control as determinants of subjective well-being. *European Journal of Personality, 15,* 29–47.

Knowles, E. S., & Nathan, K. T. (1997). Acquiescent responding in self-reports: Cognitive style or social concern? *Journal of Research in Personality, 31,* 293–301.

Kobasa, S. C. (1979). Stressful life events, personality, and health: An inquiry into hardiness. *Journal of Personality and Social Psychology, 37,* 1–11.

Koenig, L. J., Isaacs, A. M., & Schwartz, J. A. J. (1994). Sex differences in adolescent depression and loneliness: Why are boys lonelier if girls are more depressed? *Journal of Research in Personality, 28,* 27–43.

Konecni, V. J., & Doob, A. N. (1972). Catharsis through displacement of aggression. *Journal of Personality and Social Psychology, 23,* 379–387.

Korabik, K. (1982). Sex-role orientation and impressions: A comparison of differing genders and sex roles. *Personality and Social Psychology Bulletin, 8,* 25–30.

Koriat, A., Melkman, R., Averill, J. R., & Lazarus, R. S. (1972). The self-control of emotional reactions to a stressful film. *Journal of Personality, 40,* 601–619.

Korn, J. H., Davis, R., & Davis, S. F. (1991). Historians' and chairpersons' judgments of eminence among psychologists. *American Psychologist, 46,* 789–792.

Kram, M. L., Kramer, G. L., Steciuk, M., Ronan, P. J., & Petty, F. (2000). Effects of learned helplessness on brain GABA receptors. *Neuroscience Research, 38,* 193–196.

Krantz, D. S., & McCeney, M. K. (2002). Effects of psychological and social factors on organic disease: A critical assessment of research on coronary heart disease. *Annual Review of Psychology, 53,* 341–369.

Kraus, S. J. (1995). Attitudes and the prediction of behavior: A meta-analysis of the empirical literature. *Personality and Social Psychology Bulletin, 21,* 58–75.

Kring, A. M., & Gordon, A. H. (1998). Sex differences in emotion: Expression, experience, and physiology. *Journal of Personality and Social Psychology, 74,* 686–703.

Kring, A. M., Smith, D. A., & Neale, J. M. (1994). Individual differences in dispositional expressiveness: Development and validation of the Emotional Expressivity Scale. *Journal of Personality and Social Psychology, 66,* 934–949.

Krokoff, L. J. (1990). Job distress is no laughing matter in marriage, or is it? *Journal of Social and Personal Relationships, 8,* 5–25.

Kuebli, J., Butler, S., & Fivush, R. (1995). Mother-child talk about past emotions: Relations of maternal language and child gender over time. *Cognition and Emotion, 9,* 265–283.

Kuhlman, T. L. (1985). A study of salience and motivational theories of humor. *Journal of Personality and Social Psychology, 49,* 281–286.

Kuiper, N. A., & Derry, P. A. (1981). The self as a cognitive prototype: An application to person perception and depression. In N. Cantor & J. F. Kihlstrom (Eds.), *Personality, cognition, and social interaction* (pp. 215–231). Hillsdale, NJ: Erlbaum.

Kuiper, N. A., MacDonald, M. R., & Derry, P. A. (1983). Parameters of a depressive self-schema. In J. Suls & A. G. Greenwald (Eds.), *Psychological perspectives on the self* (Vol. 2, pp. 191–217). Hillsdale, NJ: Erlbaum.

Kuiper, N. A., & Martin, R. A. (1998). Laughter and stress in daily life: Relation to positive and negative affect. *Motivation and Emotion, 22,* 133–143.

Kuiper, N. A., McKenzie, S. D., & Belanger, K. A. (1995). Cognitive appraisal and individual differences in sense of humor: Motivational and affective implications. *Personality and Individual Differences, 19,* 359–372.

Kuiper, N. A., & Rogers, T. B. (1979). Encoding of personal information: Self-other differences. *Journal of Personality and Social Psychology, 37,* 499–514.

Kulick, J. A., & Harackiewicz, J. (1979). Opposite-sex interpersonal attraction as a function of the sex roles of the perceiver and the perceived. *Sex Roles, 5,* 443–452.

Kurdek, L. A., & Schmitt, J. P. (1986). Interaction of sex role self-concept with relationship quality and relationship beliefs in married, heterosexual cohabiting, gay and lesbian couples. *Journal of Personality and Social Psychology, 51,* 365–370.

Kwon, P. (2000). Hope and dysphoria: The moderating role of defense mechanisms. *Journal of Personality, 68,* 199–223.

Lacayo, R. (1994, October 24). For whom the Bell Curve tolls. *Time, 144,* 66–67.

LaGasse, L., Gruber, C., & Lipsitt, L. P. (1989). The infantile expression of activity in relation to later assessments. In J. S. Reznick (Ed.), *Perspectives on behavioral inhibition* (pp. 159–176). Chicago: University of Chicago Press.

Lai, J. C. L., & Wong, W. S. (1998). Optimism and coping with unemployment among Hong Kong Chinese women. *Journal of Research in Personality, 32,* 454–479.

Lamke, L. K., & Bell, N. J. (1982). Sex-role orientation and relationship development in same-sex dyads. *Journal of Research in Personality, 16,* 343–354.

Landau, S. F. (1988). Violent crime and its relation to subjective social stress indicators: The case of Israel. *Aggressive Behavior, 14,* 337–362.

Landau, S. F., & Raveh, A. (1987). Stress factors, social support, and violence in Israeli society: A quantitative analysis. *Aggressive Behavior, 13,* 67–85.

Landfield, A. W. (1984). Personal construct psychology: A developmental perspective. *Journal of Social and Clinical Psychology, 2,* 97–107.

Landfield, A. W., & Epting, F. R. (1987). *Personal construct psychology: Clinical and personality assessment.* New York: Human Sciences Press.

Landy, F. J., Shankster, L. J., & Kohler, S. S. (1994). Personnel selection and placement. *Annual Review of Psychology, 45,* 261–296.

Langer, E. J., & Rodin, J. (1976). The effects of choice and enhanced personal responsibility for the aged: A field experiment in an institutional setting. *Journal of Personality and Social Psychology, 34,* 191–198.

Lanning, K. (2003). Myers-Briggs Type Indicator, Form Q. In B. S. Plake, & J. C. Impara (Eds.), *The fifteenth mental measurements yearbook.* Lincoln, NE: University of Nebraska Press.

Larsen, J. T., McGraw, A. P., & Cacioppo, J. T. (2001). Can people feel happy and sad at the same time? *Journal of Personality and Social Psychology, 81,* 684–696.

Larsen, R. J. (1987). The stability of mood variability: A spectral analytic approach to daily mood assessments. *Journal of Personality and Social Psychology, 52,* 1195–1204.

Larsen, R. J. (1995). On teaching what we do: Theory and research in personality psychology. *Contemporary Psychology, 40*, 40–41.

Larsen, R. J., Billings, D. W., & Cutler, S. E. (1996). Individual differences in informational style: Associations with dispositional affect intensity. *Journal of Personality, 64*, 185–207.

Larsen, R. J., & Diener, E. (1987). Affect intensity as an individual difference characteristic: A review. *Journal of Research in Personality, 21*, 1–39.

Larsen, R. J., Diener, E., & Cropanzano, R. S. (1987). Cognitive operations associated with individual differences in affect intensity. *Journal of Personality and Social Psychology, 53*, 767–774.

Larsen, R. J., Diener, E., & Emmons, R. A. (1985). An evaluation of subjective well-being measures. *Social Indicators Research, 17*, 1–17.

Larsen, R. J., Diener, E., & Emmons, R. A. (1986). Affect intensity and reactions to daily life events. *Journal of Personality and Social Psychology, 51*, 803–814.

Larsen, R. J., & Kasimatis, M. (1990). Individual differences in entrainment of mood to the weekly calendar. *Journal of Personality and Social Psychology, 58*, 164–171.

Larsen, R. J., & Ketelaar, T. (1989). Extraversion, neuroticism and susceptibility to positive and negative mood induction procedures. *Personality and Individual Differences, 10*, 1221–1228.

Larsen, R. J., & Seidman, E. (1986). Gender schema theory and sex role inventories: Some conceptual and psychometric considerations. *Journal of Personality and Social Psychology, 50*, 205–211.

Larson, D. G., & Chastain, R. L. (1990). Self-concealment: Conceptualization, measurement, and health implications. *Journal of Social and Clinical Psychology, 9*, 439–455.

Larson, R. W. (1990). The solitary side of life: An examination of the time people spend alone from childhood to old age. *Developmental Review, 10*, 155–183.

Larson, R. W. (1997). The emergence of solitude as a constructive domain of experience in early adolescence. *Child Development, 68*, 80–93.

Larson, R. W., & Csikszentmihalyi, M. (1980). The significance of solitude in adolescents' development. *Journal of Current Adolescent Medicine, 2*, 33–40.

Larson, R. W., Csikszentmihalyi, M., & Graef, R. (1982). Time alone in daily experience: Loneliness or renewal? In L. A. Peplau & D. Perlman (Eds.), *Loneliness: A sourcebook of current theory, research and therapy* (pp. 40–53). New York: Wiley.

Larson, R. W., & Johnson, C. (1985). Bulimia: Disturbed patterns of solitude. *Addictive Behaviors, 10*, 281–290.

Larson, R. W., & Lee, M. (1996). The capacity to be alone as a stress buffer. *Journal of Social Psychology, 136*, 5–16.

Larson, R. W., & Richards, M. H. (1991). Daily companionship in late childhood and early adolescence: Changing developmental contexts. *Child Development, 62*, 284–300.

Larson, R. W., Zuzanek, J., & Mannell, R. (1985). Being alone versus being with people: Disengagement in the daily experience of older adults. *Journal of Gerontology, 40*, 375–381.

Lau, R. R., Hartman, K. A., & Ware, J. E. (1986). Health as value: Methodological and theoretical considerations. *Health Psychology, 5*, 25–43.

Lax, E. (1991). *Woody Allen: A biography.* New York: Knopf.

Lazarus, R. (1968). Emotions and adaptation. In W. J. Arnold (Ed.), *Nebraska Symposium on Motivation* (pp. 175–266). Lincoln: University of Nebraska Press.

Lazarus, R. S. (1974). Cognitive and coping processes in emotion. In B. Weiner (Ed.), *Cognitive views of human motivation* (pp. 21–32). New York: Academic Press.

Lazarus, R. S., & Folkman, S. (1984). *Stress, appraisal and coping.* New York: Springer.

Leak, G. K. (1974). Effects of hostility arousal and aggressive humor on catharsis and humor preference. *Journal of Personality and Social Psychology, 30*, 736–740.

Leary, M. R. (1983a). Social anxiousness: The construct and its measurement. *Journal of Personality Assessment, 47*, 66–75.

Leary, M. R. (1983b). *Understanding social anxiety: Social, personality, and clinical perspectives.* Beverly Hills, CA: Sage.

Leary, M. R. (1986). The impact of interactional impediments on social anxiety and self-presentation. *Journal of Experimental Social Psychology, 22*, 122–135.

Leary, M. R., & Atherton, S. C. (1986). Self-efficacy, social anxiety, and inhibition in interpersonal encounters. *Journal of Social and Clinical Psychology, 4*, 256–267.

Leary, M. R., Knight, P. D., & Johnson, K. A. (1987). Social anxiety and dyadic conversation: A verbal response analysis. *Journal of Social and Clinical Psychology, 5*, 34–50.

Leary, M. R., & Kowalski, R. M. (1995). *Social anxiety.* New York: Guilford.

Leary, M. R., & Meadows, S. (1991). Predictors, elicitors, and concomitants of social blushing. *Journal of Personality and Social Psychology, 60*, 254–262.

Lee, Y-T., & Seligman, M. E. P. (1997). Are Americans more optimistic than the Chinese? *Personality and Social Psychology Bulletin, 23,* 32–40.

Leedham, B., Meyerowitz, B. E., Muirhead, J., & Frist, W. H. (1995). Positive expectations predict health after heart transplant. *Health Psychology, 14,* 74–79.

Leeds, J. (2001, January 17). Surgeon Gen. links TV, real violence. *Los Angeles Times,* p. A-1.

Lefcourt, H. M. (1982). *Locus of control: Current trends in theory and research* (2nd ed.). Hillsdale, NJ: Erlbaum.

Lefcourt, H. M., Davidson, K., Prkachin, K. M., & Mills, D. E. (1997). Humor as a stress moderator in the prediction of blood pressure obtained during five stressful tasks. *Journal of Research in Personality, 31,* 523–542.

Lefkowitz, M. M., Eron, L. D., Walder, L. O., & Huesmann, L. R. (1977). *Growing up to be violent: A longitudinal study of the development of aggression.* New York: Pergamon.

Lenney, E. (1991). Sex roles: The measurement of masculinity, femininity, and androgyny. In J. P. Robinson, P. R. Shaver, & L. S. Wrightsman (Eds.), *Measures of personality and social psychological attitudes* (pp. 573–660). San Diego, CA: Academic Press.

Leon, G. R., Gillum, B., Gillum, R., & Gouze, M. (1979). Personality stability and change over a 30-year period—middle age to old age. *Journal of Consulting and Clinical Psychology, 47,* 517–524.

Lepore, S. J. (1997). Expressive writing moderates the relation between intrusive thoughts and depressive symptoms. *Journal of Personality and Social Psychology, 73,* 1030–1037.

Lepore, S. J., Ragan, J. D., & Jones, S. (2000). Talking facilitates cognitive-emotional processes of adaptation to an acute stressor. *Journal of Personality and Social Psychology, 78,* 499–508.

Lerner, J. V. (1983). The role of temperament in psychosocial adaptation in early adolescents: A test of a "goodness of fit" model. *Journal of Genetic Psychology, 143,* 149–157.

Lerner, J. V., Lerner, R. M., & Zabski, S. (1985). Temperament and elementary school children's actual and rated academic performance: A test of a "goodness of fit" model. *Journal of Child Psychology and Psychiatry, 26,* 125–136.

Lerner, P., & Lerner, H. (1990). Rorschach measures of psychoanalytic theories of defense. In J. N. Butcher & C. D. Spielberger (Eds.), *Advances in personality assessment* (Vol. 8, pp. 121–160). Hillsdale, NJ: Erlbaum.

Leventhal, E. A., Hansell, S., Diefenbach, M., Leventhal, H., & Glass, D. C. (1996). Negative affect and self-report of physical symptoms: Two longitudinal studies of older adults. *Health Psychology, 15,* 193–199.

Levin, I., & Stokes, J. P. (1986). An examination of the relation of individual difference variables to loneliness. *Journal of Personality, 54,* 717–733.

Levy, K. N., Blatt, S. J., & Shaver, P. R. (1998). Attachment styles and parental representations. *Journal of Personality and Social Psychology, 74,* 407–419.

Lewin, K. (1938). *The conceptual representation and measurement of psychological forces.* Durham, NC: Duke University Press.

Lewinsohn, P. M., Joiner, T. E., & Rohde, P. (2001). Evaluation of cognitive diathesis-stress models in predicting major depressive disorder in adolescents. *Journal of Abnormal Psychology, 110,* 203–215.

Lewis-Fernandez, R., & Kleinman, A. (1994). Culture, personality, and psychopathology. *Journal of Abnormal Psychology, 103,* 67–71.

Lindsay, J. L., & Anderson, C. A. (2000). From antecedent conditions to violent actions: A general affective aggression model. *Personality and Social Psychology Bulletin, 26,* 533–547.

Littig, L. W., & Yeracaris, C. A. (1965). Achievement motivation and intergenerational occupational mobility. *Journal of Personality and Social Psychology, 1,* 386–389.

Lloyd, G. G., & Lishman, W. R. (1975). Effect of depression on the speed of recall of pleasant and unpleasant experiences. *Psychological Medicine, 5,* 173–180.

Lochman, J. E. (1987). Self- and peer perceptions and attributional biases of aggressive and nonaggressive boys in dyadic interactions. *Journal of Consulting and Clinical Psychology, 55,* 404–410.

Loehlin, J. C. (1992). *Genes and the environment in personality development.* Newbury Park, NJ: Sage.

Loehlin, J. C., McCrae, R. R., & Costa, P. T. (1998). Heritabilities of common and measure-specific components of the Big Five personality factors. *Journal of Research in Personality, 32,* 431–453.

Loehlin, J. C., Willerman, L., & Horn, J. M. (1982). Personality resemblances between unwed mothers and their adopted-away offspring. *Journal of Personality and Social Psychology, 42,* 1089–1099.

Loehlin, J., Willerman, L., & Horn, J. M. (1987). Personality resemblance in adoptive families: A 10-year follow-up. *Journal of Personality and Social Psychology, 53,* 961–969.

Loftus, E. F. (1993). The reality of repressed memories. *American Psychologist, 48,* 518–537.

Long, B. C., & Sangster, J. I. (1993). Dispositional optimism/pessimism and coping strategies: Predictors of psychosocial adjustment of rheumatoid and osteoarthritis patients. *Journal of Applied Social Psychology, 23,* 1069–1091.

Lord, C. G. (1980). Schemas and images as memory aids: Two modes of processing social information. *Journal of Personality and Social Psychology, 38,* 257–269.

Lucas, R. E., & Diener, E. (2001). Understanding extraverts' enjoyment of social situations: The importance of pleasantness. *Journal of Personality and Social Psychology, 81,* 343–356.

Lucas, R. E., Diener, E., Grob, A., Suh, E. M., & Shao, L. (2000). Cross-cultural evidence for the fundamental features of extraversion. *Journal of Personality and Social Psychology, 79,* 452–468.

Lucas, R. E., & Fujita, F. (2000). Factors influencing the relation between extraversion and pleasant affect. *Journal of Personality and Social Psychology, 79,* 1039–1056.

Lyness, S. A. (1993). Predictors of differences between Type A and B individuals in heart rate and blood pressure reactivity. *Psychological Bulletin, 114,* 266–295.

Lynn, R., & Martin, T. (1995). National differences for thirty-seven nations in extraversion, neuroticism, psychoticism and economic, demographic and other correlates. *Personality and Individual Differences, 19,* 403–406.

Lynn, S. J. (1978). Three theories of self-disclosure exchange. *Journal of Experimental Social Psychology, 14,* 466–479.

Lynn, S. J., & Sherman, S. J. (2000). The clinical importance of sociocognitive models of hypnosis: Response set theory and Milton Erickson's strategic interventions. *American Journal of Clinical Hypnosis, 42,* 294–315.

Lynn, S. J., Weekes, J. R., Neufeld, V., Zivney, O., Brentar, J., & Weiss, F. (1991). Interpersonal climate and hypnotizability level: Effects on hypnotic performance, rapport, and archaic involvement. *Journal of Personality and Social Psychology, 60,* 739–743.

Lytton, H. (1977). Do parents create, or respond to, differences in twins? *Developmental Psychology, 13,* 456–459.

MacDonald, D. A. (2000). Spirituality: Description, measurement, and relation to the five factor model of personality. *Journal of Personality, 68,* 153–197.

Mackie, M. (1983). The domestication of self: Gender comparisons of self-imagery and self-esteem. *Social Psychology Quarterly, 46,* 343–350.

Maddux, J. E., Brawley, L., & Boykin, A. (1995). Self-efficacy and healthy behavior: Prevention, promotion, and detection. In J. E. Maddux (Ed.), *Self-efficacy, adaptation, and adjustment: Theory, research, and application* (pp. 173–202). New York: Plenum.

Maddux, J. E., Norton, L. W., & Leary, M. R. (1988). Cognitive components of social anxiety: An investigation of the integration of self-presentation theory and self-efficacy theory. *Journal of Social and Clinical Psychology, 6,* 180–190.

Magnus, K., Diener, E., Fujita, F., & Pavot, W. (1993). Extraversion and neuroticism as predictors of objective life events: A longitudinal analysis. *Journal of Personality and Social Psychology, 65,* 1046–1053.

Magnusson, D. (1990). Personality development from an interactional perspective. In L. A. Pervin (Ed.), *Handbook of personality: Theory and research* (pp. 193–222). New York: Guilford.

Mahalik, J. R., Cournoyer, R. J., DeFranc, W., Cherry, M., & Napolitano, J. M. (1998). Men's gender role conflict and use of psychological defenses. *Journal of Counseling Psychology, 45,* 247–255.

Mahoney, M. J., & Arnkoff, D. B. (1979). Self-management. In O. F. Pomerleau & J. P. Brady (Eds.), *Behavioral medicine: Theory and practice* (pp. 75–96). Baltimore: Williams & Wilkins.

Maier, S. F. (2001). Exposure to the stressor environment prevents the temporal dissipation of behavioral depression/learned helplessness. *Biological Psychiatry, 49,* 763–773.

Maier, S. F., & Seligman, M. E. P. (1976). Learned helplessness: Theory and evidence. *Journal of Experimental Psychology: General, 105,* 3–46.

Major, B., Carnevale, P. J. D., & Deaux, K. (1981). A different perspective on androgyny: Evaluations of masculine and feminine personality characteristics. *Journal of Personality and Social Psychology, 41,* 988–1001.

Mallon, S. D., Kingsley, D., Affleck, G., & Tennen, H. (1998). Methodological trends in *Journal of Personality:* 1970–1995. *Journal of Personality, 66,* 671–685.

Marcus-Newhall, A., Pedersen, W. C., Carlson, M., & Miller, N. (2000). Displaced aggression is alive and well: A meta-analytic review. *Journal of Personality and Social Psychology, 78,* 670–689.

Markey, P. M., Markey, C. N., Tinsley, B. J., & Ericksen, A. J. (2002). A preliminary validation of preadolescents' self-reports using the five-factor model of personality. *Journal of Research in Personality, 36,* 173–181.

Marks, G., Richardson, J. L., Graham, J. W., & Levine, A. (1986). Role of health locus of control beliefs and expectations of treatment efficacy in adjustment to cancer. *Journal of Personality and Social Psychology, 51,* 443–450.

Markus, H. (1977). Self-schemata and processing information about the self. *Journal of Personality and Social Psychology, 35,* 63–78.

Markus, H. (1983). Self-knowledge: An expanded view. *Journal of Personality, 51,* 543–565.

Markus, H., Crane, M., Bernstein, S., & Siladi, M. (1982). Self-schemas and gender. *Journal of Personality and Social Psychology, 42,* 38–50.

Markus, H. R., & Kitayama, S. (1991). Culture and the self: Implications for cognition, emotion, and motivation. *Psychological Review, 98,* 224–253.

Markus, H. R., & Kitayama, S. (1994). A collective fear of the collective: Implications for selves and theories of selves. *Personality and Social Psychology Bulletin, 20,* 568–579.

Markus, H., & Kunda, Z. (1986). Stability and malleability of the self-concept. *Journal of Personality and Social Psychology, 51,* 858–866.

Markus, H., & Nurius, P. (1986). Possible selves. *American Psychologist, 41,* 954–969.

Markus, H., & Sentis, K. (1982). The self and social information processing. In J. Suls (Ed.), *Psychological perspectives on the self* (Vol. 1, pp. 41–70). Hillsdale, NJ: Erlbaum.

Markus, H., & Smith, J. (1981). The influence of self-schemata on the perception of others. In N. Cantor & J. F. Kihlstrom (Eds.), *Personality, cognition, and social interaction* (pp. 233–262). Hillsdale, NJ: Erlbaum.

Marsh, H. W., Antill, J. K., & Cunningham, J. D. (1987). Masculinity, femininity, and androgyny: Relations to self-esteem and social desirability. *Journal of Personality, 55,* 661–683.

Marsh, H. W., & Byrne, B. M. (1991). Differentiated additive androgyny model: Relations between masculinity, femininity, and multiple dimensions of self-concept. *Journal of Personality and Social Psychology, 61,* 811–828.

Marshall, G. N. (1991). A multidimensional analysis of internal health locus of control beliefs: Separating the wheat from the chaff? *Journal of Personality and Social Psychology, 61,* 483–491.

Marshall, G. N., Wortman, C. B., Vickers, R. R., Kusulas, J. W., & Hervig, L. K. (1994). The five-factor model of personality as a framework for personality-health research. *Journal of Personality and Social Psychology, 67,* 278–286.

Martin, R., & Watson, D. (1997). Style of anger expression and its relation to daily experience. *Personality and Social Psychology Bulletin, 23,* 285–294.

Martin, R. P. (1985). Temperament: A review of research with implications for the school psychologist. *School Psychology Review, 12,* 266–275.

Martin, R. P. (1989). Activity level, distractability, and persistence: Critical characteristics in early schooling. In G. A. Kohnstamm, J. E. Bates, & M. K. Rothbart (Eds.), *Temperament in childhood* (pp. 451–461). New York: Wiley.

Martinez, J. C. (1994). Perceived control and feedback in judgment and memory. *Journal of Research in Personality, 28,* 374–381.

Maslow, A. H. (1968). *Toward a psychology of being* (2nd ed.). New York: Van Nostrand.

Maslow, A. H. (1970). *Motivation and personality* (2nd ed.). New York: Harper & Row.

Maslow, A. H. (1971). *The farther reaches of human nature.* New York: Viking.

Mastrangelo, P. M. (2001). Myers-Briggs Type Indicator, Form M. In B. S. Plake, & J. C. Impara (Eds.), *The fourteenth mental measurements yearbook* (pp. 818–819). Lincoln, NE: University of Nebraska Press.

Matthews, K. A., & Haynes, S. G. (1986). Type A behavior pattern and coronary risk: Update and critical evaluation. *American Journal of Epidemiology, 123,* 923–960.

Matthews, K. A., Helmreich, R. L., Beane, W. E., & Lucker, G. W. (1980). Pattern A, achievement striving, and scientific merit: Does Pattern A help or hinder? *Journal of Personality and Social Psychology, 39,* 962–967.

Matthews, K. A., & Saal, F. E. (1978). The relationship of the Type A coronary-prone behavior pattern to achievement, power, and affiliation motives. *Psychosomatic Medicine, 40,* 631–636.

Matto, H. C. (2002). Investigating the validity of the Draw-A-Person: Screening procedure for emotional disturbance: A measurement validation study with high-risk youth. *Personality Assessment, 14,* 221–225.

Mayer, J. D. (1998). A systems framework for the field of personality. *Psychological Inquiry, 9,* 118–144.

Mayer, J. D., & Gaschke, Y. N. (1988). The experience and meta-experience of mood. *Journal of Personality and Social Psychology, 55,* 102–111.

Mayne, T. J., Norcross, J. C., & Sayette, M. A. (1994). Admission requirements, acceptance rates, and financial assistance in clinical psychology programs: Diversity across the practice-research continuum. *American Psychologist, 49,* 806–811.

Mayo, P. R. (1983). Personality traits and the retrieval of positive and negative memories. *Personality and Individual Differences, 4,* 465–471.

McAdams, D. P., & Emmons, R. A. (Eds.). (1995). Levels and domains in personality [Special issue]. *Journal of Personality, 63*(3).

McCarthy, E. D., Langner, T. S., Gersten, J. C., Eisenberg, J. G., & Orzeck, L. (1975). Violence and behavior disorders. *Journal of Communication, 25,* 71–85.

McCaul, K. D., & Maki, R. H. (1984). Self-reference versus desirability ratings and memory for traits. *Journal of Personality and Social Psychology, 47,* 953–955.

McCauley, C., Woods, K., Coolidge, C., & Kulick, W. (1983). More aggressive cartoons are funnier. *Journal of Personality and Social Psychology, 44,* 817–823.

McClelland, D. C. (1961). *The achieving society.* Princeton, NJ: Van Nostrand.

McClelland, D. C. (1965). Achievement and entrepreneurship: A longitudinal study. *Journal of Personality and Social Psychology, 1,* 389–392.

McClelland, D. C. (1980). Motive dispositions: The merits of operant and respondent measures. In L. Wheeler (Ed.), *Review of personality and social psychology* (Vol. 1, pp. 10–41). Beverly Hills, CA: Sage.

McClelland, D. C. (1985). How motives, skill, and values determine what people do. *American Psychologist, 40,* 812–825.

McClelland, D. C., Atkinson, J. W., Clark, R. A., & Lowell, E. L. (1953). *The achievement motive.* New York: Appleton-Century-Crofts.

McClelland, D. C., & Boyatzis, R. E. (1982). Leadership motive pattern and long-term success in management. *Journal of Applied Psychology, 67,* 737–743.

McClelland, D. C., & Pilon, D. A. (1983). Sources of adult motives in patterns of parent behavior in early childhood. *Journal of Personality and Social Psychology, 44,* 564–574.

McClure, E. B. (2000). A meta-analytic review of sex differences in facial expression processing and their development in infants, children, and adolescents. *Psychological Bulletin, 126,* 424–453.

McCrae, R. R. (1993). Moderated analysis of longitudinal personality stability. *Journal of Personality and Social Psychology, 65,* 577–585.

McCrae, R. R. (2001). 5 years of progress: A reply to Block. *Journal of Research in Personality, 35,* 108–113.

McCrae, R. R., & Costa, P. T., Jr. (1983). Social desirability scales: More substance than style. *Journal of Consulting and Clinical Psychology, 51,* 882–888.

McCrae, R. R., & Costa, P. T. (1986a). Personality, coping, and coping effectiveness in an adult sample. *Journal of Personality, 54,* 385–405.

McCrae, R. R., & Costa, P. T. (1986b). Clinical assessment can benefit from recent advances in personality psychology. *American Psychologist, 41,* 1001–1003.

McCrae, R. R., & Costa, P. T. (1987). Validation of the five-factor model of personality across instruments and observers. *Journal of Personality and Social Psychology, 52,* 81–90.

McCrae, R. R., & Costa, P. T. (1990). *Personality in adulthood.* New York: Guilford.

McCrae, R. R., & Costa, P. T. (1995). Positive and negative valence within the five-factor model. *Journal of Research in Personality, 29,* 443–460.

McCrae, R. R., & Costa, P. T. (1997). Personality trait structure as a human universal. *American Psychologist, 52,* 509–516.

McCrae, R. R., Costa, P. T., & Busch, C. M. (1986). Evaluating comprehensiveness in personality systems: The California Q-Set and the five-factor model. *Journal of Personality, 54,* 430–446.

McCrae, R. R., Jang, K. L., Livesley, W. J., Riemann, R., & Angleitner, A. (2001). Sources of structure: Genetic, environmental and artifactual influences on the covariation of personality traits. *Journal of Personality, 69,* 511–535.

McDowall, J. (1984). Recall of pleasant and unpleasant words in depressed subjects. *Journal of Abnormal Psychology, 93,* 401–407.

McFarlin, D. B., & Blascovich, J. (1981). Effects of self-esteem and performance feedback on future affective preferences and cognitive expectations. *Journal of Personality and Social Psychology, 40,* 521–531.

McGhee, P. E. (1979). *Humor: Its origin and development.* San Francisco: W. H. Freeman.

McGrath, M. J., & Cohen, D. B. (1978). REM sleep facilitation of adaptive waking behavior: A review of the literature. *Psychological Bulletin, 85,* 24–57.

McGue, M., & Christensen, K. (1997). Genetic and environmental contributions to depression symptomatology: Evidence from Danish twins 75 years of age and older. *Journal of Abnormal Psychology, 106,* 439–448.

McGuire, M. T., & Troisi, A. (1990). Anger: An evolutionary view. In R. Plutchik & H. Kellerman (Eds.), *Emotion: Theory, research, and experience* (Vol. 5, pp. 43–57). San Diego, CA: Academic Press.

McGuire, P. A. (1999, March). Therapists see new sense in use of humor. *APA Monitor,* pp. 1, 10.

McGuire, W. J., & McGuire, C. V. (1982). Significant others in self-space: Sex differences and developmental trends in the social self. In J. Suls (Ed.), *Psychological perspectives on the self* (Vol. 1, pp. 71–96). Hillsdale, NJ: Erlbaum.

Meeker, W. B., & Barber, T. X. (1971). Toward an explanation of stage hypnosis. *Journal of Abnormal Psychology, 77,* 61–70.

Meichenbaum, D. H. (1977). *Cognitive behavior modification: An integrative approach.* New York: Plenum.

Meichenbaum, D. H. (1985). *Stress inoculation training.* New York: Pergamon.

Meichenbaum, D. H., & Cameron, R. (1983). Stress inoculation training: Toward a general paradigm for training coping skills. In D. Meichenbaum & M. E. Jaemko (Eds.), *Stress reduction and prevention* (pp. 115–157). New York: Plenum.

Meichenbaum, D. H., & Deffenbacher, J. L. (1988). Stress inoculation training. *Counseling Psychologist, 16,* 69–90.

Meissner, W. W. (1984). *Psychoanalysis and religious experience.* New Haven, CT: Yale University Press.

Meleshko, K. G. A., & Alden, L. E. (1993). Anxiety and self-disclosure: Toward a motivational model. *Journal of Personality and Social Psychology, 64,* 1000–1009.

Melges, F. T., & Weisz, A. E. (1971). The personal future and suicidal ideation. *Journal of Nervous and Mental Disease, 153,* 244–250.

Mendolia, M. (1999). Repressors' appraisals of emotional stimuli in threatening and nonthreatening positive emotional contexts. *Journal of Research in Personality, 33,* 1–26.

Mendolia, M., Moore, J., & Tesser, A. (1996). Dispositional and situational determinants of repression. *Journal of Personality and Social Psychology, 70,* 856–867.

Mershon, B., & Gorsuch, R. L. (1988). Number of factors in the personality sphere: Does increase in factors increase predictability of real-life criteria? *Journal of Personality and Social Psychology, 55,* 675–680.

Mestel, R. (2000, October 13). New doubt cast on fiber in averting cancer. *Los Angeles Times,* p. A-30.

Metalsky, G. I., Halberstadt, L. J., & Abramson, L. Y. (1987). Vulnerability to depressive mood reactions: Toward a more powerful test of the diathesis-stress and causal mediation components of the reformulated theory of depression. *Journal of Personality and Social Psychology, 52,* 386–393.

Mettlin, C. (1976). Occupational careers and the prevention of coronary-prone behavior. *Social Science and Medicine, 10,* 367–372.

Meyer, G. J. (1997). Assessing reliability: Critical corrections for a critical examination of the Rorschach Comprehensive System. *Psychological Assessment, 9,* 480–489.

Meyer, G. J., & Shack, J. R. (1989). The structural convergence of mood and personality: Evidence for old and new directions. *Journal of Personality and Social Psychology, 57,* 691–706.

Michalski, R. L., & Shackelford, T. K. (2002). An attempted replication of the relationships between birth order and personality. *Journal of Research in Personality, 36,* 182–188.

Mickelson, K. D., Kessler, R. C., & Shaver, P. R. (1997). Adult attachment in a nationally representative sample. *Journal of Personality and Social Psychology, 73,* 1092–1106.

Mikulincer, M., & Nachshon, O. (1991). Attachment styles and patterns of self-disclosure. *Journal of Personality and Social Psychology, 61,* 321–331.

Miles, D. R., & Carey, G. (1997). Genetic and environmental architecture of human aggression. *Journal of Personality and Social Psychology, 72,* 207–217.

Miller, C. T. (1984). Self-schemas, gender, and social comparison: A clarification of the related attributes hypothesis. *Journal of Personality and Social Psychology, 46,* 1222–1229.

Miller, I. W., & Norman, W. H. (1979). Learned helplessness in humans: A review and attribution theory model. *Psychological Bulletin, 86,* 93–118.

Miller, N. E. (1941). The frustration-aggression hypothesis. *Psychological Review, 48,* 337–346.

Miller, T. Q., Smith, T. W., Turner, C. W., Guijarro, M. L., & Hallet, A. J. (1996). A meta-analytic review of research on hostility and physical health. *Psychological Bulletin, 119,* 322–348.

Mills, C. J. (1983). Sex-typing and self schemata effects on memory and response latency. *Journal of Personality and Social Psychology, 45,* 163–172.

Mischel, W. (1968). *Personality and assessment.* New York: Wiley.

Mischel, W. (1973). Toward a cognitive social learning reconceptualization of personality. *Psychological Review, 80,* 252–283.

Mischel, W. (1979). On the interface of cognition and personality: Beyond the person-situation debate. *American Psychologist, 34,* 740–754.

Mischel, W. (1980). George Kelly's anticipation of psychology: A personal tribute. In M. J. Mahoney (Ed.), *Psychotherapy process.* New York: Plenum.

Many Americans fed up with diet advice. (2001, January 2). *New York Times,* p. F-10.

Mischel, W. (1983). Alternatives in the pursuit of the predictability and consistency of persons: Stable data that yield unstable interpretations. *Journal of Personality, 51,* 578–604.

Mischel, W. (1990). Personality dispositions revisited and revised: A view after three decades. In L. A. Pervin (Ed.),

Handbook of personality: Theory and research (pp. 111–134). New York: Guilford.

Mischel, W., & Peake, P. K. (1982). Beyond déjà vu in the search for cross-situational consistency. *Psychological Review, 89,* 730–755.

Mischel, W., & Peake, P. K. (1983). Some facets of consistency: Replies to Epstein, Funder, and Bem. *Psychological Review, 90,* 394–402.

Mischel, W., & Shoda, Y. (1995). A cognitive-affective system theory of personality: Reconceptualizing situations, dispositions, dynamics, and invariance in personality structure. *Psychological Review, 102,* 246–268.

Mitchell, R. E., Cronkite, R. C., & Moos, R. H. (1983). Stress, coping, and depression among married couples. *Journal of Abnormal Psychology, 92,* 433–448.

Moilanen, D. L. (1993). Depressive information processing among nonclinic, nonreferred college students. *Journal of Counseling Psychology, 40,* 340–347.

Monat, A., & Lazarus, R. S. (1985). Stress and coping: Some current issues and controversies. In A. Monat & R. S. Lazarus (Eds.), *Stress and coping: An anthology* (2nd ed., pp. 1–12). New York: Columbia University Press.

Moneta, G. B., & Csikszentmihalyi, M. (1996). The effect of perceived challenges and skills on the quality of subjective experience. *Journal of Personality, 64,* 275–310.

Moretti, M. M., Segal, Z. V., McCann, C. D., Shaw, B. F., Miller, D. T., & Vella, D. (1996). Self-referent versus other-referent information processing in dysphoric, clinically depressed, and remitted depressed subjects. *Personality and Social Psychology Bulletin, 22,* 68–80.

Morfei, M. Z., Hooker, K., Fiese, B. H., & Cordeiro, A. M. (2001). Continuity and change in parenting possible selves: A longtitudinal follow-up. *Basic and Applied Social Psychology, 23,* 217–223.

Morton, T. L. (1978). Intimacy and reciprocity of exchange: A comparison of spouses and strangers. *Journal of Personality and Social Psychology, 36,* 72–81.

Mount, M. K., Barrick, M. R., & Strauss, J. P. (1994). Validity of observer ratings of the Big Five personality factors. *Journal of Applied Psychology, 79,* 272–280.

Moustakas, C. E. (1961). *Loneliness.* Englewood Cliffs, NJ: Prentice-Hall.

Moustakas, C. E. (1968). *Individuality and encounter.* Cambridge, MA: Doyle.

Mundorf, N., Bhatia, A., Zillmann, D., Lester, P., & Robertson, S. (1988). Gender differences in humor appreciation. *Humor, 1,* 231–243.

Murray, B. (1998, June). Study says TV violence still seen as heroic, glamorous. *APA Monitor,* p. 16.

Murray, E. J., Lamnin, A. D., & Carver, C. S. (1989). Emotional expression in written essays and psychotherapy. *Journal of Social and Clinical Psychology, 8,* 414–429.

Murray, H. A. (1938). *Explorations in personality: A clinical and experimental study of fifty men of college age.* New York: Oxford University Press.

Murray, H. A. (1967). Henry A. Murray. In E. G. Boring & G. Lindzey (Eds.), *A history of psychology in autobiography* (Vol. 5, pp. 285–310). New York: Appleton-Century-Crofts.

Murray, J. A., & Terry, D. J. (1999). Parental reactions to infant death: The effects of resources and coping strategies. *Journal of Social and Clinical Psychology, 18,* 341–369.

Musante, L., MacDougall, J. M., Dembroski, T. M., & Costa, P. T. (1989). Potential for hostility and dimensions of anger. *Health Psychology, 8,* 343–354.

Myers, D. G. (1992). *The pursuit of happiness: Who is happy—and why.* New York: Morrow.

Myers, L. B. (2000). Identifying repressors: A methodological issue for health psychology. *Psychology and Health, 15,* 205–214.

Myers, M. B., & McCaulley, M. H. (1985). *Manual: A guide to the development and use of the Myers-Briggs Type Indicator.* Palo Alto, CA: Consulting Psychologists Press.

Nadon, R., Hoyt, I. P., Register, P. A., & Kihlstrom, J. F. (1991). Absorption and hypnotizability: Context effects reexamined. *Journal of Personality and Social Psychology, 60,* 144–153.

Nasby, W., & Read, N. W. (1997). The life voyage of a solo circumnavigator: Integrating theoretical and methodological perspectives. *Journal of Personality, 65,* 785–1068.

Nash, M. (1987). What, if anything, is regressed about hypnotic age regression? A review of the empirical literature. *Psychological Bulletin, 102,* 42–52.

National Institute of Mental Health (1982). *Television and behavior: Ten years of scientific progress and implications for the eighties* (Vol. 1). Washington, DC: U.S. Department of Health and Human Services.

Neale, M. C., Rushton, P., & Fulker, D. W. (1986). Heritability of item responses on the Eysenck Personality Questionnaire. *Personality and Individual Differences, 7,* 771–779.

Neale, M. C., & Stevenson, J. (1989). Rater bias in the EASI Temperament Scales: A twin study. *Journal of Personality and Social Psychology, 56,* 446–455.

Neimeyer, G. J. (1984). Cognitive complexity and marital satisfaction. *Journal of Social and Clinical Psychology, 2,* 258–263.

Neimeyer, R. A. (2001). Repertory Grid Technique. In W. E. Craighead & C. B. Nemeroff (Eds.), *The Corsini encyclopedia of psychology and behavioral science* (3rd ed.) (Vol. 4, pp. 1394–1395). New York: Wiley.

Neisser, U., Boodoo, G., Bourchard, T. J., Boykin, A. W., Brody, N., Ceci, S. J., Halpern, D. F., Loehlin, J. C., Perloff, R., Sternberg, R. J., & Urbina, S. (1996). Intelligence: Knowns and unknowns. *American Psychologist, 51,* 77–101.

Nevid, J. S., & Spencer, S. A. (1978). Multivariate and normative data pertaining to the RAS with the college population. *Behavior Therapy, 9,* 675.

Nevo, O., & Nevo, B. (1983). What do you do when asked to answer humorously? *Journal of Personality and Social Psychology, 44,* 188–194.

Newman, L. S., Duff, K. J., & Baumeister, R. F. (1997). A new look at defensive projection: Thought suppression, accessibility, and biased person perception. *Journal of Personality and Social Psychology, 72,* 980–1001.

Newman, L. S., & McKinney, L. C. (2002). Repressive coping and threat-avoidance: An idiographic Stroop study. *Personality and Social Psychology Bulletin, 28,* 409–422.

Newton, T. L., & Contrada, R. J. (1992). Repressive coping and verbal-autonomic response dissociation: The influence of social content. *Journal of Personality and Social Psychology, 62,* 159–167.

Niaura, R., Herbert, P. N., McMahon, N., & Sommerville, L. (1992). Repressive coping and blood lipids in men and women. *Psychosomatic Medicine, 54,* 698–706.

Nicholson, I. A. M. (1997). To "Correlate Psychology and Social Ethics": Gordon Allport and the first course in American personality psychology. *Journal of Personality, 65,* 733–742.

Nicholson, R. A., Mouton, G. J., Bagby, R. M., Buis, T., Peterson, S. A., & Buigas, R. A. (1997). Utility of MMPI-2 indicators of response distortion: Receiver operating characteristic analysis. *Psychological Assessment, 9,* 471–479.

Nikles, C. D., Brecht, D. L., Klinger, E., & Bursell, A. L. (1998). The effects of current-concern- and nonconcern-related waking suggestions on nocturnal dream content. *Journal of Personality and Social Psychology, 75,* 242–255.

Nisbett, R. E., & Ross, L. D. (1980). *Human inference: Strategies and shortcomings of social judgment.* Englewood Cliffs, NJ: Prentice-Hall.

Nolen-Hoeksema, S. (1987). Sex differences in unipolar depression: Evidence and theory. *Psychological Bulletin, 101,* 259–282.

Nolen-Hoeksema, S. (2000). The role of rumination in depressive disorders and mixed anxiety/depressive symptoms. *Journal of Abnormal Psychology, 109,* 504–511.

Noll, R. (1997). *The Aryan Christ: The secret life of Carl Jung.* New York: Random House.

Noller, P. (1984). *Nonverbal communication and marital interaction.* Oxford: Pergamon.

Noller, P., Law, H., & Comrey, A. L. (1987). Cattell, Comrey, and Eysenck personality factors compared: More evidence for the five robust factors? *Journal of Personality and Social Psychology, 53,* 775–782.

Norem, J. K. (1989). Cognitive strategies as personality: Effectiveness, specificity, flexibility, and change. In D. M. Buss & N. Cantor (Eds.), *Personality psychology: Recent trends and emerging directions* (pp. 45–60). New York: Springer-Verlag.

Norem, J. K. (2001). *The positive power of negative thinking: Using defensive pessimism to harness anxiety and perform at your peak.* Cambridge, MA: Basic Books.

Norem, J. K., & Cantor, N. (1986a). Anticipatory and post hoc cushioning strategies: Optimism and defensive pessimism in "risky" situations. *Cognitive Therapy and Research, 10,* 347–362.

Norem, J. K., & Cantor, N. (1986b). Defensive pessimism: Harnessing anxiety as motivation. *Journal of Personality and Social Psychology, 51,* 1208–1217.

Norem, J. K., & Illingworth, K. S. S. (1993). Strategy-dependent effects of reflecting on self and tasks: Some implications of optimism and defensive pessimism. *Journal of Personality and Social Psychology, 65,* 822–835.

Norman, P., & Bennett, P. (1996). Health locus of control. In M. Conner & P. Norman (Eds.), *Predicting health behaviour: Research and practice within social cognition models* (pp. 62–94). Buckingham, England: Open University Press.

Nunnally, J. C. (1978). *Psychometric theory* (2nd ed.). New York: McGraw-Hill.

O'Brien, M., Peyton, V., Mistry, R., Hruda, L., Jacobs, A., Caldera, Y., et al. (2000). Gender-role cognition in three-year-old boys and girls. *Sex Roles, 42,* 1007–1025.

Ochse, R., & Plug, C. (1986). Cross-cultural investigation of the validity of Erikson's theory of personality development. *Journal of Personality and Social Psychology, 50,* 1240–1252.

O'Connor, B. P., & Dyce, J. A. (2001). Rigid and extreme: A geometric representation of personality disorders in five-factor model space. *Journal of Personality and Social Psychology, 81,* 1119–1130.

O'Connor, S. C., & Rosenblood, L. K. (1996). Affiliation motivation in everyday experience: A theoretical comparison. *Journal of Personality and Social Psychology, 70,* 513–522.

O'Heron, C. A., & Orlofsky, J. L. (1990). Stereotypic and nonstereotypic sex role trait and behavior orientations, gender identity, and psychological adjustment. *Journal of Personality and Social Psychology, 58,* 134–143.

Oishi, S., & Diener, E. (2001). Goals, culture, and subjective well-being. *Personality and Social Psychology Bulletin, 27,* 1674–1682.

Okazaki, S. (1997). Sources of ethnic differences between Asian American and White American college students on measures of depression and social anxiety. *Journal of Abnormal Psychology, 106,* 52–60.

Oosterwegel, A., Field, N., Hart, D., & Anderson, K. (2001). The relation of self-esteem variability to emotion variability, mood, personality traits, and depressive tendencies. *Journal of Personality, 69,* 689–708.

Orgler, H. (1963). *Alfred Adler: The man and his work.* New York: Liveright.

Orlofsky, J. L., & O'Heron, C. A. (1987). Stereotypic and nonstereotypic sex role trait and behavior orientations: Implications for personal adjustment. *Journal of Personality and Social Psychology, 52,* 1034–1042.

Ortega, D. F., & Pipal, J. E. (1984). Challenge seeking and the Type A coronary-prone behavior pattern. *Journal of Personality and Social Psychology, 46,* 1328–1334.

Ovcharchyn, C. A., Johnson, H. H., & Petzel, T. P. (1981). Type A behavior, academic aspirations, and academic success. *Journal of Personality, 49,* 248–256.

Overmier, J. B., & Seligman, M. E. P. (1967). Effects of inescapable shock upon subsequent escape and avoidance learning. *Journal of Comparative and Physiological Psychology, 63,* 28–33.

Oyserman, D., & Markus, H. R. (1990). Possible selves and delinquency. *Journal of Personality and Social Psychology, 59,* 112–125.

Oyserman, D., & Saltz, E. (1993). Competence, delinquency, and attempts to attain possible selves. *Journal of Personality and Social Psychology, 65,* 360–374.

Pace, T. M., & Dixon, D. N. (1993). Changes in depressive self-schemata and depressive symptoms following cognitive therapy. *Journal of Counseling Psychology, 40,* 288–294.

Paik, H., & Comstock, G. (1994). The effects of television violence on antisocial behavior: A meta-analysis. *Communication Research, 21,* 516–546.

Papsdorf, M., & Alden, L. (1998). Mediators of social rejection in social anxiety: Similarity, self-disclosure, and overt signs of anxiety. *Journal of Research in Personality, 32,* 351–369.

Parch, L. (1997, October). Testing . . . 1, 2, 3. *Working Woman, 22,* 74.

Parker, D. R., & Rogers, R. W. (1981). Observation and performance of aggression: Effects of multiple models and frustration. *Personality and Social Psychology Bulletin, 7,* 302–308.

Parker, K. C. H., Hanson, R. K., & Hunsley, J. (1988). MMPI, Rorschach, and WAIS: A meta-analytic comparison of reliability, stability, and validity. *Psychological Bulletin, 103,* 367–373.

Parker, W. D. (1998). Birth order effects in the academically talented. *Gifted Child Quarterly, 42,* 29–38.

Parton, D. A., & Geshuri, Y. (1971). Learning of aggression as a function of presence of a human model, response intensity, and target of the response. *Journal of Experimental Child Psychology, 20,* 304–318.

Paulhus, D. (1983). Sphere-specific measures of perceived control. *Journal of Personality and Social Psychology, 44,* 1253–1265.

Paulhus, D. L. (1984). Two-component models of socially desirable responding. *Journal of Personality and Social Psychology, 46,* 598–609.

Paulhus, D. L. (1991). Measurement and control of response bias. In J. P. Robinson, P. S. Shaver, & L. S. Wrightsman (Eds.), *Measures of personality and social psychological attitudes* (Vol. 1, pp. 17–59). San Diego, CA: Academic Press.

Paulhus, D. L., & Christie, R. (1981). Spheres of control: An interactionist approach to assessment of perceived control. In H. Lefcourt (Ed.), *Research with the locus of control construct* (Vol. 1, pp. 161–188). New York: Academic Press.

Paulhus, D. L., & Martin, C. L. (1987). The structure of personality capabilities. *Journal of Personality and Social Psychology, 52,* 354–365.

Paulhus, D. L., & Morgan, K. L. (1997). Perception of intelligence in leaderless groups: The dynamic effects of shyness and acquaintance. *Journal of Personality and Social Psychology, 72,* 581–591.

Paunonen, S. V. (1998). Hierarchical organization of personality and prediction of behavior. *Journal of Personality and Social Psychology, 74,* 538–556.

Paunonen, S. V., & Ashton, M. C. (2001a). Big Five predictors of academic achievement. *Journal of Research in Personality, 35,* 78–90.

Paunonen, S. V., & Ashton, M. C. (2001b). Big Five factors and facets and the prediction of behavior. *Journal of Personality and Social Psychology, 81,* 524–539.

Paunonen, S. V., & Jackson, D. N. (2000). What is beyond the Big Five? Plenty! *Journal of Personality, 68,* 821–835.

Paunonen, S. V., Jackson, D. N., Trzebinski, J., & Forsterling, F. (1992). Personality structure across cultures: A multimethod evaluation. *Journal of Personality and Social Psychology, 62,* 447–456.

Payne, T. J., Connor, J. M., & Colletti, G. (1987). Gender-based schematic processing: An empirical investigation and reevaluation. *Journal of Personality and Social Psychology, 52,* 937–945.

Peabody, D., & Goldberg, L. R. (1989). Some determinants of factor structures from personality-trait descriptors. *Journal of Personality and Social Psychology, 57,* 552–567.

Peacock, E. J., & Wong, P. T. P. (1996). Anticipatory stress: The relation of locus of control, optimism, and control appraisals to coping. *Journal of Research in Personality, 30,* 204–222.

Pedersen, D. M. (1999). Model for types of privacy by privacy functions. *Journal of Environmental Psychology, 19,* 397–405.

Pedersen, N. L., Plomin, R., McClearn, G. E., & Friberg, L. (1988). Neuroticism, extraversion, and related traits in adult twins reared apart and reared together. *Journal of Personality and Social Psychology, 55,* 950–957.

Pedersen, W. C., Gonzales, C., & Miller, N. (2000). The moderating effect of trivial triggering provocation on displaced aggression. *Journal of Personality and Social Psychology, 78,* 913–927.

Pedhazur, E. J., & Tetenbaum, T. J. (1979). Bem Sex Role Inventory: A theoretical and methodological critique. *Journal of Personality and Social Psychology, 37,* 996–1016.

Pennebaker, J. W. (1989). Confession, inhibition, and disease. In L. Berkowitz (Ed.), *Advances in experimental social psychology* (Vol. 22, pp. 211–244). New York: Academic Press.

Pennebaker, J. W., & Beall, S. K. (1986). Confronting a traumatic event: Toward an understanding of inhibition and disease. *Journal of Abnormal Psychology, 95,* 274–281.

Pennebaker, J. W., Colder, M., & Sharp, L. K. (1990). Accelerating the coping process. *Journal of Personality and Social Psychology, 58,* 528–537.

Pennebaker, J. W., & O'Heeron, R. C. (1984). Confiding in others and illness rates among spouses of suicide and accidental-death victims. *Journal of Abnormal Psychology, 93,* 473–476.

Peplau, L. A., Russell, D., & Heim, M. (1979). The experience of loneliness. In I. Frieze, D. Bar-Tel, & J. Carroll (Eds.), *New approaches to social problems* (pp. 53–78). San Francisco: Jossey-Bass.

Perrig-Chiello, P., Perrig, W. G., & Staehelin, H. B. (1999). Health control beliefs in old age: Relationship with subjective and objective health, and health behaviour. *Psychology, Health and Medicine, 4,* 83–94.

Perry, D. G., & Bussey, K. (1979). The social learning theory of sex differences: Imitation is alive and well. *Journal of Personality and Social Psychology, 37,* 1699–1712.

Perry, H. S. (1984). *Psychiatrist of America: The life of Harry Stack Sullivan.* Cambridge, MA: Belknap.

Peterson, C., & Bossio, L. M. (2001). Optimism and physical well-being. In E. C. Chang (Ed.), *Optimism and pessimism: Implications for theory, research, and practice* (pp. 127–145). Washington, DC: American Psychological Association.

Peterson, C., Maier, S. F., & Seligman, M. E. P. (1993). *Learned helplessness: A theory for the age of personal control.* New York: Oxford University Press.

Peterson, C., & Seligman, M. E. P. (1984). Causal explanations as a risk factor for depression: Theory and evidence. *Psychological Review, 91,* 347–374.

Peterson, C., & Seligman, M. E. P. (1987). Explanatory style and illness. *Journal of Personality, 55,* 237–265.

Peterson, C., Seligman, M. E. P., & Vaillant, G. E. (1988). Pessimistic explanatory style is a risk factor for physical illness: A thirty-five-year longitudinal study. *Journal of Personality and Social Psychology, 55,* 23–27.

Peterson, C., Seligman, M. E. P., Yurko, K. H., Martin, L. R., & Friedman, H. S. (1998). Catastrophizing and untimely death. *Psychological Science, 9,* 127–130.

Peterson, C., Semmel, A., von Baeyer, C., Abramson, L. Y., Metalsky, G. I., & Seligman, M. E. P. (1982). The Attributional Style Questionnaire. *Cognitive Therapy and Research, 6,* 287–300.

Peterson, C., & Villanova, P. (1988). An expanded Attributional Style Questionnaire. *Journal of Abnormal Psychology, 97,* 87–89.

Peterson, C., Villanova, P., & Raps, C. S. (1985). Depression and attributions: Factors responsible for inconsistent results in the published literature. *Journal of Abnormal Psychology, 94,* 165–168.

Peterson, R. S., Owens, P. D., & Martorana, P. V. (1999). The group dynamics Q-sort in organizational research: A new method for studying familiar problems. *Organizational Research Methods, 2,* 107–139.

Petrie, K. J., Booth, R. J., & Pennebaker, J. W. (1998). The immunological effects of thought suppression. *Journal of Personality and Social Psychology, 75,* 1264–1272.

Phares, E. J. (1976). *Locus of control in personality.* Morristown, NJ: General Learning Press.

Phillips, D. P. (1983). The impact of mass media violence on U.S. homicides. *American Sociological Review, 48,* 560–568.

Phillips, S. D., & Bruch, M. A. (1988). Shyness and dysfunction in career development. *Journal of Counseling Psychology, 35,* 159–165.

Piccione, C., Hilgard, E. R., & Zimbardo, P. G. (1989). On the degree of stability of measured hypnotizability over a 25-year period. *Journal of Personality and Social Psychology, 56,* 289–295.

Piedmont, R. L. (1999). Does spirituality represent the sixth factor of personality? Spiritual transcendence and the five-factor model. *Journal of Personality, 67,* 985–1013.

Piedmont, R. L., McCrae, R. R., Riemann, R., & Angleitner, A. (2000). On the invalidity of validity scales: Evidence from self-reports and observer ratings in volunteer samples. *Journal of Personality and Social Psychology, 78,* 582–593.

Pilkonis, P. A. (1977a). Shyness, public and private, and its relationship to other measures of social behavior. *Journal of Personality, 45,* 585–595.

Pilkonis, P. A. (1977b). The behavioral consequences of shyness. *Journal of Personality, 45,* 596–611.

Pinderhughes, E. E., & Zigler, E. (1985). Cognitive and motivational determinants of children's humor responses. *Journal of Research in Personality, 19,* 185–196.

Pinquart, M., & Sorensen, S. (2001). Influences on loneliness in older adults: A meta-analysis. *Basic and Applied Social Psychology, 23,* 245–266.

Piotrowski, C., & Keller, J. W. (1989). Psychological testing in outpatient mental health facilities: A national study. *Professional Psychology: Research and Practice, 20,* 423–425.

Piotrowski, C., & Zalewski, C. (1993). Training in psychodiagnostic testing in APA-approved PsyD and PhD clinical psychology programs. *Journal of Personality Assessment, 61,* 394–405.

Pistole, M. C. (1989). Attachment in adult romantic relationships: Style of conflict resolution and relationship satisfaction. *Journal of Social and Personal Relationships, 6,* 505–510.

Pittner, M. S., & Houston, B. K. (1980). Response to stress, cognitive coping strategies, and the Type A behavior pattern. *Journal of Personality and Social Psychology, 39,* 147–157.

Pittner, M. S., Houston, B. K., & Spiridigliozzi, G. (1983). Control over stress, Type A behavior pattern, and response to stress. *Journal of Personality and Social Psychology, 44,* 627–637.

Plomin, R., Chipuer, H. M., & Loehlin, J. C. (1990). Behavioral genetics and personality. In L. A. Pervin (Ed.), *Handbook of personality: Theory and research* (pp. 225–243). New York: Guilford.

Plomin, R., & Crabbe, J. (2000). DNA. *Psychological Bulletin, 126,* 806–828.

Plomin, R., Corley, R., Caspi, A., Fulker, D. W., & DeFries, J. (1998). Adoption results for self-reported personality: Evidence for nonadditive genetic effects? *Journal of Personality and Social Psychology, 75,* 211–218.

Plomin, R., & DeFries, J. C. (1998, May). Genetics of cognitive abilities and disabilities. *Scientific American,* 62–69.

Pomerleau, A., Bolduc, D., Malcuit, G., & Cossette, L. (1990). Pink or blue: Environmental gender stereotypes in the first two years of life. *Sex Roles, 22,* 359–367.

Porter, L. S. Marco, C. A., Schwartz, J. E., Neale, J. M., Shiffman, S., & Stone, A. A. (2000). Gender differences in coping: A comparison of trait and momentary assessments. *Journal of Social and Clinical Psychology, 19,* 480–498.

Powch, I. G., & Houston, B. K. (1996). Hostility, anger-in, and cardiovascular reactivity in white women. *Health Psychology, 15,* 200–208.

Pozo, C., Carver, C. S., Wellens, A. R., & Scheier, M. F. (1991). Social anxiety and social perception: Construing others' reactions to the self. *Personality and Social Psychology Bulletin, 17,* 355–362.

Prager, K. J. (1986). Intimacy status: Its relationship to locus of control, self-disclosure, and anxiety in adults. *Personality and Social Psychology Bulletin, 12,* 91–109.

Pratto, F., & John, O. P. (1991). Automatic vigilance: The attention-grabbing power of negative social information. *Journal of Personality and Social Psychology, 67,* 159–167.

Price, R. A., Vandenberg, S. G., Iyer, H., & Williams, J. S. (1982). Components of variation in normal personality. *Journal of Personality and Social Psychology, 43,* 328–340.

Ptacek, J. T., Smith, R. E., & Dodge, K. L. (1994). Gender differences in coping with stress: When stressor and appraisals do not differ. *Personality and Social Psychology Bulletin, 20,* 421–430.

Puca, R. M., & Schmalt, H-D. (2001). The influence of the achievement motive on spontaneous thoughts in pre- and postdecisional action phases. *Personality and Social Psychology Bulletin, 27,* 302–308.

Raag, T., & Rackliff, C. L. (1998). Preschoolers' awareness of social expectations of gender: Relationships to toy choices. *Sex Roles, 38,* 685–700.

Raikkonen, K., Matthews, K. A., Flory, J. D., & Owens, J. F. (1999). Effects of hostility on ambulatory blood pressure and mood during daily living in healthy adults. *Health Psychology, 18,* 44–53.

Raikkonen, K., Matthews, K. A., Flory, J. D., Owens, J. F., & Gump, B. B. (1999). Effects of optimism, pessimism, and trait anxiety on ambulatory blood pressure and mood during everyday life. *Journal of Personality and Social Psychology, 76,* 104–113.

Ralph, J. A., & Mineka, S. (1998). Attributional style and self-esteem: The prediction of emotional distress following a midterm exam. *Journal of Abnormal Psychology, 107,* 203–215.

Rathus, S. A. (1973). A 30-item schedule for assessing assertive behavior. *Behavior Therapy, 4,* 398–406.

Ravaja, N., Keltikangas-Jarvinen, L., & Keskivaara, P. (1996). Type A factors as predictors of changes in the metabolic syndrome precursors in adolescents and young adults: A 3-year follow-up study. *Health Psychology, 15,* 18–29.

Rawsthorne, L. J., & Elliot, A. J. (1999). Achievement goals and intrinsic motivation: A meta-analytic review. *Personality and Social Psychology Review, 3,* 326–344.

"Raymond B. Cattell." (1997). *American Psychologist, 52,* 797–799.

Reich, J. W., & Zautra, A. J. (1997). Locus of control influences diathesis-stress effects in rheumatoid arthritis patients. *Journal of Research in Personality, 31,* 423–438.

Reilly, R. R., & Chao, G. T. (1982). Validity and fairness of some alternative employee selection procedures. *Personnel Psychology, 35,* 1–62.

Reise, S. P., & Waller, N. G. (1993). Traitedness and the assessment of response pattern scalability. *Journal of Personality and Social Psychology, 65,* 143–151.

Rescorla, R. A. (1988). Pavlovian conditioning: It's not what you think it is. *American Psychologist, 43,* 151–160.

Reynolds, S. K., & Clark, L. A. (2001). Predicting dimensions of personality disorder from domains and facets of the five-factor model. *Journal of Personality, 69,* 199–222.

Reznick, J. S., Kagan, J., Snidman, N., Gersten, M., Baak, K., & Rosenberg, A. (1986). Inhibited and uninhibited children: A follow-up study. *Child Development, 57,* 660–680.

Rhee, S. H., & Waldman, I. D. (2002). Genetic and environmental influences on antisocial behavior: A meta-analysis of twin and adoption studies. *Psychological Bulletin, 128,* 490–529.

Rhodewalt, F., & Comer, R. (1982). Coronary-prone behavior and reactance: The attractiveness of an eliminated choice. *Personality and Social Psychology Bulletin, 8,* 152–158.

Rhodewalt, F., & Davison, J. (1983). Reactance and the coronary-prone behavior pattern: The role of self-attribution in responses to reduced behavioral freedom. *Journal of Personality and Social Psychology, 44,* 220–228.

Rhodewalt, F., Morf, C., Hazlett, S., & Fairfield, M. (1991). Self-handicapping: The role of discounting and augmentation in the preservation of self-esteem. *Journal of Personality and Social Psychology, 61,* 122–131.

Rholes, W. S., Simpson, J. A., Campbell, L., & Grich, J. (2001). Adult attachment and transition to parenthood. *Journal of Personality and Social Psychology, 81,* 421–435.

Riemann, R., Angleitner, A., & Strelau, J. (1997). Genetic and environmental influences on personality: A study of twins reared together using the self- and peer-report NEO-FFI Scales. *Journal of Personality, 65,* 449–475.

Richards, J. C., Hof, A., & Alvarenga, M. (2000). Serum lipids and their relationships with hostility and angry affect and behaviors in men. *Health Psychology, 19,* 393–398.

Riordan, C. A., & Tedeschi, J. T. (1983). Attraction in aversive environments: Some evidence for classical conditioning and negative reinforcement. *Journal of Personality and Social Psychology, 44,* 683–692.

Ritts, V., & Patterson, M. L. (1996). Effects of social anxiety and action identification on impressions and thoughts in interaction. *Journal of Social and Clinical Psychology, 15,* 191–205.

Robbins, P. R., Tanck, R. H., & Houshi, F. (1985). Anxiety and dream symbolism. *Journal of Personality, 53,* 17–22.

Roberts, B., & Hogan, R. (2001). *Personality psychology in the workplace.* Washington, DC: American Psychological Association.

Roberts, B. W., & Del Vecchio, W. F. (2000). The rank-order consistency of personality traits from childhood to old age: A quantitative review of longitudinal studies. *Psychological Bulletin, 126,* 3–25.

Roberts, J. E., & Monroe, S. M. (1992). Vulnerable self-esteem and depressive symptoms: Prospective findings comparing three alternative conceptualizations. *Journal of Personality and Social Psychology, 62,* 804–835.

Robins, C. J. (1988). Attributions and depression: Why is the literature so inconsistent? *Journal of Personality and Social Psychology, 54,* 880–889.

Robins, R. W., Gosling, S. D., & Craik, K. H. (1999). An empirical analysis of trends in psychology. *American Psychologist, 54,* 117–128.

Robinson-Whelen, S., Kim, C., MacCallum, R. C., & Kiecolt-Glaser, J. K. (1997). Distinguishing optimism from pessimism in older adults: Is it more important to be optimistic or not to be pessimistic? *Journal of Personality and Social Psychology, 73,* 1345–1353.

Roche, S. M., & McConkey, K. M. (1990). Absorption: Nature, assessment, and correlates. *Journal of Personality and Social Psychology, 59,* 91–101.

Rodgers, J. L., Cleveland, H. H., van den Oord, E., & Rowe, D. C. (2000). Resolving the debate over birth order, family size, and intelligence. *American Psychologist, 55,* 599–612.

Rodin, J., & Langer, E. J. (1977). Long-term effects of a control-relevant intervention with the institutionalized aged. *Journal of Personality and Social Psychology, 35,* 897–902.

Rogers, C. R. (1947). The case of Mary Jane Tildon. In W. U. Snyder (Ed.), *Casebook of nondirective counseling* (pp. 128–203). Cambridge, MA: Houghton Mifflin.

Rogers, C. R. (1951). *Client-centered therapy: Its current practice, implications, and theory.* Boston: Houghton Mifflin.

Rogers, C. R. (1954). The case of Mrs. Oak: A research analysis. In C. R. Rogers & R. F. Dymond (Eds.), *Psychotherapy and personality change* (pp. 259–348). Chicago: University of Chicago Press.

Rogers, C. R. (1961). *On becoming a person: A therapist's view of psychotherapy.* Boston: Houghton Mifflin.

Rogers, C. R. (1967). Carl R. Rogers. In E. G. Boring & G. Lindzey (Eds.), *A history of psychology in autobiography* (Vol. 5, pp. 341–384). New York: Appleton-Century-Crofts.

Rogers, C. R. (1969). *Freedom to learn: A view of what education might become.* Columbus, OH: Merrill.

Rogers, C. R. (1970). *Carl Rogers on encounter groups.* New York: Harper & Row.

Rogers, C. R. (1977). *Carl Rogers on personal power.* New York: Delacorte.

Rogers, C. R. (1982, August). Nuclear war: A personal response. *APA Monitor,* pp. 6–7.

Rogers, T. B., Kuiper, N. A., & Kirker, W. S. (1977). Self-reference and the encoding of personal information. *Journal of Personality and Social Psychology, 35,* 677–688.

Rokach, A. (1998). The relation of cultural background to the causes of loneliness. *Journal of Social and Clinical Psychology, 17,* 75–88.

Rook, K. S., & Peplau, L. A. (1982). Perspectives on helping the lonely. In L. A. Peplau & D. Perlman (Eds.), *Loneliness* (pp. 351–378). New York: Wiley.

Roos, P. E., & Cohen, L. H. (1987). Sex roles and social support as moderators of life stress adjustment. *Journal of Personality and Social Psychology, 52,* 576–585.

Rose, R. J. (1988). Genetic and environmental variance in content dimensions of the MMPI. *Journal of Personality and Social Psychology, 55,* 302–311.

Rose, R. J., Koskenvuo, M., Kaprio, J., Sarna, S., & Langinvainio, H. (1988). Shared genes, shared experiences, and similarity of personality: Data from 14,288 adult Finnish co-twins. *Journal of Personality and Social Psychology, 54,* 161–171.

Rosen, J., & Lane, C. (1994, October 31). Neo-Nazis! *New Republic, 210,* 15.

Rosenman, R. H. (1986). Current and past history of Type A behavior pattern. In T. H. Schmidt, T. M. Dembroski, & G. Blumchen (Eds.), *Biological and psychological factors in cardiovascular disease* (pp. 15–40). New York: Springer-Verlag.

Rosenman, R. H., Brand, R. J., Jenkins, C. D., Friedman, M., Straus, R., & Wurm, M. (1975). Coronary heart disease in the western collaborative group study: Final follow-up experience of 8-1/2 years. *Journal of the American Medical Association, 233,* 872–877.

Rosenthal, R. (1979). The "file drawer problem" and tolerance for null results. *Psychological Bulletin, 86,* 638–641.

Rosenthal, R. (1990). How are we doing in soft psychology? *American Psychologist, 45,* 775–777.

Ross, M., & Holmberg, D. (1992). Are wives' memories for events in relationships more vivid than their husbands' memories? *Journal of Social and Personal Relationships, 9,* 585–604.

Rosse, J. G., Stecher, M. D., Miller, J. L., & Levin, R. A. (1998). The impact of response distortion on preemployment personality testing and hiring decisions. *Journal of Applied Psychology, 83,* 634–644.

Rotenberg, K. J. (1994). Loneliness and interpersonal trust. *Journal of Social and Clinical Psychology, 13,* 152–173.

Rotenberg, K. J. (1997). Loneliness and the perception of the exchange of disclosures. *Journal of Social and Clinical Psychology, 16,* 259–276.

Roth, S. (1980). A revised model of learned helplessness in humans. *Journal of Personality, 48,* 103–133.

Rothbart, M. K., & Ahadi, S. A. (1994). Temperament and the development of personality. *Journal of Abnormal Psychology, 103,* 55–66.

Rothbart, M. K., Ahadi, S. A., & Evans, D. E. (2000). Temperament and personality: Origins and outcomes. *Journal of Personality and Social Psychology, 78,* 122–135.

Rotter, J. B. (1954). *Social learning and clinical psychology.* Englewood Cliffs, NJ: Prentice-Hall.

Rotter, J. B. (1966). Generalized expectancies for internal versus external control of reinforcement. *Psychological Monographs, 80*(1).

Rotter, J. B. (1982). *The development and applications of social learning theory: Selected papers.* New York: Praeger.

Rotter, J. B., Chance, J. E., & Phares, E. J. (Eds.). (1972). *Applications of a social learning theory of personality.* New York: Holt, Rinehart & Winston.

Rowe, D. C. (1987). Resolving the person-situation debate: Invitation to an interdisciplinary dialogue. *American Psychologist, 42,* 218–227.

Rubenstein, C. M., & Shaver, P. (1980). Loneliness in two northern cities. In J. Hartog, J. R. Andy, & Y. A. Cohen (Eds.), *The anatomy of loneliness* (pp. 319–337). New York: International Universities Press.

Rubin, J. A., Provenzano, F. J., & Luria, Z. (1974). The eye of the beholder: Parents' views of sex of newborns. *American Journal of Orthopsychiatry, 44,* 512–519.

Rubin, Z., & Shenker, S. (1978). Friendship, proximity, and self-disclosure. *Journal of Personality, 46,* 1–22.

Rubins, J. L. (1978). *Karen Horney: Gentle rebel of psychoanalysis.* New York: Dial.

Ruble, D. N., & Stangor, C. (1986). Stalking the elusive schema: Insights from developmental and social-psychological analyses of gender schemas. *Social Cognition, 4,* 227–261.

Rudich, E. A., & Vallacher, R. R. (1999). To belong or to self-enhance? Motivational bases for choosing interaction partners. *Personality and Social Psychology Bulletin, 25,* 1387–1404.

Russell, D., Peplau, L. A., & Cutrona, C. E. (1980). The revised UCLA Loneliness Scale: Concurrent and discriminant validity. *Journal of Personality and Social Psychology, 39,* 472–480.

Russell, J. A., & Carroll, J. M. (1999). On the bipolarity of positive and negative affect. *Psychological Bulletin, 125,* 3–30.

Rusting, C. L. (1998). Personality, mood, and cognitive processing of emotional information: Three conceptual frameworks. *Psychological Bulletin, 124,* 165–196.

Rusting, C. L. (1999). Interactive effects of personality and mood on emotion-congruent memory and judgment. *Journal of Personality and Social Psychology, 77,* 1073–1086.

Rusting, C. L., & Larsen, R. J. (1998). Personality and cognitive processing of affective information. *Personality and Social Psychology Bulletin, 24,* 200–213.

Ruvolo, A. P., & Markus, H. R. (1992). Possible selves and performance: The power of self-relevant imagery. *Social Cognition, 10,* 95–124.

Sadalla, E. K., Kenrick, D. T., & Vershure, B. (1987). Dominance and heterosexual attraction. *Journal of Personality and Social Psychology, 52,* 730–738.

Sadler, W. A., & Johnson, T. B. (1980). From loneliness to anomie. In J. Hartog, J. R. Audy, & Y. A. Cohen (Eds.), *The anatomy of loneliness* (pp. 34–64). New York: International Universities Press.

Salgado, J. F. (1997). The five factor model of personality and job performance in the European community. *Journal of Applied Psychology, 82,* 30–43.

Salili, F. (1994). Age, sex, and cultural differences in the meaning and dimensions of achievement. *Personality and Social Psychology Bulletin, 20,* 635–648.

Sanford, S., & Eder, D. (1984). Adolescent humor during peer interaction. *Social Psychology Quarterly, 47,* 235–243.

Sanna, L. J., & Meier, S. (2000). Looking for clouds in a silver lining: Self-esteem, mental simulations, and temporal confidence changes. *Journal of Research in Personality, 34,* 236–251.

Sansone, C., & Harackiewicz, J. M. (1998). "Reality" is complicated. *American Psychologist, 53,* 673–674.

Saragovi, C., Koestner, R., Di Dio, L., & Aube, J. (1997). Agency, communion, and well-being: Extending Helgeson's (1994) model. *Journal of Personality and Social Psychology, 73,* 593–609.

Sarason, I. G., Sarason, B. R., & Pierce, G. R. (Eds.). (1996). The future of personality [Special issue]. *Journal of Research in Personality, 30*(3).

Sarbin, T. R. (1950). Contributions to role-taking theory: I. Hypnotic behavior. *Psychological Review, 57,* 225–270.

Sarbin, T. R., & Coe, W. C. (1972). *Hypnosis: A social psychological analysis of influence communication.* New York: Holt, Rinehart & Winston.

Sarbin, T. R., & Coe, W. C. (1979). Hypnosis and psychopathology: Replacing old myths with fresh metaphors. *Journal of Abnormal Psychology, 88,* 506–526.

Saucier, G., & Goldberg, L. R. (1998). What is beyond the Big Five? *Journal of Personality, 66,* 495–524.

Saucier, G., & Goldberg, L. R. (2001). Lexical studies of indigenous personality factors: Premises, products, and prospects. *Journal of Personality, 69,* 847–879.

Savickas, M. L. (1997). Constructivist career counseling: Models and methods. In G. J. Neimeyer & R. A. Neimeyer (Eds.), *Advances in personal construct psychology* (Vol. 4, pp. 149–182). Greenwich, CN: JAI Press.

Sayers, S. L., Baucom, D. H., & Tierney, A. M. (1993). Sex roles, interpersonal control, and depression: Who can get their way? *Journal of Research in Personality, 27,* 377–395.

Scarr, S. (1969). Social introversion-extraversion as a heritable response. *Child Development, 40,* 823–832.

Scarr, S., & Carter-Saltzman, L. (1979). Twin method: Defense of a critical assumption. *Behavior Genetics, 9,* 527–542.

Scarr, S., Webber, P. L., Weinberg, R. A., & Wittig, M. A. (1981). Personality resemblances among adolescents and their parents in biologically related and adoptive families. *Journal of Personality and Social Psychology, 40,* 885–898.

Scarr, S., & Weinberg, R. A. (1976). IQ test performance of black children adopted by white families. *American Psychologist, 31,* 726–739.

Scarr-Salapatek, S. (1971). Race, social class, and IQ. *Science, 174,* 1286–1295.

Scheier, M. F., & Carver, C. S. (1985). Optimism, coping, and health: Assessment and implications of generalized outcome expectancies. *Health Psychology, 4,* 219–247.

Scheier, M. F., & Carver, C. S. (1987). Dispositional optimism and physical well-being: The influence of generalized outcome expectancies on health. *Journal of Personality, 55,* 169–210.

Scheier, M. F., Carver, C. S., & Bridges, M. W. (2001). Optimism, pessimism, and psychological well-being. In E. C. Chang (Ed.), *Optimism and pessimism: Implications for theory, research, and practice* (pp. 189–216). Washington, DC: American Psychological Association.

Scheier, M. F., Matthews, K. A., Owens, J. F., Magovern, G. J., Lefebvre, R. C., Abbott, R. A., & Carver, C. S. (1989). Dispositional optimism and recovery from coronary artery bypass surgery: The beneficial effects on physical and psychological well-being. *Journal of Personality and Social Psychology, 57,* 1024–1040.

Scheier, M. F., Weintraub, J. K., & Carver, C. S. (1986). Coping with stress: Divergent strategies of optimists and pessimists. *Journal of Personality and Social Psychology, 51,* 1257–1264.

Schimmack, U., & Diener, E. (1997). Affect intensity: Separating intensity and frequency in repeatedly measured affect. *Journal of Personality and Social Psychology, 73,* 1313–1329.

Schimmack, U., & Hartmann, K. (1997). Individual differences in the memory representation of emotional episodes: Exploring the cognitive processes in repression. *Journal of Personality and Social Psychology, 73,* 1064–1079.

Schimmack, U., Oishi, S., Diener, E., & Suh, E. (2000). Facets of affective experiences: A framework for investigations of trait affect. *Personality and Social Psychology Bulletin, 26,* 655–668.

Schlenker, B. R., & Britt, T. W. (1996). Depression and the explanation of events that happen to self, close others, and strangers. *Journal of Personality and Social Psychology, 71,* 180–192.

Schlenker, B. R., & Leary, M. R. (1982). Social anxiety and self-presentation: A conceptualization and model. *Psychological Bulletin, 92,* 641–669.

Schlenker, B. R., Weigold, M. F., & Hallam, J. R. (1990). Self-serving attributions in social context: Effects of self-esteem and social pressure. *Journal of Personality and Social Psychology, 58,* 855–863.

Schmalt, H-D. (1999). Assessing the achievement motive using the grid technique. *Journal of Research in Personality, 33,* 109–130.

Schmidt, N., Gooding, R. Z., Noe, R. A., & Kirsch, M. (1984). Meta-analyses of validity studies published between 1964 and 1982 and the investigation of study characteristics. *Personnel Psychology, 37,* 407–422.

Schmidt, N., & Sermat, V. (1983). Measuring loneliness in different relationships. *Journal of Personality and Social Psychology, 44,* 1038–1047.

Schulz, R., & Heckhausen, J. (1999). Aging, culture and control: Setting a new research agenda. *Journal of Gerontology: Psychological Sciences, 54B,* 139–145.

Schuyler, B. A., & Coe, W. C. (1981). A physiological investigation of volitional and nonvolitional experience during posthypnotic amnesia. *Journal of Personality and Social Psychology, 40,* 1160–1169.

Schwartz, C. E., Snidman, N., & Kagan, J. (1999). Adolescent social anxiety as an outcome of inhibited temperament in childhood. *Journal of the American Academy of Child and Adolescent Psychiatry, 38,* 1008–1015.

Schwartz, D. P., Burish, T. G., O'Rourke, D. F., & Holmes, D. S. (1986). Influence of personal and universal failure on the subsequent performance of persons with Type A and Type B behavior patterns. *Journal of Personality and Social Psychology, 51,* 459–462.

Schwartz, R. D., & Higgins, R. L. (1979). Differential outcome from automated assertion training as a function of locus of control. *Journal of Consulting and Clinical Psychology, 47,* 686–694.

Sears, R. R. (1941). Non-aggressive reactions to frustration. *Psychological Review, 48,* 343–346.

Segal, D. L., & Murray, E. J. (1993). Emotional processing in cognitive therapy and vocal expression of feeling. *Journal of Social and Clinical Psychology, 13,* 189–206.

Segal, Z. V., Gemar, M., & Williams, S. (1999). Differential cognitive response to a mood challenge following successful cognitive therapy or pharmacotherapy for unipolar depression. *Journal of Abnormal Psychology, 108,* 3–10.

Segall, M. H., Lonner, W. J., & Berry, J. W. (1998). Cross-cultural psychology as a scholarly discipline: On the flowering of culture in behavioral research. *American Psychologist, 53,* 1101–1110.

Segerstrom, S. C., Taylor, S. E., Kemeny, M. E., & Fahey, J. L. (1998). Optimism is associated with mood, coping, and immune change in response to stress. *Journal of Personality and Social Psychology, 74,* 1646–1655.

Segrin, C. (1999). Social skills, stressful life events, and the development of psychosocial problems. *Journal of Social and Clinical Psychology, 18,* 14–34.

Segrin, C., & Flora, J. (2000). Poor social skills are a vulnerability factor in the development of psychosocial problems. *Human Communication Research, 26,* 489–514.

Seidlitz, L., & Diener, E. (1998). Sex differences in the recall of affective experiences. *Journal of Personality and Social Psychology, 74,* 262–271.

Seligman, M. E. P. (1975). *Helplessness: On depression, development and death.* San Francisco: W. H. Freeman.

Seligman, M. E. P. (1976). *Learned helplessness and depression in animals and men.* Morristown, NJ: General Learning Press.

Seligman, M. E. P. (1991). *Learned optimism.* New York: Random House.

Seligman, M. E. P., & Csikszentmihalyi, M. (2000). Positive psychology: An introduction. *American Psychologist, 55,* 5–14.

Seligman, M. E. P., & Hager, J. L. (Eds.). (1972). *Biological boundaries of learning.* Englewood Cliffs, NJ: Prentice-Hall.

Seligman, M. E. P., & Maier, S. F. (1967). Failure to escape traumatic shock. *Journal of Experimental Psychology, 74,* 1–9.

Seligman, M. E. P., & Schulman, P. (1986). Explanatory style as a predictor of productivity and quitting among life insurance sales agents. *Journal of Personality and Social Psychology, 50,* 832–838.

Sevrens, J. (1999, January 22). Fiber just latest victim of nutrition flip-flops. *San Jose Mercury News,* pp. 1A, 20A.

Shah, J., & Higgins, E. T. (2001). Regulatory concerns and appraisal efficiency: The general impact of promotion and prevention. *Journal of Personality and Social Psychology, 80,* 693–705.

Shaw, J. S. (1982). Psychological androgyny and stressful life events. *Journal of Personality and Social Psychology, 43,* 145–153.

Shedler, J., Mayman, M., & Manis, M. (1993). The illusion of mental health. *American Psychologist, 48,* 1117–1131.

Sheldon, K. M. (1994). Emotionality differences between artists and scientists. *Journal of Research in Personality, 28,* 481–491.

Sheldon, W. H. (1942). *The varieties of temperament: A psychology of constitutional differences.* New York: Harper & Row.

Sheppard, L. C., & Teasdale, J. D. (2000). Dysfunctional thinking in major depressive disorder: A deficit in meta-cognitive monitoring? *Journal of Abnormal Psychology, 109,* 768–776.

Shepperd, J. A., & Arkin, R. M. (1990). Shyness and self-presentation. In W. R. Crozier (Ed.), *Shyness and embarrassment: Perspectives from social psychology* (pp. 286–314). Cambridge: Cambridge University Press.

Shepperd, J. A., Maroto, J. J., & Pbert, L. A. (1996). Dispositional optimism as a predictor of health changes among cardiac patients. *Journal of Research in Personality, 30,* 517–534.

Sherman, R. C., Buddie, A. M., Dragan, K. L., End, C. M., & Finney, L. J. (1999). Twenty years of PSPB: Trends in content, design, and analysis. *Personality and Social Psychology Bulletin, 25,* 177–187.

Shiffman, S. (1985). Coping with temptations to smoke. In S. Shiffman & T. A. Wills (Eds.), *Coping and substance use* (pp. 223–242). New York: Academic Press.

Shiffman, S., Balabanis, M. H., Paty, J. A., Engberg, J., Gwaltney, C. J., Liu, K. S., et al. (2000). Dynamic effects of self-efficacy on smoking lapse and relapse. *Health Psychology, 19,* 315–323.

Shiner, R. L. (1998). How shall we speak of children's personalities in middle childhood? A preliminary taxonomy. *Psychological Bulletin, 124,* 308–332.

Shoda, Y., & Mischel, W. (1996). Toward a unified, intra-individual dynamic conception of personality. *Journal of Research in Personality, 30,* 414–428.

Showers, C. (1992). The motivational and emotional consequences of considering positive and negative possibilities for an upcoming event. *Journal of Personality and Social Psychology, 63,* 474–484.

Showers, C., & Ruben, C. (1990). Distinguishing defensive pessimism from depression: Negative expectations and positive coping mechanisms. *Cognitive Therapy and Research, 14,* 385–399.

Shrauger, J. S., & Rosenberg, S. E. (1970). Self-esteem and the effects of success and failure feedback on performance. *Journal of Personality, 38,* 404–417.

Shrauger, J. S., & Sorman, P. B. (1977). Self-evaluations, initial success and failure, and improvement as determinants of persistence. *Journal of Consulting and Clinical Psychology, 45,* 784–795.

Shurcliff, A. (1968). Judged humor, arousal, and the relief theory. *Journal of Personality and Social Psychology, 4,* 360–363.

Siegler, I. C. (1994). Hostility and risk: Demographic and lifestyle variables. In A. W. Siegman & T. W. Smith (Eds.), *Anger, hostility, and the heart* (pp. 199–214). Hillsdale, NJ: Erlbaum.

Siegman, A. W. (1994). From Type A to hostility to anger: Reflections on the history of coronary-prone behavior. In A. W. Siegman & T. W. Smith (Eds.), *Anger, hostility, and the heart* (pp. 1–21). Hillsdale, NJ: Erlbaum.

Siem, F. M. (1998). Metatraits and self-schemata: Same or different? *Journal of Personality, 66,* 783–803.

Simoni, J. M., & Ng, M. T. (2002). Abuse, health locus of control, and perceived health among HIV-positive women. *Health Psychology, 21,* 89–93.

Simpson, J. A. (1990). Influence of attachment styles on romantic relationships. *Journal of Personality and Social Psychology, 59,* 971–980.

Simpson, J. A., Ickes, W., & Grich, J. (1999). When accuracy hurts: Reactions of anxious-ambivalent dating partners to a relationship threatening situation. *Journal of Personality and Social Psychology, 76,* 754–769.

Simpson, J. A., Rholes, W. S., & Nelligan, J. S. (1992). Support seeking and support giving within couples in an anx-iety-provoking situation: The role of attachment styles. *Journal of Personality and Social Psychology, 62,* 434–446.

Simpson, J. A., Rholes, W. S., Orina, M. M., & Grich, J. (2002). Working models of attachment, support giving, and support seeking in a stressful situation. *Personality and Social Psychology Bulletin, 28,* 598–608.

Simpson, J. A., Rholes, W. S., & Phillips, D. (1996). Conflict in close relationships: An attachment perspective. *Journal of Personality and Social Psychology, 71,* 899–914.

Simpson, T. L., & Arroyo, J. A. (1998). Coping patterns associated with alcohol-related negative consequences among college women. *Journal of Social and Clinical Psychology, 17,* 150–166.

Singer, J. L. (1988). Reinterpreting the transference. In D. C. Turk & P. Salovey (Eds.), *Reasoning, inference, and judgment in clinical psychology* (pp. 182–205). New York: Free Press.

Singer, J. L., & Singer, D. G. (1981). *Television, imagination, and aggression: A study of preschoolers.* Hillside, NJ: Erlbaum.

Sitharthan, T., & Kavanaugh, D. J. (1990). Role of self-efficacy in predicting outcomes from a program for controlled drinking. *Drug and Alcohol Dependence, 27,* 87–94.

Skinner, B. F. (1967). B. F. Skinner. In E. G. Boring & G. Lindzey (Eds.), *A history of psychology in autobiography* (Vol. 5, pp. 387–413). New York: Appleton-Century-Crofts.

Skinner, B. F. (1971). *Beyond freedom and dignity.* New York: Bantam.

Skinner, B. F. (1974). *About behaviorism.* New York: Vintage Books.

Skinner, B. F. (1983). *A matter of consequences.* New York: Knopf.

Slater, J., & Depue, R. A. (1981). The contribution of environmental events and social support to serious suicide attempts in primary depressive disorder. *Journal of Abnormal Psychology, 90,* 275–285.

Slavkin, M., & Stright, A. D. (2000). Gender role differences in college students from one- and two-parent families. *Sex Roles, 42,* 23–37.

Slife, B., & Rychlak, J. F. (1982). Role of affective assessment in modeling aggressive behavior. *Journal of Personality and Social Psychology, 43,* 861–868.

Sloan, W. W., & Solano, C. H. (1984). The conversational styles of lonely males with strangers and roommates. *Personality and Social Psychology Bulletin, 10,* 293–301.

Smith, C. A., Wallston, K. A., & Dwyer, K. A. (1995). On babies and bathwater: Disease impact and negative affectivity in the self-reports of persons with rheumatoid arthritis. *Health Psychology, 14,* 64–73.

Smith, C. E., Fernengel, K., Holcroft, C., Gerald, K., & Marien, M. (1994). Meta-analysis of the associations between social support and health outcomes. *Annals of Behavioral Medicine, 16,* 352–362.

Smith, D. (1982). Trends in counseling and psychotherapy. *American Psychologist, 37,* 802–809.

Smith, R. E. (1989). Effects of coping skills training on generalized self-efficacy and locus of control. *Journal of Personality and Social Psychology, 56,* 228–233.

Smith, S. L., & Donnerstein, E. (1998). Harmful effects of exposure to media violence: Learning of aggression, emotional desensitization, and fear. In R. G. Geen & E. Donnerstein (Eds.), *Human aggression: Theories, research, and implications for social policy* (pp. 167–202). San Diego: Academic Press.

Smith, W. P., & Rossman, B. B. R. (1986). Developmental changes in trait and situational denial under stress during childhood. *Journal of Child Psychiatry, 27,* 227–235.

Smyth, J., True, N., & Souto, J. (2001). Effects of writing about traumatic experiences: The necessity for narrative structuring. *Journal of Social and Clinical Psychology, 20,* 161–172.

Snyder, C. R. (1988). From defenses to self-protection: An evolutionary perspective. *Journal of Social and Clinical Psychology, 6,* 155–158.

Solano, C. H., Batten, P. G., & Parish, E. A. (1982). Loneliness and patterns of self-disclosure. *Journal of Personality and Social Psychology, 43,* 524–531.

Solano, C. H., & Koester, N. H. (1989). Loneliness and communication problems: Subjective anxiety or objective skills? *Personality and Social Psychology Bulletin, 15,* 126–133.

Soldz, S., & Vaillant, G. E. (1999). The Big Five personality traits and the life course: A 45-year longitudinal study. *Journal of Research in Personality, 33,* 208–232.

Solomon, Z., Avitzur, E., & Mikulincer, M. (1989). Coping resources and social functioning following combat stress reaction: A longitudinal study. *Journal of Social and Clinical Psychology, 8,* 87–96.

Solomon, Z., Mikulincer, M., & Avitzur, E. (1988). Coping, locus of control, social support, and combat-related posttraumatic stress disorder: A prospective study. *Journal of Personality and Social Psychology, 55,* 279–285.

Solomon, Z., Weisenberg, M., Schwarzwald, J., & Mikulincer, M. (1988). Combat stress reaction and posttraumatic stress disorder as determinants of perceived self-efficacy in battle. *Journal of Social and Clinical Psychology, 6,* 356–370.

Somer, O., & Goldberg, L. R. (1999). The structure of Turkish trait-descriptive adjectives. *Journal of Personality and Social Psychology, 76,* 431–450.

Spangler, W. D., & House, R. J. (1991). Presidential effectiveness and the leadership motive profile. *Journal of Personality and Social Psychology, 60,* 439–455.

Spanos, N. P. (1991). A sociocognitive approach to hypnosis. In S. J. Lynn & J. W. Rhue (Eds.), *Theories of hypnosis: Current models and perspectives* (pp. 324–361). New York: Guilford.

Spanos, N. P., Burgess, C. A., Roncon, V., Wallace-Capretta, S., & Cross, P. (1993). Surreptitiously observed hypnotic responding in simulators and in skill-trained and untrained high hypnotizables. *Journal of Personality and Social Psychology, 65,* 391–398.

Spanos, N. P., & Hewitt, E. C. (1980). The hidden observer in hypnotic analgesia: Discovery or experimental creation? *Journal of Personality and Social Psychology, 39,* 1201–1214.

Spanos, N. P., & Katsanis, J. (1989). Effects of instructional set on attributions of nonvolition during hypnotic and nonhypnotic analgesia. *Journal of Personality and Social Psychology, 56,* 182–188.

Spanos, N. P., Liddy, S. J., Baxter, C. E., & Burgess, C. A. (1994). Long-term and short-term stability of behavioral and subjective indexes of hypnotizability. *Journal of Research in Personality, 28,* 301–313.

Spanos, N. P., Radtke, H. L., & Dubreuil, D. L. (1982). Episodic and semantic memory in posthypnotic amnesia: A reevaluation. *Journal of Personality and Social Psychology, 43,* 565–573.

Spanos, N. P., Robertson, L. A., Menary, E. P., Brett, P. J., & Smith, J. (1987). Effects of repeated baseline testing on cognitive-skill-training-induced increments in hypnotic susceptibility. *Journal of Personality and Social Psychology, 52,* 1230–1235.

Spector, P. E. (1982). Behavior in organizations as a function of employee's locus of control. *Psychological Bulletin, 91,* 482–497.

Spector, P. E., Cooper, C. L., Sanchez, J. L., O'Driscoll, M., Sparks, K., Bernin, P. et al. (2001). Do national levels of individualism and internal locus of control relate to well-being: An ecological level international study. *Journal of Organizational Behavior, 22,* 815–832.

Speed, A., & Gangestad, S. W. (1997). Romantic popularity and mate preferences: A peer-nomination study. *Personality and Social Psychology Bulletin, 23,* 928–935.

Spence, J. T. (1993). Gender-related traits and gender ideology: Evidence for a multifactorial theory. *Journal of Personality and Social Psychology, 64,* 624–635.

Spence, J. T., & Helmreich, R. L. (1983). Achievement-related motives and behaviors. In J. T. Spence (Ed.), *Achievement and achievement motives: Psychological and sociological approaches* (pp. 7–74). San Francisco: W. H. Freeman.

Spence, J. T., Helmreich, R. L., & Stapp, J. (1974). The Personal Attributes Questionnaire: A measure of sex-role stereotypes and masculinity-femininity. *JSAS Catalog of Selected Documents in Psychology, 4,* 127 (Ms. No. 617).

Spencer, S. M., & Norem, J. K. (1996). Reflection and distraction: Defensive pessimism, strategic optimism, and performance. *Personality and Social Psychology Bulletin, 22,* 354–365.

Spett, M. C. (1983). All psychologists are not members of Divisions 12 and 17. *American Psychologist, 38,* 498.

Sprecher, S., Sullivan, Q., & Hatfield, E. (1994). Mate selection preferences: Gender differences examined in a national sample. *Journal of Personality and Social Psychology, 66,* 1074–1080.

Staats, A. W. (1975). *Social behaviorism.* Homewood, IL: Dorsey.

Staats, A. W. (1981). Paradigmatic behaviorism, unified theory, unified theory construction methods, and the Zeitgeist of separatism. *American Psychologist, 36,* 239–256.

Staats, A. W. (1996). *Behaviorism and personality: Psychological behaviorism.* New York: Springer.

Stajkovic, A. D., & Luthans, F. (1998). Self-efficacy and work-related performance: A meta-analysis. *Psychological Bulletin, 124,* 240–261.

Stake, J. E. (2000). When situations call for instrumentality *and* expressiveness: Resource appraisal, coping strategy choice, and adjustment. *Sex Roles, 42,* 865–885.

Stake, J. E., Huff, L., & Zand, D. (1995). Trait self-esteem, positive and negative events, and event-specific shifts in self-evaluation and affect. *Journal of Research in Personality, 29,* 223–241.

Stanton, A. L., Kirk, S. B., Cameron, C. L., & Danoff-Burg, S. (2000). Coping through emotional approach: Scale construction and validation. *Journal of Personality and Social Psychology, 78,* 1150–1169.

Stava, L. J., & Jaffa, M. (1988). Some operationalizations of the neodissociation concept and their relationship to hypnotic susceptibility. *Journal of Personality and Social Psychology, 54,* 989–996.

Stein, G. L., Kimiecik, J. C., Daniels, J., & Jackson, S. A. (1995). Psychological antecedents of flow in recreational sports. *Personality and Social Psychology Bulletin, 21,* 125–135.

Stelmack, R. M. (1990). Biological bases of extraversion: Psychophysiological evidence. *Journal of Personality, 58,* 293–311.

Stelmack, R. M., & Pivik, R. T. (1996). Extraversion and the effects of exercise on spinal motoneuronal excitability. *Personality and Individual Differences, 21,* 69–76.

Stephenson, W. (1953). *The study of behavior: Q-technique and its methodology.* Chicago: University of Chicago Press.

Steptoe, A., & Wardle, J. (2001). Locus of control and health behaviour revisited: A multivariate analysis of young adults from 18 countries. *British Journal of Psychology, 92,* 659–672.

Stewart, A. J. (1982). *Motivation and society.* San Francisco: Jossey-Bass.

Stoolmiller, M. (1999). Implications of the restricted range of family environments for estimates of heritability and nonshared environment in behavior-genetic adoption studies. *Psychological Bulletin, 125,* 392–409.

Storr, A. (1988). *Solitude: A return to the self.* New York: Free Press.

Story, A. L. (1998). Self-esteem and memory for favorable and unfavorable personality feedback. *Personality and Social Psychology Bulletin, 24,* 51–64.

Strauman, T. J. (1996). Stability within the self: A longitudinal study of the structural implications of self-discrepancy theory. *Journal of Personality and Social Psychology, 71,* 1142–1153.

Strauman, T. J., & Higgins, E. T. (1987). Automatic activation of self-discrepancies and emotional syndromes: When cognitive structures influence affect. *Journal of Personality and Social Psychology, 53,* 1004–1014.

Strelau, J. (1987). Emotion as a key concept in temperament research. *Journal of Research in Personality, 21,* 510–528.

Strentz, T., & Auerbach, S. M. (1988). Adjustment to the stress of simulated captivity: Effects of emotion-focused versus problem-focused preparation on hostages differing in locus of control. *Journal of Personality and Social Psychology, 55,* 652–660.

Strickland, B. R. (1978). Internal-external expectancies and health-related behaviors. *Journal of Consulting and Clinical Psychology, 46,* 1192–1211.

Strickland, B. R. (1989). Internal-external control expectancies: From contingency to creativity. *American Psychologist, 44,* 1–12.

Strube, M. J. (1982). Time urgency and Type A behavior: A methodological note. *Personality and Social Psychology Bulletin, 8,* 563–565.

Strube, M. J., Berry, J. M., & Moergen, S. (1985). Relinquishment of control and the Type A behavior pattern: The role of performance evaluation. *Journal of Personality and Social Psychology, 49,* 831–842.

Suedfeld, P. (1980). *Restricted environmental stimulation: Research and clinical applications.* New York: Wiley.

Suedfeld, P. (1982). Aloneness as a healing experience. In L. A. Peplau & D. Perlman (Eds.), *Loneliness: A sourcebook of current theory, research and therapy* (pp. 54–67). New York: Wiley.

Suinn, R. M. (2001). The terrible twos—anger and anxiety: Hazardous to your health. *American Psychologist, 56,* 27–36.

Suh, E., Diener, E., Oishi, S., & Triandis, H. C. (1998). The shifting basis of life satisfaction judgments across cultures: Emotions versus norms. *Journal of Personality and Social Psychology, 74,* 482–493.

Sullivan, H. S. (1953). *The interpersonal theory of psychiatry.* New York: Norton.

Suls, J., & Fletcher, B. (1985). The relative efficacy of avoidant and nonavoidant coping strategies: A meta-analysis. *Health Psychology, 4,* 249–288.

Suls, J., Green, P., & Hillis, S. (1998). Emotional reactivity to everyday problems, affective inertia, and Neuroticism. *Personality and Social Psychology Bulletin, 24,* 127–136.

Suls, J., & Wan, C. K. (1989). The relation between Type A behavior and chronic emotional distress: A meta-analysis. *Journal of Personality and Social Psychology, 57,* 503–512.

Swan, G. E., & MacDonald, M. L. (1978). Behavior therapy in practice: A national survey of behavior therapists. *Behavior Therapy, 9,* 799–807.

Sweeney, P. D., Anderson, K., & Bailey, S. (1986). Attributional style in depression: A meta-analytic review. *Journal of Personality and Social Psychology, 50,* 974–991.

Swendsen, J. D. (1998). The helplessness-hopelessness theory and daily mood experience: An idiographic and cross-situational perspective. *Journal of Personality and Social Psychology, 74,* 1398–1408.

Swickert, R. J., & Gilliland, K. (1998). Relationship between the brainstem auditory evoked response and extraversion, impulsivity, and sociability. *Journal of Research in Personality, 32,* 314–330.

Tafarodi, R. W., & Vu, C. (1997). Two-dimensional self-esteem and reactions to success and failure. *Personality and Social Psychology Bulletin, 23,* 626–635.

Tamres, L. K., Janicki, D., & Helgeson, V. S. (2002). Sex differences in coping behavior: A meta-analytic review and an examination of relative coping. *Personality and Social Psychology Review, 6,* 2–30.

Tarlow, E. M., & Haaga, D. A. F. (1996). Negative self-concept: Specificity to depressive symptoms and relation to positive and negative affectivity. *Journal of Research in Personality, 30,* 120–127.

Taubes, G. (1998, May–June). Telling time by the second hand. *Technology Review, 101,* 76.

Taylor, D. A., & Belgrave, F. Z. (1986). The effects of perceived intimacy and valence on self-disclosure reciprocity. *Personality and Social Psychology Bulletin, 12,* 247–255.

Taylor, M. C., & Hall, J. A. (1982). Psychological androgyny: Theories, methods and conclusions. *Psychological Bulletin, 92,* 347–366.

Taylor, S. E. (1989). *Positive illusions: Creative self-deception and the healthy mind.* New York: Basic Books.

Taylor, S. E., & Brown, J. D. (1988). Illusion and well-being: A social psychological perspective on mental health. *Psychological Bulletin, 103,* 193–210.

Tellegen, A., & Atkinson, G. (1974). Openness to absorbing and self-altering experiences ("absorption"), a trait related to hypnotic susceptibility. *Journal of Abnormal Psychology, 83,* 268–277.

Tellegen, A., Lykken, D. T., Bouchard, T. J., Wilcox, K. J., Segal, N. L., & Rich, S. (1988). Personality similarity in twins raised apart and together. *Journal of Personality and Social Psychology, 54,* 1031–1039.

Terry, D. J. (1994). Determinants of coping: The role of stable and situational factors. *Journal of Personality and Social Psychology, 66,* 895–910.

Terry, D. J., & Hynes, G. J. (1998). Adjustment to a low-control situation: Reexamining the role of coping responses. *Journal of Personality and Social Psychology, 74,* 1078–1092.

Tett, R. P., Jackson, D. N., & Rothstein, M. (1991). Personality measures as predictors of job performance: A meta-analytic review. *Personnel Psychology, 44,* 703–739.

Thomas, A., & Chess, S. (1977). *Temperament and development.* New York: Brunner/Mazel.

Thorndike, E. L. (1911). *Animal intelligence: Experimental studies.* New York: Macmillan.

Tice, D. M. (1991). Esteem protection or enhancement? Self-handicapping motives and attributions differ by trait self-esteem. *Journal of Personality and Social Psychology, 60,* 711–725.

Tice, D. M. (1993). The social motivations of people with low self-esteem. In R. F. Baumeister (Ed.), *Self-esteem: The puzzle of low self-regard* (pp. 37–53). New York: Plenum.

Tice, D. M., & Baumeister, R. F. (1990). Self-esteem, self-handicapping, and self-presentation: The strategy of inadequate practice. *Journal of Personality, 58,* 443–464.

Tidwell, M-C. O., Reis, H. T., & Shaver, P. R. (1996). Attachment, attractiveness, and social interaction: A diary study. *Journal of Personality and Social Psychology, 71,* 729–745.

Timmers, M., Fischer, A. H., & Manstead, A. S. R. (1998). Gender differences in motives for regulating emotions. *Personality and Social Psychology Bulletin, 24,* 974–985.

Triandis, H. C. (1989). The self and social behavior in differing cultural contexts. *Psychological Review, 96,* 506–520.

Triandis, H. C. (2001). Individualism-collectivism and personality. *Journal of Personality, 69,* 907–924.

Trivers, R. L. (1972). Parental investment and sexual selection. In B. Campbell (Ed.), *Sexual selection and the descent of man: 1871–1971* (pp. 136–179). Chicago: Aldine.

Trull, T. J., Widiger, T. A., & Burr, R. (2001). A structured interview for the assessment of the five-factor model of personality: Facet-level relations to the Axis II personality disorder. *Journal of Personality, 69,* 175–198.

Tucker, J. S., & Anders, S. L. (1999). Attachment style, interpersonal perception accuracy, and relationship satisfaction in dating couples. *Personality and Social Psychology Bulletin, 15,* 403–412.

Tuerlinckx, F., De Boeck, P., & Lens, W. (2002). Measuring needs with the Thematic Apperception Test: A psychometric study. *Journal of Personality and Social Psychology, 82,* 448–461.

Tunnell, G. (1981). Sex role and cognitive schemata: Person perception in feminine and androgynous women. *Journal of Personality and Social Psychology, 40,* 1126–1136.

Twenge, J. M. (1997). Changes in masculine and feminine traits over time: A meta-analysis. *Sex Roles, 36,* 305–325.

Twenge, J. M. (2000). The age of anxiety? Birth cohort change in anxiety and neuroticism, 1952–1993. *Journal of Personality and Social Psychology, 79,* 1007–1021.

Uchino, B. N., Cacioppo, J. T., & Kiecolt-Glaser, J. K. (1996). The relationship between social support and physiological processes: A review with emphasis on underlying mechanisms and implications for health. *Psychological Bulletin, 119,* 488–531.

Ungerer, J. A., Waters, B., & Barnett, B. (1997). Defense style and adjustment in interpersonal relationships. *Journal of Research in Personality, 31,* 375–384.

Urbina, S. P., & Grey, A. (1975). Cultural and sex differences in the sex distribution of dream characters. *Journal of Cross-Cultural Psychology, 6,* 358–364.

Urdan, T. C. (1997). Achievement goal theory: Past results, future directions. In M. Maehr & P. Pintrich (Eds.), *Advances in motivation and achievement* (pp. 99–141). Greenwich, CT: JAI Press.

Vaillant, G. E. (1977). *Adaptation to life.* Boston: Little, Brown.

Vaillant, G. E. (1992). *Ego mechanisms of defense: A guide for clinicians and researchers.* Washington, DC: American Psychiatric Press.

Valentiner, D. P., Foa, E. B., Riggs, D. S., & Gershuny, B. S. (1996). Coping strategies and posttraumatic stress disorder in female victims of sexual and nonsexual assault. *Journal of Abnormal Psychology, 105,* 455–458.

Van Egeren, L. F. (1979). Cardiovascular changes during social competition in a mixed-motive game. *Journal of Personality and Social Psychology, 37,* 858–864.

Veroff, J., Depner, C., Kulka, R., & Douvan, E. (1980). Comparison of American motives: 1957 versus 1976. *Journal of Personality and Social Psychology, 39,* 1249–1262.

Viglione, D. J. (1999). A review of recent research addressing the utility of the Rorschach. *Psychological Assessment, 11,* 251–265.

Viglione, D. J., & Hilsenroth, M. J. (2001). The Rorschach: Facts, fictions, and future. *Psychological Assessment, 13,* 452–471.

Vitaliano, P. P., DeWolfe, D. J., Maiuro, R. D., Russo, J., & Katon, W. (1990). Appraised changeability of a stressor as a modifier of the relationship between coping and depression: A test of the hypothesis of fit. *Journal of Personality and Social Psychology, 59,* 582–592.

Vitkus, J., & Horowitz, L. M. (1987). Poor social performance of lonely people: Lacking a skill or adopting a role? *Journal of Personality and Social Psychology, 52,* 1266–1273.

Voelz, C. J. (1985). Effects of gender role disparity on couples' decision-making processes. *Journal of Personality and Social Psychology, 49,* 1532–1540.

Vogel, D. A., Lake, M. A., Evans, S., & Karraker, K. H. (1991). Children's and adults' sex-stereotyped perceptions of infants. *Sex Roles, 24,* 605–616.

Vogel, G. W. (1975). Review of REM sleep deprivation. *Archives of General Psychiatry, 32,* 749–761.

Von Dras, D. D., & Siegler, I. C. (1997). Stability in Extraversion and aspects of social support at midlife. *Journal of Personality and Social Psychology, 72,* 233–241.

Wachtel, P. L. (1981). Transference, schema, and assimilation: The relevance of Piaget to the psychoanalytic theory of transference. *The Annual of Psychoanalysis, 8,* 59–76.

Waller, N. G., & Ben-Porath, Y. S. (1987). Is it time for clinical psychology to embrace the five-factor model of personality? *American Psychologist, 42,* 887–889.

Wallston, K. A. (1992). Hocus-pocus, the focus isn't strictly on locus: Rotter's social learning theory modified for health. *Cognitive Therapy and Research, 16,* 183–199.

Wallston, K. A., Maides, S., & Wallston, B. S. (1976). Health-related information seeking as a function of health-related locus of control and health value. *Journal of Research in Personality, 10,* 215–222.

Wallston, K. A., & Smith, M. S. (1994). Issues of control and health: The action is in the interaction. In G. N. Penney, P. Bennett, & M. Herbert (Eds.), *Health psychology: A lifespan perspective* (pp. 153–168). London, England: Harwood.

Wallston, K. A., & Wallston, B. S. (1981). Health locus of control scales. In H. M. Lefcourt (Ed.), *Research with the locus of control construct* (Vol. 1, pp. 189–243). New York: Academic Press.

Ward, C. H., & Eisler, R. M. (1987). Type A behavior, achievement striving, and a dysfunctional self-evaluation system. *Journal of Personality and Social Psychology, 53,* 318–326.

Watkins, C. E., Campbell, V. L., Nieberding, R., & Hallmark, R. (1995). Contemporary practice of psychological assessment by clinical psychologists. *Professional Psychology: Research and Practice, 26,* 54–60.

Watson, D. (1988). Intraindividual and interindividual analyses of positive and negative affect: Their relation to health complaints, perceived stress, and daily activities. *Journal of Personality and Social Psychology, 54,* 1020–1030.

Watson, D., & Clark, L. A. (1991). Self- versus peer-ratings of specific emotional traits: Evidence of convergent and discriminant validity. *Journal of Personality and Social Psychology, 60,* 927–940.

Watson, D., Clark, L. A., & Carey, G. (1988). Positive and negative affectivity and their relation to anxiety and depressive disorders. *Journal of Abnormal Psychology, 97,* 346–353.

Watson, D., Clark, L. A., McIntyre, C. W., & Hamaker, S. (1992). Affect, personality, and social activity. *Journal of Personality and Social Psychology, 63,* 1011–1025.

Watson, D., Clark, L. A., & Tellegen, A. (1988). Development and validation of brief measures of positive and negative affect: The PANAS Scales. *Journal of Personality and Social Psychology, 54,* 1063–1070.

Watson, D., Hubbard, B., & Wiese, D. (2000). Self-other agreement in personality and affectivity: The role of acquaintanceship, trait visibility, and assumed similarity. *Journal of Personality and Social Psychology, 78,* 546–558.

Watson, D., & Pennebaker, J. W. (1989). Health complaints, stress, and distress: Exploring the central role of negative affectivity. *Psychological Review, 96,* 234–254.

Watson, D., & Tellegen, A. (1985). Toward a consensual structure of mood. *Psychological Bulletin, 98,* 219–235.

Watson, D., Wiese, D., Vaidya, J., & Tellegen, A. (1999). The two general activation systems of affect: Structural findings, evolutionary considerations, and psychobiological evidence. *Journal of Personality and Social Psychology, 76,* 820–838.

Watson, J. B. (1936). John Broadus Watson. In C. Murchison (Ed.), *A history of psychology in autobiography* (Vol. 3, pp. 271–281). Worcester, MA: Clark University Press.

Watson, J. B. (1924/1970). *Behaviorism.* New York: Norton.

Watson, J. B., & Rayner, R. (1920). Conditioned emotional reactions. *Journal of Experimental Psychology, 3,* 1–14.

Webb, S. D. (1978). Privacy and psychosomatic stress: An empirical analysis. *Social Behavior and Personality, 6,* 227–234.

Weeks, D. G., Michela, J. L., Peplau, L. A., & Bragg, M. E. (1980). Relation between loneliness and depression: A structural equation analysis. *Journal of Personality and Social Psychology, 39,* 1238–1244.

Weidner, G., & Matthews, K. A. (1978). Reported physical symptoms elicited by unpredictable events and the Type A coronary-prone behavior pattern. *Journal of Personality and Social Psychology, 36,* 1213–1220.

Weinberger, D. A. (1998). Defenses, personality structure, and development: Integrating psychodynamic theory into a typological approach to personality. *Journal of Personality, 66,* 1061–1080.

Weinberger, D. A., & Davidson, M. N. (1994). Styles of inhibiting emotional expression: Distinguishing repressive coping from impression management. *Journal of Personality, 62,* 587–613.

Weinberger, D. A., & Schwartz, G. E. (1990). Distress and restraint as superordinate dimensions of self-reported adjustment: A typological perspective. *Journal of Personality, 58*, 381–417.

Weinberger, D. A., Schwartz, G. E., & Davidson, R. J. (1979). Low-anxious, high-anxious, and repressive coping styles: Psychometric patterns and behavioral and physiological responses to stress. *Journal of Abnormal Psychology, 88*, 369–380.

Weiner, B. (1979). A theory of motivation for some classroom experiences. *Journal of Educational Psychology, 71*, 3–25.

Weiner, B. (1985). An attributional theory of achievement motivation and emotion. *Psychological Bulletin, 92*, 548–573.

Weiner, B. (1990). Attribution in personality psychology. In L. A. Pervin (Ed.), *Handbook of personality: Theory and research* (pp. 465–485). New York: Guilford.

Weiner, I. B. (1995). Methodological considerations in Rorschach research. *Psychological Assessment, 7*, 330–337.

Weiner, I. B. (1996). Some observations on the validity of the Rorschach inkblot method. *Psychological Assessment, 8*, 206–213.

Weiner, I. B. (2001). Advancing the science of psychological assessment: The Rorschach inkblot method as exemplar. *Psychological Assessment, 13*, 423–432.

Wender, P. H., Kety, S. S., Rosenthal, D., Schulsinger, F., Ortmann, J., & Lunde, I. (1986). Psychiatric disorders in the biological and adoptive families of adopted individuals with affective disorders. *Archives of General Psychiatry, 92*, 923–929.

Wenzlaff, R. M., Wegner, D. M., & Roper, D. W. (1988). Depression and mental control: Resurgence of unwanted negative thoughts. *Journal of Personality and Social Psychology, 55*, 882–892.

Westen, D. (1988). Transference and information processing. *Clinical Psychology Review, 8*, 161–179.

Westen, D. (1996). A model and a method for uncovering the nomothetic from the idiographic: An alternative to the five-factor model? *Journal of Research in Personality, 30*, 400–413.

Westen, D. (1998). The scientific legacy of Sigmund Freud: Toward a psychodynamically informed psychological science. *Psychological Bulletin, 124*, 333–371.

Wheeler, R. E., Davidson, R. J., & Tomarken, A. J. (1993). Frontal brain asymmetry and emotional reactivity: A biological substrate of affective style. *Psychophysiology, 30*, 82–89.

Whiting, R. (1989). *You gotta have Wa*. New York: Vintage.

Whitley, B. E. (1983). Sex-role orientation and self-esteem: A critical meta-analytic review. *Journal of Personality and Social Psychology, 44*, 765–778.

Whitley, D. (2002, March 31). Former major leaguer confronts painful past. *San Jose Mercury News*, p. 16D.

Whyte, L. L. (1978). *The unconscious before Freud*. New York: St. Martin's.

Wicker, F. W., Barron, W. L., & Willis, A. C. (1980). Disparagement humor: Dispositions and resolutions. *Journal of Personality and Social Psychology, 39*, 701–709.

Wiggins, J. S. (1997). In defense of traits. In R. Hogan, J. Johnson, & S. Briggs (Eds.), *Handbook of personality psychology* (pp. 95–115). San Diego, CA: Academic Press.

Williams, J. E., Nieto, F. J., Sanford, C. P., Couper, D. J., & Tyroler, H. A. (2002). The association between trait anger and incident stroke risk: The Atheroslerosis Risk in Communities (ARIC) study. *Stroke, 33*, 13–20.

Williams, J. E., Nieto, F. J., Sanford, C. P., & Tyroler, H. A. (2001). Effects of an angry temperament on coronary heart disease risk: The Atherosclerosis Risk in Communities study. *American Journal of Epidemiology, 154*, 230–235.

Williams, J. E., Paton, C. C., Seigler, I. C., Eigenbrodt, M. L., Nieto, F. J., & Tyroler, H. A. (2000). Anger proneness predicts coronary heart disease risk: Prospective analysis from the Atherosclerosis Risk in Communities (ARIC) study. *Circulation, 101*, 2034–2039.

Williams, J. E., & Best, D. L. (1982). *Measuring sex stereotypes: A thirty-nation study*. Beverly Hills, CA: Sage.

Williams, J. G., & Solano, C. H. (1983). The social reality of feeling lonely: Friendship and reciprocation. *Personality and Social Psychology Bulletin, 9*, 237–242.

Williams, S. L. (1995). Self-efficacy and anxiety and phobic disorders. In J. E. Maddux (Ed.), *Self-efficacy, adaptation, and adjustment: Theory, research, and application* (pp. 69–108). New York: Plenum.

Wilson, T. D., & Linville, P. W. (1982). Improving the academic performance of college freshmen: Attribution therapy revisited. *Journal of Personality and Social Psychology, 42*, 367–376.

Wilson, T. D., & Linville, P. W. (1985). Improving the performance of college freshmen with attributional techniques. *Journal of Personality and Social Psychology, 49*, 287–293.

Windle, M., & Windle, R. C. (1996). Coping strategies, drinking motives, and stressful life events among middle adolescents: Associations with emotional and behavioral problems and with academic functioning. *Journal of Abnormal Psychology, 105,* 551–560.

Wittenberg, M. T., & Reis, H. T. (1986). Loneliness, social skills, and social perception. *Personality and Social Psychology Bulletin, 12,* 121–130.

Wolfe, R. N., & Kasmer, J. A. (1988). Type versus trait: Extraversion, impulsivity, sociability, and preferences for cooperative and competitive activities. *Journal of Personality and Social Psychology, 54,* 864–871.

Wolfle, L. M., & Robertshaw, D. (1982). Effects of college attendance on locus of control. *Journal of Personality and Social Psychology, 43,* 802–810.

Won-Doornink, M. J. (1985). Self-disclosure and reciprocity in conversation: A cross-national study. *Social Psychology Quarterly, 48,* 97–107.

Wong, M. M., & Csikszentmihalyi, M. (1991). Motivation and academic achievement: The effects of personality traits and the quality of experience. *Journal of Personality, 59,* 539–574.

Wood, J. M., Garb, H. N., Lilienfeld, S. O., & Nezworski, M. T. (2002). Clinical assessment. *Annual Review of Psychology, 53,* 519–543.

Wood, J. M., Nezworski, M. T., & Stejskal, W. J. (1996). Thinking critically about the Comprehensive System for the Rorschach: A reply to Exner. *Psychological Science, 7,* 14–17.

Wood, J. M., Nezworski, M. T., & Stejskal, W. J. (1997). The reliability of the Comprehensive System for the Rorschach: A comment on Meyer (1997). *Psychological Assessment, 9,* 490–494.

Wood, J. V., Giordano-Beech, M., Taylor, K. L., Michela, J. L., & Gaus, V. (1994). Strategies of social comparison among people with low self-esteem: Self-protection and self-enhancement. *Journal of Personality and Social Psychology, 67,* 713–731.

Wood, W., Wong, F. Y., & Chachere, J. G. (1991). Effects of media violence on viewers' aggression in unconstrained social interaction. *Psychological Bulletin, 109,* 371–383.

Worell, J. (1978). Sex roles and psychological well-being: Perspectives on methodology. *Journal of Consulting and Clinical Psychology, 46,* 777–791.

Wortman, C. B., & Brehm, J. W. (1975). Responses to uncontrollable outcomes: An integration of reactance theory and the learned helplessness model. In L. Berkowitz (Ed.), *Advances in experimental social psychology* (Vol. 8, pp. 277–336). New York: Academic Press.

Wu, J., Kramer, G. L., Kram, M., Steciuk, M., Crawford, I. L., & Petty, F. (1999). Serotonin and learned helplessness: A regional study of 5-HT$_{1A}$, 5-HT$_{2A}$ receptors and the serotonin transport site in rat brain. *Journal of Psychiatric Research, 33,* 17–22.

Wykes, S. L. (1993, January 24). Therapists accused of implanting memories of abuse. *San Jose Mercury News,* pp. 1A, 21A.

Wykes, S. L. (1996, January 16). Franklin to be retried for killing. *San Jose Mercury News,* pp. 1B, 4B.

Yang, K., & Bond, M. H. (1990). Exploring implicit personality theories with indigenous or imported constructs: The Chinese case. *Journal of Personality and Social Psychology, 58,* 1087–1095.

Yarnold, P. R., Mueser, K. T., & Grimm, L. G. (1985). Interpersonal dominance of Type As in group discussions. *Journal of Abnormal Psychology, 94,* 233–236.

Yik, M. S. M., Bond, M. H., & Paulhus, D. L. (1998). Do Chinese self-enhance or self-efface? *Personality and Social Psychology Bulletin, 24,* 399–406.

Yik, M. S. M., Russell, J. A., & Barrett, L. F. (1999). Structure of self-reported current affect: Integration and beyond. *Journal of Personality and Social Psychology, 77,* 600–619.

Young, J. E. (1982). Loneliness, depression and cognitive therapy: Theory and application. In L. A. Peplau & D. Perlman (Eds.), *Loneliness* (pp. 379–405). New York: Wiley.

Zadra, A. L., O'Brien, S. A., & Donderi, D. C. (1998). Dream content, dream recurrence and well-being: A replication with a younger sample. *Imagination, Cognition and Personality, 17,* 293–311.

Zajonc, R. B. (2001). The family dynamics of intellectual development. *American Psychologist, 56,* 490–496.

Zajonc, R. B., & Mullally, P. R. (1997). Birth order: Reconciling conflicting effects. *American Psychologist, 52,* 685–699.

Zammichieli, M. E., Gilroy, F. D., & Sherman, M. F. (1988). Relations between sex-role orientation and marital satisfaction. *Personality and Social Psychology Bulletin, 14,* 747–754.

Zautra, A. J., Reich, J. W., Davis, M. C., Potter, P. T., & Nicolson, N. A. (2000). The role of stressful events in the relationship between positive and negative affects: Evidence from field and experimental studies. *Journal of Personality, 68,* 927–951.

Zeidner, M., & Hammer, A. L. (1992). Coping with missile attack: Resources, strategies, and outcomes. *Journal of Personality, 60,* 709–746.

Zelli, A., Cervone, D., & Huesmann, L. R. (1996). Behavioral experience and social inference: Individual differences in aggressive experience and spontaneous versus deliberate trait inference. *Social Cognition, 14,* 165–190.

Zernike, K. (2000, August 25). Academic race gap grows again. *San Jose Mercury News,* p. 21A.

Zillmann, D. (1979). *Hostility and aggression.* Hillsdale, NJ: Erlbaum.

Zillmann, D., Bryant, J., & Cantor, J. R. (1974). Brutality of assault in political cartoons affecting humor appreciation. *Journal of Research in Personality, 7,* 334–345.

Zimbardo, P. G. (1977). *Shyness.* Reading, MA: Addison-Wesley.

Zimbardo, P. G. (1986). The Stanford Shyness Project. In W. H. Jones, J. M. Cheek, & S. R. Briggs (Eds.), *Shyness: Perspectives on research and treatment* (pp. 17–25). New York: Plenum.

Zuckerman, M., Kuhlman, D. M., Joireman, J., Teta, P., & Kraft, M. (1993). A comparison of three structural models for personality: The Big Three, the Big Five, and the alternative five. *Journal of Personality and Social Psychology, 65,* 757–768.

Name Index

Subject Index